Chevrolet Malibu Automotive Repair Manual

by Jeff Killingsworth

Models covered:
Malibu - 2013 through 2019

Does not include information specific to diesel or hybrid models

Haynes Publishing Group
Sparkford Nr Yeovil
Somerset BA22 7JJ England

Haynes North America, Inc
859 Lawrence Drive
Newbury Park, CA 91320 USA

www.haynes.com

ABCDE
FGHIJ
KLMNO
PQRST

Acknowledgements

Wiring diagrams provided exclusively for Haynes North America, Inc. by HaynesPro BV. Technical writers who contributed to this project include Demian Hurst and Scott "Gonzo" Weaver. Mechanical work and photography was provided by Mark Henderson.

© **Haynes North America, Inc. 2020**

With permission from J.H. Haynes & Co. Ltd.

A book in the Haynes Automotive Repair Manual Series

Printed in Malaysia

ISBN-10: 1-62092-385-8
ISBN-13: 978-1-62092-385-6

Library of Congress Control Number: 2020949022

While every attempt is made to ensure that the information in this manual is correct, no liability can be accepted by the authors or publishers for loss, damage or injury caused by any errors in, or omissions from, the information given.

Contents

Haynes mechanic and photographer with a 2018 Chevrolet Malibu

About this manual

Its purpose

The purpose of this manual is to help you get the best value from your vehicle. It can do so in several ways. It can help you decide what work must be done, even if you choose to have it done by a dealer service department or a repair shop; it provides information and procedures for routine maintenance and servicing; and it offers diagnostic and repair procedures to follow when trouble occurs.

We hope you use the manual to tackle the work yourself. For many simpler jobs, doing it yourself may be quicker than arranging an appointment to get the vehicle into a shop and making the trips to leave it and pick it up. More importantly, a lot of money can be saved by avoiding the expense the shop must pass on to you to cover its labor and overhead costs. An added benefit is the sense of satisfaction and accomplishment that you feel after doing the job yourself.

Using the manual

The manual is divided into Chapters. Each Chapter is divided into numbered Sections, which are headed in bold type between horizontal lines. Each Section consists of consecutively numbered paragraphs.

The reference numbers used in illustration captions pinpoint the pertinent Section and the Step within that Section. That is, illustration 3.2 means the illustration refers to Section 3 and Step (or paragraph) 2 within that Section.

Procedures, once described in the text, are not normally repeated. When it's necessary to refer to another Chapter, the reference will be given as Chapter and Section number. Cross references given without use of the word "Chapter" apply to Sections and/or paragraphs in the same Chapter. For example, "see Section 8" means in the same Chapter.

References to the left or right side of the vehicle assume you are sitting in the driver's seat, facing forward.

Even though we have prepared this manual with extreme care, neither the publisher nor the author can accept responsibility for any errors in, or omissions from, the information given.

NOTE

A **Note** provides information necessary to properly complete a procedure or information which will make the procedure easier to understand.

CAUTION

A **Caution** provides a special procedure or special steps which must be taken while completing the procedure where the Caution is found. Not heeding a Caution can result in damage to the assembly being worked on.

WARNING

A **Warning** provides a special procedure or special steps which must be taken while completing the procedure where the Warning is found. Not heeding a Warning can result in personal injury.

Introduction to the Chevrolet Malibu (2013 - 2019)

This manual covers the Chevrolet Malibu. This vehicle features several engines: 1.5L turbocharged four-cylinder, 2.0L turbocharged four-cylinder or a 2.5L normally aspirated four-cylinder. The engine drives the front wheels via independent driveaxles.

2016 and earlier Front Wheel Drive (FWD) models are equipped with a fully electronic, six-speed (6T40/45) automatic transaxle. 2017 and 2018 1.5L models are equipped with a fully electronic, six-speed (6T40) automatic transaxle and 2017 and 2018 2.0L models are equipped with a fully electronic, nine-speed (9T50) automatic transaxle. 2019 and later 1.5L models are equipped with a (VT40) Continuously Variable Transmission (CVT) and 2.0L models are equipped with a fully electronic, nine-speed (9T50) automatic transaxle.

Suspension is independent at all four wheels, with MacPherson struts used at the front and coil springs with shock absorbers at the rear. The rack-and-pinion steering unit is mounted on the subframe. All models are equipped with Electronic Power Steering (EPS).

The brakes are disc at the front and rear, with power assist standard. All models are equipped with an Anti-Lock Brake System (ABS).

Vehicle identification numbers

Modifications are a continuing and unpublicized process in vehicle manufacturing. Since spare parts lists and manuals are compiled on a numerical basis, the individual vehicle numbers are necessary to correctly identify the component required.

Vehicle Identification Number (VIN)

This very important identification number is stamped on a plate attached to the dashboard inside the windshield on the driver's side of the vehicle (see illustration). The VIN also appears on the Vehicle Certificate of Title and Registration. It contains information such as where and when the vehicle was manufactured, the model year and the body style.

On the vehicles covered by this manual the model year codes are:

D   2013
E   2014
F   2015
G   2016
H   2017
J   2018
K   2019

On the vehicles covered by this manual the engine codes are:

T   1.5L four-cylinder (LFV) turbocharged engine with high-pressure direct fuel injection (SIDI), DOHC, VVT - 2016 and later models

X   2.0L four-cylinder (LTG) turbocharged engine with high-pressure direct fuel injection (SIDI), DOHC, VVT - 2013 and later models

A   2.5L four-cylinder (LCV) engine with high-pressure direct fuel injection (SIDI), DOHC, VVT - 2013 and 2016 (Limited) models

L   2.5L four-cylinder (LKW) engine with high pressure direct fuel injection (SIDI), DOHC, VVT - 2014 and 2015 models

Certification Label

The certification label is attached to the driver's door pillar (see illustration). The label contains the name of the manufacturer, the month and year of production, the Gross Vehicle Weight Rating (GVWR), the Gross Axle Weight Rating (GAWR) and the certification statement.

Engine number

On all except 1.5L models, the engine identification number is on a sticker attached to the drivebelt end of the cylinder head, or etched on the left side of the engine, on the oil filter flange. On 1.5L models the engine sticker/etching is on the flat area of the cylinder block where it meets the transaxle (see illustration).

Transaxle number

The transaxle identification number has important information, such as the transaxle type and build date, on a label that is attached to the left top end of the transaxle (see illustrations) or the side of the transaxle near the top.

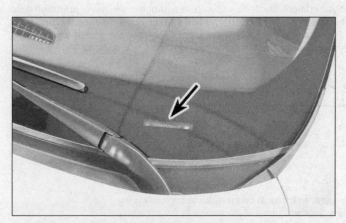

The Vehicle Identification Number (VIN) is located on a plate on top of the dash (visible through the windshield)

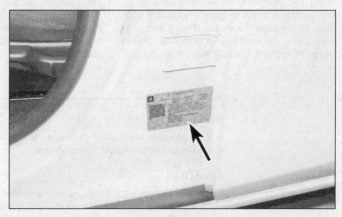

The Certification label is located on the door post between the doors

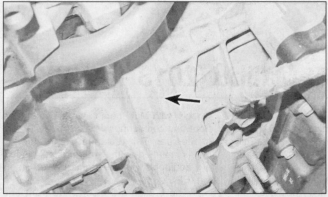

Location of the engine identification number - 1.5L four-cylinder engines

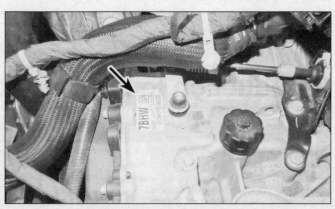

Location of the transaxle identification label (battery and battery tray removed)

Recall information

Vehicle recalls are carried out by the manufacturer in the rare event of a possible safety-related defect. The vehicle's registered owner is contacted at the address on file at the Department of Motor Vehicles and given the details of the recall. Remedial work is carried out free of charge at a dealer service department.

If you are the new owner of a used vehicle which was subject to a recall and you want to be sure that the work has been carried out, it's best to contact a dealer service department and ask about your individual vehicle - you'll need to furnish them your Vehicle Identification Number (VIN).

The table below is based on information provided by the National Highway Traffic Safety Administration (NHTSA), the body which oversees vehicle recalls in the United States. The recall database is updated constantly. For the latest information on vehicle recalls, check the NHTSA website at www.nhtsa.gov, www.safercar.gov, or call the NHTSA hotline at 1-888-327-4236.

Recall date	Recall campaign number	Model(s) affected	Concern
May 18, 2012	12V224000	2013 Malibu	On some models, after an event of hard braking, the Sensing and Diagnostic Module (SDM) may reset itself. If this occurs during an aggressive turning maneuver, and then afterwards a potential vehicle rollover event is sensed, the roof rail airbag may unintentionally deploy. Additionally, the airbags and or seatbelt pre-tensioners may not deploy during a severe crash, increasing the risk of personal injury.
Oct 04, 2012	12V484000	2013 Malibu	On some models equipped with two turn signal bulbs in each front turn signal, if one of the two front turn signal bulbs burn out in either front turn signal lamp, there is no indication to the driver. If the driver is not aware that a turn signal is not functioning properly, the driver may continue to drive the vehicle. If half of a turn signal is not illuminating, other drivers may not be aware that the affected vehicle is turning, thereby increasing the risk of a crash.
Jan 23, 2013	13V024000	2013 Malibu	On certain models, one or more rear suspension bolts may not have been tightened to the specified torque. This may lead to sudden changes in vehicle handling. Sudden changes in the vehicle handling may increase the risk of a crash.
Nov 13, 2013	13V566000	2013 Malibu	On some models equipped with the 8-way power adjustable front seat, the wiring harness for the power seat may contact the seat frame which may chafe the harness. If the harness is chafed enough to expose the wires, a short circuit could occur, resulting in unintended movement of the seat, the seat to become inoperative, sparking under the seat, flickering lights, smoke or possibly a fire.
Nov 13, 2013	13V567000	2014 Malibu	On some models, the heating, ventilation, and air conditioning (HVAC) control unit may intermittently become inoperable when the vehicle is started, preventing the windshield defroster from working. The inability to turn on the windshield defroster may decrease the driver's visibility thereby increasing the risk of a crash.

Recall date	Recall campaign number	Model(s) affected	Concern
Feb 21, 2014	14V092000	2014 Malibu	On some models, the transmission shift cable adjuster may disengage from the transmission shift lever. If a vehicle's shift cable disengages from the transmission shift lever, a driver may be unable to shift the gear positions and the indicated shift position may not represent the gear position the vehicle is in. Should a disengagement occur while the vehicle is being driven, when the driver goes to stop and park the vehicle, the driver may be able to shift the lever to the "PARK" position, but the vehicle transmission may not be in the "PARK" gear position. If the vehicle is not in the "PARK" position there is a risk the vehicle will roll away as the driver and other occupants exit the vehicle or anytime thereafter. A vehicle rollaway increases the risk of injury to exiting occupants and bystanders.
May 14, 2014	14V247000	2013, 2014 Malibu	Some models equipped with a 2.5L engine with the auto stop/start option may experience a complete loss of brake vacuum assist, disabling the hydraulic boost assist. If the hydraulic boost assist is disabled, slowing or stopping the vehicle will require additional brake pedal effort and a lengthened stopping distance. Both of these effects increase the risk of a crash.
Mar 23, 2015	15V164000	2013, 2014, 2015 Malibu	On some models, the Slide or Tilt switch for the roof panel may not be adequately recessed to prevent the switch from inadvertently being pressed. The Slide or Tilt roof panel switch may inadvertently be pressed and the roof panel may auto-close unexpectedly, increasing the risk of pinch injury.
Apr 24, 2015	15V245000	2013 Malibu	On some models, the console transmission gear selection indicator may not illuminate the shift position selected. If the console shift indicator does not illuminate the transmission gear selection, a driver could inadvertently select a transmission position other than the position the driver intended, increasing the risk of a crash.
Oct 16, 2015	15V666000	2015 Malibu	Some models may have front seat-mounted side impact airbags whose inflator may rupture upon its deployment. In the event of a crash necessitating deployment of one or both of the side impact airbags, the airbag's inflator may rupture and the airbag may not properly inflate. The rupture could cause metal fragments to strike the vehicle occupants, potentially resulting in serious injury or death. Additionally, if the airbag does not properly inflate, the driver or passenger is at an increased risk of injury.
Feb 11, 2016	16V084000	2016 Malibu	On some models, the radio may intermittently fail to provide an audio warning when the key has been left in the ignition and the door is opened or when the driver does not fasten their seat belt. An unbelted driver is at greater risk of injury in a crash.
Mar 2, 2016	16V125000	2016 Malibu	On some models, the driver's frontal airbag may improperly inflate during second-stage deployment in the event of a high-speed crash. An improperly inflated airbag increases the risk of injury.

Recall date	Recall campaign number	Model(s) affected	Concern
Mar 11, 2016	16V151000	2016 Malibu	On some modes, the two weld studs that secure the front and rear side impact airbags may fracture and separate from the airbag during deployment. Fractured weld studs may allow the side airbag to move out of position during deployment, increasing the risk of injury.
May 5, 2016	16V272000	2016 Malibu	On some models, the memory chip in the Electronic Brake Control Module (EBCM) may fail and cause the loss of electronically controlled brake systems including anti-lock brakes (ABS) and Electronic Stability Control (ESC). If the EBCM fails, the primary braking system will still function, but the loss of the ABS and ESC increases the risk of a crash.
July 05, 2016	16V502000	2013, 2016 Malibu	Some models may have been serviced with similar defective replacement electronic park lock levers. If the key is removed without the transmission in PARK, the vehicle may roll away as occupants are exiting, increasing the risk of injury.
Oct 26, 2016	16V781000	2016 Malibu	On some models, the fabric of the side-impact airbag cushion may tear during deployment. If the airbag tears during deployment, it might not perform as designed, increasing the risk of injury in the event of a crash.
Dec 2, 2016	16V87000	2017 Malibu	On some models, the right-hand rear side airbag inflator manifold may have insufficient welds. Insufficient welds could cause the inflator to separate and propel airbag debris into the cabin during a crash. Also, the inflator could fail to inflate during a crash, increasing the risk of injury.
May 31, 2018	18V358000	2016, 2017, 2018 Malibu	On some models, the high-pressure fuel pump may detach from its mounting flange, possibly resulting in the pump damaging the high-pressure fuel line. A damaged fuel line can create a fuel leak, increasing the risk of a fire.
Jun 14, 2018	18V400000	2016, 2017, 2018 Malibu	On some models, a Passenger Presence System (PPS) may have been installed that was not correctly calibrated to the vehicle's seat type. As a result, the PPS may not properly identify an adult passenger from a child passenger in the front passenger seat, potentially causing the airbag to not deploy when it should, or causing the airbag to deploy when it shouldn't. In the event of a crash, improper airbag deployment can increase the risk of injury.
Aug 30, 2018	18V576000	2018, 2019 Malibu	On some models, the rear brake caliper pistons may have an insufficient coating, causing gas pockets to form, potentially reducing rear brake performance. A reduction of braking performance can increase the risk of a crash.
Sep 06, 2019	19V642000	2018 Malibu	On models equipped with 1.5L turbocharged engines, an error in the Engine Control Module (ECM) software may result in the fuel injectors being disabled. Disabled fuel injectors would prevent the engine from starting or cause a stall, increasing the risk of a crash.

Buying parts

Replacement parts are available from many sources. Our advice concerning them is as follows:

Retail auto parts stores: Good auto parts stores will stock frequently needed components which wear out relatively fast, such as clutch components, exhaust systems, brake parts, tune-up parts, etc. These stores often supply new or reconditioned parts on an exchange basis, which can save a considerable amount of money. Discount auto parts stores are often very good places to buy materials and parts needed for general vehicle maintenance such as oil, grease, filters, spark plugs, belts, touch-up paint, bulbs, etc. They also usually sell tools and general accessories, have convenient hours, charge lower prices and can give you knowledgeable answers to your questions. To be sure of obtaining the correct parts, have engine and chassis numbers available and, if possible, take the old parts along for positive identification.

Authorized dealer parts department: This is the best source for parts which are unique to the vehicle and not generally available elsewhere. Prices for most parts tend to be higher than at retail auto parts stores.

Auto recyclers or salvage yards: Auto recyclers and salvage yards are good sources for components that are specific to the vehicle and not subject to wear, such as fenders, bumpers, trim pieces, etc. You can expect substantial savings by going this route, and self-service salvage yards offer still more savings if you're willing to bring your own tools and pull the part(s) yourself.

Warranty information: If the vehicle is still covered under warranty, be sure that any replacement parts purchased - regardless of the source - do not invalidate the warranty! In most cases, replacement parts, even from aftermarket suppliers, are designed to meet manufacturer specifications. If in doubt, check with the parts supplier.

Because of a Federally mandated extended warranty that covers the emissions control system components, check with your dealer about warranty coverage before working on any emissions-related systems.

Discount auto parts stores provide a wide variety of parts, and the knowledgeable counter-people found there are an excellent resource

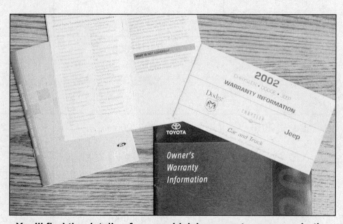

You'll find the details of your vehicle's warranty coverage in the warranty book provided by the manufacturer

Maintenance techniques, tools and working facilities

Maintenance techniques

There are a number of techniques involved in maintenance and repair that will be referred to throughout this manual. Application of these techniques will enable the home mechanic to be more efficient, better organized and capable of performing the various tasks properly, which will ensure that the repair job is thorough and complete.

Fasteners

Fasteners are nuts, bolts, studs and screws used to hold two or more parts together. There are a few things to keep in mind when working with fasteners. Almost all of them use a locking device of some type, either a lockwasher, locknut, locking tab or thread adhesive. All threaded fasteners should be clean and straight, with undamaged threads and undamaged corners on the hex head where the wrench fits. Develop the habit of replacing all damaged nuts and bolts with new ones. Special locknuts with nylon or fiber inserts can only be used once. If they are removed, they lose their locking ability and must be replaced with new ones.

Rusted nuts and bolts should be treated with a penetrating fluid to ease removal and prevent breakage. Some mechanics use turpentine in a spout-type oil can, which works quite well. After applying the rust penetrant, let it work for a few minutes before trying to loosen the nut or bolt. Badly rusted fasteners may have to be chiseled or sawed off or removed with a special nut breaker, available at tool stores.

If a bolt or stud breaks off in an assembly, it can be drilled and removed with a special tool commonly available for this purpose. Most automotive machine shops can perform this task, as well as other repair procedures, such as the repair of threaded holes that have been stripped out.

Flat washers and lockwashers, when removed from an assembly, should always be replaced exactly as removed. Replace any damaged washers with new ones. Never use a lockwasher on any soft metal surface (such as aluminum), thin sheet metal or plastic.

Fastener sizes

For a number of reasons, automobile manufacturers are making wider and wider use of metric fasteners. Therefore, it is important to be able to tell the difference between standard (sometimes called U.S. or SAE) and metric hardware, since they cannot be interchanged.

All bolts, whether standard or metric, are sized according to diameter, thread pitch and length. For example, a standard 1/2 - 13 x 1 bolt is 1/2 inch in diameter, has 13 threads per inch and is 1 inch long. An M12 - 1.75 x 25 metric bolt is 12 mm in diameter, has a thread pitch of 1.75 mm (the distance between threads) and is 25 mm long. The two bolts are nearly identical, and easily confused, but they are not interchangeable.

In addition to the differences in diameter, thread pitch and length, metric and standard bolts can also be distinguished by examining the bolt heads. To begin with, the distance across the flats on a standard bolt head is measured in inches, while the same dimension on a metric bolt is sized in millimeters (the same

is true for nuts). As a result, a standard wrench should not be used on a metric bolt and a metric wrench should not be used on a standard bolt. Also, most standard bolts have slashes radiating out from the center of the head to denote the grade or strength of the bolt, which is an indication of the amount of torque that can be applied to it. The greater the number of slashes, the greater the strength of the bolt. Grades 0 through 5 are commonly used on automobiles. Metric bolts have a property class (grade) number, rather than a slash, molded into their heads to indicate bolt strength. In this case, the higher the number, the stronger the bolt. Property class numbers 8.8, 9.8 and 10.9 are commonly used on automobiles.

Strength markings can also be used to distinguish standard hex nuts from metric hex nuts. Many standard nuts have dots stamped into one side, while metric nuts are marked with a number. The greater the number of dots, or the higher the number, the greater the strength of the nut.

Metric studs are also marked on their ends according to property class (grade).

Larger studs are numbered (the same as metric bolts), while smaller studs carry a geometric code to denote grade.

It should be noted that many fasteners, especially Grades 0 through 2, have no distinguishing marks on them. When such is the case, the only way to determine whether it is standard or metric is to measure the thread pitch or compare it to a known fastener of the same size.

Standard fasteners are often referred to as SAE, as opposed to metric. However, it should be noted that SAE technically refers to a non-metric fine thread fastener only. Coarse thread non-metric fasteners are referred to as USS sizes.

Since fasteners of the same size (both standard and metric) may have different strength ratings, be sure to reinstall any bolts, studs or nuts removed from your vehicle in their original locations. Also, when replacing a fastener with a new one, make sure that the new one has a strength rating equal to or greater than the original.

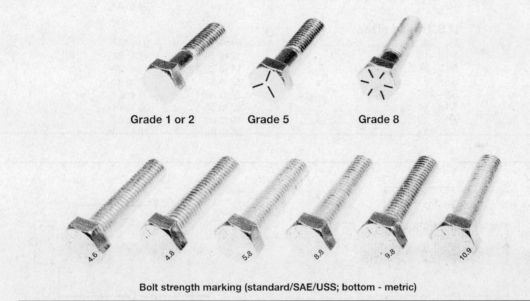

Grade 1 or 2   Grade 5   Grade 8

Bolt strength marking (standard/SAE/USS; bottom - metric)

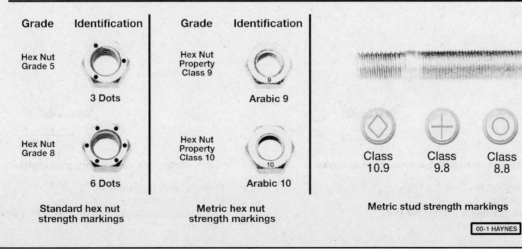

Grade	Identification
Hex Nut Grade 5	3 Dots
Hex Nut Grade 8	6 Dots

Standard hex nut strength markings

Grade	Identification
Hex Nut Property Class 9	Arabic 9
Hex Nut Property Class 10	Arabic 10

Metric hex nut strength markings

Class 10.9   Class 9.8   Class 8.8

Metric stud strength markings

Tightening sequences and procedures

Most threaded fasteners should be tightened to a specific torque value (torque is the twisting force applied to a threaded component such as a nut or bolt). Overtightening the fastener can weaken it and cause it to break, while undertightening can cause it to eventually come loose. Bolts, screws and studs, depending on the material they are made of and their thread diameters, have specific torque values, many of which are noted in the Specifications at the beginning of each Chapter. Be sure to follow the torque recommendations closely. For fasteners not assigned a specific torque, a general torque value chart is presented here as a guide. These torque values are for dry (unlubricated) fasteners threaded into steel or cast iron (not aluminum). As was previously mentioned, the size and grade of a fastener determine the amount of torque that can safely be applied to it. The figures listed here are approximate for Grade 2 and Grade 3 fasteners. Higher grades can tolerate higher torque values.

Fasteners laid out in a pattern, such as cylinder head bolts, oil pan bolts, differential cover bolts, etc., must be loosened or tightened in sequence to avoid warping the component. This sequence will normally be shown in the appropriate Chapter. If a specific pattern is not given, the following procedures can be used to prevent warping.

Initially, the bolts or nuts should be assembled finger-tight only. Next, they should be tightened one full turn each, in a criss-cross or diagonal pattern. After each one has been tightened one full turn, return to the first one and tighten them all one-half turn, following the same pattern. Finally, tighten each of them one-quarter turn at a time until each fastener has been tightened to the proper torque. To loosen and remove the fasteners, the procedure would be reversed.

Metric thread sizes	Ft-lbs	Nm
M-6	6 to 9	9 to 12
M-8	14 to 21	19 to 28
M-10	28 to 40	38 to 54
M-12	50 to 71	68 to 96
M-14	80 to 140	109 to 154

Pipe thread sizes		
1/8	5 to 8	7 to 10
1/4	12 to 18	17 to 24
3/8	22 to 33	30 to 44
1/2	25 to 35	34 to 47

U.S. thread sizes		
1/4 - 20	6 to 9	9 to 12
5/16 - 18	12 to 18	17 to 24
5/16 - 24	14 to 20	19 to 27
3/8 - 16	22 to 32	30 to 43
3/8 - 24	27 to 38	37 to 51
7/16 - 14	40 to 55	55 to 74
7/16 - 20	40 to 60	55 to 81
1/2 - 13	55 to 80	75 to 108

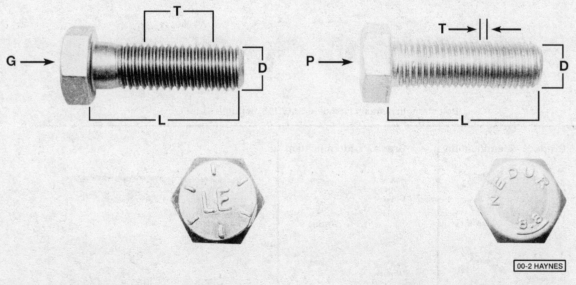

Standard (SAE and USS) bolt dimensions/grade marks

G   Grade marks (bolt strength)
L   Length (in inches)
T   Thread pitch (number of threads per inch)
D   Nominal diameter (in inches)

Metric bolt dimensions/grade marks

P   Property class (bolt strength)
L   Length (in millimeters)
T   Thread pitch (distance between threads in millimeters)
D   Diameter

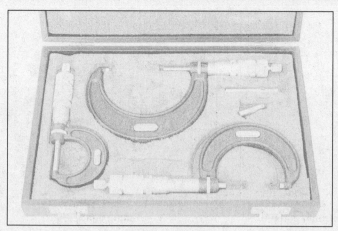

Micrometer set

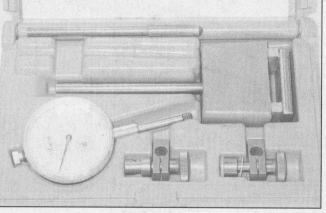

Dial indicator set

Component disassembly

Component disassembly should be done with care and purpose to help ensure that the parts go back together properly. Always keep track of the sequence in which parts are removed. Make note of special characteristics or marks on parts that can be installed more than one way, such as a grooved thrust washer on a shaft. It is a good idea to lay the disassembled parts out on a clean surface in the order that they were removed. It may also be helpful to make sketches or take instant photos of components before removal.

When removing fasteners from a component, keep track of their locations. Sometimes threading a bolt back in a part, or putting the washers and nut back on a stud, can prevent mix-ups later. If nuts and bolts cannot be returned to their original locations, they should be kept in a compartmented box or a series of small boxes. A cupcake or muffin tin is ideal for this purpose, since each cavity can hold the bolts and nuts from a particular area (i.e. oil pan bolts, valve cover bolts, engine mount bolts, etc.). A pan of this type is especially helpful when working on assemblies with very small parts, such as the carburetor, alternator, valve train or interior dash and trim pieces. The cavities can be marked with paint or tape to identify the contents.

Whenever wiring looms, harnesses or connectors are separated, it is a good idea to identify the two halves with numbered pieces of masking tape so they can be easily reconnected.

Gasket sealing surfaces

Throughout any vehicle, gaskets are used to seal the mating surfaces between two parts and keep lubricants, fluids, vacuum or pressure contained in an assembly.

Many times these gaskets are coated with a liquid or paste-type gasket sealing compound before assembly. Age, heat and pressure can sometimes cause the two parts to stick together so tightly that they are very difficult to separate. Often, the assembly can be loosened by striking it with a soft-face hammer near the mating surfaces. A regular hammer can be used if a block of wood is placed between the hammer and the part. Do not hammer on cast parts or parts that could be easily damaged. With any particularly stubborn part, always recheck to make sure that every fastener has been removed.

Avoid using a screwdriver or bar to pry apart an assembly, as they can easily mar the gasket sealing surfaces of the parts, which must remain smooth. If prying is absolutely necessary, use an old broom handle, but keep in mind that extra clean up will be necessary if the wood splinters.

After the parts are separated, the old gasket must be carefully scraped off and the gasket surfaces cleaned. Stubborn gasket material can be soaked with rust penetrant or treated with a special chemical to soften it so it can be easily scraped off. **Caution:** *Never use gasket removal solutions or caustic chemicals on plastic or other composite components.* A scraper can be fashioned from a piece of copper tubing by flattening and sharpening one end. Copper is recommended because it is usually softer than the surfaces to be scraped, which reduces the chance of gouging the part. Some gaskets can be removed with a wire brush, but regardless of the method used, the mating surfaces must be left clean and smooth. If for some reason the gasket surface is gouged, then a gasket sealer thick enough to fill scratches will have to be used during reassembly of the components. For most applications, a non-drying (or semi-drying) gasket sealer should be used.

Hose removal tips

Warning: *If the vehicle is equipped with air conditioning, do not disconnect any of the A/C hoses without first having the system depressurized by a dealer service department or a service station.*

Hose removal precautions closely parallel gasket removal precautions. Avoid scratching or gouging the surface that the hose mates against or the connection may leak. This is especially true for radiator hoses. Because of various chemical reactions, the rubber in hoses can bond itself to the metal spigot that the hose fits over. To remove a hose, first loosen the hose clamps that secure it to the spigot. Then, with slip-joint pliers, grab the hose at the clamp and rotate it around the spigot. Work it back and forth until it is completely free, then pull it off. Silicone or other lubricants will ease removal if they can be applied between the hose and the outside of the spigot. Apply the same lubricant to the inside of the hose and the outside of the spigot to simplify installation.

As a last resort (and if the hose is to be replaced with a new one anyway), the rubber can be slit with a knife and the hose peeled from the spigot. If this must be done, be careful that the metal connection is not damaged.

If a hose clamp is broken or damaged, do not reuse it. Wire-type clamps usually weaken with age, so it is a good idea to replace them with screw-type clamps whenever a hose is removed.

Tools

A selection of good tools is a basic requirement for anyone who plans to maintain and repair his or her own vehicle. For the owner who has few tools, the initial investment might seem high, but when compared to the spiraling costs of professional auto maintenance and repair, it is a wise one.

To help the owner decide which tools are needed to perform the tasks detailed in this manual, the following tool lists are offered: *Maintenance and minor repair, Repair/overhaul* and *Special.*

The newcomer to practical mechanics should start off with the *maintenance and minor repair* tool kit, which is adequate for the simpler jobs performed on a vehicle. Then, as confidence and experience grow, the owner can tackle more difficult tasks, buying additional tools as they are needed. Eventually the basic kit will be expanded into the *repair and overhaul* tool set. Over a period of time, the experienced do-it-yourselfer will assemble a tool set complete enough for most repair and overhaul procedures and will add tools from the special category when it is felt that the expense is justified by the frequency of use.

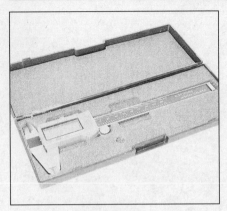

Digital caliper

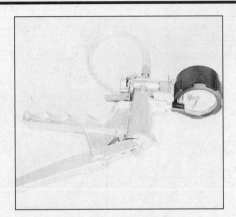

Hand-operated vacuum pump

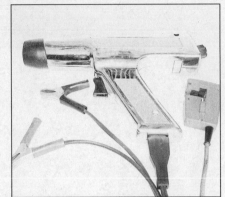

Timing light

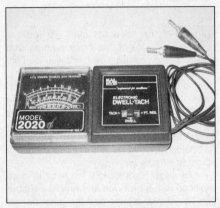

Tachometer and dwellmeter

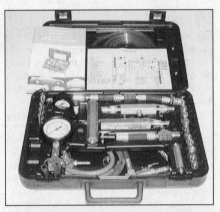

Fuel pressure guage set

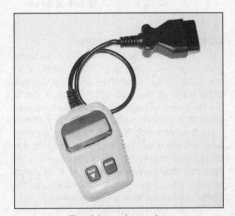

Trouble code reader

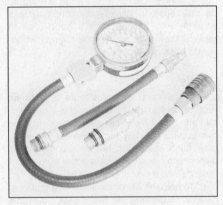

Compression gauge

Cooling system pressure tester

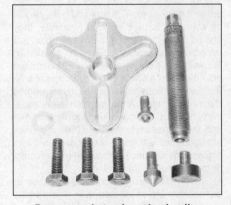

Damper and steering wheel puller

Maintenance and minor repair tool kit

The tools in this list should be considered the minimum required for performance of routine maintenance, servicing and minor repair work. We recommend the purchase of combination wrenches (box-end and open-end combined in one wrench). While more expensive than open end wrenches, they offer the advantages of both types of wrench.

Combination wrench set
(1/4-inch to 1 inch or 6 mm to 19 mm)
Adjustable wrench, 8 inch

Spark plug wrench with rubber insert
Spark plug gap adjusting tool
Feeler gauge set
Brake bleeder wrench
Standard screwdriver
(5/16-inch x 6 inch)
Phillips screwdriver (No. 2 x 6 inch)
Combination pliers - 6 inch
Hacksaw and assortment of blades
Tire pressure gauge
Grease gun
Oil can
Fine emery cloth
Wire brush

Battery post and cable cleaning tool
Oil filter wrench
Funnel (medium size)
Safety goggles
Jackstands (2)
Drain pan

Note: *If basic tune-ups are going to be part of routine maintenance, it will be necessary to purchase a good quality stroboscopic timing light and combination tachometer/dwell meter. Although they are included in the list of special tools, it is mentioned here because they are absolutely necessary for tuning most vehicles properly.*

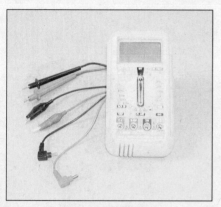

Electrical multimeter

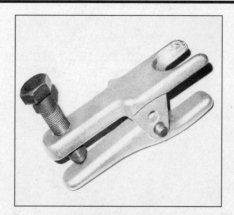

Balljoint separator

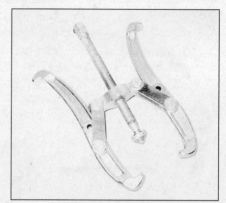

General purpose puller

Brake hold-down spring tool

Impact screwdriver

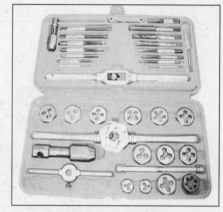

Tap and die set

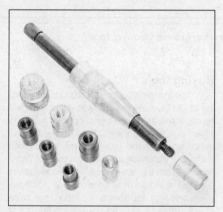

Clutch plate alignment tool

Torque angle gauge

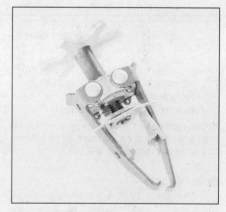

Valve spring compressor

Repair and overhaul tool set

These tools are essential for anyone who plans to perform major repairs and are in addition to those in the maintenance and minor repair tool kit. Included is a comprehensive set of sockets which, though expensive, are invaluable because of their versatility, especially when various extensions and drives are available. We recommend the 1/2-inch drive over the 3/8-inch drive. Although the larger drive is bulky and more expensive, it has the capacity of accepting a very wide range of large sockets. Ideally, however, the mechanic should have a 3/8-inch drive set and a 1/2-inch drive set.

Socket set(s)
Reversible ratchet
Extension - 10 inch
Universal joint
Torque wrench
 (same size drive as sockets)
Ball peen hammer - 8 ounce
Soft-face hammer (plastic/rubber)
Standard screwdriver (1/4-inch x 6 inch)
Standard screwdriver (stubby - 5/16-inch)
Phillips screwdriver (No. 3 x 8 inch)
Phillips screwdriver (stubby - No. 2)
Pliers - vise grip

Pliers - lineman's
Pliers - needle nose
Pliers - snap-ring (internal and external)
Cold chisel (1/2-inch)
Scribe
Scraper (made from flattened
 copper tubing)
Centerpunch
Pin punches (1/16, 1/8, 3/16-inch)
Steel rule/straightedge (12 inch)
Allen wrench set (1/8 to 3/8-inch or
 4 mm to 10 mm)
A selection of files

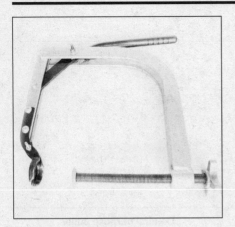

Valve spring compressor

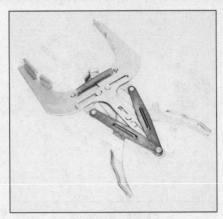

Piston ring removal and installation tool

Piston ring compressor

Cylinder hone

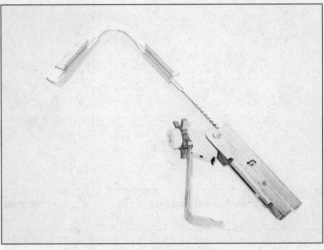

Piston ring groove cleaning tool

Wire brush (large)
Jackstands (second set)
Jack (scissor or hydraulic type)

Note: *Another tool which is often useful is an electric drill with a chuck capacity of 3/8-inch and a set of good quality drill bits.*

Special tools

The tools in this list include those which are not used regularly, are expensive to buy, or which need to be used in accordance with their manufacturer's instructions. Unless these tools will be used frequently, it is not very economical to purchase many of them. A consideration would be to split the cost and use between yourself and a friend or friends. In addition, most of these tools can be obtained from a tool rental shop on a temporary basis.

This list primarily contains only those tools and instruments widely available to the public, and not those special tools produced by the vehicle manufacturer for distribution to dealer service departments. Occasionally, references to the manufacturer's special tools are included in the text of this manual. Generally, an alternative method

of doing the job without the special tool is offered. However, sometimes there is no alternative to their use. Where this is the case, and the tool cannot be purchased or borrowed, the work should be turned over to the dealer service department or an automotive repair shop.

Valve spring compressor
Piston ring groove cleaning tool
Piston ring compressor
Piston ring installation tool
Cylinder compression gauge
Cylinder ridge reamer
Cylinder surfacing hone
Cylinder bore gauge
Micrometers and/or dial calipers
Hydraulic lifter removal tool
Balljoint separator
Universal-type puller
Impact screwdriver
Dial indicator set
Stroboscopic timing light (inductive pickup)
Hand operated vacuum/pressure pump
Tachometer/dwell meter
Universal electrical multimeter
Cable hoist
Brake spring removal and installation tools
Floor jack

Buying tools

For the do-it-yourselfer who is just starting to get involved in vehicle maintenance and repair, there are a number of options available when purchasing tools. If maintenance and minor repair is the extent of the work to be done, the purchase of individual tools is satisfactory. If, on the other hand, extensive work is planned, it would be a good idea to purchase a modest tool set from one of the large retail chain stores. A set can usually be bought at a substantial savings over the individual tool prices, and they often come with a tool box. As additional tools are needed, add-on sets, individual tools and a larger tool box can be purchased to expand the tool selection. Building a tool set gradually allows the cost of the tools to be spread over a longer period of time and gives the mechanic the freedom to choose only those tools that will actually be used.

Tool stores will often be the only source of some of the special tools that are needed, but regardless of where tools are bought, try to avoid cheap ones, especially when buying screwdrivers and sockets, because they won't last very long. The expense involved in replacing cheap tools will eventually be greater than the initial cost of quality tools.

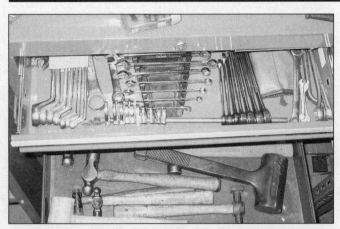

Keep your tools clean and organized – you'll spend less time under the hood, and the time spent will be more pleasant

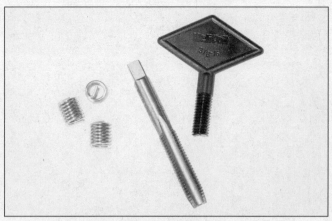

Thread repair kits like this one can be purchased at your local auto parts store

Care and maintenance of tools

Good tools are expensive, so it makes sense to treat them with respect. Keep them clean and in usable condition and store them properly when not in use. Always wipe off any dirt, grease or metal chips before putting them away. Never leave tools lying around in the work area. Upon completion of a job, always check closely under the hood for tools that may have been left there so they won't get lost during a test drive.

Some tools, such as screwdrivers, pliers, wrenches and sockets, can be hung on a panel mounted on the garage or workshop wall, while others should be kept in a tool box or tray. Measuring instruments, gauges, meters, etc. must be carefully stored where they cannot be damaged by weather or impact from other tools.

When tools are used with care and stored properly, they will last a very long time. Even with the best of care, though, tools will wear out if used frequently. When a tool is damaged or worn out, replace it. Subsequent jobs will be safer and more enjoyable if you do.

How to repair damaged threads

Sometimes, the internal threads of a nut or bolt hole can become stripped, usually from overtightening. Stripping threads is an all-too-common occurrence, especially when working with aluminum parts, because aluminum is so soft that it easily strips out.

Usually, external or internal threads are only partially stripped. After they've been cleaned up with a tap or die, they'll still work. Sometimes, however, threads are badly damaged. When this happens, you've got three choices:

1) *Drill and tap the hole to the next suitable oversize and install a larger diameter bolt, screw or stud.*
2) *Drill and tap the hole to accept a threaded plug, then drill and tap the plug to the original screw size. You can also buy a plug already threaded to the original size. Then you simply drill a hole to the specified size, then run the threaded plug into the hole with a bolt and jam nut. Once the plug is fully seated, remove the jam nut and bolt.*

3) *The third method uses a patented thread repair kit like Heli-Coil or Slimsert. These easy-to-use kits are designed to repair damaged threads in straight-through holes and blind holes. Both are available as kits which can handle a variety of sizes and thread patterns. Drill the hole, then tap it with the special included tap. Install the Heli-Coil and the hole is back to its original diameter and thread pitch.*

Regardless of which method you use, be sure to proceed calmly and carefully. A little impatience or carelessness during one of these relatively simple procedures can ruin your whole day's work and cost you a bundle if you wreck an expensive part.

Working facilities

Not to be overlooked when discussing tools is the workshop. If anything more than routine maintenance is to be carried out, some sort of suitable work area is essential.

It is understood, and appreciated, that many home mechanics do not have a good workshop or garage available, and end up removing an engine or doing major repairs outside. It is recommended, however, that the overhaul or repair be completed under the cover of a roof.

A clean, flat workbench or table of comfortable working height is an absolute necessity.

The workbench should be equipped with a vise that has a jaw opening of at least four inches.

As mentioned previously, some clean, dry storage space is also required for tools, as well as the lubricants, fluids, cleaning solvents, etc. which soon become necessary.

Sometimes waste oil and fluids, drained from the engine or cooling system during normal maintenance or repairs, present a disposal problem. To avoid pouring them on the ground or into a sewage system, pour the used fluids into large containers, seal them with caps and take them to an authorized disposal site or recycling center. Plastic jugs, such as old antifreeze containers, are ideal for this purpose.

Always keep a supply of old newspapers and clean rags available. Old towels are excellent for mopping up spills. Many mechanics use rolls of paper towels for most work because they are readily available and disposable. To help keep the area under the vehicle clean, a large cardboard box can be cut open and flattened to protect the garage or shop floor.

Whenever working over a painted surface, such as when leaning over a fender to service something under the hood, always cover it with an old blanket or bedspread to protect the finish. Vinyl covered pads, made especially for this purpose, are available at auto parts stores.

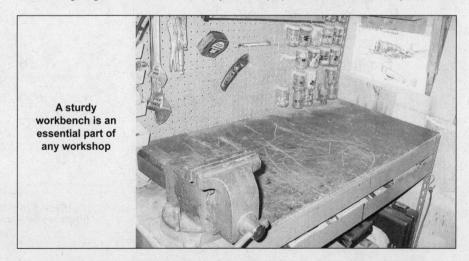

A sturdy workbench is an essential part of any workshop

Jacking and towing

Jacking

The jack supplied with the vehicle should only be used for raising the vehicle for changing a tire or placing jackstands under the frame.

Warning: *Never crawl under the vehicle or start the engine when the jack is being used as the only means of support.*

All vehicles are supplied with a scissors-type jack located under the spare tire **(see illustration)**.

When jacking the vehicle, it should be engaged with the rocker panel flange **(see illustration)**.

The vehicle should be on level ground with the wheels blocked and the transmission in Park (automatic). Pry off the hub cap (if equipped) using the tapered end of the lug wrench. Loosen the lug nuts one-half turn and leave them in place until the wheel is raised off the ground.

Place the jack under the side of the vehicle in the indicated position. Use the supplied wrench to turn the jackscrew clockwise until the wheel is raised off the ground. Remove the lug nuts, pull off the wheel and replace it with the spare.

With the beveled side in, reinstall the lug nuts and tighten them until snug. Lower the vehicle by turning the jackscrew counterclockwise. Remove the jack and tighten the nuts in a diagonal pattern to the torque listed in the Chapter 1 Specifications. If a torque wrench is not available, have the torque checked by a service station as soon as possible. Replace the hubcap by placing it in position and using the heel of your hand or a rubber mallet to seat it.

Towing

These models can be towed with all four wheels on the ground, from the front; this is known as "Dinghy towing." The transmission must be in Neutral, and the ignition key in the ACC position. If the vehicle is being towed more than a few hours, the engine should be run for five minutes and the shifter cycled through each gear position to ensure the proper lubrication of the transaxle. If the engine can't be run at least five minutes a day, the vehicle should not be towed by this method.

Note: *To prevent the battery from draining, remove the BATT1 (50-amp) fuse from the underhood fuse/relay box.*

These models can also be towed with the front wheels on a dolly.

Caution: *Don't tow a FWD vehicle with the front tires on the ground if the compact spare tire is installed on one of the front wheels - the transaxle could be damaged.*

In an emergency, the vehicle can be towed a short distance with a cable or chain attached to one of the towing eyelets located under the front or rear bumpers. The driver must remain in the vehicle to operate the steering and brakes (remember that power steering and power brakes will not work with the engine off).

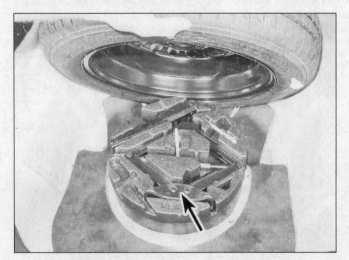

Locate the scissors-type jack under the spare tire

The jack fits in the cutout of the rocker panel flange (there are two jacking points on each side of the vehicle) - front shown, rear identical

Booster battery (jump) starting

Observe these precautions when using a booster battery to start a vehicle:

a) Before connecting the booster battery, make sure the ignition switch is in the Off position.
b) Turn off the lights, heater and other electrical loads.
c) Your eyes should be shielded. Safety goggles are a good idea.
d) Make sure the booster battery is the same voltage as the dead one in the vehicle.
e) The two vehicles MUST NOT TOUCH each other!
f) Make sure the transaxle is in Neutral (manual) or Park (automatic).

g) If the booster battery is not a maintenance-free type, remove the vent caps and lay a cloth over the vent holes.

Connect the red jumper cable to the positive (+) terminals of each vehicle (see illustrations).
Note: On 2016 and later models, the battery is located in the trunk or rear hatch area. A remote positive terminal for jump starting is located under the hood, at the rear of the fuse/relay box near the coolant expansion tank. A grounding lug for the negative jumper cable is located on the left (driver's side) strut tower.

Connect one end of the black jumper cable to the negative (-) terminal of the booster battery. The other end of this cable should be connected to a good ground on the vehicle to be started, such as a bolt or bracket on the body.

Start the engine using the booster battery, then, with the engine running at idle speed, disconnect the jumper cables in the reverse order of connection.

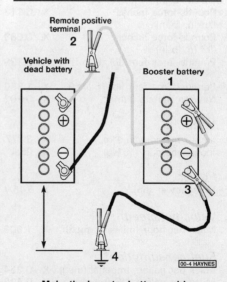

Make the booster battery cable connections in the numerical order shown (note that the negative cable of the booster battery is NOT attached to the negative terminal of the dead battery)

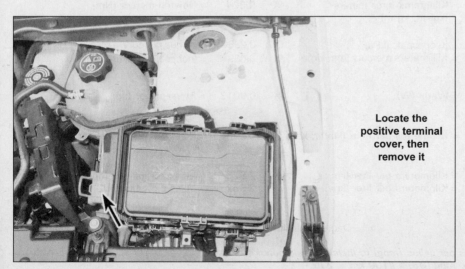

Locate the positive terminal cover, then remove it

Conversion factors

Length (distance)

Inches (in)	X	25.4	= Millimeters (mm)	X	0.0394	= Inches (in)
Feet (ft)	X	0.305	= Meters (m)	X	3.281	= Feet (ft)
Miles	X	1.609	= Kilometers (km)	X	0.621	= Miles

Volume (capacity)

Cubic inches (cu in; in³)	X	16.387	= Cubic centimeters (cc; cm³)	X	0.061	= Cubic inches (cu in; in³)
Imperial pints (Imp pt)	X	0.568	= Liters (l)	X	1.76	= Imperial pints (Imp pt)
Imperial quarts (Imp qt)	X	1.137	= Liters (l)	X	0.88	= Imperial quarts (Imp qt)
Imperial quarts (Imp qt)	X	1.201	= US quarts (US qt)	X	0.833	= Imperial quarts (Imp qt)
US quarts (US qt)	X	0.946	= Liters (l)	X	1.057	= US quarts (US qt)
Imperial gallons (Imp gal)	X	4.546	= Liters (l)	X	0.22	= Imperial gallons (Imp gal)
Imperial gallons (Imp gal)	X	1.201	= US gallons (US gal)	X	0.833	= Imperial gallons (Imp gal)
US gallons (US gal)	X	3.785	= Liters (l)	X	0.264	= US gallons (US gal)

Mass (weight)

Ounces (oz)	X	28.35	= Grams (g)	X	0.035	= Ounces (oz)
Pounds (lb)	X	0.454	= Kilograms (kg)	X	2.205	= Pounds (lb)

Force

Ounces-force (ozf; oz)	X	0.278	= Newtons (N)	X	3.6	= Ounces-force (ozf; oz)
Pounds-force (lbf; lb)	X	4.448	= Newtons (N)	X	0.225	= Pounds-force (lbf; lb)
Newtons (N)	X	0.1	= Kilograms-force (kgf; kg)	X	9.81	= Newtons (N)

Pressure

Pounds-force per square inch (psi; lbf/in²; lb/in²)	X	0.070	= Kilograms-force per square centimeter (kgf/cm²; kg/cm²)	X	14.223	= Pounds-force per square inch (psi; lbf/in²; lb/in²)
Pounds-force per square inch (psi; lbf/in²; lb/in²)	X	0.068	= Atmospheres (atm)	X	14.696	= Pounds-force per square inch (psi; lbf/in²; lb/in²)
Pounds-force per square inch (psi; lbf/in²; lb/in²)	X	0.069	= Bars	X	14.5	= Pounds-force per square inch (psi; lbf/in²; lb/in²)
Pounds-force per square inch (psi; lbf/in²; lb/in²)	X	6.895	= Kilopascals (kPa)	X	0.145	= Pounds-force per square inch (psi; lbf/in²; lb/in²)
Kilopascals (kPa)	X	0.01	= Kilograms-force per square centimeter (kgf/cm²; kg/cm²)	X	98.1	= Kilopascals (kPa)

Torque (moment of force)

Pounds-force inches (lbf in; lb in)	X	1.152	= Kilograms-force centimeter (kgf cm; kg cm)	X	0.868	= Pounds-force inches (lbf in; lb in)
Pounds-force inches (lbf in; lb in)	X	0.113	= Newton meters (Nm)	X	8.85	= Pounds-force inches (lbf in; lb in)
Pounds-force inches (lbf in; lb in)	X	0.083	= Pounds-force feet (lbf ft; lb ft)	X	12	= Pounds-force inches (lbf in; lb in)
Pounds-force feet (lbf ft; lb ft)	X	0.138	= Kilograms-force meters (kgf m; kg m)	X	7.233	= Pounds-force feet (lbf ft; lb ft)
Pounds-force feet (lbf ft; lb ft)	X	1.356	= Newton meters (Nm)	X	0.738	= Pounds-force feet (lbf ft; lb ft)
Newton meters (Nm)	X	0.102	= Kilograms-force meters (kgf m; kg m)	X	9.804	= Newton meters (Nm)

Vacuum

Inches mercury (in. Hg)	X	3.377	= Kilopascals (kPa)	X	0.2961	= Inches mercury
Inches mercury (in. Hg)	X	25.4	= Millimeters mercury (mm Hg)	X	0.0394	= Inches mercury

Power

Horsepower (hp)	X	745.7	= Watts (W)	X	0.0013	= Horsepower (hp)

Velocity (speed)

Miles per hour (miles/hr; mph)	X	1.609	= Kilometers per hour (km/hr; kph)	X	0.621	= Miles per hour (miles/hr; mph)

Fuel consumption*

Miles per gallon, Imperial (mpg)	X	0.354	= Kilometers per liter (km/l)	X	2.825	= Miles per gallon, Imperial (mpg)
Miles per gallon, US (mpg)	X	0.425	= Kilometers per liter (km/l)	X	2.352	= Miles per gallon, US (mpg)

Temperature

Degrees Fahrenheit = (°C x 1.8) + 32

Degrees Celsius (Degrees Centigrade; °C) = (°F - 32) x 0.56

*It is common practice to convert from miles per gallon (mpg) to liters/100 kilometers (l/100km),
where mpg (Imperial) x l/100 km = 282 and mpg (US) x l/100 km = 235

DECIMALS to MILLIMETERS

Decimal	mm	Decimal	mm
0.001	0.0254	0.500	12.7000
0.002	0.0508	0.510	12.9540
0.003	0.0762	0.520	13.2080
0.004	0.1016	0.530	13.4620
0.005	0.1270	0.540	13.7160
0.006	0.1524	0.550	13.9700
0.007	0.1778	0.560	14.2240
0.008	0.2032	0.570	14.4780
0.009	0.2286	0.580	14.7320
0.010	0.2540	0.590	14.9860
0.020	0.5080		
0.030	0.7620		
0.040	1.0160	0.600	15.2400
0.050	1.2700	0.610	15.4940
0.060	1.5240	0.620	15.7480
0.070	1.7780	0.630	16.0020
0.080	2.0320	0.640	16.2560
0.090	2.2860	0.650	16.5100
0.100	2.5400	0.660	16.7640
0.110	2.7940	0.670	17.0180
0.120	3.0480	0.680	17.2720
0.130	3.3020	0.690	17.5260
0.140	3.5560		
0.150	3.8100		
0.160	4.0640	0.700	17.7800
0.170	4.3180	0.710	18.0340
0.180	4.5720	0.720	18.2880
0.190	4.8260	0.730	18.5420
0.200	5.0800	0.740	18.7960
0.210	5.3340	0.750	19.0500
0.220	5.5880	0.760	19.3040
0.230	5.8420	0.770	19.5580
0.240	6.0960	0.780	19.8120
0.250	6.3500	0.790	20.0660
0.260	6.6040		
0.270	6.8580	0.800	20.3200
0.280	7.1120	0.810	20.5740
0.290	7.3660	0.820	20.8280
0.300	7.6200	0.830	21.0820
0.310	7.8740	0.840	21.3360
0.320	8.1280	0.850	21.5900
0.330	8.3820	0.860	21.8440
0.340	8.6360	0.870	22.0980
0.350	8.8900	0.880	22.3520
0.360	9.1440	0.890	22.6060
0.370	9.3980		
0.380	9.6520		
0.390	9.9060	0.900	22.8600
0.400	10.1600	0.910	23.1140
0.410	10.4140	0.920	23.3680
0.420	10.6680	0.930	23.6220
0.430	10.9220	0.940	23.8760
0.440	11.1760	0.950	24.1300
0.450	11.4300	0.960	24.3840
0.460	11.6840	0.970	24.6380
0.470	11.9380	0.980	24.8920
0.480	12.1920	0.990	25.1460
0.490	12.4460	1.000	25.4000

FRACTIONS to DECIMALS to MILLIMETERS

Fraction	Decimal	mm	Fraction	Decimal	mm
1/64	0.0156	0.3969	33/64	0.5156	13.0969
1/32	0.0312	0.7938	17/32	0.5312	13.4938
3/64	0.0469	1.1906	35/64	0.5469	13.8906
1/16	0.0625	1.5875	9/16	0.5625	14.2875
5/64	0.0781	1.9844	37/64	0.5781	14.6844
3/32	0.0938	2.3812	19/32	0.5938	15.0812
7/64	0.1094	2.7781	39/64	0.6094	15.4781
1/8	0.1250	3.1750	5/8	0.6250	15.8750
9/64	0.1406	3.5719	41/64	0.6406	16.2719
5/32	0.1562	3.9688	21/32	0.6562	16.6688
11/64	0.1719	4.3656	43/64	0.6719	17.0656
3/16	0.1875	4.7625	11/16	0.6875	17.4625
13/64	0.2031	5.1594	45/64	0.7031	17.8594
7/32	0.2188	5.5562	23/32	0.7188	18.2562
15/64	0.2344	5.9531	47/64	0.7344	18.6531
1/4	0.2500	6.3500	3/4	0.7500	19.0500
17/64	0.2656	6.7469	49/64	0.7656	19.4469
9/32	0.2812	7.1438	25/32	0.7812	19.8438
19/64	0.2969	7.5406	51/64	0.7969	20.2406
5/16	0.3125	7.9375	13/16	0.8125	20.6375
21/64	0.3281	8.3344	53/64	0.8281	21.0344
11/32	0.3438	8.7312	27/32	0.8438	21.4312
23/64	0.3594	9.1281	55/64	0.8594	21.8281
3/8	0.3750	9.5250	7/8	0.8750	22.2250
25/64	0.3906	9.9219	57/64	0.8906	22.6219
13/32	0.4062	10.3188	29/32	0.9062	23.0188
27/64	0.4219	10.7156	59/64	0.9219	23.4156
7/16	0.4375	11.1125	15/16	0.9375	23.8125
29/64	0.4531	11.5094	61/64	0.9531	24.2094
15/32	0.4688	11.9062	31/32	0.9688	24.6062
31/64	0.4844	12.3031	63/64	0.9844	25.0031
1/2	0.5000	12.7000	1	1.0000	25.4000

Automotive chemicals and lubricants

A number of automotive chemicals and lubricants are available for use during vehicle maintenance and repair. They include a wide variety of products ranging from cleaning solvents and degreasers to lubricants and protective sprays for rubber, plastic and vinyl.

Cleaners

Carburetor cleaner and choke cleaner is a strong solvent for gum, varnish and carbon. Most carburetor cleaners leave a dry-type lubricant film which will not harden or gum up. Because of this film it is not recommended for use on electrical components.

Brake system cleaner is used to remove brake dust, grease and brake fluid from the brake system, where clean surfaces are absolutely necessary. It leaves no residue and often eliminates brake squeal caused by contaminants.

Electrical cleaner removes oxidation, corrosion and carbon deposits from electrical contacts, restoring full current flow. It can also be used to clean spark plugs, carburetor jets, voltage regulators and other parts where an oil-free surface is desired.

Demoisturants remove water and moisture from electrical components such as alternators, voltage regulators, electrical connectors and fuse blocks. They are non-conductive and non-corrosive.

Degreasers are heavy-duty solvents used to remove grease from the outside of the engine and from chassis components. They can be sprayed or brushed on and, depending on the type, are rinsed off either with water or solvent.

Lubricants

Motor oil is the lubricant formulated for use in engines. It normally contains a wide variety of additives to prevent corrosion and reduce foaming and wear. Motor oil comes in various weights (viscosity ratings) from 0 to 50. The recommended weight of the oil depends on the season, temperature and the demands on the engine. Light oil is used in cold climates and under light load conditions. Heavy oil is used in hot climates and where high loads are encountered. Multi-viscosity oils are designed to have characteristics of both light and heavy oils and are available in a number of weights from 0W-20 to 20W-50.

Gear oil is designed to be used in differentials, manual transmissions and other areas where high-temperature lubrication is required.

Chassis and wheel bearing grease is a heavy grease used where increased loads and friction are encountered, such as for wheel bearings, balljoints, tie-rod ends and universal joints.

High-temperature wheel bearing grease is designed to withstand the extreme temperatures encountered by wheel bearings in disc brake equipped vehicles. It usually contains molybdenum disulfide (moly), which is a dry-type lubricant.

White grease is a heavy grease for metal-to-metal applications where water is a problem. White grease stays soft under both low and high temperatures (usually from -100 to +190-degrees F), and will not wash off or dilute in the presence of water.

Assembly lube is a special extreme pressure lubricant, usually containing moly, used to lubricate high-load parts (such as main and rod bearings and cam lobes) for initial start-up of a new engine. The assembly lube lubricates the parts without being squeezed out or washed away until the engine oiling system begins to function.

Silicone lubricants are used to protect rubber, plastic, vinyl and nylon parts.

Graphite lubricants are used where oils cannot be used due to contamination problems, such as in locks. The dry graphite will lubricate metal parts while remaining uncontaminated by dirt, water, oil or acids. It is electrically conductive and will not foul electrical contacts in locks such as the ignition switch.

Moly penetrants loosen and lubricate frozen, rusted and corroded fasteners and prevent future rusting or freezing.

Heat-sink grease is a special electrically non-conductive grease that is used for mounting electronic ignition modules where it is essential that heat is transferred away from the module.

Sealants

RTV sealant is one of the most widely used gasket compounds. Made from silicone, RTV is air curing, it seals, bonds, waterproofs, fills surface irregularities, remains flexible, doesn't shrink, is relatively easy to remove, and is used as a supplementary sealer with almost all low and medium temperature gaskets.

Anaerobic sealant is much like RTV in that it can be used either to seal gaskets or to form gaskets by itself. It remains flexible, is solvent resistant and fills surface imperfections. The difference between an anaerobic sealant and an RTV-type sealant is in the curing. RTV cures when exposed to air, while an anaerobic sealant cures only in the absence of air. This means that an anaerobic sealant cures only after the assembly of parts, sealing them together.

Thread and pipe sealant is used for sealing hydraulic and pneumatic fittings and vacuum lines. It is usually made from a Teflon compound, and comes in a spray, a paint-on liquid and as a wrap-around tape.

Chemicals

Anti-seize compound prevents seizing, galling, cold welding, rust and corrosion in fasteners. High-temperature anti-seize, usually made with copper and graphite lubricants, is used for exhaust system and exhaust manifold bolts.

Anaerobic locking compounds are used to keep fasteners from vibrating or working loose and cure only after installation, in the absence of air. Medium strength locking compound is used for small nuts, bolts and screws that may be removed later. High-strength locking compound is for large nuts, bolts and studs which aren't removed on a regular basis.

Oil additives range from viscosity index improvers to chemical treatments that claim to reduce internal engine friction. It should be noted that most oil manufacturers caution against using additives with their oils.

Gas additives perform several functions, depending on their chemical makeup. They usually contain solvents that help dissolve gum and varnish that build up on carburetor, fuel injection and intake parts. They also serve to break down carbon deposits that form on the inside surfaces of the combustion chambers. Some additives contain upper cylinder lubricants for valves and piston rings, and others contain chemicals to remove condensation from the gas tank.

Miscellaneous

Brake fluid is specially formulated hydraulic fluid that can withstand the heat and pressure encountered in brake systems. Care must be taken so this fluid does not come in contact with painted surfaces or plastics. An opened container should always be resealed to prevent contamination by water or dirt.

Weatherstrip adhesive is used to bond weatherstripping around doors, windows and trunk lids. It is sometimes used to attach trim pieces.

Undercoating is a petroleum-based, tar-like substance that is designed to protect metal surfaces on the underside of the vehicle from corrosion. It also acts as a sound-deadening agent by insulating the bottom of the vehicle.

Waxes and polishes are used to help protect painted and plated surfaces from the weather. Different types of paint may require the use of different types of wax and polish. Some polishes utilize a chemical or abrasive cleaner to help remove the top layer of oxidized (dull) paint on older vehicles. In recent years many non-wax polishes that contain a wide variety of chemicals such as polymers and silicones have been introduced. These non-wax polishes are usually easier to apply and last longer than conventional waxes and polishes.

Safety first!

Regardless of how enthusiastic you may be about getting on with the job at hand, take the time to ensure that your safety is not jeopardized. A moment's lack of attention can result in an accident, as can failure to observe certain simple safety precautions. The possibility of an accident will always exist, and the following points should not be considered a comprehensive list of all dangers. Rather, they are intended to make you aware of the risks and to encourage a safety conscious approach to all work you carry out on your vehicle.

Essential DOs and DON'Ts

DON'T rely on a jack when working under the vehicle. Always use approved jackstands to support the weight of the vehicle and place them under the recommended lift or support points.

DON'T attempt to loosen extremely tight fasteners (i.e. wheel lug nuts) while the vehicle is on a jack - it may fall.

DON'T start the engine without first making sure that the transmission is in Neutral (or Park where applicable) and the parking brake is set.

DON'T remove the radiator cap from a hot cooling system - let it cool or cover it with a cloth and release the pressure gradually.

DON'T attempt to drain the engine oil until you are sure it has cooled to the point that it will not burn you.

DON'T touch any part of the engine or exhaust system until it has cooled sufficiently to avoid burns.

DON'T siphon toxic liquids such as gasoline, antifreeze and brake fluid by mouth, or allow them to remain on your skin.

DON'T inhale brake lining dust - it is potentially hazardous (see *Asbestos* below).

DON'T allow spilled oil or grease to remain on the floor - wipe it up before someone slips on it.

DON'T use loose fitting wrenches or other tools which may slip and cause injury.

DON'T push on wrenches when loosening or tightening nuts or bolts. Always try to pull the wrench toward you. If the situation calls for pushing the wrench away, push with an open hand to avoid scraped knuckles if the wrench should slip.

DON'T attempt to lift a heavy component alone - get someone to help you.

DON'T rush or take unsafe shortcuts to finish a job.

DON'T allow children or animals in or around the vehicle while you are working on it.

DO wear eye protection when using power tools such as a drill, sander, bench grinder, etc. and when working under a vehicle.

DO keep loose clothing and long hair well out of the way of moving parts.

DO make sure that any hoist used has a safe working load rating adequate for the job.

DO get someone to check on you periodically when working alone on a vehicle.

DO carry out work in a logical sequence and make sure that everything is correctly assembled and tightened.

DO keep chemicals and fluids tightly capped and out of the reach of children and pets.

DO remember that your vehicle's safety affects that of yourself and others. If in doubt on any point, get professional advice.

Steering, suspension and brakes

These systems are essential to driving safety, so make sure you have a qualified shop or individual check your work. Also, compressed suspension springs can cause injury if released suddenly - be sure to use a spring compressor.

Airbags

Airbags are explosive devices that can **CAUSE** injury if they deploy while you're working on the vehicle. Follow the manufacturer's instructions to disable the airbag whenever you're working in the vicinity of airbag components.

Asbestos

Certain friction, insulating, sealing, and other products - such as brake linings, brake bands, clutch linings, torque converters, gaskets, etc. - may contain asbestos or other hazardous friction material. Extreme care must be taken to avoid inhalation of dust from such products, since it is hazardous to health. If in doubt, assume that they do contain asbestos.

Fire

Remember at all times that gasoline is highly flammable. Never smoke or have any kind of open flame around when working on a vehicle. But the risk does not end there. A spark caused by an electrical short circuit, by two metal surfaces contacting each other, or even by static electricity built up in your body under certain conditions, can ignite gasoline vapors, which in a confined space are highly explosive. Do not, under any circumstances, use gasoline for cleaning parts. Use an approved safety solvent.

Always disconnect the battery ground (-) cable at the battery before working on any part of the fuel system or electrical system. Never risk spilling fuel on a hot engine or exhaust component. It is strongly recommended that a fire extinguisher suitable for use on fuel and electrical fires be kept handy in the garage or workshop at all times. Never try to extinguish a fuel or electrical fire with water.

Fumes

Certain fumes are highly toxic and can quickly cause unconsciousness and even death if inhaled to any extent. Gasoline vapor falls into this category, as do the vapors from some cleaning solvents. Any draining or pouring of such volatile fluids should be done in a well ventilated area.

When using cleaning fluids and solvents, read the instructions on the container carefully. Never use materials from unmarked containers.

Never run the engine in an enclosed space, such as a garage. Exhaust fumes contain carbon monoxide, which is extremely poisonous. If you need to run the engine, always do so in the open air, or at least have the rear of the vehicle outside the work area.

The battery

Never create a spark or allow a bare light bulb near a battery. They normally give off a certain amount of hydrogen gas, which is highly explosive.

Always disconnect the battery ground (-) cable at the battery before working on the fuel or electrical systems.

If possible, loosen the filler caps or cover when charging the battery from an external source (this does not apply to sealed or maintenance-free batteries). Do not charge at an excessive rate or the battery may burst.

Take care when adding water to a non maintenance-free battery and when carrying a battery. The electrolyte, even when diluted, is very corrosive and should not be allowed to contact clothing or skin.

Always wear eye protection when cleaning the battery to prevent the caustic deposits from entering your eyes.

Household current

When using an electric power tool, inspection light, etc., which operates on household current, always make sure that the tool is correctly connected to its plug and that, where necessary, it is properly grounded. Do not use such items in damp conditions and, again, do not create a spark or apply excessive heat in the vicinity of fuel or fuel vapor.

Secondary ignition system voltage

A severe electric shock can result from touching certain parts of the ignition system (such as the spark plug wires) when the engine is running or being cranked, particularly if components are damp or the insulation is defective. In the case of an electronic ignition system, the secondary system voltage is much higher and could prove fatal.

Hydrofluoric acid

This extremely corrosive acid is formed when certain types of synthetic rubber, found in some O-rings, oil seals, fuel hoses, etc. are exposed to temperatures above 750-degrees F (400-degrees C). The rubber changes into a charred or sticky substance containing the acid. *Once formed, the acid remains dangerous for years. If it gets onto the skin, it may be necessary to amputate the limb concerned.*

When dealing with a vehicle which has suffered a fire, or with components salvaged from such a vehicle, wear protective gloves and discard them after use.

Troubleshooting

Contents

This section provides an easy reference guide to the more common problems which may occur during the operation of your vehicle. These problems and their possible causes are grouped under headings denoting various components or systems, such as Engine, Cooling system, etc. They also refer you to the chapter and/or section which deals with the problem.

Remember that successful troubleshooting is not a mysterious black art practiced only by professional mechanics. It is simply the result of the right knowledge combined with an intelligent, systematic approach to the problem. Always work by a process of elimination, starting with the simplest solution and working through to the most complex - and never overlook the obvious. Anyone can run the gas tank dry or leave the lights on overnight, so don't assume that you are exempt from such oversights.

Finally, always establish a clear idea of why a problem has occurred and take steps to ensure that it doesn't happen again. If the electrical system fails because of a poor connection, check the other connections in the system to make sure that they don't fail as well. If a particular fuse continues to blow, find out why - don't just replace one fuse after another. Remember, failure of a small component can often be indicative of potential failure or incorrect functioning of a more important component or system.

Engine

1 Engine will not rotate when attempting to start

1   Battery terminal connections loose or corroded (Chapter 1).
2   Battery discharged or faulty (Chapters 1 and 5).
3   Automatic transaxle not completely engaged in Park (Chapter 7A) or clutch pedal not completely depressed (Chapter 6).
4   Broken, loose or disconnected wiring in the starting circuit (Chapters 5 and 12).
5   Starter motor pinion jammed in flywheel ring gear (Chapter 5).
6   Starter solenoid faulty (Chapter 5).
7   Starter motor faulty (Chapter 5).
8   Ignition switch faulty (Chapter 12).
9   Starter pinion or flywheel teeth worn or broken (Chapter 5).

2 Engine rotates but will not start

1   Fuel tank empty.
2   Battery discharged (engine rotates slowly) (Chapter 5).
3   Battery terminal connections loose or corroded (Chapter 1).
4   Leaking fuel injector(s), faulty fuel pump, pressure regulator, etc. (Chapter 4).
5   Broken timing chain (Chapter 2A).
6   Ignition components damp or damaged (Chapter 5).
7   Worn, faulty or incorrectly-gapped spark plugs (Chapter 1).
8   Broken, loose or disconnected wiring in the starting circuit (Chapter 5).
9   Broken, loose or disconnected wires at the ignition coil or faulty coil (Chapter 5).
10   Defective crankshaft or camshaft sensor (Chapter 6).

3 Engine hard to start when cold

1   Battery discharged or low (Chapter 1).
2   Malfunctioning fuel system (Chapter 4).
3   Faulty coolant temperature sensor or intake air temperature sensor (Chapter 6).
4   Faulty ignition system (Chapter 5).

4 Engine hard to start when hot

1   Air filter clogged (Chapter 1).
2   Fuel not reaching the fuel injection rail (Chapter 4).
3   Corroded battery connections (Chapter 1).
4   Faulty coolant temperature sensor or intake air temperature sensor (Chapter 6).

5 Starter motor noisy or excessively rough in engagement

1   Pinion or flywheel gear teeth worn or broken (Chapter 5).
2   Starter motor mounting bolts loose or missing (Chapter 5).

6 Engine starts but stops immediately

1   Insufficient fuel reaching the fuel injector(s) (Chapters 1 and 4).
2   Vacuum leak at the gasket between the intake manifold/plenum and throttle body (Chapter 4).

7 Oil puddle under engine

1   Oil pan gasket and/or oil pan drain bolt washer leaking (Chapter 2A).
2   Oil pressure sending unit leaking (Chapter 2A).
3   Valve cover leaking (Chapter 2A).
4   Engine oil seals leaking (Chapter 2A).
5   Timing chain cover leaking (Chapter 2A).

8 Engine lopes while idling or idles erratically

1   Vacuum leakage (Chapters 2A and 4).
2   Leaking EGR valve (Chapter 6).
3   Air filter clogged (Chapter 1).
4   Malfunction in the fuel injection or engine control system (Chapters 4 and 6).
5   Leaking head gasket (Chapter 2A).
6   Timing chain and/or sprockets worn (Chapter 2A).
7   Camshaft lobes worn (Chapter 2A).

9 Engine misses at idle speed

1   Spark plugs worn or not gapped properly (Chapter 1).
2   Faulty coil(s) (Chapter 1).
3   Vacuum leaks (Chapter 1).
4   Uneven or low compression (Chapter 2A).
5   Problem with the fuel injection system (Chapter 4).

10 Engine misses throughout driving speed range

1   Fuel filter clogged and/or impurities in the fuel system (Chapters 1 and 4).
2   Low fuel pressure (Chapter 4).
3   Faulty or incorrectly gapped spark plugs (Chapter 1).
4   Faulty engine management system components (Chapter 6).
5   Low or uneven cylinder compression pressures (Chapter 2A).
6   Weak or faulty ignition system (Chapter 5).
7   Vacuum leak in fuel injection system, intake manifold, air control valve or vacuum hoses (Chapters 4 and 6).

11 Engine stumbles on acceleration

1   Spark plugs fouled (Chapter 1).
2   Problem with fuel injection or engine control system (Chapters 4 and 6).
3   Fuel filter clogged (Chapters 1 and 4).
4   Intake manifold air leak (Chapters 2A and 4).
5   Problem with the emissions control system (Chapter 6).

12 Engine surges while holding accelerator steady

1   Intake air leak (Chapter 4).
2   Fuel pump or fuel pressure regulator faulty (Chapter 4).
3   Problem with the fuel injection system (Chapter 4).
4   Problem with the emissions control system (Chapter 6).

13 Engine stalls

1   Idle speed incorrect (Chapter 1).
2   Fuel filter clogged and/or water and impurities in the fuel system (Chapters 1 and 4).
3   Faulty emissions system components (Chapter 6).
4   Faulty or incorrectly gapped spark plugs (Chapter 1).
5   Vacuum leak in the fuel injection system, intake manifold or vacuum hoses (Chapters 2A and 4).

14 Engine lacks power

1   Obstructed exhaust system (Chapter 4).
2   Faulty or incorrectly gapped spark plugs (Chapter 1).
3   Problem with the fuel injection system (Chapter 4).
4   Dirty air filter (Chapter 1).
5   Brakes binding (Chapter 9).
6   Automatic transaxle fluid level incorrect (Chapter 1).
7   Clutch slipping (Chapter 8).
8   Fuel filter clogged and/or impurities in the fuel system (Chapters 1 and 4).
9   Emission control system not functioning properly (Chapter 6).
10 Low or uneven cylinder compression pressures (Chapter 2A).

15 Engine backfires

1   Emission control system not functioning properly (Chapter 6).
2   Problem with the fuel injection system (Chapter 4).
3   Vacuum leak at fuel injector(s), intake manifold or vacuum hoses (Chapters 2A and 4).
4   Valve sticking (Chapter 2A).

16 Pinging or knocking engine sounds during acceleration or uphill

1   Incorrect grade of fuel.
2   Fuel injection system faulty (Chapter 4).
3   Improper or damaged spark plugs or wires (Chapter 1).
4   Knock sensor defective (Chapter 6).
5   EGR valve not functioning (Chapter 6).
6   Vacuum leak (Chapters 2A and 4).

17 Engine runs with oil pressure light on

1   Low oil level (Chapter 1).
2   Idle rpm below specification (Chapter 1).
3   Short in wiring circuit (Chapter 12).
4   Faulty oil pressure sender (Chapter 2A).

5   Worn engine bearings and/or oil pump (Chapter 2A).

18 Engine continues to run after switching off

1   Defective ignition switch (Chapter 12).
2   Faulty Powertrain Control Module (Chapter 6).
3   Faulty Body Control Module.
4   Leaking fuel injector (Chapter 4).

Engine electrical systems

19 Battery will not hold a charge

1   Drivebelt or tensioner defective (Chapter 1).
2   Battery electrolyte level low (Chapter 1).
3   Battery terminals loose or corroded (Chapter 1).
4   Alternator not charging properly (Chapter 5).
5   Loose, broken or faulty wiring in the charging circuit (Chapter 5).
6   Short in vehicle wiring (Chapter 12).
7   Internally defective battery (Chapters 1 and 5).

20 Alternator light fails to go out

1   Faulty alternator or charging circuit (Chapter 5).
2   Drivebelt or tensioner defective (Chapter 1).

21 Alternator light fails to come on when key is turned on

1   Instrument cluster defective (Chapter 12).
2   Fault in the wiring harness (Chapter 12).

Fuel system

22 Excessive fuel consumption

1   Dirty air filter element (Chapter 1).
2   Emissions system not functioning properly (Chapter 6).
3   Fuel injection system not functioning properly (Chapter 4).
4   Low tire pressure or incorrect tire size (Chapter 1).

23 Fuel leakage and/or fuel odor

1   Leaking fuel line (Chapters 1 and 4).
2   Tank overfilled.

3   Evaporative emissions control system problem (Chapters 1 and 6).
4   Problem with the fuel injection system (Chapter 4).

Cooling system

24 Overheating

1   Insufficient coolant in system (Chapter 1).
2   Water pump drivebelt defective or out of adjustment (Chapter 1).
3   Radiator core blocked or grille restricted (Chapter 3).
4   Thermostat faulty (Chapter 3).
5   Electric cooling fan inoperative or blades broken (Chapter 3).
6   Expansion tank cap not maintaining proper pressure (Chapter 3).

25 Overcooling

1   Faulty thermostat (Chapter 3).
2   Inaccurate temperature gauge sending unit (Chapter 3).

26 External coolant leakage

1   Deteriorated/damaged hoses; loose clamps (Chapters 1 and 3).
2   Water pump defective (Chapter 3).
3   Leakage from radiator core or coolant expansion tank (Chapter 3).
4   Engine drain or water jacket core plugs leaking (Chapter 2A).

27 Internal coolant leakage

1   Leaking cylinder head gasket (Chapter 2A).
2   Cracked cylinder bore or cylinder head (Chapter 2A).

28 Coolant loss

1   Too much coolant in reservoir (Chapter 1).
2   Coolant boiling away because of overheating (Chapter 3).
3   Internal or external leakage (Chapter 3).
4   Faulty radiator cap (Chapter 3).

29 Poor coolant circulation

1   Inoperative water pump (Chapter 3).
2   Restriction in cooling system (Chapters 1 and 3).
3   Drivebelt or tensioner defective (Chapter 1).
4   Thermostat sticking (Chapter 3).

Clutch

30 Pedal travels to floor - no pressure or very little resistance

1   Master or release cylinder faulty (Chapter 8).
2   Hose/pipe burst or leaking (Chapter 8).
3   Connections leaking (Chapter 8).
4   No fluid in reservoir (Chapter 8).
5   If fluid level in reservoir rises as pedal is depressed, master cylinder center valve seal is faulty (Chapter 8).
6   Broken release bearing or fork (Chapter 8).
7   Faulty pressure plate diaphragm spring (Chapter 8).

31 Fluid in area of master cylinder dust cover and on pedal

Piston primary seal failure in master cylinder (Chapter 8).

32 Fluid on release cylinder

Release cylinder plunger seal faulty (Chapter 8).

33 Pedal feels spongy when depressed

Air in system (Chapter 8).

34 Unable to select gears

1   Faulty transaxle (Chapter 7A).
2   Faulty clutch disc or pressure plate (Chapter 8).
3   Faulty release lever or release bearing (Chapter 8).
4   Faulty shift lever assembly or control cables (Chapter 8).

35 Clutch slips (engine speed increases with no increase in vehicle speed)

1   Clutch plate worn (Chapter 8).
2   Clutch plate is oil soaked by leaking rear main seal (Chapters 2A and 8).
3   Clutch plate not seated (Chapter 8).
4   Warped pressure plate or flywheel (Chapter 8).
5   Weak diaphragm springs (Chapter 8).
6   Clutch plate overheated. Allow to cool.

36 Grabbing (chattering) as clutch is engaged

1   Oil on clutch plate lining, burned or glazed facings (Chapter 8).
2   Worn or loose engine or transaxle mounts (Chapter 2A).
3   Worn splines on clutch plate hub (Chapter 8).
4   Warped pressure plate or flywheel (Chapter 8).
5   Burned or smeared resin on flywheel or pressure plate (Chapter 8).

37 Transaxle rattling (clicking)

1   Release lever loose (Chapter 8).
2   Clutch plate damper spring failure (Chapter 8).

38 Noise in clutch area

1   Fork shaft improperly installed (Chapter 8).
2   Faulty bearing (Chapter 8).

39 Clutch pedal stays on floor

1   Clutch master cylinder piston binding in bore (Chapter 8).
2   Broken release bearing or fork (Chapter 8).

40 High pedal effort

1   Piston binding in bore (Chapter 8).
2   Pressure plate faulty (Chapter 8).
3   Incorrect size master or release cylinder (Chapter 8).

Manual transaxle

41 Knocking noise at low speeds

Worn input shaft bearing (Chapter 7A).*

42 Noise most pronounced when turning

Rear differential gear noise (Chapter 10).*

43 Clunk on acceleration or deceleration

1   Loose engine or transaxle mounts (Chapter 2A).

2   Worn differential pinion shaft in case.*
3   Worn side gear shaft counterbore in rear differential case (Chapter 10).*

44 Clicking noise in turns

Worn or damaged outboard CV joint (Chapter 8).

45 Vibration

1   Rough wheel bearing (Chapter 10).
2   Damaged driveshaft (Chapter 8).
3   Out-of-round tires (Chapter 1).
4   Tire out of balance (Chapters 1 and 10).
5   Worn driveshaft joints (Chapter 8).

46 Noisy in neutral with engine running

1   Damaged input gear bearing (Chapter 7A).*
2   Damaged clutch release bearing (Chapter 8).

47 Noisy in one particular gear

1   Damaged or worn constant mesh gears (Chapter 7A).*
2   Damaged or worn synchronizers (Chapter 7A).*
3   Bent reverse fork (Chapter 7A).*
4   Damaged fourth/fifth speed gear or output gear (Chapter 7A).*
5   Worn or damaged reverse idler gear or idler bushing (Chapter 7A).*

48 Noisy in all gears

1   Insufficient lubricant (Chapter 7A).
2   Damaged or worn bearings (Chapter 7A).*
3   Worn or damaged input gear shaft and/or output gear shaft (Chapter 7A).*

49 Slips out of gear

1   Worn or improperly adjusted linkage (Chapter 7A).
2   Shift linkage does not work freely, binds (Chapter 7A).
3   Input gear bearing retainer broken or loose (Chapter 7A).*
4   Worn or bent shift fork (Chapter 7A).*

50 Leaks lubricant

1 Side gear shaft seals worn (Chapter 7A).
2 Excessive amount of lubricant in transaxle (Chapters 1 and 7A).
3 Loose or broken input gear shaft bearing retainer (Chapter 7A).*
4 Input gear bearing retainer O-ring and/or lip seal damaged (Chapter 7A).*

51 Locked in gear

1 Lock pin or interlock pin missing (Chapter 7A).*
* Although the corrective action necessary to remedy the symptoms described is beyond the scope of this manual, the above information should be helpful in isolating the cause of the condition so that the owner can communicate clearly with a professional mechanic.

Automatic transaxle

52 Fluid leakage

1 Automatic transmission fluid is a deep red color. Fluid leaks should not be confused with engine oil, which can easily be blown onto the transaxle by air flow.
2 To pinpoint a leak, first remove all built-up dirt and grime from the transaxle housing with degreasing agents and/or steam cleaning. Then drive the vehicle at low speeds so air flow will not blow the leak far from its source. Raise the vehicle and determine where the leak is coming from. Common areas of leakage are:
Transaxle oil lines (Chapter 7A).
Speed sensor (Chapter 6).
Driveaxle oil seal (Chapter 7A).

53 Transmission fluid brown or has a burned smell

Transmission fluid overheated (Chapter 1).

54 General shift mechanism problems

1 Chapter 7A , Part B, deals with checking and adjusting the shift linkage on automatic transaxles. Common problems which may be attributed to poorly adjusted linkage are:
Engine starting in gears other than Park or Neutral.
Indicator on shifter pointing to a gear other than the one actually being used.
Vehicle moves when in Park.
2 Refer to Chapter 7B for the shift linkage adjustment procedure.

55 Transaxle slips, shifts roughly, is noisy or has no drive in forward or reverse gears

There are many probable causes for the above problems, but the home mechanic should be concerned with only one possibility - fluid level. Before taking the vehicle to a repair shop, check the level and condition of the fluid as described in Chapter 1. Correct the fluid level as necessary or change the fluid and filter if needed. If the problem persists, have a professional diagnose the cause.

Driveaxles

56 Clicking noise in turns

Worn or damaged outboard CV joint (Chapter 8).

57 Shudder or vibration during acceleration

1 Excessive toe-in (Chapter 10).
2 Worn or damaged inboard or outboard CV joints (Chapter 8).
3 Sticking inboard CV joint assembly (Chapter 8).

58 Vibration at highway speeds

1 Out-of-balance front wheels and/or tires (Chapters 1 and 10).
2 Out-of-round front tires (Chapters 1 and 10).
3 Worn CV joint(s) (Chapter 8).

Brakes

59 Vehicle pulls to one side during braking

1 Incorrect tire pressures (Chapter 1).
2 Front end out of alignment (have the front end aligned).
3 Front, or rear, tire sizes not matched to one another.
4 Restricted brake lines or hoses (Chapter 9).
5 Malfunctioning caliper assembly (Chapter 9).
6 Loose suspension parts (Chapter 10).
7 Excessive wear of pad material or disc on one side (Chapter 9).
8 Contamination (grease or brake fluid) of brake pad material or disc on one side (Chapter 9).

60 Noise (high-pitched squeal or grinding when the brakes are applied)

Brake pads or shoes worn out. Replace pads or shoes with new ones immediately. Also inspect the discs/drums (Chapter 9).

61 Brake roughness or chatter (pedal pulsates)

1 Excessive lateral runout (Chapter 9).
2 Uneven pad wear (Chapter 9).
3 Defective disc (Chapter 9).

62 Excessive brake pedal effort required to stop vehicle

1 Malfunctioning power brake booster (Chapter 9).
2 Malfunctioning vacuum pump (Chapter 9).
3 Partial system failure (Chapter 9).
4 Excessively worn pads (Chapter 9).
5 Piston in caliper stuck or sluggish (Chapter 9).
6 Brake pads contaminated with oil or grease (Chapter 9).
7 Brake disc grooved and/or glazed (Chapter 9).

63 Excessive brake pedal travel

1 Partial brake system failure (Chapter 9).
2 Insufficient fluid in master cylinder (Chapters 1 and 9).
3 Air trapped in system (Chapter 9).

64 Dragging brakes

1 Incorrect adjustment of brake light switch (Chapter 9).
2 Master cylinder pistons not returning correctly (Chapter 9).
3 Caliper piston stuck (Chapter 9).
4 Restricted brakes lines or hoses (Chapter 9).
5 Incorrect parking brake adjustment (Chapter 9).

65 Grabbing or uneven braking action

1 Malfunction of proportioning valve (Chapter 9).
2 Binding brake pedal mechanism (Chapter 9).
3 Contaminated brake linings (Chapter 9).

66 Brake pedal feels spongy when depressed

1   Air in hydraulic lines (Chapter 9).
2   Master cylinder mounting bolts loose (Chapter 9).
3   Master cylinder defective (Chapter 9).

67 Brake pedal travels to the floor with little resistance

1   Little or no fluid in the master cylinder reservoir caused by leaking caliper piston(s) or wheel cylinder(s) (Chapter 9).
2   Loose, damaged or disconnected brake lines (Chapter 9).

68 Parking brake does not hold

Parking brake improperly adjusted (Chapter 9).

Suspension and steering systems

69 Vehicle pulls to one side

1   Mismatched or uneven tires (Chapter 10).
2   Broken or sagging springs (Chapter 10).
3   Wheel alignment incorrect. Have the wheels professionally aligned.
4   Front brake dragging (Chapter 9).

70 Abnormal or excessive tire wear

1   Wheel alignment out-of-specification. Have the wheels aligned.
2   Sagging or broken springs (Chapter 10).
3   Tire out-of-balance (Chapter 10).
4   Worn strut damper or shock absorber (Chapter 10).
5   Overloaded vehicle.
6   Tires not rotated regularly.

71 Wheel makes a thumping noise

1   Blister or bump on tire (Chapter 10).
2   Improper strut damper action (Chapter 10).

72 Shimmy, shake or vibration

1   Tire or wheel out-of-balance or out-of-round (Chapter 10).
2   Loose or worn wheel bearings (Chapter 10).
3   Worn tie-rod ends (Chapter 10).
4   Worn balljoints (Chapters 1 and 10).
5   Excessive wheel runout (Chapter 10).
6   Blister or bump on tire (Chapter 10).

73 Hard steering

1   Worn balljoints and/or tie-rod ends (Chapter 10).
2   Wheel alignment out-of-specifications. Have the wheels professionally aligned.
3   Low tire pressure(s) (Chapter 1).
4   Worn steering gear (Chapter 10).

74 Poor returnability of steering to center

1   Worn balljoints or tie-rod ends (Chapter 10).
2   Worn steering gear assembly (Chapter 10).
3   Wheel alignment out-of-specifications. Have the wheels professionally aligned.

75 Abnormal noise at the front end

1   Worn balljoints or tie-rod ends (Chapter 10).
2   Damaged shock absorber mounting (Chapter 10).
3   Worn control arm bushings or tie-rod ends (Chapter 10).
4   Loose stabilizer bar (Chapter 10).
5   Loose wheel nuts (Chapter 1).
6   Loose suspension bolts (Chapter 10).

76 Wander or poor steering stability

1   Mismatched or uneven tires (Chapter 10).
2   Worn balljoints or tie-rod ends (Chapters 1 and 10).
3   Worn struts or shock absorbers (Chapter 10).
4   Broken or sagging springs (Chapter 10).
5   Wheels out of alignment. Have the wheels professionally aligned.

77 Erratic steering when braking

1   Wheel bearings worn (Chapter 10).
2   Broken or sagging springs (Chapter 10).
3   Leaking wheel cylinder or caliper (Chapter 10).
4   Excessive brake disc runout (Chapter 9).

78 Excessive pitching and/or rolling around corners or during braking

1   Loose stabilizer bar or worn stabilizer bar bushings (Chapter 10).
2   Worn strut dampers or mountings (Chapter 10).
3   Broken or sagging springs (Chapter 10).
4   Overloaded vehicle.

79 Suspension bottoms

1   Overloaded vehicle.
2   Sagging springs (Chapter 10).

80 Cupped tires

1   Wheel alignment out-of-specifications. Have the wheels professionally aligned.
2   Worn shock absorbers (Chapter 10).
3   Wheel bearings worn (Chapter 10).
4   Excessive tire or wheel runout (Chapter 10).
5   Worn balljoints (Chapter 10).

81 Excessive tire wear on outside edge

1   Inflation pressures incorrect (Chapter 1).
2   Excessive speed in turns.
3   Wheel alignment incorrect (excessive toe-in). Have professionally aligned.
4   Suspension arm bent or twisted (Chapter 10).

82 Excessive tire wear on inside edge

1   Inflation pressures incorrect (Chapter 1).
2   Wheel alignment incorrect (toe-out). Have professionally aligned.
3   Loose or damaged steering components (Chapter 10).

83 Tire tread worn in one place

1   Tires out-of-balance.
2   Damaged or buckled wheel. Inspect and replace if necessary.
3   Defective tire (Chapter 1).

84 Excessive play or looseness in steering system

1   Wheel bearing(s) worn (Chapter 10).
2   Tie-rod end loose (Chapter 10).
3   Steering gear loose (Chapter 10).
4   Worn or loose steering intermediate shaft U-joint (Chapter 10).

85 Rattling or clicking noise in steering gear

1   Steering gear loose (Chapter 10).
2   Steering gear defective.

Notes

Chapter 1
Tune-up and routine maintenance

Contents

Specifications

Recommended lubricants and fluids

Note: *Listed here are manufacturer recommendations at the time this manual was written. Manufacturers occasionally upgrade their fluid and lubricant specifications, so refer to your vehicle owner's manual or check with your local auto parts store for current recommendations.*

Engine oil type	API "certified for gasoline engines"
Engine oil viscosity	5W-30
Fuel	Unleaded fuel, 87-octane minimum
Automatic transaxle fluid	
6T40/70 6-speed (2018 and earlier models)	DEXRON-VI automatic transmission fluid
VT40 CVT (1.5L engines)	HP CVT automatic transmission fluid
9T50 9-speed (2.0L engines)	DEXRON-VI automatic transmission fluid
Brake fluid	DOT 3 brake fluid
Engine coolant	50/50 mixture of DEX-COOL coolant and demineralized water
Parking brake mechanism grease	White lithium-based grease NLGI no. 2
Chassis lubrication grease	NLGI no. 2 GC or GC-LB chassis grease
Hood, door and trunk hinge lubricant	Lubriplate lubricant aerosol spray
Door check spring grease	NLGI no. 2 multi-purpose grease
Key lock cylinder lubricant	Graphite spray
Hood latch assembly lubricant	Lubriplate lubricant aerosol spray
Door latch lubricant	NLGI no. 2 multi-purpose grease or equivalent

Capacities*

Engine oil (including filter)

1.5L engines	4.2 quarts	4.0 liters
2.0L engines	5.0 quarts	4.7 liters
2.5L engines	5.0 quarts	4.7 liters

Cooling system

1.5L engines

2017 and earlier models	6.4 quarts	6.1 liters
2018 models	6.6 quarts	6.3 liters
2019 and later models	6.9 quarts	6.5 liters

2.0L engines

2016 and earlier models	7.7 quarts	7.3 liters
2017 and later models	7.2 quarts	6.8 liters
2.5L engines	7.8 quarts	7.4 liters

Automatic transaxle (drain and refill)**

6-speed, 6T40/70	4.2 to 6.3 quarts	4 to 6 liters
9-speed, 9T50	5.3 to 6.3 quarts	5 to 6 liters
VT40 CVT transaxle (dry, without cooler)	8.8 quarts	8.4 liters

All capacities are approximate. Add as necessary to bring to appropriate level.
This is an initial-fill specification. Check the fluid level (see Section 6).

Brakes

Disc brake pad wear limit	3/32 inch	2.38 mm

Ignition system

Spark plug type

1.5L engines	AC Delco 41-156 (iridium) or equivalent
2.0L engines	AC Delco 41-125 (iridium) or equivalent
2.5L engines	AC Delco 41-115 (iridium) or equivalent

Spark plug gap

1.5L engines	0.028 inch	0.70 mm
2.0L engines	0.035 inch	0.90 mm
2.5L engines	0.043 inch	1.10 mm
Firing order	1-3-4-2	

Cylinder locations

Torque specifications

Note: *One foot-pound (ft-lb) of torque is equivalent to 12 inch-pounds (in-lbs) of torque. Torque values below approximately 15 ft-lbs are expressed in inch-pounds, since most foot-pound torque wrenches are not accurate at these smaller values.*

	Ft-lbs (unless otherwise indicated)	Nm
Engine oil drain plug	18	25
Automatic transaxle drain plug		
6-speed (6T40)	106 in-lbs	12
9-speed (9T50)	106 in-lbs	12
CVT (VT40)	93 in-lbs	10.5
Automatic transaxle fluid level check/fill plug		
6-speed (6T40)	106 in-lbs	12
9-speed (9T50)	30	40
CVT (VT40)	93 in-lbs	10.5
Drivebelt tensioner bolt(s)		
1.5L engines	36 to 49	49 to 67
2.0L and 2.5L engines	43	58
Spark plugs		
1.5L engines	156 in-lbs	17
2.0L and 2.5L engines	15	20
Wheel lug nuts		
2015 and earlier models	111	150
2016 and later models	103	140

1 Maintenance schedule

1   The following maintenance intervals are based on the assumption that the vehicle owner will be doing the maintenance or service work, as opposed to having a dealer service department do the work. These are the minimum maintenance intervals recommended by the factory for vehicles that are driven daily. If you wish to keep your vehicle in peak condition at all times, you may wish to perform some of these procedures even more often. Because frequent maintenance enhances the efficiency, performance and resale value of your vehicle, we encourage you to do so. If you drive in dusty areas, tow a trailer, idle or drive at low speeds for extended periods or drive for short distances (less than four miles) in below freezing temperatures, shorter intervals are also recommended.

2   When the vehicle is new, follow the maintenance schedule to the letter, record the maintenance performed in your owner's manual and keep all receipts to protect the new vehicle warranty. In many cases the initial maintenance check is done at no cost to the owner (check with your dealer service department for more information).

Every 250 miles or weekly, whichever comes first

Check the engine oil level (Section 4)
Check the coolant level (Section 4)
Check the windshield washer fluid level (Section 4)
Check the brake fluid level (Section 4)
Check the tires and tire pressures (Section 5)

Every 3,000 miles or 3 months, whichever comes first

Note: *All items listed above, plus:*
Change the engine oil and filter (Section 7)

Every 6,000 miles or 6 months, whichever comes first

Note: *All items listed above, plus:*
Check the seat belts (Section 8)
Inspect the windshield wiper blades (Section 9)
Check and service the battery (Section 10)
Check the engine drivebelt (Section 11)
Inspect underhood hoses (Section 12)
Check the cooling system (Section 13)
Rotate the tires (Section 14)

Every 15,000 miles or 12 months, whichever comes first

Note: *All items listed above, plus:*
Replace the interior ventilation filter (Section 15)
Check the driveaxle boots (Section 16)
Check the fuel system (Section 17)
Check the brake system (Section 18)*
Check the exhaust system (Section 19)

Every 30,000 miles or 30 months, whichever comes first

Note: *All items listed above, plus:*
Change the brake fluid (Section 20)
Replace the air filter (Section 21)
Replace the spark plugs (non-platinum or iridium type) (Section 22)
Check the steering and suspension components (Section 23)
Change the automatic transaxle fluid and filter (Section 24)**

Every 100,000 miles or 60 months, whichever comes first

Note: *All items listed above, plus:*
Change the brake fluid (Section 20)
Replace the air filter (Section 21)
Replace the spark plugs (non-platinum or iridium type) (Section 22)
Check the steering and suspension components (Section 23)
Change the automatic transaxle fluid and filter (Section 24)**

Note: * *This item is affected by severe operating conditions, as described below. If the vehicle is operated under severe conditions, perform all maintenance indicated with an asterisk (*) at half the indicated intervals. Severe conditions exist if you mainly operate the vehicle. . .*
a) In dusty areas
b) Towing a trailer
c) Idling for extended periods
d) Driving at low speeds when outside temperatures remain below freezing, and most trips are less than four miles long

Note: ** *Perform this procedure at half the recommended interval if operated under one or more of the following conditions:*
a) In heavy city traffic where the outside temperature regularly reaches 90-degrees F or higher
b) In hilly or mountainous terrain
c) Frequent trailer towing
d) If the vehicle has been driven through deep water

2   Introduction

1   This Chapter is designed to help the home mechanic maintain the Chevrolet Malibu with the goals of maximum performance, economy, safety and reliability in mind.

2   Included is a master maintenance schedule, followed by procedures dealing specifically with each item on the schedule. Visual checks, adjustments, component replacement and other helpful items are included. Refer to the **accompanying illustrations** of the engine compartment and the underside of the vehicle for the locations of various components.

3   Servicing your vehicle in accordance with the mileage/time maintenance schedule and the step-by-step procedures will result in a planned maintenance program that should produce a long and reliable service life. Keep in mind that it's a comprehensive plan, so maintaining some items but not others at the specified intervals will produce the same results.

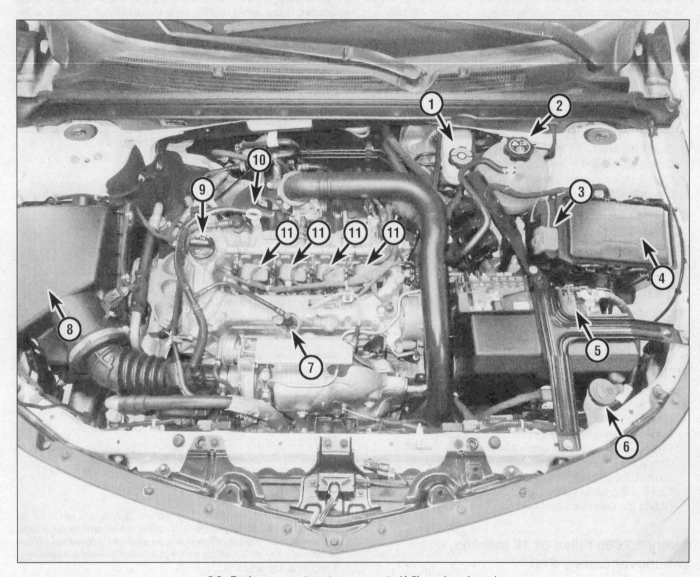

2.2a Engine compartment components (1.5L engine shown)

1	Brake fluid reservoir	5	Battery (under cover)
2	Coolant expansion tank	6	Windshield washer fluid reservoir
3	Remote positive jump start terminal	7	Positive Crankcase Ventilation (PCV) valve
4	Underhood fuse/relay box		

8	Air filter housing
9	Engine oil filler cap
10	Engine oil dipstick
11	Ignition coil/spark plug

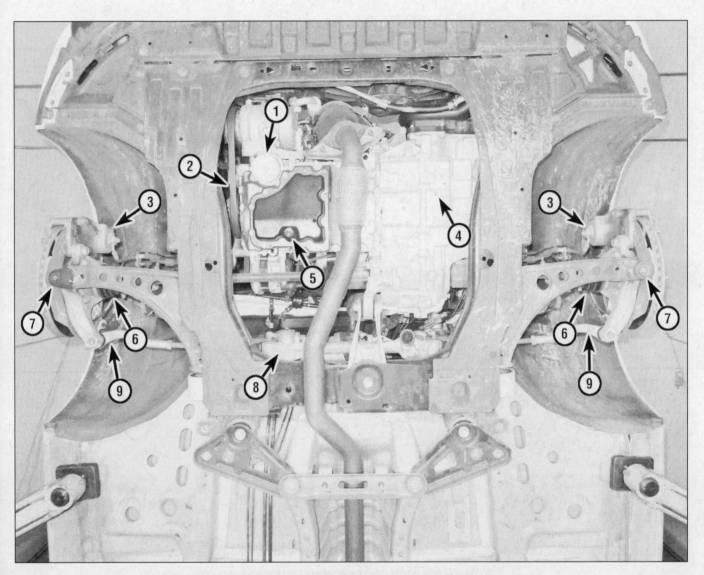

2.2b Typical engine compartment underside components (2018 model shown)

1	Engine oil filter	4	Automatic transaxle drain plug	7	Balljoint
2	Drivebelt	5	Engine oil drain plug	8	Steering gear
3	Brake caliper	6	Outer driveaxle boot	9	Tie-rod end

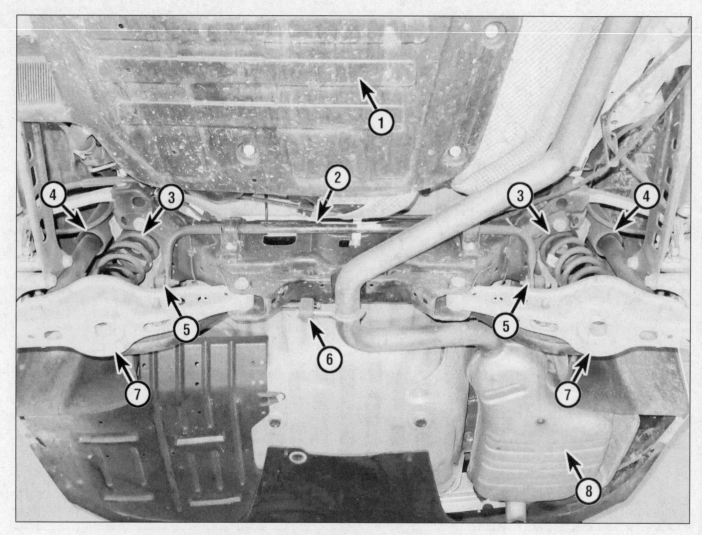

2.2c Typical rear underside components (2018 model shown)

1	Fuel tank shield/fuel tank	4	Shock absorber	7	Lower control arm
2	Stabilizer bar	5	Stabilizer bar link	8	Muffler
3	Coil spring	6	Exhaust system hanger		

4 As you service your vehicle, you will discover that many of the procedures can - and should - be grouped together because of the nature of the particular procedure you're performing or because of the close proximity of two otherwise unrelated components to one another.

5 For example, if the vehicle is raised for chassis lubrication, you should inspect the exhaust, suspension, steering and fuel systems while you're under the vehicle. When you're rotating the tires, it makes good sense to check the brakes since the wheels are already removed. Finally, let's suppose you have to borrow or rent a torque wrench. Even if you only need it to tighten the spark plugs, you might as well check the torque of as many critical fasteners as time allows.

6 The first step in this maintenance program is to prepare you before the actual work begins. Read through all the procedures you're planning to do, then gather up all the parts and tools needed. If it looks like you might run into problems during a particular job, seek advice from a mechanic or an experienced do-it-yourselfer.

Owner's manual and VECI label information

7 Your vehicle owner's manual was written for your year and model and contains very specific information on component locations, specifications, fuse ratings, part numbers, etc. The owner's manual is an important resource for the do-it-yourselfer to have; if one was not supplied with your vehicle, it can generally be ordered from a dealer parts department.

8 Among other important information, the Vehicle Emissions Control Information (VECI) label describes emissions control equipment installed on the vehicle. This data often varies by intended operating altitude, local emissions regulations, month of manufacture, etc.

9 This Chapter contains procedural details, safety information and more ambitious maintenance intervals than you might find in the manufacturer's literature. However, you may also find procedures and specifications in your owner's manual that differ with what's printed here. In these cases, the owner's manual can be considered correct, since it is specific to your particular vehicle.

3 Tune-up general information

1 The term tune-up is used in this manual to represent a combination of individual operations rather than one specific procedure that will maintain a gasoline engine in proper tune.

2 If, from the time the vehicle is new, the routine maintenance schedule is followed closely and frequent checks are made of fluid levels and high wear items, as suggested throughout this manual, the engine will be kept in relatively good running condition and the need for additional work will be minimized.

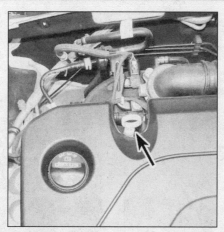

4.2 The engine oil dipstick is located on the back side of the engine - 1.5L model shown, other models similar

3 More likely than not, however, there may be times when the engine is running poorly due to lack of regular maintenance. This is even more likely if a used vehicle, which has not received regular and frequent maintenance checks, is purchased. In such cases, an engine tune-up will be needed outside of the regular routine maintenance intervals.

4 The first step in any tune-up or diagnostic procedure to help correct a poor running engine is a cylinder compression check. A compression check (see Chapter 2B) will help determine the condition of internal engine components and should be used as a guide for tune-up and repair procedures. If, for instance, the compression check indicates serious internal engine wear, a conventional tune-up won't improve the performance of the engine and would be a waste of time and money. Because of its importance, the compression check should only be performed by someone with the right equipment and the knowledge to use it properly.

5 The following procedures are those most often needed to bring a generally poor running engine back into a proper state of tune.

Minor tune-up
Check all engine-related fluids (Section 4)
Clean, inspect and test the battery (Section 10)
Check the drivebelt (Section 11)
Check all underhood hoses (Section 12)
Check the cooling system (Section 13)
Check the air filter (Section 21)

Major tune-up
Note: *All items listed under Minor tune-up, plus. . .*
Replace the air filter (Section 21)
Replace the spark plugs (Section 22)
Check the ignition system (Chapter 5)
Check the charging system (Chapter 5)

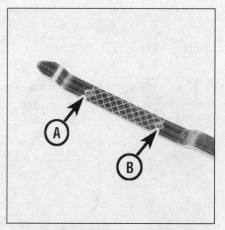

4.4 The oil level should be in the safe range - if it's below the MIN or ADD mark (A), add enough oil to bring it up to or near the MAX or FULL mark (B)

4 Fluid level checks (every 250 miles or weekly)

Note: *The following are fluid level checks to be done on a 250 mile or weekly basis. Additional fluid level checks can be found in specific maintenance procedures that follow. Regardless of intervals, be alert to fluid leaks under the vehicle, which would indicate a fault to be corrected immediately.*

1 Fluids are an essential part of the lubrication, cooling, brake and windshield washer systems. Because the fluids gradually become depleted and/or contaminated during normal operation of the vehicle, they must be periodically replenished. See Recommended lubricants and fluids in this Chapter's Specifications before adding fluid to any of the following components.

Note: *The vehicle must be on level ground when fluid levels are checked.*

Engine oil

2 The engine oil level is checked with a dipstick that extends down into the oil pan at the bottom of the engine **(see illustration)**.

3 The oil level should be checked before the vehicle has been driven, or about 5 minutes after the engine has been shut off. If the oil is checked immediately after driving the vehicle, some of the oil will remain in the upper engine components, resulting in an inaccurate reading on the dipstick.

4 Pull the dipstick out of the tube and wipe all the oil from the end with a clean rag or paper towel. Insert the clean dipstick all the way back into the tube, then pull it out again. Note the oil at the end of the dipstick. Add oil as necessary to keep the level within the cross-hatched zone on the dipstick **(see illustration)**.

5 Do not overfill the engine by adding too much oil since this may result in oil-fouled spark plugs, oil leaks or oil seal failures.

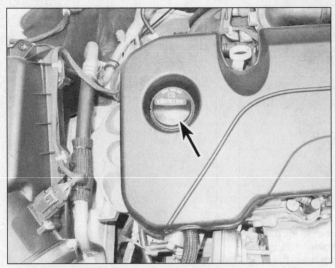

4.6 To prevent dirt from contaminating the engine, always make sure the area around the cap is clean before removing it

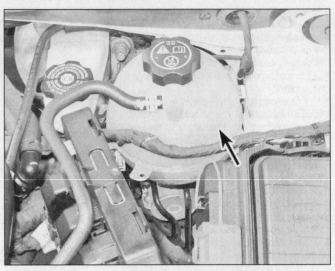

4.8 The coolant expansion tank is located on the rear left side of the engine compartment

6   Oil is added to the engine after unscrewing a cap from the valve cover **(see illustration)**. A funnel will help to reduce spills.

7   Checking the oil level is an important preventive maintenance step. A consistently low oil level indicates oil leakage through damaged seals, defective gaskets or past worn rings or valve guides. If the oil looks milky or has water droplets in it, the cylinder head gasket(s) may be blown or the head(s) or block may be cracked. The engine should be checked immediately. The condition of the oil should also be checked. Whenever you check the oil level, slide your thumb and index finger up the dipstick before wiping off the oil. If you see small dirt or metal particles clinging to the dipstick, the oil should be changed (see Section 7).

Engine coolant

Warning: *Do not allow antifreeze to come in contact with your skin or painted surfaces of the vehicle. Rinse off spills immediately with*

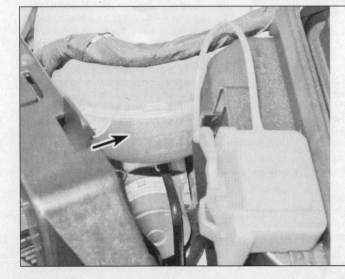

4.10 Keep the level above the COLD zone - DO NOT remove the tank cap until the engine has cooled completely

plenty of water. Antifreeze is highly toxic if ingested. Never leave antifreeze lying around in an open container or in puddles on the floor; children and pets are attracted by its sweet smell and may drink it. Check with local authorities on disposing of used antifreeze. Many communities have collection centers that will see that antifreeze is disposed of safely.

Caution: *Never mix green-colored ethylene glycol antifreeze and orange-colored DEX-COOL silicate-free coolant because doing so will destroy the efficiency of the DEX-COOL coolant, which is designed to last for 100,000 miles or five years.*

Note: *Non-toxic antifreeze is now manufactured and available at auto parts stores, but even this type should be disposed of properly.*

8   All vehicles covered by this manual are equipped with a pressurized coolant expansion tank, located in the left rear corner of the engine compartment **(see illustration)**.

9   The coolant level in the expansion tank should be checked regularly. When the

engine is cold, the coolant level should be at or slightly above the COLD FILL mark. If it isn't, add coolant to the tank.

Warning: *Never unscrew the expansion tank cap when the engine is warm. Only remove the cap when the engine and cooling system is cool.*

10   To add coolant, open the cap and add a 50/50 mixture of DEX-COOL coolant and water until the level is up to the COLD FILL mark **(see illustration)** (see the Caution at the beginning of this Section).

11   Drive the vehicle and recheck the coolant level. If only a small amount of coolant is required to bring the system up to the proper level, water can be used. However, repeated additions of water will dilute the antifreeze and water solution. In order to maintain the proper ratio of antifreeze and water, always top up the coolant level with the correct mixture. An empty plastic milk jug or bleach bottle makes an excellent container for mixing coolant. Do not use rust inhibitors or additives.

12   If the coolant level drops consistently, there may be a leak in the system. Inspect the radiator, hoses, filler cap, drain plugs and water pump (see Section 13). If no leaks are noted, have the pressure cap tested by a service station.

13   Check the condition of the coolant as well. It should be relatively clear. If it is brown or rust colored, the system should be drained, flushed and refilled. Even if the coolant appears to be normal, the corrosion inhibitors wear out, so it must be replaced at the specified intervals. If the system is filled with standard green coolant/water, it must be flushed and replaced more frequently than if the original DEX-COOL coolant is retained.

Windshield washer fluid

14   Fluid for the windshield washer system is located in a plastic reservoir in the left side of the engine compartment (2010 and later

4.14 The windshield washer fluid tank is located at the left front corner of the engine compartment

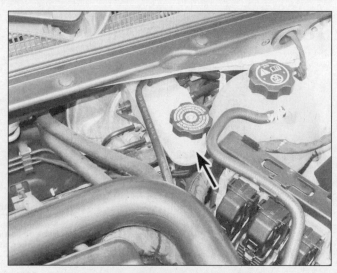

4.19 The brake fluid reservoir is located at the left side of the firewall

models) **(see illustration)** or the right side of the engine compartment (2009 and earlier models).

15   In milder climates, plain water can be used in the reservoir, but it should be kept no more than 2/3 full to allow for expansion if the water freezes. In colder climates, use windshield washer system antifreeze, available at any auto parts store, to lower the freezing point of the fluid. Mix the antifreeze with water in accordance with the manufacturer's directions on the container.

Caution: *Don't use cooling system antifreeze - it will damage the vehicle's paint.*

16   To help prevent icing in cold weather, warm the windshield with the defroster before using the washer.

Battery electrolyte

17   These vehicles are equipped with a battery which is permanently sealed (except for vent holes) and has no filler caps. Water doesn't have to be added to these batteries at any time. If a maintenance-type battery is installed, the caps on the top of the battery should be removed periodically to check for a low electrolyte level. If the level is low, add only distilled water until the level is above the plates.

Brake fluid

18   The brake master cylinder is mounted on the left side of the engine compartment firewall.

19   The translucent plastic reservoir allows the fluid inside to be checked without removing the cap **(see illustration)**. Wipe the cap and reservoir with a clean rag to prevent contamination of the brake system before removing it.

20   When adding fluid, pour it carefully into the reservoir to avoid spilling it on surrounding painted surfaces. Be sure the specified fluid is used, since mixing different types of

brake fluid can cause damage to the system. See Recommended lubricants and fluids in this Chapter's Specifications or your owner's manual.

Warning: *Brake fluid can harm your eyes and damage painted surfaces, so use extreme caution when handling or pouring it. Do not use brake fluid that has been standing open or is more than one year old. Brake fluid absorbs moisture from the air. Moisture in the system can cause a dangerous loss of brake performance.*

21   At this time, the fluid and master cylinder can be inspected for contamination. The system should be drained and refilled if deposits, dirt particles or water droplets are seen in the fluid.

22   After filling the reservoir to the proper level, make sure the cap is installed securely to prevent fluid leakage.

23   The brake fluid level in the master cylinder will drop slightly as the pads at the front wheels wear down during normal operation. If the master cylinder requires repeated additions to keep it at the proper level, it's an indication of leakage in the brake system, which

should be corrected immediately. Check all brake lines and connections (see Section 18 for more information).

24   If, upon checking the master cylinder fluid level, you discover the reservoir empty or nearly empty, the brake system should be bled and thoroughly inspected (see Chapter 9).

---

5   Tire and tire pressure checks (every 250 miles or weekly)

1   Periodic inspection of the tires may spare you the inconvenience of being stranded with a flat tire. It can also provide you with vital information regarding possible problems in the steering and suspension systems before major damage occurs.

2   The original tires on this vehicle are equipped with 1/2-inch wide wear bands that will appear when tread depth reaches 1/16-inch, at which point the tires can be considered worn out. Tread wear can be monitored with a simple, inexpensive device known as a tread depth indicator **(see illustration)**.

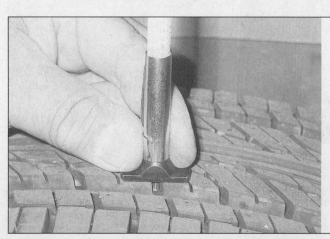

5.2 Use a tire tread depth indicator to monitor tire wear - they are available at auto parts stores and service stations and cost very little

UNDERINFLATION

CUPPING

OVERINFLATION

**INCORRECT TOE-IN
OR EXTREME CAMBER**

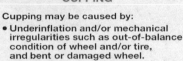

Cupping may be caused by:
- Underinflation and/or mechanical irregularities such as out-of-balance condition of wheel and/or tire, and bent or damaged wheel.
- Loose or worn steering tie-rod or steering idler arm.
- Loose, damaged or worn front suspension parts.

**FEATHERING DUE
TO MISALIGNMENT**

5.3 This chart will help you determine the condition of the tires and the probable cause(s) of abnormal wear

3   Note any abnormal tread wear **(see illustration)**. Tread pattern irregularities such as cupping, flat spots and more wear on one side than the other are indications of front end alignment and/or balance problems. If any of these conditions are noted, take the vehicle to a tire shop or service station to correct the problem.

4   Look closely for cuts, punctures and embedded nails or tacks. Sometimes a tire will hold air pressure for a short time or leak down very slowly after a nail has embedded itself in the tread. If a slow leak persists, check the valve stem core to make sure it's tight **(see illustration)**. Examine the tread for an object that may have embedded itself in the tire or for a plug that may have begun to leak (radial tire punctures are repaired with a plug that's installed in a puncture). If a puncture is suspected, it can be easily verified by spraying a solution of soapy water onto the puncture area **(see illustration)**. The soapy solution will bubble if there's a leak. Unless the puncture is unusually large, a tire shop or service station can usually repair the tire.

5   Carefully inspect the inner sidewall of each tire for evidence of brake fluid leakage. If you see any, inspect the brakes immediately.

6   Correct air pressure adds miles to the lifespan of the tires, improves mileage and enhances overall ride quality. Tire pressure cannot be accurately estimated by looking at a tire, especially if it's a radial. A tire pressure gauge is essential. Keep an accurate gauge in the vehicle. The pressure gauges attached to the nozzles of air hoses at gas stations are often inaccurate.

7   Always check tire pressure when the tires are cold. Cold, in this case, means the vehicle has not been driven over a mile in the three hours preceding a tire pressure check. A pressure rise of four to eight pounds is not uncommon once the tires are warm.

8   Unscrew the valve cap protruding from the wheel or hubcap and push the gauge firmly onto the valve stem **(see illustration)**. Note the reading on the gauge and compare the figure to the recommended tire pressure shown on the placard on the driver's side door pillar. Reinstall the valve cap to keep dirt and moisture out of the valve stem mechanism. Check all four tires and, if necessary, add enough air to bring them up to the recommended pressure.

5.4a If a tire loses air on a steady basis, check the valve stem core first to make sure it's snug (special inexpensive wrenches are commonly available at auto parts stores)

5.4b If the valve stem core is tight, raise the corner of the vehicle with the low tire and spray a soapy water solution onto the tread as the tire is turned slowly - leaks will cause small bubbles to appear

5.8 To extend the life of the tires, check the air pressure at least once a week with an accurate gauge (don't forget the spare!)

9 Don't forget to keep the spare tire inflated to the specified pressure (see your owner's manual or the tire sidewall).

6 Automatic transaxle fluid level check

1 Checking the automatic transaxle fluid level is not a routine maintenance procedure on these vehicles. The only reason the fluid level would drop would be due to a leak.

2 Checking the fluid level is necessary when the transaxle fluid is drained and refilled. The fluid level checking procedure is included in Section 24.

7 Engine oil and filter change (every 3000 miles or 3 months)

Note: *These vehicles are equipped with an oil life indicator system that illuminates a light on the instrument panel when the system deems it necessary to change the oil. A number of factors are taken into consideration to determine when the oil should be considered worn out. Generally, this system will allow the vehicle to accumulate more miles between oil changes than the traditional 3000 mile interval, but we believe that frequent oil changes are cheap insurance and will prolong engine life. If you do decide not to change your oil every 3000 miles and rely on the oil life indicator instead, make sure you don't exceed 10,000 miles before the oil is changed, regardless of what the oil life indicator shows.*

1 Frequent oil changes are the most important preventive maintenance procedures that can be done by the home mechanic. As engine oil ages, it becomes diluted and contaminated, which leads to premature engine wear.

2 Although some sources recommend oil filter changes every other oil change, we feel that the minimal cost of an oil filter and the relative ease with which it is installed dictate that a new filter be installed every time the oil is changed.

3 Gather together all necessary tools and materials before beginning this procedure **(see illustration).**

4 You should have plenty of clean rags and newspapers handy to mop up any spills. Access to the underside of the vehicle may be improved if the vehicle can be lifted on a hoist, driven onto ramps or supported by jackstands. **Warning:** *Do not work under a vehicle which is supported only by a jack.*

5 If this is your first oil change, familiarize yourself with the locations of the oil drain plug and the oil filter.

6 Warm the engine to normal operating temperature. If new oil or any tools are needed, use this warm-up time to gather everything necessary for the job. The correct type of oil for your application can be found in *Recommended lubricants and fluids* in this Chapter's Specifications.

7 With the engine oil warm (warm engine oil will drain better and more built-up sludge will be removed with it), raise and support the vehicle. Make sure it's safely supported!

8 Remove the under-vehicle splash shield. Move all necessary tools, rags and newspapers under the vehicle. Set the drain pan under the drain plug. Keep in mind that the oil will initially flow from the pan with some force; position the pan accordingly.

9 Being careful not to touch any of the hot exhaust components, use a wrench to remove the drain plug near the bottom of the oil pan **(see illustration).** Depending on how hot the oil is, you may want to wear gloves while unscrewing the plug the final few turns.

10 Allow the oil to drain into the pan. It may be necessary to move the pan as the oil flow slows to a trickle.

11 After all the oil has drained, wipe off the drain plug with a clean rag. Small metal particles may cling to the plug and would immediately contaminate the new oil.

12 Clean the area around the drain plug opening and reinstall the plug. Tighten the plug securely with the wrench. If a torque wrench is available, use it to tighten the plug to the torque listed in this Chapter's Specifications.

13 Move the drain pan into position under the oil filter.

14 Use an oil filter wrench to loosen the oil filter **(see illustration).**

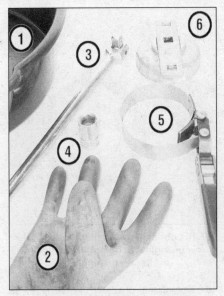

7.3 These tools are required when changing the engine oil and filter

1 **Drain pan** - *It should be fairly shallow in depth, but wide to prevent spills*

2 **Rubber gloves** - *When removing the drain plug and filter, you will get oil on your hands (the gloves will prevent burns)*

3 **Breaker bar** - *Sometimes the oil drain plug is tight, and a long breaker bar is needed to loosen it*

4 **Socket** – *To be used with the breaker bar or a ratchet (must be the correct size to fit the drain plug - six-point preferred)*

5 **Filter wrench** - *This is a metal band-type wrench, which requires clearance around the filter to be effective*

6 **Filter wrench** - *This type fits on the bottom of the filter and can be turned with a ratchet or breaker bar (different-size wrenches are available for different types of filters)*

7.9 Use a proper size box-end wrench or socket to remove the oil drain plug and avoid rounding it off

7.14 Since the oil filter is on very tight, you'll need a special wrench for removal - DO NOT use the wrench to tighten the new filter

7.18 Lubricate the oil filter gasket with clean engine oil before installing the filter on the engine

15   Completely unscrew the old filter. Be careful; it's full of oil. Empty the oil inside the filter into the drain pan.
16   Compare the old filter with the new one to make sure they're the same type.
17   Use a clean rag to remove all oil, dirt and sludge from the area where the oil filter mounts to the engine. Check the old filter to make sure the rubber gasket isn't stuck to the engine. If the gasket is stuck to the engine, remove it.
18   Apply a light coat of clean oil to the rubber gasket on the new oil filter **(see illustration)**.
19   Attach the new filter to the engine, following the tightening directions printed on the filter canister or packing box. Most filter manufacturers recommend against using a filter wrench due to the possibility of overtightening and damage to the seal.
20   Remove all tools, rags, etc., from under the vehicle, being careful not to spill the oil in the drain pan, then lower the vehicle.
21   Move to the engine compartment and locate the oil filler cap.
22   Refer to the engine oil capacity in this Chapter's Specifications and add the proper

amount of fresh oil into the engine. Wait a few minutes to allow the oil to drain into the pan, then check the level on the oil dipstick (see Section 4, if necessary). If the oil level is above the upper mark, start the engine and allow the new oil to circulate.
23   Run the engine for only about a minute and then shut it off. Immediately look under the vehicle and check for leaks at the oil pan drain plug and around the oil filter.
24   Wait about five minutes. With the new oil circulated and the filter now completely full, recheck the level on the dipstick and add more oil as necessary.
25   During the first few trips after an oil change, make it a point to check frequently for leaks and proper oil level.
26   The old oil drained from the engine cannot be reused in its present state and should be disposed of. Check with your local auto parts store, disposal facility or environmental agency to see if they will accept the oil for recycling. After the oil has cooled it can be drained into a container (capped plastic jugs, topped bottles, milk cartons, etc.) for transport to one of these disposal sites. Don't dispose of the oil by pouring it on the ground or down a drain!

Oil life monitor

27   The Oil Life Monitor is a function of the PCM that tracks engine operating temperature and rpm. If the PCM determines that your engine's oil has been used long enough, an indicator that shows "Change Engine Oil Soon" will light on the instrument panel.
28   When you change your engine oil and filter, whether you change it at the interval recommended in Section 1 or only when the light comes on, you will have to reset the system to make the indicator go out.
29   Reset the system whenever the engine oil is changed so that the system can calculate the next engine oil change.

To reset the oil life monitor system on 2016 and earlier models

30   Turn the ignition to the On or Run position

without starting the engine. Press the Driver Information Center (DIC) Menu button on the turn signal lever to enter the vehicle information menu on the display. Use the band (thumb wheel) to scroll through the menu until you see the REMAINING OIL LIFE. Press the SET/CLR button (oil life reset) button until 100% is shown. Turn the ignition to the Off or Lock position. The system is now reset. If the CHANGE ENGINE OIL SOON message comes back on now, or when the engine is started, the engine oil life system has not been reset, and the procedure will need to be repeated.

To reset the oil life monitor system on 2017 and later models using the Driver Information Center (DIC) buttons

31   Turn the ignition to the On or Run position without starting the engine. Use the left and right arrows on the Drivers Information Controls (DIC) on the right side of the steering wheel, to display REMAINING OIL LIFE on the (DIC). Press the center select or check button on the Drivers information Controls (DIC) and hold the button down for a few seconds to clear the CHANGE ENGINE OIL SOON message and reset the oil life at 100%.
Note: *Be careful to not accidentally reset the oil life display at any time other than after an oil changed. Once it is set, it cannot be reset accurately until the next oil change.*

---

8   Seat belt check (every 6000 miles or 6 months)

1   Check seat belts, buckles, latch plates, and guide loops for obvious damage and signs of wear.
2   Where the seat belt receptacle bolts to the floor of the vehicle, check that the bolts are secure.
3   See if the seat belt reminder light comes on when the key is turned to the Run or Start position. A chime should also sound.

9.4a To release the blade holder, use a small blade screwdriver to pry the release tab up...

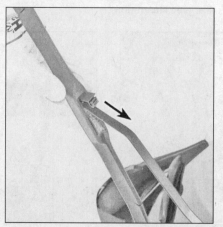

9.4b... slide the wiper blade assembly down the arm until the pivot is out of the hook in the end of the arm...

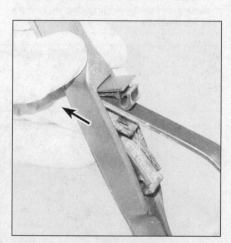

9.4c... then pull the wiper blade in the direction of the windshield to separate it from the arm

9 Wiper blade inspection and replacement (every 6000 miles or 6 months)

1 The windshield wiper and blade assembly should be inspected periodically for damage, loose components and cracked or worn blade elements.

2 Road film can build up on the wiper blades and affect their efficiency, so they should be washed regularly with a mild detergent solution.

3 If the wiper blade elements are cracked, worn or warped, or no longer clean adequately, they should be replaced with new ones.

4 Lift the arm assembly away from the glass for clearance, release the tab and slide the wiper blade assembly down the arm until the pivot is out of the hook in the end of the arm, then slide the blade assembly off of the arm (see illustrations).

5 Attach the new wiper to the arm. Connection can be confirmed by an audible click and press the release tab down into the locked position.

10 Battery check, maintenance and charging (every 6000 miles or 6 months)

Warning: *Certain precautions must be followed when checking and servicing the battery. Hydrogen gas, which is highly flammable, is always present in the battery cells, so keep lighted tobacco and all other open flames and sparks away from the battery. The electrolyte inside the battery is actually dilute sulfuric acid, which will cause injury if splashed on your skin or in your eyes. It will also ruin clothes and painted surfaces. When removing the battery cables, always detach the negative cable first and hook it up last!*
Note: *The battery has a protective cover that must be removed to access the battery and battery terminals (see Chapter 5).*

1 A routine preventive maintenance program for the battery in your vehicle is the only way to ensure quick and reliable starts. But before performing any battery maintenance, make sure that you have the proper equipment necessary to work safely around the battery (see illustration).

2 There are also several precautions that should be taken whenever battery maintenance is performed. Before servicing the battery, always turn the engine and all accessories off and disconnect the cable from the negative terminal of the battery.

3 The battery produces hydrogen gas, which is both flammable and explosive. Never create a spark, smoke or light a match around the battery. Always charge the battery in a ventilated area.

4 Electrolyte contains poisonous and corrosive sulfuric acid. Do not allow it to get in

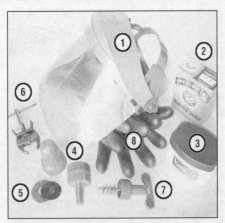

10.1 Tools and materials required for battery maintenance

1 **Face shield/safety goggles** - *When removing corrosion with a brush, the acidic particles can easily fly up into your eyes*
2 **Baking soda** - *A solution of baking soda and water can be used to neutralize corrosion*
3 **Petroleum jelly** - *A layer of this on the battery posts will help prevent corrosion*
4 **Battery post/cable cleaner** - *This wire brush cleaning tool will remove all traces of corrosion from the battery posts and cable clamps*
5 **Treated felt washers** - *Placing one of these on each post, directly under the cable clamps, will help prevent corrosion*
6 **Puller** - *Sometimes the cable clamps are very difficult to pull off the posts, even after the nut/bolt has been completely loosened. This tool pulls the clamp straight up and off the post without damage*
7 **Battery post/cable cleaner** - *Here is another cleaning tool which is a slightly different version of Number 4 above, but it does the same thing*
8 **Rubber gloves** - *Another safety item to consider when servicing the battery; remember that's acid inside the battery!*

your eyes, on your skin or on your clothes. Never ingest it. Wear protective safety glasses when working near the battery. Keep children away from the battery.

5 Note the external condition of the battery. If the positive terminal and cable clamp on your vehicle's battery is equipped with a rubber protector, make sure that it's not torn or damaged. It should completely cover the terminal. Look for any corroded or loose connections, cracks in the case or cover or loose hold-down clamps. Also check the entire length of each cable for cracks and frayed conductors.

10.6a Battery terminal corrosion usually appears as light, fluffy powder

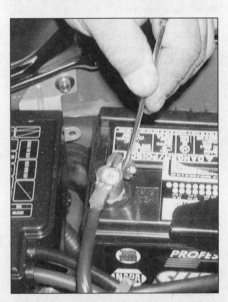

10.6b Removing a cable from the battery post with a wrench - sometimes a pair of special battery pliers are required for this procedure if the corrosion has caused deterioration of the nut hex (always remove the ground (-) cable first and hook it up last!)

6 If corrosion, which looks like white, fluffy deposits is evident, particularly around the terminals, the battery should be removed for cleaning. Loosen the cable bolts with a wrench, being careful to remove the ground cable first, and slide them off the terminals (see illustrations). Then remove the hold-down clamp and lift the battery from the engine compartment.

10.7a A tool like this one (available at auto parts stores) is used to clean the side-terminal type battery cable contact area

10.7b Use the brush side of the tool to finish the job

7   Clean the cable ends thoroughly with a battery brush or a terminal cleaner and a solution of warm water and baking soda. Wash the terminals and the side of the battery case with the same solution but make sure that the solution doesn't get into the battery. When cleaning the cables, terminals and battery case, wear safety goggles and rubber gloves to prevent any solution from coming in contact with your eyes or hands. Wear old clothes too - even diluted, sulfuric acid splashed onto clothes will burn holes in them. If the terminals have been corroded, clean them up with a terminal cleaner **(see illustrations)**. Thoroughly wash all cleaned areas with plain water.

8   Make sure that the battery tray is in good condition and the hold-down clamp is tight. If the battery is removed from the tray, make sure no parts remain in the bottom of the tray when the battery is reinstalled. When reinstalling the hold-down clamp bolts, do not overtighten them.

9   Any metal parts of the vehicle damaged by corrosion should be covered with a zinc-based primer, then painted.

10   Information on removing and installing the battery can be found in Chapter 5. Information on jump starting can be found at the front of this manual. For more detailed battery checking procedures, refer to the Haynes Automotive Electrical Manual.

Charging

Warning: *When batteries are being charged, hydrogen gas, which is very explosive and flammable, is produced. Do not smoke or allow open flames near a charging or a recently charged battery. Wear eye protection when near the battery during charging. Also, make sure the charger is unplugged before connecting or disconnecting the battery from the charger.*
Note: *The manufacturer recommends the battery be removed from the vehicle for charging because the gas that escapes during this pro-*

cedure can damage the paint. Fast charging with the battery cables connected can result in damage to the electrical system.

11   Slow-rate charging is the best way to restore a battery that's discharged to the point where it will not start the engine. It's also a good way to maintain the battery charge in a vehicle that's only driven a few miles between starts. Maintaining the battery charge is particularly important in the winter when the battery must work harder to start the engine and electrical accessories that drain the battery are in greater use.

12   It's best to use a one or two-amp battery charger (sometimes called a trickle charger). They are the safest and put the least strain on the battery. They are also the least expensive. For a faster charge, you can use a higher amperage charger, but don't use one rated more than 1/10th the amp/hour rating of the battery. Rapid boost charges that claim to restore the power of the battery in one to two hours are hardest on the battery and can damage batteries not in good condition. This type of charging should only be used in emergency situations.

13   The average time necessary to charge a battery should be listed in the instructions that come with the charger. As a general rule, a trickle charger will charge a battery in 12 to 16 hours.

14   Remove all the cell caps (if equipped) and cover the holes with a clean cloth to prevent spattering electrolyte. Disconnect the negative battery cable and hook the battery charger cable clamps up to the battery posts (positive to positive, negative to negative), then plug in the charger. Make sure it is set at 12-volts if it has a selector switch.

15   If you're using a charger with a rate higher than two amps, check the battery regularly during charging to make sure it doesn't overheat. If you're using a trickle charger, you can safely let the battery charge overnight after you've checked it regularly for the first couple of hours.

16   If the battery has removable cell caps, measure the specific gravity with a hydrometer every hour during the last few hours of the charging cycle. Hydrometers are available inexpensively from auto parts stores - follow the instructions that come with the hydrometer. Consider the battery charged when there's no change in the specific gravity reading for two hours and the electrolyte in the cells is gassing (bubbling) freely. The specific gravity reading from each cell should be very close to the others. If not, the battery probably has a bad cell(s).

17   Some batteries with sealed tops have built-in hydrometers on the top that indicate the state of charge by the color displayed in the hydrometer window. Normally, a bright-colored hydrometer indicates a full charge and a dark hydrometer indicates the battery still needs charging.

18   If the battery has a sealed top and no built-in hydrometer, you can hook up a digital voltmeter across the battery terminals to check the charge. A fully charged battery should read 12.5 volts or higher.

19   Further information on the battery and jump-starting can be found in at the front of this manual and in Chapter 5.

11 Drivebelt and tensioner check and replacement (every 6000 miles or 6 months)

1   A serpentine drivebelt is located at the front of the engine and plays an important role in the overall operation of the engine and its components. Due to its function and material makeup, the belt is prone to wear and should be periodically inspected. The serpentine belt drives the alternator, power steering pump, water pump and air conditioning compressor.

2   With the engine off, open the hood and use your fingers (and a flashlight, if necessary), to move along the belt checking for cracks and separation of the belt plies. Also check for fraying and glazing, which gives the belt a shiny appearance **(see illustration)**. Both sides of the belt must be inspected.

3   Check the ribs on the underside of the belt. They should all be the same depth, with none of the surface uneven.

4   The tension of the belt is maintained by a spring-loaded tensioner assembly and isn't adjustable. Replace the belt at the specified intervals (see Section 1), or any time it is damaged or worn.

5   Loosen the right-front wheel lug nuts. Raise the vehicle and support it securely on jackstands, then remove the right-front wheel and inner fenderwell splash shield **(see illustration)**.

6   Insert a 3/8-inch drive ratchet or breaker bar into the square hole in the tensioner, then rotate the tensioner away from the belt to release belt tension **(see illustration)**.
Note: *If your ratchet or breaker bar is too thick to fit in the space between the tensioner and*

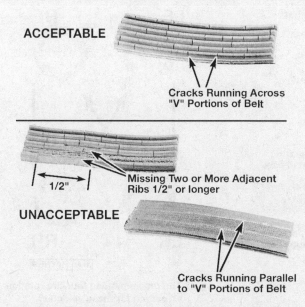

ACCEPTABLE

Cracks Running Across
"V" Portions of Belt

1/2"

Missing Two or More Adjacent
Ribs 1/2" or longer

UNACCEPTABLE

Cracks Running Parallel
to "V" Portions of Belt

11.2 Check ribbed (serpentine) belts for signs of wear like these - if it looks worn, replace it

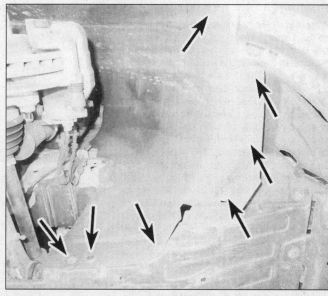

11.5 Remove the inner splash shield fasteners and secure the front section of the splash shield out of the way

the chassis, special drivebelt tensioner tools are available at most auto parts stores.

7   Noting how it's routed, remove the belt from the tensioner and auxiliary components, then slowly release the tensioner.

8   After verifying the new belt is the same length as the original belt, route the new belt over the various pulleys, again rotating the tensioner to allow the belt to be installed, then release the belt tensioner.

Tensioner replacement

9   Remove the drivebelt.

10   Remove the tensioner mounting bolt **(see illustration)** and detach the tensioner from the engine.

11   Installation is the reverse of removal. Tighten the mounting bolt(s) to the torque listed in this Chapter's Specifications.

---

12   Underhood hose check and replacement (every 6000 miles or 6 months)

Warning: *Replacement of air conditioning hoses must be left to a dealer service department or air conditioning shop that has the equipment to depressurize the system safely and recover the refrigerant. Never remove air conditioning components or hoses until the system has been depressurized.*

1   High temperatures in the engine compartment can cause the deterioration of the rubber and plastic hoses used for engine, accessory and emission systems operation. Periodic inspection should be made for cracks, loose clamps, material hardening and leaks. Information specific to the cooling system hoses can be found in Section 13.

11.6 Insert a square-drive tool of the proper size into the square hole in the tensioner, then rotate the tensioner away from the belt - 1.5L model shown, others similar

2   Some, but not all, hoses are secured to their fittings with clamps. Where clamps are used, check to be sure they haven't lost their tension, allowing the hose to leak. If clamps aren't used, make sure the hose has not expanded and/or hardened where it slips over the fitting, allowing it to leak.

Vacuum hoses

3   It's quite common for vacuum hoses, especially those in the emissions system, to be color-coded or identified by colored stripes molded into them. Various systems require hoses with different wall thickness, collapse resistance and temperature resistance. When replacing hoses, be sure the new ones are made of the same material.

11.10 Remove the tensioner mounting bolt

4   Often the only effective way to check a hose is to remove it completely from the vehicle. If more than one hose is removed, label the hoses and fittings to ensure correct installation.

5   When checking vacuum hoses, be sure to include any plastic T-fittings in the check. Inspect the fittings for cracks and the hose where it fits over the fitting for distortion, which could cause leakage.

6   A small piece of vacuum hose (1/4-inch inside diameter) can be used as a stethoscope to detect vacuum leaks. Hold one end of the hose to your ear and probe around vacuum hoses and fittings, listening for the hissing sound characteristic of a vacuum leak. **Warning:** *When probing with the vacuum hose stethoscope, be very careful not to come into contact with moving engine components such as the drivebelt, cooling fan, etc.*

Fuel hose

Warning: *Gasoline is extremely flammable, so take extra precautions when you work on any part of the fuel system. Don't smoke or allow open flames or bare light bulbs near the work area, and don't work in a garage where a gas-type appliance (such as a water heater or clothes dryer) is present. Since gasoline is carcinogenic, wear fuel-resistant gloves when there's a possibility of being exposed to fuel, and, if you spill any fuel on your skin, rinse it off immediately with soap and water. Mop up any spills immediately and do not store fuel-soaked rags where they could ignite. When you perform any kind of work on the fuel system, wear safety glasses and have a Class B type fire extinguisher on hand. The fuel system is under pressure, so if any lines must be disconnected, the pressure in the system must be relieved first (see Chapter 4 for more information).*

7   Check all rubber fuel lines for deterioration and chafing. Check especially for cracks in areas where the hose bends and just before fittings, such as where a hose attaches to the fuel filter and fuel injection unit.

8   High quality fuel line, specifically designed for high-pressure fuel injection applications, must be used for fuel line replacement. Never, under any circumstances, use regular fuel line, unreinforced vacuum line, clear plastic tubing or water hose for fuel lines.

9   Spring-type (pinch) clamps are commonly used on fuel lines. These clamps often lose their tension over a period of time, and can be sprung during removal. Replace all spring-type clamps with screw clamps whenever a hose is replaced.

Metal lines

10   Sections of metal line are routed along the frame, between the fuel tank and the engine. Check carefully to be sure the line has not been bent or crimped and no cracks have started in the line.

11   If a section of metal fuel line must be replaced, only seamless steel tubing should be used, since copper and aluminum tubing don't have the strength necessary to withstand normal engine vibration.

12   Check the metal brake lines where they enter the master cylinder and brake proportioning unit for cracks in the lines or loose fittings. Any sign of brake fluid leakage calls for an immediate and thorough inspection of the brake system.

---

13   Cooling system check
(every 6000 miles or 6 months)

Caution: *Never mix green-colored ethylene glycol antifreeze and orange-colored DEX-COOL silicate-free coolant because doing so will destroy the efficiency of the DEX-COOL coolant, which is designed to last for 100,000 miles or five years.*

1   Many major engine failures can be attributed to a faulty cooling system. If the vehicle

Check for a chafed area that could fail prematurely.

Check for a soft area indicating the hose has deteriorated inside.

Overtightening the clamp on a hardened hose will damage the hose and cause a leak.

Check each hose for swelling and oil-soaked ends. Cracks and breaks can be located by squeezing the hose.

13.3 Hoses, like drivebelts, have a habit of failing at the worst possible time - to prevent the inconvenience of a blown radiator or heater hose, inspect them carefully as shown here

---

is equipped with an automatic transaxle, the cooling system also cools the transmission fluid and thus plays an important role in prolonging transmission life. The cooling system should be checked with the engine cold. Do this before the vehicle is driven for the day or after it has been shut off for at least three hours.

2   Slowly remove the coolant reservoir cap; if you hear any hissing sounds (indicating there is still pressure in the system), wait until it stops. If there is no hissing sound, continue unscrewing it. Thoroughly clean the cap, inside and out, with clean water. Also clean the opening on the coolant reservoir neck. All traces of corrosion should be removed. The coolant inside the coolant reservoir should be relatively transparent. If it is rust colored, the system should be drained and refilled (see Section 25). If the coolant level is not up to the COLD FILL mark on the reservoir, add additional antifreeze/coolant mixture (see Section 4).

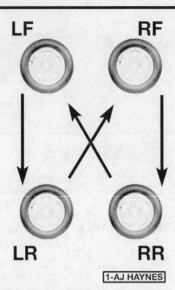

14.2 The recommended four-tire rotation pattern for these vehicles

---

3   Carefully check the large upper and lower radiator hoses along with any smaller diameter heater hoses that run from the engine to the firewall. Inspect each hose along its entire length, replacing any hose that is cracked, swollen or shows signs of deterioration. Cracks may become more apparent if the hose is squeezed **(see illustration)**.

4   Make sure all hose connections are tight. A leak in the cooling system will usually show up as white or rust-colored deposits on the areas adjoining the leak. If wire-type clamps are used at the ends of the hoses, it may be wise to replace them with more secure, screw-type clamps.

5   Use compressed air or a soft brush to remove bugs, leaves, etc., from the front of the radiator or air conditioning condenser. Be careful not to damage the delicate cooling fins or cut yourself on them.

6   Every other inspection, or at the first indication of cooling system problems, have the cap and system pressure tested. If you don't have a pressure tester, most gas stations and repair shops will do this for a minimal charge.

---

14   Tire rotation
(every 6000 miles or 6 months)

1   The tires should be rotated at the specified intervals and whenever uneven wear is noticed.

2   Tires must be rotated in the recommended pattern **(see illustration)**.

3   Refer to the information in the front of this manual of *Jacking and towing* for the proper procedures to follow when raising the vehicle and changing a tire. If the brakes are to be checked, don't apply the parking brake as stated. Make sure the tires are blocked to prevent the vehicle from rolling as it's raised.

4   Preferably, the entire vehicle should be raised at the same time. This can be done

15.3 Pull the dampener arm towards the large end of the slot on the door, then pull the tab of the dampener arm out of the slot on the glove box

15.5 Release the retaining clips and open the filter door. . .

15.6. . . then pull the filter out of the housing

on a hoist or by jacking up each corner and then lowering the vehicle onto jackstands placed under the frame rails. Always use four jackstands and make sure the vehicle is safely supported.

5   After rotation, check and adjust the tire pressures as necessary. Tighten the lug nuts to the torque listed in this Chapter's Specifications.

15   Interior ventilation filter replacement (every 15,000 miles or 12 months)

1   Open the glove box door.
2   On 2015 and earlier models, disconnect the door dampener string and slide a pen or pencil through the loop to keep the string from being pulled back into the door.
3   On 2016 and later models, pull the dampener arm towards the front of the door then unhook the dampener from the door **(see illustration)**.
4   Squeeze both sides of the glove box door until the stops can clear the sides of the opening and lower the door.
5   Release the filter door clips and remove the door **(see illustration)**.
6   Pull the filter out of the housing **(see illustration)**.
7   Slide the filter back into the housing, then close the door and reinstall the fasteners.
Note: *Make sure the airflow arrows on the filter are pointing downward.*
8   The remainder of installation is the reverse of removal.

16   Driveaxle boot check (every 15,000 miles or 12 months)

1   The driveaxle boots are very important because they prevent dirt, water and foreign material from entering and damaging the con-

stant velocity (CV) joints. Oil and grease can cause the boot material to deteriorate prematurely, so it's a good idea to wash the boots with soap and water. Because it constantly pivots back and forth following the steering action of the front hub, the outer CV boot wears out sooner and should be inspected regularly.
2   Inspect the boots for tears and cracks as well as loose clamps **(see illustration)**. If there is any evidence of cracks or leaking lubricant, they must be replaced (see Chapter 8).

17   Fuel system check (every 15,000 miles or 12 months)

Warning: *Gasoline is extremely flammable, so take extra precautions when you work on any part of the fuel system. Don't smoke or allow open flames or bare light bulbs near the work area, and don't work in a garage where a gas-type appliance (such as a water heater or clothes dryer) is present. Since gasoline is carcinogenic, wear fuel-resistant gloves when there's a possibility of being exposed to fuel, and, if you spill any fuel on your skin, rinse it off immediately with soap and water. Mop up any spills immediately and do not store fuel-soaked rags where they could ignite. When you perform any kind of work on the fuel system, wear safety glasses and have a Class B type fire extinguisher on hand. The fuel system is under constant pressure, so before any lines are disconnected, the fuel system pressure must be relieved (see Chapter 4).*
1   If you smell gasoline while driving or after the vehicle has been sitting in the sun, inspect the fuel system immediately.
2   Remove the gas filler cap and inspect it for damage and corrosion. The gasket should have an unbroken sealing imprint. If the gasket is damaged or corroded, install a new cap.
3   Inspect the fuel feed and return lines for cracks. Make sure that the connections between the fuel lines and the fuel injection system are tight.
Warning: *Your vehicle is fuel injected, so you*

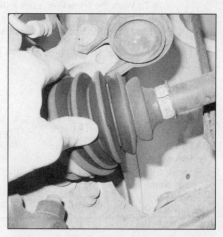

16.2 Inspect the inner and outer driveaxle boots for loose clamps, cracks or signs of leaking lubricant (AWD models also have driveaxles at the rear)

must relieve the fuel system pressure before servicing fuel system components (see Chapter 4).
4   Since some components of the fuel system - the fuel tank and the fuel feed line, for example - are underneath the vehicle, they can be inspected more easily with the vehicle raised on a hoist. If that's not possible, raise the vehicle and support it on jackstands.
5   With the vehicle raised and safely supported, inspect the gas tank and filler neck for punctures, cracks and other damage. The connection between the filler neck and the tank is particularly critical. Sometimes a rubber filler neck will leak because of loose clamps or deteriorated rubber. Inspect all fuel tank mounting brackets and straps to be sure that the tank is securely attached to the vehicle.
6   Carefully check all rubber hoses and metal lines leading away from the fuel tank. Check for loose connections, deteriorated hoses, crimped lines and other damage. Repair or replace damaged sections as necessary (see Section 12).

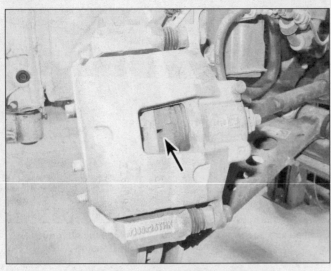

**18.7a With the wheel off, check the thickness
of the inner pad through the inspection hole in the caliper
(front caliper shown, rear caliper similar)**

**18.7b The outer pad is more easily checked
at the edge of the caliper**

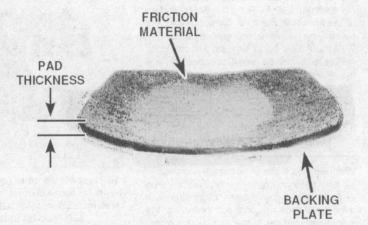

**18.9 If a
more precise
measurement of
pad thickness
is necessary,
remove the
pads and
measure
the remaining
friction material**

PAD
THICKNESS

FRICTION
MATERIAL

BACKING
PLATE

5   Remove the wheels.

6   There are two pads (an outer and an inner) in each caliper. The pads are visible with the wheels removed.

7   Check the pad thickness by looking at each end of the caliper and through the inspection window in the caliper body **(see illustrations)**. If the lining material is less than the thickness listed in this Chapter's Specifications, replace the pads.

Note: Keep in mind that the lining material is riveted or bonded to a metal backing plate and the metal portion is not included in this measurement.

8   If it is difficult to determine the exact thickness of the remaining pad material by the above method, or if you are at all concerned about the condition of the pads, remove the caliper(s), then remove the pads from the calipers for further inspection (see Chapter 9).

9   Once the pads are removed from the calipers, clean them with brake cleaner and re-measure them with a ruler or a vernier caliper **(see illustration)**.

10   Measure the disc thickness with a micrometer to make sure that it still has service life remaining. If any disc is thinner than the specified minimum thickness, replace it (see Chapter 9). Even if the disc has service life remaining, check its condition. Look for scoring, gouging and burned spots. If these conditions exist, remove the disc and have it resurfaced (see Chapter 9).

11   Before installing the wheels, check all brake lines and hoses for damage, wear, deformation, cracks, corrosion, leakage, bends and twists, particularly in the vicinity of the rubber hoses at the calipers **(see illustration)**. Check the clamps for tightness and the connections for leakage. Make sure that all hoses and lines are clear of sharp edges, moving parts and the exhaust system. If any of the above conditions are noted, repair, reroute or replace the lines and/or fittings as necessary (see Chapter 9).

7   The evaporative emissions control system can also be a source of fuel odors. The function of the system is to store fuel vapors from the fuel tank in a charcoal canister until they can be routed to the intake manifold where they mix with incoming air before being burned in the combustion chambers.

8   The most common symptom of a faulty evaporative emissions system is a strong odor of fuel coming from the area of the charcoal canister which is mounted next to the fuel tank. If a fuel odor has been detected, and you have already checked the areas described above, check the charcoal canister and the hoses connected to it (see Chapter 6).

18   Brake system check (every 15,000 miles or 12 months)

Warning: *The dust created by the brake system is harmful to your health. Never blow it out*

with compressed air and don't inhale any of it. An approved filtering mask should be worn when working on the brakes. Do not, under any circumstances, use petroleum-based solvents to clean brake parts. Use brake system cleaner only!

Note: *For detailed photographs of the brake system, refer to Chapter 9*

1   In addition to the specified intervals, the brakes should be inspected every time the wheels are removed or whenever a defect is suspected.

2   Any of the following symptoms could indicate a potential brake system defect: The vehicle pulls to one side when the brake pedal is depressed; the brakes make squealing or dragging noises when applied; brake pedal travel is excessive; the pedal pulsates; or brake fluid leaks, usually onto the inside of the tire or wheel.

3   Loosen the wheel lug nuts.

4   Looen the wheel lug nuts, then raise the vehicle and support it securely on jackstands.

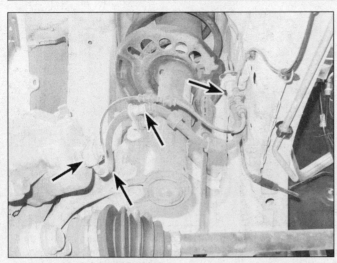

18.11 Check along the brake hoses and at each fitting for deterioration, cracks and leakage

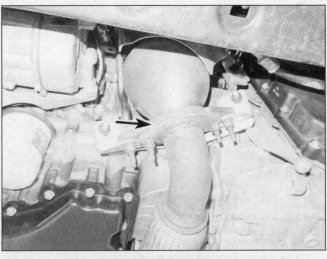

19.2a Inspect all flanged joints for signs of exhaust gas leakage

Brake booster check

12   Sit in the driver's seat and perform the following sequence of tests:

13   With the brake fully depressed, start the engine - the pedal should move down a little when the engine starts.

14   With the engine running, depress the brake pedal several times - the travel distance should not change.

15   Depress the brake, stop the engine and hold the pedal in for about 30 seconds - the pedal should neither sink nor rise.

16   Restart the engine, run it for about a minute and turn it off. Then firmly depress the brake several times - the pedal travel should decrease with each application.

17   If your brakes do not operate as described, the brake booster has failed. Refer to Chapter 9 for the replacement procedure.

Parking brake

18   One method of checking the parking brake is to park the vehicle on a steep hill with the parking brake set and the transaxle in Neutral (be sure to stay in the vehicle for this check). If the parking brake cannot prevent the vehicle from rolling, it's in need of attention (see Chapter 9).

19   Exhaust system check (every 15,000 miles or 12 months)

1   With the engine cold (at least three hours after the vehicle has been driven), check the complete exhaust system from the manifold to the end of the tailpipe. Be careful around the catalytic converter, which may be hot even after three hours. The inspection should be done with the vehicle on a hoist to permit unrestricted access. If a hoist isn't available, raise the vehicle and support it securely on jackstands.

2   Check the exhaust pipes and connections for signs of leakage and/or corrosion indicating a potential failure. Make sure that

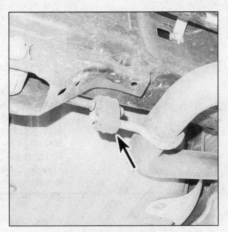

19.2b Inspect the exhaust pipe and all hangers. . .

all brackets and hangers are in good condition and tight **(see illustrations)**.

3   Inspect the underside of the body for holes, corrosion, open seams, etc., which may allow exhaust gasses to enter the passenger compartment. Seal all body openings with silicone sealant or body putty.

4   Rattles and other noises can often be traced to the exhaust system, especially the hangers, mounts and heat shields. Try to move the pipes, mufflers and catalytic converter. If the components can come in contact with the body or suspension parts, secure the exhaust system with new brackets and hangers.

20   Brake fluid change (every 30,000 miles or 24 months)

Warning: *Brake fluid can harm your eyes and damage painted surfaces, so use extreme caution when handling or pouring it. Do not use brake fluid that has been standing open or is more than one year old. Brake fluid absorbs moisture from*

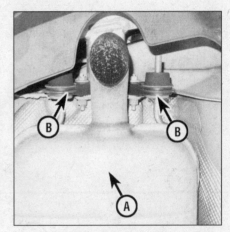

19.2c. . . the muffler (A) and all hangers (B) for signs of deterioration

the air. Excess moisture can cause a dangerous loss of braking effectiveness.

1   At the specified intervals, the brake fluid should be drained and replaced. Since the brake fluid may drip or splash when pouring it, place plenty of rags around the master cylinder to protect any surrounding painted surfaces.

2   Before beginning work, purchase the specified brake fluid (see this Chapter's Specifications).

3   Remove the cap from the master cylinder reservoir.

4   Using a hand suction pump or similar device, withdraw the fluid from the master cylinder reservoir.

5   Add new fluid to the master cylinder until it rises to the line indicated on the reservoir.

6   Bleed the brake system at all four brakes until new and uncontaminated fluid is expelled from the bleeder screw (see Chapter 9). Maintain the fluid level in the master cylinder as you perform the bleeding process. If you allow the master cylinder to run dry, air will enter the system.

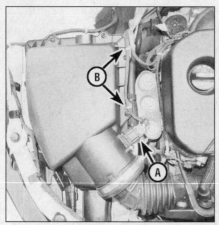

21.3 Disconnect the electrical connector from the MAF/IAT sensor (A), then disengage the harness retainers (B) from the top cover - 1.5L models shown, other models similar

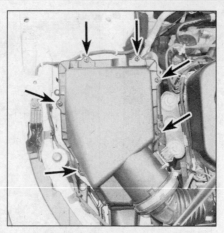

21.4 Air filter housing upper cover fasteners - 1.5L models shown, other models similar

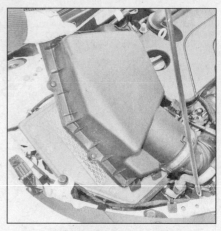

21.5 Lift up the cover and remove the filter element - 1.5L models shown, other models similar

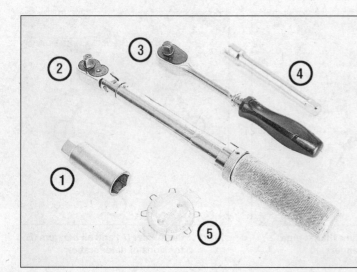

22.2 Tools required for changing spark plugs

1   **Spark plug socket** - This will have special padding inside to protect the spark plug's porcelain insulator
2   **Torque wrench** - Although not mandatory, using this tool is the best way to ensure the plugs are tightened properly
3   **Ratchet** - Standard hand tool to fit the spark plug socket
4   **Extension** - Depending on model and accessories, you may need special extensions and universal joints to reach one or more of the plugs
5   **Spark plug gap gauge** - This gauge for checking the gap comes in a variety of styles. Make sure the gap for your engine is included

7   Refill the master cylinder with fluid and check the operation of the brakes. The pedal should feel solid when depressed, with no sponginess.
Warning: *Do not operate the vehicle if you are at all in doubt about the effectiveness of the brake system.*

21   Air filter replacement (every 30,000 miles or 24 months)

1   At the specified intervals, the air filter element should be replaced with a new one.
2   The air filter is housed in a black plastic box mounted on the right side of the engine compartment.
3   Disconnect the electrical connector from the Mass Air Flow/Intake Air Temperature (MAF/IAT) sensor, then use a trim tool to remove the harness retainers from the cover **(see illustration)**.
4   Remove the screws around the perimeter of the upper cover **(see illustration)**.

Note: *It is possible to lift the cover up enough to remove the filter without disconnecting the inlet duct.*
5   Pull up the housing cover, then lift the air filter element out of the housing **(see illustration)**. Wipe out the inside of the air filter housing with a clean rag.
6   Installation is the reverse of removal.

22   Spark plug replacement (see maintenance schedule for service intervals)

1   The spark plugs are threaded into the top of each cylinder head on all engines.
Note: *The engine cover (see Chapter 4) must be removed first to access the ignition coils and spark plugs.*
2   In most cases, the tools necessary for spark plug replacement include a spark plug socket which fits onto a ratchet (spark plug sockets are padded inside to prevent damage to the porcelain insulators on the new plugs),

various extensions and a gap gauge to check and adjust the gaps on the new plugs **(see illustration)**. A torque wrench should be used to tighten the new plugs.
3   The best approach when replacing the spark plugs is to purchase the new ones in advance, adjust them to the proper gap and replace them one at a time. When buying the new spark plugs, be sure to obtain the correct plug type for your particular engine. This information can be found in your owner's manual and in this Chapter's Specifications.
4   Allow the engine to cool completely before attempting to remove any of the plugs. While you're waiting for the engine to cool, check the new plugs for defects and adjust the gaps.
5   The gap is checked by inserting the proper-thickness gauge between the electrodes at the tip of the plug **(see illustration)**. The gap between the electrodes should be the same as the one specified in this Chapter's Specifications. The gauge should just slide between the electrodes with a slight amount of drag. If the gap is incorrect, use

22.5 Spark plug manufacturers recommend using a wire-type gauge when checking the gap - the wire should slide between the electrodes with a slight drag

22.8 Use a socket and extension to unscrew the spark plugs - various length extensions and perhaps a flex-joint may be required to reach some plugs - 1.5L engine shown, other models similar

A **normally worn** spark plug should have light tan or gray deposits on the firing tip.

A **carbon fouled** plug, identified by soft, sooty, black deposits, may indicate an improperly tuned vehicle. Check the air cleaner, ignition components and engine control system.

An **oil fouled** spark plug indicates an engine with worn piston rings and/or bad valve seals allowing excessive oil to enter the chamber.

This spark plug has been **left in the engine too long**, as evidenced by the extreme gap- Plugs with such an extreme gap can cause misfiring and stumbling accompanied by a noticeable lack of power.

A **physically damaged** spark plug may be evidence of severe detonation in that cylinder. Watch that cylinder carefully between services, as a continued detonation will not only damage the plug, but could also damage the engine.

A **bridged or almost bridged** spark plug, identified by a build-up between the electrodes caused by excessive carbon or oil build-up on the plug.

22.9 Common spark plug conditions

the adjuster on the gauge body to bend the curved side electrode slightly until the proper gap is obtained. If the side electrode is not exactly over the center electrode, bend it with the adjuster until it is. Check for cracks in the porcelain insulator (if any are found, the plug should not be used).

Note: *Be careful not to scrape the thin platinum or iridium coating from the electrodes, as this would dramatically shorten the life of the plugs.*

6   Remove the ignition coils (see Chapter 5).

7   If compressed air is available, use it to blow any dirt or foreign material away from around the spark plugs. The idea here is to eliminate the possibility of debris falling into the cylinder as the spark plug is removed.

8   Place the spark plug socket over the plug and turn it counterclockwise to remove it from the engine **(see illustration)**.

9   Compare the spark plug with the accompanying chart to get an indication of the general running condition of the engine **(see illustration)**.

10   Thread one of the new plugs into the hole until you can no longer turn it with your fingers, then tighten it with a torque wrench (if available) or the ratchet. It's a good idea to slip a short length of rubber hose over the end of the plug to use as a tool to thread it into place **(see illustration)**. The hose will grip the plug well enough to turn it, but will start to slip if the plug begins to cross-thread in the hole - this will prevent damaged threads and the accompanying repair costs.

11   Reinstall the spark plug wires or ignition coils.

12   Repeat the procedure for the remaining spark plugs.

22.10 A length of snug-fitting rubber hose will save time and prevent damaged threads when installing the spark plugs

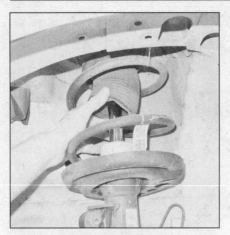

23.6 Check for signs of fluid leakage at this point on struts/shock absorbers (front strut shown)

23.9a Examine the mounting points for the control arms on the front suspension at the front. . .

23.9b. . . and the rear of the control arms on the front suspension

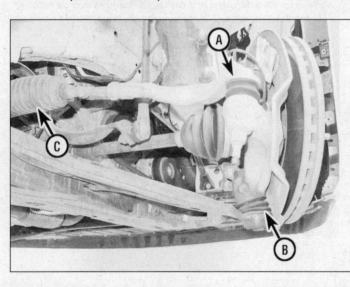

23.9c Inspect the tie-rod ends (A), the balljoints (B) and the steering gear boots (C)

10   Clean the lower end of the steering knuckle. Have an assistant grasp the lower edge of the tire and move the wheel in-and-out while you look for movement at the steering knuckle-to-control arm balljoint. If there is any movement the balljoint must be replaced.

11   Grasp each front tire at the front and rear edges, push in at the front, pull out at the rear and feel for play in the steering system components. If any freeplay is noted, check the tie-rod ends for looseness or wear.

12   Additional steering and suspension system information and illustrations can be found in Chapter 10.

24   Automatic transaxle fluid change (every 30,000 miles or 30 months)

Fluid change

1   At the specified intervals, the transmission fluid should be drained and replaced. Since the fluid will remain hot long after driving, perform this procedure only after the engine has cooled down completely.

2   Before beginning work, purchase the specified transmission fluid (see this Chapter's Specifications).

3   Other tools necessary for this job include a floor jack, jackstands to support the vehicle in a raised position, a drain pan capable of holding at least eight quarts, newspapers and clean rags.

4   Raise the vehicle and support it securely on jackstands.

5   Before beginning work, purchase the specified transaxle fluid (see this Chapter's Specifications) and a new filter.

6   Place the drain pan underneath the transaxle drain plug. Remove the drain plug and allow the fluid to drain **(see illustration)**.

7   Install the drain plug and tighten it to the torque listed in this Chapter's Specifications.

8   Lower the vehicle.

23   Suspension and steering check (every 30,000 miles or 30 months)

Note: *The steering linkage and suspension components should be checked periodically. Worn or damaged suspension and steering linkage components can result in excessive and abnormal tire wear, poor ride quality and vehicle handling and reduced fuel economy. For detailed illustrations of the steering and suspension components, refer to Chapter 10.*

Strut and shock absorber check

1   Park the vehicle on level ground, turn the engine off and set the parking brake. Check the tire pressures.

2   Push down at one corner of the vehicle, then release it while noting the movement of the body. It should stop moving and come to rest in a level position within one or two bounces.

3   If the vehicle continues to move up-and-down or if it fails to return to its original position, a worn or weak shock absorber is probably the reason.

4   Repeat the above check at each of the three remaining corners of the vehicle.

5   Raise the vehicle and support it securely on jackstands.

6   Check the struts/shock absorbers for evidence of fluid leakage **(see illustration)**. A light film of fluid is no cause for concern. Make sure that any fluid noted is from the struts/shocks and not from some other source. If leakage is noted, replace the struts/shocks as a set.

7   Check the struts/shocks to be sure that they are securely mounted and undamaged. Check the upper mounts for damage and wear. If damage or wear is noted, replace the struts/shocks as a set (front or rear).

8   If the struts/shocks must be replaced, refer to Chapter 10 for the procedure.

Steering and suspension check

9   Visually inspect the steering and suspension components (front and rear) for damage and distortion. Look for damaged seals, boots and bushings and leaks of any kind. Examine the bushings where the control arms meet the chassis **(see illustrations)**.

24.6 Location of the transaxle drain plug

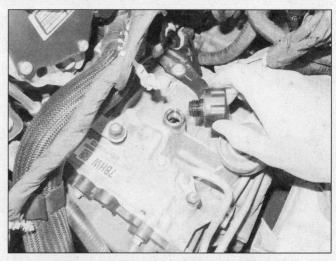

24.9 Automatic transaxle fluid filler cap - battery and battery tray removed for clarity

9 Remove the fluid filler cap **(see illustration)** and add approximately 4-1/2 quarts of the specified type of automatic transmission fluid. Reinstall the cap.

Fluid level check

Note: *The automatic transaxle fluid level should be carefully maintained. Low fluid level can lead to slipping or loss of drive, while over-filling can cause foaming and loss of fluid.*

10 Raise the vehicle on a hoist or support it on four jackstands; the vehicle must be level, with the engine running and the transaxle in Park.

11 Start the engine. With the brake pedal depressed, slowly shift through each gear range, then place the shifter in Park. Let the engine idle for one minute.

12 Using the Driver Information Center, display the transmission fluid temperature. On VT40 (CVT) models, if the fluid temperature is between 140 and 176-degrees F, proceed to the next Step. On 6T40 and 9T50 models, if the fluid temperature is between 185 and 203-degrees F, proceed to the next Step. If the temperature is not warm enough, drive the vehicle until it is. If it's above the maximum temperature, wait until the fluid has cooled back down and falls within the temperature range.

Note: *Some scan tools are capable of displaying transmission fluid temperature.*

13 With the engine running, remove the fluid level check plug on the side of the transaxle and allow the fluid to drain out **(see illustration)**.

14 Allow the fluid to flow out in a steady stream until it begins to drip out. Once the fluid is at a drip, install the plug and tighten it to the torque listed this Chapter's Specifications.

15 If no fluid comes out, add fluid until it begins to drip out. Once the fluid is at a drip, install the plug and tighten it to the torque listed this Chapter's Specifications

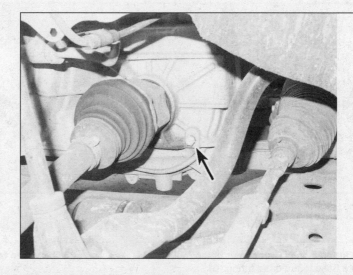

24.13 The transaxle fluid level check plug is located on the left side of the case, just to the rear of the driveaxle

25 Cooling system servicing (draining, flushing and refilling) (every 100,000 miles or 60 months)

Warning: *Wait until the engine is completely cool before beginning this procedure.*

Warning: *Do not allow engine coolant (antifreeze) to come in contact with your skin or painted surfaces of the vehicle. Rinse off spills immediately with plenty of water. Antifreeze is highly toxic if ingested. Never leave antifreeze lying around in an open container or in puddles on the floor; children and pets are attracted by its sweet smell and may drink it. Check with local authorities about disposing of used antifreeze. Many communities have collection centers which will see that antifreeze is disposed of safely.*

Caution: *Never mix green-colored ethylene glycol antifreeze and orange-colored DEX-COOL silicate-free coolant because doing so*

will destroy the efficiency of the DEX-COOL coolant, which is designed to last for 100,000 miles or five years.

Note: *Non-toxic coolant is available at ocal auto parts stores. Although the coolant is non-toxic when fresh, proper disposal is still required.*

1 Periodically, the cooling system should be drained, flushed and refilled to replenish the antifreeze mixture and prevent formation of rust and corrosion, which can impair the performance of the cooling system and cause engine damage. When the cooling system is serviced, all hoses and the coolant reservoir cap should be checked and replaced if necessary.

Draining

2 Apply the parking brake and block the wheels. If the vehicle has just been driven, wait several hours to allow the engine to cool down before beginning this procedure.

3 Once the engine is completely cool, remove the expansion tank cap (see Section 13).

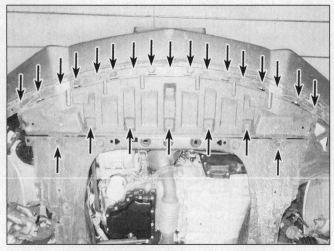

**25.4a Radiator splash shield fastener locations -
2018 model shown, other models similar**

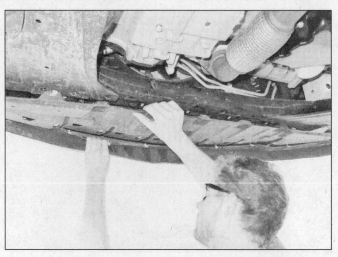

**25.4b Pull the front bumper cover down to allow the
radiator splash shield to be removed**

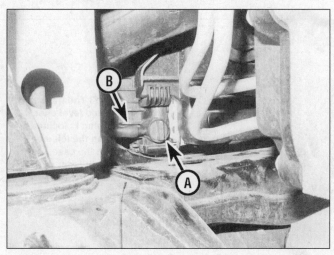

**25.5a Locate the drain fitting at the lower corner of the radiator (A)
and attach a hose to the drain fitting (B). . .**

**25.5b. . . then feed the hose down and out so that it
may drain into the container**

4   Raise the vehicle and support it securely on jackstands, then remove the radiator splash shield **(see illustrations)** from under the vehicle.

5   Move a large container under the radiator drain to catch the coolant. Attach a 3/8-inch diameter hose to the drain fitting to direct the coolant into the container, then open the drain fitting (a pair of pliers may be required to turn it) **(see illustrations)**.

6   While the coolant is draining, check the condition of the radiator hoses, heater hoses and clamps (see Section 13).

7   Reconnect the hose to the radiator and tighten the clamp securely.

Flushing

8   Fill the cooling system with clean water, following the Refilling procedure (see Steps 14 through 17).

9   Start the engine and allow it to reach normal operating temperature, then rev up the engine a few times.

10   Turn the engine off and allow it to cool completely, then drain the system as described earlier.

11   Repeat Steps 8 through 10 until the water being drained is free of contaminants.

12   In severe cases of contamination or clogging of the radiator, remove the radiator (see Chapter 3) and have a radiator repair facility clean and repair it if necessary.

13   Many deposits can be removed by the chemical action of a cleaner available at auto parts stores. Follow the procedure outlined in the manufacturer's instructions.

Note: *When the coolant is regularly drained and the system refilled with the correct antifreeze/water mixture, there should be no need to use chemical cleaners or descalers.*

Refilling

14   Close the radiator drain fitting. Place the heater temperature control in the maximum heat position.

15   Slowly add new coolant/water mixture to the radiator until it's visible in the filler neck.

16   Install the cap and run the engine in a well-ventilated area until the thermostat opens (coolant will begin flowing through the radiator and the upper radiator hose will become hot; the engine cooling fan will turn on). Allow the engine to run long enough for the cooling fan to cycle on and off twice.

17   Turn the engine off and let it cool. Add more coolant mixture if necessary, until it is 1/2-inch above the COLD FILL mark.

18   Start the engine, allow it to reach normal operating temperature and check for leaks.

Chapter 2 Part A
Four-cylinder engines

Contents

Specifications

General

Firing order	1-3-4-2
Compression ratio	
1.5L (LFV)	10.0: 1
2.0L (LTG)	9.50: 1
2.5L (LCV, LKW)	11.20: 1
Compression pressure	See Chapter 2B
Displacement	
1.5L	92 cubic inches
2.0L	122 cubic inches
2.5L	152 cubic inches
Oil pressure	See Chapter 2B

FRONT OF VEHICLE → ① ② ③ ④

Cylinder locations and firing order

Camshafts

Lobe lift	Not available
Endplay	
1.5L engine	0.0016 to 0.0260 inch (0.040 to 0.660 mm)
2.0L and 2.5L engines	0.0016 to 0.0121 inch (0.040 to 0.307 mm)
Journal diameter	
1.5L engine	
Journal No. 1	1.2179 to 1.2189 inches (30.935 to 30.960 mm)
Journal No. 2 through No. 6	0.9423 to 0.9433 inch (23.935 to 23.960 mm)
2.0L and 2.5L engines	
Journal No. 1	1.3754 to 1.3764 inches (34.935 to 34.960 mm)
Journal No. 2 through No. 5	1.0604 to 1.0614 inches (26.935 to 26.960 mm)
Camshaft bearing oil clearance	
1.5L engine	0.0016 to 0.0033 inch (0.040 to 0.085 mm)
2.0L and 2.5L engines	Not available
Camshaft thrust bearing width	
1.5L engine	
With camshaft phaser installed	1.3061 to 1.3199 inches (33.175 to 33.525 mm)
Cylinder head	1.2939 to 1.3045 inches (32.865 to 33.135 mm)
2.0L and 2.5L engines	
With camshaft phaser installed	1.1821 to 1.1880 inches (30.025 to 30.175 mm)
Cylinder head	1.1759 to 1.1768 inches (29.868 to 29.890 mm)

Torque specifications

	Ft-lbs (unless otherwise indicated)	Nm

Note: *One foot-pound (ft-lb) of torque is equivalent to 12 inch-pounds (in-lbs) of torque. Torque values below approximately 15 ft-lbs are expressed in inch-pounds, because most foot-pound torque wrenches are not accurate at these smaller values.*

	Ft-lbs	Nm
Camshaft actuator sprocket bolts (intake and exhaust)		
1.5L engine		
Step 1	15	20
Step 2	Tighten an additional 90-degrees	
2.0L and 2.5L engines		
Step 1	22	30
Step 2	Tighten an additional 100-degrees	
Camshaft bearing cap bolts **(in sequence see illustration 11.23a or 11.23b)**		
1.5L engine	106 in-lbs	12
2.0L and 2.5L engines	89 in-lbs	10
Crankshaft pulley bolt*		
1.5L engine		
Step 1	74	100
Step 2	Tighten an additional 180-degrees	
2.0L and 2.5L engines		
Step 1	111	150
Step 2	Tighten an additional 140-degrees	
Cylinder head bolts* **(in sequence - see illustration 12.21a or 12.21b)**		
Step 1	22	30
Step 2		
1.5L engine	Tighten an additional 240-degrees	
2.0L and 2.5L engines	Tighten an additional 190-degrees	
Drivebelt tensioner bolt	See Chapter 1	
Driveplate bolts		
Step 1	15	20
Step 2	22	30
Step 3		
1.5L engine	Tighten an additional 70-degrees	
2.0L and 2.5L engines	Tighten an additional 40-degrees	
Right side engine mount		
Engine mount-to-chassis bolts		
1.5L and 2016 and later 2.0L engines		
Step 1	74	100
Step 2		
1.5L engine	Tighten an additional 70-degrees	
2.0L engine	Tighten an additional 75-degrees	
2015 and earlier 2.0L and all 2.5L engines	46	62
Engine mount brace nut/bolt	16	22
Engine mount-to-engine bracket bolts		
1.5L and 2016 and later 2.0L engines		
Step 1	74	100
Step 2	Tighten an additional 75-degrees	
2015 and earlier 2.0L and all 2.5L engines	46	62
Engine mount bracket-to-engine bolts (1.5L engine)		
Step 1	43	58
Step 2	Tighten an additional 60-degrees	
Engine mount bracket brace bolts (1.5L engine)		
Small bolt	80 in-lbs	9
Large bolt	16	22
Left-side transaxle mount		
1.5L and 2016 and later 2.0L engines		
Mount-to-chassis bolts	74	100
Mount-to-transmission bolts		
Step 1	74	100
Step 2	Tighten an additional 60 to 75-degrees	
Brace bolts		
Step 1	16	22
Step 2	16	22
Transaxle front mount (2015 and earlier 2.0L and all 2.5L engines)		
Mount through-bolt	74	100
Mount-to-transmission bolts	46	62

Torque specifications (continued)

	Ft-lbs (unless otherwise indicated)	Nm
Rear transaxle mount		
1.5L and 2016 and later 2.0L engines		
Mount-to-subframe bolt		
Step 1	74	100
Step 2	Tighten an additional 120 to 135-degrees	
Transaxle bracket bolts		
Step 1	74	100
Step 2	Tighten an additional 60 to 70-degrees	
Mount through-bolt		
Step 1	52	70
Step 2	Tighten an additional 90 to 105-degrees	
2015 and earlier 2.0L and all 2.5L engines		
Mount-to-subframe bolts/nuts		
Step 1	74	100
Step 2	Tighten an additional 120 to 130-degrees	
Transaxle bracket bolts	74	100
Mount through bolt	74	100
Mount brace bolts		
Brace-to-block bolt	37	50
Brace-to-mount bracket bolt/nut	74	100
Exhaust manifold-to-cylinder head bolts		
2.0L and 2.5L engines		
Step 1	15	20
Step 2	15	20
Step 3 (2.0L engine only)	15	20
Exhaust manifold support bracket bolt/nuts (2.0L engines)	18	25
Exhaust manifold heat shield bolts	80 in-lbs	9
Exhaust pipe-to-manifold nuts	22	30
Engine front cover perimeter bolts	18	24
Engine front cover water pump bolt	18	24
Intake manifold bolts/nuts		
1.5L engines (in sequence - see illustration 5.15)	106 in-lbs	12
2.0L and 2.5L engines (in sequence - see illustration 5.34)		
Step 1	106 in-lbs	12
Step 2	106 in-lbs	12
Engine oil cooler bolts (1.5L engine)	89 in-lbs	10
Lower oil pan bolts		
1.5L engine (in sequence - see illustration 13.8)	89 in-lbs	10
2.0L and 2.5L engines	89 in-lbs	10
Upper oil pan bolts		
1.5L engines (in sequence - see illustration 13.27a)		
Step 1	Hand-tighten	
Step 2	89 in-lbs	10
Step 3, oil pan-to-transmission bolts	43	58
2.0L and 2.5L engines (in sequence - see illustration 13.27b)		
Step 1	Hand-tighten	
Step 2, bolts 1-11	18	25
Step 3, bolts 12 and 13	89 in-lbs	10
Step 4	Repeat Step 2 and Step 3	
Step 5, oil pan-to-transmission bolts	44	60
Oil pump-to-balance shaft module bolts (2.0L and 2.5L engines)	89 in-lbs	10
Oil pump pickup tube bolts (2.0L and 2.5L engines)	89 in-lbs	
Oil pump mounting bolts (1.5L engines)	89 in-lbs	10
Oil pump drive chain tensioner bolt	89 in-lbs	10
Balance shaft module		
Step 1	43	58
Step 2	43	58
Balance shaft driven sprocket bolt		
Step 1	30	40
Step 2	Tighten an additional 50-degrees	
Balance shaft chain tensioner	89 in-lbs	10
Balance shaft chain guides	89 in-lbs	10
Timing chain tensioner	18	25
Timing chain guides		
1.5L engines	89 in-lbs	10
2.0L and 2.5L engines	18	25

Torque specifications (continued) Ft-lbs (unless otherwise indicated) Nm

Note: *One foot-pound (ft-lb) of torque is equivalent to 12 inch-pounds (in-lbs) of torque. Torque values below approximately 15 ft-lbs are expressed in inch-pounds, because most foot-pound torque wrenches are not accurate at these smaller values.*

	Ft-lbs (unless otherwise indicated)	Nm
Timing chain oiling nozzle bolt	132 in-lbs	15
Timing chain guide access hole plug	55	75
Timing chain cover		
1.5L engine **(in sequence - see illustration 7.20a)**		
Step 1, all bolts	44 in-lbs	5
Step 2, bolts 1 and 3 through 14	133 in-lbs	15
Step 3, bolts 2 and 15	43	58
2.0L and 2.5L engines **(in sequence - see illustration 7.20b)**		
Step 1, bolts 1 through 3	132 in-lbs	15
Step 2, bolts 1 through 3	Tighten an additional 130-degrees	
Step 3, bolts 4 through 15	18	25
Step 4, bolts 16 and 17	89 in-lbs	10
Step 5, bolts 18 and 19	89 in-lbs	10
Step 6, bolt 20	18	25
Double-end studs (cylinder head-to-turbocharger) 1.5L engine	89 in-lbs	10
Vacuum pump bolts		
1.5L engine		
Step 1	132 in-lbs	15
Step 2	18	25
2.0L and 2.5L engines	89 in-lbs	10
Valve cover bolts/stud bolts		
1.5L engine	132 in-lbs	15
2.0L and 2.5L engines	89 in-lbs	10
Water outlet housing bolts		
1.5L engine	89 in-lbs	10
Water pump sprocket housing-to-rear housing bolts	89 in-lbs	10
Water pump rear housing-to-engine block bolts	18	25

Caution: * *Bolt(s) must be replaced.*

1   General Information

1   The Chevrolet Malibu has been equipped with either a 1.5L, 2.0L or a 2.5L engine. This Chapter is devoted to in-vehicle repair procedures for these DOHC (Double Overhead Camshaft) four-cylinder engines. Information concerning engine removal and installation and engine overhaul can be found in Part B of this Chapter.

2   All models are equipped with a single timing chain to drive the camshafts and single chain to drive the dual balance shaft assembly and oil pump. The balance shaft chain is mounted directly behind the camshaft timing chain.

3   The Specifications included in this Chapter apply only to the procedures contained in this Part. Specifications related to engine removal and installation or overhaul can be found in Chapter 2B.

2   Repair operations possible with the engine in the vehicle

1   Many major repair operations can be accomplished without removing the engine from the vehicle.

2   Clean the engine compartment and the exterior of the engine with some type of degreaser before any work is done. It will make the job easier and help keep dirt out of the internal areas of the engine.

3   Depending on the components involved, it may be helpful to remove the hood to improve access to the engine as repairs are performed (refer to Chapter 11 if necessary). Cover the fenders to prevent damage to the paint. Special pads are available, but an old bedspread or blanket will also work.

4   If vacuum, exhaust, oil or coolant leaks develop, indicating a need for gasket or seal replacement, the repairs can generally be made with the engine in the vehicle. The intake and exhaust manifold gaskets, oil pan gasket, crankshaft oil seals and cylinder head gasket are all accessible with the engine in place.

5   Exterior engine components, such as the intake and exhaust manifolds, the oil pan, the oil pump/balance shaft, the water pump, the starter motor, the alternator and the fuel system components can be removed for repair with the engine in place.

6   Since the cylinder head can be removed without pulling the engine, camshaft and valve component servicing can also be accomplished with the engine in the vehicle. Replacement of the timing chain or timing belt, and sprockets is also possible with the engine in the vehicle.

7   In extreme cases caused by a lack of necessary equipment, repair or replacement of piston rings, pistons, connecting rods and rod bearings is possible with the engine in the vehicle. However, this practice is not recommended because of the cleaning and preparation work that must be done to the components involved.

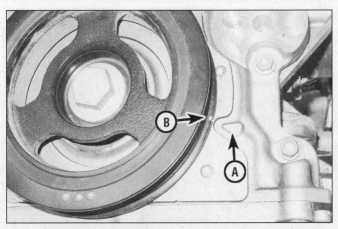

3.4 Align the cast pointer on the timing chain cover (A) with the notch in the crankshaft pulley (B) - drivebelt tensioner removed for clarity

4.5 PCV fresh air tube quick-connectors locations

4.7 PCV dirty air tube fastener location

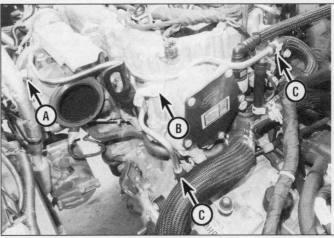

4.8 Turbocharger coolant return pipe details

A Turbocharger coolant return pipe banjo bolt fitting
B Coolant return pipe bracket bolt
C Coolant pipe hose clamps

---

3 Top Dead Center (TDC) for number one piston - locating

1 Top Dead Center (TDC) is the highest point in the cylinder that each piston reaches as it travels up-and-down during crankshaft rotation. Each piston reaches TDC on the compression stroke and again on the exhaust stroke, but TDC generally refers to piston position on the compression stroke.

2 Positioning the piston(s) at TDC is an essential part of certain other repair procedures discussed in this manual.

3 Before beginning this procedure, place the transmission in Park or Neutral and apply the parking brake or block the rear wheels. Remove the spark plugs (see Chapter 1).

4 Insert a compression gauge into the number one cylinder spark plug hole. Turn the crankshaft using a ratchet or breaker bar and socket (normal direction of rotation is clockwise) until compression registers on the gauge, then turn it slowly until the notch on the crankshaft pulley is aligned with the pointer on the timing chain cover **(see illustration)**.

5 After the number one piston has been positioned at TDC on the compression stroke, TDC for any of the remaining pistons can be located by turning the crankshaft and following the firing order. Divide the crankshaft pulley into two equal sections with chalk marks at each point, each indicating 180-degrees of crankshaft rotation. Rotating the engine past TDC no. 1 to the next mark will place the engine at TDC for cylinder no. 3.

---

4 Valve cover - removal and installation

Warning: *Wait until the engine is completely cool before beginning this procedure.*

1.5L engines
Removal

1 Relieve the fuel system pressure (see Chapter 5).

2 Disconnect the cable from the negative battery terminal (see Chapter 4).

3 Remove the oil filler cap, then remove engine cover fastener **(see illustration 5.4)** and lift the cover off of the ballstuds.

4 Remove the intake manifold sound insulator **(see illustration 5.5)**.

5 Disconnect the PCV fresh air tube quick-connectors, then remove the tube **(see illustration)**.
Caution: *The PCV valve and tube assembly are not reusable. If removing the valve cover, do not remove the PCV valve and tube assembly from the valve camshaft cover. Disconnect them at the quick connect fittings.*

6 Remove the ignition coil assembly from the valve cover (see Chapter 5).

7 Remove the PCV dirty air tube fastener **(see illustration)** and pull the tube fitting out of the turbocharger, then move the tube back and secure it out of the way. Make sure to cover the opening in the turbocharger, and make sure the O-ring on the tube fitting is not damaged.
Caution: *The PCV valve and tube assembly are not reusable. If removing the valve cover, do not remove the PCV valve and tube assembly from the valve camshaft cover. Disconnect the tube fitting from the turbocharger.*

8 Drain the coolant (see Chapter 1), disconnect the turbocharger coolant pipe clamps, banjo bolt and tube bracket bolt, then remove the coolant line **(see illustration)**.

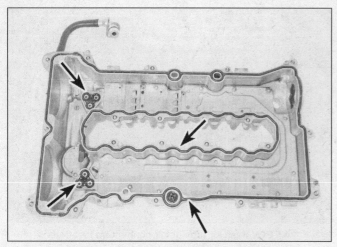

4.14 Install the gaskets into the grooved recesses in the valve cover - 1.5L engine shown

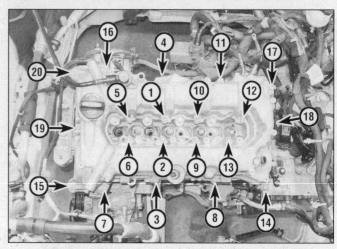

4.15 Valve cover bolt tightening sequence - 1.5L engine

9   Remove the fuel rail and injectors (see Chapter 4).
10   Remove the vacuum pump (see Chapter 9).
11   Disconnect the electrical connectors from the camshaft position sensors, the camshaft position actuator solenoids, release the harness retainers and move the harness out of the way, then remove the camshaft position sensors and actuators (see Chapter 6).
12   Remove the valve cover bolts **(see illustration 4.15)** making note of their locations, then lift the valve cover off. Tap gently with a soft-faced hammer, if necessary, to break the gasket seal.

Installation
13   Clean the gasket surfaces on the cylinder head and valve cover. Use a shop rag and brake cleaner to wipe off all residue and gasket material from the sealing surfaces.
14   Insert new valve cover gaskets into the grooved recesses in the valve cover. Make sure the gaskets are positioned properly in their grooves **(see illustration)**.
15   Install the valve cover and hand-tighten the bolts. Tighten the valve cover bolts in the

recommended sequence **(see illustration)** to the torque listed in this Chapter's Specifications.
16   The remainder of installation is the reverse of removal.
17   Refill the cooling system (see Chapter 1) and reconnect the battery (see Chapter 5).

2.0L and 2.5L engines
Removal
18   Disconnect the cable from the negative battery terminal (see Chapter 5). If you're working on a 2.0L model, drain the cooling system (see Chapter 1).
19   Remove the oil filler cap, then remove engine cover fastener and lift the cover off of the ballstuds.
20   Remove the ignition coil assembly from the valve cover (see Chapter 5).
21   Disconnect the PCV fresh air tube quick-connectors, then remove the tube.
Caution: *The PCV valve and tube assembly are not reusable. If removing the valve cover, do not remove the PCV valve and tube assembly from the valve camshaft cover. Disconnect them at the quick connect fittings.*
22   Remove the vacuum pump (see Chapter 9).

23   On 2.0L engines, remove the turbocharger heat shield fasteners and shield.
24   On 2.0L engines, remove the PCV dirty air tube fastener and pull the tube fitting out of the turbocharger, then move the tube back so it can be removed with the valve cover. Make sure to cover the opening in the turbocharger and the O-ring on the tube fitting is not damaged.
Caution: *The PCV valve and tube assembly are not reusable. If removing the valve cover, do not remove the PCV valve and tube assembly from the valve camshaft cover. Disconnect the tube fitting from the turbocharger.*
25   Drain the coolant (see Chapter 1), then remove the turbocharger coolant return pipe (see Chapter 4).
26   Remove the oil dipstick from the tube (see Chapter 1).
27   On 2.0L engines, remove the coolant air bleed pipe fastener, then remove the pipe from the top of the cover and replace the O-ring.
28   Disconnect the electrical connectors from the camshaft position sensors and the camshaft position actuator solenoids. Release the harness retainers and move the harness out of the way, then remove the camshaft sensors and actuators (see Chapter 6).
29   Remove the valve cover heat shield fasteners and heat shield.
30   Remove the valve cover bolts **(see illustration 4.33)**, making note of their locations, then lift the valve cover off. Tap gently with a soft-faced hammer, if necessary, to break the gasket seal.
Note: *The center four bolts are longer than the remaining perimeter bolts.*

Installation
31   Clean the gasket surfaces on the cylinder head and valve cover. Use a shop rag and brake cleaner to wipe off all residue and gasket material from the sealing surfaces.
32   Insert new valve cover gaskets into the grooved recesses in the valve cover. Make sure the gaskets are positioned properly in their grooves **(see illustration 4.14)**.
33   The remainder of installation is the reverse of removal. On 2.0L engines, tighten

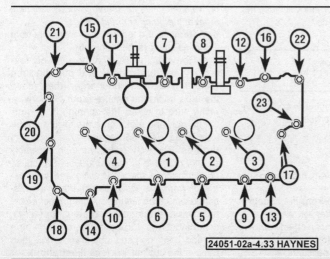

4.33 Valve cover bolt tightening sequence - 2.0L engine

24051-02a-4.33 HAYNES

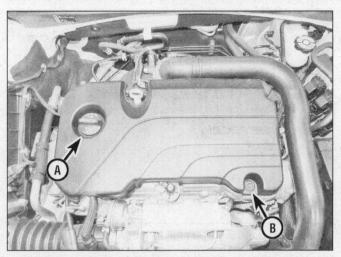

5.4 Remove the oil filler cap (A) and the engine cover
fastener (B) - 1.5L engine shown

5.5 Lift the intake manifold sound insulator off
the top on the engine

the valve cover bolts in the recommended
sequence **(see illustration)** to the torque
listed in this Chapter's Specifications. If you're
working on a 2.5L engine, tighten the valve
cover bolts evenly, starting with the center
bolts and working outward, to the torque listed
in this Chapter's Specifications.
34   On 2.0L engines, refill the cooling system (see Chapter 1).
35   Reconnect the battery (see Chapter 5).

5   Intake manifold - removal and installation

Warning: *Wait until the engine is completely
cool before beginning this procedure.*
1   Relieve the fuel system pressure (see
Chapter 4).
2   Disconnect the cable from the negative
battery terminal (see Chapter 5).
3   If you're working on a 2.0L engine, drain
the cooling system (see Chapter 1).

1.5L engine

Removal
4   Remove the oil filler cap, then remove
the engine cover fastener **(see illustration)**
and lift the cover off of the ballstuds.
5   Remove the intake manifold sound insulator **(see illustration)**.
6   Detach the charge air cooler outlet pipe
from the throttle body (see Chapter 4).
7   Remove the fuel feed line and bracket
from the intake manifold (see Chapter 4).
8   Disconnect the canister purge line quick-
connector from the throttle body **(see illustration)**, then remove the bracket and electrical
connectors to the throttle body and intake air
pressure sensor.
9   Disconnect the canister purge solenoid
electrical connector then unclip the solenoid
(see illustration) from the bottom of the
intake manifold and secure the solenoid and
hose out of the way.

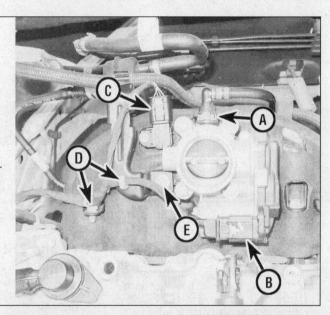

5.8 Disconnect
the canister purge
solenoid line quick-
connect fitting

A   Canister purge line
     quick connector
B   Throttle body
     electrical connector
C   Intake air pressure
     sensor connector
D   Harness retainers
E   Canister purge fuel
     line bracket
     fastener

5.9 Slide the
canister purge
solenoid off of the
intake manifold
bracket tab

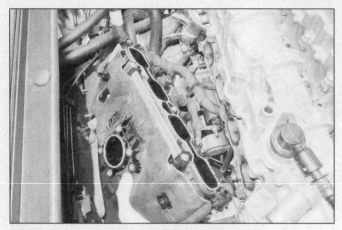

5.12 Remove the intake manifold
from the cylinder head

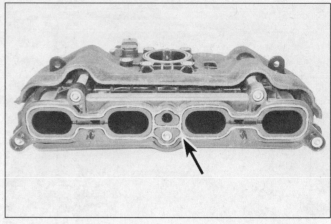

5.13 Install the gasket into the grooved recess in the
intake manifold - 1.5L engine shown

5.15 Intake manifold bolt tightening sequence (1.5L engine)

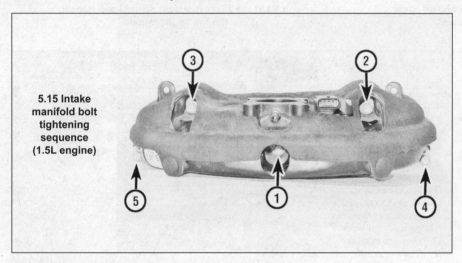

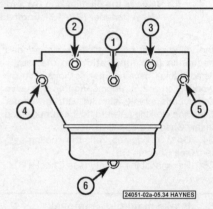

5.34 Intake manifold tightening sequence -
2.0L and 2.5L engines

10 Disconnect any remaining electrical connectors that would interfere with manifold removal. Open the wiring harness clips and detach all wiring harnesses from the manifold.
11 Loosen the intake manifold captive mounting bolts **(see illustration 5.15)**.
Note: *The intake manifold bolts are captive bolts, do not try and remove the bolts from the intake manifold.*
12 Carefully detach the intake manifold from the cylinder head **(see illustration)**.

Installation

13 Insert a new intake manifold gasket into the grooved recess in the intake manifold. Make sure the gasket is positioned properly in the groove **(see illustration)**.
Note: *Make sure the mating surfaces of the manifold and cylinder head are clean.*
14 Place the manifold against the cylinder head and tighten the bolts, but only finger-tight.
15 Tighten the bolts in sequence **(see illustration)** to the torque listed in this Chapter's Specifications.
16 The remainder of installation is the reverse of removal.
17 Reconnect the battery (see Chapter 5).
18 Run the engine and check for vacuum and fuel leaks.

2.0L and 2.5L engines
Removal

19 On 2.0L engines, detach the charge air cooler outlet pipe from the throttle body (see Chapter 4).
20 Disconnect the fuel feed pipe quick-connect fitting (see Chapter 4).
21 On 2.0L engines, disconnect the coolant air bleed pipe hose then plug the hose and cap the pipe.
22 Remove the air intake duct, throttle body, fuel rail and fuel injectors (see Chapter 4).
23 Disconnect the power brake booster vacuum line (see Chapter 9).
24 Disconnect the PCV fresh air tube quick-connectors, then remove the tube.
Caution: *The PCV valve and tube assembly are not reusable. If removing the intake manifold, do not remove the PCV valve and tube assembly from the valve camshaft cover. Disconnect them at the quick connect fittings.*
25 Remove the EVAP canister purge solenoid valve (see Chapter 6).
26 Remove the throttle body (see Chapter 4).
27 Remove the high-pressure fuel pump (see Chapter 4).
28 Disengage the intake manifold cover clips and remove the cover from the intake manifold.

29 Disconnect any electrical connectors that would interfere with manifold removal. Open the wiring harness clips and detach all wiring harnesses from the manifold.
30 Loosen the intake manifold mounting bolts **(see illustration 5.34)**.
Note: *On 2.0L engines, the intake manifold bolts are captive bolts - do not try to remove the bolts from the intake manifold.*
31 Separate the intake manifold from the cylinder head to access the fuel pressure sensor, then disconnect the sensor electrical connector and remove the intake manifold.

Installation

32 Insert the new intake manifold gasket into the grooved recess in the intake manifold. Make sure the gasket is positioned properly in the grooves **(see illustration 5.13)**.
Note: *Make sure the mating surfaces of the manifold and cylinder head are clean.*
33 Place the manifold close to the cylinder head and reconnect the fuel pressure sensor electrical connector, then place the manifold against the cylinder head and finger-tighten the bolts.
34 Tighten the bolts in sequence **(see illustration)** to the torque listed in this Chapter's Specifications.

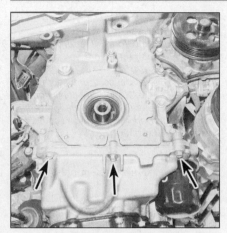

7.13 Oil pan-to-timing chain cover bolts

7.14a Remove the lower bolts. . .

7.14b. . . and the upper bolts - 1.5L engine shown

35 The remainder of installation is the reverse of removal.

36 Reconnect the battery (see Chapter 5).

37 Run the engine and check for vacuum and fuel leaks.

6 Exhaust manifold - removal and installation

Warning: *Wait until the engine is completely cool before starting this procedure.*

Note: *On 1.5L engines, the exhaust manifold has been integrated into the turbocharger (see Chapter 4).*

2.0L engine

Removal

1 Disconnect the cable from the negative terminal of the battery (see Chapter 5).

2 Remove the exhaust manifold heat shield, then remove the turbocharger (see Chapter 4).

3 Remove the exhaust manifold support bracket mounting nuts and bolts, then detach the bracket from the manifold and the block.

4 Remove the exhaust manifold mounting bolts and detach the manifold from the cylinder head.

Installation

5 Using a scraper, thoroughly clean the mating surfaces on the cylinder head, manifold and exhaust pipe. Remove the residue with brake system cleaner.

6 Check that the mating surfaces are perfectly flat and not damaged in any way. A warped or damaged manifold may require machining or, if severe enough, replacement. Install the new gasket to the cylinder head and place the manifold on the head. Install new exhaust manifold bolts and tighten the bolts evenly, working from the center outwards, to the torque listed in this Chapter's Specifications.

Note: *The new exhaust manifold bolts have adhesive coating and must be tightened to final torque within five minutes of tightening the bolts.*

7 The remainder of installation is the reverse of removal.

8 Reconnect the battery (see Chapter 5).

9 Run the engine and check for exhaust leaks.

2.5L engines

Removal

10 Disconnect the cable from the negative battery terminal (see Chapter 5).

11 Remove the exhaust manifold heat shield.

12 Raise the vehicle and support it securely on jackstands.

13 Soak the catalytic converter-to-manifold retaining nuts with penetrating oil, then unscrew them and detach the catalytic converter from the exhaust manifold.

14 Follow the lead from the oxygen sensor up to its electrical connector, then unplug the connector. Also detach the lead from its retaining clip.

15 Remove the exhaust manifold mounting bolts and detach the manifold from the cylinder head.

Installation

16 Using a scraper, thoroughly clean the mating surfaces on the cylinder head, manifold and exhaust pipe. Remove the residue with brake system cleaner.

17 Check that the mating surfaces are perfectly flat and not damaged in any way. A warped or damaged manifold may require machining or, if severe enough, replacement. Install the new gasket to the cylinder head and place the manifold on the head. Tighten the bolts evenly, working from the center outwards, to the torque listed in this Chapter's Specifications.

18 Connect the catalytic converter to the manifold and tighten the bolts evenly to the torque listed in this Chapter's Specifications.

19 The remainder of installation is the reverse of removal.

20 Reconnect the battery (see Chapter 5).

21 Run the engine and check for exhaust leaks.

7 Timing chain cover - removal and installation

Warning: *The engine must be completely cool before beginning this procedure.*

Removal

1 Relieve the fuel system pressure (see Chapter 4).

2 Disconnect the cable from the negative battery terminal (see Chapter 5).

3 Remove the air filter housing (see Chapter 4).

4 Set the engine to TDC (see Section 3).

5 Loosen the right front wheel lug nuts, then raise the front of the vehicle and support it securely on jackstands. Remove the right front wheel.

6 Drain the engine oil and coolant (see Chapter 1).

7 Remove the valve cover (see Section 4).

8 Remove the drivebelt and tensioner (see Chapter 1).

9 Remove the alternator (see Chapter 5).

10 Support the engine with an engine hoist or engine support fixture, or place a block of wood between the jack head and the oil pan **(see illustration 17.8)**. Carefully raise the engine or transaxle just enough to take the weight off the mounts.

11 Remove the right engine mount (see Section 17).

12 Remove the crankshaft pulley (see Section 10).

13 On 1.5L engines, remove the oil pan-to-timing chain cover bolts **(see illustration)**.

14 Loosen the timing chain cover bolts gradually and evenly, then remove them **(see illustrations)**.

Note: *Draw a sketch of the engine cover and cover fasteners. Identify the location of all bolts for installation in their original locations.*

15 If necessary, insert a prybar between the cylinder head and the front cover prying

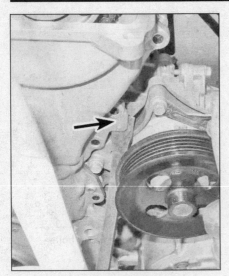

**7.15 Front prying point location -
1.5L engine**

points and separate the cover **(see illustration)**.

16   Remove the timing chain cover.

Installation

17   Inspect and clean all sealing surfaces of the timing chain cover, the upper oil pan on 1.5L engines and the block.

Note: *Be very careful when scraping on aluminum engine parts. Aluminum is soft and gouges easily. Severely gouged parts may require replacement.*

18   If necessary, replace the crankshaft front oil seal (see Section 10).

19   On 1.5L engines, apply a 4 mm bead of RTV sealant around the sealing surface

of the timing chain cover, then apply a 3 mm dab of sealant where the cylinder head and engine block meet. On 2.0L and 2.5L engines, apply a 5 mm bead of RTV sealant around the sealing surface of the timing chain cover, then apply a 14 mm dab of sealant where the cylinder head and engine block meet.

Note: *Once the sealant has been applied, the timing chain cover must be installed within a 20 minute period and the final torque competed within 60 minutes or the sealant must be removed and applied again.*

20   Install the cover and the bolts into their original locations and tighten them hand-tight, then tighten them in sequence **(see illustrations)** to the torque listed in this Chapter's Specifications.

Caution: *On 2.0L and 2.5L engines, the #3, #5 and #6 bolts must be replaced with new bolts.*

21   Reinstall the remaining parts in the reverse order of removal.

22   Fill the crankcase with the recommended oil (see Chapter 1).

23   Reconnect the battery (see Chapter 5).

24   Refill the cooling system (see Chapter 1).

25   Start the engine and check for leaks. Check all fluid levels.

---

8   Timing chain, oil pump drive chain and sprockets - removal, inspection and installation

---

Caution: *The timing system is complex. Severe engine damage will occur if you make any mistakes. Do not attempt this procedure unless you are highly experienced*

with this type of repair. If you are at all unsure of your abilities, consult an expert. Double-check all your work and be sure everything is correct before you attempt to start the engine.

Caution: *This is a difficult procedure. Read through the entire Section and obtain the necessary tools before beginning the procedure. New camshaft sprocket bolts must be purchased ahead of time.*

Removal

1   Relieve the fuel system pressure (see Chapter 4).

2   Remove the spark plugs (see Chapter 1), then set the engine to TDC (see Section 3).

3   Disconnect the cable from the negative battery terminal (see Chapter 5).

4   Remove the valve cover (see Section 4).

5   Drain the engine oil (see Chapter 1).

6   Remove the drivebelt and drivebelt tensioner (see Chapter 1).

7   Remove the timing chain cover (see Section 7).

Timing chain

8   Remove the upper timing chain guide bolts and guide from the top of the cylinder head **(see illustration)**.

9   If the tensioner has a lever on the front, press down on the lever and compress the plunger **(see illustration)**. Insert a drill bit or small Allen wrench through the lever and into the hole in the tensioner body to hold the plunger in the retracted position. Some models may use a retaining clip instead of a lever; on those models, press the clip and depress the plunger, then insert a drill bit into the hole in the tensioner body to hold the plunger in the retracted position.

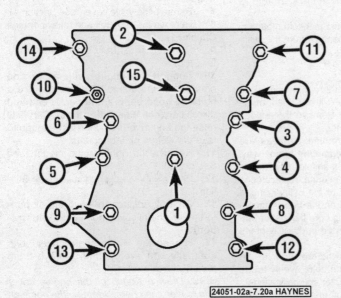

24051-02a-7.20a HAYNES

**7.20a Timing chain cover tightening sequence -
1.5L engines**

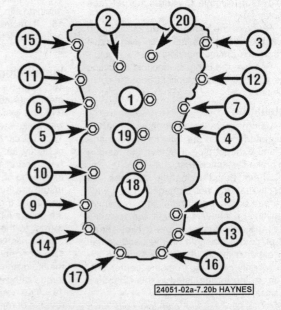

24051-02a-7.20b HAYNES

**7.20b Timing chain cover tightening sequence -
2.0L and 2.5L engines**

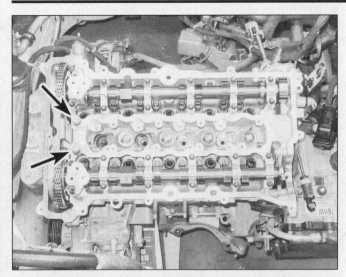

8.8 Upper timing chain guide bolts - 1.5L engine shown, 2.0L and 2.5L similar

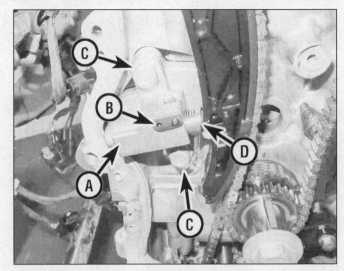

8.9 Tensioner details - 1.5L engine shown, 2.0L and 2.5L similar

A	Tensioner body	C	Tensioner mounting bolts
B	Tensioner lever and hole	D	Tensioner plunger

10 With the tensioner locked in the compressed position remove the tensioner mounting bolts, tensioner and gasket.

11 Remove the rear timing chain guide bolts and guide (see illustration).

12 Remove the front timing chain guide bolt from the bottom of the guide and remove the guide (see illustration 8.11).

13 Remove the timing chain from the crankshaft sprocket and camshaft actuator sprockets.

14 Remove the timing chain tensioner bolts and tensioner.

15 Using an Allen wrench, remove the timing chain oil nozzle from the block.

16 Use a wrench on the intake or exhaust cam hex to hold the camshaft, and remove the camshaft sprocket bolt(s), then slide the sprocket(s) off the end of the camshaft(s).

Discard the bolt and install a new one on reassembly.
Note: On 2.0L and 2.5L engines, to replace the balance shaft chain, see Section 9 .

Oil pump drive chain - 1.5L engines

17 Remove the upper oil pan (see Section 13) and oil pump (see Section 14).

18 Remove the timing chain (see Steps 1 through 14).

19 Press the oil pump drive chain tensioner away from the chain, then insert a drill bit or Allen wrench into the hole on the tensioner arm to lock it into the retracted position (see illustration).

20 Remove the oil pump drive chain tensioner mounting bolt and remove the tensioner.

21 Lift the oil pump chain off the oil pump

sprocket, then the crankshaft sprocket and remove the chain.

Inspection

22 Clean all parts with solvent and dry with compressed air, if available.

23 Inspect the chain tensioner for excessive wear or other damage. Drain all the oil out of the chain tensioner if it is to be reused.

24 Inspect the timing chain guides for deep grooves, excessive wear, or other damage.

25 Inspect the timing chain for excessive wear or damage.

26 Inspect the crankshaft and camshaft sprockets for chipped or broken teeth, excessive wear, or damage.

27 Replace any component that is in questionable condition.

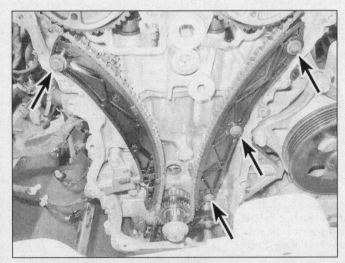

8.11 Timing chain guide bolt locations - 1.5L engine shown, 2.0L and 2.5L similar

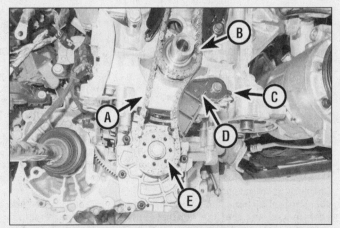

8.19 Oil pump drive chain and tensioner details - 1.5L engines

A	Oil pump drive chain	D	Oil pump drive chain
B	Crankshaft sprocket		tensioner
C	Oil pump drive chain tensioner locking hole	E	Oil pump drive sprocket

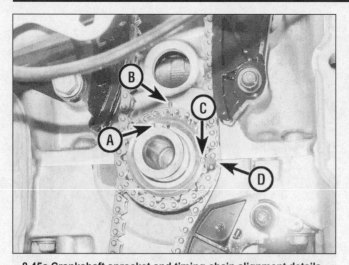

**8.45a Crankshaft sprocket and timing chain alignment details -
1.5L engine shown, 2.0L and 2.5L engines similar**

A　*Crankshaft key way - 12 o'clock position*
B　*TDC timing mark*
C　*Crankshaft sprocket timing mark*
D　*Timing chain colored link for the crankshaft*

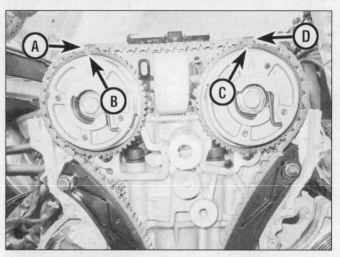

**8.45b Camshaft sprockets and timing chain alignment details -
1.5L engine shown, 2.0L and 2.5L engines similar**

A　*Timing chain colored link - intake sprocket*
B　*Intake camshaft actuator sprocket timing mark*
C　*Exhaust camshaft actuator sprocket timing mark*
D　*Timing chain colored link - exhaust sprocket*

Installation

Caution: *Before starting the engine, carefully rotate the crankshaft by hand through at least two full revolutions (use a socket and breaker bar on the crankshaft pulley center bolt). If you feel any resistance, STOP! There is something wrong; most likely valves are contacting the pistons. You must find the problem before proceeding.*

Oil pump drive chain - 1.5L engines

28　Place the oil pump drive chain over the crankshaft sprocket.

29　Install the oil pump (see Section 14).

30　Install the oil pump drive chain tensioner making sure the tensioner spring is retained in the correct position before installing it.

31　Install the oil pump tensioner bolt and tighten it to the torque listed in this Chapter's Specifications.

32　Release the oil pump tensioner retaining tool and allow the tensioner to seat against the chain.

33　Install the upper oil pan (see Section 13).

34　Remaining installation is the reverse of removal.

Timing chain

Note: *On 2.0L and 2.5L engines, install the balance shaft chain if removed (see Section 9).*

35　Install the timing chain oil nozzle into the block and tighten it to the torque listed in this Chapter's Specifications.

36　Verify that both camshafts have not been moved and that the notches in the ends of the camshafts are at the 12 o'clock positions.

37　Slide the camshaft sprockets onto the end of the camshafts, then install new camshaft sprocket bolts and tighten the bolts by hand.

38　Hold the intake or exhaust camshaft with a wrench on the camshaft's hex to prevent it from turning, then tighten the camshaft actuator sprocket bolt to the torque listed in this Chapter's Specifications.

39　Slide the crankshaft sprocket onto the end of the crankshaft, if removed, and verify that the crankshaft keyway is at the 12 o'clock position **(see illustration 8.45a)**.

40　Place the timing chain under the crankshaft sprocket and over the camshaft actuator sprockets and align the timing marks **(see illustration 8.45b)**.

41　Install the front timing chain guide and guide bolts, then tighten the bolts to the torque listed in this Chapter's Specifications.

42　Install the right-side timing chain guide and guide bolts, then tighten the bolts to the torque listed in this Chapter's Specifications.

43　Install the timing chain tensioner and tighten the bolts to the torque listed in this Chapter's Specifications.

44　Push the rear guide towards the tensioner until the locking pin can be removed, then pull the pin out from the tensioner **(see illustration 8.9)**.

45　Verify the timing chain colored links are still aligned with the crankshaft sprocket and camshaft sprockets **(see illustrations)**.

46　Install the timing chain cover (see Section 7).

47　Install the valve cover (see Section 4).

48　The remainder of installation is the reverse of removal. Install a new oil filter and refill the crankcase with oil (see Chapter 1).

49　Reconnect the battery (see Chapter 5).

50　Refill the cooling system (see Chapter 1).

51　Run the engine and check for leaks.

9　Balance shaft chain and balance module assembly (2.0L and 2.5L engines) - removal, inspection and installation

Warning: *The engine must be completely cool before beginning this procedure.*

Removal

1　Disconnect the cable from the negative battery terminal (see Chapter 5).

2　Drain the engine oil (see Chapter 1).

3　Position the engine at Top Dead Center (TDC) for cylinder number 1 (see Section 3).

4　Remove the timing chain, timing chain guides and sprockets (see Section 8).

5　Remove the balance shaft chain tensioner.

6　Once the tensioner is removed, insert special tool #EN-50837 into the lever arm and push the arm in a counterclockwise rotation.

7　Compress the tensioner while holding the lever arm from rotating. Slowly release the lever arm on the tensioner until the tensioner extends 3 ratchet "audible clicks" and hold it in this position.

8　Rotate the lever arm clockwise, using special tool #EN-50837 until the hole in the lever arm aligns with the hole in the tensioner body. Once in this position, insert the tool through the lever arm and into the tensioner assembly, locking the tensioner in place.

9　Remove the balance shaft chain guide bolts and chain guide.

10　Temporarily reinstall the crankshaft pulley and original bolt and tighten the bolt securely. Install the special tool to hold the crankshaft pulley from rotating (see Section 10). While preventing the crankshaft pulley from rotating, loosen the balance shaft sprocket bolt.

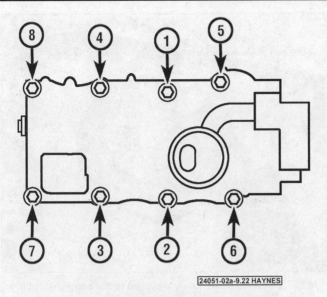

9.22 Balance shaft module tightening sequence -
2.0L and 2.5L engines

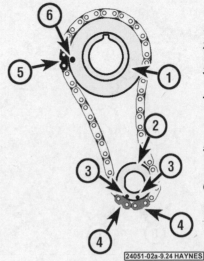

1 Crankshaft sprocket
2 Balance shaft driven
   sprocket
3 Driven sprocket
   timing marks
4 Balance shaft
   chain colored links
   (driven sprocket
   double links)
5 Balance shaft
   chain colored link
   (crankshaft single link)
6 Crankshaft sprocket
   timing mark

9.24 Balance shaft timing chain alignment details -
2.0 and 2.5L engines

11 Remove the crankshaft pulley tool, pulley and bolt, then remove the balance shaft sprocket bolt.

12 Remove the crankshaft sprocket, balance shaft chain and balance shaft sprocket as an assembly, then set the assembly on a workbench.

13 Remove the balance shaft bolts and lower the balance shaft module from the engine block.
Caution: *If you're replacing the oil pump, see Section 14.*

Inspection

14 Clean all parts with clean solvent and dry with compressed air, if available.

15 Inspect the chain tensioners for excessive wear or other damage.

16 Inspect the balance shaft chain guides for deep grooves, excessive wear, or other damage.

17 Inspect the balance shaft chain for excessive wear or damage.

18 Inspect the oil pump (see Section 14).

19 Replace any component that is damaged.

Installation

20 Install the oil pump to the balance shaft module (see Section 14), if necessary.

21 Install the balance shaft module assembly to the engine, then install the mounting bolts hand-tight.

22 Tighten the balance shaft module bolts, in sequence **(see illustration)** to the torque listed in this Chapter's Specifications.

23 Before installing the balance shaft chain, make sure the crankshaft timing key way is at TDC (12 o'clock) position.

24 Place the crankshaft sprocket and balance shaft driven sprocket into the balance shaft chain. Verify the colored timing chain link lines up with the timing mark on the

crankshaft sprocket, and both timing marks on the balance shaft driven sprocket line up with colored links on the timing chain **(see illustration)**.

25 Install the chain and gear as an assembly and verify that the timing marks are aligned properly.

26 Temporarily reinstall the crankshaft pulley and original bolt, then tighten the bolt securely. Install the special tool to hold the crankshaft pulley from rotating (see Section 10). While preventing the crankshaft pulley from rotating, tighten the new balance shaft sprocket bolt to the torque listed this Chapter's Specifications.

27 Remove the crankshaft pulley tool, pulley and bolt.

28 Install the balancer chain guide with the long end pointing towards the crankshaft and the flat edge against the chain, then install the guide bolts and tighten the bolts to the torque listed in this Chapter's Specifications.

29 Install the balancer chain tensioner and bolts, then tighten the tensioner bolts to the torque listed in this Chapter's Specifications.

30 Remove the special tool EN-50837 retaining pin from the tensioner arm and allow the tensioner arm to expand against the chain.

31 Recheck all the balance shaft chain timing marks **(see illustration 9.24)**.

32 Install the timing chain (see Section 8) and timing chain cover (see Section 7).

33 Install the upper oil pan (see Section 13).

34 Remaining installation is the reverse of removal.

35 Reconnect the battery (see Chapter 5).

36 Install a new oil filter and refill the crankcase with oil (see Chapter 1).

37 Refill the cooling system (see Chapter 1).

38 Run the engine and check for leaks.

10 Crankshaft pulley and front oil seal - removal and installation

Crankshaft pulley

1 Raise the vehicle and support it securely on jackstands.

2 Remove the under-vehicle splash shield.

3 Remove the drivebelt and, on 1.5L engines, remove the drivebelt tensioner (see Chapter 1).

4 Prevent the pulley from turning by holding it with special tool #EN-4426-1 for 1.5L engines or EN-51577-1 for 2.0L and 2.5L engines, or a large universal pin spanner. Alternatively, wrap the crankshaft pulley with a shop rag and use a chain wrench to hold the pulley, then use a large ratchet or breaker bar and socket to unscrew the crankshaft pulley center bolt **(see illustration)**.
Caution: *Using the chain wrench method can potentially damage the vibration damper portion of the pulley. Be sure to inspect the rubber damper portion of the pulley and make sure*

10.4 With a shop rag around the pulley, use a chain wrench to hold the pulley from rotating while the bolt is loosened

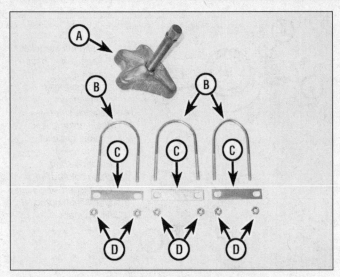

10.5a To make the tool, loop the U-bolts around the hub spokes and through the pulley slots, then tighten the nuts securely. . .

A   *Three-spoke crankshaft puller*   C   *Metal straps*
B   *U-bolts*   D   *Nuts*

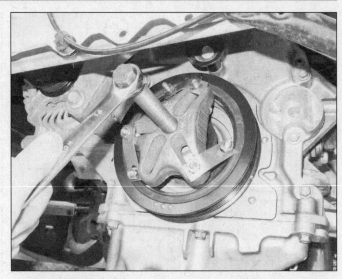

10.5b. . . with the puller firmly mounted to the crankshaft pulley hub, tighten the puller center bolt and remove the pulley

10.13 Use a seal puller to remove the old crankshaft seal, taking care not to damage the crankshaft or the seal bore in the cover

10.15 Drive the new seal in with a seal driver until the seal is flush with the surface of the timing chain cover

the outer ring of the pulley has not shifted in relation to the hub.

Caution: *Obtain a new bolt for installation, but save the old bolt for the first stage of pulley installation.*

5   Remove the crankshaft pulley with special tool #EN-4426-1. Alternatively, you can attach a standard crankshaft pulley puller using exhaust U-clamps **(see illustrations)**. Place the U-bolts around the hub spokes on the pulley, then place the puller onto the crankshaft pulley, allowing one end of the U-bolt to go through the puller. Place the straps on the U-bolts and tighten the nuts.

6   Slide the pulley off the nose of the crankshaft.

7   If you're replacing the crankshaft front oil seal, proceed to Step 13.

8   Lubricate the hub of the pulley with clean engine oil, then slide it onto the crankshaft. The pulley flange must fit into the hexagon section of the oil pump rotor and to the flats of the crankshaft. The TDC markings on crankshaft pulley and timing marks on the timing chain cover must align. Carefully press the pulley into position, using the old bolt if necessary. When installed, the distance between the timing chain cover and the edge of the crankshaft pulley should be 7/32-inch (5.5 mm).

9   Install a NEW bolt and, holding the pulley with a pin spanner to immobilize it, tighten the bolt to the torque listed in this Chapter's Specifications.

10   The remainder of installation is the reverse of removal.

11   Reconnect the battery (see Chapter 5).

Crankshaft front oil seal replacement

12   Remove the crankshaft pulley.

13   Use a seal removal tool to pry the seal out **(see illustration)**.

14   Clean the seal bore and check it for nicks or gouges. Also examine the area of the hub that rides in the seal for signs of abnormal wear or scoring.

15   Coat the lip of the new seal with clean engine oil and drive it into the bore with a seal driver **(see illustration)**. The open side of the seal faces into the engine.

16   Using clean engine oil, lubricate the sealing surface of the crankshaft pulley hub.

17   Install the crankshaft pulley.

11.8 Remove each rocker arm

11.9 Store the rocker arms in an organized manner so they can be returned to their original locations

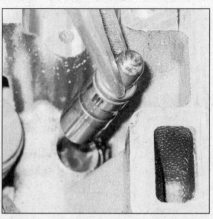

11.10 Pull the lash adjusters from their bores in the head and store them along with their corresponding rocker arms

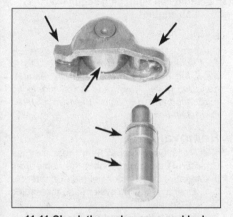

11.11 Check the rocker arms and lash adjusters for wear at the indicated points

11.14 Check the cam lobes for pitting, excessive wear, and scoring. If scoring is excessive, as shown here, replace the camshaft

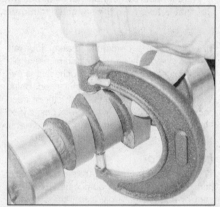

11.15 Measure each camshaft lobe height with a micrometer

11 Camshafts and hydraulic lash adjusters - removal, inspection and installation

Caution: *This is a difficult procedure, involving special tools. Read through the entire Section and obtain the necessary tools before beginning the procedure. New camshaft sprocket bolts must be purchased for installation.*

1   Relieve the fuel system pressure (see Chapter 4).
2   Disconnect the cable from the negative battery terminal (see Chapter 5).
3   Remove the valve cover (see Section 4) and high-pressure fuel pump (see Chapter 4).

Removal

4   Remove the drivebelt and drivebelt tensioner (see Chapter 1).
5   Set the engine to TDC (see Section 3).
6   Remove the timing chain cover (see Section 7), the timing chain and and camshaft sprockets (see Section 8).
7   Each camshaft cap should be marked for location and direction prior to disassembly. A little at time, loosen each bearing cap bolt

slowly and evenly in reverse order of the tightening sequence **(see illustration 11.23a or 11.23b)**. Lift the camshaft(s) from the cylinder head, parallel to the head surface.
Caution: *The caps must be installed in their original locations. Keep all parts from each camshaft together - never mix parts from one camshaft with those for another.*
8   Remove the rocker arms **(see illustration)**.
9   Place the rocker arms in a suitable container, in order, so they can be reinstalled in their original positions **(see illustration)**.
10   Remove the hydraulic lash adjusters from their bores in the cylinder head **(see illustration)**. Store these with their corresponding rocker arms so they can be reinstalled in their original locations.

Inspection

11   Check each hydraulic lash adjuster for excessive wear, scoring, pitting, or an out-of-round condition **(see illustration)**. Replace as necessary.
12   If the adjusters or the cylinder head bores are excessively worn, new adjusters or a new cylinder head, or both, may be

required. If the valvetrain is noisy, particularly if the noise persists after a cold start, you can suspect a faulty lash adjuster.
13   Inspect the rocker arms for signs of wear or damage. The areas of wear are the tip that contacts the valve stem, the socket that contacts the lash adjuster and the roller that contacts the camshaft **(see illustration 11.11)**.
14   Examine the camshaft lobes for scoring, pitting, galling (wear due to rubbing), and evidence of overheating (blue, discolored areas). Look for flaking of the hardened surface layer of each lobe **(see illustration)**. If any such wear is evident, replace the camshaft.
15   Measure the lobe height of each cam lobe on the intake camshaft, and record your measurements **(see illustration)**. Compare the measurements for excessive variation; if the lobe heights vary more than 0.00 inch (0.125 mm), replace the camshaft. Compare the lobe height measurements on the exhaust camshaft and follow the same procedure. Do not compare intake camshaft lobe heights with exhaust camshaft lobe heights, as they are different. Only compare intake lobes with intake lobes and exhaust lobes with exhaust lobes.

11.16 Measure each journal diameter with a micrometer. If any journal is less than the specified minimum, replace the camshaft

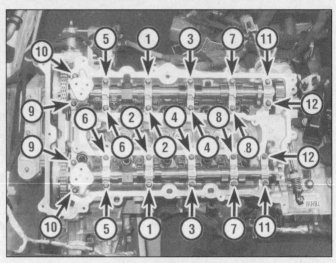

11.23a Camshaft bearing cap tightening sequence - 1.5L engines

16 Inspect the camshaft bearing journals and the cylinder head bearing surfaces for pitting or excessive wear. If any such wear is evident, replace the component concerned. Using a micrometer, measure the diameter of each camshaft bearing journal at several points **(see illustration)**. If the diameter of any journal is less than specified, replace the camshaft.

Installation

17 Lubricate the rocker arms and hydraulic lash adjusters with engine assembly lubricant or fresh engine oil. Install the adjusters into their original bores, then install the rocker arms in their correct locations.
18 Lubricate the camshaft(s) with camshaft installation lubricant or clean engine oil.
19 With the camshaft notch at the front of the camshaft in the 12 o'clock position, install the camshaft into the cylinder head.
20 Rotate the oil seal in the groove of the number one camshaft journal so the split line

is at approximately the 12 o'clock position before installing the camshaft caps.
21 Lubricate the camshaft bearing caps, then install the bearing caps into their original locations.
22 Install the camshaft bearing cap bolts and hand-start the bolts.
23 Tighten the bolts in sequence **(see illustrations)**, a little at a time, to the torque listed in this Chapter's Specifications.
24 Install the camshaft actuator sprockets and timing chain (see Section 8), and the timing chain cover (see Section 7).
25 The remainder of installation is the reverse of removal.

12   Cylinder head - removal and installation

Warning: *The engine must be completely cool before beginning this procedure.*

Caution: *The engine must be completely cool when the head is removed. Failure to allow the engine to cool off could result in head warpage. New head bolts should be purchased ahead of time - they are required for installation.*

Removal

1 Relieve the fuel system pressure (see Chapter 4), then disconnect the cable from the negative battery terminal (see Chapter 5).
2 Drain the cooling system and the engine oil (see Chapter 1).
3 Remove the Powertrain Control Module (PCM) (see Chapter 6).
4 Disconnect the hose clamps and hoses **(see illustration)** from the coolant outlet housing, then remove the housing bolts and housing.
5 Remove the valve cover (see Section 4).
6 Remove the turbocharger assembly (see Chapter 4).

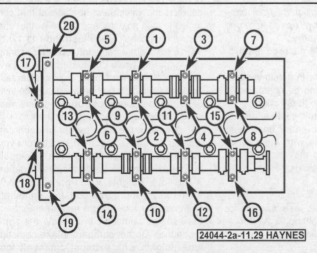

11.23b Camshaft bearing cap tightening sequence - 2.0L and 2.5L engines

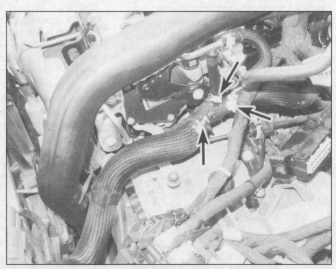

12.4 Disconnect the hoses from the coolant outlet housing - 1.5L engine shown, other models similar

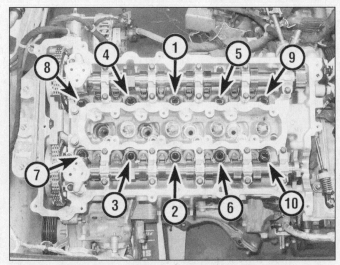

12.21a Cylinder head bolt tightening sequence - 1.5L engine

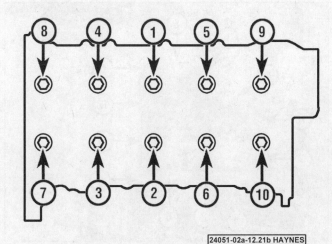

24051-02a-12.21b HAYNES

12.21b Cylinder head bolt tightening sequence - 2.0L and 2.5L engines

7   Remove the intake manifold (see Section 5).

8   On 2.0L and 2.5L engines, remove the exhaust manifold (see Section 6).

9   Remove the timing chain cover (see Section 7) and timing chain (see Section 8). **Caution:** *Support the engine from below using a block of wood and a floor jack while the engine mount is removed* **(see illustration 17.8)**.

10   Remove the high-pressure fuel pump (see Chapter 4).

11   On 2.0L and 2.5L engines, remove the camshaft position actuators and camshafts (see Chapter 6).

12   Label and disconnect the electrical connectors from the cylinder head that will interfere with removal. Use tape and mark each connector to insure correct reassembly.

13   Remove the cylinder head bolts following the tightening sequence **(see illustration 12.21a or 12.21b)**. Loosen the bolts in sequence 1/4-turn then a 1/2-turn at a time. If the head is to be completely overhauled, refer to Section 11 for removal of the camshafts, rocker arms and hydraulic lash adjusters or lifters.

14   Use a prybar at the corners of the head-to-block mating surface to break the gasket seal. Do not pry between the cylinder head and engine block in the gasket sealing area.

15   Attach an engine hoist lifting bracket and chains to the cylinder head, then lift the cylinder head off the engine. If resistance is felt, place a wood block against the end and strike the wood block with a hammer. Store the cylinder head on wood blocks to prevent damage to the gasket sealing surfaces. **Caution:** *In order to prevent damage to the valves and fuel injectors during cylinder head removal, set the cylinder head on blocks.*

16   Remove the old cylinder head gasket. Before removing, note the correct orientation of the gasket for correct installation.

Installation

17   The mating surfaces of the cylinder head and block must be perfectly clean when the head is installed. Use a gasket scraper to remove all traces of carbon and old gasket material, then clean the mating surfaces with brake system cleaner. If there's oil on the mating surfaces when the cylinder head is installed, the gasket may not seal correctly and leaks may develop. When working on the engine block, cover the open areas of the engine with shop rags to keep debris out during repair and reassembly. Use a vacuum cleaner to remove any debris that falls into the cylinders.

18   Check the engine block and cylinder head mating surfaces for nicks, deep scratches and other damage.

19   Use a tap of the correct size to chase the threads in the cylinder head bolt holes. Dirt, corrosion, sealant and damaged threads will affect torque readings.

20   Make sure the new gasket is located on the dowels in the block.

21   Carefully position the cylinder head on the engine block without disturbing the gasket. Install new cylinder head bolts and, following the recommended sequence **(see illustrations)**, tighten the bolts to the torque listed in this Chapter's Specifications. **Note:** *The method used for the head bolt tightening procedure is referred to as a "torque-angle" method. A special torque angle gauge (available at most auto parts stores) is available to attach to a breaker bar and socket for better accuracy during the tightening procedure.*

22   Install the timing chain (see Section 8).

23   Install the turbocharger (see Chapter 4) or exhaust manifold (see Section 6).

24   Install the intake manifold (see Section 5).

25   The remaining installation steps are the reverse of removal.

26   Reconnect the battery (see Chapter 5).

27   Change the engine oil and filter and refill the cooling system (see Chapter 1), then start the engine and check carefully for oil and coolant leaks.

13   Oil pans - removal and installation

1   Raise the front of the vehicle and support it securely on jackstands.

2   Drain the engine oil (see Chapter 1).

Lower oil pan

Removal

3   On 2.0L and 2.5L engines, disconnect the front exhaust pipe from the exhaust manifold, then from the rear portion of the exhaust system, and remove the front exhaust pipe.

4   Loosen the oil pan bolts a little at a time, in a criss-cross pattern, until they can be removed. **Caution:** *On 1.5L engines, the lower oil pan must be replaced with a new one once it's removed. The lower oil pan becomes damaged during removal and oil leaks may occur if it is not replaced with a new oil pan.*

5   Carefully remove the lower oil pan from the upper oil pan.

Installation

6   Using a gasket scraper, thoroughly clean all old gasket material from the upper oil pan (and lower oil pan on 2.0L and 2.5L models). Remove residue and oil film with a solvent such as brake system cleaner.

7   Apply an approximate 3/16-inch (4.25 mm) bead of sealant on 1.5L engines or a 5/64-inch (2.25 mm) bead of sealant on 2.0L and 2.5L engines to the perimeter of the lower oil pan, inboard of the bolt holes. **Caution:** *Install the pan within 10 minutes of applying the sealant. The final torque must be must be done within 60 minutes of applying the sealant.*

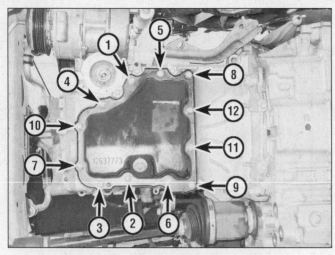

**13.8 Lower oil pan bolt tightening sequence
- 1.5L engines**

**13.14 Oil flow control valve solenoid electrical connector location
- 1.5L engine shown, other models similar**

**13.20 Oil pan-to-transmission bolt locations
- 1.5L engines shown, other models similar**

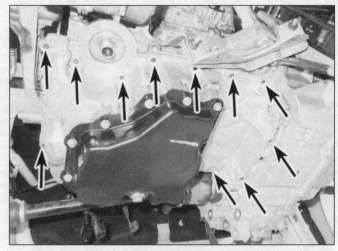

**13.21 Upper oil pan bolt locations - 11 of 16 bolts shown
(1.5L engines shown, other models similar)**

8   Install the oil pan and bolts, tightening them hand-tight. On 1.5L engines tighten the oil pan bolts in sequence **(see illustration)** to the torque listed in this Chapter's Specifications and on 2.0L and 2.5L engines tighten the bolts in a circular pattern, working from the center bolts outward, to the torque listed in this Chapter's Specifications.

9   Remaining installation is the reverse of removal.

10   Refill the engine with oil and install a new oil filter (see Chapter 1), then run the engine and check for leaks.

Upper oil pan
Removal

11   On 2.0L and 2.5L engines, support the engine from above using an engine support fixture.

12   Disconnect the front exhaust pipe from the exhaust manifold, then from the rear portion of the exhaust system, and remove the front exhaust pipe.

13   On 2.0L and 2.5L engines, remove the timing chain cover (see Section 7).

14   Remove the oil pump flow control heat shield fasteners and heat shield, then disconnect the oil flow control valve solenoid electrical connector **(see illustration)**.

15   On 2.0L and 2.5L engines, remove the air conditioning compressor (see Chapter 3) without disconnecting the refrigerant lines and secure it out of the way, then remove the air conditioning compressor bracket bolts and bracket.

16   On 2.0L and 2.5L engines, remove the transmission rear mount-to-transmission bolts and through-bolt.

Caution: *The transmission rear mount bracket bolts and through-bolts must be replaced with new ones once they are removed.*

17   On 2.0L and 2.5L engines, remove the catalytic converter support bracket bolts and bracket, then remove the bracket from the side of the oil pan.

18   On 2.0L and 2.5L engines, remove the

right-side driveaxle support bearing bolt (see Chapter 8).

19   On 2.0L engines, remove the engine oil cooler (see Chapter 3, Section 19).

20   Remove the oil pan to transmission bolts **(see illustration)**.

21   Remove the upper oil pan bolts, noting their original locations, because the bolts are different lengths **(see illustration)**.

22   Locate the prying points on the upper oil pan **(see illustrations)**, then carefully pry at the points to separate the upper oil pan from the engine block.

Caution: *If the oil pan is difficult to separate from the crankcase, use a rubber mallet or a block of wood and a hammer to jar it loose. If it's stubborn and still won't come off, pry carefully on the casting protrusions shown (not the mating surfaces!).*

23   Once the seal is broken, lower the oil pan and, on 1.5L engines, disconnect the electrical connector from the oil flow control solenoid on the oil pump **(see illustration)**. Remove the upper oil pan.

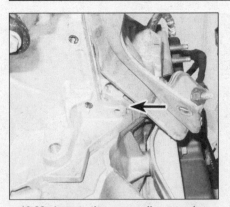

13.22a Locate the upper oil pan prying locations at the rear. . .

13.22b. . . the front. . .

13.22c. . . and the back side of the upper oil pan - 1.5L engines shown, other models similar

13.23 Lower the oil pan down until the electrical connector can be disconnected from the oil flow control solenoid - 1.5L engines

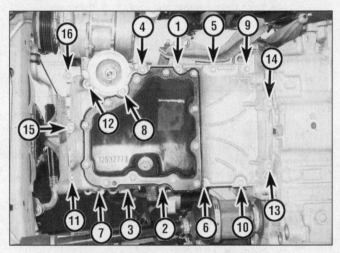

13.27a Upper oil pan tightening sequence - 1.5L engines

Installation

24   Using a gasket scraper, thoroughly clean all old gasket material from the lower crankcase and oil pan. Remove residue and oil film with a solvent such as brake system cleaner.
Caution: *The lower crankcase surface must be oil free before applying the sealant.*
25   Apply an approximate 3/16-inch (4.25 mm) bead of sealant to the perimeter of the upper oil pan, inboard of the bolt holes.
Caution: *Install the pan within 10 minutes of applying the sealant. The final torque must be done within 60 minutes of applying the sealant.*
26   On 2.0L and 2.5L engines, also apply a bead of sealant to the groove at the bottom of the timing chain cover.
27   Install the oil pan and bolts, tightening them in sequence **(see illustrations)** to the torque listed in this Chapter's Specifications.
28   Install and tighten the oil pan-to-transaxle bolts to the torque listed in this Chapter's Specifications.
29   The remaining installation is the reverse of removal.
30   Refill the engine with oil and install a new oil filter (see Chapter 1), then run the engine and check for leaks.

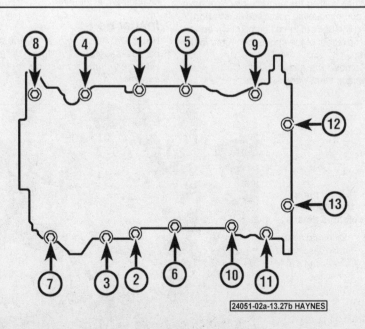

13.27b Upper oil pan tightening sequence - 2.0L and 2.0L engines

14.4 Push the tensioner arm away from the chain and lock it in place

14.5 Oil pump mounting bolt locations - 1.5L engines

14 Oil pump - removal, inspection and installation

Removal

1   Raise the vehicle and support it securely on jackstands.
2   Drain the engine oil (see Chapter 1).
3   Remove the lower oil pan and the upper oil pan as an assembly (see Section 13).

1.5L engine

Note: *If the oil pump drive chain, drive gear or tensioner need to be replaced, see Section 8.*
4   Make matching marks on the oil pump sprocket and chain, then push the oil pump drive chain tensioner away from the chain **(see illustration)** and secure it in place using an Allen wrench or drill bit.
5   While holding the pump in place, remove the oil pump mounting bolts **(see illustration)**.
6   Tilt the back of the oil pump down and lift the sprocket out of the chain, then remove the oil pump.
7   Remove the two oil pump O-ring seals and replace them with new ones.

8   If you're replacing the oil pump, remove the oil pump flow control solenoid retaining clip **(see illustration)**, then pull the solenoid from the oil pump.

2.0L and 2.5L engines

Note: *On 2.0L and 2.5L models, the oil pump is mounted to the balance shaft assembly. The oil pump can be removed and replaced once the balance shaft assembly has been removed.*
9   Remove the balance shaft module assembly (see Section 9).
10   Remove the oil pump pickup tube bolts, gasket and tube from the oil pump. Always replace the oil pump pickup tube gasket.
11   Remove the oil pump assembly and the oil pump cover from the balance shaft module making note where the oil pump locating pin is installed.

Inspection

Note: *On 1.5L engines, the oil pump can't be disassembled, if there is a problem with the pump, it must be replaced as an assembly.*

2.0L and 2.5L engines

12   Thoroughly clean and dry the components.
13   Inspect the oil pump assembly, the oil pump cover and all threaded holes for obvious wear or damage. If damaged, the complete oil pump assembly must be replaced.
14   If the oil pump components are in acceptable condition, lubricate them with a small amount of clean engine oil and install the locating pin to the balance shaft module, then place the oil pump cover and the oil pump assembly on to the module. Install the mounting bolts and tighten them to the torque listed in this Chapter's Specifications. Install the oil pump pickup tube gasket and pickup tube, then tighten the bolts to the torque listed in this Chapter's Specifications.

Installation

1.5L engine

15   Install new oil pump seals into the grooves in the oil pump body.
16   Tilt the back of the pump down and set the shaft sprocket into the drive chain, aligning the marks made in Step 4, then lift the oil pump up and into place.
17   Install the mounting bolts hand-tight. Once all of the bolts are installed, tighten them to the torque listed in this Chapter's Specifications.
18   Install the oil pump flow control solenoid valve, if removed **(see illustration 14.8)**.
19   Push the tensioner arm back, then remove the Allen wrench or drill bit and release the oil pump chain tensioner arm.
20   Install the upper oil pan assembly (see Section 13).
21   The remainder of installation is the reverse of removal.

2.0L and 2.5L engines

22   Install the balance shaft/oil pump assembly (see Section 9).
23   Install the upper oil pan assembly (see Section 13).
24   Remaining installation is the reverse of removal.

14.8 Oil pump flow control solenoid details

A   *Oil pump flow control solenoid*
B   *Retaining clip*

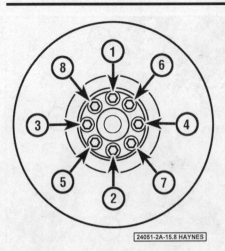

15.8 Driveplate bolt tightening sequence

17.8 Place a block of wood between the jack head and the oil pan

All models

25   Refill the engine with oil and install a new oil filter (see Chapter 1).

26   Start the engine and check for leaks.

Caution: *Run the engine and make sure oil pressure comes up to normal quickly. If it doesn't, stop the engine and find out the cause. Severe engine damage can result from running an engine with insufficient oil pressure!*

15   Driveplate - removal and installation

Removal

1   Raise the vehicle and support it securely on jackstands, then remove the transaxle (see Chapter 7). If it's leaking, now would be a very good time to replace the front pump seal/O-ring.

2   Use a center punch or paint to make alignment marks on the driveplate and crankshaft to ensure correct alignment during reinstallation.

3   Remove the bolts that secure the driveplate to the crankshaft. If the crankshaft turns, wedge a screwdriver in the ring gear teeth.

4   Remove the driveplate from the crankshaft. If there is a spacer between the crankshaft and the driveplate, note which way it is installed.

Installation

5   Inspect the surface of the driveplate for cracks.

6   Clean and inspect the mating surfaces of the driveplate and the crankshaft. If the crankshaft rear seal is leaking, replace it before reinstalling the driveplate (see Section 16).

7   Position the driveplate against the crankshaft, installing the spacer if one was present originally. Align the mating marks made during removal. Note that some engines have an

alignment dowel or staggered bolt holes to ensure correct installation. Before installing the bolts, apply thread locking compound to the threads.

8   Wedge a screwdriver in the ring gear teeth to keep the driveplate from turning, then tighten the bolts in sequence **(see illustration)** to the torque listed in this Chapter's Specifications. Work up to the final torque in three or four steps.

9   The remainder of installation is the reverse of removal.

16   Rear main oil seal - replacement

1   The one-piece rear main oil seal is pressed into the engine block and the lower crankcase. Remove the transaxle (see Chapter 7) and the driveplate (see Section 15).

2   On 1.5L engines, remove the crankshaft position sensor reluctor ring from the end of the crankshaft, noting the reluctor ring alignment hole location - it must be installed in the same orientation.

3   Pry out the old seal with a special seal removal tool or a flat-blade screwdriver.

Caution: *To prevent an oil leak after the new seal is installed, be very careful not to scratch or otherwise damage the crankshaft sealing surface or the bore of the lower crankcase and the engine block.*

4   Clean the crankshaft and seal bore in the block thoroughly and de-grease these areas by wiping them with a rag soaked in brake system cleaner. Lubricate the lip of the new seal and the outer diameter of the crankshaft with engine oil.

5   On 1.5L engines, apply a small amount of RTV sealant where the lower crankcase and the engine block meet in the rear main seal bore.

6   Position the new seal onto the crankshaft. Make sure the edges of the new oil seal are not rolled over. Use a special rear main oil

seal installation tool or a socket with the exact diameter of the seal to drive the seal in place. Make sure the seal is not off-set; it must be flush along the entire circumference of the engine block and the crankcase reinforcement section.

Note: *When installing the new seal, if so marked, the words THIS SIDE OUT on the seal must face out, toward the rear of the engine.*

7   The remainder of installation is the reverse of removal.

17   Powertrain mounts - check and replacement

Check

1   Engine mounts seldom require attention, but broken or deteriorated mounts should be replaced immediately or the added strain placed on the driveline components may cause damage or wear.

2   During the check, the engine must be raised slightly to remove the weight from the mounts.

3   Raise the vehicle and support it securely on jackstands, then position a jack under the engine oil pan. Place a large block of wood between the jack head and the oil pan, then carefully raise the engine just enough to take the weight off the mounts.

Warning: *DO NOT place any part of your body under the engine when it's supported only by a jack!*

4   Check the mounts to see if the rubber is cracked, hardened or separated from the bushing in the center of the mount.

5   Check for relative movement between the mount and the engine or frame (use a large screwdriver or prybar to attempt to move the mounts). If movement is noted, tighten the mount fasteners.

Replacement

6   Disconnect the negative battery cable (see Chapter 5). If you're replacing the right-side engine mount, remove the air filter housing (see Chapter 4). If you're replacing the left-side transaxle mount, remove the battery and the battery tray (see Chapter 5) and the underhood fuse and relay center (see Chapter 12).

7   If you're replacing the front or rear transaxle mount, raise the vehicle and support it securely on jackstands.

8   Place a block of wood between the jack head and the oil pan **(see illustration)**, then carefully raise the engine or transaxle just enough to take the weight off the mounts.

Caution: *Do not disconnect more than one mount at a time unless the engine will be removed from the vehicle.*

Note: *On 2.5L and 2015 and earlier 2.0L engines, the left-side transaxle mount is located on the front side of the transaxle and is called the front transaxle mount.*

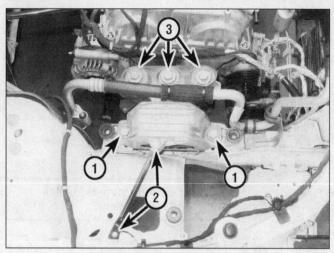

**17.9a Right-side engine mounting fasteners -
1.5L engine shown, other models similar**

1 *Mount-to-body bolts*
2 *Brace bolts*
3 *Mount bracket-to-engine bracket bolts*

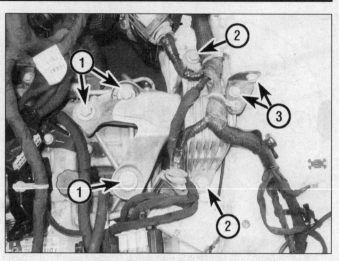

**17.9b Left-side transaxle mounting fasteners -
1.5L engine shown, other models similar**

1 *Mount-to-transaxle bolts*
2 *Mount-to-chassis bolts*
3 *Chassis brace-to-mount and chassis bolts*

9 Refer to the accompanying illustrations for the locations of the powertrain mount fasteners **(see illustrations)**.
10 Remove the fasteners holding the mount to the bracket.
11 Installation is the reverse of removal. Proceed to Step 12.

Powertrain/mount balancing

Note: *The engine/transaxle assembly must be aligned and balanced in its weight distribution among the powertrain mounts, before the mounting bolts are tightened.*
12 Raise the vehicle and support it securely on jackstands, if not already done.
13 Loosen the front and rear transaxle mount through-bolts **(see illustration 17.9c)**.
14 Lower the vehicle, then using two floor jacks, support the engine and transaxle.
Caution: *Place blocks of wood on the heads of the floor jacks to protect the engine and transaxle.*
15 Loosen the transaxle mount-to-transaxle bolts **(see illustration 17.9b)**.
16 Loosen the engine mount-to-mount bracket bolts **(see illustration 17.9a)**.
17 Lower the floor jacks so there is a 1/4-inch gap between the engine mount and its bracket and the transaxle mount and the transaxle.
18 The front and rear transaxle mounts must be centered in their brackets; if not,

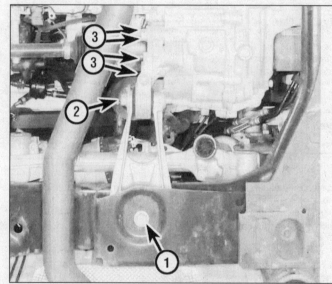

**17.9c Transaxle rear
mount fasteners -
1.5L engine shown,
other models similar**

1 *Mount-to-subframe
   bolt*
2 *Through-bolt*
3 *Bracket-to-transaxle
   bolts*

use a prybar to adjust the powertrain to achieve this.
19 Once alignment has been achieved, tighten the transaxle mount-to-transaxle bolts to the torque listed in this Chapter's Specifications.
20 Tighten the engine mount-to-mount bracket to the torque listed in this Chapter's Specifications.

21 Lower the floor jacks, then raise the vehicle and support it securely on jackstands.
22 Shake the engine and transaxle back and forth. Tighten the transaxle rear through-bolt to the torque listed in this Chapter's Specifications.
23 Install the under-vehicle splash shield, then lower the vehicle.

Chapter 2 Part B
General engine overhaul procedures

Contents

Specifications

General

Displacement
1.5L (LFV)	92 cubic inches
2.0L (LTG)	122 cubic inches
2.5L, VIN A (LCV)	152 cubic inches
2.5L, VIN L (LKW)	152 cubic inches

Bore
1.5L	2.91 inches (74 mm)
2.0L	3.3855 to 3.3861 inches (85.992 to 86.008 mm)
2.5L	3.4642 to 3.4649 inches (87.992 to 88.008 mm)

Stroke
1.5L	3.409 inches (86.6 mm)
2.0L	3.386 inches (86.0 mm)
2.5L	3.976 inches (101 mm)
Cylinder compression	Lowest cylinder must be within 70 percent of highest cylinder

Oil pressure, engine at operating temperature 212-degrees F (100-degrees C)
1.5L engine, at 1500 rpm	29 to 36 psi (200 to 250 kPa)
2.0L engine, at 700 rpm	20 to 29 psi (140 to 200 kPa)
2.5L engine, at 700 rpm	20 to 28 psi (135 to 190 kPa)

Torque specifications

Note: *One foot-pound (ft-lb) of torque is equivalent to 12 inch-pounds (in-lbs) of torque. Torque values below approximately 15 ft-lbs are expressed in inch-pounds, since most foot-pound torque wrenches are not accurate at these smaller values.*

	Ft-lbs (unless otherwise indicated)	Nm
Connecting rod bearing cap bolts*		
1.5L engine		
Step 1	18	25
Step 2	Tighten an additional 75-degrees	
2.0L and 2.5L engines		
Step 1	18	25
Step 2	Tighten an additional 110-degrees	
Lower crankcase bolts* (see illustration 10.19a or 10.19b)		
1.5L engine		
Step 1	132 in-lbs	15
Step 2	Tighten an additional 180-degrees	
2.0L and 2.5L engines		
Step 1		
2016 and earlier 2.0L models	132 in-lbs	15
2017 and later 2.0L and all 2.5L models	15	20
Step 2	Tighten an additional 140-degrees	
Lower crankcase perimeter bolts (see illustration 10.30a or 10.30b)	18	25
1.5L engines		
Step 1	44 in-lbs	5
Step 2	89 in-lbs	10
2.0L and 2.5L engines	18	25

Bolt(s) must be replaced.

1.10a An engine block being bored. An engine rebuilder will use special machinery to recondition the cylinder bores

1.10b If the cylinders are bored, the machine shop will normally hone the engine on a machine like this

1   General information - engine overhaul

1   Included in this portion of Chapter 2B are general information and diagnostic testing procedures for determining the overall mechanical condition of your engine.

2   The information ranges from advice concerning preparation for an overhaul and the purchase of replacement parts and/or components to detailed, step-by-step procedures covering removal and installation.

3   The following Sections have been written to help you determine whether your engine needs to be overhauled and how to remove and install it once you've determined it needs to be rebuilt. For information concerning in-vehicle engine repair, see Chapter 2A.

4   The Specifications included in this Part are general in nature and include only those necessary for testing the oil pressure, checking the engine compression, and bottom-end torque specifications. Refer to Chapter 2A for additional engine Specifications.

5   It's not always easy to determine when, or if, an engine should be completely overhauled, because a number of factors must be considered.

6   High mileage is not necessarily an indication that an overhaul is needed, while low mileage doesn't preclude the need for an overhaul. Frequency of servicing is probably the most important consideration. An engine that's had regular and frequent oil and filter changes, as well as other required maintenance, will most likely give many thousands of miles of reliable service. Conversely, a neglected engine may require an overhaul very early in its service life.

7   Excessive oil consumption is an indication that piston rings, valve seals and/or valve guides are in need of attention. Make sure that oil leaks aren't responsible before deciding that the rings and/or guides are bad. Perform a cylinder compression check to determine the extent of the work required (see

Section 3). Also check the vacuum readings under various conditions (see Section 4).

8   Check the oil pressure with a gauge installed in place of the oil pressure sending unit and compare it to this Chapter's Specifications. If it's extremely low, the bearings and/or oil pump are probably worn out (see Chapter 2A).

9   Loss of power, rough running, knocking or metallic engine noises, excessive valve train noise and high fuel consumption rates may also point to the need for an overhaul, especially if they're all present at the same time.

10   An engine overhaul involves restoring the internal parts to the specifications of a new engine. During an overhaul, the piston rings are replaced and the cylinder walls are reconditioned (rebored and/or honed) **(see illustrations 1.10a and 1.10b)**. If a rebore is done by an automotive machine shop, new oversize pistons will also be installed. The main bearings, connecting rod bearings and camshaft bearings are generally replaced with new ones and, if necessary, the crankshaft may be reground to restore the journals **(see illustration 1.10c)**. Generally, the valves are serviced as well, since they're usually in less-than-perfect condition at this point. While the engine is being overhauled, other com-

ponents, such as the distributor, starter and alternator, can be rebuilt as well. The end result should be similar to a new engine that will give many trouble free miles.

Note: *Critical cooling system components such as the hoses, drivebelts, thermostat and water pump should be replaced with new parts when an engine is overhauled. The radiator should be checked carefully to ensure that it isn't clogged or leaking (see Chapter 1, Section 13). If you purchase a rebuilt engine or short block, some rebuilders will not warrantee their engines unless the radiator has been professionally flushed. Also, we don't recommend overhauling the oil pump - always install a new one when an engine is rebuilt.*

11   Overhauling the internal components on today's engines is a difficult and time-consuming task which requires a significant amount of specialty tools and is best left to a professional engine rebuilder **(see illustrations 1.11a, 1.11b and 1.11c)**. A competent engine rebuilder will handle the inspection of your old parts and offer advice concerning the reconditioning or replacement of the original engine; never purchase parts or have machine work done on other components until the block has been thoroughly inspected by a professional machine shop. As a general rule, time is the primary cost

1.10c A crankshaft having a main bearing journal ground

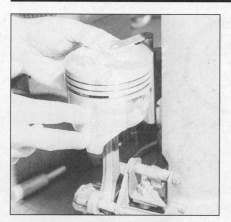

1.11a A machinist checks for a bent connecting rod, using specialized equipment

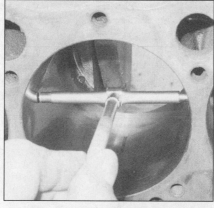

1.11b A bore gauge being used to check a cylinder bore

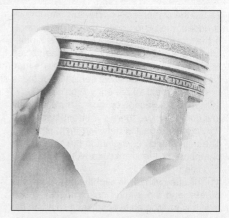

1.11c Uneven piston wear like this indicates a bent connecting rod

of an overhaul, especially since the vehicle may be tied up for a minimum of two weeks or more. Be aware that some engine builders only have the capability to rebuild the engine you bring them while other rebuilders have a large inventory of rebuilt exchange engines in stock. Also be aware that many machine shops could take as much as two weeks' time to completely rebuild your engine depending on shop workload. Sometimes it makes more sense to simply exchange your engine for another engine that's already rebuilt to save time.

2 Oil pressure check

1   Low engine oil pressure can be a sign of an engine in need of rebuilding. A low oil pressure indicator (often called an "idiot light") is not a test of the oiling system. Such indicators only come on when the oil pressure is dangerously low. Even a factory oil pressure gauge in the instrument panel is only a relative indication, although much better for driver information than a warning light. A better test is with a mechanical (not electrical) oil pressure gauge.

2   Locate the oil pressure sending unit. On the 1.5L engine it is located on the back side of the engine block just below the cylinder head towards the rear of the engine **(see illustration)**. On 2.0L and 2.5L engines it is located on the back side of the engine block just below the cylinder head and towards the front (right end, or passenger's side) of the engine.

3   Unscrew and remove the oil pressure sending unit and screw in the hose for your oil pressure gauge. If necessary, install an adapter fitting. Use Teflon tape or thread sealant on the threads of the adapter and/or the fitting on the end of your gauge's hose.

4   Connect an accurate tachometer to the engine, according to the tachometer manufacturer's instructions.

5   Check the oil pressure with the engine running (normal operating temperature) at the specified engine speed, and compare it to this

Chapter's Specifications. If it's extremely low, the bearings and/or oil pump are probably worn out.

3 Cylinder compression check

1   A compression check will tell you what mechanical condition the upper end of your engine (pistons, rings, valves, head gaskets) is in. Specifically, it can tell you if the compression is down due to leakage caused by worn piston rings, defective valves and seats or a blown head gasket. **Note:** *The engine must be at normal operating temperature and the battery must be fully charged for this check.*

2   Begin by cleaning the area around the spark plugs before you remove them (compressed air should be used, if available). The idea is to prevent dirt from getting into the cylinders as the compression check is being done.

3   Remove all of the spark plugs from the engine (see Chapter 1, Section 22).

4   Disable the fuel system by unplugging the electrical connector in the harness to the fuel

injectors or by removing the fuel pump control module fuses (see Chapter 4, Section 3).

5   Install a compression gauge in the spark plug hole **(see illustration)**.

6   Have an assistant hold the accelerator pedal to the floor and crank the engine over at least seven compression strokes while you watch the gauge. The compression should build up quickly in a healthy engine. Low compression on the first stroke, followed by gradually increasing pressure on successive strokes, indicates worn piston rings. A low compression reading on the first stroke, which doesn't build up during successive strokes, indicates leaking valves or a blown head gasket (a cracked head could also be the cause). Deposits on the undersides of the valve heads can also cause low compression. Record the highest gauge reading obtained.

7   Repeat the procedure for the remaining cylinders and compare the results to this Chapter's Specifications.

8   Add some engine oil (about three squirts from a plunger-type oil can) to each cylinder, through the spark plug hole, and repeat the test.

2.2 On the 1.5L engine, the oil pressure sending unit is located on the right rear side of the engine block

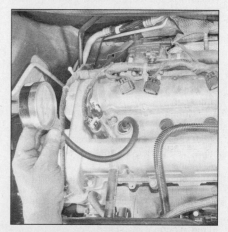

3.5 Use a compression gauge with a threaded fitting for the spark plug hole, not the type that requires hand pressure to maintain the seal

9   If the compression increases after the oil is added, the piston rings are definitely worn. If the compression doesn't increase significantly, the leakage is occurring at the valves or head gasket. Leakage past the valves may be caused by burned valve seats and/or faces or warped, cracked or bent valves.

10   If two adjacent cylinders have equally low compression, there's a strong possibility that the head gasket between them is blown. The appearance of coolant in the combustion chambers or the crankcase would verify this condition.

11   If one cylinder is slightly lower than the others, and the engine has a slightly rough idle, a worn lobe on the camshaft could be the cause.

12   If the compression is unusually high, the combustion chambers are probably coated with carbon deposits. If that's the case, the cylinder head(s) should be removed and decarbonized.

13   If compression is way down or varies greatly between cylinders, it would be a good idea to have a leak-down test performed by an automotive repair shop. This test will pinpoint exactly where the leakage is occurring and how severe it is.

4   Vacuum gauge diagnostic checks

1   A vacuum gauge provides inexpensive but valuable information about what is going on in the engine. You can check for worn rings or cylinder walls, leaking head or intake manifold gaskets, incorrect carburetor adjustments, restricted exhaust, stuck or burned valves, weak valve springs, improper ignition or valve timing and ignition problems.

2   Unfortunately, vacuum gauge readings are easy to misinterpret, so they should be used in conjunction with other tests to confirm the diagnosis.

3   Both the absolute readings and the rate of needle movement are important for accurate interpretation. Most gauges measure vacuum in inches of mercury (in-Hg). The following references to vacuum assume the diagnosis is being performed at sea level. As elevation increases (or atmospheric pressure decreases), the reading will decrease. For every 1,000 foot increase in elevation above approximately 2,000 feet, the gauge readings will decrease about one inch of mercury.

4   Connect the vacuum gauge directly to intake manifold vacuum, not to ported (throttle body) vacuum. Be sure no hoses are left disconnected during the test or false readings will result.

5   Before you begin the test, allow the engine to warm up completely. Block the wheels and set the parking brake. With the transaxle in Park, start the engine and allow it to run at normal idle speed.

Warning: *Keep your hands and the vacuum gauge clear of the fans.*

6   Read the vacuum gauge; an average, healthy engine should normally produce

Low, steady reading   **Low, fluctuating needle**   **Regular drops**

Irregular drops   **Rapid vibration**

Large fluctuation   **Slow fluctuation**

STD-O-OBR HAYNES

4.6 Typical vacuum gauge readings

about 17 to 22 in-Hg with a fairly steady needle **(see illustration)**. Refer to the following vacuum gauge readings and what they indicate about the engine's condition:

7   A low steady reading usually indicates a leaking gasket between the intake manifold and cylinder head(s) or throttle body, a leaky vacuum hose, late ignition timing or incorrect camshaft timing. Check ignition timing with a timing light and eliminate all other possible causes, utilizing the tests provided in this Chapter before you remove the timing chain cover to check the timing marks.

8   If the reading is three to eight inches below normal and it fluctuates at that low reading, suspect an intake manifold gasket leak at an intake port or a faulty fuel injector.

9   If the needle has regular drops of about two-to-four inches at a steady rate, the valves are probably leaking. Perform a compression check or leak-down test to confirm this.

10   An irregular drop or down-flick of the needle can be caused by a sticking valve or an ignition misfire. Perform a compression check or leak-down test and read the spark plugs.

11   A rapid vibration of about four in-Hg vibration at idle combined with exhaust smoke indicates worn valve guides. Perform a leak-down test to confirm this. If the rapid vibration occurs with an increase in engine speed, check for a leaking intake manifold gasket or head gasket, weak valve springs, burned valves or ignition misfire.

12   A slight fluctuation, say one inch up and down, may mean ignition problems. Check all the usual tune-up items and, if necessary, run the engine on an ignition analyzer.

13   If there is a large fluctuation, perform a compression or leak-down test to look for a weak or dead cylinder or a blown head gasket.

14   If the needle moves slowly through a wide range, check for a clogged PCV system, incorrect idle fuel mixture, throttle body or intake manifold gasket leaks.

15   Check for a slow return after revving the engine by quickly snapping the throttle open until the engine reaches about 2,500 rpm and let it shut. Normally the reading should drop to near zero, rise above normal idle reading (about 5 in-Hg over) and return to the previous idle reading. If the vacuum returns slowly and doesn't peak when the throttle is snapped shut, the rings may be worn. If there is a long delay, look for a restricted exhaust system (often the muffler or catalytic converter). An easy way to check this is to temporarily disconnect the exhaust ahead of the suspected part and redo the test.

5   Engine rebuilding alternatives

1   The do-it-yourselfer is faced with a number of options when purchasing a rebuilt engine. The major considerations are cost, warranty, parts availability and the time required for the rebuilder to complete the project. The decision to replace the engine block, piston/connecting rod assemblies and crankshaft depends on the final inspection results of your engine. Only then can you make a cost effective decision whether to have your engine overhauled or simply purchase an exchange engine for your vehicle.

6.3a After tightly wrapping water-vulnerable components, use a spray cleaner on everything, with particular concentration on the greasiest areas, usually around the valve cover and lower edges of the block. If one section dries out, apply more cleaner

6.3b Depending on how dirty the engine is, let the cleaner soak in according to the directions and hose off the grime and cleaner. Get the rinse water down into every area you can get at; then dry important components with a hair dryer or paper towels

2   Some of the rebuilding alternatives include:

Individual parts - *If the inspection procedures reveal that the engine block and most engine components are in reusable condition, purchasing individual parts and having a rebuilder rebuild your engine may be the most economical alternative. The block, crankshaft and piston/connecting rod assemblies should all be inspected carefully by a machine shop first.*

Short block - *A short block consists of an engine block with a crankshaft and piston/connecting rod assemblies already installed. All new bearings are incorporated and all clearances will be correct. The existing camshafts, valve train components, cylinder head and external parts can be bolted to the short block with little or no machine shop work necessary.*

Long block - *A long block consists of a short block plus an oil pump, oil pan, cylinder head, valve cover, camshaft and valve train components, timing sprockets and chain or gears and timing cover. All components are installed with new bearings, seals and gaskets incorporated throughout. The installation of manifolds and external parts is all that's necessary.*

Low mileage used engines - *Some companies now offer low mileage used engines which is a very cost effective way to get your vehicle up and running again. These engines often come from vehicles that have been in totaled in accidents or come from other countries that have a higher vehicle turnover rate. A low mileage used engine also usually has a similar warranty like the newly remanufactured engines.*

3   Give careful thought to which alternative is best for you and discuss the situation with local automotive machine shops, auto parts dealers and experienced rebuilders before ordering or purchasing replacement parts.

6   Engine removal - methods and precautions

1   If you've decided that an engine must be removed for overhaul or major repair work, several preliminary steps should be taken. Read all removal and installation procedures carefully prior to committing to this job.
2   Locating a suitable place to work is extremely important. Adequate work space, along with storage space for the vehicle, will be needed. If a shop or garage isn't available, at the very least a flat, level, clean work surface made of concrete or asphalt is required.
3   Cleaning the engine compartment and engine before beginning the removal procedure will help keep tools clean and organized **(see illustrations)**.
4   An engine hoist will also be necessary. Make sure the hoist is rated in excess of the combined weight of the engine and transaxle. Safety is of primary importance, considering the potential hazards involved in removing the engine from the vehicle.
5   A vehicle hoist will be necessary for engine removal, too, since on these models the engine and transaxle assembly must be lowered from the engine compartment, then the vehicle is raised and the powertrain unit is removed from under the vehicle. If the necessary equipment is not available, the engine will have to be removed by a qualified automotive repair facility.
6   If you're a novice at engine removal, get at least one helper. One person cannot easily do all the things you need to do to remove a big heavy engine and transaxle assembly from the engine compartment. Also helpful is to seek advice and assistance from someone who's experienced in engine removal.
7   Plan the operation ahead of time. Arrange for or obtain all of the tools and equipment you'll need prior to beginning the job **(see illustration)**. Some of the equipment necessary to perform engine removal and installation safely and with relative ease are (in addition to a vehicle hoist and an engine hoist) a heavy duty floor jack (preferably fitted with a transaxle jack head adapter), complete sets of wrenches and sockets as described in the front of this manual, wooden blocks, plenty of rags and cleaning solvent for mopping up spilled oil, coolant and gasoline.
8   Plan for the vehicle to be out of use for quite a while. A machine shop can do the work that is beyond the scope of the home mechanic. Machine shops often have a busy schedule, so before removing the engine, consult the shop for an estimate of how long it will take to rebuild or repair the components that may need work.

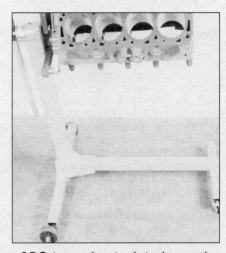

6.7 Get an engine stand sturdy enough to firmly support the engine while you're working on it. Stay away from three-wheeled models; they have a tendency to tip over more easily, so get a four-wheeled unit

7   Engine - removal and installation

Warning: *Gasoline is extremely flammable, so take extra precautions when you work on any part of the fuel system. Don't smoke or allow open flames or bare light bulbs near the work area, and don't work in a garage where a gas-type appliance (such as a water heater or clothes dryer) is present. Since gasoline is carcinogenic, wear fuel-resistant gloves when there's a possibility of being exposed to fuel, and, if you spill any fuel on your skin, rinse it off immediately with soap and water. Mop up any spills immediately and do not store fuel-soaked rags where they could ignite. The fuel system is under constant pressure, so, if any fuel lines are to be disconnected, the fuel pressure in the system must be relieved first (see Chapter 4 for more information). When you perform any kind of work on the fuel system, wear safety glasses and have a Class B type fire extinguisher on hand.*

Warning: *The engine must be completely cool before beginning this procedure.*

Note: *Read through the entire Section before beginning this procedure. On 1.5L engines, the transaxle must be supported from below with a floor jack, then the transaxle and torque converter fasteners removed to separate the transaxle from the engine, leaving the transaxle in place in the vehicle.*

Note: *On 2.0L and 2.5L models, engine removal is a difficult job, especially for the do-it-yourself mechanic working at home. Because of the vehicle's design, the manufacturer states that the engine and transaxle have to be removed as a unit from the bottom of the vehicle, not the top. With a floor jack and jackstands, the vehicle can't be raised high enough and supported safely enough for the engine/transaxle assembly to slide out from underneath. The manufacturer recommends that removal of the engine transaxle assembly only be performed on a frame-contact type vehicle hoist.*

Removal

1   On 2.0L and 2.5L engines, have the air conditioning refrigerant recovered by a qualified air conditioning technician.

2   On 2.0L and 2.5L models, loosen the front wheel lug nuts and driveaxle hub nuts, then raise the vehicle and support it securely on jackstands. Position the steering wheel so the front wheels point straight ahead. Remove the front wheels.

3   Relieve the fuel system pressure (see Chapter 4), then disconnect the cable from the negative terminal of the battery (see Chapter 5).

4   Remove the hood (see Chapter 11). Cover the fenders with fender covers.

5   Remove the air filter housing and the air intake duct (see Chapter 4).

6   On 1.5L and 2.0L engines, disconnect and remove the turbocharger and charge air cooler inlet and outlet hoses (see Chapter 4).

7   Disconnect the fuel line from the fuel rail (see Chapter 4).

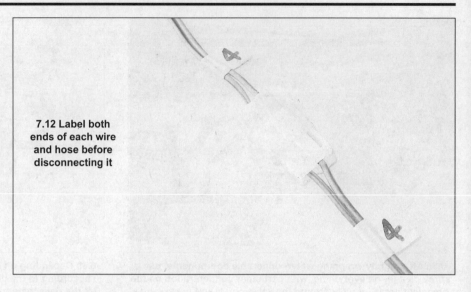

7.12 Label both ends of each wire and hose before disconnecting it

8   Remove the lower splash shield and inner fender splash shields.

9   Drain the cooling system (see Chapter 1). Support the radiator/condenser assembly to the body with wire or large plastic tie-wraps, and remove the expansion tank and its hoses.

10   Remove the upper radiator hose and disconnect the coolant hoses at the engine oil cooler, the thermostat housing, then remove the coolant reservoir (see Chapter 3).

11   Follow the heater hoses from the firewall and detach them from the pipes on the engine.

12   Clearly label and disconnect all vacuum lines, emissions hoses, wiring harness connectors and fuel lines. Masking tape and/or a touch-up paint applicator work well for marking items **(see illustration)**. Take photos or sketch the locations of components and brackets. Move the wiring harness out of the way.

13   Remove the drivebelt and drain the engine oil (see Chapter 1).

14   On 1.5L engines, remove the air conditioning compressor and secure the compressor out of the way without disconnecting the lines from the compressor (see Chapter 3).

15   On 2.0L and 2.5L engines, remove the air conditioning compressor from the vehicle (see Chapter 3).

16   Remove the PCM (see Chapter 6).

17   Disconnect the electrical connectors to the TCM (see Chapter 7).

18   Remove the lower radiator hose.

19   Remove the battery and battery tray (see Chapter 5).

20   Unbolt the exhaust pipe from the exhaust manifold or catalytic converter (see Chapter 4). Disconnect the oxygen sensor electrical connectors.

21   Remove the starter (see Chapter 5).

22   Mark the torque converter to the driveplate and remove the driveplate-to-torque converter bolts.

23   Disconnect the shift cable(s) from the transaxle (see Chapter 7). Also disconnect any wiring harness connectors from the transaxle and cable brackets from the engine.

1.5L engines

24   Support the engine from above with an engine hoist securely attached by heavy-duty chains to the engine lifting brackets. Support the transaxle from below with a floor jack, preferably one equipped with a transmission jack head adapter. Loosen all the engine and transaxle mount fasteners. With the hoist taking the weight off the mounts, remove the engine mounts (see Chapter 2A, Section 17).

25   Push the torque converter back towards the transaxle.

26   Disconnect the transaxle and separate the transaxle from the engine, leaving the transaxle in place in the vehicle.

27   With an assistant to help, carefully lift the engine out from the top of the vehicle.

28   Remove the driveplate (see Chapter 2A) and mount the engine on an engine stand.

2.0L and 2.5L models

29   Disconnect the stabilizer bar links from the stabilizer bar, the tie-rod ends from the steering knuckles, and the steering intermediate shaft from the steering gear (see Chapter 10).

Caution: *Don't allow the steering shaft to rotate after the intermediate shaft has been disconnected, as damage to the airbag clockspring could occur.*

30   Disconnect the electrical connectors from the steering gear.

31   Disconnect the control arms from the steering knuckles (see Chapter 10) and remove the driveaxles (see Chapter 8).

32   Support the engine/transaxle assembly from above with an engine hoist securely attached by heavy-duty chains to the engine lifting brackets. Place blocks of wood between the engine/transaxle and the subframe, then loosen all the engine and transaxle mount fasteners. With the hoist taking the weight off the mounts, remove the engine/transaxle mounts.

Warning: *DO NOT place any part of your body under the engine when it's supported only by a hoist or other lifting device.*

33   Recheck to be sure nothing is still connecting the engine/transaxle to the vehicle. Disconnect anything still remaining.

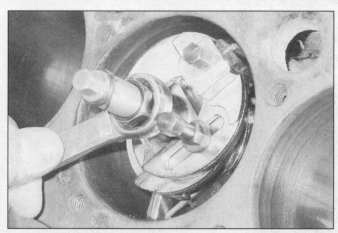

9.1 Before you try to remove the pistons, use a ridge reamer to remove the raised material (ridge) from the top of the cylinders

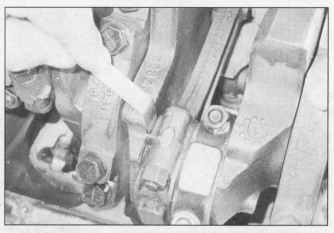

9.3 Checking the connecting rod endplay (side clearance)

34   Scribe or make paint marks where the subframe meets the chassis for installation alignment purposes.

35   Lower the vehicle and support the subframe with two floor jacks - one positioned under each side of the subframe. Remove the subframe bolts (see Chapter 10).

36   With an assistant to help, carefully and slowly lower each jack until the subframe is down far enough to be slid out from under the vehicle.

37   Inspect the engine/transaxle assembly thoroughly once more to make sure that nothing is still attached, then slowly lower the powertrain down out of the engine compartment and onto the floor. Check carefully to make sure nothing is hanging up as this is done.

38   Once the powertrain is on the floor, disconnect the engine lifting chains and move the engine hoist out of the way, then raise the vehicle hoist until the vehicle clears the powertrain.

39   Reconnect the engine hoist to the engine, raise the engine/transaxle up a little and support the engine with blocks of wood. Support the transaxle with a floor jack, preferably one with a transmission adapter. Secure the transaxle to the jack with safety chains.

40   Remove the bolts and the engine-to-transaxle brace, if equipped. Remove engine-to-transaxle mounting bolts and separate the engine from the transaxle.

41   Remove the driveplate (see Chapter 2A) and mount the engine on an engine stand.

Installation

42   Installation is the reverse of removal, noting the following points:

a) *Check the engine/transaxle mounts. If they're worn or damaged, replace them (See Chapters 2A and 7).*

b) *On 2.0L and 2.5L engines, attach the transaxle to the engine following the procedure described in Chapter 7. On 1.5L engines the transaxle is attached after the engine is installed into the vehicle. Tighten the driveplate and transaxle-to-engine fasteners to the torque listed in this Chapter's Specifications.*

c) *When installing the subframe, align the marks made during removal, then tighten the subframe mounting bolts to the torque listed in Chapter 10.*

d) *Add coolant, oil and transaxle fluids as needed (see Chapter 1).*

e) *Reconnect the battery (see Chapter 5).*

f) *Run the engine and check for proper operation and leaks. Shut off the engine and recheck fluid levels.*

g) *Have the air conditioning system recharged and leak tested, if it was discharged.*

8   Engine overhaul - disassembly sequence

1   It's much easier to remove the external components if the engine is mounted on a portable engine stand. A stand can often be rented quite cheaply from an equipment rental yard. Before the engine is mounted on a stand, the flywheel/driveplate should be removed from the engine.

2   If a stand isn't available, it's possible to remove the external engine components with it blocked up on the floor. Be extra careful not to tip or drop the engine when working without a stand.

3   If you're going to obtain a rebuilt engine, all external components must come off first, to be transferred to the replacement engine. These components include:

• *Driveplate*
• *Ignition system components*
• *Emissions-related components*
• *Engine mounts and mount brackets*
• *Engine rear cover (spacer plate between flywheel/driveplate and engine block)*
• *Intake/exhaust manifolds*
• *Turbocharger*
• *Fuel injection components*
• *Oil filter*
• *Thermostat and housing assembly*
• *Water pump*

Note: *When removing the external components from the engine, pay close attention to details that may be helpful or important during installation. Note the installed position of gaskets, seals, spacers, pins, brackets, washers, bolts and other small items.*

4   If you're going to obtain a short block (assembled engine block, crankshaft, pistons and connecting rods), then remove the timing chain, cylinder head, oil pan, oil pump pick-up tube, oil pump and water pump from your engine so that you can turn in your old short block to the rebuilder as a core. See *Engine rebuilding alternatives* for additional information regarding the different possibilities to be considered.

9   Pistons and connecting rods - removal and installation

Removal

Note: *Prior to removing the piston/connecting rod assemblies, remove the cylinder head and oil pan (see Chapter 2A).*

1   Use your fingernail to feel if a ridge has formed at the upper limit of ring travel (about 1/4-inch down from the top of each cylinder). If carbon deposits or cylinder wear have produced ridges, they must be completely removed with a special tool **(see illustration)**. Follow the manufacturer's instructions provided with the tool. Failure to remove the ridges before attempting to remove the piston/connecting rod assemblies may result in piston breakage.

2   After the cylinder ridges have been removed, turn the engine so the crankshaft is facing up.

3   Before the main bearing cap assembly and connecting rods are removed, check the connecting rod endplay with feeler gauges. Slide them between the first connecting rod and the crankshaft throw until the play is removed **(see illustration)**. Repeat this procedure for each connecting rod. The endplay is equal to the thickness of the feeler gauge(s). Check with an automotive machine shop for the end-

9.4 If the connecting rods and caps are not marked, use permanent ink to mark the caps to the rods by cylinder number (for example, this would be the No. 4 connecting rod)

9.13 Install the piston ring into the cylinder then push it down into position using a piston so the ring will be square in the cylinder

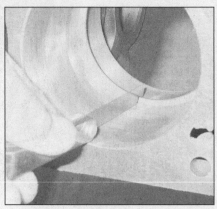

9.14 With the ring square in the cylinder, measure the ring end gap with a feeler gauge

play service limit (a typical endplay limit should measure between 0.005 to 0.015 inch [0.127 to 0.381 mm]). If the play exceeds the service limit, new connecting rods will be required. If new rods (or a new crankshaft) are installed, the endplay may fall under the minimum allowable. If it does, the rods will have to be machined to restore it. If necessary, consult an automotive machine shop for advice.

4   Check the connecting rods and caps for identification marks. If they aren't plainly marked, use paint or marker to clearly identify each rod and cap (1, 2, 3, etc., depending on the cylinder they're associated with) **(see illustration)**.

5   Remove the connecting rod cap bolts from the number one connecting rod.

Note: *New connecting rod cap bolts must be used when reassembling the engine, but save the old bolts - they'll be used during the bearing oil clearance check during reassembly.*

6   Remove the number one connecting rod cap and bearing insert. Don't drop the bearing insert out of the cap.

7   Remove the bearing insert and push the connecting rod/piston assembly out through the top of the engine. Use a

wooden dowel to push on the connecting rod. If resistance is felt, double-check to make sure that all of the ridge was removed from the cylinder.

8   Repeat the procedure for the remaining cylinders.

9   After removal, reassemble the connecting rod caps and bearing inserts in their respective connecting rods and install the cap bolts finger-tight. Leaving the old bearing inserts in place until reassembly will help prevent the connecting rod bearing surfaces from being accidentally nicked or gouged.

10   The pistons and connecting rods are now ready for inspection and overhaul at an automotive machine shop.

Piston ring installation

11   Before installing the new piston rings, the ring end gaps must be checked. It's assumed that the piston ring side clearance has been checked and verified correct.

12   Lay out the piston/connecting rod assemblies and the new ring sets so the ring sets will be matched with the same piston and cylinder during the end gap measurement and engine assembly.

13   Insert the top (number one) ring into the first cylinder and square it up with the cylinder walls by pushing it in with the top of the piston **(see illustration)**. The ring should be near the bottom of the cylinder, at the lower limit of ring travel.

14   To measure the end gap, slip feeler gauges between the ends of the ring until a gauge equal to the gap width is found **(see illustration)**. The feeler gauge should slide between the ring ends with a slight amount of drag. A typical ring gap should fall between 0.010 and 0.020 inch [0.25 to 0.50 mm] for compression rings and up to 0.030 inch [0.76 mm] for the oil ring steel rails. If the gap is larger or smaller than specified, double-check to make sure you have the correct rings before proceeding.

15   If the gap is too small, it must be enlarged or the ring ends may come in contact with each other during engine operation, which can cause serious damage to the engine. If necessary, increase the end gaps by filing the ring ends very carefully with a fine file. Mount the file in a vise equipped with soft jaws, slip the ring over the file with the ends contacting the file face and slowly move the

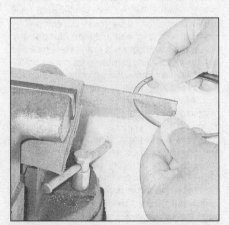

9.15 If the ring end gap is too small, clamp a file in a vise as shown and file the piston ring ends - remove all raised material

9.19a Installing the spacer/expander in the oil ring groove

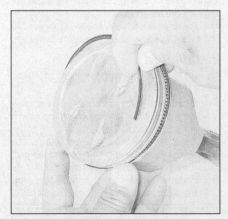

9.19b DO NOT use a piston ring installation tool when installing the oil ring side rails

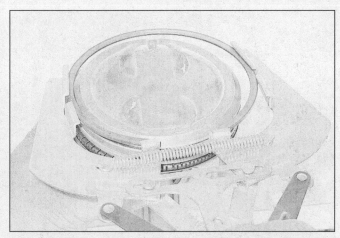

9.22 Use a piston ring installation tool to install the number 2 and the number 1 (top) rings - be sure the directional mark on the piston ring(s) is facing toward the top of the piston

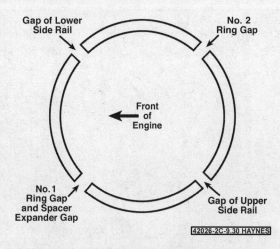

9.30 Position the piston ring end gaps as shown

ring to remove material from the ends. When performing this operation, file only by pushing the ring from the outside end of the file towards the vise (see illustration).

16   Excess end gap isn't critical unless it's greater than 0.040 inch (1.01 mm). Again, double-check to make sure you have the correct ring type.

17   Repeat the procedure for each ring that will be installed in the first cylinder and for each ring in the remaining cylinders. Remember to keep rings, pistons and cylinders matched up.

18   Once the ring end gaps have been checked/corrected, the rings can be installed on the pistons.

19   The oil control ring (lowest one on the piston) is usually installed first. It's composed of three separate components. Slip the spacer/expander into the groove (see illustration). If an anti-rotation tang is used, make sure it's inserted into the drilled hole in the ring groove. Next, install the upper side rail in the same manner (see illustration). Don't use a piston ring installation tool on the oil ring side rails, as they may be damaged. Instead, place one end of the side rail into the groove between the spacer/expander and the ring land, hold it firmly in place and slide a finger around the piston while pushing the rail into the groove. Finally, install the lower side rail.

20   After the three oil ring components have been installed, check to make sure that both the upper and lower side rails can be rotated smoothly inside the ring grooves.

21   The number two (middle) ring is installed next. It's usually stamped with a mark, which must face up, toward the top of the piston. Do not mix up the top and middle rings, as they have different cross-sections.

Note: Always follow the instructions printed on the ring package or box - different manufacturers may require different approaches.

22   Use a piston ring installation tool and make sure the identification mark is facing the top of the piston, then slip the ring into the middle groove on the piston (see illustra-

tion). Don't expand the ring any more than necessary to slide it over the piston.

23   Install the number one (top) ring in the same manner. Make sure the mark is facing up. Be careful not to confuse the number one and number two rings.

24   Repeat the procedure for the remaining pistons and rings.

Installation

Note: For final assembly, the pistons and rods are installed after the lower crankcase (or bedplate) has been installed and torqued in sequence.

25   Before installing the piston/connecting rod assemblies, the cylinder walls must be perfectly clean, the top edge of each cylinder bore must be chamfered, and the crankshaft must be in place.

26   Remove the cap from the end of the number one connecting rod (refer to the marks made during removal). Remove the original bearing inserts and wipe the bearing surfaces of the connecting rod and cap with a clean, lint-free cloth. They must be kept spotlessly clean.

Connecting rod bearing oil clearance check

27   Clean the back side of the new upper bearing insert, then lay it in place in the connecting rod.

28   Make sure the tab on the bearing fits into the recess in the rod. Don't hammer the bearing insert into place and be very careful not to nick or gouge the bearing face. Don't lubricate the bearing at this time.

29   Clean the back side of the other bearing insert and install it in the rod cap. Again, make sure the tab on the bearing fits into the recess in the cap, and don't apply any lubricant. It's critically important that the mating surfaces of the bearing and connecting rod are perfectly clean and oil free when they're assembled.

30   Position the piston ring gaps at the specified intervals around the piston as shown (see illustration).

31   Lubricate the piston and rings with clean engine oil and attach a piston ring compressor to the piston. Leave the skirt protruding about 1/4-inch to guide the piston into the cylinder. The rings must be compressed until they're flush with the piston.

32   Rotate the crankshaft until the number one connecting rod journal is at BDC (Bottom Dead Center) and apply a liberal coat of engine oil to the cylinder walls.

33   With the arrow on top of the piston facing the front (timing belt end or timing chain) of the engine, gently insert the piston/connecting rod assembly into the number one cylinder bore and rest the bottom edge of the ring compressor on the engine block. Install the pistons with the cavity mark(s) or arrow facing toward the timing belt or timing chain end of the engine.

34   Tap the top edge of the ring compressor to make sure it's contacting the block around its entire circumference.

35   Gently tap on the top of the piston with the end of a wooden or plastic hammer handle (see illustration) while guiding the end of the connecting rod into place on the crankshaft journal (a pair of wooden dowels would be helpful for this). The piston rings may try to pop out of the ring compressor just before

9.35 Use a plastic or wooden hammer handle to push the piston into the cylinder

9.37 Place Plastigage on each connecting rod bearing journal, parallel to the crankshaft centerline

9.41 Use the scale on the Plastigage package to determine the bearing oil clearance - measure the widest part of the Plastigage and use the correct scale; it comes with both standard and metric scales

entering the cylinder bore, so keep some downward pressure on the ring compressor. Work slowly, and if any resistance is felt as the piston enters the cylinder, stop immediately. Find out what's hanging up and fix it before proceeding. Do not force the piston into the cylinder - you might break a ring and/or the piston.

Caution: *On 1.5L engines, the connecting rod bearing anti-rotation tab grooves should be pointing toward the right-hand side of the engine.*

36　Once the piston/connecting rod assembly is installed, the connecting rod bearing oil clearance must be checked before the rod cap is permanently installed.

37　Cut a piece of the appropriate size Plastigage slightly shorter than the width of the connecting rod bearing and lay it in place on the number one connecting rod journal, parallel with the journal axis **(see illustration)**.

38　Clean the connecting rod cap bearing face and install the rod cap. Make sure the mating mark on the cap is on the same side as the mark on the connecting rod **(see illustration 9.4)**.

39　Install the old rod bolts at this time, and tighten them to the torque listed in this Chapter's Specifications.

Note: *Use a thin-wall socket to avoid erroneous torque readings that can result if the socket is wedged between the rod cap and the bolt. If the socket tends to wedge itself between the fastener and the cap, lift up on it slightly until it no longer contacts the cap. DO NOT rotate the crankshaft at any time during this operation.*

40　Remove the fasteners and detach the rod cap, being very careful not to disturb the Plastigage. Discard the cap bolts at this time as they cannot be reused.

41　Compare the width of the crushed Plastigage to the scale printed on the Plastigage

envelope to obtain the oil clearance **(see illustration)**. The connecting rod oil clearance is usually about 0.001 to 0.002 inch. Consult an automotive machine shop for the clearance specified for the rod bearings on your engine.

42　If the clearance is not as specified, the bearing inserts may be the wrong size (which means different ones will be required). Before deciding that different inserts are needed, make sure that no dirt or oil was between the bearing inserts and the connecting rod or cap when the clearance was measured. Also, recheck the journal diameter. If the Plastigage was wider at one end than the other, the journal may be tapered. If the clearance still exceeds the limit specified, the bearing will have to be replaced with an undersize bearing.

Note: *When installing a new crankshaft always use a standard size bearing.*

Final installation

43　Carefully scrape all traces of the Plastigage material off the rod journal and/or bearing face. Be very careful not to scratch the bearing - use your fingernail or the edge of a plastic card.

44　Make sure the bearing faces are perfectly clean, then apply a uniform layer of clean moly-base grease or engine assembly lube to both of them. You'll have to push the piston into the cylinder to expose the face of the bearing insert in the connecting rod.

45　Slide the connecting rod back into place on the journal, install the rod cap, install the new bolts and tighten them to the torque listed in this Chapter's Specifications.

Note: *Install new connecting rod cap bolts. Do NOT reuse old bolts - they have stretched and cannot be reused.*

46　Repeat the entire procedure for the remaining pistons/connecting rods.

47　The important points to remember are:

a) *Keep the back sides of the bearing inserts and the insides of the connecting rods and caps perfectly clean when assembling them.*

b) *Make sure you have the correct piston/rod assembly for each cylinder.*

c) *The arrow or mark on the piston must face the front (timing chain end) of the engine.*

d) *Lubricate the cylinder walls liberally with clean oil.*

e) *Lubricate the bearing faces when installing the rod caps after the oil clearance has been checked.*

48　After all the piston/connecting rod assemblies have been correctly installed, rotate the crankshaft a number of times by hand to check for any obvious binding.

49　As a final step, check the connecting rod endplay, as described in Step 3. If it was correct before disassembly and the original crankshaft and rods were reinstalled, it should still be correct. If new rods or a new crankshaft were installed, the endplay may be inadequate. If so, the rods will have to be removed and taken to an automotive machine shop for resizing.

10　Crankshaft - removal and installation

Removal

Note: *The crankshaft can be removed only after the engine has been removed from the vehicle. It's assumed that the flywheel or driveplate, crankshaft pulley, timing chain, oil pan, balancer shaft with oil pump body, oil filter and piston/connecting rod assemblies have already been removed. The rear main oil seal is removed.*

1　Before the crankshaft is removed, measure the endplay. Mount a dial indicator with

**10.1 Checking crankshaft endplay with
a dial indicator**

**10.3 Checking the crankshaft endplay with feeler gauges
at the thrust bearing journal**

the indicator in line with the crankshaft and just touching the end of the crankshaft as shown **(see illustration)**.

2   Pry the crankshaft all the way to the rear and zero the dial indicator. Next, pry the crankshaft to the front as far as possible and check the reading on the dial indicator. The distance traveled is the endplay. A typical crankshaft endplay will fall between 0.003 to 0.010 inch (0.076 to 0.254 mm). If it is greater than that, check the crankshaft thrust surfaces for wear after it's removed. If no wear is evident, new main bearings should correct the endplay.

3   If a dial indicator isn't available, feeler gauges can be used. Gently pry the crankshaft all the way to the front of the engine. Slip feeler gauges between the crankshaft and the front face of the thrust bearing or washer to determine the clearance **(see illustration)**.

4   Loosen the lower crankcase perimeter bolts and the lower crankcase center bolts 1/4-turn at a time each, until they can be removed by hand. Follow the reverse of the tightening sequence **(see illustrations 10.30a or 10.30b and 10.19a or 10.19b)**.
Caution: *All 10 lower crankcase center bolts must be replaced with new ones upon installation. Save the old bolts, however, as they will be used for the main bearing oil clearance check.*

5   Remove the lower crankcase. Try not to drop the bearing inserts if they come out with the lower crankcase or bearing caps.

6   Carefully lift the crankshaft out of the engine. It may be a good idea to have an assistant available, since the crankshaft is quite heavy and awkward to handle. With the bearing inserts in place inside the engine block and the lower crankcase, reinstall the lower crankcase onto the engine block and tighten the bolts finger-tight.

Installation

7   Crankshaft installation is the first step in engine reassembly. It's assumed at this point that the engine block and crankshaft

have been cleaned, inspected and repaired or reconditioned.

8   Position the engine block with the bottom facing up.

9   Remove the mounting bolts and lift off the lower crankcase or bearing caps.

10   If they're still in place, remove the original bearing inserts from the block and from the lower crankcase. Wipe the bearing surfaces of the block and lower crankcase saddle with a clean, lint-free cloth. They must be kept spotlessly clean. This is critical for determining the correct bearing oil clearance.

Main bearing oil clearance check

11   Without mixing them up, clean the back sides of the new upper main bearing inserts (with grooves and oil holes) and lay one in each main bearing saddle in the engine block. Each upper bearing (engine block) has an oil groove and oil hole in it.
Caution: *The oil holes in the block must line up with the oil holes in the engine block inserts. The thrust washer or thrust bearing insert must be installed in the correct location.*
Caution: *Do not hammer the bearing insert into place and don't nick or gouge the bearing faces. DO NOT apply any lubrication at this time.*
Note: *The thrust bearing is located on the en-*

gine block number 4 journal for 1.5L engines and the number 2 journal for 2.0L and 2.5L engines. Clean the back sides of the lower main bearing inserts and lay them in the corresponding location in the lower crankcase saddles. Make sure the tab on the bearing insert fits into the recess in the block or lower crankcase saddles.

12   Clean the faces of the bearing inserts in the block and the crankshaft main bearing journals with a clean, lint-free cloth.

13   Check or clean the oil holes in the crankshaft, as any dirt here can go only one way - straight through the new bearings.

14   Once you're certain the crankshaft is clean, carefully lay it in position in the cylinder block.

15   Before the crankshaft can be permanently installed, the main bearing oil clearance must be checked.

16   Cut several strips of the appropriate size of Plastigage. They must be slightly shorter than the width of the main bearing journal.

17   Place one piece on each crankshaft main bearing journal, parallel with the journal axis as shown **(see illustration)**.

18   Clean the faces of the bearing inserts in the lower crankcase. Hold the bearing inserts in place and install the lower crankcase onto the crankshaft and cylinder block. DO NOT disturb the Plastigage.

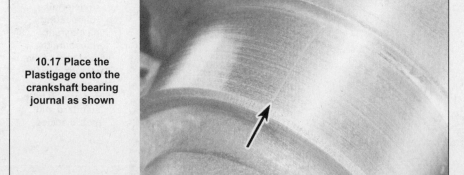

10.17 Place the Plastigage onto the crankshaft bearing journal as shown

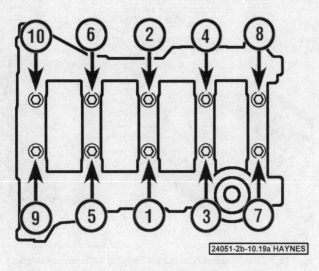

10.19a Lower crankcase center bolt tightening sequence - 1.5L engine

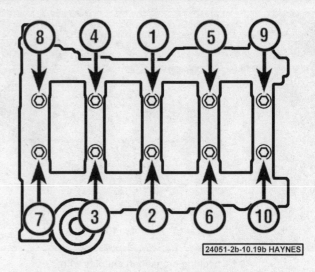

10.19b Lower crankcase center bolt tightening sequence - 2.0L and 2.5L engines

19   Apply clean engine oil to all bolt threads prior to installation, then install all bolts finger-tight. Tighten the lower crankcase bolts or main bearing cap bolts in the sequence shown **(see illustrations)** progressing in steps, to the torque listed in this Chapter's Specifications. DO NOT rotate the crankshaft at any time during this operation.

20   Remove the bolts in the reverse order of the tightening sequence and carefully lift the lower crankcase straight up and off the block. Do not disturb the Plastigage or rotate the crankshaft.

21   Compare the width of the crushed Plastigage on each journal to the scale printed on the Plastigage envelope to determine the main bearing oil clearance **(see illustration)**. Check with an automotive machine shop for the oil clearance for your engine.

22   If the clearance is not correct, the bearing inserts may be the wrong size (which means different ones will be required). Before deciding if different inserts are needed, make sure that no dirt or oil was between the bearing inserts and the caps or block when the clearance was measured. If the Plastigage was wider at one end than the other, the crankshaft journal may be tapered. If the clearance still exceeds the limit specified, the bearing insert(s) will have to be replaced with an undersize bearing insert(s).

Caution: *When installing a new crankshaft always install a standard bearing insert set.*

23   Carefully scrape all traces of the Plastigage material off the main bearing journals and/or the bearing insert faces. Remove all residue from the oil holes. Use your fingernail or the edge of a plastic card - don't nick or scratch the bearing faces.

Final installation

24   Carefully lift the crankshaft out of the cylinder block. If the crankshaft position sensor reluctor wheel ring was removed, install the ring and tighten the bolts to the torque listed in this Chapter's Specifications 2B.

25   Clean the bearing insert faces in the cylinder block, then apply a thin, uniform layer of moly-base grease or engine assembly lube to each of the bearing surfaces. Coat the thrust faces as well as the journal face of the thrust bearing.

26   Make sure the crankshaft journals are clean, then lay the crankshaft back in place in the cylinder block.

27   Clean the bearing insert faces and apply the same lubricant to them. Clean the engine block and the mating surface of the lower crankcase thoroughly. The surfaces must be free of oil residue. Install the lower crankcase.

28   Prior to installation, apply clean engine oil to all bolt threads, wiping off any excess, then install all bolts finger-tight.

Caution: *Remember, new bolts must be used.*

29   Tighten the bolts to the torque listed in this Chapter's Specifications following the correct torque sequence **(see illustration 10.19a or 10.19b)**.

30   Install the lower crankcase perimeter bolts and tighten them, in sequence, to the torque listed in this Chapter's Specifications **(see illustrations)**.

31   Recheck the crankshaft endplay with a feeler gauge or a dial indicator. The endplay should be correct if the crankshaft thrust faces aren't worn or damaged and if new bearings have been installed.

32   Rotate the crankshaft a number of times by hand to check for any obvious binding. It should rotate with a running torque of 50 in-lbs or less. If the running torque is too high, correct the problem at this time.

33   Install the new rear main oil seal (see Chapter 2A).

10.21 Use the scale on the Plastigage package to determine the bearing oil clearance - measure the widest part of the Plastigage and use the correct scale; it comes with both standard and metric scales

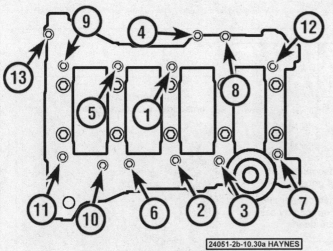

10.30a Lower crankcase perimeter bolt tightening sequence - 1.5L engine

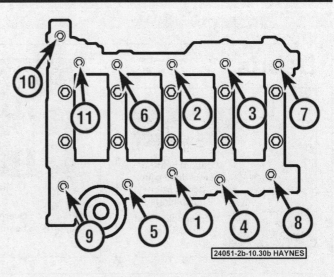

10.30b Lower crankcase perimeter bolt tightening sequence - 2.0L and 2.5L engines

11 Engine overhaul - reassembly sequence

1   Before beginning engine reassembly, make sure you have all the necessary new parts, gaskets and seals as well as the following items on hand:

- *Common hand tools*
- *A 3/8-inch and 1/2-inch drive torque wrench*
- *New engine oil*
- *Gasket sealant*
- *Thread locking compound*

2   If you obtained a short block it will be necessary to install the cylinder head, the oil pump and pick-up tube, the oil pan, the water pump, the timing chain and timing cover, and the valve cover (see Chapter 2A). In order to save time and avoid problems, the external components must be installed in the following general order:

- *Thermostat and housing cover*
- *Water pump*
- *Intake and exhaust manifolds*
- *Turbocharger*
- *Fuel injection components*
- *Emission control components*
- *Spark plugs*
- *Ignition coils*
- *Oil filter*
- *Engine mounts and mount brackets*
- *Driveplate (automatic transaxle)*

12 Initial start-up and break-in after overhaul

Warning: *Have a fire extinguisher handy when starting the engine for the first time.*

1   Once the engine has been installed in the vehicle, double-check the engine oil and coolant levels.

2   With the spark plugs out of the engine and the ignition system and fuel pump disabled, crank the engine until oil pressure registers on the gauge or the light goes out.

3   Install the spark plugs, coil pack or coils and restore the ignition system and fuel pump functions.

4   Start the engine. It may take a few moments for the fuel system to build up pressure, but the engine should start without a great deal of effort.

5   After the engine starts, it should be allowed to warm up to normal operating temperature. While the engine is warming up, make a thorough check for fuel, oil and coolant leaks.

6   Shut the engine off and recheck the engine oil and coolant levels.

7   Drive the vehicle to an area with minimum traffic, accelerate from 30 to 50 mph, then allow the vehicle to slow to 30 mph with the throttle closed. Repeat the procedure 10 or 12 times. This will load the piston rings and cause them to seat properly against the cylinder walls. Check again for oil and coolant leaks.

8   Drive the vehicle gently for the first 500 miles (no sustained high speeds) and keep a constant check on the oil level. It is not unusual for an engine to use oil during the break-in period.

9   At approximately 500 to 600 miles, change the oil and filter.

10   For the next few hundred miles, drive the vehicle normally. Do not pamper it or abuse it.

11   After 2,000 miles, change the oil and filter again and consider the engine broken in.

ENGINE BEARING ANALYSIS

Debris

Babbitt bearing embedded with debris from machinings

Microscopic detail of debris

Microscopic detail of gouges

Overplated copper alloy bearing gouged by cast iron debris

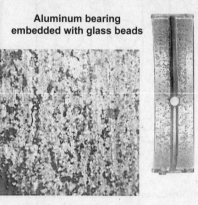

Aluminum bearing embedded with glass beads

Microscopic detail of glass beads

Damaged lining caused by dirt left on the bearing back

Misassembly

Result of a lower half assembled as an upper - blocking the oil flow

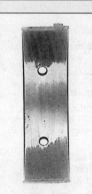

Excessive oil clearance is indicated by a short contact arc

Polished and oil-stained backs are a result of a poor fit in the housing bore

Result of a wrong, reversed, or shifted cap

Overloading

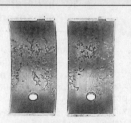

Damage from excessive idling which resulted in an oil film unable to support the load imposed

Damaged upper connecting rod bearings caused by engine lugging; the lower main bearings (not shown) were similarly affected

The damage shown in these upper and lower connecting rod bearings was caused by engine operation at a higher-than-rated speed under load

Misalignment

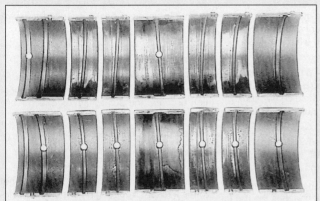

A warped crankshaft caused this pattern of severe wear in the center, diminishing toward the ends

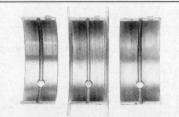

A poorly finished crankshaft caused the equally spaced scoring shown

A tapered housing bore caused the damage along one edge of this pair

A bent connecting rod led to the damage in the "V" pattern

Lubrication

Result of dry start: The bearings on the left, farthest from the oil pump, show more damage

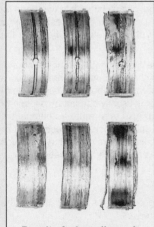

Result of a low oil supply or oil starvation

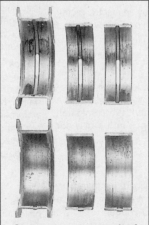

Severe wear as a result of inadequate oil clearance

Corrosion

Microscopic detail of corrosion

Corrosion is an acid attack on the bearing lining generally caused by inadequate maintenance, extremely hot or cold operation, or inferior oils or fuels

Microscopic detail of cavitation

Example of cavitation - a surface erosion caused by pressure changes in the oil film

Damage from excessive thrust or insufficient axial clearance

Bearing affected by oil dilution caused by excessive blow-by or a rich mixture

COMMON ENGINE OVERHAUL TERMS

B

Backlash - The amount of play between two parts. Usually refers to how much one gear can be moved back and forth without moving the gear with which it's meshed.

Bearing Caps - The caps held in place by nuts or bolts which, in turn, hold the bearing surface. This space is for lubricating oil to enter.

Bearing clearance - The amount of space left between shaft and bearing surface. This space is for lubricating oil to enter.

Bearing crush - The additional height which is purposely manufactured into each bearing half to ensure complete contact of the bearing back with the housing bore when the engine is assembled.

Bearing knock - The noise created by movement of a part in a loose or worn bearing.

Blueprinting - Dismantling an engine and reassembling it to EXACT specifications.

Bore - An engine cylinder, or any cylindrical hole; also used to describe the process of enlarging or accurately refinishing a hole with a cutting tool, as to bore an engine cylinder. The bore size is the diameter of the hole.

Boring - Renewing the cylinders by cutting them out to a specified size. A boring bar is used to make the cut.

Bottom end - A term which refers collectively to the engine block, crankshaft, main bearings and the big ends of the connecting rods.

Break-in - The period of operation between installation of new or rebuilt parts and time in which parts are worn to the correct fit. Driving at reduced and varying speed for a specified mileage to permit parts to wear to the correct fit.

Bushing - A one-piece sleeve placed in a bore to serve as a bearing surface for shaft, piston pin, etc. Usually replaceable.

C

Camshaft - The shaft in the engine, on which a series of lobes are located for operating the valve mechanisms. The camshaft is driven by gears or sprockets and a timing chain. Usually referred to simply as the cam.

Carbon - Hard, or soft, black deposits found in combustion chamber, on plugs, under rings, on and under valve heads.

Cast iron - An alloy of iron and more than two percent carbon, used for engine blocks and heads because it's relatively inexpensive and easy to mold into complex shapes.

Chamfer - To bevel across (or a bevel on) the sharp edge of an object.

Chase - To repair damaged threads with a tap or die.

Combustion chamber - The space between the piston and the cylinder head, with the piston at top dead center, in which air-fuel mixture is burned.

Compression ratio - The relationship between cylinder volume (clearance volume) when the piston is at top dead center and cylinder volume when the piston is at bottom dead center.

Connecting rod - The rod that connects the crank on the crankshaft with the piston. Sometimes called a con rod.

Connecting rod cap - The part of the connecting rod assembly that attaches the rod to the crankpin.

Core plug - Soft metal plug used to plug the casting holes for the coolant passages in the block.

Crankcase - The lower part of the engine in which the crankshaft rotates; includes the lower section of the cylinder block and the oil pan.

Crank kit - A reground or reconditioned crankshaft and new main and connecting rod bearings.

Crankpin - The part of a crankshaft to which a connecting rod is attached.

Crankshaft - The main rotating member, or shaft, running the length of the crankcase, with offset throws to which the connecting rods are attached; changes the reciprocating motion of the pistons into rotating motion.

Cylinder sleeve - A replaceable sleeve, or liner, pressed into the cylinder block to form the cylinder bore.

D

Deburring - Removing the burrs (rough edges or areas) from a bearing.

Deglazer - A tool, rotated by an electric motor, used to remove glaze from cylinder walls so a new set of rings will seat.

E

Endplay - The amount of lengthwise movement between two parts. As applied to a crankshaft, the distance that the crankshaft can move forward and back in the cylinder block.

F

Face - A machinist's term that refers to removing metal from the end of a shaft or the face of a larger part, such as a flywheel.

Fatigue - A breakdown of material through a large number of loading and unloading cycles. The first signs are cracks followed shortly by breaks.

Feeler gauge - A thin strip of hardened steel,

ground to an exact thickness, used to check clearances between parts.

Free height - The unloaded length or height of a spring.

Freeplay - The looseness in a linkage, or an assembly of parts, between the initial application of force and actual movement. Usually perceived as slop or slight delay.

Freeze plug - See Core plug.

G

Gallery - A large passage in the block that forms a reservoir for engine oil pressure.

Glaze - The very smooth, glassy finish that develops on cylinder walls while an engine is in service.

H

Heli-Coil - A rethreading device used when threads are worn or damaged. The device is installed in a retapped hole to reduce the thread size to the original size.

I

Installed height - The spring's measured length or height, as installed on the cylinder head. Installed height is measured from the spring seat to the underside of the spring retainer.

J

Journal - The surface of a rotating shaft which turns in a bearing.

K

Keeper - The split lock that holds the valve spring retainer in position on the valve stem.

Key - A small piece of metal inserted into matching grooves machined into two parts fitted together - such as a gear pressed onto a shaft - which prevents slippage between the two parts.

Knock - The heavy metallic engine sound, produced in the combustion chamber as a result of abnormal combustion - usually detonation. Knock is usually caused by a loose or worn bearing. Also referred to as detonation, pinging and spark knock. Connecting rod or main bearing knocks are created by too much oil clearance or insufficient lubrication.

L

Lands - The portions of metal between the piston ring grooves.

Lapping the valves - Grinding a valve face and its seat together with lapping compound.

Lash - The amount of free motion in a gear train, between gears, or in a mechanical assembly, that occurs before movement can begin. Usually refers to the lash in a valve train.

Lifter - The part that rides against the cam to transfer motion to the rest of the valve train.

M

Machining - The process of using a machine to remove metal from a metal part.

Main bearings - The plain, or babbit, bearings that support the crankshaft.

Main bearing caps - The cast iron caps, bolted to the bottom of the block, that support the main bearings.

O

O.D. - Outside diameter.

Oil gallery - A pipe or drilled passageway in the engine used to carry engine oil from one area to another.

Oil ring - The lower ring, or rings, of a piston; designed to prevent excessive amounts of oil from working up the cylinder walls and into the combustion chamber. Also called an oil-control ring.

Oil seal - A seal which keeps oil from leaking out of a compartment. Usually refers to a dynamic seal around a rotating shaft or other moving part.

O-ring - A type of sealing ring made of a special rubberlike material; in use, the O-ring is compressed into a groove to provide the sealing action.

Overhaul - To completely disassemble a unit, clean and inspect all parts, reassemble it with the original or new parts and make all adjustments necessary for proper operation.

P

Pilot bearing - A small bearing installed in the center of the flywheel (or the rear end of the crankshaft) to support the front end of the input shaft of the transmission.

Pip mark - A little dot or indentation which indicates the top side of a compression ring.

Piston - The cylindrical part, attached to the connecting rod, that moves up and down in the cylinder as the crankshaft rotates. When the fuel charge is fired, the piston transfers the force of the explosion to the connecting rod, then to the crankshaft.

Piston pin (or wrist pin) - The cylindrical and usually hollow steel pin that passes through the piston. The piston pin fastens the piston to the upper end of the connecting rod.

Piston ring - The split ring fitted to the groove in a piston. The ring contacts the sides of the ring groove and also rubs against the cylinder wall, thus sealing space between piston and wall. There are two types of rings: Compression rings seal the compression pressure in the combustion chamber; oil rings scrape excessive oil off the cylinder wall.

Piston ring groove - The slots or grooves cut in piston heads to hold piston rings in position.

Piston skirt - The portion of the piston below the rings and the piston pin hole.

Plastigage - A thin strip of plastic thread, available in different sizes, used for measuring clearances. For example, a strip of plastigage is laid across a bearing journal and mashed as parts are assembled. Then parts are disassembled and the width of the strip is measured to determine clearance between journal and bearing. Commonly used to measure crankshaft main-bearing and connecting rod bearing clearances.

Press-fit - A tight fit between two parts that requires pressure to force the parts together. Also referred to as drive, or force, fit.

Prussian blue - A blue pigment; in solution, useful in determining the area of contact between two surfaces. Prussian blue is commonly used to determine the width and location of the contact area between the valve face and the valve seat.

R

Race (bearing) - The inner or outer ring that provides a contact surface for balls or rollers in bearing.

Ream - To size, enlarge or smooth a hole by using a round cutting tool with fluted edges.

Ring job - The process of reconditioning the cylinders and installing new rings.

Runout - Wobble. The amount a shaft rotates out-of-true.

S

Saddle - The upper main bearing seat.

Scored - Scratched or grooved, as a cylinder wall may be scored by abrasive particles moved up and down by the piston rings.

Scuffing - A type of wear in which there's a transfer of material between parts moving against each other; shows up as pits or grooves in the mating surfaces.

Seat - The surface upon which another part rests or seats. For example, the valve seat is the matched surface upon which the valve face rests. Also used to refer to wearing into a good fit; for example, piston rings seat after a few miles of driving.

Short block - An engine block complete with crankshaft and piston and, usually, camshaft assemblies.

Static balance - The balance of an object while it's stationary.

Step - The wear on the lower portion of a ring land caused by excessive side and back-clearance. The height of the step indicates the ring's extra side clearance and the length of the step projecting from the back wall of the groove represents the ring's back clearance.

Stroke - The distance the piston moves when traveling from top dead center to bottom dead center, or from bottom dead center to top dead center.

Stud - A metal rod with threads on both ends.

T

Tang - A lip on the end of a plain bearing used to align the bearing during assembly.

Tap - To cut threads in a hole. Also refers to the fluted tool used to cut threads.

Taper - A gradual reduction in the width of a shaft or hole; in an engine cylinder, taper usually takes the form of uneven wear, more pronounced at the top than at the bottom.

Throws - The offset portions of the crankshaft to which the connecting rods are affixed.

Thrust bearing - The main bearing that has thrust faces to prevent excessive endplay, or forward and backward movement of the crankshaft.

Thrust washer - A bronze or hardened steel washer placed between two moving parts. The washer prevents longitudinal movement and provides a bearing surface for thrust surfaces of parts.

Tolerance - The amount of variation permitted from an exact size of measurement. Actual amount from smallest acceptable dimension to largest acceptable dimension.

U

Umbrella - An oil deflector placed near the valve tip to throw oil from the valve stem area.

Undercut - A machined groove below the normal surface.

Undersize bearings - Smaller diameter bearings used with re-ground crankshaft journals.

V

Valve grinding - Refacing a valve in a valve-refacing machine.

Valve train - The valve-operating mechanism of an engine; includes all components from the camshaft to the valve.

Vibration damper - A cylindrical weight attached to the front of the crankshaft to minimize torsional vibration (the twist-untwist actions of the crankshaft caused by the cylinder firing impulses). Also called a harmonic balancer.

W

Water jacket - The spaces around the cylinders, between the inner and outer shells of the cylinder block or head, through which coolant circulates.

Web - A supporting structure across a cavity.

Woodruff key - A key with a radiused backside (viewed from the side).

Notes

Chapter 3
Cooling, heating and air conditioning systems

Contents

Specifications

General

Cooling system cap pressure rating	Refer to top of cap
Thermostat rating (opening temperature range)....................	195 degrees F (92 degrees C)
Cooling system capacity...	See Chapter 1
HVAC refrigerant type	
2016 and earlier models..	R-134a
2017 and later models...	R-1234yf
Refrigerant capacity and type..	Refer to HVAC specification tag

Warning: *Do not mix R-134a with R-1234yf or the air conditioning components will be contaminated, requiring replacement of all of the components in the system.*

Torque specifications

	Ft-lbs (unless otherwise indicated)	Nm

Note: *One foot-pound (ft-lb) of torque is equivalent to 12 inch-pounds (in-lbs) of torque. Torque values below approximately 15 ft-lbs are expressed in inch-pounds, since most foot-pound torque wrenches are not accurate at these smaller values.*

	Ft-lbs (unless otherwise indicated)	Nm
Thermostat housing bolts (all)	89 in-lbs	10
Thermostat bypass pipe bolts	89 in-lbs	10
Water pump-to-housing mounting bolts		
1.5L engines	N/A	
2.0L and 2.5L engines	N/A	
Water pump housing-to-block bolts		
1.5L engines	18	25
2.0L and 2.5L engines		
Step 1	18	25
Step 2	18	25
Air conditioning compressor refrigerant line nut	16	22
Air conditioning compressor bracket bolts and nut	16	22
Air conditioning condenser refrigerant line nut(s)	16	22
Air conditioning compressor bolt/nut	16	22
Air conditioning compressor stud	80 in-lbs	9
Receiver-drier plug	108 in-lbs	12
Refrigerant pressure sensor	62 in-lbs	7
Thermal Expansion Valve (TXV) mounting fastener-to-evaporator		
2015 and earlier 2.0L models and all 2.5L models	62 in-lbs	7
2016 and later 1.5L and 2.0L models	42 in-lbs	4.7
Engine oil cooler		
1.5L engines		
Larger bolts	18	25
Small bolts	89 in-lbs	10
2.0L engines (center hollow bolt)	37	50

1　General information

Warning: *Do not allow antifreeze to come in contact with your skin or painted surfaces of the vehicle. Rinse off spills immediately with plenty of water. Antifreeze is highly toxic if ingested. Never leave antifreeze lying around in an open container or in puddles on the floor; children and pets are attracted by its sweet smell and may drink it. Check with local authorities about disposing of used antifreeze. Many communities have collection centers which will see that antifreeze is disposed of safely. Never dump used antifreeze on the ground or pour it into drains.*

Engine cooling system

1　All modern vehicles employ a pressurized engine cooling system with thermostatically controlled coolant circulation. The cooling system consists of a radiator, an expansion tank or coolant reservoir, a pressure cap (located on the expansion tank or radiator), a thermostat, a cooling fan, and a water pump.

2　The water pump circulates coolant through the engine. The coolant flows around each cylinder and around the intake and exhaust ports, near the spark plug areas and in close proximity to the exhaust valve guides.

3　A thermostat controls engine coolant temperature. During warm up, the closed thermostat prevents coolant from circulating through the radiator. As the engine nears normal operating temperature, the thermostat opens and allows hot coolant to travel through the radiator, where it's cooled before returning to the engine.

Heating system

4　The heating system consists of a blower fan and heater core located in a housing under the dash, the hoses connecting the heater core to the engine cooling system and the heater/air conditioning control head on the dashboard. Hot engine coolant is circulated through the heater core. When the heater mode is activated, a flap door in the housing opens to expose the heater core to the passenger compartment through air ducts. A fan switch on the control head activates the blower motor, which forces air through the core, heating the air.

Air conditioning system

5　The air conditioning system consists of a condenser mounted in front of the radiator, an evaporator mounted adjacent to the heater core, a compressor mounted on the engine, a receiver-drier or accumulator and the plumbing connecting all of the above components.

6　A blower fan forces the warmer air of the passenger compartment through the evaporator core (sort of a radiator-in-reverse), transferring the heat from the air to the refrigerant. The liquid refrigerant boils off into low pressure vapor, taking the heat with it when it leaves the evaporator.

2　Troubleshooting

Coolant leaks

1　A coolant leak can develop anywhere in the cooling system, but the most common causes are:

  a) A loose or weak hose clamp
  b) A defective hose
  c) A faulty pressure cap
  d) A damaged radiator
  e) A bad heater core
  f) A faulty water pump
  g) A leaking gasket at any joint that carries coolant

2　Coolant leaks aren't always easy to find. Sometimes they can only be detected when the cooling system is under pressure. Here's where a cooling system pressure tester comes in handy. After the engine has cooled completely, the tester is attached in place of the pressure cap, then pumped up to the pressure value equal to that of the pressure cap rating **(see illustration)**. Now, leaks that only exist when the engine is fully warmed up will become apparent. The tester can be left connected to locate a nagging slow leak.

Coolant level drops, but no external leaks

3　If you find it necessary to keep adding coolant, but there are no external leaks, the probable causes include:

  a) A blown head gasket

2.2 The cooling system pressure tester is connected in place of the pressure cap, then pumped up to pressurize the system

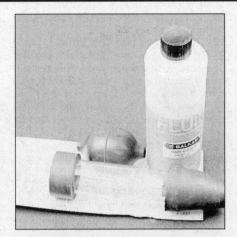

2.5a The combustion leak detector consists of a bulb syringe and test fluid

2.5b Place the tester over the cooling system filler neck and use the bulb to draw a sample into the tester

b) *A leaking intake manifold gasket (only on engines that have coolant passages in the manifold), or a cracked cylinder head or cylinder block*

4 Any of the above problems will also usually result in contamination of the engine oil, which will cause it to take on a milkshake-like appearance. A bad head gasket or cracked head or block can also result in engine oil contaminating the cooling system.

5 Combustion leak detectors (also known as block testers) are available at most auto parts stores. These work by detecting exhaust gases in the cooling system, which indicates a compression leak from a cylinder into the coolant. The tester consists of a large bulb-type syringe and bottle of test fluid **(see illustration)**. A measured amount of the fluid is added to the syringe. The syringe is placed over the cooling system filler neck and, with the

engine running, the bulb is squeezed and a sample of the gases present in the cooling system are drawn up through the test fluid **(see illustration)**. If any combustion gases are present in the sample taken, the test fluid will change color.

6 If the test indicates combustion gas is present in the cooling system, you can be sure that the engine has a blown head gasket or a crack in the cylinder head or block, and will require disassembly to repair.

Pressure cap

Warning: *Wait until the engine is completely cool before beginning this check.*

7 The cooling system is sealed by a spring-loaded cap, which raises the boiling point of the coolant. If the cap's seal or spring are worn out, the coolant can boil and escape past the cap. With the engine completely cool, remove the cap and check the

seal; if it's cracked, hardened or deteriorated in any way, replace it with a new one.

8 Even if the seal is good, the spring might not be; this can be checked with a cooling system pressure tester **(see illustration)**. If the cap can't hold a pressure within approximately 1-1/2 lbs of its rated pressure (which is marked on the cap), replace it with a new one.

9 The cap is also equipped with a vacuum relief spring. When the engine cools off, a vacuum is created in the cooling system. The vacuum relief spring allows air back into the system, which will equalize the pressure and prevent damage to the radiator (the radiator tanks could collapse if the vacuum is great enough). If, after turning the engine off and allowing it to cool down you notice any of the cooling system hoses collapsing, replace the pressure cap with a new one.

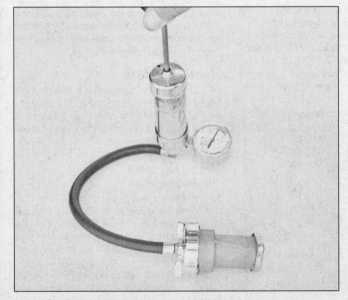

2.8 Checking the cooling system pressure cap with a cooling system pressure tester

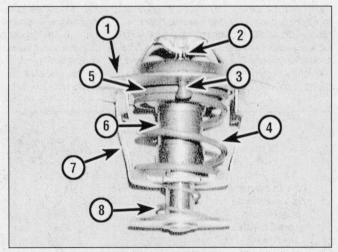

2.10 Typical thermostat

1	*Flange*	5	*Valve seat*
2	*Piston*	6	*Valve*
3	*Jiggle valve*	7	*Frame*
4	*Main coil spring*	8	*Secondary coil spring*

Thermostat

10   Before assuming the thermostat (**see illustration**) is responsible for a cooling system problem, check the coolant level (see Chapter 1), drivebelt tension (see Chapter 1) and temperature gauge (or light) operation.

11   If the engine takes a long time to warm up (as indicated by the temperature gauge or heater operation), the thermostat is probably stuck open. Replace the thermostat with a new one.

12   If the engine runs hot or overheats, a thorough test of the thermostat should be performed.

13   Definitive testing of the thermostat can only be made when it is removed from the vehicle. If the thermostat is stuck in the open position at room temperature, it is faulty and must be replaced.

Caution: *Do not drive the vehicle without a thermostat. The computer may stay in open loop and emissions and fuel economy will suffer.*

14   To test a thermostat, suspend the (closed) thermostat on a length of string or wire in a pot of cold water.

15   Heat the water on a stove while observing the thermostat. The thermostat should fully open before the water boils.

16   If the thermostat doesn't open and close as specified, or sticks in any position, replace it.

Cooling fan

Electric cooling fan

17   If the engine is overheating and the cooling fan is not coming on when the engine temperature rises to an excessive level, unplug the fan motor electrical connector(s) and connect the motor directly to the battery with fused jumper wires. If the fan motor doesn't come on, replace the motor.

18   If the radiator fan motor is okay, but it isn't coming on when the engine gets hot, the fan relay might be defective. A relay is used to control a circuit by turning it on and off in response to a control decision by the Powertrain Control Module (PCM). These control circuits are fairly complex, and checking them should be left to a qualified automotive technician. Sometimes, the control system can be fixed by simply identifying and replacing a bad relay.

19   Locate the fan relays in the engine compartment fuse/relay box.

20   Test the relay (see Chapter 12).

21   If the relay is okay, check all wiring and connections to the fan motor. Refer to the wiring diagrams at the end of this manual. If no obvious problems are found, the problem could be the Engine Coolant Temperature (ECT) sensor or the Powertrain Control Module (PCM). Have the cooling fan system and circuit diagnosed by a dealer service department or repair shop with the proper diagnostic equipment .

Belt-driven cooling fan

22   Disconnect the cable from the negative battery terminal (see Chapter 5) and rock the fan back and forth by hand to check for excessive bearing play.

23   With the engine cold (and not running), turn the fan blades by hand. The fan should turn freely.

24   Visually inspect for substantial fluid leakage from the clutch assembly. If problems are noted, replace the clutch assembly.

25   With the engine completely warmed up, turn off the ignition switch and disconnect the cable from the negative battery terminal. Turn the fan by hand. Some drag should be evident. If the fan turns easily, replace the fan clutch.

Water pump

26   A failure in the water pump can cause serious engine damage due to overheating.

Drivebelt-driven water pump

27   There are two ways to check the operation of the water pump while it's installed on the engine. If the pump is found to be defective, it should be replaced with a new or rebuilt unit.

28   Water pumps are equipped with weep (or vent) holes (**see illustration**). If a failure occurs in the pump seal, coolant will leak from the hole.

29   If the water pump shaft bearings fail, there may be a howling sound at the pump while it's running. Shaft wear can be felt with the drivebelt removed if the water pump pulley is rocked up and down (with the engine off). Don't mistake drivebelt slippage, which causes a squealing sound, for water pump bearing failure.

Timing chain or timing belt-driven water pump

30   Water pumps driven by the timing chain or timing belt are located underneath the timing chain or timing belt cover.

31   Checking the water pump is limited because of where it is located. However, some basic checks can be made before deciding to remove the water pump. If the pump is found to be defective, it should be replaced with a new or rebuilt unit.

32   One sign that the water pump may be failing is that the heater (climate control) may not work well. Warm the engine to normal operating temperature, confirm that the coolant level is correct, then run the heater and check for hot air coming from the ducts.

33   Check for noises coming from the water pump area. If the water pump impeller shaft or bearings are failing, there may be a howling sound at the pump while the engine is running. **Note:** *Be careful not to mistake drivebelt noise (squealing) for water pump bearing or shaft failure.*

34   It you suspect water pump failure due to noise, wear can be confirmed by feeling for play at the pump shaft. This can be done by rocking the drive sprocket on the pump shaft up and down. To do this you will need to remove the tension on the timing chain or belt as well as access the water pump.

All water pumps

35   In rare cases or on high-mileage vehicles, another sign of water pump failure may be the presence of coolant in the engine oil. This condition will adversely affect the engine in varying degrees. **Note:** *Finding coolant in the engine oil could indicate other serious issues besides a failed water pump, such as a blown head gasket or a cracked cylinder head or block.*

36   Even a pump that exhibits no outward signs of a problem, such as noise or leakage, can still be due for replacement. Removal for close examination is the only sure way to tell. Sometimes the fins on the back of the impeller can corrode to the point that cooling efficiency is diminished significantly.

Heater system

37   Little can go wrong with a heater. If the fan motor will run at all speeds, the electrical part of the system is okay. The three basic heater problems fall into the following general categories:

a) *Not enough heat*
b) *Heat all the time*
c) *No heat*

38   If there's not enough heat, the control valve or door is stuck in a partially open position, the coolant coming from the engine isn't hot enough, or the heater core is restricted. If the coolant isn't hot enough, the thermostat in the engine cooling system is stuck open, allowing coolant to pass through the engine so rapidly that it doesn't heat up quickly enough. If the vehicle is equipped with a temperature gauge

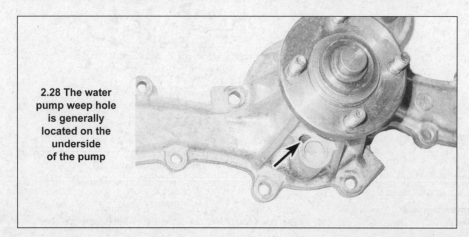

2.28 The water pump weep hole is generally located on the underside of the pump

instead of a warning light, watch to see if the engine temperature rises to the normal operating range after driving for a reasonable distance.

39 If there's heat all the time, the control valve or the door is stuck wide open.

40 If there's no heat, coolant is probably not reaching the heater core, or the heater core is plugged. The likely cause is a collapsed or plugged hose, core, or a frozen heater control valve. If the heater is the type that flows coolant all the time, the cause is a stuck door or a broken or kinked control cable.

Air conditioning system

41 If the cool air output is inadequate:
a) Inspect the condenser coils and fins to make sure they're clear
b) Check the compressor clutch for slippage
c) Check the blower motor for proper operation
d) Inspect the blower discharge passage for obstructions
e) Check the system air intake filter for clogging

42 If the system provides intermittent cooling air:
a) Check the circuit breaker, blower switch and blower motor for a malfunction
b) Make sure the compressor clutch isn't slipping
c) Inspect the plenum door to make sure it's operating properly
d) Inspect the evaporator to make sure it isn't clogged
e) If the unit is icing up, it may be caused by excessive moisture in the system, incorrect super heat switch adjustment, or low thermostat adjustment

43 If the system provides no cooling air:
a) Inspect the compressor drivebelt; make sure it isn't loose or broken
b) Make sure the compressor clutch engages; if it doesn't, check for a blown fuse
c) Inspect the wire harness for broken or disconnected wires
d) If the compressor clutch doesn't engage, bridge the terminals of the AC pressure switch(es) with a jumper wire; if the clutch now engages, and the system is properly charged, the pressure switch is bad
e) Make sure the blower motor is not disconnected or burned out
f) Make sure the compressor isn't partially or completely seized
g) Inspect the refrigerant lines for leaks
h) Check the components for leaks
i) Inspect the receiver-drier/accumulator or expansion valve/tube for clogged screens

44 If the system is noisy:
a) Look for loose panels in the passenger compartment
b) Inspect the compressor drivebelt; it may be loose or worn

c) Check the compressor mounting bolts; they should be tight
d) Listen carefully to the compressor; it may be worn out
e) Listen to the idler pulley and bearing, and the clutch; either may be defective
f) The winding in the compressor clutch coil or solenoid may be defective
g) The compressor oil level may be low
h) The blower motor fan bushing or the motor itself may be worn out
i) If there is an excessive charge in the system, you'll hear a rumbling noise in the high pressure line, a thumping noise in the compressor, or see bubbles or cloudiness in the sight glass
j) If there is a low charge in the system, you might hear hissing in the evaporator case at the expansion valve, or see bubbles or cloudiness in the sight glass

---

3   Air conditioning and heating system - check and maintenance

---

Air conditioning system

Warning: *The air conditioning system is under high pressure. Do not loosen any hose fittings or remove any components until after the system has been discharged. Air conditioning refrigerant should be properly discharged into an EPA-approved recovery/ recycling unit at a dealer service department or an automotive air conditioning repair facility. Always wear eye protection when disconnecting air conditioning system fittings.*

Caution: *All models covered by this manual use environmentally friendly R-134a. This refrigerant (and its appropriate refrigerant oils) are not compatible with R-12 refrigerant system components and must never be mixed or the components will be damaged.*

Caution: *When replacing entire components, additional refrigerant oil should be added equal to the amount that is removed with the component being replaced. Be sure to read the can before adding any oil to the system, to make sure it is compatible with the R-134a system.*

1 The following maintenance checks should be performed on a regular basis to ensure that the air conditioning continues to operate at peak efficiency.

a) Inspect the condition of the drivebelt. If it is worn or deteriorated, replace it (see Chapter 1).
b) Check the drivebelt tension (see Chapter 1).
c) Inspect the system hoses. Look for cracks, bubbles, hardening and deterioration. Inspect the hoses and all fittings for oil bubbles or seepage. If there is any evidence of wear, damage or leakage, replace the hose(s).
d) Inspect the condenser fins for leaves, bugs and any other foreign material that may have embedded itself in the fins. Use a fin comb or compressed air to remove debris from the condenser.

e) Make sure the system has the correct refrigerant charge.
f) If you hear water sloshing around in the dash area or have water dripping on the carpet, check the evaporator housing drain tube and insert a piece of wire into the opening to check for blockage **(see illustration)**.

2 It's a good idea to operate the system for about ten minutes at least once a month. This is particularly important during the winter months because long term non-use can cause hardening, and subsequent failure, of the seals. Note that using the Defrost function operates the compressor.

3 If the air conditioning system is not working properly, proceed to Step 6 and perform the general checks outlined below.

4 Because of the complexity of the air conditioning system and the special equipment necessary to service it, in-depth troubleshooting and repairs beyond checking the refrigerant charge and the compressor clutch operation are not included in this manual. However, simple checks and component replacement procedures are provided in this Chapter. For more complete information on the air conditioning system, refer to the *Haynes Automotive Heating and Air Conditioning Manual*.

5 The most common cause of poor cooling is simply a low system refrigerant charge. If a noticeable drop in system cooling ability occurs, one of the following quick checks will help you determine if the refrigerant level is low.

Checking the refrigerant charge

6 Warm the engine up to normal operating temperature.

7 Place the air conditioning temperature selector at the coldest setting and put the blower at the highest setting.

8 After the system reaches operating temperature, feel the larger pipe exiting the evaporator at the firewall. The outlet pipe should be cold (the tubing that leads back to the compressor). If the evaporator outlet pipe is warm, the system probably needs a charge.

3.1 The evaporator drain tube exits the HVAC housing and is attached to a fitting on the passenger's side floor. To access it from underneath, it may be necessary to remove a heat shield

3.9 Insert a thermometer in the center vent, turn on the air conditioning system and wait for it to cool down; depending on the humidity, the output air should be 35 to 40 degrees cooler than the ambient air temperature

3.11 Typcal automotive air conditioning charging kit

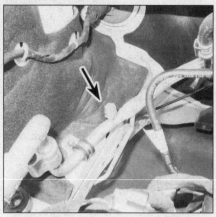

3.13 Location of the low-side charging port (right-rear corner of the engine compartment)

9   Insert a thermometer in the center air distribution duct while operating the air conditioning system at its maximum setting - the temperature of the output air should be 35 to 40 degrees F below the ambient air temperature (down to approximately 40 degrees F). If the ambient (outside) air temperature is very high, say 110 degrees F, the duct air temperature may be as high as 60 degrees F, but generally the air conditioning is 35 to 40 degrees F cooler than the ambient air **(see illustration)**.

10   Further inspection or testing of the system requires special tools and techniques and is beyond the scope of the home mechanic.

Adding refrigerant

Caution: *Make sure any refrigerant, refrigerant oil or replacement component you purchase is designated as compatible with R-134a or R1234yf systems, as applicable.*

Caution: *Never add more than one can of refrigerant to the system. If more refrigerant than that is required, the system should be evacuated and leak tested.*

11   Purchase the proper type of air conditioning charging kit at an auto parts store (either R-134a or R-1234yf, depending on model - see this Chapter's Specifications). A charging kit includes a can of refrigerant, a tap valve and a short section of hose that can be attached between the tap valve and the system low side service valve **(see illustration)**.

Warning: *Wear protective eyewear when dealing with pressurized refrigerant cans.*

12   Back off the valve handle on the charging kit and screw the kit onto the refrigerant can, making sure first that the O-ring or rubber seal inside the threaded portion of the kit is in place.

13   Remove the dust cap from the low-side charging port and attach the hose's quick-connect fitting to the port **(see illustration)**. The fittings on the charging kit are designed to fit only on the low side of the system.

Warning: *DO NOT hook the charging kit hose to the system high side!*

14   Warm up the engine and turn On the air conditioning. Keep the charging kit hose away from the fan and other moving parts.

Note: *The charging process requires the compressor to be running. If the clutch cycles off, you can put the air conditioning switch on High and leave the car doors open to keep the clutch on and compressor working. The compressor can be kept on during the charging by removing the connector from the pressure switch and bridging it with a paper clip or jumper wire during the procedure.*

15   Turn the valve handle on the kit until the stem pierces the can, then back the handle out to release the refrigerant. You should be able to hear the rush of gas. Keep the can upright at all times, but shake it occasionally. Allow stabilization time between each addition.

Note: *The charging process will go faster if you wrap the can with a hot-water-soaked rag to keep the can from freezing up.*

16   If you have an accurate thermometer, you can place it in the center air conditioning duct inside the vehicle and keep track of the output air temperature. A charged system that is working properly should cool down to approximately 40 degrees F. If the ambient (outside) air temperature is very high, say 110 degrees F, the duct air temperature may be as high as 60 degrees F, but generally the air conditioning is 35 to 40 degrees F cooler than the ambient air.

17   When the can is empty, turn the valve handle to the closed position and release the connection from the low-side port. Reinstall the dust cap.

18   Remove the charging kit from the can and store the kit for future use with the piercing valve in the UP position, to prevent inadvertently piercing the can on the next use.

Heating systems

19   If the carpet under the heater core is damp, or if antifreeze vapor or steam is coming through the vents, the heater core is leaking. Remove it (see Section 12) and install a new unit (most radiator shops will not repair a leaking heater core).

20   If the air coming out of the heater vents isn't hot, the problem could stem from any of the following causes:

a) *The thermostat is stuck open, preventing the engine coolant from warming up enough to carry heat to the heater core. Replace the thermostat (see Section 4).*

b) *There is a blockage in the system, preventing the flow of coolant through the heater core. Feel both heater hoses at the firewall. They should be hot. If one of them is cold, there is an obstruction in one of the hoses or in the heater core, or the heater control valve is shut. Detach the hoses and back flush the heater core with a water hose. If the heater core is clear but circulation is impeded, remove the two hoses and flush them out with a water hose.*

c) *If flushing fails to remove the blockage from the heater core, the core must be replaced (see Section 12).*

Eliminating air conditioning odors

21   Unpleasant odors that often develop in air conditioning systems are caused by the growth of a fungus, usually on the surface of the evaporator core. The warm, humid environment there is a perfect breeding ground for mildew to develop.

22   The evaporator core on most vehicles is difficult to access, and factory dealerships have a lengthy, expensive process for eliminating the fungus by opening up the evaporator case and using a powerful disinfectant and rinse on the core until the fungus is gone. You can service your own system at home, but it takes something much stronger than basic household germ-killers or deodorizers.

23   Aerosol disinfectants for automotive air conditioning systems are available in most auto parts stores, but remember when shopping for them that the most effective treatments are also the most expensive. The basic procedure for using these sprays is to start by running the system in the RECIRC mode

3.24 Insert the nozzle of the disinfectant can into the return-air intake behind the glove box

4.6 Detach the radiator hose from the thermostat housing

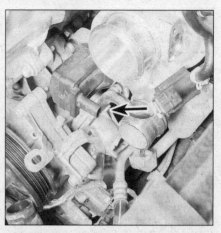

4.7a Thermostat housing top bolt shown (lower bolt is at the bottom of the housing)

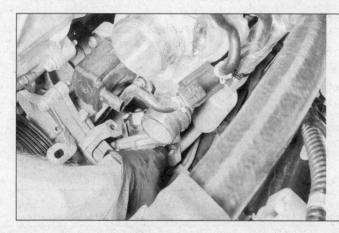

4.7b Once the housing is separated from the engine, carefully work the housing out towards the front of the engine until it can be removed

for ten minutes with the blower on its highest speed. Use the highest heat mode to dry out the system and keep the compressor from engaging by disconnecting the wiring connector at the compressor.

24 The disinfectant can usually comes with a long spray hose. Insert the nozzle into an intake port inside the cabin, and spray according to the manufacturer's recommendations **(see illustration)**. Try to cover the whole surface of the evaporator core, by aiming the spray up, down and sideways. Follow the manufacturer's recommendations for the length of spray and waiting time between applications.

25 Once the evaporator has been cleaned, the best way to prevent the mildew from coming back again is to make sure your evaporator housing drain tube is clear.

Automatic heating and air conditioning systems

26 Some vehicles are equipped with an optional automatic climate control system. This system has its own computer that receives inputs from various sensors in the heating and air conditioning system. This computer, like the PCM, has self-diagnostic capabilities to help pinpoint problems or faults within the system. Vehicles equipped with automatic heating and air conditioning systems are very complex and considered beyond the scope of the home mechanic. Vehicles equipped with automatic heating and air conditioning systems should be taken to a dealer service department or other qualified facility for repair.

---

4   Thermostat - replacement

Warning: *Do not allow antifreeze to come in contact with your skin or painted surfaces of the vehicle. Rinse off spills immediately with plenty of water. Antifreeze is highly toxic if ingested. Never leave antifreeze lying around in an open container or in puddles on the floor; children and pets are attracted by its sweet smell and may drink it. Check with local author-*

ities about disposing of used antifreeze. Many communities have collection centers which will see that antifreeze is disposed of safely.
Warning: *The engine must be completely cool before beginning this procedure.*
Note: *On all engines, the thermostat and thermostat housing are replaced as a unit only.*

1 Disconnect the cable from the negative battery terminal (see Chapter 5).
2 Drain the cooling system (see Chapter 1). If the coolant is relatively new or in good condition, save it and reuse it.
3 Remove the engine cover (if equipped).
4 Remove the air filter outlet duct (see Chapter 4).

1.5L engine

5 Remove the charge air cooler inlet air tube (see Chapter 4).
6 Squeeze the hose clamps and slide it back on the hose, then detach the radiator hose from the thermostat housing **(see illustration)**.
7 Unscrew the bolts and lift off the thermostat housing and maneuver the housing out of the engine **(see illustration)**.
8 Clean the housing and cover mating surfaces.
9 Install a new gasket to the cylinder block, the thermostat housing and mounting bolts, then tighten the bolts to the torque

listed in this Chapter's Specifications.
10 The remainder of the installation is the reverse of the removal.
11 Refill the cooling system (see Chapter 1).
12 Start the engine and allow it to reach normal operating temperature. Check for leaks and proper thermostat operation.

2.0L and 2.5L engines

13 Remove the exhaust manifold heat shield bolts and shield (see Chapter 2A).
14 Locate the radiator outlet hose on the right side of the radiator and squeeze the hose clamps, slide them back on the hose, then detach the radiator hose from the thermostat housing.
15 Remove the thermostat housing bolts and the housing from the front side of the engine.
16 Clean the housing and cover mating surfaces.
17 Install a new gasket to the cylinder block, the thermostat housing and mounting bolts, then tighten the bolts to the torque listed in this Chapter's Specifications.
18 Refill the cooling system (see Chapter 3).
19 Start the engine and allow it to reach normal operating temperature. Check for leaks and proper thermostat operation.

5   Engine cooling fans - removal and installation

Warning: *Do not allow antifreeze to come in contact with your skin or painted surfaces of the vehicle. Rinse off spills immediately with plenty of water. Antifreeze is highly toxic if ingested. Never leave antifreeze lying around in an open container or in puddles on the floor; children and pets are attracted by its sweet smell and may drink it. Check with local authorities about disposing of used antifreeze. Many communities have collection centers which will see that antifreeze is disposed of safely.*

Warning: *To avoid possible injury or damage, DO NOT operate the engine with a damaged fan. Do not attempt to repair fan blades - replace a damaged fan with a new one.*

Warning: *The engine must be completely cool before beginning this procedure.*

1   Disconnect the cable from the negative terminal of the battery (see Chapter 5).

2015 and earlier models and all 2.5L engines
Fan shroud and motor

2   Drain the cooling system (see Chapter 1) below the upper radiator hose level. If the coolant is relatively new or in good condition, save it and reuse it.

3   Remove the engine cover fasteners and the cover, if equipped.

4   Loosen the hose clamp and slide the clamp back on the upper hose, then disconnect the upper radiator hose from the radiator.

5   On 2.5L engines, remove the front bumper fascia, radiator support trim panel and hood latch (see Chapter 11), then radiator support fasteners and radiator support.

6   Disconnect the electrical connectors to the cooling fans, then disengage the wiring harness retainers from the shroud and move the harness out of the way.

7   Disengage the transaxle cooler lines from the retainers on the shroud.

8   Remove the fan shroud mounting bolts at the top corners of the shroud, then tilt the shroud back towards the engine and lift the shroud assembly up and off of the radiator.

9   Remove the fan shroud to radiator fasteners and clips then separate the fan shroud from the radiator.

Motor replacement

10   Remove the shroud and fan assembly.

11   Remove the retainer from the fan motor shaft and detach the fan blade from the motor.

12   Remove the fan motor mounting bolts and detach the motor from the shroud.

13   Installation is the reverse of removal.

All 2016 and later models (except 2.5L engines)
Fan shroud and motor

14   Remove the radiator and cooling fan module (see Section 7).

15   Remove the fan shroud-to-radiator fasteners and clips, then separate the fan shroud from the radiator.

6.3 Coolant reservoir/expansion tank fastener location (2016 and later models)

Motor replacement

16   Remove the shroud and fan assembly.

17   Remove the retainer from the fan motor shaft and detach the fan blade from the motor.

18   Remove the fan motor mounting bolts and detach the motor from the shroud.

19   Installation is the reverse of removal.

6   Coolant reservoir/expansion tank - removal and installation

Warning: *Do not allow antifreeze to come in contact with your skin or painted surfaces of the vehicle. Rinse off spills immediately with plenty of water. Antifreeze is highly toxic if ingested. Never leave antifreeze lying around in an open container or in puddles on the floor; children and pets are attracted by its sweet smell and may drink it. Check with local authorities about disposing of used antifreeze. Many communities have collection centers which will see that antifreeze is disposed of safely.*

Warning: *Wait until the engine is completely cool before beginning this procedure.*

1   Drain the cooling system (see Chapter 1). If the coolant is relatively new and still in good condition, it can be saved and reused.

2   On 2015 and earlier models, remove the retaining clip and unclip the coolant reservoir/expansion tank from the mounting bracket.

3   On 2016 and later models, remove the coolant reservoir/expansion tank mounting fastener **(see illustration)**.

4   Loosen the clamps and move them back on the hoses, then detach the hoses **(see illustration)**.

5   Remove the expansion tank from its mount.

6   Clean the tank with soapy water and a brush to remove any deposits inside. Inspect the tank carefully for cracks; if any are found, replace it.

7   Installation is the reverse of removal. Refill the cooling system (see Chapter 1).

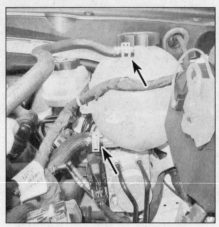

6.4 Expansion tank inlet and outlet hoses (2016 and later models shown)

7   Radiator - removal and installation

Warning: *The air conditioning system is under high pressure. DO NOT loosen any fittings or remove any components until after the system has been discharged. Air conditioning refrigerant must be properly discharged into an EPA-approved container at a dealer service department or an automotive air conditioning repair facility. Always wear eye protection when disconnecting air conditioning system fittings.*

Warning: *Do not allow antifreeze to come in contact with your skin or painted surfaces of the vehicle. Rinse off spills immediately with plenty of water. Antifreeze is highly toxic if ingested. Never leave antifreeze lying around in an open container or in puddles on the floor; children and pets are attracted by its sweet smell and may drink it. Check with local authorities about disposing of used antifreeze. Many communities have collection centers which will see that antifreeze is disposed of safely.*

Warning: *Wait until the engine is completely cool before beginning this procedure.*

2015 and earlier 2.0L engines
Removal

1   Have the air conditioning system discharged by an automotive air conditioning technician (see Warning above).

2   Disconnect the cable from the negative battery terminal (see Chapter 5).

3   Raise the vehicle and support it securely on jackstands, then drain the cooling system (see Chapter 1). If the coolant is relatively new or in good condition, save it and reuse it.

4   Have the air conditioning system discharged by an automotive air conditioning technician (see Warning above).

5   Remove the air filter housing (see Chapter 4), the intake duct and resonator.

6   Remove the engine cooling fan assembly (see Section 5).

7   Loosen the hose clamps and slide them back on the hoses, then disconnect the radiator hoses from the radiator.

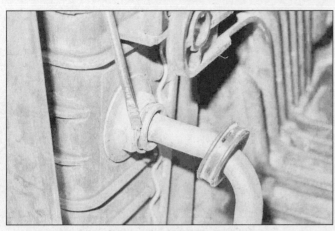

7.12 Remove the spring clips to disconnect the transaxle fluid cooler lines from the radiator

7.36 Radiator bracket details

a)	Right-side upper bracket	c)	Left-side upper bracket
b)	Right-side upper bracket fasteners		fasteners
		d)	Left-side upper bracket

8 Remove the radiator upper bracket mounting bolts and brackets.
9 Remove the condenser (see Section 14).
10 Remove the charge air cooler (see Chapter 4).
11 Disengage the left and right radiator support brackets, then lift the condenser up and off of the radiator.
12 Detach the automatic transaxle fluid cooler lines from the radiator **(see illustration)**.
13 Remove the radiator air seal, then tilt the radiator forward and lift it out of the vehicle.

Installation
14 Installation is the reverse of removal. Make sure the radiator seats properly in its mounts and the condenser tabs engage with the radiator. Tighten the fasteners securely.
15 Fill the cooling system with the proper mixture of antifreeze and water (see Chapter 1).
16 Start the engine and check for leaks. Allow the engine to reach normal operating temperature. Re-check the coolant level and add more if necessary.
17 Check the transaxle fluid level and add some, if necessary (see Chapter 1).
18 Have the system evacuated, recharged and leak tested by the shop that discharged it.

2.5L engines
Removal
19 Remove the air filter housing (see Chapter 4), the intake duct and resonator.
20 Disconnect the electrical connectors to the engine cooling fan assembly (see Section 5).
21 Loosen the hose clamps and slide them back on the hoses, then disconnect the radiator hoses from the radiator.
22 Detach the automatic transaxle fluid cooler lines from the radiator **(see illustration 7.12)**.
23 Lift the condenser off of the retainers on the radiator, then support the condenser without damaging the fins or the lines.

24 Remove the front bumper cover (see Chapter 11).
25 Remove the radiator lower bracket mounting bolts and brackets.
26 Lower the radiator and fan shroud down and out from the bottom of the vehicle.

Installation
27 Installation is the reverse of removal. Make sure the radiator seats properly in its mounts and the condenser tabs engage with the radiator. Tighten the fasteners securely.
28 Fill the cooling system with the proper mixture of antifreeze and water (see Chapter 1).
29 Start the engine and check for leaks. Allow the engine to reach normal operating temperature. Re-check the coolant level and add more if necessary.
30 Check the transaxle fluid level and add some, if necessary (see Chapter 1).

1.5L engines and 2016 and later 2.0L engines
Removal
31 Have the air conditioning system discharged by an automotive air conditioning technician (see Warning above).
32 Disconnect the cable from the negative battery terminal (see Chapter 5).
33 Raise the vehicle and support it securely on jackstands, then drain the cooling system (see Chapter 1). If the coolant is relatively new or in good condition, save it and reuse it.
34 Remove the front bumper cover (see Chapter 11).
35 Remove the condenser (see Section 14).
36 Remove the radiator upper bracket fasteners and brackets **(see illustration)**.
37 Remove the air filter inlet and outlets ducts (see Chapter 4).
38 Remove the charge air cooler (see Chapter 4).
39 Detach the automatic transaxle fluid cooler lines from the radiator **(see illustration 7.12)**.

40 Loosen the hose clamps and slide them back on the hoses, then disconnect the radiator hoses from the radiator.
41 Detach the automatic transaxle fluid cooler lines from the retaining clip on the fan shroud **(see illustration)**.
42 Disconnect the electrical connectors to the cooling fans.
43 Lift the radiator and cooling fan module assembly up and out of the vehicle.

Installation
44 Install the cooling fan shroud to the radiator and tighten the fasteners securely.
45 Installation is the reverse of removal. Make sure the radiator seats properly in its mounts and the condenser tabs engage with the radiator. Tighten the fasteners securely.
46 Fill the cooling system with the proper mixture of antifreeze and water (see Chapter 1).
47 Start the engine and check for leaks. Allow the engine to reach normal operating temperature. Re-check the coolant level and add more if necessary.
48 Check the transaxle fluid level and add some, if necessary (see Chapter 1).
49 Have the system evacuated, recharged and leak tested by the shop that discharged it.

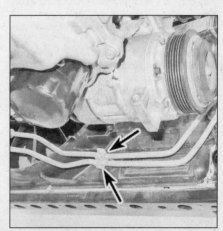

7.41 Detach the automatic transaxle fluid cooler lines from the retaining clip

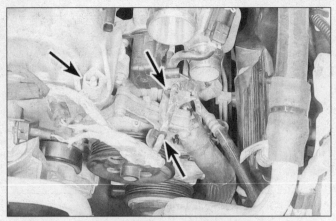

8.5 Use a trim tool to disengage the wiring harness retainers

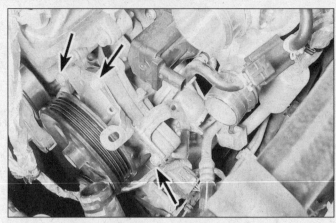

8.6a Remove the water pump upper bolts. . .

8.6b. . . and the lower bolts

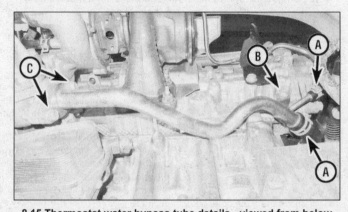

8.15 Thermostat water bypass tube details - viewed from below

A	Hose clamps and hoses	C Tube-to-water pump
B	Tube bracket bolt	housing bolts

8   Water pump - replacement

Warning: *Do not allow antifreeze to come in contact with your skin or painted surfaces of the vehicle. Rinse off spills immediately with plenty of water. Antifreeze is highly toxic if ingested. Never leave antifreeze lying around in an open container or in puddles on the floor; children and pets are attracted by its sweet smell and may drink it. Check with local authorities about disposing of used antifreeze. Many communities have collection centers which will see that antifreeze is disposed of safely.*

Warning: *The engine must be completely cool before beginning this procedure.*

1   Drain the cooling system (see Chapter 1). If the coolant is relatively new and still in good condition, it can be saved and reused.

2   Loosen the right front wheel lug nuts. Raise the vehicle and support it securely on jackstands. Remove the wheel and the inner fender splash shield (see Chapter 11).

3   Remove the drivebelt (see Chapter 1).

1.5L engines

4   Remove the drivebelt tensioner (see Chapter 1).

5   Disengage the wiring harness retainers and move the wiring harness away from the water pump **(see illustration)**.

Water pump

6   Remove the water pump and pulley housing bolts **(see illustration)** and remove the water pump from the water pump housing. If the water pump is stuck, gently tap it with a soft-faced hammer to break the seal.

7   Remove all traces of the old gasket seal from the mounting surface on the water pump housing and the water pump (if the pump is going to be re-installed).

8   Clean the mounting bolt threads and threaded holes on the water pump housing to remove corrosion and sealant, if necessary.

9   Compare the replacement pump with the old one to make sure that they're identical.

10   Use a new gasket when installing the water pump. Install the mounting bolts to align the water pump and finger-tighten them.

11   Tighten the water pump-to-water pump housing bolts to the torque listed in this Chapter's Specifications.

12   The remainder of installation is the reverse of removal. Refill the cooling system with the proper concentration of antifreeze (see Chapter 1). Start the engine and allow it to reach normal operating temperature while inspecting the system for leaks.

Water pump housing

13   Remove the charge air cooler inlet air tube (see Chapter 4).

14   Remove the thermostat housing (see Section 4).

15   Disconnect the hose clamps and hoses from the thermostat water bypass tube, then remove the tube bracket bolt, tube-to-water pump housing bolts and remove the tube with the gasket from the backside of the water pump **(see illustration)**.

16   Remove the turbocharger oil feed pipe retaining clip, then disconnect the pipe and move the pipe out of the way (see Chapter 4).

17   Remove the engine oil cooler (see Section 19).

18   Remove the turbocharger coolant inlet pipe (see Chapter 4).

19   Remove the water pump housing bolts **(see illustration)** and remove the water pump housing. If the water pump housing is stuck, gently tap it with a soft-faced hammer to break the seal.

20   Remove all traces of the old gasket seal from the engine surface and on the water pump housing.

21   Use a new gasket when installing the water pump housing. Install the mounting bolts to align the water pump housing and finger-tighten them.

22   Tighten the water pump housing bolts to the torque listed in this Chapter's Specifications.

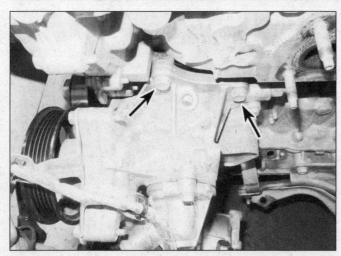

8.19 Water pump housing bolt locations

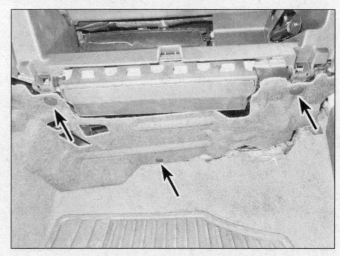

10.2 Remove the fasteners under the glove box
in the passenger's footwell

23   The remainder of installation is the reverse of removal. Refill the cooling system with the proper concentration of antifreeze (see Chapter 1). Start the engine and allow it to reach normal operating temperature while inspecting the system for leaks.

2.0L and 2.5L engines

24   Remove the exhaust manifold heat shield bolts and shield.
25   Remove the thermostat housing (see Section 4).
26   Disengage the wiring harness retainers and move the wiring harness away from the water pump.
27   Remove the thermostat bypass tube fasteners from the top of the water pump housing, then remove the tube.
28   Remove the thermostat bypass tube gasket from the top of the water pump housing.
29   Remove the water pump housing bolts and remove the water pump housing from the side of the engine block. If the water pump housing is stuck, gently tap it with a soft-faced hammer to break the seal.
30   Thoroughly clean the mating surface of the engine (and the water pump if it's going to be reinstalled).
31   Compare the replacement pump with the old one to make sure that they're identical.
32   Place the gasket and water pump into position. Install the new mounting bolts until they are all finger-tight.
33   Tighten the water pump housing mounting bolts a little at a time, in a criss-cross pattern, to the torque listed in this Chapter's Specifications.
34   The remainder of installation is the reverse of removal. Tighten the water pump pulley bolts to the torque listed in this Chapter's Specifications. Refill the cooling system with the proper concentration of antifreeze (see Chapter 1). Start the engine and allow it to reach normal operating temperature while inspecting the system for leaks.

9   Coolant temperature sending unit - check

Warning: *Wait until the engine is completely cool before beginning this procedure.*

1   The coolant temperature indicator system consists of a temperature gauge on the dash and a sensor mounted on the engine. The Engine Coolant Temperature (ECT) sensor (see Chapter 6) provides a signal to the Powertrain Control Module (PCM) and Body Control Module (BCM), which operate the temperature gauge.
2   If an overheating condition has occurred, first check the coolant level in the system (see Chapter 1) and that the coolant mixture is correct (see Chapter 1, Specifications). Also, refer to the Troubleshooting section at the front of this manual before assuming that the temperature indicator is faulty.
3   If the temperature gauge does not move from the C position, check the wiring harness connections going to the instrument cluster.
4   If there is a problem with the ECT sensor, it is very likely that the CHECK ENGINE light will come on and the sensor will need replacing or the circuit will need repair (see Chapter 6).

10   Blower motor module and blower motor - replacement

Warning: *The models covered by this manual are equipped with a Supplemental Restraint System (SRS), more commonly known as airbags. Always disarm the airbag system before working in the vicinity of any airbag system component to avoid the possibility of accidental deployment of the airbag, which could cause personal injury (see Chapter 12). Do not use a memory saving device to preserve the PCM's memory when working on or near airbag system components.*

10.5 Remove the control module mounting screws (2015 and earlier models, and all 2.5L engines)

1   Disconnect the cable from the negative battery terminal (see Chapter 5).
2   Remove the insulating panel from below the dash and under the glove box in the passenger's side footwell **(see illustration)**.
3   On 2015 and earlier models, and all 2.5L engines remove the right side floor air duct fastener and air outlet duct.

Blower motor control module

Note: *On 2015 and later 1.5L and 2.0L models, the blower control module is incorporated into the HVAC control assembly (see Section 11).*

4   On 2015 and earlier models, and all 2.5L engines, disconnect the electrical connector at the blower motor control module.
5   On 2015 and earlier models, and all 2.5L engines, remove the control module mounting screws **(see illustration)**.
6   Installation is the reverse of removal.
Note: *If a new control module is being installed, the unit will have to be programmed and setup by a dealer service department or other qualified repair shop.*

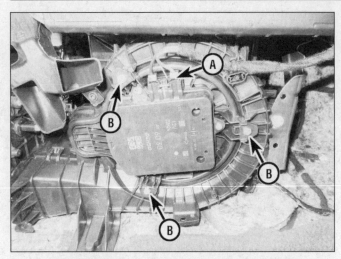

10.9 Disconnect the blower motor electrical connector (A) and remove the blower mounting fasteners (B) - 2018 model shown, all other models similar

11.7 Pry the heater and air conditioner control assembly out from the instrument panel (2016 and later models shown)

11.8 Disconnect the electrical connectors on the back of the control assembly

Blower motor

7   Remove the insulating panel from below the dash and under the glove box in the passenger's side footwell **(see illustration 10.2)**.
8   On 2015 and earlier models, and all 2.5L engines remove the right side floor air duct fastener and air outlet duct.
9   Disconnect the blower motor electrical connector. Remove the mounting fasteners and lower the motor assembly out of the housing **(see illustration)**.
10   Installation is the reverse of removal.

---

11   Heater and air conditioner control assembly - removal and installation

Warning: *The models covered by this manual are equipped with a Supplemental Restraint System (SRS), more commonly known as airbags. Always disarm the airbag system before working in the vicinity of any airbag system component to avoid the possibility of acci-*

dental deployment of the airbag, which could cause personal injury (see Chapter 12). Do not use a memory saving device to preserve the PCM's memory when working on or near airbag system components.
Note: *If the heater and air conditioner control assembly is replaced, a special scan tool is required to program the replacement unit.*
1   Disconnect the cable from the negative battery terminal (see Chapter 5).
2   On 2015 and earlier 2.0L models and all 2.5L models, remove the center trim panel around the radio, heater and air conditioning control assembly using a trim stick (see Chapter 11).
3   On 2015 and earlier 2.0L models and all 2.5L models, remove the center console left and right extension panels (see Chapter 11).
4   On 2015 and earlier 2.0L models and all 2.5L models, remove the instrument panel trim plate fasteners and remove the trim plate from the bottom of the instrument panel and top of the floor console.
5   On 2016 and later 1.5L and 2.0L models, remove the instrument panel right side center

trim panel using a trim stick (see Chapter 11).
6   On 2015 and earlier 2.0L models and all 2.5L models, remove the heater and air conditioner control assembly fasteners and pull out the control unit.
7   On 2016 and later 1.5L and 2.0L models, use a trim stick to pry the heater and air conditioner control assembly out enough to disengage the clips and pull out the control unit **(see illustration)**.
8   Disconnect the electrical connectors on the back of the control assembly **(see illustration)** and remove the assembly.
9   Installation is the reverse of removal.

---

12   Heater core - replacement

Warning: *The models covered by this manual are equipped with a Supplemental Restraint System (SRS), more commonly known as airbags. Always disarm the airbag system before working in the vicinity of any airbag system component to avoid the possibility of accidental deployment of the airbag, which could cause personal injury (see Chapter 12). Do not use a memory saving device to preserve the PCM's memory when working on or near airbag system components.*
Note: *Before disconnecting the battery, move the power seat(s) fully to the rear.*

2015 and earlier 2.0L models and all 2.5L models

Removal

1   Disconnect the cable from the negative battery terminal (see Chapter 5).
2   Drain the cooling system (see Chapter 1). If the coolant is relatively new or in good condition, save it and reuse it.
3   Release the clamps holding the heater hoses at the firewall, then disconnect the heater hoses.

12.5 Pull back the front carpet to expose the heater core

12.7 On 2015 and earlier models, unclip the heater core hose clamps

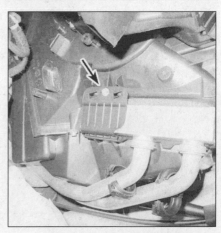

12.8 Heater core bracket fastener

12.9 Disconnect the tubes from the heater core

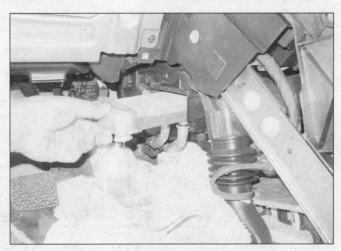

12.10 Remove the heater core from the vehicle

4   Remove the left-side insulating panel mounted below the dash, and the driver's knee bolster (see Chapter 11).

5   Pull back the front carpet to expose the heater core **(see illustration)**.

6   Remove the driver's side rear floor duct fasteners, and remove the duct.

7   Unclip the heater core tube clamps **(see illustration)**.

8   Remove the heater core bracket fasteners, and remove the bracket **(see illustration)**.

9   Disconnect the tubes from the heater core **(see illustration)**.

Caution: *Before disconnecting the heater core hoses, have towels or rags handy to catch any coolant that may spill out during this step.*

10   Carefully remove the heater core from the vehicle **(see illustration)**. Avoid damaging the heater core or spilling coolant on the interior.

Installation

11   Installation is the reverse of removal, noting the following:

a)   *Fill the cooling system with the proper mixture of antifreeze and water (see Chapter 1).*

b)   *Start the engine and check for leaks. Allow the engine to reach normal operating temperature. Re-check the coolant level and add more if necessary.*

2016 and later 1.5L and 2.0L models

Warning: *The air conditioning system is under high pressure. DO NOT loosen any fittings or remove any components until after the system has been discharged. Air conditioning refrigerant must be properly discharged into an EPA-approved container at a dealer service department or an automotive air conditioning repair facility. Always wear eye protection when disconnecting air conditioning system fittings.*

Removal

12   Have the air conditioning system discharged by an automotive air conditioning technician (see Warning above).

13   Disconnect the cable from the negative battery terminal (see Chapter 5).

14   Drain the cooling system (see Chapter 1). If the coolant is relatively new or in good condition, save it and reuse it.

15   Release the clamps holding the heater hoses at the firewall, and disconnect the heater hoses **(see illustration)**.

16   Disconnect the line from the TXV valve (see Section 17).

17   Remove the instrument panel and tie bar (see Chapter 11).

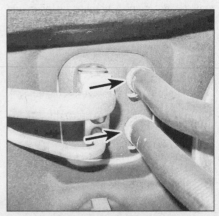

12.15 Use hose clamp pliers to release the heater hose clamps, then disconnect the hoses

13.6 Air conditioning compressor electrical connector locations - 1.5L engine shown, other models similar

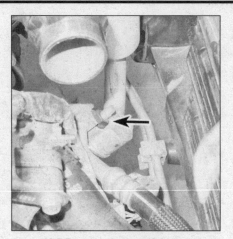

13.7 Remove the manifold nut and disconnect the lines from the compressor

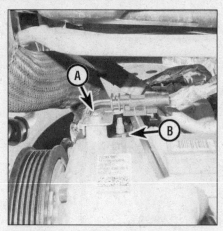

13.8 Remove the electrical connector bracket retaining screw (A) and bracket, then the compressor upper stud / nut (B)

13.9 Air conditioning compressor lower mounting bolt locations

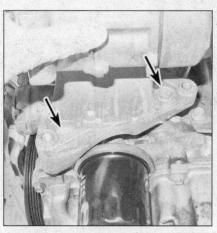

13.10 Compressor bracket lower mounting bolt locations

18 Remove the brake and accelerator pedal assembly fasteners and remove the assembly.

19 Remove the HVAC housing fasteners from the engine compartment side.

20 Remove the heater tube seals, then remove the support bracket fastener and open up the bracket on the HVAC housing.

21 With the tubes free of the bracket side remove the heater core out of the side of the HVAC housing.

Installation

22 Installation is the reverse of removal, noting the following:

a) *Fill the cooling system with the proper mixture of antifreeze and water (see Chapter 1).*

b) *Start the engine and check for leaks. Allow the engine to reach normal operating temperature. Re-check the coolant level and add more if necessary.*

c) *Have the system evacuated, recharged and leak tested by the shop that discharged it.*

---

13 Air conditioning compressor - removal and installation

Warning: *The air conditioning system is under high pressure. DO NOT loosen any fittings or remove any components until after the system has been discharged. Air conditioning refrigerant must be properly discharged into an EPA-approved container at a dealer service department or an automotive air conditioning repair facility. Always wear eye protection when disconnecting air conditioning system fittings.*

Note: *If the compressor is being replaced with a new unit due to major internal damage, you must also replace the refrigerant filter in the condenser (see Section 15) and the rest of the system should be flushed by a technician to remove the particles of contaminant.*

Note: *When a compressor is removed or replaced the oil in the compressor must be balanced.*

Removal

1 Have the air conditioning system discharged by an automotive air conditioning technician (see Warning above).

Note: *When the system is being discharged make sure the technician gives you the oil totals that were removed. This information is needed when replacing an air conditioning compressor.*

2 Remove the drivebelt (see Chapter 1).

3 Loosen the right front wheel lug nuts. Raise the front of the vehicle and support it securely on jackstands. Remove the wheel.

4 Remove the inner fender splash shield (see Chapter 11).

5 On 1.5L engines, remove the air filter housing inlet hose (see Chapter 4).

6 Remove the heat shield fasteners and shield if equipped, then disconnect the electrical connectors from the compressor **(see illustration)**.

7 Disconnect the compressor refrigerant line fitting from the compressor **(see illustration)**. Note: Plug all open lines and fittings to prevent contamination of the air conditioning system.

Caution: *Discard the old sealing O-rings. If the old ones are reused, leaks may occur.*

Note: *The stud can be unscrewed using an 5/16-inch (8 mm) socket or box-end wrench.*

8 Remove the electrical connector bracket, then the upper mounting nut and stud from the compressor **(see illustration)**.

9 Remove the compressor lower mounting bolts and slowly lower the compressor down **(see illustration)**.

10 Remove the compressor mounting bracket fasteners and remove the compressor mounting bracket **(see illustration)**, if necessary.

Installation

11 If a new compressor is being installed, the oil in the compressor must be balanced (see Steps 17 through 20) (or follow the directions with the compressor regarding the draining of excess oil prior to installation).

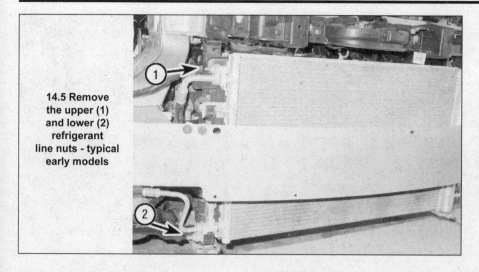

14.5 Remove the upper (1) and lower (2) refrigerant line nuts - typical early models

14.10 With the electrical connector for the shutter motor disconnected, disengage the harness retainer

12   In the unlikely event that the replacement compressor is not equipped with a clutch, have the clutch from the original compressor transferred to the new one by a shop that specializes in air conditioning service.

13   Before connecting the refrigerant line fitting to the compressor, discard all old O-rings and replace them with new ones lubricated with compatible refrigerant oil.

14   Use a floor jack to raise the compressor into the correct position, then tighten the mounting bolts to the torque listed in this Chapter's Specifications.

15   The remainder of installation is the reverse of removal.

16   Have the system evacuated, recharged and leak tested by the shop that discharged it.

Oil balancing

17   With the old compressor removed, remove the compressor drain plug and allow the oil to drain into a graduated container. Tilt the compressor over to allow both ports to drain into the same container.
Caution: *Turn the compressor shaft to make sure all of the oil drains out.*

18   Once all the oil is drained from the compressor, record the amount that you measured and add the total to any amount measured when the system was evacuated in Step 1.

19   If the total amount of oil drained from the old (removed) compressor and the amount of oil removed during refrigerant recovery is less than the oil volume in the replacement compressor, no balancing is required. Refill the replacement compressor with the amount of oil removed then go to Step 13.

20   If the total amount of oil drained from the old (removed) compressor and the amount of oil removed during refrigerant recovery is more than the oil volume in the replacement compressor, additional oil is required. Subtract the oil volume in the replacement compressor from the total removed oil (oil drained + oil recovered). The difference in the amount of oil is what

14.11 Lower air baffle assembly-to-bumper impact bar fastener locations

needs to be added to the replacement compressor. Add the additional oil needed and install the replacement compressor, then go to Step 13.

14   Air conditioning condenser - removal and installation

Warning: *The air conditioning system is under high pressure. DO NOT loosen any fittings or remove any components until after the system has been discharged. Air conditioning refrigerant must be properly discharged into an EPA-approved container at a dealer service department or an automotive air conditioning repair facility. Always wear eye protection when disconnecting air conditioning system fittings.*

Removal

1   Have the air conditioning system discharged by an automotive air conditioning technician (see Warning above).

2015 and earlier 2.0L models and all 2.5L models

2   Remove the headlight housings (see Chapter 12).

3   Remove the front bumper cover (see

Chapter 11), then remove the bumper impact bar bolts and impact bar.

4   Remove the radiator upper and side air deflector plastic push-pins, then remove the air deflectors.

5   Remove the upper and lower refrigerant line nuts; disconnect the refrigerant lines from the condenser **(see illustration)**.

6   Remove the air conditioning refrigerant pressure sensor (see Section 16).
Caution: *Discard the old sealing O-rings. If the old ones are re-used, leaks may occur.*
Note: *Plug all open lines and fittings to prevent contamination of the air conditioning system.*

7   Disengage the left and right radiator support brackets then lift the condenser up and off of the radiator.

2016 and later 1.5L and 2.0L models

8   Remove the front bumper cover (see Chapter 11).

9   Disconnect the electrical connector to the upper shutter, then remove the fasteners and remove the shutter assembly, if equipped.

10   Disconnect the electrical connector to the lower shutter then remove the harness retainer **(see illustration)**.

11   Remove the lower air baffle assembly-to-bumper impact bar fasteners **(see illustration)**.

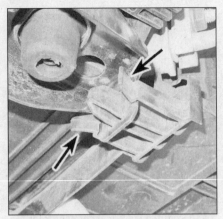

14.12 Disengage the clips of the lower air baffle by pulling the locking tabs apart on each retainer (1 of 2 shown)

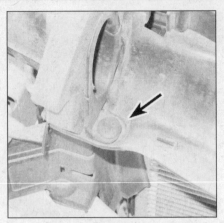

14.13a Remove the air inlet-to-baffle push-pin. . .

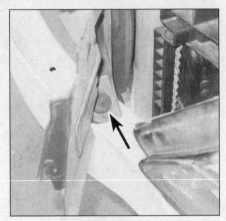

14.13b. . . then the left side. . .

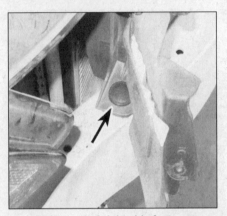

14.13c. . . and right side fastener

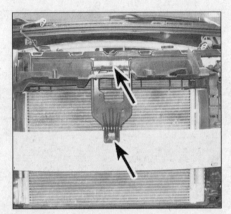

14.15a Remove the fasteners from the front. . .

sor connector (see Section 16).

17   On 2019 and later models, push the transaxle auxiliary cooler inlet line in slightly, then use a small screwdriver to pry out the E-retaining clip and disconnect the transaxle cooler fluid line, if equipped.

All models

18   Remove the condenser from the vehicle; avoid damaging the fins during removal.

19   Carefully guide the condenser out of the engine compartment.

20   Remove and discard all of the sealing washers from the fittings and tubes; new ones must be used on installation.

Installation

21   Installation is the reverse of removal, noting the following:

22   Lubricate the new O-rings with compatible refrigerant oil.

23   Use new sealing washers when reconnecting the refrigerant lines to the condenser.

24   Have the system evacuated, recharged and leak tested by the shop that discharged it.

12   Disengage the clips of the lower air baffle by pulling the locking tabs apart, disconnecting the retainer clip from the bracket **(see illustration)** and remove the lower air baffle assembly from the vehicle.

13   Remove the plastic push-pin fasteners for the radiator upper air baffle assembly **(see illustration)**.

14   Disconnect the hood release cable (see Chapter 11) and electrical connector from the hood release

15   Remove the fasteners for the radiator air upper baffle assembly **(see illustration)**.

16   Disconnect the refrigerant lines from the condenser **(see illustration)**, then disconnect the air conditioning refrigerant pressure sen-

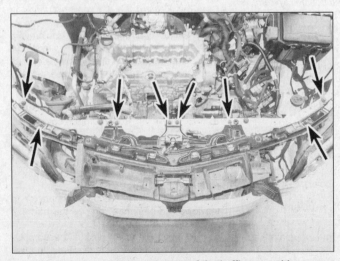

14.15b. . . and along the top of the baffle assembly

14.15c Carefully lift the baffle assembly off the front of the vehicle

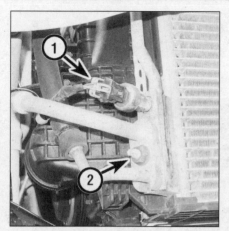

14.16 Disconnect the pressure switch then the condenser line retaining nut from the condenser

1   *Air conditioning pressure switch*
2   *Condenser line retaining nut*

15   Air conditioning receiver-drier and filter removal and installation

Warning: *The air conditioning system is under high pressure. DO NOT loosen any fittings or remove any components until after the system has been discharged. Air conditioning refrigerant must be properly discharged into an EPA-approved container at a dealer service department or an automotive air conditioning repair facility. Always wear eye protection when disconnecting air conditioning system fittings.*

Removal

Note: *The receiver-drier cartridge housing is integrated to the condenser. If the housing is damaged, the condenser must be replaced.*

1   Have the air conditioning system discharged by an automotive air conditioning technician (see Warning above).
2   On 2015 and earlier models, remove the bumper cover (see Chapter 11).
3   On 2015 and earlier models, support the condenser and radiator on the passenger's side using wire or sturdy line. Remove the driver's side radiator support bracket fasteners and remove the bracket.
4   On 2016 and later models, raise the vehicle and support it securely on jackstands, then remove the radiator splash shield fasteners and shield from under the vehicle.
5   Remove the receiver-drier plug and O-ring **(see illustration)**.
6   Remove the refrigerant filter and drier from the receiver-drier cartridge housing.

Installation

7   Installation is the reverse of removal, noting the following:
a) *Lubricate the new O-rings with compatible refrigerant oil.*
b) *Have the system evacuated, recharged and leak tested by the shop that discharged it.*

15.5 The receiver-drier plug can be accessed from under the vehicle - 2016 and later models shown, other models similar

16   Air conditioning refrigerant pressure sensor - replacement

Note: *The air conditioning pressure sensor is used to monitor excessively high and low system pressures and will prevent the system from operating if either condition occurs.*
Note: *The air conditioning pressure sensor is threaded onto a Schrader valve. Therefore, it is not necessary to discharge the air conditioning system to replace it.*

Removal

1   Remove the front bumper cover (see Chapter 11).
2   Unplug the electrical connector from the sensor **(see illustration)**.
3   Unscrew the sensor from the Schrader valve. Use a back-up wrench on the fitting for the sensor.
Caution: *Discard the old sealing O-rings. If the old ones are reused, leaks may occur.*
Note: *Plug all open lines and fittings to prevent contamination of the air conditioning system.*

Installation

4   Installation is the reverse of removal, noting the following:
5   Lubricate the new O-rings with compatible refrigerant oil.
6   Screw the new sensor onto the threads and tighten it securely.

17   Thermal expansion valve (TXV)

Warning: *The air conditioning system is under high pressure. DO NOT loosen any fittings or remove any components until after the system has been discharged. Air conditioning refrigerant must be properly discharged into an EPA-approved container at a dealer service department or an automotive air conditioning repair facility. Always wear eye protection when disconnecting air conditioning system fittings.*

16.2 The pressure sensor is located at the lower right corner of the condenser

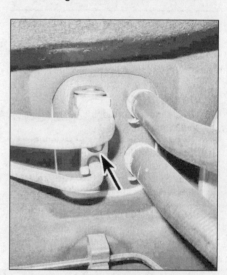

17.3 TXV refrigerant line retaining nut location

1   Have the air conditioning system discharged by an automotive air conditioning technician (see Warning above).
2   Detach the fuel and brake lines and move them aside for access to the TXV, if necessary.
3   Remove the refrigerant line fitting nut **(see illustration)** and detach the line fitting from the TXV.
4   Remove TXV insulation, then remove the TXV-to-firewall mounting bolts, then remove the valve.
Caution: *Discard the old sealing O-rings. If reused, leaks may occur.*
Note: *Plug all open lines and fittings to prevent contamination of the air conditioning system.*
5   Installation is the reverse of removal. Use new O-rings or seals lubricated with refrigerant oil as necessary.
6   Have the system evacuated, recharged and leak tested by the shop that discharged it.

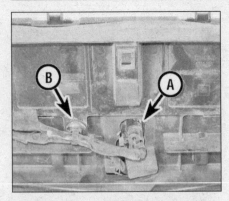

18.6 Disconnect the electrical connector from the shutter motor, then disengage the harness retainer

A   Shutter motor electrical connector
B   Wiring harness retainer

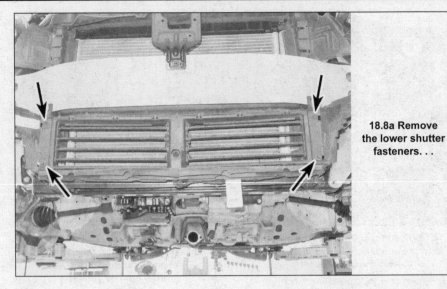

18.8a Remove the lower shutter fasteners. . .

18   Front bumper shutter - removal and installation

1   Remove the front bumper cover (see Chapter 11).

Upper shutter

2   Disconnect the electrical connector to the shutter motor.
3   Remove the upper shutter fasteners.
4   Using a small screwdriver, release the retaining tabs and remove the upper shutter from the radiator upper air baffle assembly.
5   Installation is the reverse of removal.

Lower shutter

6   Disconnect the electrical connector to the shutter motor, then disengage the harness retainer **(see illustration)**.
7   Remove the radiator lower air baffle assembly (see Section 14).
8   Remove the lower shutter fasteners **(see illustration)** and the shutter assembly from the lower air baffle **(see illustration)**.
9   To disassemble a shutter assembly,

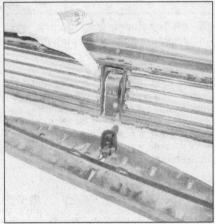

18.8b. . . then the shutter assembly from the lower air baffle

remove the shutter retaining brackets (the individual shutters can be removed) **(see illustration)**.
10   To remove the shutter motor, remove the

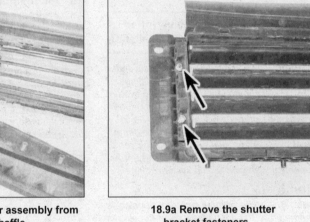

18.9a Remove the shutter bracket fasteners. . .

shutters from both sides (see Step 9) then remove the shutter motor fastener **(see illustration)** and motor from the housing.
11   Installation is the reverse of removal.

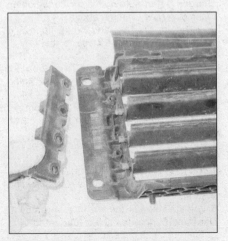

18.9b. . . then remove the shutter bracket from the ends of the shutters

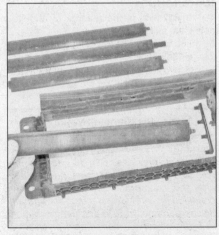

18.9c Slide the shutters out of the shutter housing, making sure to mark the shutters' original locations

18.10 Shutter motor fastener location

19   Engine oil cooler

Warning: *The air conditioning system is under high pressure. DO NOT loosen any fittings or remove any components until after the system has been discharged. Air conditioning refrigerant must be properly discharged into an EPA-approved container at a dealer service department or an automotive air conditioning repair facility. Always wear eye protection when disconnecting air conditioning system fittings.*

Warning: *Wait until the engine is completely cool before beginning this procedure.*

1   Drain the cooling system (see Chapter 1).
2   Drain the engine oil (see Chapter 1).

1.5L engines

3   Remove the air conditioning compressor (see Section 13) without disconnecting the refrigerant lines **(see illustration 13.10)**, then secure the compressor out of the way.
4   Remove the air conditioning compressor bracket bolts and bracket **(see illustration 13.10b)**.
5   Disconnect the turbocharger oil feed pipe (see Chapter 4) from the engine block.
6   Remove the engine oil cooler mounting bolts **(see illustration)**, then remove the cooler and gaskets.
7   Install a new gasket and the oil cooler to the engine, then install the mounting bolts and tighten the bolts to the torque listed in this Chapter's Specifications.
Caution: *Discard the old gasket. If reused, leaks may occur.*

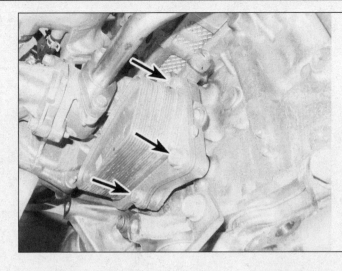

19.6 Engine cooler mounting bolt locations - 1.5L engines (3 of 4 bolts shown)

8   Installation is the reverse of removal.
9   Fill the engine with the proper engine oil and the cooling system with the proper mixture of antifreeze and water (see Chapter 1).

2.0L engines

10   Remove the catalytic converter (see Chapter 6).
11   Remove the oil pump flow control valve heat shield fasteners and shield.
12   Squeeze the hose clamps and slide them back on the hoses, then detach the oil cooler hoses from the oil cooler pipes.
13   Once the oil cooler hoses are disconnected, remove the oil cooler hose retaining bracket fastener.

14   Remove the oil cooler pipe center fastener and unscrew the pipe from the engine, then lower the oil cooler down from the engine.
15   Remove the oil cooler O-ring seal and clean the sealing surfaces of the oil cooler.
16   Install a new O-ring seal into the groove in the oil cooler then install the oil cooler and tighten the oil cooler center pipe to the torque listed in this Chapter's Specifications.
17   Remaining installation is the reverse of removal.
18   Fill the engine with the proper engine oil and the cooling system with the proper mixture of antifreeze and water (see Chapter 1).

Notes

Chapter 4
Fuel and exhaust systems

Contents

Specifications

Fuel pressure

Fuel pressure (primary in-tank fuel pump)*		
Key on, engine off	50 to 100 psi	345 to 689 kPa
Engine running	43 to 58 psi	296 to 400 kPa
Fuel pressure leakdown (one minute after turning key to OFF)	No more than 5 psi (35 kPa) drop	

Secondary fuel pressure for direct injection pump cannot be tested.

Torque specifications

Note: *One foot-pound (ft-lb) of torque is equivalent to 12 inch-pounds (in-lbs) of torque. Torque values below approximately 15 ft-lbs are expressed in inch-pounds, since most foot-pound torque wrenches are not accurate at these smaller values.*

	Ft-lbs (unless otherwise indicated)	Nm
Throttle body mounting bolts/nuts	89 in-lbs	10
Fuel feed line fuel pressure sensor	80 in-lbs	9
Fuel rail pressure sensor	24	32
High-pressure fuel pump bolts		
1.5L	18	25
2.0L, 2.5L		
Step 1	71 in-lbs	8
Step 2	Tighten an additional 50 degrees	
High-pressure fuel pipe fittings		
Step 1	132 in-lbs	15
Step 2	22	30
High-pressure fuel line bracket bolts	28	50
Fuel rail mounting bolts		
1.5L	89 in-lbs	10
2.0L, 2.5L	18	25
Fuel injector screws (1.5L)	44 in-lbs	5
Turbocharger		
Turbocharger-to-manifold nuts		
Step 1	22	30
Step 2	Tighten an additional 90 degrees	
Coolant/oil feed pipe bolts	24	35
Coolant return pipe bolt	24	35
Oil return pipe bolts	89 in-lbs	10

1   General information

Fuel system warnings

Warning: *Gasoline is extremely flammable and repairing fuel system components can be dangerous. Consider your automotive repair knowledge and experience before attempting repairs which may be better suited for a professional mechanic.*

- *Don't smoke or allow open flames or bare light bulbs near the work area*
- *Don't work in a garage with a gas-type appliance (water heater, clothes dryer)*
- *Use fuel-resistant gloves. If any fuel spills on your skin, wash it off immediately with soap and water*
- *Clean up spills immediately*
- *Do not store fuel-soaked rags where they could ignite*
- *Prior to disconnecting any fuel line, you must relieve the fuel pressure (see Section 3).*
- *Wear safety glasses*
- *Have a proper fire extinguisher on hand*

Fuel system

1   The fuel system consists of the fuel tank, electric fuel pump/fuel level sending unit (located in the fuel tank), fuel pump control module, fuel rail and fuel injectors. Fuel pressure is increased greatly by a camshaft-driven high-pressure fuel pump, which supplies high-pressure fuel to the direct fuel injectors (which spray fuel directly into the combustion chambers). The fuel injection system is a multi-port system; multi-port fuel injection uses timed impulses to inject the fuel directly into the intake port of each cylinder or, as previously stated, into the combustion chambers on Direct Injection systems. The Powertrain Control Module (PCM) controls the injectors. The PCM monitors various engine parameters and delivers the exact amount of fuel required into the intake ports.
2   Fuel is delivered from the fuel pump in the fuel tank to the fuel rail through fuel lines running along the underside of the vehicle. Various sections of the fuel line are either rigid metal or nylon, or flexible fuel hose. The various sections of the fuel hose are connected either by quick-connect fittings or threaded metal fittings.

Exhaust system

3   The exhaust system consists of the exhaust manifold, catalytic converter, muffler, tailpipe and all connecting pipes, flanges and clamps. The catalytic converter is an emission control device added to the exhaust system to reduce pollutants. Some models are quipped with a turbocharger system.

2   Troubleshooting

Fuel pump

1   The low pressure fuel pump is located inside the fuel tank. Sit inside the vehicle with the windows closed, turn the ignition key to On

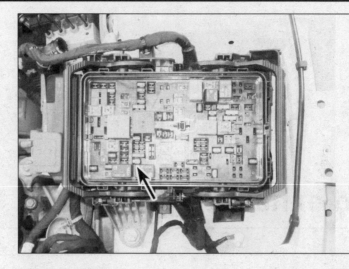

2.2 Check the fuse in the underhood fuse/relay box fuse no. 36 (2016 and later models shown - except Malibu Limited)

(not Start) and listen for the sound of the fuel pump as it's briefly activated. You will only hear the sound for a second or two, but that sound tells you that the pump is working. Alternatively, have an assistant listen at the fuel filler cap.
2   If the pump does not come on, check the fuse for the fuel pump control module in the underhood fuse and relay box **(see illustration)**. If the fuse is okay, check the wiring back to the fuel pump. If the fuse and wiring are okay, the fuel pump is probably defective, but the problem could also lie in the Powertrain Control Module (PCM) or the Fuel Pump Flow Control Module (FPFCM). If the pump runs continuously with the ignition key in the On position, the PCM or FPFCM is probably defective. Have the circuit checked by a professional mechanic, because if the PCM is defective, the new one will have to be programmed with a special proprietary scan tool.
Note: *The fuel pump control module fuse is fuse no. 67 on 2015 and earlier models and 2016 Malibu Limited models, and fuse no. 36 on 2016 and later models (except Malibu Limited).*

Fuel injection system

Note: *The following procedure is based on the assumption that the fuel pump is working and the fuel pressure is adequate (see Section 4).*
3   Check all electrical connectors that are related to the system. Check the ground wire connections for tightness.
4   Verify that the battery is fully charged (see Chapter 5).
5   Inspect the air filter element (see Chapter 1).
6   Check all fuses.
7   Check the air induction system between the throttle body and the intake manifold for air leaks. Also inspect the condition of all vacuum hoses connected to the intake manifold and to the throttle body.
8   Remove the air intake duct from the throttle body and look for dirt, carbon, varnish, or other residue in the throttle body, particularly around the throttle plate. If it's dirty, clean it with carb cleaner, a toothbrush and a clean shop towel.

9   Check to see if any trouble codes are stored in the PCM (see Chapter 6).

3   Fuel pressure relief procedure

Warning: *Gasoline is extremely flammable, so take extra precautions when you work on any part of the fuel system. See Fuel system warnings in Section 1.*
Warning: *The fuel delivery system is made up of a low-pressure system and a high-pressure system. Once the pressure on the low-pressure side of the system has been relieved (as described here), wait at least two hours before loosening any fuel line fittings in the engine compartment.*
Warning: *After the fuel pressure has been relieved, it's a good idea to lay a shop towel over any fuel connection to be disassembled, to absorb the residual fuel that may leak out when servicing the fuel system.*
Note: *The fuel system pressure can be relieved using a compatible scan tool. If a scan tool is not available, perform the procedure below to relieve fuel pressure.*
1   The fuel system referred to in this Chapter is defined as the fuel tank and tank-mounted fuel pump/fuel gauge sender unit, the fuel filter, the fuel injectors and the metal pipes and flexible hoses of the fuel lines between these components. All these components contain fuel, which is pressurized as soon as the ignition key is turned to On, and remains pressurized while the engine is running. And because the pressure remains for some time after the ignition has been switched off, it must be relieved before any fuel lines are disconnected.
2   Remove the fuel filler cap to relieve any pressure built-up in the fuel tank.
3   Open the fuse and relay panel inside the engine compartment and locate the fuel pump control module fuse **(see illustration 2.2)**. Pull the fuel pump control module fuse, start the engine and allow it to run until it stalls (it might not even start). Once it has stalled (or has failed to start), crank the starter for three more seconds, then turn off the ignition key.
Note: *The fuel pump control module fuse*

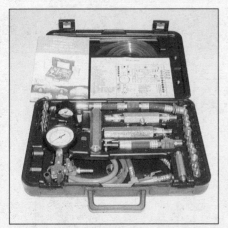

4.1 This fuel pressure testing kit contains all the necessary fittings and adapters, along with the pressure gauge, to test most automotive systems

4.3 Attach the fuel pressure gauge adapter between the fuel feed line and the high-pressure fuel pump

is fuse no. 67 on 2015 and earlier models and 2016 Malibu Limited models, and fuse no. 36 on 2016 and later models (except Malibu Limited).

Warning: *After removing the fuel pump control module fuse, verify that the fuel pump does not run when the ignition key is turned to the On position, and that the engine stalls or won't start.*

4   The fuel pressure on the low-pressure side of the system is now relieved. Disconnect the cable from the negative terminal of the battery before working on any fuel system component (see Chapter 5).

Warning: *Wait at least two hours before working on the high-pressure side of the system.*

Warning: *This procedure merely relieves the pressure that the engine needs to run. But remember that fuel is still present in the system components, and take precautions accordingly before disconnecting any of them.*

4   Fuel pressure check

Warning: *Gasoline is extremely flammable, so take extra precautions when you work on any part of the fuel system. See Fuel system warnings in Section 1.*

Warning: *Do not attempt to measure the fuel pressure on the high-pressure side of the system.*

Note: *The following procedures apply to the in-tank fuel pump and low-pressure side of the system. These procedures do not cover the high-pressure fuel system.*

Note: *Fuel pressure can be checked by monitoring the Fuel Pressure Sensor (FPS) data using a scan tool. If a scan tool is not available, perform the following procedure.*

1   To measure the fuel pressure you'll need a fuel pressure gauge compatible with high-pressure (up to 100 psi) fuel injection systems, and a hose and fitting suitable for connecting the gauge to the Schrader valve-type test port on the fuel feed line **(see illustration)**.

2   Relieve the fuel pressure (see Section 3).
3   Disconnect the fuel feed line (low-pressure quick-connect fitting) at the high-pressure fuel pump and connect a fuel pressure gauge between the fuel line and the fuel pump **(see illustration)**.
4   Start the engine and allow it to idle. Note the gauge reading as soon as the pressure stabilizes, and compare it with the pressure listed in this Chapter's Specifications.

- *If the pressure is lower than specified, check for a restriction in the fuel system. Two likely suspects are the fuel inlet strainer at the base of the fuel pump module in the left fuel tank, or a faulty fuel pressure regulator. Neither of these components can be inspected or replaced separately. It's also possible that there is a restriction in the fuel line (a blockage or a kink).*
- *If the fuel pressure is higher than specified, replace the fuel pressure regulator, which is part of the fuel pump module (see Section 7).*

5   Turn off the engine. Verify that the fuel pressure loses no more than 5 psi for five minutes after the engine is turned off.
6   Relieve the fuel pressure (see Section 3), then disconnect the fuel pressure gauge and reconnect the fuel line to the high-pressure fuel pump. Clean up any spilled gasoline.
7   Start the engine and verify that there are no fuel leaks.

5   Fuel lines and fittings - general information and disconnection

Warning: *Gasoline is extremely flammable. See Fuel system warnings in Section 1.*
1   Relieve the fuel pressure before servicing fuel lines or fittings (see Section 3), then disconnect the cable from the negative battery terminal (see Chapter 5) before proceeding.
2   The fuel supply line connects the fuel pump in the fuel tank to the fuel rail on the engine. The

Evaporative Emission (EVAP) system lines connect the fuel tank to the EVAP canister, and connect the canister to the intake manifold.
3   Whenever you're working under the vehicle, inspect all fuel and evaporative emission lines for leaks, kinks, dents and other damage. Always replace a damaged fuel or EVAP line immediately.
4   If you find signs of dirt in the lines during disassembly, disconnect all lines and blow them out with compressed air. Inspect the fuel strainer on the fuel pump pick-up unit for damage and deterioration.

Steel tubing
5   It is critical that the fuel lines be replaced with lines of equivalent type and specification.
6   Some steel fuel lines have threaded fittings. When loosening these fittings, hold the stationary fitting with a wrench while turning the tube nut.

Plastic tubing
Warning: *When removing or installing plastic fuel line tubing, be careful not to bend or twist it too much, which can damage it. Also, plastic fuel tubing is NOT heat resistant, so keep it away from excessive heat.*
7   When replacing fuel system plastic tubing, use only original equipment replacement plastic tubing.

Flexible hoses
8   When replacing fuel system flexible hoses, use only original equipment replacements.
9   Don't route fuel hoses (or metal lines) within four inches of the exhaust system or within ten inches of the catalytic converter. Make sure that no rubber hoses are installed directly against the vehicle, particularly in places where there is any vibration. If allowed to touch some vibrating part of the vehicle, a hose can easily become chafed and it might start leaking. A good rule of thumb is to maintain a minimum of 1/4-inch clearance around a hose (or metal line) to prevent contact with the vehicle underbody.

Disconnecting Fuel Line Fittings

Two-tab type fitting; depress both tabs with your fingers, then pull the fuel line and the fitting apart

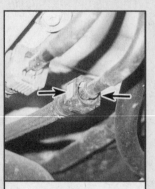

On this type of fitting, depress the two buttons on opposite sides of the fitting, then pull it off the fuel line

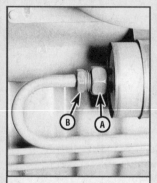

Threaded fuel line fitting; hold the stationary portion of the line or component (A) while loosening the tube nut (B) with a flare-nut wrench

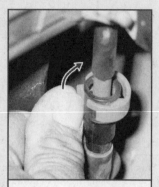

Plastic collar-type fitting; rotate the outer part of the fitting

Metal collar quick-connect fitting; pull the end of the retainer off the fuel line and disengage the other end from the female side of the fitting . . .

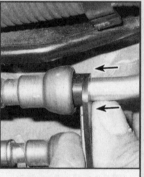

. . . insert a fuel line separator tool into the female side of the fitting, push it into the fitting and pull the fuel line off the pipe

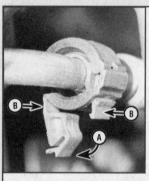

Some fittings are secured by lock tabs. Release the lock tab (A) and rotate it to the fully-opened position, squeeze the two smaller lock tabs (B) . . .

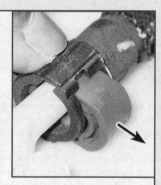

. . . then push the retainer out and pull the fuel line off the pipe

Spring-lock coupling; remove the safety cover, install a coupling release tool and close the tool around the coupling . . .

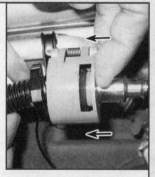

. . . push the tool into the fitting, then pull the two lines apart

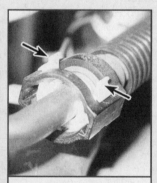

Hairpin clip type fitting: push the legs of the retainer clip together, then push the clip down all the way until it stops and pull the fuel line off the pipe

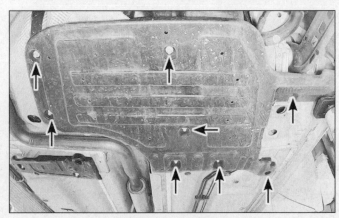

**6.4 Fuel tank shield fasteners
(2016 and later model shown, others similar)**

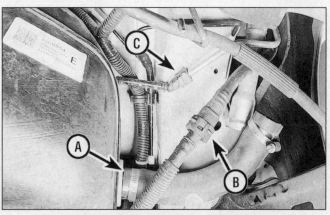

**6.6 Remove the fuel tank filler hose (A) and disconnect
the EVAP canister filter line (B) and vent line (C)
(2016 and later model shown)**

6 Fuel tank - removal and installation

Warning: *Gasoline is extremely flammable, so take extra precautions when you work on any part of the fuel system. See* Fuel system warnings *in Section 1.*

Warning: *Before disconnecting or opening any part of the fuel system, relieve the fuel system pressure (see Section 3), and equalize the pressure inside the fuel tank by removing the fuel filler cap.*

1   Relieve the fuel system pressure (see Section 3).

2   Disconnect the cable from the negative battery terminal (see Chapter 5).

Note: *It's easier to remove the fuel tank when it's nearly empty. There is no fuel tank drain plug, so if there's still a lot of fuel in the tank, siphon or hand-pump the remaining fuel from the tank through the tank filler neck pipe.*

Warning: *Don't start the siphoning action by mouth! Use a siphoning kit (available at most auto parts stores).*

3   Raise the vehicle and support it securely on jackstands.

4   Remove the fuel tank shield **(see illustration)**.

5   It's a good idea to remove the exhaust system that's underneath the fuel tank (on models where it interferes) (see Section 16). It will make lowering the tank much easier.

Note: *It's possible to lower the tank by removing the rubber exhaust hangers and supporting the exhaust system so that it's out of the way, but you'll have more room to maneuver if you remove the rear part of the exhaust system (everything behind the rear mounting flange of the catalytic converter).*

6   Remove the fuel tank filler hose. Locate the EVAP canister filter line and vent line and disconnect them **(see illustration)**. If you're unfamiliar with quick-connect fittings, refer to Section 5.

7   Disconnect the fuel feed line quick-connect fitting **(see illustration)**.

8   Disconnect the EVAP canister purge line quick-connect fitting **(see illustration)**.

9   On 2015 and earlier models (and 2016 Malibu Limited), disconnect the fuel pressure sensor connector.

10   On 2015 and earlier models (and 2016 Malibu Limited), remove the fasteners from the front of the right-rear inner fender splash shield. On all models, unplug the electrical connector for the fuel pump module wiring harness.

11   Support the fuel tank with a floor jack.

12   The fuel tank is supported by two longitudinal straps. On 2015 and earlier models (and 2016 Malibu Limited), remove the bolts from the end of the straps and swing the straps down. On 2016 and later models (except Malibu Limited), remove the bolts from both ends of the straps and remove the straps **(see illustration)**.

13   Lower the tank and remove it from the vehicle with the EVAP canister connected.

14   Installation is the reverse of removal. Check for leaks after installation.

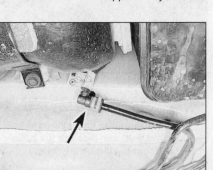

**6.7 Disconnect the fuel feed line
(2016 and later model shown)**

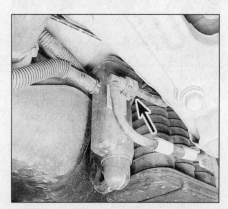

**6.8 Disconnect the canister purge line
(2016 and later model shown)**

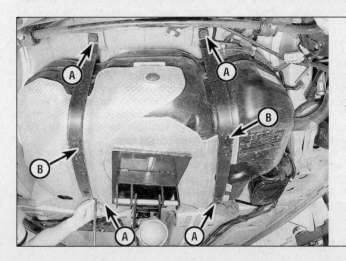

6.12 Remove the bolts from the two fuel tank straps (A), then remove the straps (B) (2016 and later models [except Malibu Limited] shown)

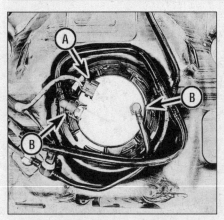

7.4 Disconnect the electrical connector(s) (A), fuel line and EVAP lines (B) from the fuel pump module (2016 and later models [except Malibu Limited] shown, others similar)

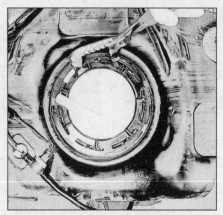

7.6a Use a large pair of water pump pliers to loosen and unscrew the fuel pump lock ring; if the lock ring is too tight to loosen this way, carefully tap it loose with a hammer and a brass punch. . .

7.6b. . . and remove the lock ring from the tank

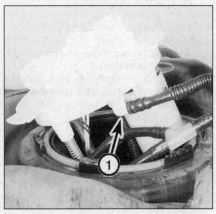

7.7a Carefully remove the fuel pump/fuel level sensor module from the fuel tank and (if equipped) disconnect the vent tube (1) from under the module top. . .

7.7b. . . once the module has cleared the mounting hole in the tank, angle it as shown to work the fuel level sensor float and float arm through the hole without damaging anything

7.8 Install a new fuel pump module O-ring

7   Fuel pump module - removal and installation

Warning: *Gasoline is extremely flammable, so take extra precautions when you work on any part of the fuel system. See* Fuel system warnings *in Section 1.*

1   Relieve the system fuel pressure (see Section 3), and equalize tank pressure by removing the fuel filler cap.

2   Disconnect the cable from the negative battery terminal (see Chapter 5).

3   Remove the fuel tank (see Section 6).

4   Disconnect the electrical connector, fuel supply line and EVAP hoses from the fuel pump/fuel level sending unit module **(see illustration)**. Use a shop rag to soak up any spilled fuel.

5   Mark the orientation of the fuel pump in relation to the fuel tank to ensure that the fuel pump is correctly realigned when you install it again.

Note: *If you're going to install a new pump, note the location of your alignment mark on*

the old pump and make a mark at the same spot on the new unit.

6   Using a pair of large water pump pliers, unscrew the fuel pump/fuel level sending unit module lock ring by turning it counterclockwise **(see illustration)**. If the lock ring is tight, use a hammer and a brass punch to loosen it (don't use a steel punch, which could produce sparks when struck by the hammer). Remove the lock ring from the tank **(see illustration)**.

7   Remove the pump assembly **(see illustration)**, taking care not to damage the fuel level sensor float arm and float **(see illustration)**.

8   Before installing the pump, replace the O-ring **(see illustration)**.

9   Installation is the reverse of removal.

Note: *Align the fuel pump/fuel level sending unit module with its hole in the tank and carefully insert it into the tank. Make sure that you don't damage the float arm or the float during installation. If the float arm is bent, the fuel level that is indicated on the fuel level gauge on the instrument cluster will be incorrect.*

8   Fuel level sensor - replacement

Note: *You can purchase the complete fuel pump/fuel level sensor module, or you can purchase either the fuel pump or the fuel level sensor separately. If only one component fails, use this procedure to separate the two components, then reassemble the good component and the new replacement component.*

1   Remove the fuel pump/fuel level sensor module (see Section 7) and place it on a clean work bench.

2   Pry both locking tabs outward and slide the sensor up and off of the fuel pump module **(see illustration)**.

3   On 2015 and earlier models (and 2016 Malibu Limited), use a pick to remove the electrical terminals from the fuel level sensor.

4   On 2016 and later models (except Malibu Limited), disconnect the electrical connector from under the top of the module housing.

5   On all models, to install the fuel level sensor on the fuel pump module, insert the

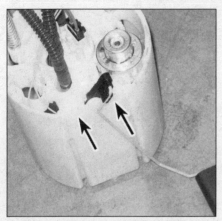

8.2 Pry the locking tabs to remove the fuel level sensor (2015 and earlier model shown, others similar)

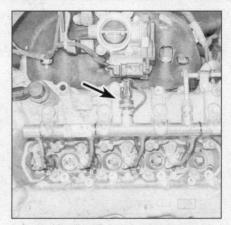

9.4 Fuel rail pressure sensor location (1.5L engine shown, others similar)

9.9 The fuel line pressure sensor is located in the fuel feed line near the fuel tank (2015 and earlier models and 2016 Malibu Limited)

terminals, then slide the sensor unit into place until you hear a click, then gently pull on the sensor unit to verify that it's locked into place.

6   Installation is otherwise the reverse of removal.

9   Fuel pressure sensors - replacement

Warning: *Gasoline is extremely flammable. See* Fuel system warnings *in Section 1.*
Warning: *The manufacturer states that the fuel pressure sensor must be replaced with a new one whenever it is removed.*
Note: *There are two fuel pressure sensors: one located on the fuel rail, and another located in the fuel feed line near the fuel tank.*

1   Relieve the fuel system pressure (see Section 3).
2   Disconnect the cable from the negative battery terminal (see Chapter 5).
Warning: *Have rags ready to catch any fuel that is remaining in the fuel rail/line.*

Fuel rail sensor

Warning: *If you're removing the fuel rail pressure sensor, wait at least two hours before proceeding to let the fuel pressure in the high-pressure side of the system to bleed down.*

3   Remove the intake manifold (see Chapter 2A, Section 5).
4   Locate and disconnect the electrical connector from the sensor **(see illustration)**.
5   Unscrew the sensor from the fuel rail.
Note: *Insect the O-ring and replace if damaged.*
6   Installation is the reverse of removal. Tighten the sensor to the torque listed in this Chapter's Specifications.

Fuel feed pipe sensor

2015 and earlier models (and 2016 Malibu Limited)

7   Raise and support the rear of the vehicle on jackstands.

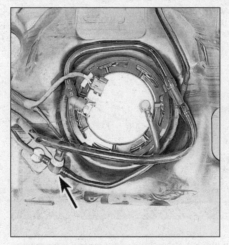

9.12 The fuel line pressure sensor is located in the fuel feed line near the fuel pump module (2016 and later model shown - except Malibu Limited)

8   Remove the protective cover from the passenger's side front corner of the fuel tank.
9   Locate and disconnect the electrical connector from the sensor **(see illustration)**.
10   Unscrew the sensor from the fuel feed line.
Note: *Inspect the O-ring and replace if damaged.*

2016 and later models (except Malibu Limited)

Note: *The fuel pressure sensor is part of the fuel feed pipe and not serviceable separately.*

11   Remove the fuel tank (see Section 6).
12   Locate and disconnect the fuel pressure sensor electrical connector **(see illustration)**.
13   Replace the fuel pressure sensor and fuel feed pipe as an assembly.

All models

14   Installation is the reverse of removal.

10.3 Depress the tab and pivot the connector lock up to unplug the connector (2015 and earlier models/2016 Malibu Limited)

Tighten the sensor to the torque listed in this Chapter's Specifications.

10   Fuel Pump Flow Control Module (FPFCM) - removal and installation

1   Disconnect the cable from the negative terminal of the battery (see Chapter 5).

2015 and earlier models (and 2016 Malibu Limited)

Note: *The FPFCM is located inside the trunk behind the right-side trim panel, to the rear of the wheel well.*

2   Remove the right-side trim panel in the trunk.
3   Disconnect the electrical connector from the FPFCM **(see illustration)**.

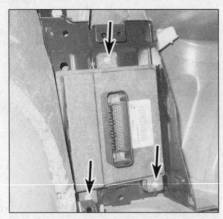

10.4 Fuel Pump Flow Control Module fasteners (2015 and earlier models/2016 Malibu Limited)

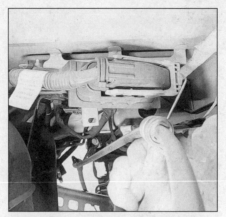

10.7 Slide the locking tab out and pivot the connector lock up to unplug the connector (2016 and later model shown, except Malibu Limited)

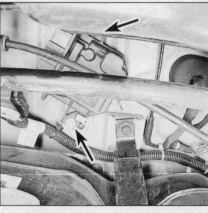

10.8 FPFCM retaining bolts (2016 and later model shown, except Malibu Limited)

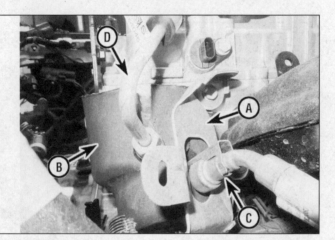

11.5 High Pressure Fuel Pump (HPFP) Components 1 of 2 (1.5L engine shown)

A   Bracket
B   Noise insulator
C   Low-pressure fuel supply line from fuel tank
D   High-pressure fuel pipe to fuel rail

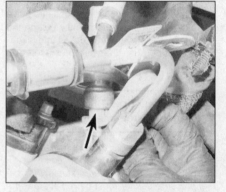

11.6 Disconnect the fuel supply line quick-connect fitting (1.5L engine shown)

4   Remove the FPFCM retaining bolts and detach the module from its mounting bracket **(see illustration)**.

2016 and later models (except Malibu Limited)

Note: *The FPFCM is located under the vehicle, between the fuel tank and the rear suspension.*
5   Raise and support the rear of the vehicle on jackstands.
6   Remove the fuel tank under cover.
7   Locate the FPFCM above the rear of the tank and disconnect the electrical connector **(see illustration)**.
8   Remove the FPFCM retaining bolts and detach the module from the vehicle **(see illustration)**.
9   Installation is the reverse of removal.

11   High-pressure fuel pump - removal and installation

Warning: *Gasoline is extremely flammable. See* Fuel system warnings *in Section 1.*
Warning: *Wait until the engine is completely cool before beginning this procedure.*
Warning: *The fuel delivery system is made up*

of a low-pressure system and a high-pressure system. Once the pressure of the low-pressure side of the system has been relieved, wait at least two hours before loosening any fuel fittings in the engine compartment.

Removal

1   Relieve the fuel system pressure (see Section 3).
2   Disconnect the cable from the negative battery terminal (see Chapter 5).
3   Remove the engine cover and if equipped, the noise insulation.
4   On 1.5L engines, disconnect the charge air cooler pipe from the throttle body and position to the side (see Section 15).
5   On all models, remove the bracket (1.5L engines) and noise insulation from the fuel pump **(see illustration)**.
6   Disconnect the low-pressure fuel supply line from the pump **(see illustration)**.
7   Disconnect the electrical connector from the pump **(see illustration)**.
8   Using a flare-nut wrench, unscrew the high-pressure fuel line fittings from the pump and the fuel rail **(see illustration)**.
Warning: *The manufacturer states that the line must be replaced if it has been removed.*
9   Remove the high-pressure fuel pump mounting bolts **(see illustration 11.6)** and

remove the pump. Always replace the bolts and O-ring with new ones.
10   With the pump removed, rotate the engine by hand and make sure the camshaft lobe is at its base circle before trying to install the pump.

Installation

11   Lubricate the pump roller with camshaft installation lubricant or clean engine oil, then install it in its bore.
12   Insert the new bolts though the holes in the pump and install the gasket (the gasket will hold the bolts in place).
13   Set the pump into the cylinder head and tighten the bolts evenly from side-to-side to the torque listed in this Chapter's Specifications.
Note: *As the pump bolts are tightened, it will get harder to tighten them until the spring in the pump is compressed.*
14   The remainder of installation is the reverse of removal. Clean the high-pressure fuel line fittings on the fuel rails, then apply a little clean engine oil to the threads. Install the new high-pressure fuel line, tightening the fittings to the torque listed in this Chapter's Specifications.
15   Reconnect the cable to the negative battery terminal (see Chapter 5), then start the engine and check for leaks.

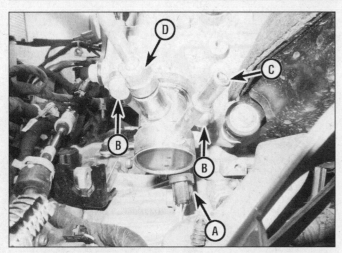

11.7 High Pressure Fuel Pump (HPFP) Components 2 of 2 (1.5L engine shown)

A   *HPFP connector*
B   *Mounting bolts*
C   *Low-pressure fuel supply fitting*
D   *High-pressure fuel pipe to fuel rail*

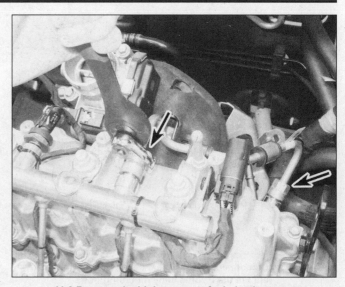

11.8 Remove the high pressure fuel pipe between the pump and fuel rail (1.5L engine shown)

12   Air filter housing - removal and installation

Air intake duct

1   Loosen the hose clamp screws at the air filter housing and turbocharger or air intake resonator (**see illustration**).
2   On 2016 and later (except Malibu Limited) remove the PCV vent hose from the duct.
3   On all models, carefully pull the intake duct from the throttle body or resonator and air filter housing.
4   On 1.5L models, set the duct to the side (with PCV hose attached).
5   Installation is the reverse of removal.

Air intake resonator (2015 and earlier models, and 2016 Malibu Limited)

6   Remove the air intake duct.
7   Remove the bolt attaching the resonator to the engine.
8   Loosen the clamp attaching the resonator hose to the throttle body.
9   Pull the resonator up and disconnect the PCV hose from the resonator or valve cover, whichever is easier.
10   Remove the resonator from the vehicle.

Air filter housing

11   Disconnect the cable from the negative terminal of the battery (see Chapter 5).
12   Remove the air intake duct.
13   Detach the electrical connector from the Mass Air Flow (MAF) sensor (**see illustration**).
14   Firmly pull the air filter housing up and out of its grommets.
15   If equipped, disconnect the secondary air injection hose.
16   Installation is the reverse of removal.

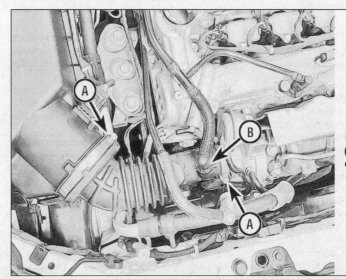

12.1 Loosen the clamps (A) and leave the PCV vent hose connected (B) (1.5L engine shown, other 2016 and later models similar)

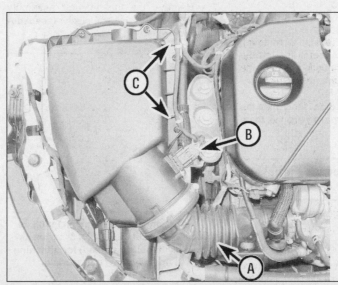

12.13 Remove the air intake duct (A) disconnect the MAF connector (B) and detach the harness (C) (2016 and later model [except Malibu Limited] shown)

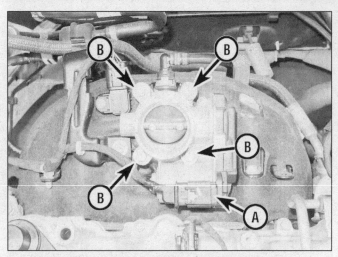

13.4 Disconnect the electrical connector (A) and remove the throttle body mounting bolts (1.5L engine shown, others similar)

14.5 Fuel rail and injector details (1.5L engines)

A	Upper fuel rail bolts	D	Fuel Rail Pressure sensor
B	Lower fuel rail bolts	E	Fuel rail harness connector
C	Fuel injectors	F	High-pressure fuel pipe

13 Throttle body - removal and installation

Warning: *Wait until the engine is completely cool before beginning this procedure.*

Removal

1   Disconnect the cable from the negative battery terminal (see Chapter 5).
2   On 1.5L and 2.0L engines, remove the charge air cooler inlet air tube (see Section 15).
3   On 2.5L engines, remove the air intake resonator (see Section 12).
4   On all engines, disconnect the throttle body electrical connector and remove the throttle body mounting bolts **(see illustration)**.
5   Remove the O-ring type throttle body gasket and inspect it. If the gasket isn't cracked, torn or otherwise deteriorated, it's okay to reuse it; if it's damaged or worn, replace it. If the vehicle is fairly old, it's a good idea to replace this gasket regardless of its apparent condition.

Installation

6   Installation is the reverse of removal. Install the gasket, then install the throttle body and tighten the mounting bolts to the torque listed in this Chapter's Specifications.
7   Start the engine, then verify that the throttle body operates correctly and that there are no air leaks.

14 Fuel rail and injectors - removal and installation

Warning: *Gasoline is extremely flammable. See Fuel system warnings in Section 1 .*

Removal

1   Relieve the fuel system pressure (see Section 3), then disconnect the cable from the negative terminal of the battery (see Chapter 5).
Warning: *Wait at least two hours before proceeding.*
Caution: *The manufacturer recommends that the O-rings and Teflon seals be replaced whenever the injectors are removed from the fuel rail or cylinder head.*
2   Remove the engine cover and insulation.
Warning: *The manufacturer states that the fuel pipe must be replaced if it has been removed.*
3   Disconnect the fuel rail pressure sensor and individual injector connectorts the move the harness out of the way.

1.5L engines

4   Remove the ignition coils (see Chapter 5, Section 6).
5   Disconnect the fuel rail harness connector **(see illustration)**.
6   Disconnect the high-pressure fuel pipe between the fuel rail and the high-pressure fuel pump (see Section 11).
7   Remove the fuel injector assembly screws. There are two per injector **(see illustration 14.5)**.

Method 1

Note: *Method 1: Factory style tools. Use special tool EN-51146-1-1 support, EN-51146-1-6 demounting screw, EN-51146-100 Plate, and EN-51146-1-3 slide hammers for the following steps.*
8   Set the EN-51146-1-6 to the same length as the injector assembly screw.
9   Attach EN-51146-1-6 together with EN-51146-1-1 and install into the injector assembly screw holes (there should be eight total). Tighten each one to 44 in-lbs (5 N.m).
10   Completely loosen, but do not remove, the upper and lower fuel rail bolts **(see illustration 14.5)**.
11   Attach EN-51146-100 to the EN-51146-1-1 and install the bolts to hold the plate in place (there should be eight total). Tighten the bolts to 44 in-lbs (5 N.m).
12   Attach the EN-21146-1-3 slide hammers to the plate (there should be two slide hammers).
13   Observe the installed angle of the fuel injectors and position the slide hammers at the same angle. Using the slide hammers at the same time, pull the injectors from the cylinder head.

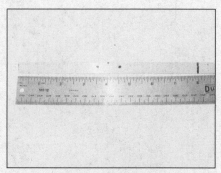

14.14a Using a suitable metal (such as aluminum), cut four 1/2" x 8" strips as shown with holes (marked) for attaching to the injectors (1.5L models)

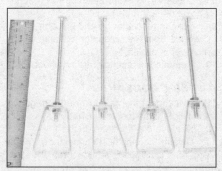

14.14b Bend the metal in the shape shown in the example and drill holes at the top for attaching bolts in the length shown. Secure the bolts to the stands (1.5L models)

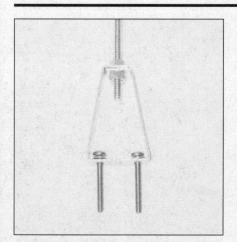

14.14c Using machine screws the same length and thread as the injector screws, insert the machine screws through the stands (1.5L models)

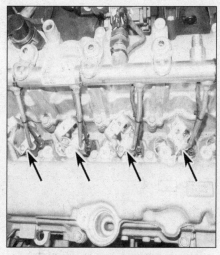

14.15 Attach the stands to the injectors using the machine screws (1.5L models)

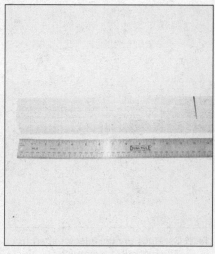

14.16a Cut a suitable piece of wood to the dimension shown (1.5L models)

Method 2

Note: *Method 2: Improvised tools. Fabricate attachments and use machine screws, bolts, a block of wood and two slide hammers.*

14 Fabricate stands using the images as a guide **(see illustrations)**.

15 Attach the stands to the injectors using the screws and tighten securely **(see illustration)**.

16 Fabricate a wooden block as shown in the examples **(see illustrations)**.

17 Remove the bolts from the stands and reinstall through the block of wood and the injector stands **(see illustrations)**.

18 Install the slide hammers to the block of wood **(see illustration)**.

19 Observe the installed angle of the fuel injectors and position the slide hammers at the same angle. Using the slide hammers at the same time, pull the injectors from the cylinder head **(see illustration)**.

Removing the injectors from the fuel rail

20 Disassemble the removal tools and remove from the injectors and fuel rail assembly.

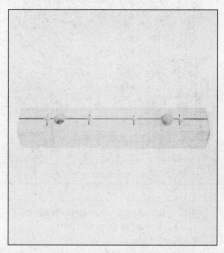

14.16b Place over the injector stand bolt and mark the locations of the bolts, then drill holes at the locations of the bolts. Drill two additional holes for the slide hammers as shown

14.17a Remove the bolts from the stands and install through the block of wood. Use nuts to secure the bolts to the wood. . .

14.17b. . . and install the bolts back onto the stands. Secure using nuts (1.5L engines)

14.18 Install the slide hammers to the block of wood (1.5L engines)

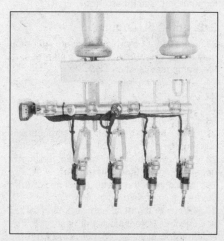

14.19 Using the slide hammers, remove the injectors and fuel rail (1.5L engines)

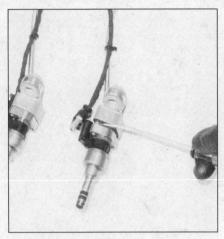

14.21 Carefully pry the injector apart from the fuel rail (1.5L models). . .

14.22. . . then twist and wiggle the injector from its bore in the rail (1.5L models)

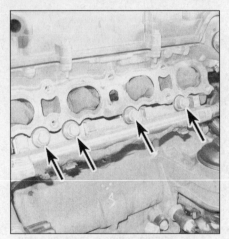

14.28 Remove the fuel rail bolts and grommets (2.5L shown)

14.34 Remove the old Teflon seal by cutting from the injector

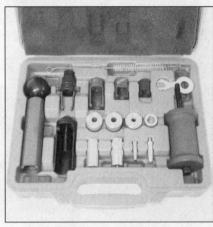

14.35 A fuel injector service kit for DI injectors is required

14.36 Wrap aluminum AC duct tape around the lower groove of the injector body until it's flush with the diameter of the injector so the seal can slide into the upper groove when installed

21 With the injectors attached to the fuel rail, carefully pry the assembly apart **(see illustration)**.

22 Pull the injector away from the fuel rail for servicing **(see illustration)**.

2.0L and 2.5L engines

23 Disconnect the high-pressure fuel pipe between the fuel rail and the high-pressure fuel pump (see Section 11).

24 Remove the intake manifold (see Chapter 2A, Section 5).

25 Remove the fuel rail noise insulation.

26 Disconnect the fuel rail harness connector.

27 Disconnect the fuel pressure sensor connector.

28 Remove the fuel rail mounting bolts and upper grommets **(see illustration)**.

29 Disconnect the electrical connector from the fuel rail harness connection.

30 Remove the bolts and work the fuel rail and injectors from the cylinder head.

Note: *If the injectors do not come from the head easily, use special tool EN-49248 or equivalent and attach to the outer fuel rail mounting bolt holes. Position the hooks of the*

tool under the fuel rail. Tighten the tool evenly on both sides to pull the fuel injectors from the cylinder head.

31 Disconnect the fuel injector electrical connectors and remove the injector harness.

32 To remove the injectors from the fuel rail, compress the injectors into the fuel rail and remove the retaining pin.

Note: *Special tool EN-50791 or equivalent can be used to compress the injectors.*

33 Pull each injector from its bore in the fuel rail. Twist if necessary to hep with removal.

Injector service

Teflon seal removal

34 Remove the Teflon seal by cutting it from the injector **(see illustration)**.

Caution: *Be careful not to scratch the injector.*

Teflon seal installation with special tools

Note: *The following procedure shows replacing injectors with two Teflon seals.*

35 A fuel injector service kit specifically for direct injection (DI) fuel injectors is needed for the following procedure **(see illustration)**.

36 With the teflon seals removed, using aluminum AC ducting tape, cut a thin piece and wrap around the lower injector seal groove as shown **(see illustration)**. This allows a seal to be positioned into the upper groove.

37 Install the seal onto the injector body using the injector service tool **(see illustrations)**.

38 Remove the AC ducting tape from the lower groove.

39 Repeat the same steps to install the seal into the lower groove.

40 After installing the seals, compress the seals using the correct diameter compression ring (starting with larger and moving to smaller rings) **(see illustrations)**.

Injector and fuel rail installation

1.5L engines

41 Lubricate a new upper O-ring with clean engine oil and install it on the injector. Do NOT oil the new Teflon seals.

14.37a Place the expander cone injector service tool over the injector with the seal installed. . .

14.37b. . . and use the correct diameter pushing ring tool to push down and install the seal on the injector body. . .

14.37c. . . and into the upper groove

14.40a Install compression rings to compress the seals. . .

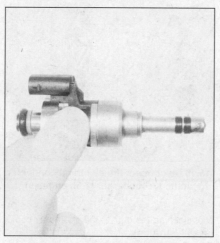

14.40b. . . to shrink them to size

14.43 Note that the upper O-ring (1) is installed above the support ring (2)

42 Insert the injectors into the fuel rail **(see illustration 14.21)**. Install the injector assembly screws, using thread locker on the threads. Tighten the screws to the torque listed in this Chapter's Specifications.

2.0L and 2.5L engines

43 Install a new support ring at the upper end of the injector. Lubricate a new upper O-ring with clean engine oil and install it on the injector. Do NOT oil the new Teflon seal. Note that the O-ring seal is installed above the support ring **(see illustration)**.
44 Install the injector on the fuel rail and compress the injector into the fuel rail to install the retaining pin.
Note: *Special tool EN-50791 or equivalent can be used to compress the injectors.*

All engines

45 Install the injector harness to the injectors and fuel rail.
46 Thoroughly clean the cylinder head injector bores with a small nylon brush.

47 Install the fuel rail and injectors in the cylinder head. Insert the injectors into their bores in the cylinder head. Press evenly on the fuel rail to start the injectors. The bore is slightly tapered, so you will encounter some resistance as the Teflon seal nears the bottom of the bore.
48 On 1.5L engines, install the fuel rail and bolts. Hand-tighten the bolts one turn at a time to seat the injectors, starting with the lower bolts, and working outwards from the center, then moving to the upper bolts and working outwards from the center. Tighten the fuel rail bolts to the torque listed in this Chapter's Specifications.
49 On 2.0L and 2.5L engines, install the fuel rail and bolts (and insulators if equipped). Hand-tighten the two outer most bolts to seat the injectors, then hand-tighten the remaining fuel rail bolts. Tighten the fuel rail bolts to the torque listed in this Chapter's Specifications.
50 The remainder of installation is the

reverse of removal. Clean the high-pressure fuel line fittings on the fuel rails, then apply a little clean engine oil to the threads. Install the new high-pressure fuel line, tightening the fittings to the torque listed in this Chapter's Specifications.
51 Turn the ignition on. Check for leaks and repair as necessary.
52 Start the engine and check for leaks.

15 Turbocharger components - removal and installation

Note: *1.5L and 2.0L engines are equipped with turbochargers.*

Turbocharger ducting

1 Raise and support the front of the vehicle on jackstands.
2 Remove the engine cover.
3 Remove the engine undercover.

15.4 Release the turbocharger duct
clip at the throttle body
(1.5L engines)

15.5 Remove the bolt attaching the
turbocharger duct bracket to the engine
(1.5L engines)

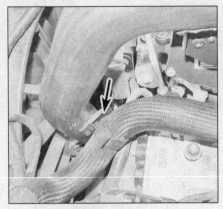

15.6 Detach the coolant hose clip
from the turbocharger duct
(1.5L engines)

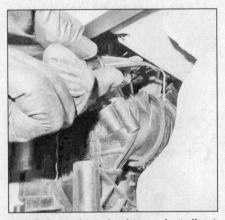

15.7 Release the turbocharger duct clip at
the charge air cooler (1.5L engines)

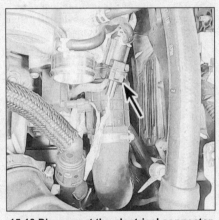

15.10 Disconnect the electrical connector
at the turbocharger (1.5L engines)

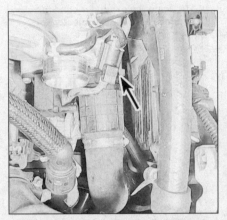

15.11 Release the turbocharger duct clip
at the turbocharger (1.5L engines)

Charge air cooler-to-throttle body (1.5L engines)

4   Release the clip attaching the duct to the throttle body **(see illustration)**.
5   Remove the bolt attaching the bracket to the engine **(see illustration)**.
6   Detach the coolant hose clip from the duct **(see illustration)**.
7   Working under the vehicle, release the clip attaching the duct to the charge air cooler **(see illustration)**.
8   Remove the duct from the vehicle.

Turbocharger-to-charge air cooler (1.5L engines)

9   Remove the air intake duct between the air filter housing and the turbocharger (see Section 12).

10   Disconnect the turbocharger electrical connector **(see illustration)**.
11   Release the clip attaching the duct to the turbocharger **(see illustration)**.
12   Working under the vehicle, release the clip attaching the duct to the charge air cooler **(see illustration)**.
13   Remove the duct through the engine compartment **(see illustration)**.

Turbocharger

Warning: *The engine must be completely cool before beginning this procedure.*
Note: *The removal and installation procedures for the turbocharger are similar between all engines.*
14   Raise and support the front of the vehicle on jackstands. Drain the engine coolant and engine oil (see Chapter 1).
Caution: While it isn't absolutely necessary to drain the oil, it is highly recommended to change the oil if the turbocharger is replaced.
15   Remove the engine cover.
16   Remove the under vehicle cover.
17   Disconnect the negative battery cable (see Chapter 5, Section 3).
18   Disconnect the PCV vent hose quick-connect fitting from the turbocharger **(see illustration)** or remove the bolt and fitting, as applicable.

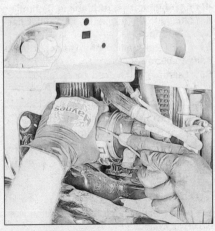

15.12 Release the turbocharger duct clip
at the charge air cooler (1.5L engines)

15.13 Pull the duct up and out through the
engine compartment (1.5L engines)

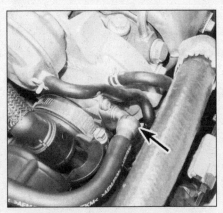

15.18 Disconnect the PCV hose quick-connect fitting at the turbo (1.5L engines)

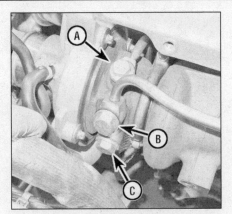

15.22 Identifying turbocharger oil and coolant pipes (1.5L engines)

A Oil feed pipe   C Coolant return pipe
B Coolant supply pipe

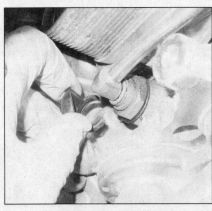

15.23a Remove the oil feed pipe clip cover. . .

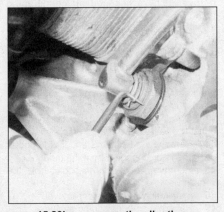

15.23b. . . remove the clip, then pull the pipe from the fitting (1.5L engines)

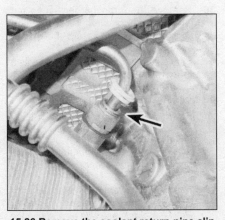

15.26 Remove the coolant return pipe clip cover and remove the clip, and pull the pipe from the fitting (1.5L engines)

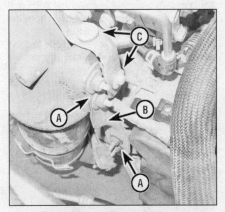

15.30 Remove the nuts (A) and bracket (B) and heat shield bolts (C) (1.5L engines)

19 Remove the air intake duct between the air filter housing and the turbocharger (see Section 12).
20 Remove the duct between the turbocharger and the charge air cooler.
21 Remove the bolts and the heat shield from the turbocharger.
22 Remove the oil feed pipe banjo bolt at the turbocharger (see illustration). Discard the sealing washers.
Note: *Place a drain pan under the turbocharger area to catch oil and coolant.*
23 Working under the vehicle, remove the oil feed pipe retainer clip, and pull the oil feed pipe out of the fitting to remove (see illustrations).
24 Remove the banjo bolt from the coolant supply pipe and secure out of the way (see illustration 15.22) or disconnect from the coolant hoses and remove. Discard the sealing washers.
25 Remove the banjo bolt from the coolant return pipe. Discard the sealing washers.
26 Working under the vehicle, remove the coolant return pipe retainer clip, then pull the coolant return pipe out of the fitting to remove (see illustration).
27 Working under the vehicle, remove the

fasteners and disconnect the exhaust pipe from the catalytic converter flange.
28 Remove the nuts attaching the catalytic converter to the lower bracket.
29 Working from the engine compartment, disconnect the oxygen sensor connectors.
30 Remove the nuts attaching the catalytic converter bracket to the catalytic converter

15.32a Loosen the band camp securing the catalytic converter to he turbocharger, then remove the catalytic converter. . .

and the engine (see illustration). Remove the bracket.
31 Remove the bolts attaching the heat shield to the catalytic converter.
32 On 1.5L engines, loosen the band clamp at the turbocharger housing, then remove the catalytic converter and seal (see illustrations).

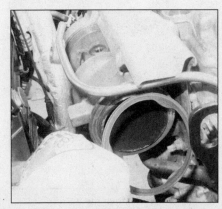

15.32b. . . and the seal (1.5L engines)

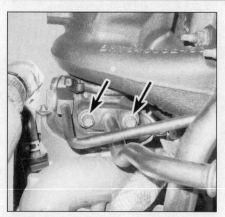

15.34a Remove the oil return pipe bolts at the turbocharger. . .

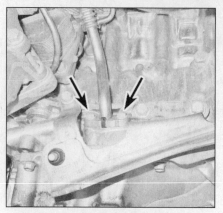

15.34b. . . and remove the clip at the engine block to remove the oil feed pipe (1.5L engines)

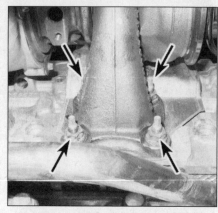

15.36 Remove the nuts and remove the turbocharger assembly from the vehicle (1.5L engines)

33 On 2.0L engines, remove the bolts and disconnect the converter assembly from the turbocharger. Discard the gasket.

34 On all models, remove the bolts and the oil return pipe **(see illustration)**. Discard the seals.

35 Disconnect any turbocharger electrical connectors.

36 Remove the turbocharger flange nuts and remove the turbocharger from the vehicle **(see illustration)**. Discard the exhaust gasket/heat shield.

37 Service the turbocharger components as necessary **(see illustrations)**.

38 Installation is reverse of removal, noting the following items:
- *Use new sealing washers on the banjo bolts.*
- *Install a new exhaust flange gasket and seal between turbocharger and exhaust manifold and turbocharger and catalytic converter flange.*
- *Use new seals for the oil return pipe.*
- *Refill the cooing system (see Chapter 1).*
- *Refill the crankcase with oil and change the oil filter (see Chapter 1).*
- *Tighten all fasteners to the torque values listed in this Chapter's Specifications.*

Charge air cooler

Note: *The charge air cooler may also be referred to as an intercooler and is located between the air conditioning condenser and the radiator.*

39 Have the air conditioning refrigerant

recovered by a licensed air conditioning technician.

40 Raise and support the front of the vehicle.

41 Remove the air conditioning condenser from the vehicle (see Chapter 3, Section 14).

42 On 2016 and later models, remove the bracket in front of the charge air cooler. The bracket is secured with clips.

43 On all models, disconnect the inlet and outlet hoses from the charge air cooler

44 Remove the fasteners and lift the cooler upwards to disengage it from the mounts.

45 Remove the charge air cooler from the vehicle.

46 Installation is reverse of removal.

47 Have the air conditioning system evacuated, leak tested and recharged by the shop that discharged it.

16 Exhaust system servicing - general information

Warning: *Allow exhaust system components to cool before inspection or repair. Also, never work under a vehicle supported*

15.37a Remove the Torx screws to service the air bypass valve (1.5L engines)

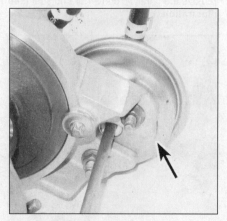

15.37b Remove the nuts. . .

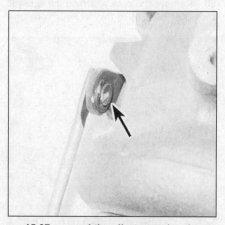

15.37c. . . and the clip to service the wastegate actuator (1.5L engines)

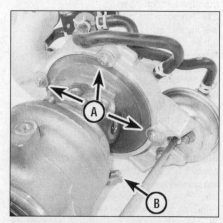

15.37d To disassemble the turbocharger housing, remove the compressor housing bolts (A) and the exhaust housing band clamp (B) (1.5L engines)

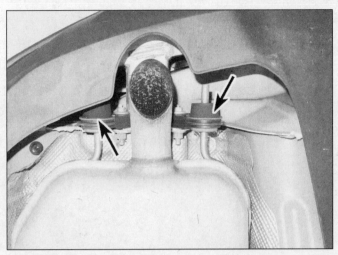

16.1a A typical exhaust system hanger supporting the muffler.
Inspect regularly and replace at the first sign of
damage or deterioration

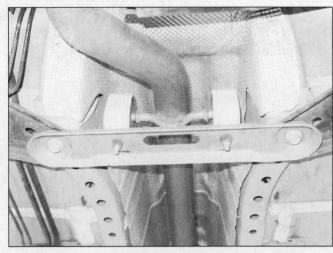

16.1b Typical exhaust system support. Inspect for damage
whenever the vehicle is raised

only by jacks, always make sure it is securely supported on jackstands.

1   The exhaust system consists of the exhaust manifolds, catalytic converter, muffler, tailpipe and all connecting pipes, flanges and clamps. The exhaust system is isolated from the vehicle body and from chassis components by a series of rubber hangers **(see illustrations)**. Periodically inspect these hangers for cracks or other signs of deterioration, replacing them as necessary.

2   Conduct regular inspections of the exhaust system to keep it safe and quiet. Look for any damaged or bent parts, open seams, holes, loose connections, excessive corrosion or other defects which could allow exhaust fumes to enter the vehicle. Do not repair deteriorated exhaust system components; replace them with new parts.

3   If the exhaust system components are extremely corroded, or rusted together, a cutting torch is the most convenient tool for removal. Consult a properly-equipped repair shop. If a cutting torch is not avail

able, you can use a hacksaw, or if you have compressed air, there are special pneumatic cutting chisels that can also be used. Wear safety goggles to protect your eyes from metal chips and wear work gloves to protect your hands.

4   Here are some simple guidelines to follow when repairing the exhaust system:

• *Work from the back to the front when removing exhaust system components.*
• *Apply penetrating oil to the exhaust system component fasteners to make them easier to remove.*
• *Use new gaskets, hangers and clamps.*
• *Apply anti-seize compound to the threads of all exhaust system fasteners during reassembly.*
• *Allow sufficient clearance between newly installed parts and all points on the underbody to avoid overheating the floor pan and possibly damaging the interior carpet and insulation. Pay particularly close attention to the catalytic converter and heat shield.*

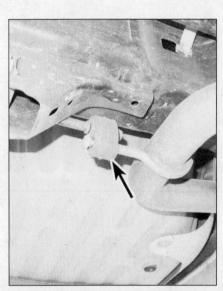

16.1c Typical exhaust system hanger.
Inspect for damage when working
on the exhaust system

Notes

Chapter 5
Engine electrical systems

Contents

Specifications

Torque specifications

Note: *One foot-pound (ft-lb) of torque is equivalent to 12 inch-pounds (in-lbs) of torque. Torque values below approximately 15 ft-lbs are expressed in inch-pounds, because most foot-pound torque wrenches are not accurate at these smaller values.*

	Ft-lbs (unless otherwise indicated)	Nm
Alternator mounting fasteners		
1.5L engine		
Stud	80 in-lbs	22
Nut and bolts	16	22
2.0L and 2.5L engines	16	22
Starter motor mounting bolts/nuts		
1.5L engine	43	58
2.0L and 2.5L engines	16	22
Ignition coil bolts	89 in-lbs	10

1   General information and precautions

General information

Ignition system

1   The electronic ignition system consists of the Crankshaft Position (CKP) sensor, the Camshaft Position (CMP) sensor, the Knock Sensor(s) (KS), the Powertrain Control Module (PCM), the ignition switch, the battery, the individual ignition coils, and the spark plugs. For more information on the CKP, CMP and KS sensors, as well as the PCM, refer to Chapter 6.

Charging system

2   The charging system includes the alternator (with an integral voltage regulator), the Powertrain Control Module (PCM), the Body Control Module (BCM), a charge indicator light on the dash, the battery, a fuse or fusible link and the wiring connecting all of these components. The charging system supplies electrical power for the ignition system, the lights, the radio, etc. The alternator is driven by a drivebelt.

Starting system

3   The starting system consists of the battery, the ignition switch, the starter relay, the Powertrain Control Module (PCM), the Body Control Module (BCM), the Transmission Range (TR) switch, the starter motor and solenoid assembly, and the wiring connecting all of the components.

Precautions

4   Always observe the following precautions when working on the electrical system:
  a) *Be extremely careful when servicing engine electrical components. They are easily damaged if checked, connected or handled improperly.*
  b) *Never leave the ignition switched on for long periods of time when the engine is not running.*
  c) *Never disconnect the battery cables while the engine is running.*
  d) *Maintain correct polarity when connecting battery cables from another vehicle during jump starting - see* Booster battery (jump) starting Section *at the front of this manual.*
  e) *Always disconnect the cable from the negative battery terminal before working on the electrical system, but read the battery disconnection procedure first (see Section 3).*

5   It's also a good idea to review the *Safety first!* section located in the front of this manual regarding the engine electrical systems before beginning any operation included in this Chapter.

2   Troubleshooting

Ignition system

1   If a malfunction occurs in the ignition system, do not immediately assume that any particular part is causing the problem. First, check the following items:
  a) *Make sure that the cable clamps at the battery terminals are clean and tight.*
  b) *Test the condition of the battery (see Steps 15 through 18). If it doesn't pass all the tests, replace it.*
  c) *Check the ignition coil or coil pack connections.*
  d) *Check any relevant fuses in the engine compartment fuse and relay box (see Chapter 12). If they're burned, determine the cause and repair the circuit.*

Check

Warning: *Because of the high voltage generated by the ignition system, use extreme care when performing a procedure involving ignition components.*
Note: *Most problems with the ignition system will result in a Diagnostic Trouble Code (DTC) being stored in the Powertrain Control; Module (PCM). See Chapter 6 for information on how to extract trouble codes from the PCM.*
Note: *You'll need a spark tester for the following test. Spark testers are available at most auto parts stores.*

2   If the engine turns over but won't start, verify that there is sufficient ignition voltage to fire the spark plugs as follows.
3   On models with a coil-over-plug type ignition system, remove a coil and install the tester between the boot at the lower end of the coil and the spark plug **(see illustration)**. On models with spark plug wires, disconnect a spark plug wire from a spark plug and install the tester between the spark plug wire boot and the spark plug.
Caution: *Do NOT crank the engine or allow it to run for more than five seconds; running the engine for more than five seconds may set a Diagnostic Trouble Code (DTC) for a cylinder misfire.*
4   Crank the engine and note whether or not the tester flashes.
5   If the tester flashes during cranking, the coil is delivering sufficient voltage to the spark plug to fire it. Repeat this test for each cylinder to verify that the other coils are OK.
6   If the tester doesn't flash, remove a coil from another cylinder and swap it for the one being tested. If the tester now flashes, you know that the original coil is bad. If the tester still doesn't flash, the PCM or wiring harness is probably defective. Have the PCM checked

out by a dealer service department or other qualified repair shop (testing the PCM is beyond the scope of the do-it-yourselfer because it requires expensive special tools).
7   If the tester flashes during cranking but a misfire code (related to the cylinder being tested) has been stored, the spark plug could be fouled or defective, or the coil could be be malfunctioning under load.

Charging system

8   If a malfunction occurs in the charging system, do not automatically assume the alternator is causing the problem. First check the following items:
  a) *Check the drivebelt tension and condition (see Chapter 1). Replace it if it's worn or deteriorated.*
  b) *Make sure the alternator mounting bolts are tight.*
  c) *Inspect the alternator wiring harness and the connectors at the alternator and voltage regulator. They must be in good condition, tight and have no corrosion.*
  d) *Check the fusible link (if equipped) or main fuse in the underhood fuse/relay box. If it is burned, determine the cause, repair the circuit and replace the link or fuse (the vehicle will not start and/or the accessories will not work if the fusible link or main fuse is blown).*
  e) *Start the engine and check the alternator for abnormal noises (a shrieking or squealing sound indicates a bad bearing).*
  f) *Check the battery. Make sure it's fully charged and in good condition (one bad cell in a battery can cause overcharging by the alternator).*
  g) *Disconnect the battery cables (negative first, then positive). Inspect the battery posts and the cable clamps for corrosion. Clean them thoroughly if necessary. Reconnect the cables (positive first, negative last).*

Check

Alternator

9   Use a voltmeter to check the battery voltage with the engine off. It should be at least 12.6 volts **(see illustration 2.15)**.
10   Start the engine and check the battery voltage again. It should now be approximately 13.5 to 15 volts.

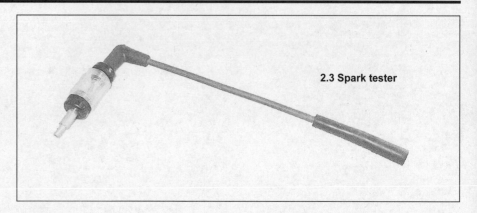

2.3 Spark tester

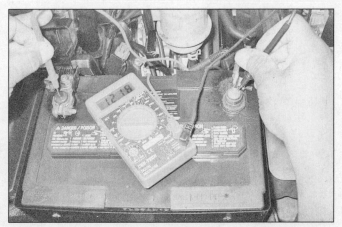

2.15 To test the open circuit voltage of the battery, touch the black probe of the voltmeter to the negative terminal and the red probe to the positive terminal of the battery; a fully charged battery should be at least 12.6 volts

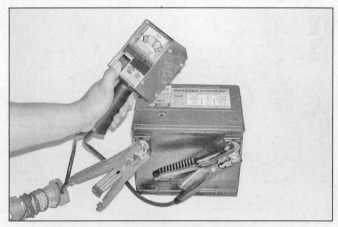

2.17 Connect a battery load tester to the battery and check the battery condition under load following the tool manufacturer's instructions

11   If the voltage reading is more or less than the specified charging voltage, the voltage regulator is probably defective, which will require replacement of the alternator (the voltage regulator is not replaceable separately). Remove the alternator and have it bench tested (most auto parts stores will do this for you).

12   The charging system (battery) light on the instrument cluster lights up when the ignition key is turned to On, but it should go out when the engine starts.

13   If the charging system light stays on after the engine has been started, there is a problem with the charging system. Before replacing the alternator, check the battery condition, alternator belt tension and electrical cable connections.

14   If replacing the alternator doesn't restore voltage to the specified range, have the charging system tested by a dealer service department or other qualified repair shop.

Battery

15   Check the battery state of charge. Visually inspect the indicator eye on the top of the battery (if equipped with one); if the indicator eye is black in color, charge the battery (see Chapter 1). Next perform an open circuit voltage test using a digital voltmeter. With the engine and all accessories Off, touch the negative probe of the voltmeter to the negative terminal of the battery and the positive probe to the positive terminal of the battery **(see illustration)**. The battery voltage should be 12.6 volts or slightly above. If the battery is less than the specified voltage, charge the battery before proceeding to the next test. Do not proceed with the battery load test unless the battery charge is correct.

Note: *The battery's surface charge must be removed before accurate voltage measurements can be made. Turn on the high beams for ten seconds, then turn them off and let the vehicle stand for two minutes.*

16   Disconnect the negative battery cable, then the positive cable from the battery.

17   Perform a battery load test. An accurate check of the battery condition can only be performed with a load tester **(see illustration)**. This test evaluates the ability of the battery to operate the starter and other accessories during periods of high current draw. Connect the load tester to the battery terminals. Load test the battery according to the tool manufacturer's instructions. This tool increases the load demand (current draw) on the battery.

18   Maintain the load on the battery for 15 seconds and observe that the battery voltage does not drop below 9.6 volts. If the battery condition is weak or defective, the tool will indicate this condition immediately.

Note: *Cold temperatures will cause the minimum voltage reading to drop slightly. Follow the chart given in the manufacturer's instructions to compensate for cold climates. Minimum load voltage for freezing temperatures (32 degrees F) should be approximately 9.1 volts.*

Starting system

The starter rotates, but the engine doesn't

19   Remove the starter (see Section 8). Check the overrunning clutch and bench test the starter to make sure the drive mechanism extends fully for proper engagement with the flywheel ring gear. If it doesn't, replace the starter.

20   Check the flywheel ring gear for missing teeth and other damage. With the ignition turned off, rotate the flywheel so you can check the entire ring gear.

The starter is noisy

21   If the solenoid is making a chattering noise, first check the battery (see Steps 15 through 18). If the battery is okay, check the cables and connections.

22   If you hear a grinding, crashing metallic sound when you turn the key to Start, check for loose starter mounting bolts. If they're tight, remove the starter and inspect the teeth on the starter pinion gear and flywheel ring gear. Look for missing or damaged teeth.

23   If the starter sounds fine when you first turn the key to Start, but then stops rotating the engine and emits a zinging sound, the problem is probably a defective starter drive that's not staying engaged with the ring gear. Replace the starter.

The starter rotates slowly

24   Check the battery (see Steps 15 through 18).

25   If the battery is okay, verify all connections (at the battery, the starter solenoid and motor) are clean, corrosion-free and tight. Make sure the cables aren't frayed or damaged.

26   Check that the starter mounting bolts are tight so it grounds properly. Also check the pinion gear and flywheel ring gear for evidence of a mechanical bind (galling, deformed gear teeth or other damage).

The starter does not rotate at all

27   Check the battery (see Steps 15 through 18).

28   If the battery is okay, verify all connections (at the battery, the starter solenoid and motor) are clean, corrosion-free and tight. Make sure the cables aren't frayed or damaged.

29   Check all of the fuses in the underhood fuse/relay box.

30   Check that the starter mounting bolts are tight so it grounds properly.

31   Check for voltage at the starter solenoid "S" terminal when the ignition key is turned to the start position. If voltage is present, replace the starter/solenoid assembly. If no voltage is present, the problem could be the starter relay, the Transmission Range (TR) switch (see Chapter 6), or with an electrical connector somewhere in the circuit (see the wiring diagrams at the end of this manual). Also, on many modern vehicles, the Powertrain Control Module (PCM) and the Body Control Module (BCM) control the voltage signal to the starter solenoid; on such vehicles a special scan tool is required for diagnosis.

3.3 To disconnect the battery negative cable, open the battery box cover, disconnect and isolate the negative battery cable

4.2a Open the battery positive cable cover and disconnect the positive (+) battery cable terminal. . .

3 Battery - disconnection and reconnection

Warning: *On models with OnStar, make absolutely sure the ignition key is in the Off position and Retained Accessory Power (RAP) has been depleted before disconnecting the cable from the negative battery terminal. Also, never remove the OnStar fuse with the ignition key in any position other than Off. If these precautions are not taken, the OnStar system's back-up battery will be activated, and remain activated, until it goes dead. If this happens, the OnStar system will not function as it should in the event that the main vehicle battery power is cut off (as might happen during a collision).*

Warning: *Always disconnect the cable from the negative battery terminal FIRST and hook it up LAST or the battery may be shorted by the tool being used to loosen the cable clamps.*

Note: *To disconnect the battery for service procedures requiring power to be cut from the vehicle, first open the driver's door to disable Retained Accessory Power (RAP), then loosen the cable end nut and disconnect the cable from the negative battery terminal. Isolate the cable end to prevent it from coming into accidental contact with the battery terminal.*

1   Some systems on the vehicle require battery power to be available at all times, either to maintain continuous operation (alarm system, power door locks, etc.), or to maintain control unit memory (radio station presets, Powertrain Control Module and other control units). When the battery is disconnected, the power that maintains these systems is cut. So, before you disconnect the battery, please note that on a vehicle with power door locks, it's a wise precaution to remove the key from the ignition and to keep it with you, so that it does not get locked inside if the power door locks should engage accidentally when the battery is reconnected!

2   Devices known as memory-savers can be used to avoid some of these problems.

4.2b. . . then unclip the mega-fuse box and move it out of the way

Precise details vary according to the device used. The typical memory saver is plugged into the cigarette lighter and is connected to a spare battery. Then the vehicle battery can be disconnected from the electrical system. The memory saver will provide sufficient current to maintain audio unit security codes, PCM memory, etc., and will provide power to always hot circuits such as the clock and radio memory circuits.

Warning: *Some memory savers deliver a considerable amount of current in order to keep vehicle systems operational after the main battery is disconnected. If you're using a memory saver, make sure that the circuit concerned is actually open before servicing it.*

Warning: *If you're going to work near any of the airbag system components, the battery MUST be disconnected and a memory saver must NOT be used. If a memory saver is used, power will be supplied to the airbag, which means that it could accidentally deploy and cause serious personal injury.*

Disconnection

3   To disconnect the battery for service procedures requiring power to be cut from the vehicle, open the battery box cover and

remove the nut attaching the negative battery cable terminal to the battery **(see illustration)**. Isolate the cable end to prevent it from coming into accidental contact with the battery terminal.

Reconnection

4   When reconnecting the battery, always connect the positive cable first and the negative cable last.

4 Battery and battery tray - removal and installation

Note: *Battery straps and handlers are available at most auto parts stores for reasonable prices. They make it easier to remove and carry the battery.*

Battery

1   Open the battery box cover and loosen the nut attaching the negative battery cable terminal to the battery **(see illustration 3.3)**.

2   Slide open the mega-fuse cover towards the rear of the vehicle and disconnect the cable from the positive battery terminal **(see illustration)**, then unclip the

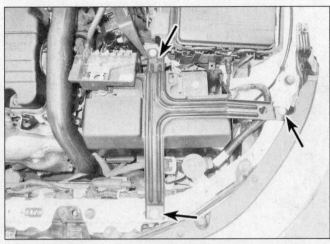

4.3 Remove the two bolts and nut and remove the battery cover hold-down

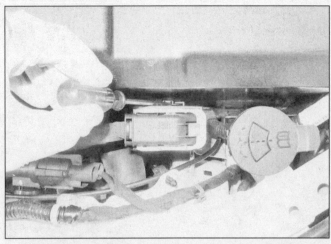

4.4 Use a screwdriver to release the tab and detach the connector from the battery cover

4.5 Pull up and remove the battery cover

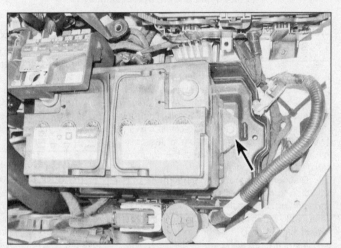

4.6 Battery hold-down clamp bolt

mega-fuse box and flip it back out of the way **(see illustration)**.

3   Remove the two bolts and nut and the battery cover hold-down **(see illustration)**.

4   Detach the connector from the side of the battery cover **(see illustration)**.

5   Remove the battery cover **(see illustration)**.

6   Remove the battery hold-down clamp **(see illustration)**.

7   Lift out the battery. Be careful - it's heavy.

8   If you are replacing the battery, make sure you get one that's identical, with the same dimensions, amperage rating, cold cranking rating, etc. Remove the heat shield from the old battery and install it on the new battery.

9   Installation is the reverse of removal. Connect the positive cable first and the negative cable last.

Battery tray

10   After removing the battery as described in the previous procedure, detach the Powertrain Control Module (PCM) bracket from the battery tray (see Chapter 6, Section 14).

11   Remove the fasteners securing the battery tray **(see illustration)**.

12   Detach the harness fasteners from the battery tray **(see illustration)** and remove the tray.

13   Installation is reverse of removal.

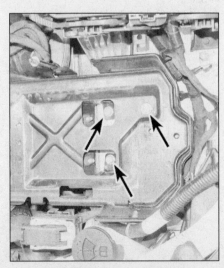

4.11 Battery tray mounting bolts

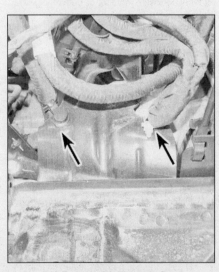

4.12 Detach the harness from the battery tray

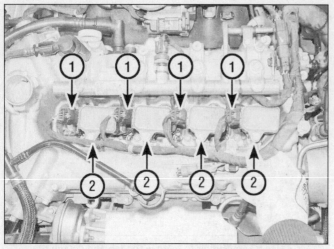

6.3 Ignition coil electrical connector (1) and mounting fastener (2) (1.5L engine shown, others similar)

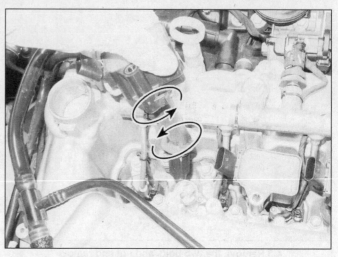

6.6 Twist and pull to remove the ignition coil

5   Battery cables - replacement

1   When removing the cables, always disconnect the cable from the negative battery terminal first and hook it up last, or you might accidentally short out the battery with the tool you're using to loosen the cable clamps. Even if you're only replacing the cable for the positive terminal, always disconnect the negative cable from the battery first.

2   Disconnect the old cables from the battery, then trace each of them to their opposite ends and disconnect them. Note the routing of each cable before disconnecting it to ensure correct installation.

3   If you are replacing any of the old cables, take them with you when buying new cables. It is vitally important that you replace the cables with identical parts.

4   Clean the threads of the solenoid or ground connection with a wire brush to remove rust and corrosion. Apply a light coat of battery terminal corrosion inhibitor or petroleum jelly to the threads to prevent future corrosion.

5   Attach the cable to the solenoid or ground connection and tighten the mounting nut/bolt securely.

6   Before connecting a new cable to the battery, make sure that it reaches the battery post without having to be stretched.

7   Connect the cable to the positive battery terminal first, then connect the ground cable to the negative battery terminal.

6   Ignition coils - replacement

1   Disconnect the cable from the negative terminal of the battery (see Section 3).

2   Remove the engine cover.

3   Disconnect the electrical connector from the coil **(see illustration)**.

4   Detach the coil harness fasteners from the valve cover and position the harness to the side.

5   Remove the ignition coil mounting fasteners.

6   Pull up and twist to remove the coil **(see illustration)**.

7   Installation is the reverse of removal.

8   Apply a little silicone dielectric compound to the inside of the coil boot before installing it.

9   Installation is reverse of removal.

7   Alternator - removal and installation

Note: *Before replacing the alternator, it is recommended to have the charging system checked prior to removal; or after removal, take the alternator to a parts store or automotive electrical repair shop to check operation.*

1   Disconnect the cable from the negative battery terminal (see Section 3).

2   Remove the engine cover.

3   Remove the air filter housing and intake duct for access to the alternator (see Chapter 4, Section 12).

4   Remove the drivebelt (see Chapter 1, Section 11).

5   Raise and support the front of the vehicle on jackstands.

6   Remove the under-vehicle splash shield.

7   Working under the vehicle, disconnect the electrical connectors from the alternator **(see illustration)**.

1.5L engine

8   Remove the alternator mounting bolts and nut, then remove the alternator from the vehicle **(see illustration)**.

Note: *If necessary for clearance, also remove the stud.*

2.0L and 2.5L engines

9   Remove the lower alternator mounting bolt.

10   Working from the top of the engine, remove the upper alternator mounting bolt and nut and remove the alternator from the vehicle.

All engines

11   Installation is reverse of removal. Tighten the alternator bolts to the torque listed in this Chapter's Specifications. Check the charging system voltage to verify proper operation.

7.7 Disconnect the alternator electrical connector (1) and remove the nut and battery cable (2) (1.5L engine shown, others similar)

7.8 Remove the bolts and nut and remove the alternator (1.5L engines)

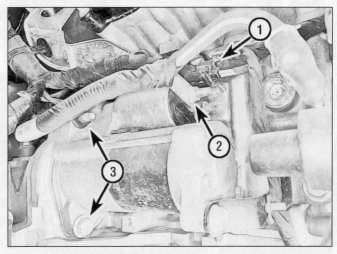

8.5 Starter electrical connector (1), battery cable (2) and mounting bolt/nut (3) (1.5L engine shown, other similar)

8   Starter motor - removal and installation

Note: *Before replacing the starter, it is recommended to have the cranking system checked prior to removal; or after removal, take the starter to a parts store or automotive electrical repair shop to check operation.*

1   Disconnect the cable from the negative battery terminal (see Section 3).

2   Raise the front of the vehicle and support it securely on jackstands.

3   Remove the under-vehicle splash shield if necessary to access the starter.

4   Remove the secondary air injection pump, if equipped (see Chapter 6, Section 18).

5   Disconnect the electrical connectors from the starter **(see illustration)**.

6   On 1.5L engines, remove the starter motor mounting bracket bolts and remove the bracket **(see illustration)**.

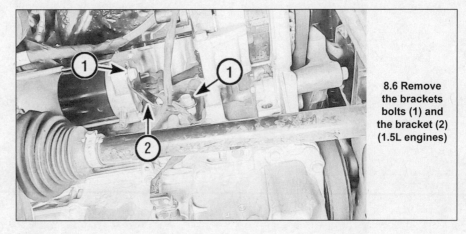

8.6 Remove the brackets bolts (1) and the bracket (2) (1.5L engines)

7   On all engines, remove the starter motor mounting bolts (and/or nuts if equipped) and remove the starter motor.

8   Installation is the reverse of removal.

Tighten the starter motor mounting bolts to the torque listed in this Chapter's Specifications.

Notes

Chapter 6
Emissions and engine control systems

Contents

Specifications

Torque specifications

Note: *One foot-pound (ft-lb) of torque is equivalent to 12 inch-pounds (in-lbs) of torque. Torque values below approximately 15 ft-lbs are expressed in inch-pounds, because most foot-pound torque wrenches are not accurate at these smaller values.*

	Ft-lbs (unless otherwise indicated)	Nm
Secondary air injection check valve bolts	16	22
Knock sensor retaining bolt	18	24
1.5L engine	18	24
2.0L engine		
2015 and earlier models	89 in-lbs	10
2016 and later models	18	24
2.5L engine	89 in-lbs	10
Oxygen sensors	30	40

1   General information

1   To prevent pollution of the atmosphere from incompletely burned and evaporating gases, and to maintain good driveability and fuel economy, a number of emission control systems are incorporated. They include the:

Catalytic converter

2   A catalytic converter is an emission control device in the exhaust system that reduces certain pollutants in the exhaust gas stream. There are two types of converters: oxidation converters and reduction converters.

3   Oxidation converters contain a monolithic substrate (a ceramic honeycomb) coated with the semi-precious metals platinum and palladium. An oxidation catalyst reduces unburned hydrocarbons (HC) and carbon monoxide (CO) by adding oxygen to the exhaust stream as it passes through the substrate, which, in the presence of high temperature and the catalyst materials, converts the HC and CO to water vapor (H_2O) and carbon dioxide (CO_2).

4   Reduction converters contain a monolithic substrate coated with platinum and rhodium. A reduction catalyst reduces oxides of nitrogen (NOx) by removing oxygen, which in the presence of high temperature and the catalyst material produces nitrogen (N) and carbon dioxide (CO_2).

5   Catalytic converters that combine both types of catalysts in one assembly are known as "three-way catalysts" or TWCs. A TWC can reduce all three pollutants.

Evaporative Emissions Control (EVAP) system

6   The Evaporative Emissions Control (EVAP) system prevents fuel system vapors (which contain unburned hydrocarbons) from escaping into the atmosphere. On warm days, vapors trapped inside the fuel tank expand until the pressure reaches a certain threshold. Then the fuel vapors are routed from the fuel tank through the fuel vapor vent valve and the fuel vapor control valve to the EVAP canister, where they're stored temporarily until the next time the vehicle is operated. When the conditions are right (engine warmed up, vehicle up to speed, moderate or heavy load on the engine, etc.), the PCM opens the canister purge valve, which allows fuel vapors to be drawn from the canister into the intake manifold. Once in the intake manifold, the fuel vapors mix with incoming air before being drawn through the intake ports into the combustion chambers where they're burned up with the rest of the air/fuel mixture. The EVAP system is complex and virtually impossible to troubleshoot without the right tools and training.

Secondary Air Injection (AIR) system

7   Some models are equipped with a Secondary Air Injection (AIR) system. The AIR system is used to reduce tailpipe emissions on initial engine start-up. The system uses an electric motor/pump assembly, relay, vacuum valve/solenoid, air shut-off valve, check valves and tubing to inject fresh air directly into the exhaust manifolds. The fresh air (oxygen) reacts with the exhaust gas in the catalytic converter to reduce HC and CO levels. The air pump and solenoid are controlled by the PCM through the AIR relay. During initial start-up, the PCM energizes the AIR relay, the relay supplies battery voltage to the air pump and the vacuum valve/solenoid, engine vacuum is applied to the air shut-off valve which opens and allows air to flow through the tubing into the exhaust manifolds. The PCM will operate the air pump until closed loop operation is reached (approximately four minutes). During normal operation, the check valves prevent exhaust backflow into the system.

Powertrain Control Module (PCM)

8   The Powertrain Control Module (PCM) is the brain of the engine management system. It also controls a wide variety of other vehicle systems. In order to program the new PCM, the dealer needs the vehicle as well as the new PCM. If you're planning to replace the PCM with a new one, there is no point in trying to do so at home because you won't be able to program it yourself.

Positive Crankcase Ventilation (PCV) system

9   The Positive Crankcase Ventilation (PCV) system reduces hydrocarbon emissions by scavenging crankcase vapors, which are rich in unburned hydrocarbons. A PCV valve or orifice regulates the flow of gases into the intake manifold in proportion to the amount of intake vacuum available.

10   The PCV system generally consists of the fresh air inlet hose, the PCV valve or orifice and the crankcase ventilation hose (or PCV hose). The fresh air inlet hose connects the air intake duct to a pipe on the valve cover. The crankcase ventilation hose (or PCV hose) connects the PCV valve or orifice in the valve cover to the intake manifold.

11   On the vehicles covered by this manual, there are no serviceable components in the PCV system.

---

2   On Board Diagnosis (OBD) system

General description

1   All models are equipped with the second generation OBD-II system. This system consists of an on-board computer known as the Powertrain Control Module (PCM), and information sensors, which monitor various functions of the engine and send data to the PCM. This system incorporates a series of diagnostic monitors that detect and identify fuel injection and emissions control system faults and store the information in the computer memory. This system also tests sensors and output actuators, diagnoses drive cycles, freezes data and clears codes.

2   The PCM is the brain of the electronically controlled fuel and emissions system. It receives data from a number of sensors and other electronic components (switches, relays, etc.). Based on the information it receives, the PCM generates output signals to control various relays, solenoids (fuel injectors) and other actuators. The PCM is specifically calibrated to optimize the emissions, fuel economy and driveability of the vehicle.

3   It isn't a good idea to attempt diagnosis or replacement of the PCM or emission control components at home while the vehicle is under warranty. Because of a federally-mandated warranty which covers the emissions system components and because any owner-induced damage to the PCM, the sensors and/or the control devices may void this warranty, take the vehicle to a dealer service department if the PCM or a system component malfunctions.

Scan tool information

4   Because extracting the Diagnostic Trouble Codes (DTCs) from an engine management system is now the first step in troubleshooting many computer-controlled systems and components, a code reader, at the very least, will be required (see illustration). More powerful scan tools can also perform many of the diagnostics once associated with expensive factory scan tools (see illustration). If you're planning to obtain a generic scan tool for your vehicle, make sure that it's compatible with OBD-II systems. If you don't plan to purchase a code reader or scan tool and don't have access to one, you can have the codes extracted by a dealer service department or an independent repair shop.

Note: *Some auto parts stores even provide this service.*

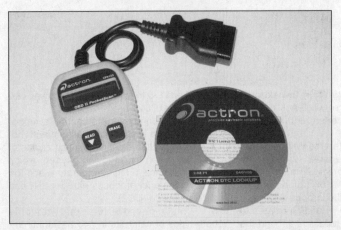

2.4a Simple code readers are an economical way to extract trouble codes when the CHECK ENGINE light comes on

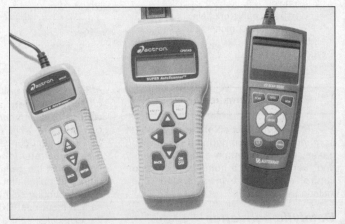

2.4b Hand-held scan tools like these can extract computer codes and also perform diagnostics

Information Sensors

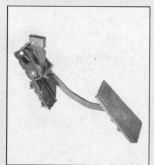

Accelerator Pedal Position (APP) sensor - as you press the accelerator pedal, the APP sensor alters its voltage signal to the PCM in proportion to the angle of the pedal, and the PCM commands a motor inside the throttle body to open or close the throttle plate accordingly

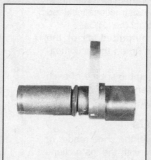

Camshaft Position (CMP) sensor - produces a signal that the PCM uses to identify the number 1 cylinder and to time the firing sequence of the fuel injectors

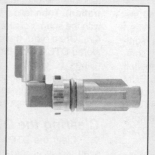

Crankshaft Position (CKP) sensor - produces a signal that the PCM uses to calculate engine speed and crankshaft position, which enables it to synchronize ignition timing with fuel injector timing, and to detect misfires

Engine Coolant Temperature (ECT) sensor - a thermistor (temperature-sensitive variable resistor) that sends a voltage signal to the PCM, which uses this data to determine the temperature of the engine coolant

Fuel tank pressure sensor - measures the fuel tank pressure and controls fuel tank pressure by signaling the EVAP system to purge the fuel tank vapors when the pressure becomes excessive

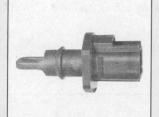

Intake Air Temperature (IAT) sensor - monitors the temperature of the air entering the engine and sends a signal to the PCM to determine injector pulse-width (the duration of each injector's on-time) and to adjust spark timing (to prevent spark knock)

Knock sensor - a piezoelectric crystal that oscillates in proportion to engine vibration which produces a voltage output that is monitored by the PCM. This retards the ignition timing when the oscillation exceeds a certain threshold

Manifold Absolute Pressure (MAP) sensor - monitors the pressure or vacuum inside the intake manifold. The PCM uses this data to determine engine load so that it can alter the ignition advance and fuel enrichment

Mass Air Flow (MAF) sensor - measures the amount of intake air drawn into the engine. It uses a hot-wire sensing element to measure the amount of air entering the engine

Oxygen sensors - generates a small variable voltage signal in proportion to the difference between the oxygen content in the exhaust stream and the oxygen content in the ambient air. The PCM uses this information to maintain the proper air/fuel ratio. A second oxygen sensor monitors the efficiency of the catalytic converter

Throttle Position (TP) sensor - a potentiometer that generates a voltage signal that varies in relation to the opening angle of the throttle plate inside the throttle body. Works with the PCM and other sensors to calculate injector pulse width (the duration of each injector's on-time)

Photos courtesy of Wells Manufacturing, except APP and MAF sensors.

3   Obtaining and clearing Diagnostic Trouble Codes (DTCs)

1   All models covered by this manual are equipped with on-board diagnostics. When the PCM recognizes a malfunction in a monitored emission or engine control system, component or circuit, it turns on the Malfunction Indicator Light (MIL) on the dash. The PCM will continue to display the MIL until the problem is fixed and the Diagnostic Trouble Code (DTC) is cleared from the PCM's memory. You'll need a scan tool to access any DTCs stored in the PCM.

2   Before outputting any DTCs stored in the PCM, thoroughly inspect ALL electrical connectors and hoses. Make sure that all electrical connections are tight, clean and free of corrosion. And make sure that all hoses are correctly connected, fit tightly and are in good condition (no cracks or tears).

Accessing the DTCs

3   The Diagnostic Trouble Codes (DTCs) can only be accessed with a code reader or scan tool. Professional scan tools are expensive, but relatively inexpensive generic code readers or scan tools **(see illustrations 2.4a and 2.4b)** are available at most auto parts stores. Simply plug the connector of the scan tool into the diagnostic connector **(see illustration)**. Then follow the instructions included with the scan tool to extract the DTCs.

4   Once you have outputted all of the stored DTCs, look them up on the accompanying DTC chart.

5   After troubleshooting the source of each DTC, make any necessary repairs or replace the defective component(s).

Clearing the DTCs

6   Clear the DTCs with the code reader or scan tool in accordance with the instructions provided by the tool's manufacturer.

Diagnostic Trouble Codes

7   The accompanying tables are a list of the Diagnostic Trouble Codes (DTCs) that can be accessed by a do-it-yourselfer working at home (there are many, many more DTCs available to professional mechanics with proprietary scan tools and software, but those codes cannot be accessed by a generic scan tool). If, after you have checked and repaired the connectors, wire

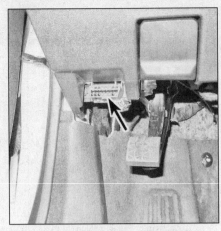

3.3 The Data Link Connector (DLC) is located under the lower edge of the dash, to the left of the steering column

harness and vacuum hoses (if applicable) for an emission-related system, component or circuit, the problem persists, have the vehicle checked by a dealer service department or other qualified repair shop.

OBD-II trouble codes

Code	Probable cause
P0008	Engine position system performance (bank 1)
P0009	Engine position system performance (bank 2)
P0010	Intake camshaft position actuator circuit open (bank 1)
P0011	"A" Camshaft position - timing over-advanced (bank 1)
P0013	"B" Camshaft position - actuator circuit malfunction (bank 1)
P0014	"B" Camshaft position - timing over-advanced (bank 1)
P0016	Crankshaft position/camshaft position, bank 1, sensor A - correlation
P0017	Crankshaft position/camshaft position, bank 1, sensor B - correlation
P0018	Crankshaft position/camshaft position, bank 2, sensor A - correlation
P0019	Crankshaft position/camshaft position, bank 2, sensor B - correlation
P0020	Intake camshaft position actuator circuit open (bank 2)
P0021	Intake camshaft position-timing over-advanced (bank 2)
P0023	"B" Camshaft position - actuator circuit (bank 2)
P0024	"B" Camshaft position - timing over-advanced or system performance problem (bank 2)
P0030	HO2S heater control circuit (bank 1, sensor 1)
P0031	HO2S heater control circuit low (bank 1, sensor 1)

Code	Probable cause
P0032	HO2S heater control circuit high (bank 1, sensor 1)
P0036	HO2S heater control circuit (bank 1 sensor 2)
P0037	HO2S heater control circuit low (bank 1, sensor 2)
P0038	HO2S heater control circuit high (bank 1, sensor 2)
P0050	HO2S heater control circuit (bank 2, sensor 1)
P0051	HO2S heater control circuit low (bank 2, sensor 1)
P0052	HO2S heater control circuit high (bank 2, sensor 1)
P0053	HO2S heater resistance (bank 1, sensor 1)
P0054	HO2S heater resistance (bank 1, sensor 2)
P0056	HO2S heater control circuit malfunction (bank 2, sensor 2)
P0057	HO2S heater control circuit low (bank 2, sensor 2)
P0058	HO2S heater control circuit high (bank 2, sensor 2)
P0068	Throttle Position (TP) sensor inconsistent with Mass Air Flow (MAF) sensor
P0100	Mass air flow or volume air flow circuit malfunction
P0101	Mass air flow or volume air flow circuit, range or performance problem
P0102	Mass air flow or volume air flow circuit, low input
P0103	Mass air flow or volume air flow circuit, high input
P0106	Manifold absolute pressure or barometric pressure circuit, range or performance problem
P0107	Manifold absolute pressure or barometric pressure circuit, low input
P0108	Manifold absolute pressure or barometric pressure circuit, high input
P0111	Intake air temperature circuit, range or performance problem
P0112	Intake air temperature circuit, low input
P0113	Intake air temperature circuit, high input
P0115	Engine coolant temperature circuit
P0116	Engine coolant temperature circuit range/performance problem
P0117	Engine coolant temperature circuit, low input
P0118	Engine coolant temperature circuit, high input
P0119	Engine coolant temperature circuit, intermittent
P0120	Throttle position or pedal position sensor/switch circuit malfunction
P0121	Throttle position or pedal position sensor/switch circuit, range or performance problem

OBD-II trouble codes (continued)

Code	Probable cause
P0122	Throttle position or pedal position sensor/switch circuit, low input
P0123	Throttle position or pedal position sensor/switch circuit, high input
P0125	Insufficient coolant temperature for closed loop fuel control
P0128	Coolant thermostat (coolant temperature below thermostat regulating temperature)
P0130	O2 sensor circuit malfunction (bank 1, sensor 1)
P0131	O2 sensor circuit, low voltage (bank 1, sensor 1)
P0132	O2 sensor circuit, high voltage (bank 1, sensor 1)
P0133	O2 sensor circuit, slow response (bank 1, sensor 1)
P0134	O2 sensor circuit - no activity detected (bank 1, sensor 1)
P0135	O2 sensor heater circuit malfunction (bank 1, sensor 1)
P0136	O2 sensor circuit (sensor 2) (5.3L V8)
P0137	O2 sensor circuit, low voltage (bank 1, sensor 2)
P0138	O2 sensor circuit, high voltage (bank 1, sensor 2)
P0139	O2 sensor circuit, slow response (bank 1, sensor 2)
P0140	O2 sensor circuit - no activity detected (bank 1, sensor 2)
P0141	O2 sensor heater circuit malfunction (bank 1, sensor 2)
P0151	O2 sensor circuit, low voltage (bank 2, sensor 1)
P0152	O2 sensor circuit, high voltage (bank 2, sensor 1)
P0153	O2 sensor circuit, slow response (bank 2, sensor 1)
P0154	O2 sensor circuit - no activity detected (bank 2, sensor 1)
P0155	O2 sensor heater circuit malfunction (bank 2, sensor 1)
P0157	O2 sensor circuit, low voltage (bank 2, sensor 2)
P0158	O2 sensor circuit, high voltage (bank 2, sensor 2)
P0160	O2 sensor circuit - no activity detected (bank 2, sensor 2)
P0161	O2 sensor heater circuit malfunction (bank 2, sensor 2)
P0171	System too lean (bank 1)
P0172	System too rich (bank 1)
P0191	Fuel rail pressure sensor performance
P0192	Fuel rail pressure sensor circuit low
P0201	Injector circuit malfunction - cylinder no. 1

Code	Probable cause
P0202	Injector circuit malfunction - cylinder no. 2
P0203	Injector circuit malfunction - cylinder no. 3
P0204	Injector circuit malfunction - cylinder no. 4
P0218	Transmission overheating condition
P0220	Throttle position or accelerator pedal position sensor/switch B circuit malfunction
P0221	Throttle position or accelerator pedal position sensor/switch B, range or performance problem
P0222	Throttle position or accelerator pedal position sensor/switch B circuit, low input
P0223	Throttle position or accelerator pedal position sensor/switch B circuit, high input
P0230	Fuel pump primary circuit malfunction
P0231	Fuel pump control circuit low
P0232	Fuel pump control circuit high
P023F	Fuel pump control circuit
P0234	Engine Overboost
P0236	Turbocharger boost sensor performance
P0237	Turbocharger boost sensor circuit low
P0238	Turbocharger boost sensor circuit high
P0243	Turbocharger wastegate solenoid valve control circuit
P0245	Turbocharger wastegate solenoid valve control circuit low
P0246	Turbocharger wastegate solenoid valve control circuit high
P0261	Cylinder no. 1 injector circuit, low
P0262	Cylinder no. 1 injector circuit, high
P0264	Cylinder no. 2 injector circuit, low
P0265	Cylinder no. 2 injector circuit, high
P0267	Cylinder no. 3 injector circuit, low
P0268	Cylinder no. 3 injector circuit, high
P0270	Cylinder no. 4 injector circuit, low
P0271	Cylinder no. 4 injector circuit, high
P0299	Engine underboost
P0300	Random/multiple cylinder misfire detected
P0301	Cylinder no. 1 misfire detected

OBD-II trouble codes (continued)

Code	Probable cause
P0302	Cylinder no. 2 misfire detected
P0303	Cylinder no. 3 misfire detected
P0304	Cylinder no. 4 misfire detected
P0315	Crankshaft position system - variation not learned
P0324	Knock control system error
P0325	Knock sensor no. 1 circuit malfunction (bank 1 or single sensor)
P0326	Knock sensor no. 1 circuit, range or performance problem (bank 1 or single sensor)
P0327	Knock sensor no. 1 circuit, low input (bank 1 or single sensor)
P0328	Knock sensor no. 1 circuit, high input (bank 1 or single sensor)
P0330	Knock sensor no. 2 circuit malfunction (bank 2)
P0331	Knock sensor no. 2 circuit, range or performance problem (bank 2)
P0332	Knock sensor no. 2 circuit, low input (bank 2)
P0333	Knock sensor no. 2 circuit, high input (bank 2)
P0335	Crankshaft position sensor "A" - circuit malfunction
P0336	Crankshaft position sensor "A" - range or performance problem
P0338	Crankshaft position sensor "A" - high input
P0340	Camshaft position sensor "A" - circuit malfunction (bank 1)
P0341	Camshaft position sensor "A" - range or performance problem (bank 1)
P0342	Camshaft position sensor "A" - low input (bank 1)
P0343	Camshaft position sensor "A" - high input (bank 1)
P0346	Camshaft position sensor "A" - range/performance problem (bank 2)
P0347	Camshaft position sensor "A" - low input (bank 2)
P0348	Camshaft position sensor "A" - range/performance problem (bank 2)
P0351	Ignition coil 1 primary or secondary circuit malfunction
P0352	Ignition coil 2 primary or secondary circuit malfunction
P0353	Ignition coil 3 primary or secondary circuit malfunction
P0354	Ignition coil 4 primary or secondary circuit malfunction
P0366	Camshaft position sensor "B" - range/performance problem (bank 1)
P0367	Camshaft position sensor "B" - low input (bank 1)
P0368	Camshaft position sensor "B" circuit high input (bank 1)

Code	Probable cause
P0391	Camshaft position sensor "B" - range/performance problem (bank 2)
P0392	Camshaft position sensor "B" - low input (bank 2)
P0393	Camshaft position sensor "B" - high input (bank 2)
P0401	Exhaust gas recirculation - insufficient flow detected
P0403	Exhaust gas recirculation - circuit malfunction
P0404	Exhaust gas recirculation - range or performance problem
P0405	Exhaust gas recirculation valve position sensor A - circuit low
P0406	Exhaust gas recirculation valve position sensor A - circuit high
P0420	Catalyst system efficiency below threshold (bank 1)
P0430	Catalyst system efficiency below threshold (bank 2)
P0442	Evaporative emission control system, small leak detected
P0443	Evaporative emission control system, purge control valve circuit malfunction
P0446	Evaporative emission control system, vent control circuit malfunction
P0449	Evaporative emission control system, vent valve/solenoid circuit malfunction
P0450	Evaporative emission control system, pressure sensor malfunction
P0451	Evaporative emission control system, pressure sensor range or performance problem
P0452	Evaporative emission control system, pressure sensor low input
P0453	Evaporative emission control system, pressure sensor high input
P0454	Evaporative emission control system, pressure sensor intermittent
P0455	Evaporative emission (EVAP) control system leak detected (no purge flow or large leak)
P0458	Evaporative emission control system, purge control valve - circuit low
P0459	Evaporative emission control system, purge control valve - circuit high
P0461	Fuel level sensor circuit, range or performance problem
P0462	Fuel level sensor circuit, low input
P0463	Fuel level sensor circuit, high input
P0464	Fuel level sensor circuit, intermittent
P0480	Cooling fan no. 1, control circuit malfunction
P0481	Cooling fan no. 2, control circuit malfunction
P0496	Evaporative emission system - high purge flow
P0497	Evaporative emission system - low purge flow

OBD-II trouble codes (continued)

Code	Probable cause
P0498	Evaporative emission system, vent control - circuit low
P0499	Evaporative emission system, vent control - circuit high
P0506	Idle control system, rpm lower than expected
P0507	Idle control system, rpm higher than expected
P0513	Incorrect immobilizer key
P0520	Engine oil pressure sensor/switch circuit malfunction
P0532	A/C refrigerant pressure sensor, low input
P0533	A/C refrigerant pressure sensor, high input
P0556	Brake booster pressure sensor performance problem
P0557	Brake booster pressure sensor circuit - low voltage
P0558	Brake booster pressure sensor circuit - high voltage
P0562	System voltage low
P0563	System voltage high
P0571	Cruise control/brake switch A, circuit malfunction
P0572	Cruise control/brake switch A, circuit low
P0573	Cruise control/brake switch A, circuit high
P0575	Cruise control system - input circuit malfunction
P0601	Internal control module, memory check sum error
P0602	Control module, programming error
P0603	Internal control module, keep alive memory (KAM) error
P0604	Internal control module, random access memory (RAM) error
P0606	PCM processor fault
P0607	Control module performance
P0615	Starter relay - circuit malfunction
P0616	Starter relay - circuit low
P0617	Starter relay - circuit high
P0621	Alternator L terminal circuit malfunction
P0622	Alternator F terminal circuit malfunction
P0625	Alternator field terminal - circuit low
P0626	Alternator field terminal - circuit high

Code	Probable cause
P0627	Fuel pump control - circuit open
P0628	Fuel pump control - circuit low
P0629	Fuel pump control - circuit high
P0633	Immobilizer key not programmed - ECM
P0634	ECM/TCM - internal temperature too high
P0638	Throttle actuator control range/performance problem (bank 1)
P0641	Sensor reference voltage A - circuit open
P0642	Engine control module (ECM), knock control - defective
P0643	Sensor reference voltage A - circuit high
P0644	Driver display, serial communication - circuit malfunction
P0645	A/C clutch relay control circuit
P0650	Malfunction indicator lamp (MIL), control circuit malfunction
P0651	Sensor reference voltage B - circuit open
P0653	Sensor reference voltage B - circuit high
P0667	ECM/TCM internal temperature sensor - circuit range/performance problem
P0668	ECM/TCM internal temperature sensor - circuit low
P0669	ECM/TCM internal temperature sensor - circuit high
P0685	ECM power relay, control - circuit open
P0686	ECM power relay control - circuit low
P0687	Engine, control relay - short to ground
P0689	ECM power relay sense - circuit low
P0690	ECM power relay sense - circuit high
P0691	Engine coolant blower motor 1 - short to ground
P0700	Transmission control system malfunction
P0703	Torque converter/brake switch B, circuit malfunction
P0705	Transmission range sensor, circuit malfunction (PRNDL input)
P0711	Transmission fluid temperature sensor circuit, range or performance problem
P0712	Transmission fluid temperature sensor circuit, low input
P0713	Transmission fluid temperature sensor circuit, high input
P0717	Input/turbine speed sensor circuit, no signal

OBD-II trouble codes (continued)

Code	Probable cause
P0722	Output speed sensor circuit, no signal
P0727	Engine speed input circuit, no signal
P0730	Incorrect gear ratio
P0731	Incorrect gear ratio, first gear
P0732	Incorrect gear ratio, second gear
P0733	Incorrect gear ratio, third gear
P0734	Incorrect gear ratio, fourth gear
P0735	Incorrect gear ratio, fifth gear
P0736	Incorrect gear ratio, reverse gear
P0741	Torque converter clutch, circuit performance problem or stuck in Off position
P0742	Torque converter clutch circuit, stuck in On position
P0762	Shift solenoid C, stuck in On position
P0962	Pressure control (PC) solenoid A - control circuit low
P0963	Pressure control (PC) solenoid A - control circuit high
P0966	Pressure control (PC) solenoid B - control circuit low
P0967	Pressure control (PC) solenoid B - control circuit high
P0970	Pressure control (PC) solenoid C - control circuit low
P0971	Pressure control (PC) solenoid C - control circuit high
P0973	Shift solenoid (SS) A - control circuit low
P0974	Shift solenoid (SS) A - control circuit high
P0976	Shift solenoid (SS) B - control circuit low
P0977	Shift solenoid (SS) B - control circuit high
P0979	Shift solenoid (SS) C - control circuit low
P0980	Shift solenoid (SS) C - control circuit high
P0982	Shift solenoid (SS) D - control circuit low
P0983	Shift solenoid (SS) D - control circuit high
P0985	Shift solenoid (SS) E - control circuit low
P0986	Shift solenoid (SS) E - control circuit high
P1176	Fuel pump driver control module 5v reference 1 circuit
P1177	Fuel pump driver control module 5v reference 2 circuit

Code	Probable cause
P2122	Accelerator position sensor 1 circuit low
P2123	Accelerator position sensor 1 circuit high
P2127	Accelerator position sensor 2 circuit low
P2128	Accelerator position sensor 2 circuit high
P2138	Accelerator position sensors 1-2 not plausable
P2199	Intake air temperature sensors 1-2 not plausible
P2227	Barometric pressure sensor performance
P2228	Barometric pressure sensor circuit low
P2229	Barometric pressure sensor circuit high
P2230	Barometric pressure sensor circuit erratic
P2261	Turbocharger bypass valve stuck (mechanical)
P2618	Crankshaft position signal output circuit low
P2619	Crankshaft position signal output circuit high

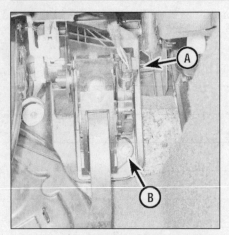

4.2 Disconnect the electrical connector (A) and remove the mounting bolt (B)

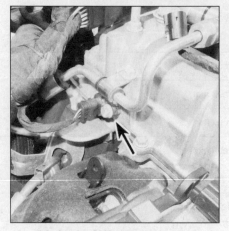

5.3a Intake CMP sensor location (1.5L engines)

5.3b Exhaust CMP sensor location (1.5L engines)

4   Accelerator Pedal Position (APP) sensor - replacement

Note: *The APP sensor is located at the top of the accelerator pedal arm. The APP sensor and the accelerator pedal are a one-piece assembly and are replaced as a unit.*

Note: *On some models, a trim panel may have to be removed to gain access to the APP sensor.*

1   Locate the APP sensor connector at the top of the accelerator pedal assembly.
2   Disconnect the electrical connector from the APP sensor **(see illustration)**.
3   Remove the APP sensor mounting bolt and rotate the bottom of the assembly upwards to remove remove from the vehicle. The sensor and accelerator pedal are a single assembly.
4   Installation is the reverse of removal. Tighten the APP sensor assembly mounting bolt securely.

5   Camshaft Position (CMP) sensor - replacement

Note: *1.5L engines use two CMP sensors: one for the intake camshaft, and one for the exhaust camshaft. The intake sensor is located at the left-rear corner of the valve cover. The exhaust sensor is located on the top of the left-front corner of the valve cover.*

Note: *2.0L and 2.5L engines use two CMP sensors: one for the intake camshaft, and one for the exhaust camshaft. The intake sensor is located at the left end of the cylinder head, above the transaxle. The exhaust sensor is located on the left front side of the cylinder head.*

1   Remove the engine cover.
2   On 2.0L engines, to access the intake CMP sensor, remove the turbocharger ducting between the throttle body and the charge air cooler (see Chapter 4, Section 15).
3   On all models, depress the tab and disconnect the CMP sensor electrical connector **(see illustrations)**.

4   Remove the CMP mounting boltand remove the sensor.
5   Inspect the CMP sensor O-ring and replace if damaged.
6   Installation is the reverse of removal. Lubricate the O-ring with a film of clean engine oil, and tighten the CMP sensor bolt securely.

6   Camshaft position actuator solenoid valve - replacement

Note: *All models use two camshaft position actuators (one intake and one exhaust). The actuators are located at the top right end of the valve cover.*

1   Remove the engine cover.
2   Disconnect the electrical connectors from the actuators **(see illustration)**.
3   Remove the solenoid mounting bolt(s) and remove the solenoid(s).
4   Inspect the O-ring and replace if damaged.
5   Installation is the reverse of removal. Lubricate the O-ring with a film of clean engine oil, and tighten the sensor bolt securely.

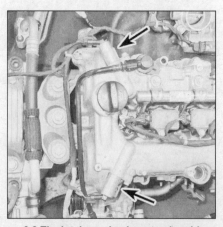

6.2 The intake and exhaust solenoid valves are located at the end of the valve cover (1.5L engine shown)

7   Crankshaft Position (CKP) sensor - replacement-

Note: *If the Malfunction Indicator Light (MIL) comes on after replacing the CKP sensor and starting the engine, drive the vehicle to a dealer or other qualified repair shop and have the crankshaft position variation learn procedure performed with a factory scan tool.*

Note: *On 1.5L engines, the CKP sensor is located in the engine block near the flywheel, facing the rear of the vehicle. On 2.0L and 2.5L engines, the CKP sensor is located in the engine block near the flywheel, facing the rear of the vehicle, behind the starter.*

1   Raise and support the front of the vehicle on jackstands.
2   On 2.0L and 2.5L engines, remove the starter to access the CKP sensor (see Chapter 5, Section 8).
3   On all models, disconnect the CKP electrical connector.
4   Remove the CKP sensor mounting bolt and remove the sensor **(see illustration)**.
5   Inspect the O-ring and replace if damaged.

7.4 Identifying the CKP sensor location (1.5L engines)

8.3a Slide the locking tab out and disconnect the electrical connector. . .

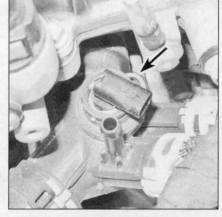

8.3b. . . and pull the clip to remove the sensor from the engine (1.5L engine shown, others similar)

8.8 Location of radiator mounted ECT sensor

6　Installation is the reverse of removal. Lubricate the O-ring with a film of clean engine oil, and tighten the sensor bolt securely.

8　Engine Coolant Temperature (ECT) sensor - replacement

Warning: *Wait until the engine is completely cool before beginning this procedure.*
Note: *The ECT sensor is installed in the water outlet at the left end of the cylinder head. Some models are equipped with a second sensor, mounted on the passenger's side of the radiator tank.*

1　Drain the cooling system to a level that's below the level of the ECT sensor (see Chapter 1).

Water oultet

2　On 1.5L engines, remove the turbocharger ducting between the throttle body and charge air cooler (see Chapter 4, Section 15).
3　Disconnect the ECT electrical connector and pull the retaining clip to remove the sensor **(see illustrations)**.
4　Inspect the O-ring and replace if damaged.
5　Installation is the reverse of removal. Refill the cooling system (see Chapter 1).

Radiator

Note: *On some models a second ECT sensor is installed in the radiator on the passenger's side lower corner.*

6　Loosen the right-front wheel lug nuts, then raise and support the front of the vehicle on jackstands.
7　Remove the wheel and the inner fender splash shield (see Chapter 11).
8　Locate the sensor in the side of the radiator tank **(see illustration)**.
9　Disconnect the ECT electrical connector and pull the retaining clip to remove the sensor.
10　Inspect the O-ring and replace if damaged.

11　Installation is the reverse of removal. Refill the cooling system (see Chapter 1).

9　Knock sensor - replacement

Warning: *Wait until the engine is completely cool before beginning this procedure.*
Note: *The knock sensors are located on the back side of the engine block.*

1　Raise the front of the vehicle and support it securely on jackstands.
2　On 2015 and earlier 2.0L and 2.5L engines, remove the secondary air injection pump (see Section 18).
3　On 2016 and later 2.0L models, to access the rear sensor, remove the starter (see Chapter 5, Section 8).
4　On all models, locate and disconnect the electrical connector from the knock sensor **(see illustration)**.
5　Remove the knock sensor retaining bolt and remove the sensor.
6　Installation is the reverse of removal. Tighten the knock sensor retaining bolt to the torque listed in this Chapter's Specifications.

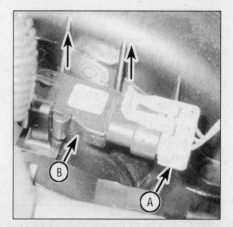

9.4 Knock sensor locations (1.5L engines)

10　Manifold Absolute Pressure (MAP) sensor - replacement

Note: *If the Malfunction Indicator Light (MIL) comes on after replacing the sensor and starting the engine, drive the vehicle to a dealer or other qualified repair shop and have the intake system learned values reset with a factory scan tool.*
Note: *On 2.0L and 2.5L engines, the MAP sensor is located on the right end of the intake manifold. 1.5L engines are not equipped with a MAP sensor.*

1　Remove the engine cover.
2　If you're working on a 2.0L model, remove the charge air cooler outlet duct (see Chapter 4, Section 15).
3　If you're working on a 2.5L engine, remove the air filter resonator and outlet duct.
4　Locate and disconnect the electrical connector from the MAP sensor.
5　Twist and pull the sensor from the intake manifold **(see illustration)**.
6　Inspect the O-ring and replace if damaged.
7　Installation is the reverse of removal.

10.5 Disconnect the electrical connector from the MAF sensor (A), then pull the sensor (B) from the intake manifold

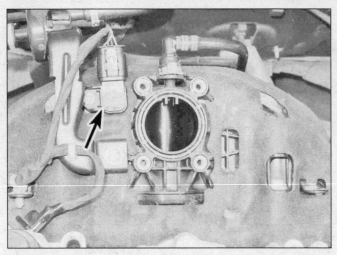

11.2 Location of the Intake Air Pressure and Temperature sensor (1.5L engines)

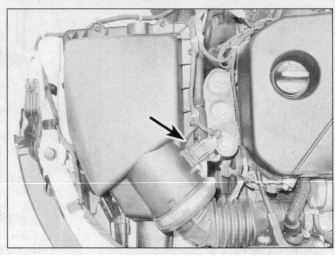

12.1 Identifying the MAF sensor location (1.5L engines)

11   Intake Air Pressure and Temperature sensor - replacement

Note: *If the Malfunction Indicator Light (MIL) comes on after replacing the sensor and starting the engine, drive the vehicle to a dealer and have the service department perform a intake system learned values reset with a factory scan tool.*

Note: *On 1.5L engines, the sensor is located on the intake manifold, next to the throttle body. On 2.0L engines, the sensor is located in the turbocharger duct just before the throttle body. 2.5L engines are not equipped with this sensor.*

1   Remove the engine cover.
2   Locate and disconnect electrical connector from the MAP sensor **(see illustration)**.
3   Remove the MAP sensor retaining screwand remove the sensor.
4   Inspect the O-ring and replace if damaged.
5   Installation is the reverse of removal.

12   Mass Air Flow (MAF) sensor - replacement

Note: *The MAF sensor is located on the air filter housing. The sensor fits into a hole in the housing.*

1   Locate and disconnect the electrical connector from the MAF sensor **(see illustration)**.
2   Remove the screws and detach the MAF sensor from the filter housing cover.
3   Installation is the reverse of removal.

13   Oxygen sensors - replacement

Caution: *Because it is installed in the exhaust manifold or pipe, both of which contract when cool, an oxygen sensor might be very difficult to loosen when the engine is cold. Rather than*

risk damage to the sensor or its mounting threads, start and run the engine for a minute or two, then shut it off. Be careful not to burn yourself during the following procedure.

Note: *All models are equipped with two oxygen sensors - upstream and downstream. On 1.5L engines, the upstream sensor is located in the turbocharger outlet elbow, and the downstream sensor is located on the side of the catalytic converter. On 2.0L engines, the upstream sensor is located in the turbo outlet just before the catalytic converter and the downstream sensor is located in the exhaust pipe just after the catalytic converter. On 2.5L engines, the upstream sensor is located in the exhaust manifold and the downstream sensor is located below the catalytic converter.*

1   Be particularly careful when servicing an oxygen sensor:
 a) *Oxygen sensors have a permanently attached pigtail and an electrical connector that cannot be removed. Damaging or removing the pigtail or electrical connector will render the sensor useless.*
 b) *Keep grease, dirt and other contaminants away from the electrical connector and the louvered end of the sensor.*

 c) *Do not use cleaning solvents of any kind on an oxygen sensor.*
 d) *Oxygen sensors are extremely delicate. Do not drop a sensor or handle it roughly.*
 e) *Make sure that the silicone boot on the sensor is installed in the correct position. Otherwise, the boot might melt and it might prevent the sensor from operating correctly.*

Upstream oxygen sensors

2   Remove the engine cover.
3   Disconnect the upstream oxygen sensor electrical connector, and unclip it from any retainers **(see illustration)**.
4   Remove the upstream oxygen sensor.
5   If you're going to install the old sensor, apply anti-seize compound to the threads of the sensor to facilitate future removal. If you're going to install a new oxygen sensor, it's necessary to apply anti-seize compound to the threads; the threads on new sensors already have anti-seize compound on them.
6   Installation is the reverse of removal. Tighten the oxygen sensor to the torque listed in this Chapter's Specifications.

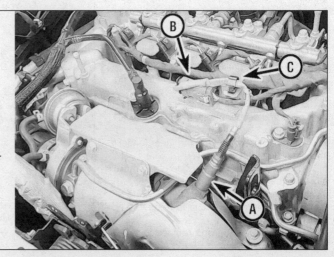

13.3 Upstream oxygen sensor located in the turbocharger outlet (1.5L engine)

A   *Oxygen Sensor*
B   *Electrical connector*
C   *Sensor harness retainer*

13.9a The downstream oxygen sensor is located in the side of the catalytic converter (1.5L engine shown)

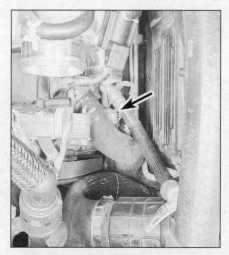

13.9b On 1.5L engines, the downstream oxygen sensor connector is accessed from the top of the engine compartment

14.6a Remove the PCM bracket retaining bolt. . .

Downstream oxygen sensors

7 Raise the vehicle and support it securely on jackstands.

8 On 1.5L engines, the turbocharger heat shield and turbocharger ducting to the throttle body needs to be removed to access the connector (see Chapter 4, Section 15).

9 Locate the downstream oxygen sensor (see illustration), then trace the lead up to the electrical connector and disconnect the connector (see illustration).

10 Unscrew the downstream oxygen sensor.

11 If you're going to install the old sensor, apply anti-seize compound to the threads of the sensor to facilitate future removal. If you're going to install a new oxygen sensor, it's not necessary to apply anti-seize compound to the threads. The threads on new sensors already have anti-seize compound on them.

12 Installation is the reverse of removal. Tighten the oxygen sensor to the torque listed in this Chapter's Specifications.

14 Powertrain Control Module (PCM) and Transmission Control Module (TCM) - removal and installation

Caution: *To avoid electrostatic discharge damage to the PCM, handle the PCM only by its case. Do not touch the electrical terminals during removal and installation. If available, ground yourself to the vehicle with an anti-static ground strap, available at computer supply stores.*

Note: *The procedures in this section apply only to disconnecting, removing and installing the PCM that is already installed in your vehicle. If, however, you need to replace the PCM or TCM, it must be programmed with new software and calibrations. This procedure requires the use of GM's TECH-2 scan tool and GM's latest PCM-programming software, so you WILL NOT BE ABLE TO REPLACE THE PCM OR TCM AT HOME.*

Note: *The PCM is located on the left side of*

the engine compartment in front of the master cylinder.

1 Disconnect the cable from the negative terminal of the battery (see Chapter 5).

2015 and earlier models (and 2016 Malibu Limited)

2 Disconnect the electrical connectors from the PCM (see illustrations 14.7a and 14.7b).

3 Release the tab and pull the PCM and bracket up and out of the vehicle.

4 Release the tab and remove the PCM from the bracket.

5 Installation is the reverse of removal.

2016 and later models (except Malibu Limited)

6 Remove the retaining bolt and lift the top of the PCM bracket off (see illustrations).

7 Disconnect the electrical connectors from the PCM (see illustrations).

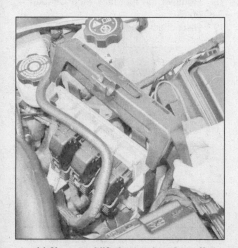

14.6b. . . and lift the top bracket off of the PCM

14.7a Slide the connector lock (A) back, depress the release tab (B). . .

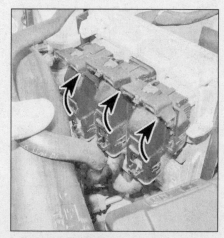

14.7b. . . swing the locking lever open, then unplug the connector

8   Remove the PCM with the bottom bracket attached (**see illustration**).
9   Remove the bracket from the PCM (**see illustration**).
10   Installation is the reverse of removal.

15   Catalytic converter - replacement

Warning: *Replace catalytic converters only after enough time has elapsed after driving the vehicle to allow the system components to cool completely. Also, when working under the vehicle, make sure it is securely supported on jackstands.*
Note: *The following is a generalized procedure for most catalytic converters on non-turbocharged engines. The specifics vary among the engines used in these vehicles. For removing the converter in turbocharged engines, see Chapter 4, Section 15.*
Note: *Many exhaust specialist shops are able to replace catalytic converters at a lower cost than what you might pay for a new one from a dealer.*
1   Raise the vehicle and support it securely on jackstands.
2   Disconnect the electrical connector from the related oxygen sensor and remove the sensor (see Section 13).
3   Support the other sections of the exhaust system as necessary.
4   Remove the retaining nuts from the front and rear catalyst mounting flanges.
Note: *Apply penetrating oil to the fasteners and allow it to soak in awhile before attempting to remove them.*
5   Remove the catalyst and pull off the gaskets.
6   Installation is the reverse of removal. Replace any rusted or damaged fasteners along with the gaskets.

16   Evaporative Emissions Control (EVAP) system - component replacement

EVAP canister purge control solenoid valve

Note: *The solenoid valve is located on the back of the intake manifold.*

14.8 Remove the PCM and lower bracket from the vehicle

1   Locate and disconnect the electrical connector from the valve (**see illustration**).
2   Disconnect the hoses (**see illustration**). See Chapter 4 for information on quick-connect fittings.
3   Slide the purge valve off its mounting bracket and remove it.
4   Installation is the reverse of removal.

EVAP canister vent solenoid valve

Note: *The EVAP vent solenoid is located on the EVAP canister.*
5   Remove the EVAP canister from the vehicle.
6   To remove the valve, twist it counterclockwise (**see illustration**).
7   Installation is the reverse of removal.

Fuel tank pressure sensor

2015 and earlier models (and 2016 Malibu Limited)

Note: *On 2015 and earlier models (and 2016 Malibu Limited), the fuel tank pressure sensor is located on the top of the fuel pump module (NU5) or on the side of the EVAP canister (NU6).*
8   To replace the sensor on NU5 models, remove the fuel tank, disconnect the sensor connector and release the tab to remove the sensor from the fuel pump module.
9   To replace the sensor on NU6 mod-

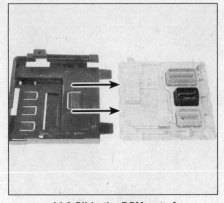

14.9 Slide the PCM out of the lower bracket

els, loosen the left-rear wheel lug nuts, then raise and support the vehicle on jackstands. Remove the wheel. Remove the under-cover below the EVAP canister. Locate the sensor on the side of the EVAP canister. Disconnect the sensor connector and release the tab to remove the sensor from the canister.
10   Inspect the O-ring and replace if damaged.
11   Installation is reverse of removal.

2016 and later models (except Malibu Limited)

Note: *On 2016 through 2018 models, the sensor is located on top of the EVAP canister. On 2019 models, the sensor is attached to the top of the fuel tank.*
12   Remove the fuel tank (see Chapter 4, Section 6).
13   Locate the sensor and remove the cover by releasing the retaining tabs (**see illustration**).
14   Disconnect the electrical connector and remove the sensor.
15   Inspect the O-ring and replace if damaged.
16   Installation is reverse of removal.

EVAP canister

17   Raise the vehicle and support it securely on jackstands.
18   Remove the fuel tank (see Chapter 4, Section 6).
19   Disconnect the electrical connector and

16.1 Identifying the location of the EVAP purge solenoid valve (1.5L engine shown)

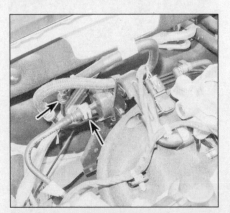

16.2 Disconnect the EVAP purge solenoid valve hoses (1.5L engine shown)

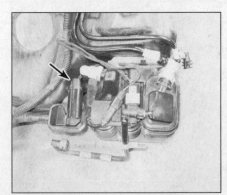

16.6 Location of the EVAP canister vent solenoid (2016 and later model shown [except Malibu Limited])

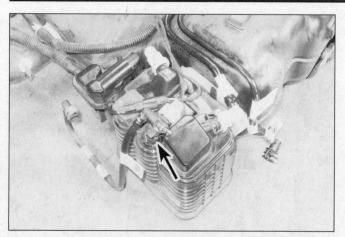

16.13 Identifying fuel tank pressure sensor on EVAP canister (2016 through 2018 models shown)

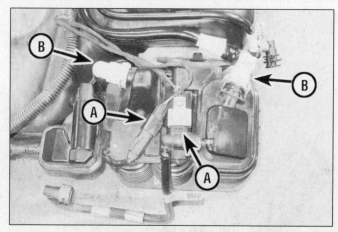

16.19 Disconnect the EVAP canister electrical connectors (A) and hoses (B) (2016 and later model shown)

hoses from the EVAP canister **(see illustration)**.

20   Use a screwdriver to pry the EVAP canister upwards and remove the canister from the fuel tank **(see illustrations)**.

21   Installation is the reverse of removal.

EVAP canister filter

Note: *2016 and later models (except Malibu Limited) are equipped with an external EVAP canister filter. The EVAP canister filter is attached to the fuel filler pipe.*

22   Loosen the right-rear wheel lug nuts, then raise and support the rear of the vehicle and secure on jackstands.

23   Remove the wheel.

24   Remove the inner fender liner (see Chapter 11).

25   Locate the canister filter and disconnect the quick-connect fitting **(see illustration)**.

26   Cut the zip-ties and remove the filter and hose.

27   Installation is reverse of removal. Use new zip-ties in the original locations to attach the filter.

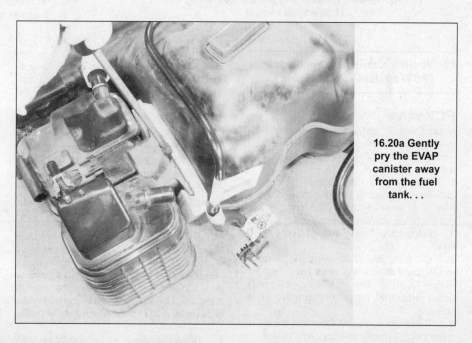

16.20a Gently pry the EVAP canister away from the fuel tank. . .

16.20b. . . and remove the EVAP canister (2016 and later model shown)

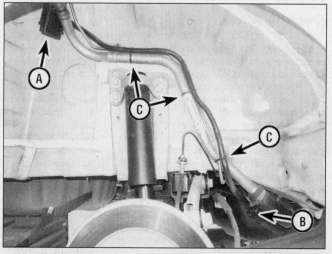

16.25 EVAP canister filter components (2016 and later models [except Malibu Limited])

A   Canister filter   B   Quick-connect fitting   C   Zip-ties

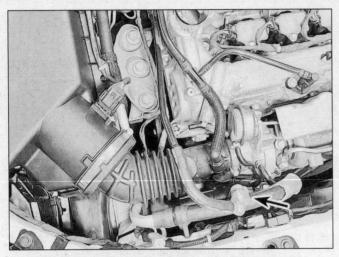

17.2 Remove the fastener and pull the PCV fitting out (1.5L engine shown)

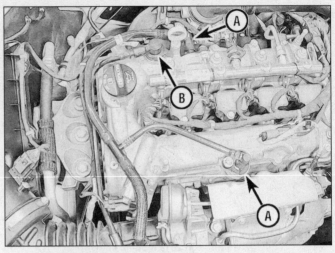

17.7 Identifying PCV components (1.5L engine shown)

A   *Fresh air valves*   B   *PCV valve*

17   Positive Crankcase Ventilation (PCV) system - replacement

PCV valve

Note: *On 2.0L and 2.5L engines, the PCV valve is broken during removal and cannot be reused. A new PCV valve and hose assembly will have to be used.*

1   Remove the engine cover.
2   Remove the bolt securing the end of the PCV hose assembly to the intake system and pull the fitting out **(see illustration)**.
3   Inspect the O-ring and replace if damaged.
4   On 2.0L and 2.5L engines, remove the PCV valve from the valve cover using a prybar type tool. The PCV valve will break apart; remove the piece from the valve cover opening.
5   Press the new PCV valve into the valve cover using firm pressure until fully seated.

Fresh air valves

Note: *1.5L engines and 2.5L engines are equipped with two fresh air valves. 2.0L engines have three fresh air valves. All fresh air valves are located on the valve cover.*

6   Remove the engine cover.
7   Locate the fresh air valves on the valve cover **(see illustration)**.
8   On 2.0L and 2.5L engines, disconnect the quick-connect fittings from the fresh air valves and remove the hose assembly. On 1.5L engines, use a sharp tool to cut the ends of the hoses to remove from the valve nipples.
Note: *On some models, the fresh air hose assembly is attached to the valve cover with a bolt.*
9   On all models, remove the fastener and pull the fresh air valve from the valve cover **(see illustration)**.
10   Inspect the O-ring and replace if damaged.
11   Remove the fresh air hose from the air

intake system. On 1.5L engines, it is recommended to leave it connected to the intake air duct. If the hose assembly requires replacement, cut the hose fitting to remove from the duct fitting.
12   Installation is the reverse of removal.

18   Secondary Air Injection Pump and Valve - component replacement

Note: *Secondary Air Injection is only used on 2014 and earlier 2.5L engines.*

Air pump

Note: *The secondary air pump and valve is mounted on the rear of the engine block. The secondary air injection pipe is located at the front of engine, just above the exhaust manifold. The secondary air injection valve is mounted on the front of the engine on the cylinder head.*

1   Raise the vehicle and support it securely on jackstands.
2   Remove the rear transaxle mount (see Chapter 7, Section 13).
3   Disconnect the secondary air injection pump feed tube by removing the feed tube bracket bolt and disconnecting the plastic collar at the pump by squeezing and pulling away from the pump.
4   Disconnect the secondary air injection pump inlet hose by disconnecting the plastic collar at the pump by squeezing and pulling away from the pump.
5   Remove the pump mounting bolts.
6   Disconnect the pump electrical connector.
7   Remove the secondary air injection pump.
8   Installation is the reverse of removal.

Check valve

9   Remove the engine cover.
10   Disconnect the secondary air injection pump feed tube by disconnecting the plastic

collar at the valve by squeezing and pulling away from the valve.
11   Remove the check valve mounting bolts.
12   Disconnect the valve electrical connector.
13   Remove the secondary air injection check valve and discard the gasket.
14   Installation is reverse of removal. Install a new gasket and tighten the bolts to the torque listed in this Chapter's Specifications.

19   Throttle Actuator Control (TAC) system - description

1   The Throttle Actuator Control (TAC) system, which is used on all vehicles, is an electronic throttle control system - there is no mechanically actuated accelerator cable. When the engine is running, the TAC system constantly monitors the position of the accelerator pedal and responds by constantly altering the position of the throttle plate inside the throttle body. The TAC system also handles cruise control functions.
2   The TAC system consists of three principal components: the Accelerator Pedal Position (APP) sensor, the Powertrain Control Module (PCM) and the throttle body. The replacement procedure for the APP sensor is covered in Section 4, the removal and installation procedure for the PCM is covered in Section 14 and the removal and installation procedure for the throttle body is covered in Chapter 4, Section 13.

20   Turbocharger boost pressure sensor - replacement

Note: *If the Malfunction Indicator Light (MIL) comes on after replacing the sensor and starting the engine, drive the vehicle to a dealer or other qualified repair shop and have the intake system learned values reset*

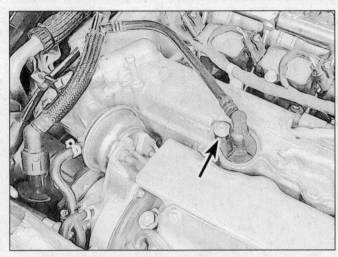

17.9 On 1.5L engines, cut a slot in the tamper proof fastener to allow removal with a screwdriver

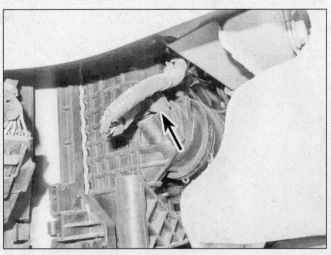

20.2 Location of the boost pressure sensor (1.5L engines)

with a factory scan tool.
Note: *On 1.5L engines, the boost pressure sensor is located on the front of the charge air cooler at the outlet. On 2.0L engines, the boost pressure sensor is located on the duct between the charge air cooler and the throttle body, under the wiper cowl.*
Note: *On 2.0L engines, the sensor also incorporates a temperature sensor.*
1   On 1.5L engines, remove the front

bumper cover to access the sensor (see Chapter 11, Section 9).
2   On all engines, locate the sensor and disconnect the electrical connector **(see illustration)**.
3   Remove the fastener and remove the sensor from the charge air cooler.
4   Inspect the O-ring and replace if damaged.
5   Installation is reverse of removal.

21 Transmission speed sensors - replacement

1   The speed sensors are incorporated with the valve body and deemed to be beyond the scope of this manual. It is therefore essential that problems with the automatic transaxle are referred to a dealer service department or other qualified repair facility for assessment.

Notes

Chapter 7
Automatic transaxle

Contents

Specifications

General

Fluid type and capacity	See Chapter 1
Transaxle and application	
6T40	1.5L engines (2016-2018), 2.5L engines
6T70	2.0L engines (2013-2015)
AF50-8	2.0L engine (2016)
9T50	2.0L engines (2017-2019)
VT40	1.5L engine (2019)

Torque specifications

Note: *One foot-pound (ft-lb) of torque is equivalent to 12 inch-pounds (in-lbs) of torque. Torque values below approximately 15 ft-lbs are expressed in inch-pounds, because most foot-pound torque wrenches are not accurate at these smaller values.*

	Ft-lbs (unless otherwise indicated)	Nm
Transaxle-to-engine bolts		
6T70	55	75
6T40, AF50-8, 9T50, VT40	43	58
Torque converter-to-driveplte bolts	46	62
Control valve solenoid body bolts *		
6T40		
M6 x 97	89 in-lbs	10
M5 x 40.5	71 in-lbs	8
6T70	106 in-lbs	12
AF50-8	89 in-lbs	10
9T50/VT40	71 in-lbs	8
Transaxle cooler line fasteners	16	22
Transaxle mount bolts		
Driver's side mount		
2015 and earlier models/2016 Malibu Limited		
Mount-to-transaxle		
Step 1	37	50
Step 2	Tighten an additional 90 degrees	
Mount-to-chassis	16	22
2016 and later models (except Malibu Limited)		
Mount-to-transaxle		
Step 1	74	100
Step 2	Tighten an additional 65 degrees	
Mount-to-chassis	74	100
Rear mount		
2015 and earlier models/2016 Malibu Limited		
Mount-to-bracket	77	105
Mount bracket-to-transaxle	74	100
Mount-to-subframe		
Step 1	74	100
Step 2	Tighten an additional 125 degrees	
2016 and later models (except Malibu Limited)		
Mount strut-to-bracket		
Step 1	74	100
Step 2	Tighten an additional 125 degrees	
Mount strut-to-subframe		
Step 1	52	70
Step 2	Tighten an additional 100 degrees	
Mount bracket-to-transaxle		
Step 1	74	100
Step 2	Tighten an additional 65 degrees	
Front mount (2015 and earlier models/2016 Malibu Limited)		
Mount-to-transaxle	46	62
Mount-to-subframe	77	105

* *Tighten by hand until snug, then tighten to specification.*

1   General information

1   Information on the automatic transaxle is included in this Chapter.

2   Because of the complexity of the automatic transaxles and the specialized equipment necessary to perform most service operations, this Chapter contains only those procedures related to general diagnosis, routine maintenance, adjustment and removal and installation.

3   If the transaxle requires major repair work, it should be left to a dealer service department or an automotive or transmission repair shop. Once properly diagnosed you can, however, remove and install the transaxle yourself and save the expense, even if the repair work is done by a transmission shop. Keep in mind, however, that transaxle removal is difficult on these models. Transmission shops are generally equipped with vehicle hoists and other specialized equipment that is necessary for transaxle removal.

2   Diagnosis - general

1   Automatic transaxle malfunctions may be caused by five general conditions:

   a) *Poor engine performance*
   b) *Improper adjustments*
   c) *Hydraulic malfunctions*
   d) *Mechanical malfunctions*
   e) *Malfunctions in the computer or its signal network*

2   Diagnosis of these problems should always begin with a check of the easily repaired items: fluid level and condition (see Chapter 1), shift cable adjustment and shift lever installation. Next, perform a road test to determine if the problem has been corrected or if more diagnosis is necessary. If the problem persists after the preliminary tests and corrections are completed, additional diagnosis should be performed by a dealer service department or other qualified transmission repair shop. Refer the *Troubleshooting section* at the front of this manual for information on symptoms of transaxle problems.

Preliminary checks

3   Drive the vehicle to warm the transaxle to normal operating temperature.

4   Check the fluid level (see Chapter 1):
If the fluid level is unusually low, add enough fluid to bring the level within the designated area of the dipstick, then check for external leaks (see following).

   a) *If the fluid level is abnormally high, drain off the excess, then check the drained fluid for contamination by coolant. The presence of engine coolant in the automatic transmission fluid indicates that a failure has occurred in the internal radiator oil cooler walls that separate the coolant from the transmission fluid (see Chapter 3).*
   b) *If the fluid is foaming, drain it and refill the transaxle, then check for coolant in the fluid, or a high fluid level.*

5   Check the engine idle speed.
Note: *If the engine is malfunctioning, do not proceed with the preliminary checks until it has been repaired and runs normally.*
6   Check and adjust the shift cable, if necessary (see Section 5).
7   If hard shifting is experienced, inspect the shift cable under the steering column and at the manual lever on the transaxle (see Section 5).

Fluid leak diagnosis

8   Most fluid leaks are easy to locate visually. Repair usually consists of replacing a seal or gasket. If a leak is difficult to find, the following procedure may help.

9   Identify the fluid. Make sure it's transmission fluid and not engine oil or brake fluid (automatic transmission fluid is a deep red color).

10   Try to pinpoint the source of the leak. Drive the vehicle several miles, then park it over a large sheet of cardboard. After a minute or two, you should be able to locate the leak by determining the source of the fluid dripping onto the cardboard.

11   Make a careful visual inspection of the suspected component and the area immediately around it. Pay particular attention to gasket mating surfaces. A mirror is often helpful for finding leaks in areas that are hard to see.

12   If the leak still cannot be found, clean the suspected area thoroughly with a degreaser or solvent, then dry it thoroughly.

13   Drive the vehicle for several miles at normal operating temperature and varying speeds. After driving the vehicle, visually inspect the suspected component again.

14   Once the leak has been located, the cause must be determined before it can be properly repaired. If a gasket is replaced but the sealing flange is bent, the new gasket will not stop the leak. The bent flange must be straightened.

15   Before attempting to repair a leak, check to make sure that the following conditions are corrected or they may cause another leak.
Note: *Some of the following conditions cannot be fixed without highly specialized tools and expertise. Such problems must be referred to a qualified transmission shop or a dealer service department.*

Gasket leaks

16   Check the pan periodically. Make sure the bolts are tight, no bolts are missing, the gasket is in good condition and the pan is flat (dents in the pan may indicate damage to the valve body inside).

17   If the pan gasket is leaking, the fluid level or the fluid pressure may be too high, the vent may be plugged, the pan bolts may be too tight, the pan sealing flange may be warped, the sealing surface of the transaxle housing may be damaged, the gasket may be damaged or the transaxle casting may be cracked or porous. If sealant instead of gasket material has been used to form a seal between the pan and the transaxle housing, it may be the wrong type of sealant.

Seal leaks

18   If a transaxle seal is leaking, the fluid level or pressure may be too high, the vent may be plugged, the seal bore may be damaged, the seal itself may be damaged or improperly installed, the surface of the shaft protruding through the seal may be damaged or a loose bearing may be causing excessive shaft movement.

19   Make sure the dipstick tube seal is in good condition and the tube is properly seated. Periodically check the area around the sensors for leakage. If transmission fluid is evident, check the seals for damage.

Case leaks

20   If the case itself appears to be leaking, the casting is porous and will have to be repaired or replaced.

21   Make sure the oil cooler hose fittings are tight and in good condition.

Fluid comes out vent pipe or fill tube

22   If this condition occurs, the possible causes are: the transaxle is overfilled, there is coolant in the fluid, the case is porous, the dipstick is incorrect, the vent is plugged or the drain-back holes are plugged.

3   Shift lever knob and boot - replacement

Warning: *These models are equipped with a Supplemental Restraint System (SRS), more commonly known as airbags. Always disable the airbag system before working in the vicinity of any airbag system component to avoid the possibility of accidental deployment of the airbag(s), which could cause personal injury (see Chapter 12).*

2015 and earlier models (and 2016 Malibu Limited)

Note: *The boot and knob are replaced as a single assembly.*
1   Squeeze the shift boot at the sides on each end, then using a trim tool or small, tape-wrapped flat-tipped screwdriver, separate the shift knob boot from the center console trim.
2   Disconnect the shift lever knob electrical connector.
3   Pull upwards on the knob while twisting to detach and remove the knob and boot assembly.
4   Installation is reverse of removal. Firmly push the shift knob onto the shift lever during installation and be sure the shift boot snaps into the console.

2016 and later models (except Malibu Limited)

5   Apply the parking brake and block the wheels so the vehicle can't roll.
6   Shift the transaxle shift lever into neutral (N) position.

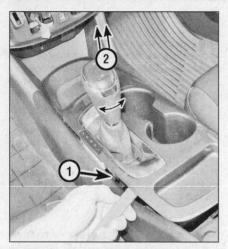

3.7 Use a trim tool to release the panel clips (1) then pull-up firmly on the shift knob while twisting slightly (2) (2016 and later models, except Malibu Limited)

3.8 Pry up the panel and disconnect the electrical connectors

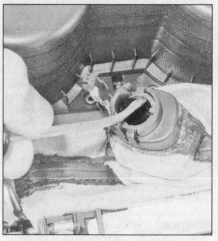

3.10 Release the clips to remove the shift knob from the boot (2016 and later models, except Malibu Limited)

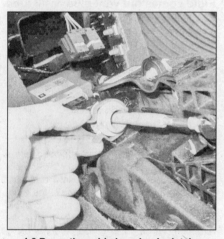

4.6 Press the cable housing lock tabs together to remove the cable from the shift lever assembly bracket (2016 and later model shown [except Malibu Limited])

4.7 Pry the shift cable from the shift lever pin (2016 and later model shown [except Malibu Limited])

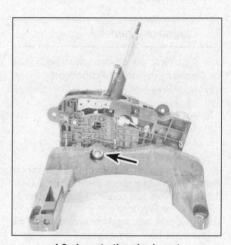

4.9a Locate the single nut and remove it. . .

7 Using a trim tool or small, tape-wrapped flat-tipped screwdriver, separate the shift knob boot trim from the center console at the rear first, then the front. Once the panel is disengaged, proceed to disengaging the shift knob by pulling it up firmly while twisting it slightly **(see illustration)**.

8 If equipped, disconnect the parking brake switch connector and the shift knob connector **(see illustration)**.

9 Remove the shift knob and shift panel together as a unit.

10 Release the clip and separate the shift knob from the boot **(see illustration)**.

11 Installation is reverse of removal.

---

4   Shift lever assembly - replacement

Warning: *These models are equipped with a Supplemental Restraint System (SRS), more commonly known as airbags. Always disable*

the airbag system before working in the vicinity of any airbag system component to avoid the possibility of accidental deployment of the airbag(s), which could cause personal injury (see Chapter 12).

Note: *On 2016 and later models (except Malibu Limited), the shift lever assembly is made up of the shift lever assembly and a floor mount bracket.*

1 Set the parking brake and chock the wheels.

2 Place the transaxle in Park.

3 Remove the shift knob and boot (see Section 3).

4 Remove the center console to expose the shift lever assembly (see Chapter 11, Section 20).

5 Remove the bolts and the driver's side center console brace.

6 Press the cable housing tabs in to disengage the cable from the shift lever assembly bracket **(see illustration)**.

7 Remove the retainer (if equipped) and pry the shift cable from the shift lever pin **(see illustration)**.

8 On 2015 and earlier models (and 2016 Malibu Limited), looking from the driver's side of the shift lever assembly, remove the single bolt below the front corner. Remove the remaining three bolts attaching the shift lever assembly to the vehicle and remove the assembly.

9 On 2016 and later models (except Malibu Limited), remove the single nut and bolt attaching the shift lever assembly to the floor mount bracket **(see illustrations)**.

10 Slide the shift lever assembly forward and up to remove **(see illustration)**.

Note: *The floor mount bracket can be removed with the shifter or separately by removing the nuts securing it to the vehicle and disconnecting the harness clips.*

11 Installation is the reverse of removal.

12 Adjust the shift cable as necessary (see Section 5).

4.9b. . . then pull the bolt from the floor mount bracket (2016 and later models [except Malibu Limited])

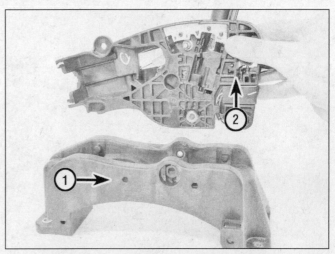

4.10 Slide the bracket forward (1) then pull the lever assembly upwards (2) to remove it from the floor bracket (2016 and later models [except Malibu Limited])

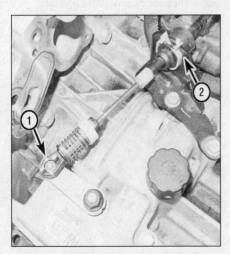

5.4 Remove the cable from the cable end (1) and squeeze the locking tabs together (2) to remove the cable from the bracket (6T40 transaxle shown)

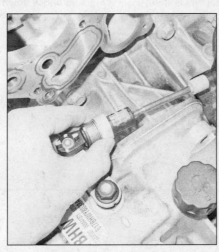

5.14a Pull back on the retainer. . .

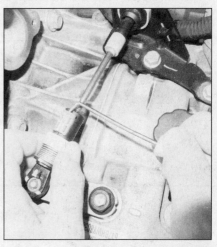

5.14b. . . then pry up on the cable lock and pull the cable out of the cable end (6T40 transaxle shown)

5   Shift cable - replacement and adjustment

Warning: *These models are equipped with a Supplemental Restraint System (SRS), more commonly known as airbags. Always disable the airbag system before working in the vicinity of any airbag system component to avoid the possibility of accidental deployment of the airbag(s), which could cause personal injury (see Chapter 12).*

Replacement

1   Set the parking brake and block the rear wheels.

2   Place the transaxle in Park.

3   Working in the engine compartment, if necessary for access, remove the turbocharger air inlet duct (see Chapter 4, Section 15) or battery (see Chapter 5, Section 4).

4   Pry the shift cable end from the ball of the transaxle shift lever arm **(see illustration)**.

5   Pinch the locking tabs and remove the cable from the shift cable bracket.

6   Remove the center console to access the shift cable at the shift lever assembly (see Chapter 11).

7   Press the cable housing tabs in to disengage the cable from the shift lever assembly bracket **(see illustration 4.6)**.

8   Remove the retainer (if equipped) and pry the shift cable from the shift lever pin **(see illustration 4.7)**.

9   Pull back the carpet on the driver's side at the firewall to expose where the cable goes through the floor pan. On 2015 and earlier models (and 2015 Malibu Limited), pull or push the shift cable grommet into the passenger compartment of the vehicle. On 2016 and later models (except Malibu Limited), remove the nuts and pull the grommet off of the studs.

10   Remove the shift cable by pulling out through the passenger compartment.

11   Installation is the reverse of removal. Ensue the rubber grommet is properly installed to prevent leaks, then adjust the cable.

Adjustment

12   Set the parking brake and block the wheels.

13   Place the shift lever in Park and ensure the transaxle shift lever is in the Park position as well.

14   Release the adjustment lock on the cable housing **(see illustrations)**. Recheck the Park position of the shift lever and transaxle shift lever. The shift cable will automatically adjust.

15   Press down on the adjustment lock. When fully locked, it will be flush with the cable housing.

16   Check the shift lever for correct operation in all ranges. If there are any problems, perform the adjustment again.

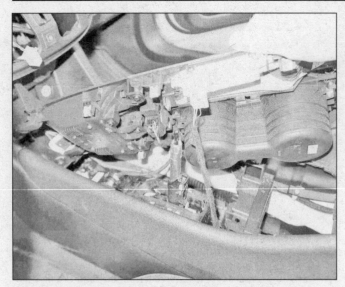

6.2 Position the console trim for access to the shift lever assembly (2016 and later models [except Malibu Limited])

6.3 Insert a small screwdriver or similar to disengage the shift interlock solenoid pin to shift out of park (2016 and later models [except Malibu Limited])

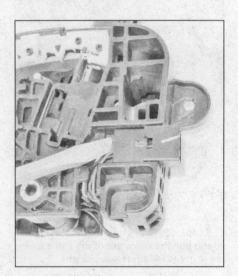

6.7a Slide the connector out. . .

6.7b. . . detach it from the shift lever assembly. . .

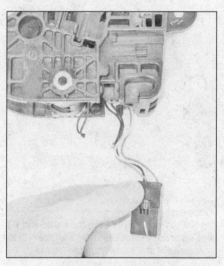

6.7c. . . then pull the harness free (2016 and later models [except Malibu Limited])

6   Brake Transmission Shift Interlock (BTSI) system - description and component replacement

Warning: *These models are equipped with a Supplemental Restraint System (SRS), more commonly known as airbags. Always disable the airbag system before working in the vicinity of any airbag system component to avoid the possibility of accidental deployment of the airbag(s), which could cause personal injury (see Chapter 12).*

Description

1   This system prevents the transmission from being shifted out of Park unless the key is turned On and the brake pedal is depressed. Before and when the vehicle is started, the BTSI is de-energized, locking the shift lever in Park; when the brake pedal is depressed, the solenoid is energized so the shift lever can be moved to another range.

Manual bypass (2016 and later models - except Malibu Limited)

2   To manually bypass the shift interlock on 2016 and later models (except Malibu Limited) to allow the vehicle to be shifted out of Park, detach the shifter center console trim and pull up to access the shift lever assembly **(see illustration)**.

3   Using a small screwdriver or similar, release the shift interlock solenoid pin **(see illustration)** and move the shift out of park.

Replacement

Note: *The following procedure applies to 2016 and later models only (except Malibu Limited). 2015 and earlier models (and 2016 Malibu Limited) require replacement of the shift lever assembly. And normally, all models require replacement of the entire shift lever assembly in the event of BTSI failure.*

4   Disconnect the cable from the negative battery terminal (see Chapter 5).

5   Ensure the transaxle is in Park.

6   Remove the shift lever assembly (see Section 4).

7   Slide the connector out and pull the harness from the shift lever assembly **(see illustrations)**.

8   Pry off the micro switch cover and carefully remove the micro switch from the shift lever assembly **(see illustrations)**.

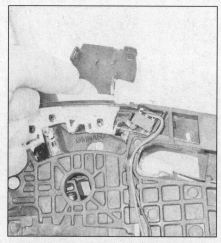

6.8a Remove the micro switch cover. . .

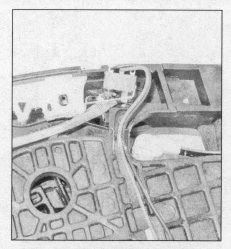

6.8b. . . and carefully remove the micro switch (2016 and later models [except Malibu Limited])

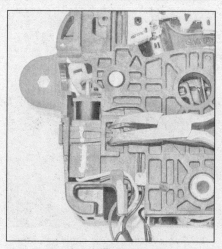

6.9a Squeeze the BTSI retaining clip with pliers. . .

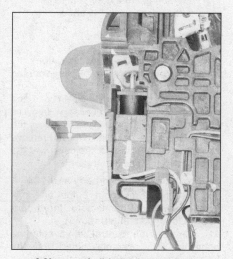

6.9b. . . and slide it out to remove (2016 and later models [except Malibu Limited])

6.10a Remove the BTSI solenoid. . .

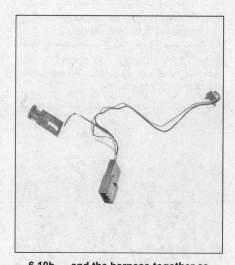

6.10b. . . and the harness together as one unit (2016 and later models [except Malibu Limited])

9 Squeeze the BTSI solenoid retaining clip using pliers and slide out to remove **(see illustrations)**.

10 Remove the solenoid and harness **(see illustrations)**.

11 Installation is the reverse of removal. Verify proper operation.

---

7 Transmission Control Module (TCM) - removal and installation

Note: *The procedures in this section apply only to disconnecting, removing and installing the TCM that is already installed in your vehicle. If, however, you need to replace the TCM, it must be programmed with new software and calibrations. This procedure requires the use of GM's TECH-2 scan tool and GM's latest PCM-programming software, so you WILL NOT BE ABLE TO REPLACE THE PCM OR TCM AT HOME.*

Note: *After replacing the TCM, a dealer or other qualified repair facility must perform a gear position "N position learn" and a learned-values reset with a factory scan tool.*

Note: *On 6T40, 6T70 transaxles, the TCM is part of the transaxle valve body (see Section 8).*

1 Disconnect the negative battery cable (see Chapter 5, Section 3).

AF50-8 transaxles

Note: *The TCM on AF50 transaxles is located on top of the transaxle, under the transaxle shift lever. The TCM also contains the Park Neutral Position (PNP) switch*

2 Remove the battery and battery tray (see Chapter 5, Section 4).

3 Disconnect the shift cable from the shift lever (see Section 5) and remove the nut attaching the shift lever to the transaxle shift shaft.

4 Disconnect the TCM electrical connector.

5 Remove the bolts and the TCM from the transaxle.

6 Installation is reverse of removal. If a new TCM was installed, have a dealer or other qualified repair facility perform the procedures mentioned at the beginning of this section.

9T50 and VT40 transaxles

Note: *On 9T50 and VT40 transaxles, the TCM is attached to the front of the transaxle on a bracket, facing the radiator fan assembly.*

7 Remove components necessary to access the TCM at the front of the transaxle.

8 Disconnect the TCM electrical connector.

9 Release the retaining tabs and remove the TCM from the bracket.

10 The bracket is attached to the transaxle with bolts, and can also be removed if necessary.

11 Installation is the reverse of removal. If a new TCM was installed, have a dealer or other qualified repair facility perform the procedures mentioned at the beginning of this section.

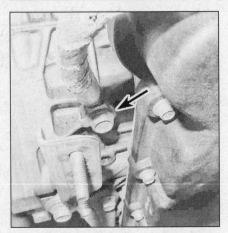

8.7 Remove the ground cable bolt from the transaxle (6T40 shown)

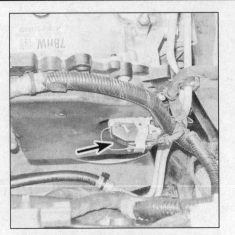

8.8 Disconnect the transaxle electrical connector (6T40 transalxe shown)

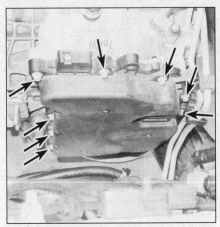

8.9 Remove the bolts attaching the cover and remove the cover from the transaxle (not all bolts visible in this photo). If necessary, adjust the transaxle position using a floor jack to get the cover out (6T40 shown)

---

8   Transmission valve body - removal and installation

Note: *The following information outlines removing the valve body for accessing the electronic shift solenoids.*

8.10a Disconnect the valve body electrical connectors at the top. . .

Removal

1   Raise and support the front of the vehicle on jackstands.
2   Drain the transaxle fluid (see Chapter 1, Section 24).
3   Place a drain pan under the front of the transaxle near the radiator.

6T40/6T70

Note: *The control valve solenoid body and TCM are a single unit, and accessed by removing the cover on the front of the transaxle.*
4   Remove the battery and battery tray (see Chapter 5, Section 4).
5   On 2015 and earlier models (and 2016 Malibu Limited), detach the transmission cooler lines from the transaxle. On 2016 and later models (except Malibu Limited), remove the cooler lines from the transaxle (see Section 11).
Note: *On turbocharged models, remove the charge air cooler outlet duct for access (see Chapter 4, Section 15).*
6   On 2015 and earlier models (and 2016 Malibu Limited), support the bottom of the transaxle using a floor jack. Remove the transaxle front mount (see Section 13).
7   Remove the bolt and disconnect the

ground at the transaxle **(see illustration)**.
8   Disconnect the transaxle connector **(see illustration)**.
9   Remove the transaxle cover bolts and remove the cover. If necessary, use the floor jack to adjust the transaxle to allow the ample clearance for cover removal. remove and discard the gasket for the cover and the TCM connector **(see illustration)**.

Control valve solenoid body and TCM

10   Disconnect the input, output and shift position electrical connectors (three connectors total) **(see illustrations)**.
11   Remove the control valve solenoid body and TCM assembly bolts. Note the bolt locations during removal to ensure proper placement during installation.
12   Remove the control valve solenoid body and TCM assembly **(see illustrations)**. Discard the plate between the component and transaxle as a new one should be used during reassembly. Check the seals for the pressure switch.

8.10b. . . and at the bottom (6T40 shown)

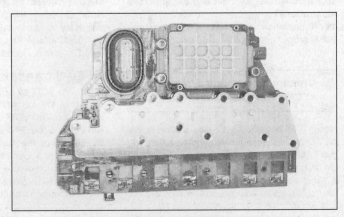

8.12a Remove the valve body/TCM from the transaxle (6T40 shown)

**8.12b Valve body solenoids
(6T40 shown)**

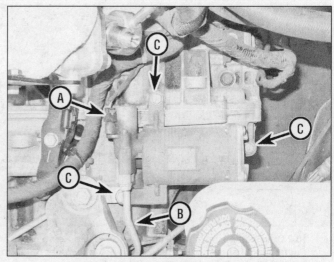

9.4 Accumulator components (6T40 shown)

A   *Electrical connector*   C   *Accumulator mounting bolts*
B   *Accumulator fluid pipe*

AF50-8

Warning: *Wait until the engine is completely cool before beginning this procedure.*

Note: *The valve body is accessed by removing the cover on the front of the transaxle.*

13   Drain the engine coolant (see Chapter 1, Section 25).

14   Remove the lower radiator hose.

15   Disconnect the transmission cooler line quick-connect fittings at the transaxle and the radiator, then remove the cooler line assembly from the vehicle.

16   Remove the transaxle cover bolts and remove the cover. Use a scraper or similar tool to carefully pry the cover off as it is attached using RTV sealant. Clean the cover and transaxle surfaces of all sealant prior to installation.

17   Remove the control valve solenoid body bolts. Note the bolt locations during removal to ensure proper placement during installation.

18   Pull the control valve solenoid body loose and disconnect the manual link.

19   Remove the control valve solenoid body. Discard the plate between the component and transaxle as a new one should be used during reassembly.

9T50

20   Remove the charge air cooler-to-throttle body duct (see Chapter 4, Section 15).

21   Remove the TCM and the TCM bracket (see Section 7).

22   Disconnect the transmission cooler lines at the transaxle by removing the bolts and pulling from the transaxle. Detach from the bracket on the transaxle and position to the side.

23   Remove the bolt and disconnect the ground at the transaxle.

24   Disconnect the transaxle electrical connector.

25   Remove the transaxle cover bolts and remove the cover.

26   Remove the bolts attaching the valve solenoid body harness. Disconnect the electrical connectors from the solenoids and remove the harness.

27   Remove control valve solenoid body bolts. Note the bolt locations during removal to ensure proper placement during installation.

28   Remove the control valve solenoid body.

VT40

Warning: *Wait until the engine is completely cool before beginning this procedure.*

29   Remove the battery and battery tray (see Chapter 5, Section 4).

30   Drain the engine coolant (see Chapter 1, Section 25).

31   Remove the upper radiator hose.

32   Remove the charge air cooler-to-throttle body duct (see Chapter 4, Section 15).

33   Remove the TCM and the TCM bracket (see Section 7).

34   Disconnect the transmission cooler line bracket from the transaxle.

35   Remove the bolt and disconnect the ground at the transaxle.

36   Disconnect the transaxle electrical connector.

37   Remove the transaxle cover bolts and remove the cover.

38   Remove the bolts attaching the valve solenoid body harness. Disconnect the electrical connectors from the solenoids and remove the harness.

39   Remove control valve solenoid body bolts. Note the bolt locations during removal to ensure proper placement during installation.

40   Remove the control valve solenoid body.

Installation - all transaxles

41   Installation is reverse of removal, noting the following items:

a) *Use new seals and plates between the components and the transaxle.*

b) *Install the bolts in the correct locations noted during removal.*

c) *Tighten the bolts for the valve body hand-tight, then tighten to the torque listed in this Chapter's Specifications.*

d) *Use new gaskets and seals or a thin bead of RTV on the transaxle cover.*

e) *Refill the transaxle to the proper fluid level and verify operation.*

f) *On models with the AF50-8 or VT40 transaxle, refill the cooling system (see Chapter 1).*

---

9   Accumulator - replacement

Warning: *The accumulator may be pressurized with transaxle fluid greater than 120 psi that may also be hot. Before servicing the accumulator, the ignition MUST be OFF a minimum of 10 minutes.*

Note: *2016 and later models equipped with 6T40 and 9T50 transaxles have an accumulator.*

1   On 9T50 models, remove the cooling system expansion tank (see Chapter 3, Section 6).

2   On 6T40 models, remove the battery and battery tray (see Chapter 5, Section 4).

3   Disconnect the shift cable from the transaxle shift lever (see Section 5).

4   On all models, disconnect the accumulator electrical connector **(see illustration)**.

5   Remove the bolts and the accumulator pipe.

6   Remove the bolts and the accumulator from the transaxle. Discard the seal between the accumulator and transaxle case.

7   Installation is the reverse of removal. Use a new seal between the accumulator and transaxle.

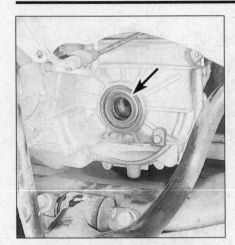

10.2 Driveaxle oil seals (2016 and later model shown, 2015 and earlier models similar)

11.6a Remove the fastener and disconnect the upper (inlet) transaxle cooler line. . .

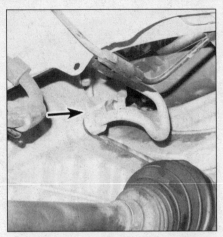

11.6b. . . and the lower (outlet) transaxle cooler line (1.5L with 6T40 shown)

10 Driveaxle oil seals - replacement

Note: *This procedure does not apply to the transfer case seals on the right side of AWD models.*

1   Oil leaks frequently occur due to wear of the driveaxle oil seals. Replacement of these seals is relatively easy since the repairs can be performed without removing the transaxle from the vehicle.

2   The seals are located on the sides of the transaxle where the driveaxles are attached **(see illustration)**. If leakage of a seal is suspected, raise the vehicle and support it securely on jackstands. If the seal is leaking, fluid will be found on the sides of the transaxle.

3   Remove the driveaxle (see Chapter 8, Section 2).

4   Note how deep the seal is installed, then use a screwdriver to carefully pry the seal from its bore. If it can't be removed with a screwdriver, a special seal removal tool (available at most auto supply stores) will be needed.

5   Compare the old seal to the new one to be sure it's correct.

6   Coat the inside and outside diameters of the new seal with transaxle fluid.

7   Using a seal installation tool or a large socket, install the new seal. Drive it into the bore squarely and make sure it's seated to its original depth.

8   Install the driveaxle.

9   Installation is the reverse of removal. Check the transaxle fluid level, adding if necessary (see Chapter 1).

11 Automatic transaxle - removal and installation

Removal

1   Remove the battery and battery tray (see Chapter 5, Section 4).

2   Disconnect the shift cable from the shift lever on the transaxle, remove the cable from the bracket and position the cable out of the way (see Section 5).

3   Disconnect all wiring from the transaxle. This includes the ground wires, harness clips, the transaxle range switch, the transaxle speed sensors and the transaxle control module.

4   Loosen the front wheel lug nuts and the driveaxle/hub nuts (see Chapter 8, Section 2), then raise the front of the vehicle and support it securely on jackstands.

5   Drain the transaxle fluid (see Chapter 1).

6   Remove the transmission cooler line fasteners and disconnect the cooler lines from the transaxle **(see illustrations)**. Disconnect the lines from the retainer. Plug and cap the lines and openings to prevent contamination.

7   Install an engine support fixture and connect the chains solidly to the lifting brackets on top of the engine **(see illustration)**. If lifting brackets are not present, connect the support chains to substantial parts of the engine (such as the threaded holes at the left ends of the cylinder heads, the exhaust manifold and the engine mount bracket).

8   Remove the uppermost transaxle-to-engine mounting bolts **(see illustration)**.

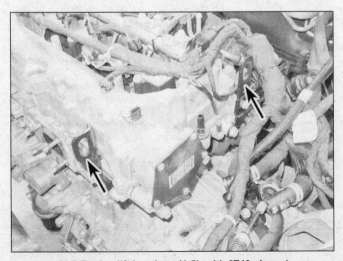

11.7 Engine lift brackets (1.5L with 6T40 shown)

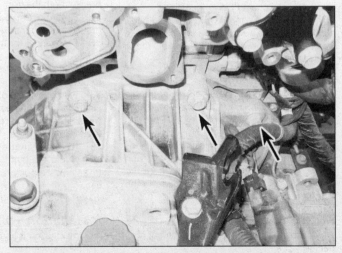

11.8 Upper transaxle-to-engine bolts (1.5L with 6T40 shown)

11.13 Mark the relationship between the torque converter and driveplate and remove the bolts (1.5L with 6T40 shown)

11.18a Remove the lower transaxle bolts...

9   Remove the subframe (see Chapter 10, Section 20).
10   Remove the driveaxles (see Chapter 8, Section 2).
11   Remove the intermediate shaft (see Chapter 8, Section 2).
12   Remove the starter (see Chapter 5, Section 8).
13   Remove the torque converter bolts through the starter opening. Make match-marks on the torque converter and driveplate so they can be assembled in the same position **(see illustration)**.
Note: *Turn the crankshaft with a large breaker bar and socket placed on the crankshaft pulley bolt.*
14   Support the transaxle with a jack - preferably one designed for this purpose. Transmission/transaxle adapters are available for most heavy duty floor jacks. If the jack is equipped with safety chains or straps, use them to secure the transaxle to the jack.
15   On turbocharged models, if necessary, remove the catalytic converter brace nuts and remove the brace.
16   On all models, remove the driver transaxle mount (see Section 13).
17   Ensure the harness is detached and disconnected from the transaxle.
18   Remove the remaining transaxle-to-engine bolts **(see illustrations)**, then pull the transaxle away from the engine until it can be lowered using the jack.
Caution: *Make sure the torque converter doesn't become detached from the transaxle. Clamping a pair of locking pliers to the transaxle case will prevent this.*
19   Lower the transaxle until it can be safely set on the ground.

Installation

20   Installation is the reverse of removal, noting the following points:
a)   *As the torque converter is reinstalled, ensure that the drive tangs at the center*

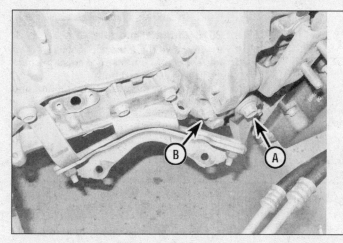

11.18b... the side bolt (A) and catalytic converter bracket bolt (B), if applicable (1.5L with 6T40 shown)

of the torque converter hub engage with the recesses in the automatic transaxle fluid pump inner gear. This can be confirmed by turning the torque converter while pushing it towards the transaxle. If it isn't fully engaged, it will clunk into place. Align the matchmarks you made on the driveplate and torque converter.
b)   *Install all of the driveplate-to-torque converter nuts before tightening any of them. Tighten the driveplate-to-torque converter bolts and transaxle mounting bolts to the torque listed in this Chapter's Specifications.*
c)   *Tighten the ttransaxle-to-engine mounting bolts to the torque listed in this Chapter's Specifications.*
d)   *Replace all O-rings with new ones.*
e)   *Tighten the wheel lug nuts to the torque listed in the Chapter 8 Specifications. Tighten the driveaxle/hub nuts to the torque listed in the Chapter 8 Specifications.*
f)   *Fill the transaxle with the correct type and amount of automatic transmission fluid (see Chapter 1).*

g)   *Adjust the shift cable (see Section 5).*

---

12   Automatic transaxle overhaul - general information

1   In the event of a problem occurring, it will be necessary to establish whether the fault is electrical, mechanical or hydraulic in nature, before repair work can be contemplated. Diagnosis requires detailed knowledge of the transaxle's operation and construction, as well as access to specialized test equipment, and so is deemed to be beyond the scope of this manual. It is therefore essential that problems with the automatic transaxle are referred to a dealer service department or other qualified repair facility for assessment.
2   Note that a faulty transaxle should not be removed before the vehicle has been diagnosed by a knowledgeable technician equipped with the proper tools, as troubleshooting must be performed with the transaxle installed in the vehicle.

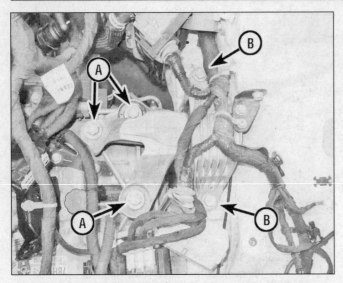

13.9 Remove the driver's side mount-to-engine (A) and mount-to-chassis (B) bolts (1.5L with 6T40 shown)

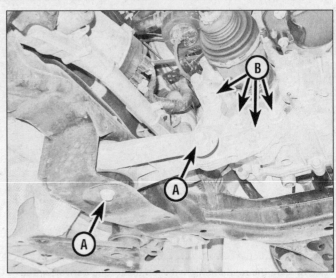

13.21 Mount through-bolts (A) and bracket-to-transaxle bolts (B) (1.5L with 6T40 shown)

13 Transaxle mount - replacement

1   Raise the vehicle and support it securely on jackstands.

2   Place a floor jack under the transaxle with a block of wood between the jack and transaxle to prevent damage.

Driver's side

2015 and earlier models

3   Remove the battery and battery tray (see Chapter 5, Section 4).

4   Remove the front transaxle mount through-bolt.

5   Remove the driver's side mount bracket-to-transaxle bolts.

6   Lower the transaxle slightly to access and remove the mount-to-chassis bolts.

7   Remove the driver's side mount and bracket.

8   Installation is the reverse of removal. Tighten all bolts to the torque listed in this Chapter's Specifications.

2016 and later models

9   Remove the transaxle mount bracket-to-transaxle and transaxle mount-to-chassis bolts **(see illustration)**.

10   Remove the transaxle mount and bracket.

11   Installation is the reverse of removal. Tighten all bolts to the torque listed in this Chapter's Specifications.

Front

Note: *2015 and earlier models are equipped with a front transaxle mount.*

12   Remove the mount-to-subframe thru bolt.

13   Remove the mount-to-transaxle bolts and remove the mount.

14   Installation is the reverse of removal. Tighten all bolts to the torque listed in this Chapter's Specifications.

Rear

2015 and earlier

15   Lower the exhaust to gain access.

16   Remove the mount-to-bracket thru bolt.

17   Remove the mount-to-subframe bolts and remove the mount.

18   Installation is the reverse of removal. Tighten all bolts to the torque listed in this Chapter's Specifications.

2016 and later

19   Raise the vehicle and support it securely on jackstands.

20   Support the rear of the drivetrain using a floor jack or jackstand.

21   Remove the rear transaxle mount through-bolts and remove the mount **(see illustration)**.

22   Remove the bracket-to-transaxle bolts and remove the bracket.

23   Installation is the reverse of removal. Tighten all bolts to the torque listed in this Chapter's Specifications.

Chapter 8
Driveline

Contents

Specifications

Torque specifications

Ft-lbs (unless otherwise indicated)   **Nm**

Note: *One foot-pound (ft-lb) of torque is equivalent to 12 inch-pounds (in-lbs) of torque. Torque values below approximately 15 ft-lbs are expressed in inch-pounds, since most foot-pound torque wrenches are not accurate at these smaller values.*

Driveaxle/hub nut*

	Ft-lbs	Nm
Step 1	111	150
Step 2	Loosen 45 degrees	
Step 3	184	250

Intermediate shaft bearing bracket fasteners

    2015 and earlier models (and 2016 Malibu Limited)

	Ft-lbs	Nm
Shaft-to-bracket bolts...	16	22
Bracket-to-engine bolts..	43	53
2016 and later models (except Malibu Limited)	43	43

* *Nut must be replaced.*

1 General information

1   The information in this Chapter deals with the components from the rear of the engine to the drive wheels, except for the transaxle, which is addressed in Chapter 7.
2   Since nearly all the procedures covered in this Chapter involve working under the vehicle, make sure it's securely supported on sturdy jackstands or on a hoist where the vehicle can be easily raised and lowered.

2 Driveaxles and intermediate shaft - removal and installation

2.2 Loosen the driveaxle/hub nut with a long breaker bar

Driveaxles

Removal

1   Loosen the wheel lug nuts, raise the vehicle and support it securely on jackstands. Remove the wheel.
2   Insert a punch into the brake disc cooling vanes and allow it to rest against the caliper mounting bracket. Break the driveaxle/hub nut loose with a socket and large breaker bar **(see illustration)**.
3   Remove the front inner fender splash shields, if necessary (see Chapter 11).
4   Disconnect the tie-rod end from the steering knuckle (see Chapter 10, Section 17).
5   Disconnect the stabilizer bar link from the stabilizer bar (see Chapter 10, Section 11).
6   Remove and discard the driveaxle/hub nut.
7   Separate the control arm balljoint from the steering knuckle (see Chapter 10, Section 5).
8   Swing the knuckle/hub assembly out (away from the vehicle) until the end of the driveaxle is free of the hub. If the driveaxle splines stick in the hub, tap on the end of the driveaxle with a plastic hammer. If the driveaxle still sticks, press it from the hub with a drive hub remover **(see illustration)**.
Note: *Support the outer end of the driveaxle with a piece of wire to avoid unnecessary*

strain on the inner CV joint **(see illustration)**.
9   Secure the strut/knuckle/hub assembly out of the way.
10   If you're removing the right driveaxle on models with an intermediate shaft, carefully pry the inner CV joint off the intermediate shaft using a large screwdriver or prybar positioned between the CV joint housing and the intermediate shaft bearing support **(see illustration 2.11)**.
11   If you're removing the left driveaxle, pry the inner CV joint out of the transaxle using a large screwdriver or prybar positioned between the transaxle and the CV joint housing **(see illustration)**. Be careful not to damage the differential seal.
12   Support the CV joints and carefully remove the driveaxle from the vehicle. If equipped, remove the washer from the outer CV end of the driveaxle and obtain a new one for installation **(see illustration)**.

Installation

13   Pry the old spring clip from the inner end of the driveaxle (left side) or outer end of the intermediate shaft (right side) and install a new one **(see illustration)**. Lubricate the dif-

ferential seal or intermediate shaft O-ring with multi-purpose grease and raise the driveaxle into position while supporting the CV joints.
Note: *Position the spring clip with the opening facing down; this will ease insertion of the driveaxle and prevent damage to the clip.*
14   Apply a light coat of multi-purpose grease to the intermediate shaft splines.
15   Push the splined end of the inner CV joint into the differential side gear (left side) or onto the intermediate shaft (right side) and make sure the spring clip locks in its groove.
16   Grasp the inner CV joint housing (not the driveaxle) and try to pull out to ensure the driveaxle retaining ring has seated securely in the transaxle or on the intermediate shaft.
17   Install the new washer on the outer CV end of the driveaxle.
18   Apply a light coat of multi-purpose grease or anti-seize compound to the outer CV joint splines, then pull out on the steering knuckle assembly and install the stub axle into the hub **(see illustration)**.
19   Insert the balljoint stud into the steering knuckle and tighten the bolt to the torque listed in the Chapter 10 Specifications.
20   Reconnect the tie-rod end and the stabi-

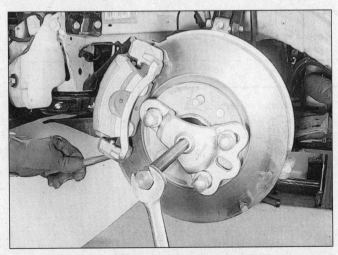

2.8a Using a drive hub remover to push the driveaxle out of the hub splines

2.8b Support the end of the driveaxle while removing the inner CV joint from the transaxle/intermediate shaft

2.11 Carefully pry the inner end of the driveaxle from the outer end of the intermediate shaft (right driveaxle), or from the transaxle (left driveaxle)

2.12 Remove he washer from the old driveaxle and transfer to the new driveaxle if necessary

lizer bar link and tighten the fasteners to the torque listed in the Chapter 10 Specifications. Install a new cotter pin if required.

21 Install the front inner fender splash shields, if removed (see Chapter 11).

22 Install a new driveaxle/hub nut and tighten it to the torque listed in this Chapter's Specifications.

23 Install the wheel and lug nuts, then lower the vehicle. Tighten the lug nuts to the torque listed in the Chapter 1 Specifications.

Intermediate shaft

Note: *2016 and later 1.5L models do not have an intermediate shaft, only 2.0L models do.*

Removal

24 Remove the right front driveaxle.

25 On 2015 and earlier models and 2016 Limited models, remove the bolts mounting the intermediate shaft bearing retainer to the engine bracket.

26 On 2016 and later models with a 2.0L engine, remove the intermediate shaft bracket bolts.

27 Pull the intermediate shaft from the transaxle.

Installation

28 Lubricate the lips of the transaxle seal with multi-purpose grease. Carefully guide the intermediate shaft into the transaxle side gear, then install the bearing support mounting bolts hand-tight. Make sure that the shaft is positively engaged into the transaxle.

29 Tighten the bolts to the torque listed in this Chapter's Specifications.

30 On 2015 and earlier models and 2016 Limited models, install a new spring clip on the right front driveaxle.

31 On 2016 and later models, install a new O-ring and spring clip on the intermediate shaft.

32 The remainder of installation is the reverse of removal.

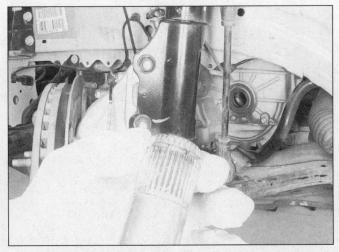

2.13 Install new spring clip on the transaxle end of the axle

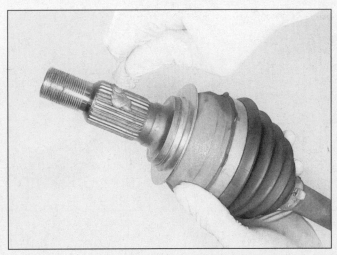

2.18 Apply a light coat of multi-purpose grease or anti-seize compound to outer CV joint splines

Notes

Chapter 9
Brakes

Contents

Specifications

General

Brake fluid type	See Chapter 1	
Disc brakes		
Minimum brake pad thickness	See Chapter 1	
Disc lateral runout limit	0.002 inch	0.05 mm
Disc minimum thickness*		
2013 through 2015 models (and 2016 Malibu Limited models)		
Front (RPO J60, J61)	1.07 in	27.0 mm
Rear		
RPO J60	0.395 in	10.0 mm
RPO J61	0.827 in	21.0 mm
2016 (non Malibu Limited) and later models		
Front	0.905 in	23.0 mm
Rear	0.393 in	10.0 mm
Brake rotor retaining screw-to-wheel hub	80 in-lbs	9 Nm

The disc minimum thickness is also cast into the disc.
RPO = Regular Production Option

Torque specifications

Note: *One foot-pound (ft-lb) of torque is equivalent to 12 inch-pounds (in-lbs) of torque. Torque values below approximately 15 ft-lbs are expressed in inch-pounds, because most foot-pound torque wrenches are not accurate at these smaller values.*

	Ft-lbs (unless otherwise indicated)	Nm
Brake line banjo bolt	30	40
Brake disc-to-hub screw		
2013 through 2015 models (and 2016 Malibu Limited models)	62 in-lbs	7
2016 (non Malibu Limited) and later models	80 in-lbs	9
Brake caliper mounting bracket bolts		
2013 through 2015 models (and 2016 Malibu Limited models)		
Front		
Step 1	111	150
Step 2	Tighten an additional 45 degrees	
Step 3	Tighten an additional 15 degrees	
Rear		
Step 1	74	100
Step 2	Tighten an additional 60 degrees	
2016 (non Malibu Limited) and later models		
Front		
Step 1	111	150
Step 2	Tighten an additional 15 to 30 degrees	
Rear		
Step 1	74	100
Step 2	Tighten an additional 15 to 30 degrees	
Caliper mounting (guide pin) bolts		
2013 through 2015 models (and 2016 Malibu Limited models)	20	27
2016 (non Malibu Limited) and later models	30	40
Master cylinder mounting nuts		
2013 through 2015 models (and 2016 Malibu Limited models)	37	50
2016 (non Malibu Limited) and later models	16	22
Master cylinder reservoir bolts		
2013 through 2015 models (and 2016 Malibu Limited models)	35 in-lbs	4
2016 (non Malibu Limited) and later models	62 in-lbs	7
Power brake booster mounting bolts		
2013 through 2015 models (and 2016 Malibu Limited models)	14	19
2016 (non Malibu Limited) and later models	14	7
Brake line to master cylinder		
2013 through 2015 models (and 2016 Malibu Limited models)	18	25
2016 (non Malibu Limited) and later models	24	32
Brake Pressure Modulator Valve (BPMV) mounting bolts	24	32
Wheel speed sensor bolts	80 in-lbs	9
Parking Brake		
Electronic Parking Brake		
Parking brake module mounting fasteners	89 in-lbs	10
Parking brake cable nut	53 in-lbs	6
Electronic Brake Control Module (EBCM)		
mounting bolts (2013 models)	26 in-lbs	3
Actuator-to-caliper mounting fasteners		
(2016 and later models)	106 in-lbs	12
Manual parking brake		
Brake cable retaining bracket fasteners	80 in-lbs	9
Cable guide bolt	16	22
Lever (console mounted) fasteners	80 in-lbs	9
Pedal (foot operated) fasteners		
Bolt	80 in-lbs	9
Nut	16	22
Vacuum pump fasteners		
2015 and earlier models/2016 Malibu Limited	89 in-lbs	10
2016 and later models (except Malibu Limited)		
1.5L engine		
Step 1	132 in-lbs	15
Step 2	18	25
2.0L engine	89 in-lbs	10
Wheel lug nuts	See Chapter 1	

1 General information

1 The vehicles covered by this manual are equipped with hydraulically operated front and rear brake systems. The front and rear brakes are disc type. Both the front and rear brakes are self adjusting. The disc brakes automatically compensate for pad wear.

Hydraulic system

2 The hydraulic system consists of two separate circuits. The master cylinder has separate reservoirs for the two circuits, and, in the event of a leak or failure in one hydraulic circuit, the other circuit will remain operative. Brake balance between the front and rear brakes is monitored and maintained by the Dynamic Rear Proportioning (DRP) function of the Anti-lock Brake System (ABS).

Power brake booster

3 The power brake booster, utilizing engine manifold vacuum and atmospheric pressure to provide assistance to the hydraulically operated brakes, is mounted on the firewall in the engine compartment. On some models, additional vacuum is provided by an electrically powered vacuum pump.

Parking brake

4 The parking brake operates the rear brakes only. It's activated by a pedal in the driver's footwell, a lever in the console, or electronically through a parking brake activation switch. On 2013 models, an electronic remote actuator with cables leading to the calipers is used. On some 2014 and later models, a lever in the console or a foot pedal is used to operate a manual parking brake system. On some 2016 and later models, an electronic rear caliper actuator mounted directly to the rear caliper is used; these actuators perform the same function as the mechanical and remote actuator systems, but without the need of parking brake cables.

Service

5 After completing any operation involving disassembly of any part of the brake system, always test drive the vehicle to check for proper braking performance before resuming normal driving. When testing the brakes, perform the tests on a clean, dry, flat surface. Conditions other than these can lead to inaccurate test results.
6 Test the brakes at various speeds with both light and heavy pedal pressure. The vehicle should stop evenly without pulling to one side or the other.
7 Tires, vehicle load and wheel alignment are factors which also affect braking performance.

Precautions

8 There are some general cautions and warnings involving the brake system on this vehicle:

a) *Use only the brake fluid listed in the Chapter 1 Specifications.*
b) *The brake pads contain fibers which are hazardous to your health if inhaled. Whenever you work on brake system components, clean all parts with brake system cleaner. Do not allow the fine dust to become airborne. Also, wear an approved filtering mask.*
c) *Safety should be paramount whenever any servicing of the brake components is performed. Do not use parts or fasteners which are not in perfect condition, and be sure that all clearances and torque specifications are adhered to. If you are at all unsure about a certain procedure, seek professional advice. Upon completion of any brake system work, test the brakes carefully in a controlled area before putting the vehicle into normal service. If a problem is suspected in the brake system, don't drive the vehicle until it's fixed. Used brake fluid is considered a hazardous waste and it must be disposed of in accordance with federal, state and local laws. DO NOT pour it down the sink, into septic tanks or storm drains, or on the ground. Clean up any spilled brake fluid immediately and then wash the area with large amounts of water. This is especially true for any finished or painted surfaces.*

Warning: *Never use reclaimed brake fluid or brake fluid from an open container. Brake fluid is hygroscopic and will absorb moisture from the air, making the fluid unsafe to use in the hydraulic brake system.*

2 Troubleshooting

PROBABLE CAUSE	CORRECTIVE ACTION
No brakes - pedal travels to floor	
1 Low fluid level 2 Air in system	1 and 2 Low fluid level and air in the system are symptoms of another problem a leak somewhere in the hydraulic system. Locate and repair the leak
3 Defective seals in master cylinder	3 Replace master cylinder
4 Fluid overheated and vaporized due to heavy braking	4 Bleed hydraulic system (temporary fix). Replace brake fluid (proper fix)
Brake pedal slowly travels to floor under braking or at a stop	
1 Defective seals in master cylinder	1 Replace master cylinder
2 Leak in a hose, line, caliper or wheel cylinder	2 Locate and repair leak
3 Air in hydraulic system	3 Bleed the system, inspect system for a leak
Brake pedal feels spongy when depressed	
1 Air in hydraulic system	1 Bleed the system, inspect system for a leak
2 Master cylinder or power booster loose	2 Tighten fasteners
3 Brake fluid overheated (beginning to boil)	3 Bleed the system (temporary fix). Replace the brake fluid (proper fix)
4 Deteriorated brake hoses (ballooning under pressure)	4 Inspect hoses, replace as necessary (it's a good idea to replace all of them if one hose shows signs of deterioration)

Troubleshooting (continued)

PROBABLE CAUSE	CORRECTIVE ACTION

Brake pedal feels hard when depressed and/or excessive effort required to stop vehicle

PROBABLE CAUSE	CORRECTIVE ACTION
1 Power booster faulty	1 Replace booster
2 Engine not producing sufficient vacuum, or hose to booster clogged, collapsed or cracked	2 Check vacuum to booster with a vacuum gauge. Replace hose if cracked or clogged, repair engine if vacuum is extremely low
3 Brake linings contaminated by grease or brake fluid	3 Locate and repair source of contamination, replace brake pads or shoes
4 Brake linings glazed	4 Replace brake pads or shoes, check discs and drums for glazing, service as necessary
5 Caliper piston(s) or wheel cylinder(s) binding or frozen	5 Replace calipers or wheel cylinders
6 Brakes wet	6 Apply pedal to boil-off water (this should only be a momentary problem)
7 Kinked, clogged or internally split brake hose or line	7 Inspect lines and hoses, replace as necessary

Excessive brake pedal travel (but will pump up)

PROBABLE CAUSE	CORRECTIVE ACTION
1 Drum brakes out of adjustment	1 Adjust brakes
2 Air in hydraulic system	2 Bleed system, inspect system for a leak

Excessive brake pedal travel (but will not pump up)

PROBABLE CAUSE	CORRECTIVE ACTION
1 Master cylinder pushrod misadjusted	1 Adjust pushrod
2 Master cylinder seals defective	2 Replace master cylinder
3 Brake linings worn out	3 Inspect brakes, replace pads and/or shoes
4 Hydraulic system leak	4 Locate and repair leak

Brake pedal doesn't return

PROBABLE CAUSE	CORRECTIVE ACTION
1 Brake pedal binding	1 Inspect pivot bushing and pushrod, repair or lubricate
2 Defective master cylinder	2 Replace master cylinder

Brake pedal pulsates during brake application

PROBABLE CAUSE	CORRECTIVE ACTION
1 Brake drums out-of-round	1 Have drums machined by an automotive machine shop
2 Excessive brake disc runout or disc surfaces out-of-parallel	2 Have discs machined by an automotive machine shop
3 Loose or worn wheel bearings	3 Adjust or replace wheel bearings
4 Loose lug nuts	4 Tighten lug nuts

Brakes slow to release

PROBABLE CAUSE	CORRECTIVE ACTION
1 Malfunctioning power booster	1 Replace booster
2 Pedal linkage binding	2 Inspect pedal pivot bushing and pushrod, repair/lubricate
3 Malfunctioning proportioning valve	3 Replace proportioning valve
4 Sticking caliper or wheel cylinder	4 Repair or replace calipers or wheel cylinders
5 Kinked or internally split brake hose	5 Locate and replace faulty brake hose

Brakes grab (one or more wheels)

PROBABLE CAUSE	CORRECTIVE ACTION
1 Grease or brake fluid on brake lining	1 Locate and repair cause of contamination, replace lining
2 Brake lining glazed	2 Replace lining, deglaze disc or drum

PROBABLE CAUSE   **CORRECTIVE ACTION**

Vehicle pulls to one side during braking

1 Grease or brake fluid on brake lining	1 Locate and repair cause of contamination, replace lining
2 Brake lining glazed	2 Deglaze or replace lining, deglaze disc or drum
3 Restricted brake line or hose	3 Repair line or replace hose
4 Tire pressures incorrect	4 Adjust tire pressures
5 Caliper or wheel cylinder sticking	5 Repair or replace calipers or wheel cylinders
6 Wheels out of alignment	6 Have wheels aligned
7 Weak suspension spring	7 Replace springs
8 Weak or broken shock absorber	8 Replace shock absorbers

Brakes drag (indicated by sluggish engine performance or wheels being very hot after driving)

1 Brake pedal pushrod incorrectly adjusted	1 Adjust pushrod
2 Master cylinder pushrod (between booster and master cylinder)	2 Adjust pushrod incorrectly adjusted
3 Obstructed compensating port in master cylinder	3 Replace master cylinder
4 Master cylinder piston seized in bore	4 Replace master cylinder
5 Contaminated fluid causing swollen seals throughout system	5 Flush system, replace all hydraulic components
6 Clogged brake lines or internally split brake hose(s)	6 Flush hydraulic system, replace defective hose(s)
7 Sticking caliper(s) or wheel cylinder(s)	7 Replace calipers or wheel cylinders
8 Parking brake not releasing	8 Inspect parking brake linkage and parking brake mechanism, repair as required
9 Improper shoe-to-drum clearance	9 Adjust brake shoes
10 Faulty proportioning valve	10 Replace proportioning valve

Brakes fade (due to excessive heat)

1 Brake linings excessively worn or glazed	1 Deglaze or replace brake pads and/or shoes
2 Excessive use of brakes	2 Downshift into a lower gear, maintain a constant slower speed (going down hills)
3 Vehicle overloaded	3 Reduce load
4 Brake drums or discs worn too thin	4 Measure drum diameter and disc thickness, replace drums or discs as required
5 Contaminated brake fluid	5 Flush system, replace fluid
6 Brakes drag	6 Repair cause of dragging brakes
7 Driver resting left foot on brake pedal	7 Don't ride the brakes

Brakes noisy (high-pitched squeal)

1 Glazed lining	1 Deglaze or replace lining
2 Contaminated lining (brake fluid, grease, etc.)	2 Repair source of contamination, replace linings
3 Weak or broken brake shoe hold-down or return spring	3 Replace springs
4 Rivets securing lining to shoe or backing plate loose	4 Replace shoes or pads
5 Excessive dust buildup on brake linings	5 Wash brakes off with brake system cleaner
6 Brake drums worn too thin	6 Measure diameter of drums, replace if necessary
7 Wear indicator on disc brake pads contacting disc	7 Replace brake pads
8 Anti-squeal shims missing or installed improperly	8 Install shims correctly

Troubleshooting (continued)

PROBABLE CAUSE	CORRECTIVE ACTION

Brakes noisy (scraping sound)

1 Brake pads or shoes worn out; rivets, backing plate or brake	1 Replace linings, have discs and/or drums machined (or replace) shoe metal contacting disc or drum

Brakes chatter

1 Worn brake lining	1 Inspect brakes, replace shoes or pads as necessary
2 Glazed or scored discs or drums	2 Deglaze discs or drums with sandpaper (if glazing is severe, machining will be required)
3 Drums or discs heat checked	3 Check discs and/or drums for hard spots, heat checking, etc. Have discs/ drums machined or replace them
4 Disc runout or drum out-of-round excessive	4 Measure disc runout and/or drum out-of-round, have discs or drums machined or replace them
5 Loose or worn wheel bearings	5 Adjust or replace wheel bearings
6 Loose or bent brake backing plate (drum brakes)	6 Tighten or replace backing plate
7 Grooves worn in discs or drums	7 Have discs or drums machined, if within limits (if not, replace them)
8 Brake linings contaminated (brake fluid, grease, etc.)	8 Locate and repair source of contamination, replace pads or shoes
9 Excessive dust buildup on linings	9 Wash brakes with brake system cleaner
10 Surface finish on discs or drums too rough after machining	10 Have discs or drums properly machined (especially on vehicles with sliding calipers)
11 Brake pads or shoes glazed	11 Deglaze or replace brake pads or shoes

Brake pads or shoes click

1 Shoe support pads on brake backing plate grooved or	1 Replace brake backing plate excessively worn
2 Brake pads loose in caliper	2 Loose pad retainers or anti-rattle clips
3 Also see items listed under Brakes chatter	

Brakes make groaning noise at end of stop

1 Brake pads and/or shoes worn out	1 Replace pads and/or shoes
2 Brake linings contaminated (brake fluid, grease, etc.)	2 Locate and repair cause of contamination, replace brake pads or shoes
3 Brake linings glazed	3 Deglaze or replace brake pads or shoes
4 Excessive dust buildup on linings	4 Wash brakes with brake system cleaner
5 Scored or heat-checked discs or drums	5 Inspect discs/drums, have machined if within limits (if not, replace discs or drums)
6 Broken or missing brake shoe attaching hardware	6 Inspect drum brakes, replace missing hardware

Rear brakes lock up under light brake application

1 Tire pressures too high	1 Adjust tire pressures
2 Tires excessively worn	2 Replace tires
3 Defective proportioning valve	3 Replace proportioning valve

Brake warning light on instrument panel comes on (or stays on)

1 Low fluid level in master cylinder reservoir (reservoirs with fluid level sensor)	1 Add fluid, inspect system for leak, check the thickness of the brake pads and shoes
2 Failure in one half of the hydraulic system	2 Inspect hydraulic system for a leak
3 Piston in pressure differential warning valve not centered	3 Center piston by bleeding one circuit or the other (close bleeder valve as soon as the light goes out)
4 Defective pressure differential valve or warning switch	4 Replace valve or switch
5 Air in the hydraulic system	5 Bleed the system, check for leaks
6 Brake pads worn out (vehicles with electric wear sensors - small probes that fit into the brake pads and ground out on the disc when the pads get thin)	6 Replace brake pads (and sensors)

PROBABLE CAUSE	CORRECTIVE ACTION

Brakes do not self adjust

Disc brakes

1 Defective caliper piston seals	1 Replace calipers. Also, possible contaminated fluid causing soft or swollen seals (flush system and fill with new fluid if in doubt)
2 Corroded caliper piston(s)	2 Same as above

Drum brakes

1 Adjuster screw frozen	1 Remove adjuster, disassemble, clean and lubricate with high-temperature grease
2 Adjuster lever does not contact star wheel or is binding	2 Inspect drum brakes, assemble correctly or clean or replace parts as required
3 Adjusters mixed up (installed on wrong wheels after brake job)	3 Reassemble correctly
4 Adjuster cable broken or installed incorrectly (cable-type adjusters)	4 Install new cable or assemble correctly

Rapid brake lining wear

1 Driver resting left foot on brake pedal	1 Don't ride the brakes
2 Surface finish on discs or drums too rough	2 Have discs or drums properly machined
3 Also see Brakes drag	

---

3   Anti-lock Brake System (ABS) - general information

General information

1   The anti-lock brake system is designed to maintain vehicle steerability, directional stability and optimum deceleration under severe braking conditions on most road surfaces. It does so by monitoring the rotational speed of each wheel and controlling the brake line pressure to each wheel during braking. This prevents the wheels from locking up.

2   The ABS system has three main components - the wheel speed sensors, the Electronic Control Unit (ECU) and the Brake Pressure Modulation Valve (BPMV) **(see illustration)**. Four wheel-speed sensors - one at each wheel - send a variable voltage signal to the control unit, which monitors these signals, compares them to its program and determines whether a wheel is about to lock up. When a wheel is about to lock up, the control unit signals the hydraulic unit to reduce hydraulic pressure (or not increase it further) at that wheel's brake caliper. Pressure modulation is handled by electrically operated solenoid valves.

3   If a problem develops within the system, an "ABS" warning light will glow on the dashboard. Sometimes, a visual inspection of the ABS system can help you locate the problem. Carefully inspect the ABS wiring harness. Pay close attention particularly to the harness and connections near each wheel. Look for signs of chafing and other damage caused by incor-

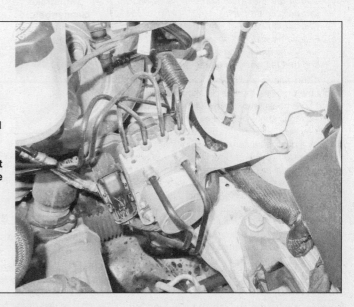

3.2 The Brake Pressure Modulation Valve (BPMV) is located to the side of the master cylinder. The hydraulic unit controls the brake line pressure to each wheel individually

rectly routed wires. If a wheel sensor harness is damaged, the sensor must be replaced.

Warning: *Do NOT try to repair an ABS wiring harness. The ABS system is sensitive to even the smallest changes in resistance. Repairing the harness could alter resistance values and cause the system to malfunction. If the ABS wiring harness is damaged in any way, it must be replaced.*

Caution: *Make sure the ignition is turned off before unplugging or reattaching any electrical connections.*

4   Some vehicles come equipped with traction control, which helps prevent wheel spin under acceleration. The Traction Control System (TCS) utilizes some of the same components as the ABS system. The wheel sensors monitor wheel rotation and transmit data through the same wiring to the ABS control module. The control module compares rotation speeds, then controls the amount of power supplied to the wheels by adjusting fuel settings to the engine.

Diagnosis and repair

5   If a dashboard warning light comes on and stays on while the vehicle is in operation, the ABS system requires attention. Although special electronic ABS diagnostic testing

3.10a Front wheel speed sensor mounting bolt

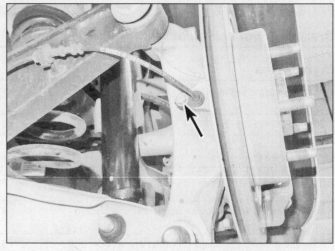

3.10b Rear wheel speed sensor mounting bolt

tools are necessary to properly diagnose the system, you can perform a few preliminary checks before taking the vehicle to a dealer service department.

a) *Check the brake fluid level in the reservoir.*

b) *Verify that the computer electrical connectors are securely connected.*

c) *Check the electrical connectors at the hydraulic control unit.*

d) *Check the fuses.*

e) *Follow the wiring harness to each wheel and verify that all connections are secure and that the wiring is undamaged.*

6   If the above preliminary checks do not rectify the problem, the vehicle should be diagnosed by a dealer service department or other qualified repair shop. Due to the complex nature of this system, all actual repair work must be done by a qualified automotive technician.

Warning: *Do not operate the vehicle if you are in doubt about the effectiveness of the brake system. It's possible for air to become trapped in the ABS hydraulic control unit, so, if the pedal continues to feel spongy after repeated bleedings or the BRAKE or ABS light stays on, have the vehicle towed to a dealer service department or other qualified repair shop to be bled.*

Wheel speed sensor - removal and installation

7   Make sure the ignition key is turned to the Off position. Loosen the wheel lug nuts, raise the vehicle and support it securely on jackstands, then remove the wheel.

8   Make sure the ignition key is turned to the Off position.

9   Trace the wiring back from the sensor, detaching all brackets and clips while noting its correct routing, then disconnect the electrical connector.

10   Remove the mounting bolt and carefully pull the sensor out from the knuckle **(see illustrations)**.

11   Installation is the reverse of removal. Tighten the mounting bolt securely.

4.5 Always wash the brakes with brake cleaner before disassembling anything

12   Install the wheel and lug nuts, tightening them securely. Lower the vehicle and tighten the lug nuts to the torque listed in the Chapter 1 Specifications.

---

4   Disc brake pads - replacement

Warning: *Disc brake pads must be replaced on both front or both rear wheels at the same time - never replace the pads on only one wheel. Also, the dust created by the brake system is harmful to your health. Never blow it out with compressed air and don't inhale any of it. An approved filtering mask should be worn when working on the brakes. Do not, under any circumstances, use petroleum-based solvents to clean brake parts. Use brake system cleaner only!*

Front brake pads

1   Remove the cap from the brake fluid reservoir. To prevent brake fluid from possibly overflowing the reservoir when the calipers are fully retracted, use a syringe or suction gun to remove brake fluid until the reservoir is approximately half full.

2   Loosen the wheel lug nuts, raise the front of the vehicle and support it securely on jackstands. Block the wheels at the opposite end.

3   Remove the wheels. Work on one brake assembly at a time, using the assembled brake for reference if necessary.

4   Inspect the brake disc carefully (see Section 6). If machining is necessary, follow the information in that Section to remove the disc, at which time the pads can be removed as well.

5   Before removing the brake caliper, wash it thoroughly with brake system cleaner and allow it to dry **(see illustration)**. Position a drain pan under the brake to catch the residue - DO NOT use compressed air to blow off the brake dust.

6   When working on the brakes, keep these points in mind:

a) *Use only hand tools to remove or install the caliper mounting bolts. Do not use air tools or the caliper could be damaged.*

b) *When removing or installing the caliper mounting (guide pin) bolts, use an open end wrench to hold the guide pin from rotating. Do not allow the open-end wrench to contact the caliper when tightening or it could cause the brakes to pulsate.*

4.8a Use a large C-clamp to depress the piston into the caliper to make room for the new pads. The caliper piston should be fully seated into the caliper body. Tighten the clamp slowly and make sure the fluid in the master cylinder reservoir doesn't overflow

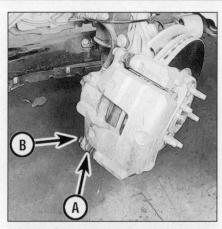

4.8b Hold the lower caliper guide pin (A) with an open-end wrench and use another wrench to unscrew the caliper guide pin bolt (B)

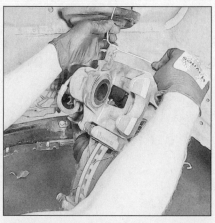

4.8c Swing the caliper up and use a length of wire to hold it out of the way. On some models, the wheel speed sensor wiring bracket may have to be unbolted in order to allow repositioning of the caliper

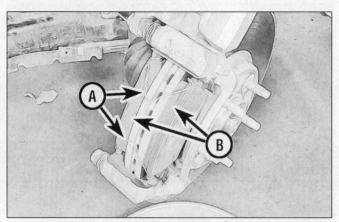

4.8d Remove the anti-rattle springs (A), and the inner and outer brake pads (B). Note which pad has the pad wear sensor (if equipped) so it can be re-assembled in the same position

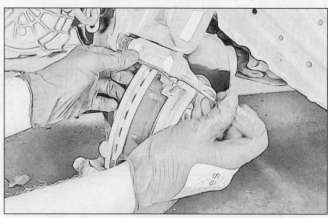

4.8e Remove the upper and lower pad support plates from the mounting bracket. If necessary, replace them. Lubricate the pad contact areas with high-temperature brake grease

c) *Do not disconnect the brake line from the caliper unless you are replacing the caliper.*

d) *If you are removing the caliper but not replacing the pads, note the position of the inner and outer pads so you can reinstall them in the same locations.*

7   Inspect the brake lines and fittings. Replace any broken clamps or brackets that hold the brake lines in place.

8   For the brake pad replacement sequence, follow the accompanying photos **(see illustrations)**. Stay in order and read the caption under each illustration.

9   Replace the pads by reversing the steps above. Clean the disassembled parts including the contact areas on the caliper bracket. Inspect the guide pins and coat them with high-temperature brake grease before installing them into the mounting bracket. Inspect the condition of the rubber boots, replacing them if they are torn or damaged, and ensure they are properly seated in the grooves on the pins **(see illustrations)**.

4.9a Remove the lower guide pin, clean it, then apply a film of high-temperature brake grease to it

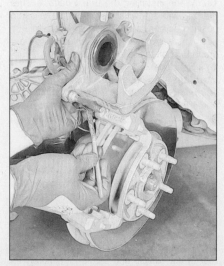

4.9b Pull the caliper and upper guide pin from the caliper mounting bracket, then clean and lubricate the upper guide pin

4.14 Always wash the brakes with brake cleaner before disassembling anything

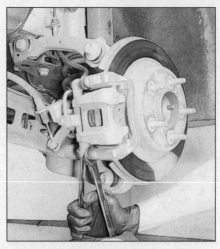

4.15 Hold the caliper guide pin with an open-end wrench and use another wrench to unscrew the caliper guide pin bolt

4.17 Support the caliper with a length of wire

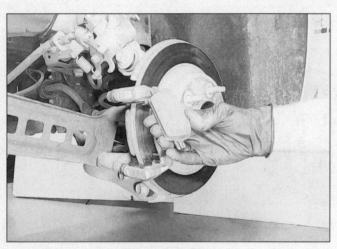

4.19a Remove the outer. . .

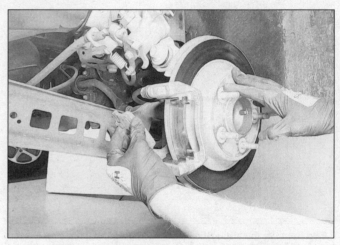

4.19b. . . and inner pad from the mounting bracket

10   When installing the brake pads, ensure the pad with the wear sensor is in the same position as before. Use new springs/retainers when installing new pads. Tighten the caliper mounting bolt to the torque listed in this Chapter's Specifications.

Warning: *New pads will not give full braking efficiency until they have bedded in. Be prepared for this and avoid hard braking as much as possible for the first hundred miles or so after pad replacement.*

Rear brake pads

11   Remove the cap from the brake fluid reservoir. To prevent brake fluid from possibly overflowing the reservoir when the calipers are fully retracted, use a syringe or suction gun to remove brake fluid until the reservoir is approximately half full.

12   Loosen the wheel lug nuts, raise the rear of the vehicle and support it securely on jackstands. Block the wheels at the opposite end. Remove the wheels.

13   If equipped with an electronic park-

ing brake, set the parking brake into service mode (see Section 12).

14   Before removing the brake caliper, wash it thoroughly with brake system cleaner and allow it to dry **(see illustration)**. Position a drain pan under the brake to catch the residue - DO NOT use compressed air to blow off the brake dust.

15   Using an open-end wrench, hold the caliper guide pin from spinning, then remove the caliper mounting bolts **(see illustration)**.

16   Remove the caliper from the caliper bracket. Hang the caliper up with a wire or a suitable strap so that it is not dangling by the brake hose.

17   Hang the caliper up with a wire so that it is not dangling by the brake hose **(see illustration)**.

18   On 2015 and earlier models with RPO J60 rear brakes, remove the caliper mounting bracket bolts.

19   Remove the brake pads from the caliper mounting bracket **(see illustrations)**.

20   Remove the brake pad support plates

from the caliper mounting bracket **(see illustration)**.

21   Install new pad support plates to the mounting bracket, then install the pads into the bracket.

Note: *Apply anti-seize compound to all the points where one piece of metal touches another piece of metal. There is no need in coating the entire surfaces. Only use the anti-seize at those points of actual metal-to-metal contact.*

22   If removed, install the caliper mounting bracket and bolts. Tighten the mounting bracket bolts to the torque listed in this Chapter's Specifications.

23   Use a caliper piston retraction tool, slowly rotate the piston clockwise until the piston is all the way into the caliper bore. Adjust the piston so the notches in the piston face align with the pins on the back of the inner brake pad - the alignment slot should be at the 12 o'clock position **(see illustrations)**.

24   Remove the caliper guide pins from the mounting bracket. Clean them, then lubricate them with high-temperature brake grease

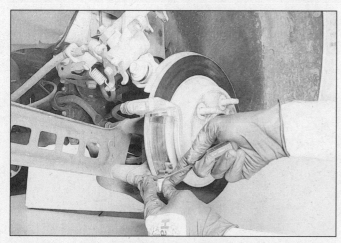

4.20 Remove and inspect the upper and lower pad support plates, replacing them if necessary

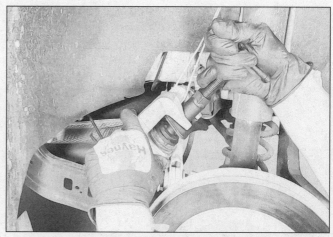

4.23a Retract the rear caliper piston by rotating it into its bore. Here, a special caliper piston retraction tool is being used. Sometimes a pair of needle-nose pliers (with the tips engaged with the notches) will work

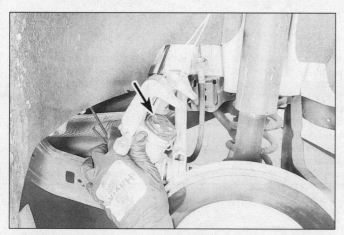

4.23b Once retracted, align the notches perpendicular (12 o'clock position) to the mounting bolt holes (the notches must align with the pins on the brake pad backing plates)

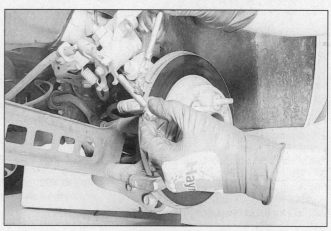

4.24 Lubricate the guide pins with high-temperature brake grease

(see illustration). Reinstall the guide pins into the mounting bracket, making sure the seals seat properly in the guide pin grooves.

25 Install the caliper over the pads, making sure the projection on the inner brake pad enages with the notch in the caliper piston. Tighten the caliper mounting bolts to the torque listed in this Chapter's Specifications **(see illustration)**. Firmly depress the brake pedal a few times to bring the pads into contact with the disc. Check the level of the brake fluid, adding some if necessary (see Chapter 1).

26 On models with an Electronic Parking Branke (EPB), follow the steps to calibrate the parking brake to the new brake pads (see Section 12).

Warning: *New pads will not give full braking efficiency until they have bedded in. Be prepared for this and avoid hard braking as much as possible for the first hundred miles or so after pad replacement.*

5   Disc brake caliper and caliper mounting bracket - removal and installation

Warning: *Dust created by the brake system is harmful to your health. Never blow it out with compressed air and don't inhale any of it. An approved filtering mask should be worn when working on the brakes. Do not, under any circumstances, use petroleum-based solvents to clean brake parts. Use brake system cleaner only.*

Note: *If replacement is indicated (usually because of fluid leakage or damage to a piston boot), it is recommended that the calipers be replaced, not overhauled. New and factory rebuilt units are available on an exchange basis, which makes this job quite easy. Always replace the calipers in pairs - never replace just one of them.*

Note: *If the caliper is just being removed to allow access to another component, do not disconnect the brake hose (or parking brake cable on rear calipers).*

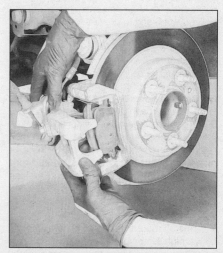

4.25 With the support plates and new pads installed, position the caliper onto the caliper bracket and install the caliper mounting bolts

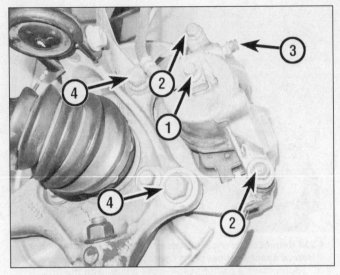

5.4a Front caliper mounting details

1	Brake hose banjo bolt	3	Caliper bleed screw
2	Caliper mounting bolts	4	Caliper mounting bracket bolts

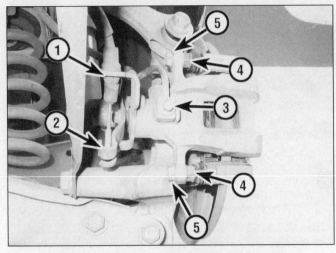

5.4b Rear caliper mounting details (models with parking brake cables)

1	Parking brake cable retaining clip	3	Brake hose banjo bolt
2	Parking brake actuator lever	4	Caliper guide pin
		5	Caliper mounting (guide pin) bolt

Removal

1   Loosen the wheel lug nuts, raise the vehicle and support it securely on jackstands. Remove the wheels.

Rear calipers

2   On models with an Electronic Parking Brake (EPB), place the parking brake actuators in service mode (see Section 12)

3   On models with parking brake cables (including 2013 models with an Electronic Parking brake), detach the parking brake cables from the calipers.

Front and rear calipers

4   Remove the banjo fitting bolt and disconnect the brake hose from the caliper **(see illustrations)**. Discard the sealing washers from each side of the hose fitting. Plug the brake hose to keep contaminants out of the brake system and to prevent losing any more brake fluid than is necessary.

5   Refer to Section 4 for the caliper removal procedure.

Caution: *If the caliper is just being removed to access another component, use a piece of wire to hang it securely out of the way. Do not let the caliper hang by the brake hose.*

6   To remove the caliper mounting bracket, remove the brake pads (see Section 4), then remove and discard the two caliper bracket mounting bolts. Clean the mating surfaces and remove any remaining thread locking material on the bracket.

Installation

7   Installation is the reverse of removal. Use a high-temperature thread locking compound on the fastener threads, and install new caliper mounting bracket bolts. Tighten the fasteners to the torque listed in this Chapter's Specifications.

8   Always use new sealing washers when re-installing the banjo fitting to the caliper.

9   If the brake hose was disconnected, bleed the brake system (see Section 9). Make sure there are no leaks from the hose connections. Test the brakes carefully before returning the vehicle to normal service.

10   If work was performed on the rear calipers, adjust the parking brake (models with parking brake cables; see Section 13). On models with an Electronic Parking Brake, enable the parking brake system.

---

6   Brake disc - inspection, removal and installation

Inspection

1   Loosen the wheel lug nuts, raise the vehicle and support it securely on jackstands.

2   Remove the brake caliper and mounting bracket (see Section 5). It isn't necessary to disconnect the brake hose. After removing the caliper, suspend it out of the way with a piece of wire.

3   Visually inspect the disc surface for score marks and other damage. Light scratches and shallow grooves are normal after use and may not always be detrimental to brake operation, but deep scoring requires disc removal and refinishing by an automotive machine shop. Check both sides of the disc **(see illustration)**. If pulsating has been noticed during application of the brakes, suspect excessive disc runout.

4   To check brake disc runout, reinstall the lug nuts (inverted if possible) and place a dial indicator at a point about 1/2-inch from the outer edge of the disc **(see illustration)**. Set the indicator to zero and

turn the disc. The indicator reading should not exceed the specified allowable runout limit. If it does, the disc should be refinished by an automotive machine shop, or replaced.

Note: *A seemingly smooth brake disc that has been previously installed should be resurfaced regardless of the dial indicator reading. This will impart a smooth finish and ensure a perfectly flat surface, eliminating any brake pedal pulsation or other undesirable symptoms related to questionable discs. At the very least, if you elect NOT to have the discs resurfaced, remove the glaze from the surface with emery cloth or sandpaper, using a swirling motion* **(see illustration)**.

5   Do NOT use a brake disc that is severely

6.3 The brake pads on this vehicle were obviously neglected, as they wore down completely and cut deep grooves into the disc - wear this severe means the disc must be replaced

6.4a To check disc runout, mount a dial indicator as shown and rotate the disc

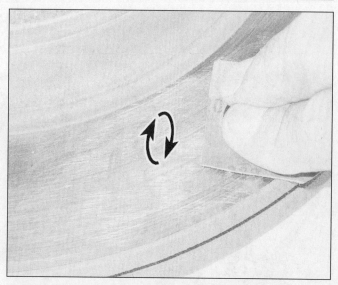

6.4b Using a swirling motion, remove the glaze from the disc surface with sandpaper or emery cloth

pitted, scarred, heavily grooved or has been machined below the minimum thickness. The minimum thickness is cast or stamped into the disc **(see illustration)**. The brake disc thickness can be checked with a micrometer **(see illustration)**.

Removal

6   Remove the caliper and the caliper mounting bracket (see Section 5). Remove the lug nuts if they were reinstalled for the runout inspection.

7   Mark the brake disc at one of the wheel studs so it can be reinstalled in the same position, then remove the disc retaining screw, if equipped. Remove the disc from the hub.

Installation

8   While the disc is off, wire-brush the backside of the disc and the center portion of the wheel hub where the disc makes contact.

9   Align the index marks and place the disc in position over the wheel studs. Tighten the retaining screw (if equipped) securely.

10   Install the caliper mounting bracket and caliper, tightening the bolts to the torque listed in this Chapter's Specifications.

11   Install the wheel, then lower the vehicle to the ground. Tighten the lug nuts to the torque listed in the Chapter 1 Specifications. Depress the brake pedal a few times to bring the brake pads into contact with the disc. Bleeding won't be necessary unless the brake hose was disconnected from the

caliper. Check the operation of the brakes carefully before driving the vehicle.

7   Master cylinder - removal and installation

Removal

Note: *Pump the brake pedal several times to remove any vacuum in the brake booster. This will prevent the O-ring sealing the master cylinder to the booster from being sucked into the booster.*

1   The master cylinder is located in the left rear corner of the engine compartment, mounted to the power brake booster.

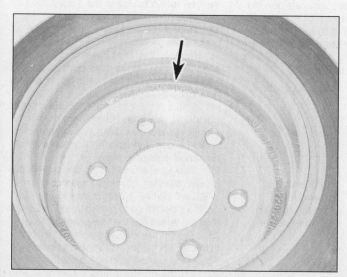

6.5a The minimum thickness dimension is cast into the front or back side of the disc

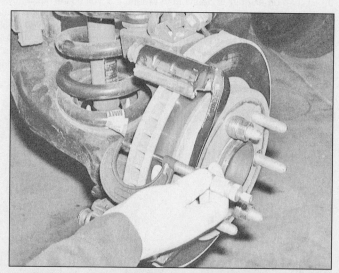

6.5b Use a micrometer to measure disc thickness. Ideally, measure the thickness in at least three different locations equally spaced around the disc

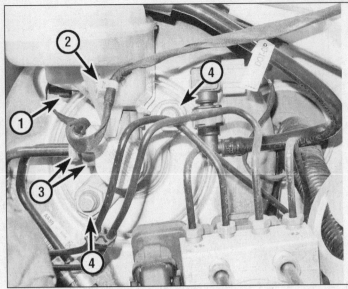

7.7 Master cylinder mounting details

1 *Fluid level sensor electrical connector*
2 *Harness clip*
3 *Fluid line fittings*
4 *Mounting nuts*

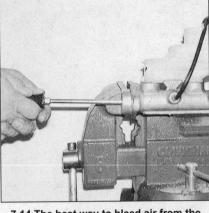

7.14 The best way to bleed air from the master cylinder before installing it on the vehicle is with a pair of bleeder tubes that direct brake fluid into the reservoir during bleeding

2   Ensure the ignition switch is turned to the Off position.

3   Depress the brake pedal several times to deplete the brake booster reserve vacuum.

4   Remove the engine cover if necessary for access.

5   Remove as much fluid as you can from the reservoir with a syringe, such as an old turkey baster.

Warning: *If a baster is used, never again use it for the preparation of food.*

6   Remove the coolant expansion tank, without disconnecting the hoses or draining any coolant, and position it to the side.

7   Disconnect the electrical connector at the brake fluid level switch on the master cylinder reservoir. **(see illustration)**.

8   Place rags under the fluid fittings and prepare caps or plastic bags to cover the ends of the lines once they are disconnected.

9   Clean off any dirt or debris from around the brake line fittings to prevent it from entering the system.

Caution: *Brake fluid will damage paint. Cover all body parts and be careful not to spill fluid during this procedure.*

10   Loosen the fittings at the ends of the brake lines where they enter the master cylinder **(see illustration 7.7)**. To prevent rounding off the corners on these nuts, the use of a flare-nut wrench, which wraps around the nut, is preferred. Pull the brake lines slightly away from the master cylinder and plug the ends to prevent contamination.

11   Remove the master cylinder-to-power booster nuts. Pull the master cylinder off the studs and out of the engine compartment. Again, be careful not to spill the fluid as this is done. Remove the O-ring seal from the booster.

12   The reservoir can be separated from the master cylinder by clamping the master cylinder in a vise and tapping out the retaining pin (clamp only the flange, do not clamp the body of the master cylinder). Some models use a retaining bolt in place of the pin. Lift the reservoir off the master cylinder. Lubricate new reservoir seals with a little brake fluid and install them on the new master cylinder. Be sure the reservoir seals are fully seated in the master cylinder. Firmly press the reservoir into place and install the retaining pin or bolt.

Warning: *Replace the retaining pin or bolt with a new one.*
Note: *Install new seals when transferring the reservoir to a new master cylinder.*

Installation

13   Bench bleed the new master cylinder before installing it. Mount the master cylinder in a vise, with the jaws of the vise clamping on the mounting flange.

14   Attach a pair of master cylinder bleeder tubes to the outlet ports of the master cylinder **(see illustration)**.

15   Fill the reservoir with brake fluid of the recommended type (see Chapter 1).

16   Slowly push the pistons into the master cylinder (a large Phillips screwdriver can be used for this) - air will be expelled from the pressure chambers and into the reservoir. Because the tubes are submerged in fluid, air can't be drawn back into the master cylinder when you release the pistons.

17   Repeat the procedure until no more air bubbles are present.

18   Remove the bleed tubes, one at a time, and install plugs in the open ports to prevent fluid leakage and air from entering. Install the reservoir cap.

19   Install a new O-ring onto the master cylinder sleeve **(see illustration)**. Install the master cylinder over the studs on the power brake booster and tighten the attaching nuts only finger-tight at this time.

20   Thread the brake line fittings into the master cylinder. Since the master cylinder is still a bit loose, it can be moved slightly in order for the fittings to thread in easily. Do not strip the threads as the fittings are tightened.

21   Tighten the mounting nuts to the torque listed in this Chapter's Specifications, then tighten the brake line fittings securely.

22   Fill the master cylinder reservoir with fluid, then bleed the master cylinder and the brake system (see Section 9). To bleed the cylinder on the vehicle, have an assistant depress the brake pedal and hold the pedal

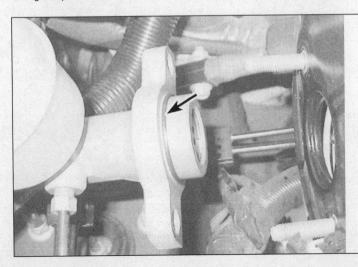

7.19 Install a new O-ring onto the master cylinder sleeve

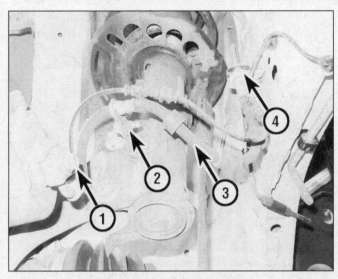

8.3a Front brake hose details

1	Banjo fitting bolt	3	Brake hose
2	Brake hose retaining bracket to strut	4	Brake hose-to-brake line fitting

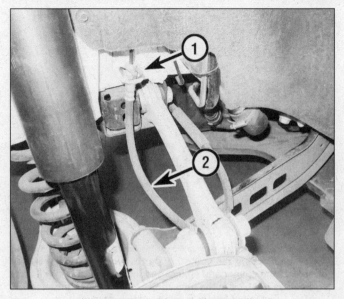

8.3b Rear brake hose details

1	Brake hose-to-brake line fitting	2	Brake hose

to the floor. Loosen the fitting to allow air and fluid to escape. Repeat this procedure on both fittings until the fluid is clear of air bubbles.
Caution: *Have plenty of rags on hand to catch the fluid - brake fluid will ruin painted surfaces. After the bleeding procedure is completed, rinse the area under the master cylinder with clean water.*
23 Test the operation of the brake system carefully before placing the vehicle into normal service.
Warning: *Do not operate the vehicle if you are in doubt about the effectiveness of the brake system. It is possible for air to become trapped in the anti-lock brake system hydraulic control unit; if the pedal continues to feel spongy after repeated bleedings or the BRAKE or ANTI-LOCK light stays on, have the vehicle towed to a dealer service department or other qualified shop to be bled with the aid of a scan tool.*

8   Brake hoses and lines - inspection and replacement

1 About every six months, with the vehicle raised and placed securely on jackstands, the flexible hoses which connect the steel brake lines with the front and rear brake assemblies should be inspected for cracks, chafing of the outer cover, leaks, blisters and other damage. These are important and vulnerable parts of the brake system and inspection should be complete. A light and mirror will be needed for a thorough check. If a hose exhibits any of the above defects, replace it with a new one.

Flexible hoses

2 Clean all dirt away from the ends of the hose.

3 To remove a brake hose, unscrew the tube nut with a flare-nut wrench, if available, to prevent rounding-off the corners of the nut, then remove the bolt(s), clip(s) or grommets securing the hose to the body (and any suspension components) **(see illustrations)**.
4 Disconnect the hose from the caliper; discard the sealing washers on either side of the fitting.
5 Using new sealing washers, attach the new brake hose to the caliper. Tighten the banjo fitting bolt to the torque listed in this Chapter's Specifications.
6 Installation is the reverse of removal, making sure the hose isn't twisted.
7 Carefully check to make sure the suspension or steering components don't make contact with the hose. Have an assistant push down on the vehicle and also turn the steering wheel lock-to-lock during inspection.
8 Bleed the brake system (see Section 9).

Metal brake lines

9 When replacing brake lines, be sure to use the correct parts. Don't use copper tubing for any brake system components. Purchase steel brake lines from a dealer parts department or auto parts store.
10 Prefabricated brake line, with the tube ends already flared and fittings installed, is available at auto parts stores and dealer parts departments. These lines can be bent to the proper shapes using a tubing bender.
11 When installing the new line, make sure it's well supported in the brackets and has plenty of clearance between moving or hot components.
12 After installation, check the master cylinder fluid level and add fluid as necessary. Bleed the brake system (see Section 9) and test the brakes carefully before placing the vehicle into normal operation.

9   Brake hydraulic system - bleeding

Warning: *If air has found its way into the hydraulic control unit, the system must be bled with the use of a scan tool. If the brake pedal feels spongy even after bleeding the brakes, or the ABS light on the instrument panel does not go off, or if you have any doubts whatsoever about the effectiveness of the brake system, have the vehicle towed to a dealer service department or other repair shop equipped with the necessary tools for bleeding the system.*
Warning: *Wear eye protection when bleeding the brake system. If the fluid comes in contact with your eyes, immediately rinse them with water and seek medical attention.*
Note: *Bleeding the brake system is necessary to remove any air that's trapped in the system when it's opened during removal and installation of a hose, line, caliper, wheel cylinder or master cylinder.*
1 It will probably be necessary to bleed the system at all four brakes if air has entered the system due to low fluid level, or if the brake lines have been disconnected at the master cylinder.
2 If a brake line was disconnected only at a wheel, then only that caliper or wheel cylinder must be bled.
3 If a brake line is disconnected at a fitting located between the master cylinder and any of the brakes, that part of the system served by the disconnected line must be bled.
4 Remove any residual vacuum (or hydraulic pressure) from the power brake booster by applying the brake several times with the engine off.
5 Remove the master cylinder reservoir cap and fill the reservoir with brake fluid. Reinstall the cap.
Note: *Check the fluid level often during the bleeding operation and add fluid as necessary*

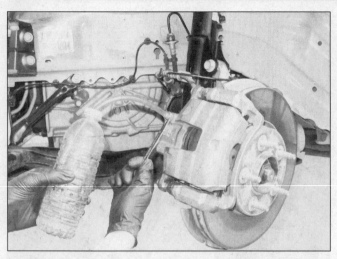

9.8 When bleeding the brakes, a hose is connected to the bleed screw at the caliper and submerged in brake fluid - air will be seen as bubbles in the tube and container (all air must be expelled before moving to the next wheel)

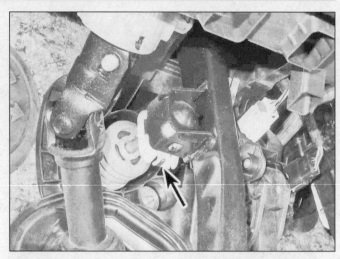

10.13a Squeeze or pry the tangs of the pushrod retainer (lower tang shown) while pulling the pedal back to detach the pushrod from the brake pedal arm

to prevent the fluid level from falling low enough to allow air bubbles into the master cylinder.

6   Have an assistant on hand, as well as a supply of new brake fluid, an empty clear plastic container, a length of plastic, rubber or vinyl tubing to fit over the bleeder valve, and a wrench to open and close the bleeder valve.

7   Beginning at the right-rear wheel, loosen the bleeder screw slightly, then tighten it to a point where it's snug but can still be loosened quickly and easily.

8   Place one end of the tubing over the bleeder screw fitting and submerge the other end in brake fluid in the container **(see illustration)**.

9   Have the assistant slowly depress the brake pedal and hold it in the depressed position.

10   While the pedal is held depressed, open the bleeder screw just enough to allow a flow of fluid to leave the valve. Watch for air bubbles to exit the submerged end of the tube. When the fluid flow slows after a couple of seconds, tighten the screw and have your assistant release the pedal.

11   Repeat Steps 9 and 10 until no more air is seen leaving the tube, then tighten the bleeder screw. Bleed the remaining calipers in the correct sequence: left front, left rear, right front.

12   Check the fluid in the master cylinder reservoir frequently.

13   Never use old brake fluid. It contains moisture which can boil, rendering the brake system inoperative.

14   Refill the master cylinder with fluid at the end of the operation.

15   Check the operation of the brakes. The pedal should feel solid when depressed, with no sponginess. If necessary, repeat the entire process.

Warning: *Do not operate the vehicle if you are in doubt about the effectiveness of the brake system. It is possible for air to become trapped*

in the anti-lock brake system hydraulic control unit, so, if the pedal continues to feel spongy after repeated bleedings or the BRAKE or ANTI-LOCK light stays on, have the vehicle towed to a dealer service department or other qualified shop to be bled with the aid of a scan tool.

10   Power brake booster - check, removal and installation

Operating check

1   Depress the brake pedal several times with the engine off and make sure that there is no change in the pedal reserve distance.

2   Depress the pedal and start the engine. If the pedal goes down slightly, operation is normal.

Airtightness check

3   Start the engine and turn it off after one or two minutes. Depress the brake pedal several times slowly. If the pedal goes down farther the first time but gradually rises after the second or third depression, the booster is airtight.

4   Depress the brake pedal while the engine is running, then stop the engine with the pedal depressed. If there is no change in the pedal reserve travel after holding the pedal for 30 seconds, the booster is airtight.

5   Before replacing the power booster unit, inspect the condition of the rubber grommet which connects the check valve or vacuum sensor to the power booster. A cracked or damaged grommet can be the cause of vacuum leaks.

Removal

Warning: *Wait until the engine is completely cool before beginning this procedure.*

6   Disassembly of the power unit requires special tools and is not ordinarily performed by the home mechanic. If a problem devel-

ops, it's recommended that a new or factory rebuilt unit be installed.

7   Set the parking brake with the vehicle parked on a level surface.

8   With the ignition switch Off, pump the brake pedal several times to deplete any remaining vacuum in the booster.

9   Disconnect the cable from the negative terminal of the battery (see Chapter 5). On 2010 and later models, remove the battery and battery tray.

10   Remove the engine cover from the top of the engine. Also remove the knee bolster panel from under the steering column (see Chapter 11).

11   Without disconnecting the hoses or draining any coolant, remove the expansion tank and position it to the side (see Chapter 3).

12   Disconnect the electrical connector from the Brake Pedal Position (BPP) sensor located on the brake pedal bracket (see Section 14).

13   Squeeze or pry the tangs of the pushrod retainer, then pull the brake pedal to the rear to release the pushrod retainer from the brake pedal arm **(see illustrations)**. Discard the retainer and use a new one on re-assembly.

14   Disconnect the power booster check valve and hose and position to the side. If equipped with a power booster vacuum sensor, disconnect the electrical connector from the sensor and remove the sensor from the power booster.

15   Disconnect the electrical connector from brake fluid level sensor located on the brake fluid reservoir.

16   Locate the Brake Pressure Modulator Valve (BPMV) assembly (or, on some models, the Electronic Brake and Traction Control Module [EBTCM] assembly) below and to the side of the master cylinder. Without disconnecting any brake lines from the valve assembly, remove the mounting fasteners and detach the assembly from its bracket to

10.13b Slide the pushrod retainer out of the
bracket to this position

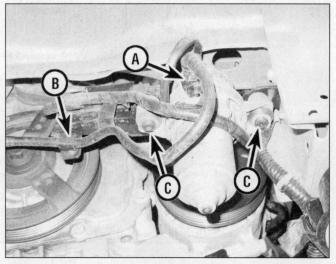

11.4 Vacuum tube quick-connect fitting (A), retaining clip (B)
and mounting bolts (C)

position it slightly forward and downward.

17 Remove the master cylinder (see Section 7).

18 Unscrew the two power booster mounting bolts from the front side of the booster and remove the booster. Note that the bolts are retained in their holes and do not come apart from the booster. If equipped, remove the gasket between the booster and the firewall.

Installation

19 Installation is the reverse of removal, noting the following:

20 Tighten fasteners to the torque listed in this Chapter's Specifications. DO NOT over tighten the power booster mounting bolts, or brake pedal movement may be impaired.

21 Inspect and, if necessary, replace the gasket between the power booster and the firewall (on models so equipped). Also, ensure the O-ring is properly positioned on the master cylinder sleeve.

22 Always install a new power booster pushrod retainer and ensure it is fully engaged in the brake pedal arm.

23 Bleed and install the master cylinder (see Section 7).

24 Bleed the brake system (see Section 9).

25 Start the engine, then depress the brake pedal several times to see if the Check Engine or Service Engine Soon light is illuminated. If so, have the vehicle towed to a dealer service department or other qualified repair shop equipped with the proper scan tool to have the brake pedal position sensorcalibrated.

26 Test the operation of the brakes before placing the vehicle in normal service.

Warning: *Do not operate the vehicle if you are in doubt about the effectiveness of the brake system. If the pedal feels spongy after repeated bleedings or the CHECK ENGINE, SERVICE ENGINE SOON, BRAKE or ANTI-LOCK light stays on, have the vehicle towed to a dealer service department or other qualified repair shop equipped with the proper scan tool.*

11 Auxiliary vacuum pump - removal and installation

Note: *Some models are equipped with an electric powered, auxiliary vacuum pump to provide additional vacuum to the brake booster. It is located in the lower left side of the engine compartment, and can be accessed through the left side wheel well.*

1 With the ignition switch in the Off position, pump the brake pedal several times to deplete any remaining vacuum.

2015 and earlier models/
2016 Malibu Limited models

2 Loosen the right front wheel lug nuts. With the parking brake applied, raise the front of the vehicle, support it securely on jackstands and remove the right front wheel.

3 Remove the right front inner fender splash shield (see Chapter 11).

4 Disconnect the vacuum tube from the vacuum pump by releasing the quick-connect fitting **(see illustration)**.

5 Disconnect the electrical connector from the vacuum pump.

6 Unscrew the fasteners and remove the vacuum pump.

7 Installation is the reverse of removal. Tighten the fasteners to the torque listed in this Chapter's Specifications and check for proper brake operation.

2016 and later models
(except Malibu Limited)

8 Remove the engine cover.

9 Remove the charge air cooler outlet tube (see Chapter 4, Section 15).

10 Detach the vacuum line fitting from the pump **(see illustration)**.

11 Remove the vacuum pump bolts and detach the pump from the valve cover and cylinder head. if the vacuum pump locating dowels remain in the cylinder head, remove them.

12 Remove the vacuum pump gasket. Clean the gasket mating surfaces.

13 Inspect the vacuum pump seal, replacing it if necessary.

**11.10 Vacuum
pump details**

1 *Vacuum line fitting*
2 *Mounting bolts*

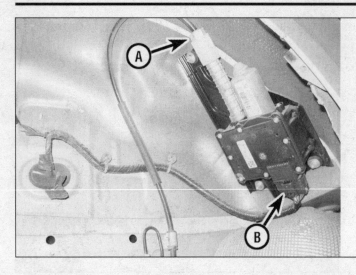

12.5 Parking brake cable nut (A) and electrical connector (B)

14   Lubricate the vacuum pump seal with clean engine oil.
15   Install the locating dowels into the vacuum pump.
16   Install a new gasket onto the vacuum pump.
17   Install the vacuum pump, making sure the drive tang engages the slot in the camshaft. Install the bolts, tightening them to the torque listed in this Chapter's Specifications.
18   The remainder of installation is the reverse of the removal procedure.

12   Electronic Parking Brake (EPB) system - component removal and installation

2013 models (remote actuator type)
Parking brake module
Note: *The parking brake module consists of apply and release actuators, a temperature sensor and the computer logic circuits to determine operating parameters.*
1   Block the front wheels and disable the electronic parking brake cable adjuster (see Section). Turn the ignition switch to the Off position.
2   Loosen the left rear wheel lug nuts, then raise the rear of the vehicle and support it securely on jackstands.
3   Remove the left rear wheel.
4   Remove the left rear inner fender liner (see Chapter 11).
5   Loosen the parking brake cable nut and remove the cable from the top of the module (**see illustration**).
6   Remove the wiring harness retainer clips if necessary and disconnect the electrical connector from the module (**see illustration 12.5**).
7   Remove the three mounting nuts and remove the parking brake module.
8   Installation is the reverse of removal.
9   Follow the procedures for module calibration (see Section 13).

Parking brake cables
10   Block the front wheels and disable the electronic parking brake cable adjuster (see Section 13). Turn the ignition switch to the Off position.
11   Loosen the left rear wheel lug nuts, then raise the rear of the vehicle and support it securely on jackstands.
12   Remove the left rear wheel.
13   Remove the rear inner fender liners (see Chapter 11).
14   Remove the cable nut from the parking brake module.
15   Remove the cable retainer from the caliper and brake hose brackets, then remove the cable.
16   Perform the same procedure for the opposite side brake caliper.
17   Remove the brake cable from the brackets on the under side of the vehicle.
18   Installation is the reverse of removal.
19   Follow the procedures for calibration (see Section 13).

Parking brake calibration
20   Block the drive wheels.
21   Turn the ignition to On (engine Off).
22   Apply the brake pedal with the transmission in park (neutral for manual transmissions), then momentarily lift and release the EPB switch.
23   Press down on the EPB switch and release it.
24   Repeat these steps to work the remote parking brake actuator from applied to disengaged an additional four to five times.
25   The parking brake is now calibrated.

2016 and later models (except Malibu Limited)
Caution: *If the Electronic Parking Brake (EPB) switch is activated at any time the rear caliper is removed and the battery was not disconnected, the EPB motor will sense this and fully extend the caliper piston outward. This will jam the piston and damage the caliper. The caliper will then have to be replaced.*
Note: *The EPB system consists of a warning light, switch, electronic controller, and two bi-*

directional motors attached to the rear calipers. The electromagnetically operated gears provide the clamping power to the rear brake pads.

Service mode (rear caliper piston retracting procedure)
Warning: *Any service work needed on the rear braking system requires the rear brake calipers to be set into "Service mode". Failure to set the caliper into the service mode before any work is performed can result in damage to the rear braking system components and possible personal injury.*
Caution: *Do not disconnect the electrical connection from the actuator before the battery is disconnected. This can cause the actuator to seek a new position when it is plugged back in. Do not reconnect the battery with the actuator removed from the caliper. This can cause a similar problem which could result in the replacement of the components.*
Note: *The caliper must be fully released in order to do any work on the rear brake pads or calipers. Perform the retract procedure before disconnecting the battery.*
26   Loosen the rear wheel lug nuts, then raise the rear of the vehicle and support it securely on jackstands. Remove the wheels.
27   Release the parking brake, then remove the parking brake actuator (see Step 34).
28   Using a Torx bit that matches the size of the brake caliper actuator shaft, rotate the caliper piston one or two turns counterclockwise.
29   Perform the needed repairs on the caliper or brake pads.
30   Using the Torx bit again, rotate the caliper piston back to the original position or as close as possible.
31   Align the actuator shaft up to the piston and reinstall the actuator retaining bolts.
32   Lower the vehicle from the jackstands and reconnect the battery.
Caution: *When the battery is reconnected, and the EPB switch is operated, the actuators will seek out their original air gap position. If you have turned the caliper piston too far, the rear brake pads will lock onto the brake disc and will not release. A scan tool will have to be utilized to re-establish the proper brake pad-to-disc clearance.*
33   Operate the EPB switch at least four times to set the air gap between the brake pads and rotors.
Note: *In some cases, after performing certain repairs to the parking brake system, a code may set indicating a false or misleading issue with the parking brake. If so, have the code checked, verified and cleared with a scanner.*

Parking brake actuator - removal and installation
Warning: *Disable the electronic parking brake before servicing the rear brake pads, and or calipers.*
34   Disconnect the cable from the negative terminal of the battery (see Chapter 5).
Warning: *If you are only removing the parking brake actuator for brake pad or caliper service, DO NOT disconnect the actuator electrical connection.*

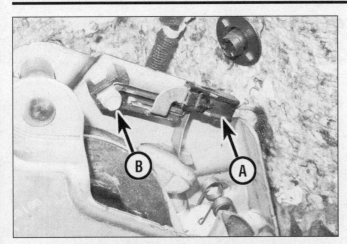

**13.24 Parking brake light switch connector (A)
and retaining bolt (B)**

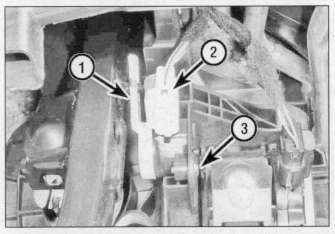

14.2 Brake Pedal Position sensor - 2010 and later models

1 *Sensor lever*   3 *Mounting bolt*
2 *Electrical connector*

35   Remove the two bolts securing the parking brake actuator to the brake caliper.
36   Pull the actuator from the brake caliper and remove the O-ring from between the caliper and actuator.
Note: *Replace the O-ring when reinstalling. The O-ring prevents dirt and moisture from collecting between the caliper and actuator moving parts.*
37   If you are replacing the actuator, disconnect the electrical connector.
38   Installation is the reverse of removal.

13   Parking brake system (manual, cable-type) - component removal and installation

Lever-operated parking brake

Lever

1   Remove the center console (see Chapter 11).
2   Disconnect the electrical connection for the parking brake lever indicator.
3   Move the parking brake adjuster rod rearward to remove tension on the parking brake cables.
4   Disconnect the parking brake cables from the equalizer bar.
5   Remove the four nuts securing the lever to the vehicle, and remove the lever.
6   Installation is the reverse of removal.

Cables

7   Remove center console (see Chapter 11).
8   Pull carpeting out of the way to expose the parking brake cables.
9   Move the parking brake adjuster rod rearward to remove tension on the parking brake cables.
10   Disconnect the parking brake cables from the equalizer bar.
11   Release the cable grommets from the vehicle and any brackets holding the cables in place.

12   Release the cable grommets from the vehicle and any brackets holding the cables in place.
13   Raise and support the vehicle on jackstands.
14   Remove any panels obstructing the brackets that are securing the cable to the vehicle.
15   Follow the cable back to the rear caliper, release any retainers or brackets along the way.
16   Disconnect the cable from the caliper lever.
17   Feed the cable through the body to remove the cable.
18   Installation is the reverse of removal.

Pedal-operated parking brake

Pedal

19   Fully release the parking brake cable.
20   Raise and support the vehicle on jackstands.
21   Locate the front and rear cable connection located on the underside of the vehicle's driver's side. Pull down on the cable to add slack, then separate the cables.
22   Lower vehicle and remove the driver's side door sill and kick panel trim.
23   Pull the driver's side carpeting out of the way to expose the parking brake cable grommet. Using a flat tipped screwdriver, pry the grommet from the vehicle.
24   Disconnect the parking brake light switch electrical connector **(see illustration)**.
25   Remove the bolt and two nuts securing the parking brake pedal assembly to the dash.
26   Guide the cable out of the vehicle as you remove the brake pedal.
27   Installation is the reverse of removal. Apply and release the parking brake several times. This will automatically adjust the cable tension for the parking brake system.

Cables

28   Raise and support the vehicle on jackstands.

29   Separate the front cable from the rear cable at the cable connection below the driver's area of the underside of the vehicle.
30   Follow the cable back along the body and remove any of the brackets and retainers securing the cable to the vehicle.
31   Remove the parking cable guide bolt located on the underside of the vehicle.
32   Disconnect the cable from the rear caliper.
33   Perform the same procedures for the opposite side.
34   Installation is the reverse of removal. Apply and release the parking brake several times. This will automatically adjust the cable tension for the parking brake system.

14   Brake Pedal Position (BPP) sensor - replacement

Note: *The manufacturer states that a special scan tool is necessary for calibrating this component when it's installed. They also state that a new component and mounting bolt are installed whenever it is removed.*
1   These vehicles do not utilize a typical brake light switch; they are equipped with a Brake Pedal Position Sensor.
2   Disconnect the brake pedal position sensor electrical connector **(see illustration)**.
3   Mark the relationship of the sensor to its mount, then remove the mounting bolt.
4   Remove the sensor.
5   Installation is the reverse of removal. Align the sensor with the marks made in Step 3.
Note: *If the sensor requires calibration after it's installed, the circuit may set a diagnostic trouble code (DTC) and a warning lamp may illuminate on the dash. The vehicle will have to be taken to a dealership service department or other qualified repair shop to calibrate the sensor and clear any codes. For more information on diagnostic trouble codes, see Chapter 6.*

Notes

Chapter 10
Suspension and steering systems

Contents

Specifications

Torque specifications

Ft-lbs (unless otherwise indicated) **Nm**

Note: *One foot-pound (ft-lb) of torque is equivalent to 12 inch-pounds (in-lbs) of torque. Torque values below approximately 15 ft-lbs are expressed in inch-pounds, since most foot-pound torque wrenches are not accurate at these smaller values.*

Front suspension
Control arm fasteners*
  2015 and earlier models (and 2016 Malibu Limited)
    Front bolts/nuts
      Step 1 ... 74 ... 100
      Step 2 ... Tighten an additional 90 to 105 degrees
    Control arm rear bushing bolt*
      Step 1 ... 41 ... 55
      Step 2 ... Tighten an additional 100 degrees
  2016 and later models (except Malibu Limited)
    Front and rear bolts/nuts
      Step 1 ... 74 ... 100
      Step 2 ... Tighten an additional 90 to 105 degrees
Balljoint
  2015 and earlier models (and 2016 Malibu Limited)
    Balljoint-to-steering knuckle pinch bolt/nut*
      Step 1 ... 37 ... 50
      Step 2 ... Loosen 120 degrees
      Step 3 ... 37 ... 50
      Step 4 ... Tighten an additional 30 to 45 degrees
  2016 and later models (except Malibu Limited)
    Step 1 ... 30 ... 40
    Step 2 ... Tighten an additional 120 to 135 degrees
Stabilizer bar*
  Link nuts
    2015 and earlier models (and 2016 Malibu Limited) ... 48 ... 65
    2016 and later models (except Malibu Limited) ... 74 ... 100
  Clamp bolts (4 used)
    2015 and earlier models (and 2016 Malibu Limited)
      Step 1 ... 16 ... 22
      Step 2 ... Tighten an additional 30 to 45 degrees
    2016 and later models (except Malibu Limited) ... 74 ... 100

Torque specifications (continued)

	Ft-lbs (unless otherwise indicated)	Nm

Note: *One foot-pound (ft-lb) of torque is equivalent to 12 inch-pounds (in-lbs) of torque. Torque values below approximately 15 ft-lbs are expressed in inch-pounds, since most foot-pound torque wrenches are not accurate at these smaller values.*

Front suspension (continued)

	Ft-lbs	Nm
Suspension strut*		
Shaft nut	52	70
Upper mounting fasteners		
2015 and earlier models (and 2016 Malibu Limited)	41	55
2016 and later models (except Malibu Limited)	26	35
Strut-to-steering knuckle bolt/nut		
2015 and earlier models (and 2016 Malibu Limited models)		
Step 1	63	85
Step 2	Tighten an additional 60 to 75 degrees	
2016 and later models (except Malibu Limited)		
Step 1	74	100
Step 2	Tighten an additional 45 to 60 degrees	
Hub and bearing assembly mounting bolts*		
Step 1	74	100
Step 2	Tighten an additional 60 to 75 degrees	
Subframe*		
Large subframe-to-chassis bolts	118	160
Small subframe-to-chassis bolts (reinforcement bracket bolts also)		
2015 and earlier models (and 2016 Malibu Limited models)		
Step 1	44	60
Step 2	Tighten an additional 30 degrees	
2016 and later models (except Malibu Limited)	44	60
Transaxle mount-to-subframe bolts	74	100

  * *Use NEW fasteners.*

Rea suspension

	Ft-lbs	Nm
Lower control arm		
Outer bolt*		
2015 and earlier models (and 2016 Malibu Limited)		
Step 1	51	70
Step 2	Tighten an additional 90 degrees	
2016 and later models (except Malibu Limited)		
Step 1	118	160
Step 2	Tighten an additional 90 to 105 degrees	
Inner nut*		
2015 and earlier models (and 2016 Malibu Limited)		
Step 1	66	90
Step 2	Tighten an additional 60 degrees	
2016 and later models (except Malibu Limited)	66	90
Upper control arm*		
2015 and earlier models models (and 2016 Malibu Limited)		
Inner		
Step 1	52	70
Step 2	Tighten an additional 60 degrees	
Outer		
Step1	111	150
Step 2	Tighten and additional 90 degrees	
2016 and later models (except Malibu Limited)*		
Outer*		
Step 1	118	160
Step 2	Tighten an additional 90 to 105 degrees	
Inner*		
Step1	118	160
Step 2	Tighten an additional 90 to 105 degrees	
Rear adjustment link bolt-to-knuckle*		
2015 and earlier models (and 2016 Malibu Limited)		
Step 1	85	115
Step 2	Tighten an additional 90 degrees	
2016 and later models (except Malibu Limited)		
Step 1	118	160
Step 2	Tighten an additional 90 to 105 degrees	
Rear inner adjustment link nut-to-frame*		
2015 and earlier models (and 2016 Malibu Limited)		
Step 1	66	90
Step 2	Tighten an additional 60 degrees	
2016 and later models (except Malibu Limited)	66	90
Trailing arm bracket bolts-to-knuckle*		
2015 and earlier models (except Malibu Limited)		
Step 1	111	150
Step 2	Tighten an additional 30 degrees	

Torque specifications (continued)

	Ft-lbs (unless otherwise indicated)	Nm
Trailing arm bracket bolts-to-knuckle* (continued)		
2016 and later models (except Malibu Limited)		
Step 1	74	100
Step 2	Tighten an additional 90 to 105 degrees	
Trailing arm to knuckle bolts*		
2015 and earlier models (and 2016 Malibu Limited)........................	Not available	
2016 and later models (except Malibu Limited)		
Step 1	118	160
Step 2	Tighten an additional 90 to 105 degrees	
Stabilizer bar..		
Clamp bolts*		
2015 and earlier models (and 2016 Malibu Limited)		
Step 1	15	22
Step 2	Tighten an additional 30 degrees	
2016 and later models (except Malibu Limited)...........................	43	58
Link nuts and bolts*		
2015 and earlier models (and 2016 Malibu Limited)....................	37	50
2016 and later models (except Malibu Limited)		
Upper		
Step 1	43	58
Step 2	Tighten an additional 45 to 60 degrees	
Lower..	43	58
Hub bearing assembly mounting bolts to knuckle*		
2015 and earlier models (and 2016 Malibu Limited)		
Step 1	66	90
Step 2	Tighten an additional 75 degrees	
2016 and later models (except Malibu Limited)		
Step 1	74	100
Step 2	Tighten an additional 15 to 30 degrees	
Shock Absorber*		
Upper mount (damper shaft) nut.......................................	15	20
Upper mounting bolts (to body)		
2015 and earlier models (and 2016 Malibu Limited)....................	74	100
2016 and later models (except Malibu Limited).........................	43	58
Lower bolt		
2015 and earlier models (and 2016 Malibu Limited)		
Step 1	111	150
Step 2	Tighten an additional 60 degrees	
2016 and later models (except 2016 Malibu Limited)		
Step 1	118	160
Step 2	Tighten an additional 90 to 105 degrees	

Use NEW fasteners.

Steering system

	Ft-lbs (unless otherwise indicated)	Nm
Ignition switch assembly screws..	62 in-lbs	7
Intermediate shaft bolts		
2015 and earlier models (and 2016 Malibu Limited)		
Upper bolt		
Step 1	18	25
Step 2	Tighten an additional 185 degrees	
Lower bolt	25	34
2016 and later models (except Malibu Limited)		
Upper bolt	29	39
Lower bolt	31	42
Steering column mounting nuts..	16	22
Steering wheel bolt*		
2015 and earlier models (and 2016 Malibu Limited)........................	22	30
2016 and later models (except Malibu limited)*	33	45
Power steering system		
Steering gear assembly mounting bolts*		
Step 1	74	100
Step 2	Tighten an additional 45 to 60 degrees	
Power steering assist motor mounting bolts*		
2015 and earlier models (and 2016 Malibu Limited)....................	71 in-lbs	8
2016 and later models (except Malibu Limited)..........................	15	22
Inner tie-rod		
2013 through 2015 models (and 2016 Malibu Limited models)....	74	100
2016 (non Malibu Limited) and later models................................	77	105
Tie-rod end-to-steering knuckle nut		
Step 1	26	35
Step 2	Tighten an additional 30 degrees	

Use NEW fasteners.

1   General information

1   The front suspension is a MacPherson strut design. The upper end of each strut is attached to the vehicle's body strut support. The lower end of the strut is connected to the upper end of the steering knuckle. The steering knuckle is attached to a balljoint mounted on the outer end of the suspension control arm. A stabilizer bar connected to each control arm and mounted to the suspension crossmember reduces body roll during cornering **(see illustration)**.
2   The rear suspension employs upper and lower control arms, adjuster link, trailing arm, a stabilizer bar, and a coil spring and shock absorber on each side **(see illustrations)**.
3   The electrically assisted rack-and-pinion steering gear is attached to the front suspension subframe. The steering gear moves the tie-rods, which are attached to the steering knuckles. The steering column is designed to collapse in the event of an accident.

Precautions

4   Frequently, when working on the suspension or steering system components, you may come across fasteners which seem impossible to loosen. These fasteners on the underside of the vehicle are continually subjected to water, road grime, mud, etc., and can become rusted or frozen in place, making them extremely difficult to remove. In order to unscrew these stubborn fasteners without damaging them (or other components), be sure to use lots of penetrating oil and allow it to soak in for a while. Using a wire brush to clean exposed threads will also ease removal of the nut or bolt and prevent damage to the threads.
5   Sometimes a sharp blow with a hammer and punch will break the bond between a nut and bolt threads, but care must be taken to prevent the punch from slipping off the fastener and ruining the threads. Heating the stuck fastener and surrounding area with a torch sometimes helps too, but isn't recommended because of the obvious dangers associated with fire. Long breaker bars and extension, or cheater pipes will increase leverage, but never use an extension pipe on a ratchet - the ratcheting mechanism could be damaged. Sometimes tightening the nut or bolt first will help to break it loose. Fasteners that require drastic measures to remove should always be replaced with new ones.
6   Most of the procedures in this Chapter involve raising the vehicle and working underneath it; a suitable jack and a good pair of jackstands will be needed. A hydraulic floor jack is the preferred type of jack to lift the vehicle, and it can also be used to support certain components during various operations.
Warning: *Never, under any circumstances, rely on a jack to support the vehicle while working on it.*
Warning: *Whenever any of the suspension or steering fasteners are loosened or removed they must be inspected and, if necessary, replaced with new ones of the same part number or of original equipment quality and design. Torque specifications must be followed for proper reassembly and component retention. Never attempt to heat or straighten any suspension or steering components. Instead, replace any bent or damaged parts with new ones.*

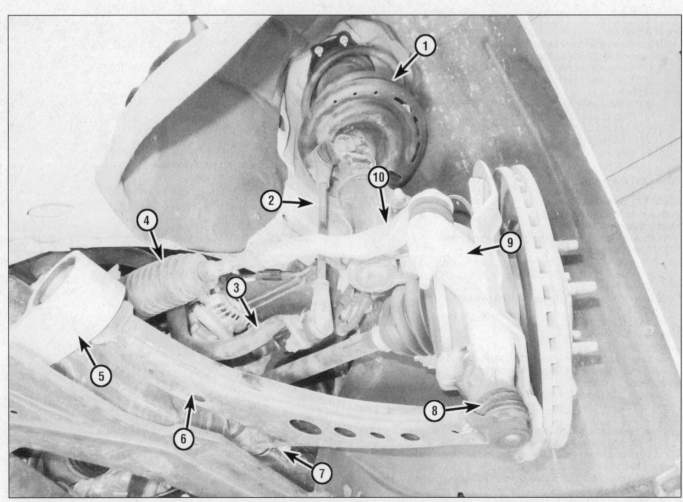

1.1 Front suspension and steering components

1	*Strut and spring assembly*	*4*	*Steering gear boot*	*7*	*Control arm front bushing*	*10*	*Tie-rod end*
2	*Stabilizer bar link*	*5*	*Control arm rear bushing*	*8*	*Balljoint*		
3	*Stabilizer bar*	*6*	*Control arm*	*9*	*Steering knuckle*		

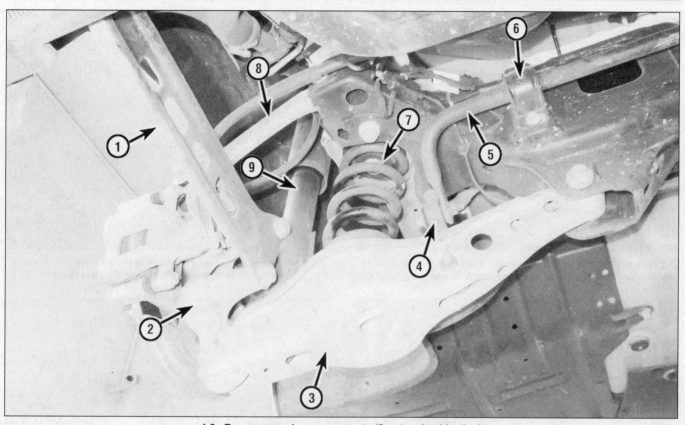

1.2a Rear suspension components (front underside view)

1	Trailing arm	4	Stabilizer bar link	7	Coil spring
2	Rear knuckle	5	Stabilizer bar	8	Adjuster link
3	Lower control arm	6	Stabilizer bar bracket	9	Shock absorber

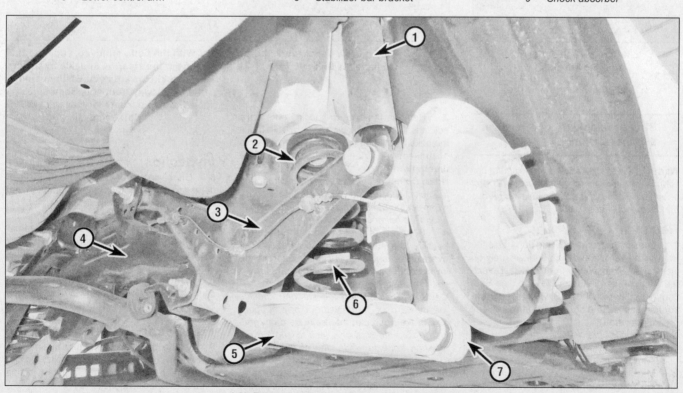

1.2b Rear suspension components (rear view)

1	Shock absorber	3	Upper control arm	5	Lower control arm	7	Rear knuckle
2	Coil spring	4	Subframe	6	Coil spring		

2.1 Remove the bolt holding the brake line to the strut as well as the clip securing the wheel speed sensor to the steering knuckle

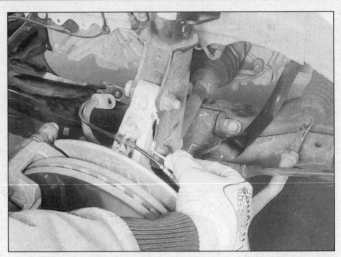

2.2 Mark the relationship of the strut to the steering knuckle and mark the fasteners on each side of the strut bracket

2.3a Tap the bolt out of the steering knuckle. . .

2.3b. . . a long narrow punch works best to drive the bolt out

2.4 With the bolts removed, separate the strut from the steering knuckle by pulling the knuckle towards you while pushing the strut away from you. Sometimes, a little help from a prybar will aid in the removal

2   Strut assembly (front) - removal and installation

Warning: *Always replace the struts and/or coil springs in pairs - never replace just one strut or one coil spring (this could cause dangerous handling peculiarities).*

Removal

1   Loosen the front wheel lug nuts, raise the front of the vehicle and support it securely on jackstands. Remove the front wheels. Detach the stabilizer bar link from the strut (see Section 4), and detach the ABS wheel speed sensor harness and the brake hose from the strut **(see illustration)**.
Note: *Support the vehicle by placing the jackstands under the frame (unibody) and not under any of the suspension components.*
2   Mark the relationship of the strut to the knuckle (these marks will be used during installation to ensure that the camber angle is returned to its original setting) **(see illustration)**.

3   Remove the strut-to-knuckle nuts while holding the bolt heads with a wrench. Remove the bolts by striking the end with a hammer to push them out of the knuckle and strut **(see illustrations)**.
Note: *Do not attempt to turn the strut mounting bolts. These bolts are serrated to fit tightly when seated against the strut mounting flange and in the holes of the knuckle.*
4   Separate the strut from the steering knuckle **(see illustration)**. Be careful not to overextend the inner CV joint. Support the lower control arm with a jack or hang it by a suitable support.
Caution: *DO NOT let the steering knuckle fall outward or hang without any support. The brake hose can internally be damaged. Use a suitable wire or a jack to support the steering knuckle while any of the suspension components have been removed.*
5   Support the strut and spring assembly with one hand and remove the upper mounting nut or bolts **(see illustrations)**. Remove the assembly from the fenderwell.

Inspection

6   Check the strut body for leaking fluid, dents, cracks and other obvious damage that would warrant repair or replacement.
7   Check the coil spring for chips or cracks in the spring coating (this can cause premature spring failure due to corrosion). Inspect the spring seat for cuts, hardness and general deterioration.
8   If any undesirable conditions exist, proceed to the strut disassembly procedure (see Section 3).

Installation

9   Guide the strut assembly up into the fenderwell and install the nut or bolts. Tighten the fastener(s) to the torque listed in this Chapter's Specifications.
Note: *On 2016 and later models (except Malibu limited), the larger ribs in the top of the strut mount must be installed facing inboard.*

2.5a On 2015 and earlier models/2016 Malibu Limited models, prevent the strut damper rod from turning by holding it with the proper size Torx or hex bit (as applicable), then unscrew the upper mounting nut with an offset box-end wrench or special socket

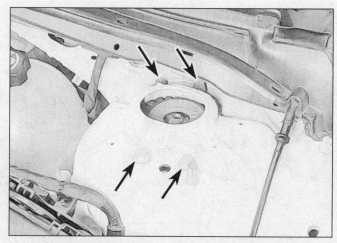

2.5b On 2016 and later models (except Malibu Limited), mark the strut in relation to the strut tower, then remove the mounting bolts while supporting the strut

3.3 Install the spring compressor following the tool manufacturer's instructions; compress the spring until all pressure is relieved from the upper spring seat (you can verify this by wiggling the spring)

3.5 Remove the upper mount after taking off the damper shaft nut

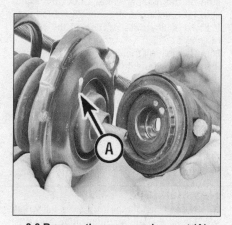

3.6 Remove the upper spring seat (A)

10   Slide the steering knuckle into the strut flange and install the two bolts using a soft-face hammer or mallet. Install the nuts, align the marks made in Step 2, then tighten the nuts to the torque listed in this Chapter's Specifications.

11   Install the wheels and lug nuts, then lower the vehicle and tighten the lug nuts to the torque listed in the Chapter 1 Specifications.

12   Have the front wheel alignment checked and, if necessary, adjusted.

3   Strut/coil spring (front) - replacement

Note: *You'll need a spring compressor for this procedure. Spring compressors can usually be rented at most auto parts stores or equipment yards.*

1   If the struts or coil springs exhibit the tell-tale signs of wear (leaking fluid, loss of damping capability, chipped, sagging or cracked coil springs) explore all options before beginning any work. The strut/coil spring components are not serviceable and must be replaced if a problem develops. However, strut assemblies, complete with springs, may be available on an exchange basis (which eliminates much time and work). Whichever route you choose to take, check on the cost and availability of parts before disassembling your vehicle.

Warning: *Disassembling a strut is potentially dangerous and utmost attention must be directed to the job, or serious injury may result. Use only a high-quality spring compressor and carefully follow the manufacturer's instructions furnished with the tool. After removing the coil spring from the strut assembly, set it aside in a safe, isolated area.*

Disassembly

2   Remove the strut and spring assembly (see Section 2). Mount the strut clevis bracket portion of the strut assembly in a vise.

Caution: *Do not clamp any other portion of*

the strut assembly in the vise as it will be damaged. Line the vise jaws with wood or rags to prevent damage to the unit and don't tighten the vise excessively.

3   Following the tool manufacturer's instructions, install the spring compressor (which can be obtained at most auto parts stores or equipment yards on a daily rental basis) on the spring and compress it sufficiently to relieve all pressure from the upper spring seat **(see illustration)**. This can be verified by wiggling the spring.

4   Hold the damper shaft from turning with an appropriate tool, and unscrew the damper shaft nut.

5   Remove the nut and upper mount **(see illustration)**. Lay the parts out in the exact order in which they are removed. Check the rubber portion of the upper mount for cracking and general deterioration. If there is any separation of the rubber, replace it.

6   Remove the upper spring seat from the damper shaft **(see illustration)**. Check the rubber portion of the spring seat for cracking and hardness; replace it if necessary. Inspect the bearing in the spring seat for smooth operation. If it doesn't turn smoothly, replace it.

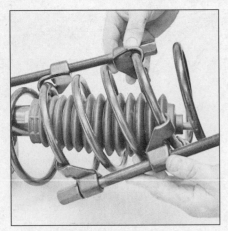

3.8 Carefully remove the compressed spring from the strut

3.10 When installing the spring, make sure the end rests against the raised stop

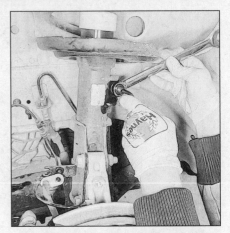

4.2 Use an Allen wrench to hold the stud while turning the wrench to remove the nut

7   Slide the dust boot and rubber bump stop off the damper shaft. Check the bump stop for cracking and general deterioration. If there is any deterioration of the rubber, replace it.

8   Carefully lift the compressed spring from the assembly **(see illustration)** and set it in a safe place.

Warning: *When removing the compressed spring, lift it off carefully and set it in a safe place. Keep the ends of the spring away from your body.*

Note: *If you are disassembling both struts, mark the springs LEFT and RIGHT so you don't mix them up (they're different).*

Reassembly

9   Extend the damper rod to its full length and install the rubber bump stop and dust boot.

10   Carefully place the compressed coil spring onto the lower seat of the damper, with the end of the spring resting against the raised stop **(see illustration)**.

11   Install the upper insulator and spring seat.

12   Install the upper mount and mounting nut and tighten the nut to the torque listed in this Chapter's Specifications.

13   Remove the spring compressor tool.

14   Install the strut/spring assembly (see Section 2).

---

4   Stabilizer bar, bushings and links (front) - removal and installation

Stabilizer bar links

1   Loosen the front wheel lug nuts, raise the front of the vehicle, support it securely on jackstands and remove the front wheels.

2   To detach the stabilizer bar link from the strut or the bar, hold the ballstud with an Allen wrench while turning the wrench to loosen and remove the nut **(see illustration)**.

3   Installation is the reverse of removal. Tighten the nuts to the torque listed this Chapter's Specifications.

4   Install the wheels and lug nuts, then lower the vehicle. Tighten the wheel lug nuts to the torque listed in the Chapter 1 Specifications.

Stabilizer bar and bushings

Note: *The stabilizer bar bushings are not serviceable separately. For stabilizer bar removal and installation, remove the links, then follow the steps for subframe removal and installation (see Section 20).*

Note: *On 2015 and earlier models (and 2016 Malibu Limited models), it isn't necessary to completely remove the subframe. Just lower it enough to allow the stabilizer bar to be removed.*

5   Once the subframe has been removed (or lowered sufficiently), remove the stabilizer bar bracket bolts and separate the bar from the subframe **(see illustrations)**.

6   Installation is the reverse of the removal procedure. Tighten the stabilizer bar clamp bolts to the torque listed in this Chapter's Specifications.

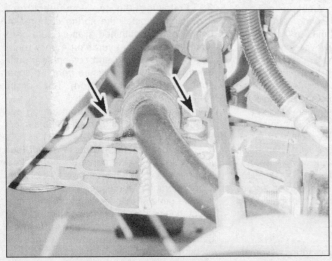

4.5a Stabilizer bar bushing bracket bolts - 2015 and later models (and 2016 Malibu Limited)

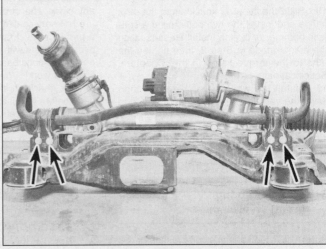

4.5b Stabilizer bar bushing bracket bolts - 2016 and later models (except 2016 Malibu Limited)

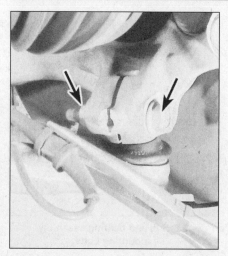

5.2a On 2015 and earlier models (and 2016 Malibu Limited models), remove the nut and pinch bolt. . .

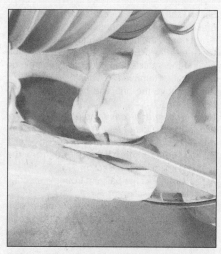

5.2b. . . then pry the balljoint stud out of the steering knuckle

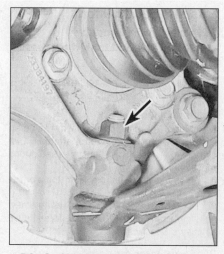

5.2c On 2016 and later models (except Malibu Limited), loosen (but don't remove) the balljoint stud nut. . .

5   Control arm (front) - removal, bushing replacement and installation

Removal and installation

1   Loosen the front wheel lug nuts, raise the front of the vehicle, support it securely on jackstands and remove the front wheel.
2   Separate the balljoint from the steering knuckle **(see illustrations)**.
3   Remove and discard the control arm-to-subframe fasteners **(see illustrations)**.
4   Remove the control arm.
5   Installation is the reverse of removal. Use new fasteners and tighten them to the torque listed in this Chapter's Specifications. Tighten the wheel lug nuts to the torque listed in the Chapter 1 Specifications.

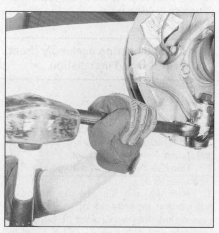

5.2d. . . then separate the balljoint from the steering knuckle. A picklefork tool like this will most likely damage the balljoint boot. . .

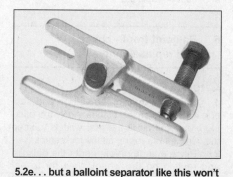

5.2e. . . but a balljoint separator like this won't

Note: *The balljoint separator tool must have jaws and opening size large enough to accommodate the stud diameter and length in order to properly and safely separate the stud from the steering knuckle - it may not be available at auto parts stores and would require it to be special ordered online*

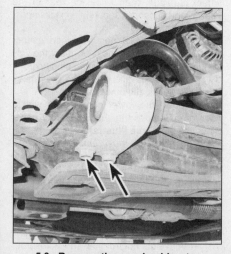

5.3a Remove the rear bushing-to-subframe nuts and bolts

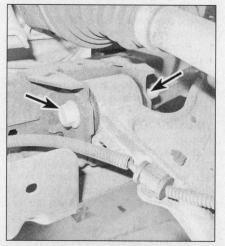

5.3b On 2015 and earlier models (and 2016 Malibu Limited models), remove the nut and pivot bolt from the front of the control arm

5.3c On 2016 and later models (except Malibu Limited), remove the two pivot shaft bolts from the front of the control arm

Bushing replacement

2015 and earlier models (and 2016 Malibu Limited models)

Front bushing

6   This bushing is not replaceable. If it is worn, the control arm must be replaced.

Rear bushing

7   Mount the control arm in a vise, then remove the bushing-to-control arm bolt. Discard the bolt - a new one must be used during reassembly.
8   Remove the bushing from the control arm shaft.
9   Install the new bushing and, using a new bolt, tighten the bolt to the torque listed in this Chapter's Specifications.

2016 and later models (except Malibu Limited)

10   Neither the front nor rear bushings are replaceable. If either are worn, the control arm must be replaced.

---

6   Balljoint front - check and replacement

Check

1   Raise the front of the vehicle and support it securely on jackstands. Apply the parking brake and block the rear wheels to keep the vehicle from rolling off the jackstands.
2   Place a large prybar under the balljoint and resting on the wheel, then try to pry the balljoint up while feeling for movement between the balljoint and steering knuckle. Now, pry between the control arm and the steering knuckle and try to lever the control arm down while feeling for movement between the balljoint and steering knuckle. If excessive movement is evident (over 0.125 inch) in either check, the balljoint is worn. Install a dial indicator and measure the amount of movement to be certain.
3   Have an assistant grasp the tire at the top and bottom and move the top of the tire in-and-out. Touch the balljoint stud nut. If excessive movement is evident (over 0.125 inch), the balljoint or knuckle is worn. Install a dial indicator and measure the amount of movement to be certain.

Replacement

4   The balljoint on these models is not serviceable separately. If the balljoint is in need of replacement, the control arm must be replaced (see Section 5).

---

7   Steering knuckle - removal and installation

Warning: *Dust created by the brake system is harmful to your health. Never blow it out with compressed air and don't inhale any of it. Do not, under any circumstances, use petroleum-*based solvents to clean brake parts. Use brake system cleaner only.
1   Loosen the driveaxle/hub nut (see Chapter 8) and the wheel lug nuts, then raise the front of the vehicle and support it securely on jackstands. Remove the wheel.
2   Remove the hub and bearing assembly (see Section 8).
Note: *Suspend the driveaxle using a length of wire or cord. Do not let it hang freely or damage to the inner CV joint may occur.*
3   Disconnect the tie-rod end from the steering knuckle (see Section 17).
4   Disconnect the balljoint from the steering knuckle (see Section 5).
5   Disconnect the ABS wheel speed sensor electrical connector and detach it from its bracket. Also, detach the ABS wire harness from the control arm, if applicable.
6   Mark the strut to the knuckle, then remove the strut-to-knuckle fasteners (see Section 2). Separate the knuckle from the strut.
7   Installation is the reverse of removal. Tighten all fasteners to the torque listed in this Chapter's Specifications.

---

8   Hub and bearing assembly (front) - removal and installation

---

Removal

1   Loosen the driveaxle/hub nut (see Chapter 8) and the wheel lug nuts, raise the front of the vehicle and support it securely on jackstands. Remove the wheel.
2   Remove the ABS wheel speed sensor (see Chapter 9).
3   Remove and discard the driveaxle/hub nut and separate the driveaxle from the steering knuckle (see Chapter 8). Support driveaxle end with a wire - DO NOT let the driveaxle hang freely.
4   Remove the brake caliper, the caliper mounting bracket and the brake disc (see Chapter 9).
Caution: *Suspend the caliper to the strut coil spring with a piece of wire. DO NOT let the caliper hang by the brake hose.*
5   Remove and discard the hub/bearing assembly mounting bolts from the back of the steering knuckle **(see illustration).**
6   Remove the hub/bearing assembly from the steering knuckle.

Installation

Warning: *New hub/bearing mounting bolts must be used for installation.*
7   Make sure that the mounting surface inside the steering knuckle and the driveaxle splines are smooth and free of burrs and nicks prior to installing the hub/bearing assembly.
8   Lubricate the driveaxle splines with multi-purpose grease. Install the hub and bearing assembly into the steering knuckle until it is fully seated.
9   Insert the driveaxle splines into the hub (see Chapter 8).

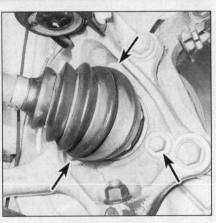

8.5 Hub and bearing assembly mounting bolts

10   Install the NEW mounting bolts. Tighten the bolts to the torque listed in this Chapter's Specifications. Install the driveaxle/hub nut, but don't tighten it completely yet.
11   Install the ABS wheel speed sensor.
12   Install the brake disc, the caliper mounting bracket and the caliper. Tighten the fasteners to the torque listed in the Chapter 9 Specifications.
13   Install the wheel and lug nuts, then lower the vehicle.
14   Tighten the driveaxle/hub nut to the torque listed in the Chapter 8 Specifications.
15   Tighten the lug nuts to the torque listed in the Chapter 1 Specifications.

---

9   Shock absorber (rear) - removal and installation

Warning: *Always replace the shock absorbers as a set - never replace just one of them.*
Warning: *Always use NEW fasteners for installation.*
1   Block the front wheels. Loosen the rear wheel lug nuts, then raise the rear of the vehicle and support it securely on jackstands. Remove the wheels.
2   Remove the fasteners from the the inner fender liner and move the liner out of the way to gain access to the upper mounting bolts.
3   If applicable, disconnect the rear shock absorber electrical connection.
4   Support the lower control arm with a floor jack. Remove the shock absorber upper mounting bolts **(see illustrations).**
Warning: *The jack must remain in this position until the shock absorber is reinstalled.*
5   Remove the shock absorber lower mounting bolt (2015 and earlier models/2016 Malibu Limited models) or nut and mounting bolt (2016 and later models except Malibu Limited) **(see illustration).**
6   Remove the shock absorber.
7   Remove the nut from the shock absorber shaft, then remove the upper mount and transfer it to the new shock absorber **(see illustrations).** Tighten the nut to the torque listed in this Chapter's Specifications.

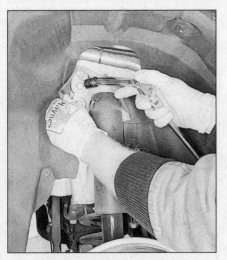

9.4a Remove the front bolt(s). . .

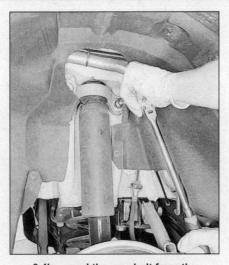

9.4b. . . and the rear bolt from the shock upper mount

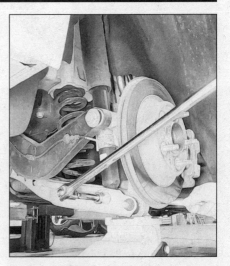

9.5 Shock absorber lower mounting bolt

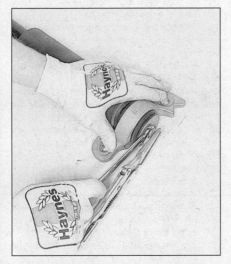

9.7a Loosen the nut from the shock absorber damper shaft - a suitable wrench or locking pliers can be used to hold the shaft upon initial loosening of the nut

9.7b Remove the nut (discard the nut - DO NOT REUSE)

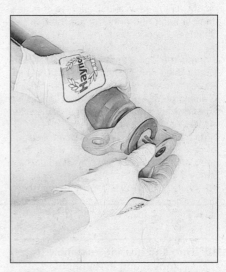

9.7c Remove the washer from the shock absorber upper mount

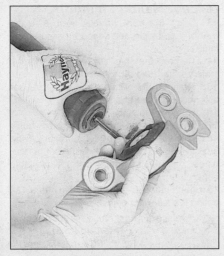

9.7d Slide the upper mount off of the shock damper shaft

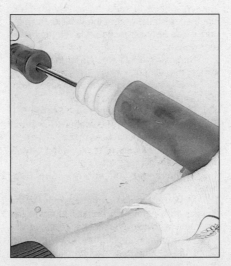

9.7e Remove the dust shield from the shock

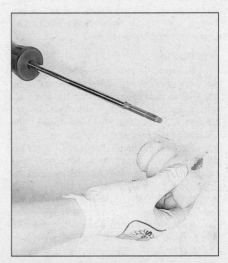

9.7f Slide the rebound cushion off of the shock

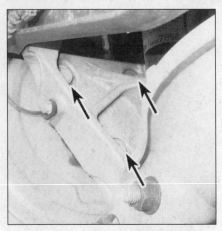

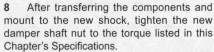

10.5 Rear hub and bearing assembly mounting bolts

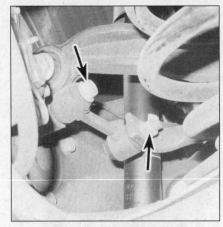

11.8 Stabilizer bar link fasteners

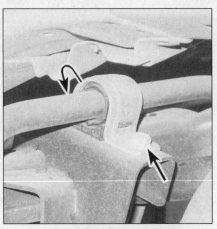

11.9 Stabilizer bar bracket bolts

8   After transferring the components and mount to the new shock, tighten the new damper shaft nut to the torque listed in this Chapter's Specifications.

9   Installation is the reverse of removal. Tighten the upper mount fasteners to the torque listed in this Chapter's Specifications. Raise the lower control arm with a floor jack to simulate normal ride height, then tighten the lower mounting fastener(s) to the torque listed in this Chapter's Specifications.

Note: *New shock absorbers are gas-filled and come compressed and retained with a fiberglass strap. Do not remove the strap until the shock is installed.*

10   Install the wheel and lug nuts, then lower the vehicle. Tighten the lug nuts to the torque listed in the Chapter 1 Specifications.

---

10   Hub and bearing assembly (rear) - removal and installation

---

Warning: *Dust created by the brake system is harmful to your health. Never blow it out with compressed air and don't inhale any of it. Do not, under any circumstances, use petroleum-based solvents to clean brake parts. Use brake system cleaner only.*

Removal

1   Loosen the rear wheel lug nuts. On AWD models, loosen the rear driveaxle/hub nut. Raise the rear of the vehicle and support it securely on jackstands, then remove the wheel. Block the front wheels to keep the vehicle from rolling off the stands.

2   Remove the brake disc (see Chapter 9).

3   If you're working on a 2015 or earlier model (or 2016 Malibu Limited), remove the upper control arm (see Section 12).

4   Remove the ABS wheel speed sensor (see Chapter 9).

5   Remove the bolts and detach the hub and bearing assembly from the knuckle **(see illustration)**. On AWD models, guide the driveaxle out of the hub splines.

Note: *If the hub and bearing assembly sticks in the knuckle, apply some penetrating oil*

and allow it to seep in between the hub and knuckle, then use a rubber mallet or block of wood and a hammer to tap it out.

Installation

6   Installation is the reverse of removal. Tighten the hub and bearing bolts to the torque listed in this Chapter's Specifications. Tighten the caliper mounting bracket bolts and caliper mounting bolts to the torque listed in the Chapter 9 Specifications. On AWD models, tighten the driveaxle/hub nut to the torque listed in the Chapter 8 Specifications.

7   Install the wheel and lug nuts. Lower the vehicle and tighten the lug nuts to the torque listed in the Chapter 1 Specifications.

---

11   Stabilizer bar, bushings and links (rear) - removal and installation

---

2015 and earlier models (and 2016 Malibu Limited models)

1   Loosen the rear wheel lug nuts. Block the front wheels to keep the vehicle from rolling, then raise the rear of the vehicle and support it securely on jackstands. Remove the rear wheels.

2   Remove the rear section of the exhaust system (see Chapter 4).

3   Remove the parking brake cables from the trailing arms (see Chapter 9).

4   Remove the coil springs (see Section 13).

5   Remove the brake calipers without disconnecting the brake hoses (see Chapter 9).

Note: *Suspend the calipers with wire or rope - don't let them hang by the hoses.*

6   Remove the coil springs (see Section 13).

7   Mark the position of the subframe to the chassis with paint or a marker. Support the subframe with two floor jacks. Remove the subframe mounting bolts, then lower the subframe just enough to access the stabilizer bar bracket bolts.

8   Detach the stabilizer bar links from the bar **(see illustration)**.

9   Remove and discard the stabilizer bar bracket bolts **(see illustration)**.

10   Remove the stabilizer bar.

11   Inspect the bushings for cracks, hardness and other signs of deterioration. If the bushings are damaged, replace them.

12   Installation is the reverse of removal, noting the following:

Caution: *Don't use petroleum or mineral-based lubricants or brake fluid to lubricate the bushings; they will lead to deterioration of the bushings. These vehicles are equipped with split-type bushings that can be installed without having to slide them onto the ends of the stabilizer bar.*

   a) *Lubricate the bushings with vegetable oil to aid in reassembly.*

   b) *Replace all suspension fasteners with new ones, tightening them to the torque listed in this Chapter's Specifications.*

   c) *Tighten the brake fasteners to the torque values listed in the Chapter 9 Specifications.*

   d) *Tighten the wheel lug nuts to the torque listed in the Chapter 1 Specifications.*

2016 and later models (except Malibu Limited)

13   Block the front wheels, then raise the rear of the vehicle and support it securely on jackstands.

14   Remove the stabilizer bar links from the stabilizer bar **(see illustration)**.

15   Remove and discard the stabilizer bar bracket bolts **(see illustration)**.

16   Remove the stabilizer bar.

17   Inspect the bushings for cracks, hardness and other signs of deterioration. If the bushings are damaged, replace the stabilizer bar (the bushings are not available separately).

18   Installation is the reverse of removal, noting the following points:

   a) *Replace all suspension fasteners with new ones, tightening them to the torque listed in this Chapter's Specifications.*

   b) *Tighten the wheel lug nuts to the torque listed in the Chapter 1 Specifications.*

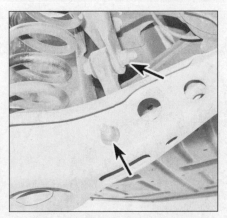

11.14 Stabilizer bar link fasteners

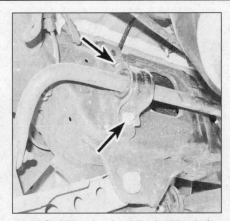

11.15 Stabilizer bar bushing bracket bolts

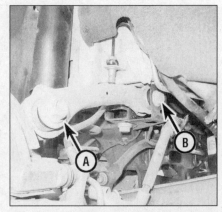

12.3 Upper control arm-to-knuckle bolt (A) and inner pivot bolt (B)

12 Suspension arms (rear) - removal and installation

Warning: *The manufacturer uses Torque-to-Yield bolts. It is recommended that all fasteners are replaced with NEW ones.*

1   Loosen the wheel lug nuts, raise the vehicle and support it securely on jackstands. Block the front wheels to prevent the vehicle from rolling. Remove the wheel.

Upper control arm

2   Detach the ABS wheel speed sensor harness clips from the control arm.

3   Support the lower control arm with a floor jack, then remove the upper control arm-to-knuckle nut and bolt **(see illustration)**.

4   Remove the inner pivot bolt.

Note: *On 2015 and earlier models (and 2016 Malibu Limited), the bolt is retained by a nut. On 2016 and later models (except Malibu Limited), the bolt threads into a welded boss on the subframe.*

5   Remove the upper control arm from the knuckle and subframe.

6   Installation is the reverse of removal. Raise the lower control arm to simulate normal ride height, then tighten the inner and outer fasteners to the torque listed in this Chapter's Specifications.

7   Install the wheel and lug nuts. Lower the vehicle and tighten the lug nuts to the torque listed in the Chapter 1 Specifications. Have the wheel alignment checked and, if necessary, adjusted.

Lower control arm

8   Remove the coil spring (see Section 13).

9   Mark the position of the adjuster cam to the subframe, then unscrew the nut **(see illustrations)**.

10   Remove the control arm-to-subframe pivot bolt and detach the arm from the subframe.

11   Installation is the reverse of removal. Raise the outer end of the control arm with a floor jack to simulate normal ride height, then tighten the fasteners to the torque listed in this Chapter's Specifications.

Note: *Be sure to align the marks on the adjuster cam and subframe before tightening the inner pivot bolt nut.*

12   Install the wheel and lug nuts. Lower the vehicle and tighten the lug nuts to the torque listed in the Chapter 1 Specifications. Have the wheel alignment checked and, if necessary, adjusted.

Trailing arm

13   If applicable, detach the ABS wheel speed sensor harness from the trailing arm.

14   On 2016 and later models (except Malibu Limited), Support the lower control arm with a floor jack. Detach the shock absorber from the control arm (see Section 9). Unbolt the lower control arm from the rear knuckle and lower the jack just enough to provide clearance for trailing arm bolt removal.

15   Remove the trailing arm-to-knuckle bolts **(see illustration)**.

16   Remove the trailing arm bracket-to-body bolts, then remove the trailing arm.

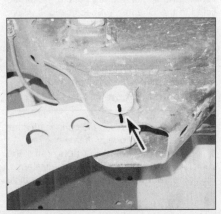

12.9a Mark the relationship of the lower control arm cam adjuster to the subframe. . .

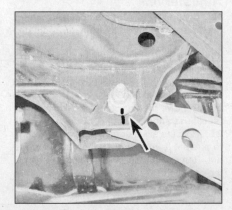

12.9b. . . then mark the nut side and unscrew the nut

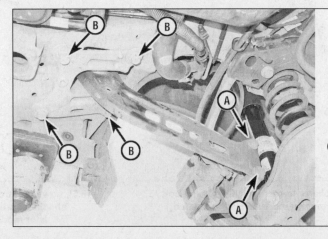

12.15 Trailing arm-to-knuckle bolts (A) and trailing arm-to-body bolts (B) - 2016 and later models shown (except Malibu Limited)

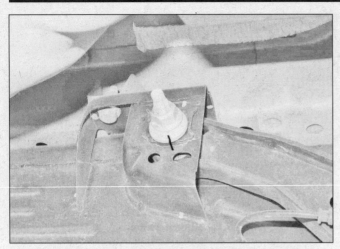

12.19 Mark the relationship of the lower control arm cam adjuster to the subframe

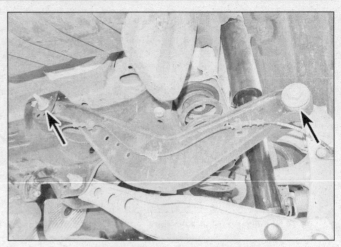

12.20 Adjuster link fastener locations

17 Installation is the reverse of removal. Use new bolts and tighten them to the torque listed in this Chapter's Specifications.
Caution: *On 2016 and later models (except Malibu Limited), raise the lower control arm with the floor jack to simulate normal ride height before tightening the shock absorber lower mounting fasteners and the control arm-to-knuckle fasteners.*

Adjuster link

18 If applicable, detach the ABS wheel speed sensor harness from the adjuster link.
19 Scribe or draw an alignment mark on the adjuster link adjuster cam to the subframe **(see illustration)**. This will help restore alignment during assembly.
20 Remove the adjuster link-to-knuckle nut **(see illustration)**.
21 Hold the adjuster cam bolt with a wrench to prevent it from turning, then unscrew the nut. Remove the nut and cam, then remove the pivot bolt.

22 Remove the adjuster link from the knuckle and subframe.
23 Installation is the reverse of removal, making sure to use new fasteners. Raise the outer end of the control arm with a floor jack to simulate normal ride height, then tighten the fasteners to the torque listed in this Chapter's Specifications.
24 Install the wheel and lug nuts. Lower the vehicle and tighten the lug nuts to the torque listed in the Chapter 1 Specifications. Have the wheel alignment checked and, if necessary, adjusted.

13 Coil spring (rear) - removal and installation

Warning: *Always replace the springs as a set - never replace just one of them.*
1 Loosen the wheel lug nuts, raise the vehicle and support it securely on jackstands. Block the front wheels to prevent the vehicle

from rolling. Remove the wheel.
2 Support the lower control arm with a floor jack.
3 On 2016 and later models (except Malibu Limited), disconnect the stabilizer bar link from the lower control arm (see Section 11).
4 On 2016 and later models (except Malibu Limited), Remove the shock absorber lower mounting nut and bolt (see Section 9).
5 Remove the lower control arm-to-knuckle nut and bolt and the upper control arm-to-lower control arm link bolt **(see illustrations)**.
6 Slowly and carefully lower the floor jack until the coil spring is fully extended, then maneuver the spring and jounce bumper out from the suspension arms. Retrieve the spring seats.
7 Inspect the spring seats and jounce bumper for wear and damage, replacing as necessary. Check the coil spring for nicks and cracks.
8 Installation is the reverse of removal, making sure to replace all fasteners with new

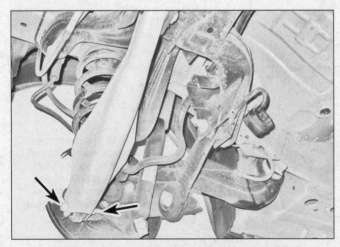

13.5a Lower control arm-to-rear knuckle nut and bolt (2015 and earlier models [and 2016 Malibu Limited])

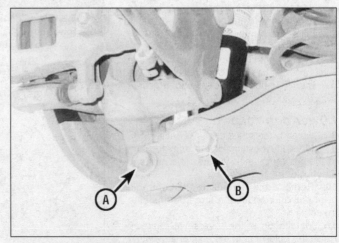

13.5b Lower control arm-to-rear knuckle nut and bolt (A) and shock absorber lower mounting bolt (B) (2016 and later models [except 2016 Malibu Limited])

ones. Raise the outer end of the lower control arm with the floor jack to simulate normal ride height, then tighten the fasteners to the torque listed in this Chapter's Specifications.

9   Install the wheel and lug nuts, then lower the vehicle. Tighten the lug nuts to the torque listed in the Chapter 1 Specifications.

15.3 The airbag module is secured by spring clips that engage three posts on the airbag (one post per side); to release them, insert a thin blunt rod (a 2.5 mm Allen wrench works best) into the small holes on each side while gently pulling the airbag away from the steering wheel

14 Knuckle (rear) - removal and installation

1   Loosen the rear wheel lug nuts. Raise the rear of the vehicle and support it securely on jackstands, then remove the wheel. Block the front wheels to keep the vehicle from rolling off the stands.

2   Support the lower control arm with a floor jack.

Warning: *The jack must remain in this position throughout the entire procedure.*

3   Remove the hub and bearing assembly (see Section 10).

4   Detach the upper control arm from the knuckle (see Section 12).

5   Detach the adjuster link from the knuckle (see Section 12).

6   On 2015 and earlier models (and 2016 Malibu Limited), detach the shock absorber (see Section 9) and stabilizer bar link (see Section 11) from the knuckle.

7   Remove the trailing arm-to-knuckle bolts (see Section 12).

8   Remove the lower control arm-to-knuckle nut and bolt (see Section 12).

9   Remove the knuckle.

10   Installation is the reverse of removal; replace all suspension fasteners with new ones and tighten all suspension fasteners to the torque values listed in this Chapter's Specifications. Tighten the brake fasteners to the torque values listed in the Chapter 9 Specifications.

Caution: *On 2016 and later models (except Malibu Limited), raise the lower control arm with the floor jack to simulate normal ride height before tightening any pivot fasteners.*

11   Install the wheel and lug nuts, then lower the vehicle. Tighten the lug nuts to the torque listed in the Chapter 1 Specifications.

15 Steering wheel - removal and installation

Warning: *These models are equipped with a Supplemental Restraint System (SRS), more commonly known as airbags. Always disable the airbag system before working in the vicinity of any airbag system component to avoid the possibility of accidental deployment of the airbag(s), which could cause personal injury (see Chapter 12).*

Warning: *Do not use a memory saving device to preserve the PCM or radio memory when working on or near airbag system components.*

Removal

1   Park the vehicle with the wheels pointing straight ahead. Disconnect the cable from the negative terminal of the battery (see Chapter 5). Disable the airbag system (see Chapter 12).

2   Remove the steering column covers (see Chapter 11).

3   Remove the airbag module by inserting a thin round tool (a 2.5 mm Allen wrench or equivalent) into the holes on the back of the steering wheel. Push slightly inward on the tools to release the retainer while gently pulling the airbag module towards you **(see illustration)**. Repeat this procedure on the other side of the steering wheel (there is one hole on each side).

4   With the airbag module released, disconnect the electrical connectors and remove the airbag module **(see illustration)**.

Note: *Be sure to notice the position of the connectors (they must be reinstalled in the same positions). Otherwise, there will be a false connection made and a diagnostic trouble code will be stored.*

Warning: *When carrying the airbag module, keep the driver's side of it away from your body, and when you set it down (in an isolated area), have the driver's side facing up.*

5   Detach the clockspring wire harness from the steering wheel hub and disconnect the electrical connector for the steering wheel switches **(see illustration)**.

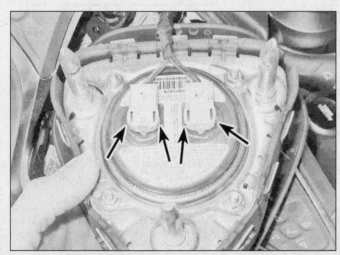

15.4 Lift up the locks on both connectors and disconnect them

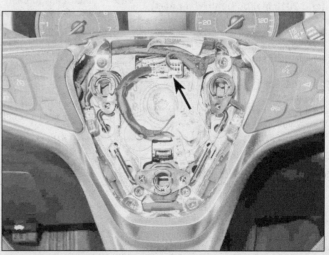

15.5 Unclip the clockspring wiring harness from the steering wheel hub

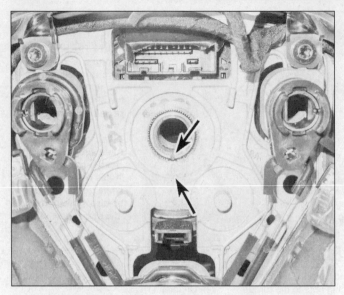

15.7 Steering wheel hub and steering shaft alignment marks. If there aren't any present, make your own

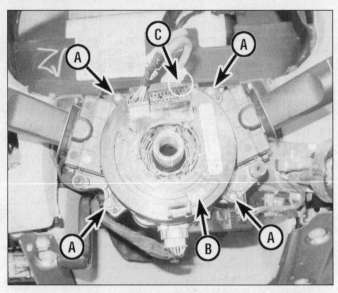

15.16 Clockspring mounting screws (A), alignment window (B) and location of alignment arrows (C)

6   Remove the steering wheel bolt from the steering shaft.

7   Note the index mark on the steering wheel hub and the steering shaft **(see illustration)**.

8   Lift the steering wheel off the shaft. If is does not come off easily, wiggle it back and forth.

Warning: *While the steering wheel is removed, DO NOT turn the steering shaft. Damage to the clockspring will occur if it's installed and the steering shaft is not centered.*

Caution: *Do not use a hammer to disengage the steering wheel from the shaft.*

Clockspring - removal and installation

9   Remove the upper and lower steering column covers (see Chapter 11).

10   Remove the steering wheel.

2013 through 2015 models (and 2016 Malibu Limited models)

11   Remove the clockspring retaining screws (four used), and electrical connections.

12   Remove the clockspring and transfer the steering angle sensor to the replacement clockspring.

13   Perform the airbag clockspring centering procedure.

14   Install the clockspring by reversing the removal procedure.

2016 and later models (except Malibu Limited)

15   Detach the clockspring locking tabs to separate the clockspring from the switch mounting bracket.

16   Remove the clockspring from the steering column **(see illustration)**.

17   Perform the airbag clockspring centering procedure.

18   Install the clockspring by reversing the removal procedure.

Airbag clockspring centering

Note: *With the steering wheel electrical connector at the 12 o'clock position and the loop (u-turn) appearing in the centering window (on 2013 to 2015 models [and 2016 Malibu Limited] the centering window is 7 o'clock position - on 2016 and later models [except Malibu Limited] the centering window is just below the 3 o'clock position).*

Note: *The centering window for each different style of clockspring must be located in the correct position before installing onto the steering shaft. Be sure the steering shaft is positioned with the front wheels pointing straight ahead.*

19   Ensure the block tooth (wide tooth) of the steering shaft is at the 6 o'clock position.

20   Hold the clockspring so you can see the centering window with the steering wheel connections at the 12 o'clock position.

21   Slowly rotate the center section of the clockspring until the it stops turning. Do NOT force it any further.

22   Slowly rotate the center section 2.5 turns in the opposite direction. Until the up-lead post is at the 12 o'clock position.

23   Visually check the centering window that the loop (u-turn) is visible.

24   Hold the coil center (to prevent it from turning) and align the clockspring with the steering column shaft and components. Slide the clockspring onto the steering shaft.

Installation

25   When installing the clockspring, make sure that the wheels are pointing straight ahead, the steering shaft is lined up in the 12 o'clock position and that the airbag clockspring is centered.

26   The remainder of the installation is the reverse of removal, noting the following:

a)   *When installing the steering wheel, align the index mark on the steering wheel hub with the mark on the shaft*

(see illustration 15.7). This will align the block-tooth on the steering wheel hub with the gap on the steering shaft splines and ensure that the steering wheel is in the proper position on the steering shaft.

b)   *Apply non-hardening threadlocking compound to the threads of the steering wheel bolt, then install the bolt and tighten it to the torque listed in this Chapter's Specifications.*

c)   *Install the airbag module on the steering wheel and push it into place until the retaining posts engage with the retaining springs.*

d)   *Enable the airbag system (see Chapter 12).*

---

16   Steering column - removal and installation

Warning: *These models are equipped with airbags. Always disable the airbag system before working in the vicinity of any airbag system component to avoid the possibility of accidental deployment of the airbag(s), which could cause personal injury (see Chapter 12).*

Warning: *Do not use a memory saving device to preserve the PCM's memory when working on or near airbag system components.*

2015 and earlier models (and 2016 Malibu Limited models) - removal and installation

Removal

1   Park the vehicle with the wheels pointing straight ahead. Disconnect the cable from the negative terminal of the battery (see Chapter 5). Disable the airbag system (see Chapter 12).

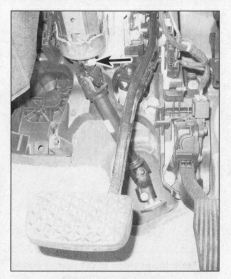

16.9 Remove and discard the pinch bolt

16.11 Steering column mounting fasteners

16.25 Remove the steering shaft dust boot

2   Make sure the steering column is locked.
3   Remove the steering column covers (see Chapter 11).
4   If the vehicle uses an ignition key, remove the lock cylinder bezel trim.
5   Remove the lower steering column filler trim (see Chapter 11).
6   Remove the steering wheel (see Section 15).
7   Remove the knee bolster (see Chapter 11) and the knee bolster support from under the steering column.
8   Disconnect the electrical connectors from the steering column switches and remove the wiring harness from the column.
9   Mark the relationship of the steering column shaft to the intermediate shaft coupler, then remove the intermediate shaft-to-steering column shaft pinch bolt **(see illustration)**.
10   Check for any remaining electrical connectors or wiring harnesses that would interfere with removal.
11   Remove the steering column-to-dash mounting fasteners, then carefully guide the column out from the instrument panel **(see illustration)**.
12   If you are replacing the steering column, remove any components that will be used on the replacement column. For removal and installation of the electrical components (near the top of the column), refer to Chapter 12.

Installation

13   Guide the column into position, connecting the steering shaft with the intermediate shaft coupler. Align the marks made in Step 9.
14   Install the mounting fasteners and them to the torque listed in this Chapter's Specifications.
15   Install the new intermediate shaft coupler pinch-bolt and tighten the nut to the torque listed in this Chapter's Specifications.
16   The remainder of installation is the reverse of removal.

17   After installation, center the steering angle sensor (see Chapter 12).

2016 and later models (except Malibu limited)

Removal

18   Park the vehicle with the wheels pointing straight ahead. Disconnect the cable from the negative terminal of the battery (see Chapter 5).
Warning: *Before working around or servicing any airbag or SRS component, disconnect the cable from the negative battery terminal (see Chapter 5) and wait at least 10 minutes for the airbag system capacitors to fully discharge. Accidental deployment of the system can cause injury or even death.*
19   With the vehicle in ACC mode, remove the fuse to UNLOCK the steering column lock control module.

20   Remove the air duct from below the steering column (see Chapter 11).
21   Remove the steering column lower trim panel (see Chapter 11).
22   Remove driver's side knee bolster trim panel (see Chapter 11).
23   Remove driver's side knee bolster trim panel (see Chapter 11).
24   Remove the instrument panel lower airbag - driver's side (see Chapter 12).
25   Rotate the steering column shaft to gain access to the intermediate shaft retaining bolt. Pull the rubber dust boot up from the floor to expose the intermediate shaft and steering column shaft connection **(see illustration)**.
26   Remove the bolt and mark the relationship of the steering column shaft to the intermediate shaft **(see illustrations)**.
27   Separate the intermediate shaft and the steering column shaft.

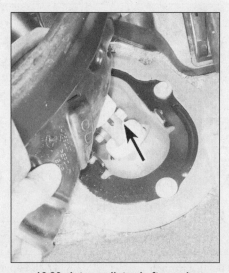

16.26a Intermediate shaft coupler pinch bolt

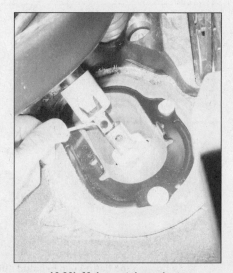

16.26b Make match marks to aid in installation

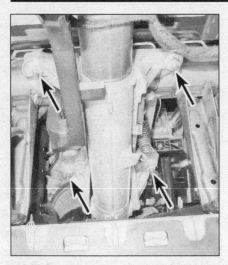

16.29 Steering column-to-dash fasteners

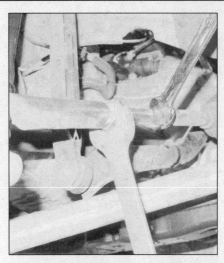

17.2 Using two wrenches, hold the tie-rod and loosen the jam nut.

17.3 Mark the position of the tie-rod end in relation to the threads

28   Disconnect the electrical connections to the steering column.

29   Remove the fasteners securing the steering column to the instrument panel support **(see illustration)**.

30   Carefully remove the steering column from the vehicle.

Installation

31   If replacing the steering column, be sure to transfer any components as needed.

32   Match mark the shaft of the replacement steering column in the same manner as the old steering column.

33   Apply non-hardening threadlocking compound to the threads of the pinch bolt. Install the bolt and tighten it to the torque listed in this Chapter's Specifications.

34   The remainder of the installation is the reverse of removal.

35   After installation, center the steering angle sensor (see Chapter 12).

17   Tie-rod ends - removal and installation

Removal

1   Apply the parking brake, loosen the front wheel lug nuts, raise the front of the vehicle and support it securely on jackstands. Remove the wheel.

2   Loosen the tie-rod end jam nut **(see illustration)**.

3   Mark the relationship of the tie-rod end to the threaded portion of the tie-rod. This will ensure the toe-in setting is restored when reassembled **(see illustration)**.

Note: *An alternative method is to count the number of turns it takes to remove the tie-rod from the linkage arm. Install the replacement tie-rod with the same amount of turns.*

4   Loosen the tie-rod end ballstud nut a

few turns, then install a puller to separate the ballstud from the steering knuckle arm **(see illustrations)**.

5   With the ballstud loose, install a balljoint puller and remove the ballstud. Then separate the tie-rod end from the steering knuckle arm.

Installation

6   Thread the tie-rod end onto the tie-rod to the marked position (or counted turns), then insert the tie-rod end ballstud into the steering knuckle arm. Install the nut onto the ballstud and tighten it to the torque listed in this Chapter's Specifications.

7   Tighten the jam nut securely and install the wheel. Lower the vehicle and tighten the lug nuts to the torque listed in the Chapter 1 Specifications.

8   Have the front end alignment checked and, if necessary, adjusted.

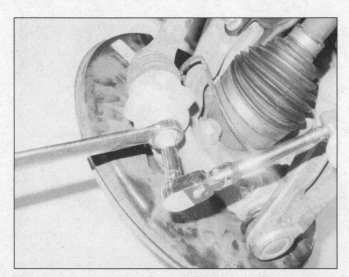

17.4a Loosen the tie-rod end ballstud nut using a wrench while holding the stud with a socket wrench

17.4b Separate the tie-rod end ballstud from the steering knuckle arm with a puller

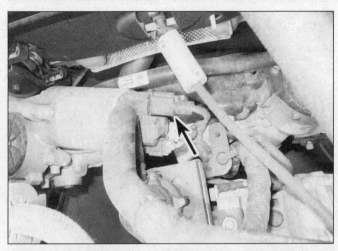

19.2 Disconnect the electrical connector from the steering gear assembly (not all connections are shown)

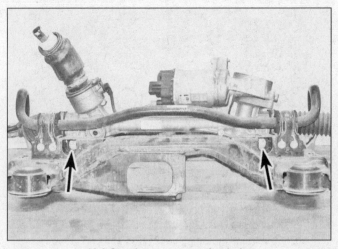

19.3 Steering gear mounting bolts

18 Steering gear boots - removal and installation

Warning: *Make sure the steering shaft is not turned while the steering gear is detached or you could damage the airbag system clockspring. To prevent the shaft from turning, place the ignition key in the LOCK position or thread the seat belt through the steering wheel and clip it into place.*

Note: *Steering gear boot removal and installation involves lowering the rear of the subframe.*

Note: *The manufacturer recommends using new subframe mounting bolts.*

1   Loosen the front wheel lug nuts, raise the front of the vehicle, support it securely on jackstands and remove the front wheels.

Warning: *Do not work below any part of the subframe unless it is supported by jackstands.*

2   Remove the tie-rod end and jam nut (see Section 17).

3   Remove the steering gear heat shield, if applicable.

4   Remove the outer steering gear boot clamp with a pair of pliers. Cut off the inner boot clamp with diagonal cutters and slide the boot off the rod.

5   Before installing the new boot, wrap the threads and splines on the end of the steering linkage with a layer of tape so the small end of the new boot isn't damaged.

6   Slide the new boot into position on the steering gear. Make sure that the breather tube is connected and in the right position, if equipped. With the boot properly positioned on the housing and seated to the tie-rod, install new clamps.

7   Remove the tape and install the tie-rod end (see Section 17).

8   Install the stabilizer bar links (see Section 4).

9   Install the wheel and lug nuts. Lower the vehicle and tighten the lug nuts to the torque listed in the Chapter 1 Specifications.

10   Have the front end alignment checked and, if necessary, adjusted.

19 Steering gear - removal and installation/assist motor and module - replacement

Warning: *During removal or installation, the components of the electronic steering gear assembly are susceptible to damage. DO NOT pry on any fasteners, connectors or metal components of the steering gear. Be sure to have the battery disconnected and remove any static charge from yourself before beginning work.*

Caution: *In order to remove or replace the power steering assist motor or control module you must first obtain the "key cycle count" from the old steering column before removal. Without the key cycle count it is IMPOSSIBLE to flash the replacement module or motor. Obtain the key cycle count with a scanner at your dealership or independent repair facility, prior to replacing the assembly.*

Warning: *If communication from the scan tool to the OLD electronic power steering gear cannot be established, DO NOT attempt to replace just the power steering assist motor or module - Replace the entire electronic power steering gear assembly.*

1   Disconnect the cable from the negative terminal of the battery (see Chapter 5).

Caution: *On 2015 and earlier (and 2016 Malibu limited models), the rear of the subframe only needs to be lowered; not completely removed - DO NOT allow the rear subframe to be lowered past 2 inches, or damage to the drivetrain components or wiring harnesses may occur.*

2   Remove the subframe (see Section 20), then remove the stabilizer bar from the subframe (see Section 4) **(see illustration)**.

3   Remove the steering gear mounting bolts and detach the steering gear from the subframe **(see illustration)**.

4   Installation is the reverse of removal.

5   Program the electronic power steering control module using the appropriate scanner at your local dealership or independent repair facility.

Power steering assist motor and control module - replacement

Caution: *In order to remove or replace the power steering assist motor or control module you must first obtain the "key cycle count" from the old steering column before removal. Without the key cycle count it is IMPOSSIBLE to flash the replacement module or motor. Obtain the key cycle count with a scanner at your dealership or independent repair facility, prior to replacing the assembly.*

Note: *The control module is part of the power steering assist motor.*

6   Remove the steering gear if not already done.

7   Disconnect the electrical connector from the motor.

8   Remove the motor-to-steering gear mounting bolts and detach the motor from the steering gear.

9   Installation is the reverse of the removal procedure, noting the following points:

a) *Install a new drive coupling and O-ring. Lubricate the O-ring with multi-purpose grease.*

b) *Install new mounting bolts and tighten them to the torque listed in this Chapter's Specifications.*

c) *Install the steering gear, then transfer the key cycle count pulled from the old steering gear control module to the new one. Have a dealer service department or qualified repair shop program / reflash the power steering motor.*

20 Subframe (front) - removal and installation

Warning: *NEW subframe mounting bolts must be used during installation.*

1   Disconnect the cable from the negative battery terminal (see Chapter 5).

2   Loosen the front wheel lug nuts, raise the front of the vehicle and support it

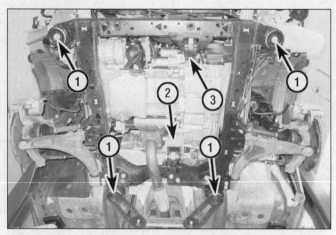

20.16 Subframe mounting bolts (2015 and earlier models [and 2016 Malibu limited])

1 *Subframe main fasteners*
2 *Rear transmission mount-to-frame fasteners*
3 *Front transmission through bolt*

20.25 Mark the relationship of the subframe to the body (typical)

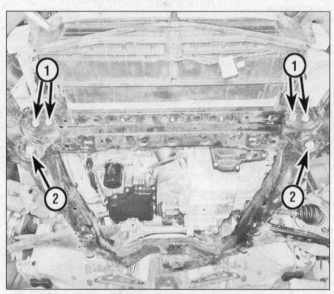

**20.28a Subframe front mounting bolts
(2016 and later models, except Malibu Limited)**

1 *Subframe reinforcement bolts*   2 *Subframe main bolts*

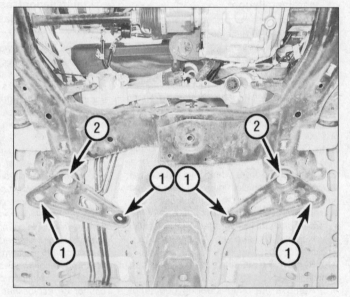

**20.28b Subframe rear mounting bolts
(2016 and later models, except Malibu Limited)**

1 *Subframe reinforcement bolts*   2 *Subframe main bolts*

securely on jackstands. Remove both front wheels.

3 With the vehicle at normal ride height, mark the relationship of the control arm to the front mounting bracket (where it attaches to the subframe).

4 Remove the front bumper cover (see Chapter 11). Remove the engine splash shield from the bottom of the front bumper.

5 Remove any remaining splash shields, air deflectors, or engine guards that are attached to the subframe.

6 Disconnect the ABS wheel speed sensors and detach the wire harness from the control arms and the subframe (where applicable). Carefully secure the harnesses out of the way.

2015 and earlier models (and 2016 Malibu Limited)

7 Using tie-downs, tie the radiator, condenser and fan shroud to the upper radiator support to prevent it from falling downward when removing the subframe. Also use suitable wire or rope to suspend the steering gear from the engine, for when the steering gear is unbolted from the subframe.

8 Remove the front section of the exhaust system (see Chapter 4).

9 Remove the front transmission mount through-bolt, and the rear transmission mount-to-frame fasteners **(see illustration 20.16)**.

10 Mark the position of the subframe in relation to the vehicle chassis **(see illustration 20.25)**.

Caution: *DO NOT allow the rear of the subframe to drop below 2 inches when removing the stabilizer bar*

11 Loosen all subframe fasteners slightly, support the rear of the subframe with jackstands, then remove the subframe rear fasteners and lower it enough to gain access to the front stabilizer bar fasteners. Remove the front stabilizer bar (see Section 4). After the stabilizer bar has been removed, temporarily reinstall the rear fasteners.

12 With the steering gear already suspended from above, remove the steering gear fasteners that attach to the subframe (see Section 19).

13   Separate the lower control arm balljoints from the steering knuckles (see Section 5).

14   Thoroughly check for wiring harnesses or anything else that may be attached to the subframe, and detach anything before continuing onto the next step.

15   Position one jack on each side of the subframe to support it. Place them midway between the front and rear mounting points, finding the center of gravity as necessary.

16   Remove the subframe mounting bolts and carefully lower the subframe along with the control arms **(see illustration)**.

17   Transfer the control arms to the new subframe assembly.

2016 and later models (except Malibu Limited)

18   Mark and disconnect the steering gear intermediate shaft (see Section 16), and disconnect the steering gear electrical connectors (see Section 19).

19   Disconnect the stabilizer bar links from the stabilizer bar (see Section 4).

20   Disconnect the tie-rod ends from the steering knuckles (see Section 17).

21   Remove the control arms (see Section 5).

22   Remove the front section of the exhaust system (see Chapter 4).

23   Attach an engine support fixture to the top of the engine/transaxle or attach an engine hoist to support the engine and transaxle (see Chapter 2A).

Caution: *If an engine support fixture is not available, a jack(s) or jackstand(s) with a block of wood on the jack or jackstand head(s) should support the engine and transaxle assembly from rocking too much and weakening the LH and RH engine mounts. If using this method, proceed with extra caution to prevent the engine from suddenly falling. DO NOT place your body directly underneath the engine or subframe.*

24   Remove the engine and transaxle mount-to-subframe fasteners (see Chapters 2A and 7).

25   Mark the position of the subframe in relation to the vehicle chassis **(see illustration)**.

26   Thoroughly check for wiring harnesses or anything else that may be attached to the subframe, and detach anything before continuing onto the next step.

27   Position one jack on each side of the subframe to support it. Place them midway between the front and rear mounting points, finding the center of gravity as necessary.

28   Remove the subframe mounting bolts **(see illustrations)**.

29   Slowly lower the floor jacks until the subframe is clear of the vehicle and the floor jacks are lowered fully.

30   Inspect the subframe mounting bushings for cracks, hardness and other signs of deterioration. If the bushings are damaged, replace them.

Note: *A special tool may be necessary to remove and install the bushings. Most automotive repair shops that specialize in front-end alignment and suspension repair will have*

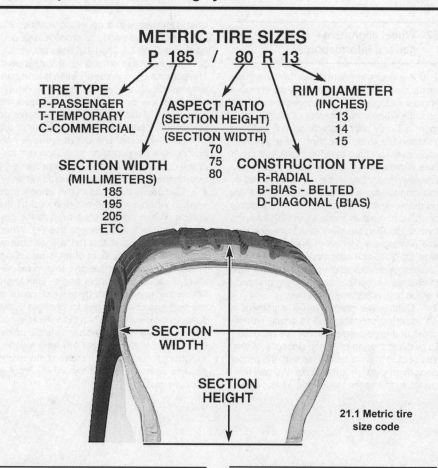

METRIC TIRE SIZES

P 185 / 80 R 13

TIRE TYPE
P-PASSENGER
T-TEMPORARY
C-COMMERCIAL

ASPECT RATIO
(SECTION HEIGHT)
—————————————
(SECTION WIDTH)
70
75
80

RIM DIAMETER
(INCHES)
13
14
15

SECTION WIDTH
(MILLIMETERS)
185
195
205
ETC

CONSTRUCTION TYPE
R-RADIAL
B-BIAS - BELTED
D-DIAGONAL (BIAS)

SECTION WIDTH

SECTION HEIGHT

21.1 Metric tire size code

the ability to press the bushings out and install new bushings.

Installation

31   Installation is the reverse of removal, noting the following:

- *Raise and support the subframe with the floor jacks while guiding the subframe into position and onto the studs for the engine and transaxle mounts. Install the subframe mounting bolts until they are all finger-tight.*
- *Raise the control arm to normal ride height before tightening the mounting fasteners.*
- *Align the subframe using the reference marks made earlier and by using a punch or drift in the alignment holes provided.*
- *Tighten the suspension fasteners to the torque listed in this Chapter's Specifications .*
- *Tighten the engine and transaxle mount fasteners to the torque listed in the Chapter 7 Specifications .*
- *Install the remaining components, splash shields, engine guards, and brackets.*
- *Tighten the wheel lug nuts to the torque listed in the Chapter 1 Specifications . Have the front end alignment checked and, if necessary, adjusted.*

32   After installation, center the steering angle sensor (see Chapter 12).

21   Wheels and tires - general information

1   All vehicles covered by this manual are equipped with metric-sized fiberglass or steel belted radial tires **(see illustration)**. Use of another size or type of tires may affect the ride and handling of the vehicle. Don't mix different types of tires, such as radials and bias belted, on the same vehicle as handling may be seriously affected. It's recommended that tires be replaced in pairs on the same axle, but if only one tire is being replaced, be sure it's the same size, structure and tread design as the other.

2   Because tire pressure has a substantial effect on handling and wear, the pressure on all tires should be checked at least once a month or before any extended trips (see Chapter 1).

3   Wheels must be replaced if they are bent, dented, leak air, have elongated bolt holes, are heavily rusted, out of vertical symmetry or if the lug nuts won't stay tight. Wheel repairs that use welding or peening are not recommended.

4   Tire and wheel balance is important in the overall handling, braking and performance of the vehicle. Unbalanced wheels can adversely affect handling and ride characteristics as well as tire life. Whenever a tire is installed on a wheel, the tire and wheel should be balanced by a shop with the proper equipment.

22   Wheel alignment -
general information

1   A wheel alignment refers to the adjustments made to the wheels so they are in proper angular relationship to the suspension and the ground. Wheels that are out of proper alignment not only affect vehicle control, but also increase tire wear. The front end angles normally measured are camber, caster and toe-in **(see illustration)**. Front camber and caster are preset at the factory on the vehicles covered by this manual; toe-in is the only adjustable angle on these vehicles. Front camber is adjustable on 2015 and earlier models (and 2016 Malibu Limited) by filing the lower strut to knuckle hole and altering the position of the knuckle in the strut. On 2016 and later models (except Malibu Limited), a special adjustment bolt is available to change the camber angle. Toe-in and camber are both adjustable at the rear.

2   Getting the proper wheel alignment is an exacting process, one in which complicated and expensive machines are necessary to perform the job properly. Because of this, you should have a technician with the proper equipment perform these tasks. We will, however, use this space to give you a basic idea of what is involved with a wheel alignment so you can better understand the process and deal intelligently with the shop that does the work.

3   Toe-in is the turning in of the wheels. The purpose of a toe specification is to ensure parallel rolling of the wheels. In a vehicle with zero toe-in, the distance between the front edges of the wheels will be the same as the distance between the rear edges of the wheels. The actual amount of toe-in is normally only a fraction of an inch. Incorrect toe-in will cause the tires to wear improperly by making them scrub against the road surface.

4   Camber is the tilting of the wheels from vertical when viewed from one end of the vehicle. When the wheels tilt out at the top, the camber is said to be positive (+). When the wheels tilt in at the top the camber is negative (-). The amount of tilt is measured in degrees from vertical and this measurement is called the camber angle. This angle affects the amount of tire tread which contacts the road and compensates for changes in the suspension geometry when the vehicle is cornering or traveling over an undulating surface.

5   Caster is the tilting of the front steering axis from the vertical. A tilt toward the rear is positive caster and a tilt toward the front is negative caster.

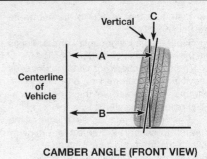

CAMBER ANGLE (FRONT VIEW)

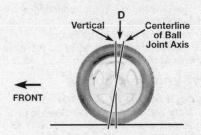

CASTER ANGLE (SIDE VIEW)

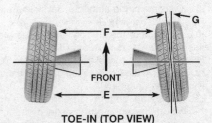

TOE-IN (TOP VIEW)

22.1 Camber, caster and toe-in angles

A minus B = C (degrees camber)
D = degrees caster
E minus F = toe-in (measured in inches)
G = toe-in (expressed in degrees)

Chapter 11
Body

Contents

Specifications

Torque specifications

Note: *One foot-pound (ft-lb) of torque is equivalent to 12 inch-pounds (in-lbs) of torque. Torque values below approximately 15 ft-lbs are expressed in inch-pounds, because most foot-pound torque wrenches are not accurate at these smaller values.*

	Ft-lbs (unless otherwise indicated)	Nm
Door hinge-to-door bolts...	18	25
Door strap bolts	16	22
Crossbeam mounting fasteners		
All crossbeam structural bolts/nuts	16	22
Crossbeam-to-HVAC housing fasteners	44 inch-lbs	5
Brake/accelerator pedal bracket-to-crossbeam bolts/nut..................	80 inch-lbs	9
Radio module (and communication interface module, if equipped)		
bracket-to-crossbeam screws.......................................	22 inch-lbs	2.5
Parking brake lever		
Bolt...	80 inch-lbs	9
Nuts	16	22

1 General Information

Warning: *The models covered by this manual are equipped with a Supplemental Restraint System (SRS), more commonly known as airbags. Always disable the air-bag system before working in the vicinity of any airbag system components to avoid the possibility of accidental deployment of the airbags, which could cause personal injury (see Chapter 12).*

1   Certain body components are particularly vulnerable to accident damage and can be unbolted and repaired or replaced. Among these parts are the hood, doors, tailgate, lift-gate, bumpers and front fenders.

2   Only general body maintenance practices and body panel repair procedures within the scope of the do-it-yourselfer are included in this Chapter.

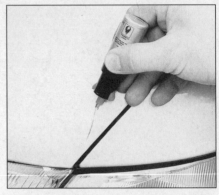

2.1a Make sure the damaged area is perfectly clean and rust free. If the touch-up kit has a wire brush, use it to clean the scratch or chip. Or use fine steel wool wrapped around the end of a pencil. Clean the scratched or chipped surface only, not the good paint surrounding it. Rinse the area with water and allow it to dry thoroughly

2.1b Thoroughly mix the paint, then apply a small amount with the touch-up kit brush or a very fine artist's brush. Brush in one direction as you fill the scratch area. Do not build up the paint higher than the surrounding paint

2   Repairing minor paint scratches

1   No matter how hard you try to keep your vehicle looking like new, it will inevitably be scratched, chipped or dented at some point. If the metal is actually dented, seek the advice of a professional. But you can fix minor scratches and chips yourself **(see illustrations)**. Buy a touch-up paint kit from a dealer service department or an auto parts store. To ensure that you get the right color, you'll need to have the specific make, model and year of your vehicle and, ideally, the paint code, which is located on a special metal plate under the hood or in the door jamb.

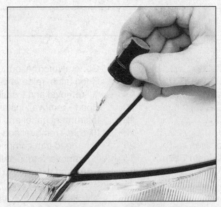

2.1c If the vehicle has a two-coat finish, apply the clear coat after the color coat has dried

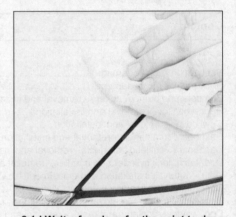

2.1d Wait a few days for the paint to dry thoroughly, then rub out the repainted area with a polishing compound to blend the new paint with the surrounding area. When you're happy with your work, wash and polish the area

3   Body repair - minor damage

Plastic body panels

1   The following repair procedures are for minor scratches and gouges. Repair of more serious damage should be left to a dealer service department or qualified auto body shop. Below is a list of the equipment and materials necessary to perform the following repair procedures on plastic body panels.

Wax, grease and silicone removing solvent
Cloth-backed body tape
Sanding discs
Drill motor with three-inch disc holder
Hand sanding block
Rubber squeegees
Sandpaper
Non-porous mixing palette
Wood paddle or putty knife
Wood paddle or putty knife
Curved-tooth body file
Flexible parts repair material

Flexible panels (bumper trim)

2   Remove the damaged panel, if necessary or desirable. In most cases, repairs can be carried out with the panel installed.

3   Clean the area(s) to be repaired with a wax, grease and silicone removing solvent applied with a water-dampened cloth.

4   If the damage is structural, that is, if it extends through the panel, clean the backside of the panel area to be repaired as well. Wipe dry.

5   Sand the rear surface about 1-1/2 inches beyond the break.

6   Cut two pieces of fiberglass cloth large enough to overlap the break by about 1-1/2 inches. Cut only to the required length.

7   Mix the adhesive from the repair kit according to the instructions included with the kit, and apply a layer of the mixture approximately 1/8-inch thick on the backside of the panel. Overlap the break by at least 1-1/2 inches.

8   Apply one piece of fiberglass cloth to the adhesive and cover the cloth with additional adhesive. Apply a second piece of fiberglass cloth to the adhesive and immediately cover the cloth with additional adhesive in sufficient quantity to fill the weave.

9   Allow the repair to cure for 20 to 30 minutes at 60-degrees to 80-degrees F.

10   If necessary, trim the excess repair material at the edge.

11   Remove all of the paint film over and around the area(s) to be repaired. The repair material should not overlap the painted surface.

12   With a drill motor and a sanding disc (or a rotary file), cut a "V" along the break line approximately 1/2-inch wide. Remove all dust and loose particles from the repair area.

13   Mix and apply the repair material. Apply a light coat first over the damaged area; then continue applying material until it reaches a level slightly higher than the surrounding finish.

14   Cure the mixture for 20 to 30 minute at 60-degrees to 80-degrees F.

15   Roughly establish the contour of the area being repaired with a body file. If low areas or pits remain, mix and apply additional adhesive.

16   Block sand the damaged area with sandpaper to establish the actual contour of the surrounding surface.

17 If desired, the repaired area can be temporarily protected with several light coats of primer. Because of the special paints and techniques required for flexible body panels, it is recommended that the vehicle be taken to a paint shop for completion of the body repair.

Steel body panels

Repairing simple dents

18 When repairing dents, the first job is to pull the dent out until the affected area is as close as possible to its original shape. There is no point in trying to restore the original shape completely as the metal in the damaged area will have stretched on impact and cannot be restored to its original contours. It is better to bring the level of the dent up to a point that is about 1/8-inch below the level of the surrounding metal. In cases where the dent is very shallow, it is not worth trying to pull it out at all.

19 If the backside of the dent is accessible, it can be hammered out gently from behind using a soft-face hammer. While doing this, hold a block of wood firmly against the opposite side of the metal to absorb the hammer blows and prevent the metal from being stretched.

20 If the dent is in a section of the body which has double layers, or some other factor makes it inaccessible from behind, a different technique is required. Drill several small holes through the metal inside the damaged area, particularly in the deeper sections. Screw long, self-tapping screws into the holes just enough for them to get a good grip in the metal. Now pulling on the protruding heads of the screws with locking pliers can pull out the dent.

21 The next stage of repair is the removal of paint from the damaged area and from an inch or so of the surrounding metal. This is easily done with a wire brush or sanding disk in a drill motor, although it can be done just as effectively by hand with sandpaper. To complete the preparation for filling, score the surface of the bare metal with a screwdriver or the tang of a file or drill small holes in the affected area. This will provide a good grip for the filler material. To complete the repair, see the Section on filling and painting.

Repair of rust holes or gashes

22 Remove all paint from the affected area and from an inch or so of the surrounding metal using a sanding disk or wire brush mounted in a drill motor. If these are not available, a few sheets of sandpaper will do the job just as effectively.

23 With the paint removed, you will be able to determine the severity of the corrosion and decide whether to replace the whole panel, if possible, or repair the affected area. New body panels are not as expensive as most people think and it is often quicker to install a new panel than to repair large areas of rust.

24 Remove all trim pieces from the affected area except those which will act as a guide to the original shape of the damaged body, such as headlight shells, etc. Using metal snips or a hacksaw blade, remove all loose metal and any other metal that is badly affected by rust. Hammer the edges of the hole in to create a slight depression for the filler material.

25 Wire-brush the affected area to remove the powdery rust from the surface of the metal. If the back of the rusted area is accessible, treat it with rust inhibiting paint.

26 Before filling is done, block the hole in some way. This can be done with sheet metal riveted or screwed into place, or by stuffing the hole with wire mesh.

27 Once the hole is blocked off, the affected area can be filled and painted. See the following subsection on filling and painting.

Filling and painting

28 Many types of body fillers are available, but generally speaking, body repair kits which contain filler paste and a tube of resin hardener are best for this type of repair work. A wide, flexible plastic or nylon applicator will be necessary for imparting a smooth and contoured finish to the surface of the filler material. Mix up a small amount of filler on a clean piece of wood or cardboard (use the hardener sparingly). Follow the manufacturer's instructions on the package, otherwise the filler will set incorrectly.

29 Using the applicator, apply the filler paste to the prepared area. Draw the applicator across the surface of the filler to achieve the desired contour and to level the filler surface. As soon as a contour that approximates the original one is achieved, stop working the paste. If you continue, the paste will begin to stick to the applicator. Continue to add thin layers of paste at 20-minute intervals until the level of the filler is just above the surrounding metal.

30 Once the filler has hardened, the excess can be removed with a body file. From then on, progressively finer grades of sandpaper should be used, starting with a 180-grit paper and finishing with 600-grit wet-or-dry paper. Always wrap the sandpaper around a flat rubber or wooden block, otherwise the surface of the filler will not be completely flat. During the sanding of the filler surface, the wet-or-dry paper should be periodically rinsed in water. This will ensure that a very smooth finish is produced in the final stage.

31 At this point, the repair area should be surrounded by a ring of bare metal, which in turn should be encircled by the finely feathered edge of good paint. Rinse the repair area with clean water until all of the dust produced by the sanding operation is gone.

32 Spray the entire area with a light coat of primer. This will reveal any imperfections in the surface of the filler. Repair the imperfections with fresh filler paste or glaze filler and once more smooth the surface with sandpaper. Repeat this spray-and-repair procedure until you are satisfied that the surface of the filler and the feathered edge of the paint are perfect. Rinse the area with clean water and allow it to dry completely.

33 The repair area is now ready for painting. Spray painting must be carried out in a warm, dry, windless and dust free atmosphere. These conditions can be created if you have access to a large indoor work area, but if you are forced to work in the open, you will have to pick the day very carefully. If you are working indoors, dousing the floor in the work area with water will help settle the dust that would otherwise be in the air. If the repair area is confined to one body panel, mask off the surrounding panels. This will help minimize the effects of a slight mismatch in paint color. Trim pieces such as chrome strips, door handles, etc., will also need to be masked off or removed. Use masking tape and several thickness of newspaper for the masking operations.

34 Before spraying, shake the paint can thoroughly, then spray a test area until the spray painting technique is mastered. Cover the repair area with a thick coat of primer. The thickness should be built up using several thin layers of primer rather than one thick one. Using 600-grit wet-or-dry sandpaper, rub down the surface of the primer until it is very smooth. While doing this, the work area should be thoroughly rinsed with water and the wet-or-dry sandpaper periodically rinsed as well. Allow the primer to dry before spraying additional coats.

35 Spray on the top coat, again building up the thickness by using several thin layers of paint. Begin spraying in the center of the repair area and then, using a circular motion, work out until the whole repair area and about two inches of the surrounding original paint is covered. Remove all masking material 10 to 15 minutes after spraying on the final coat of paint. Allow the new paint at least two weeks to harden, then use a very fine rubbing compound to blend the edges of the new paint into the existing paint. Finally, apply a coat of wax.

Repairing simple dents

36 The following photos illustrate a method of repairing simple dents. They are intended to supplement this Chapter and should not be used as the sole instructions for body repair on these vehicles.

4   Body repair - major damage

1 Major damage must be repaired by an auto body shop specifically equipped to perform body and frame repairs. These shops have the specialized equipment required to do the job properly.

2 If the damage is extensive, the frame must be checked for proper alignment or the vehicle's handling characteristics may be adversely affected and other components may wear at an accelerated rate.

3 Due to the fact that all of the major body components (hood, fenders, etc.) are separate and replaceable units, any seriously damaged components should be replaced rather than repaired. Sometimes the components can be found in a wrecking yard that specializes in used vehicle components, often at considerable savings over the cost of new parts.

These photos illustrate a method of repairing simple dents. They are intended to supplement *Body repair - minor damage* in this Chapter and should not be used as the sole instructions for body repair on these vehicles.

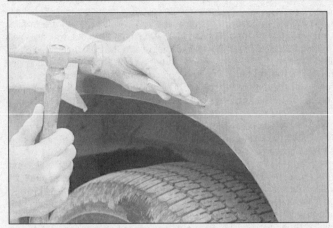

1 If you can't access the backside of the body panel to hammer out the dent, pull it out with a slide-hammer-type dent puller. In the deepest portion of the dent or along the crease line, drill or punch hole(s) at least one inch apart . . .

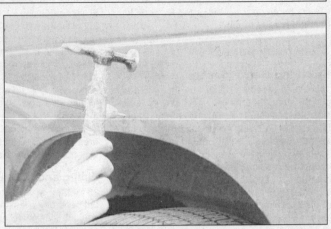

2 . . . then screw the slide-hammer into the hole and operate it. Tap with a hammer near the edge of the dent to help 'pop' the metal back to its original shape. When you're finished, the dent area should be close to its original contour and about 1/8-inch below the surface of the surrounding metal

3 Using coarse-grit sandpaper, remove the paint down to the bare metal. Hand sanding works fine, but the disc sander shown here makes the job faster. Use finer (about 320-grit) sandpaper to feather-edge the paint at least one inch around the dent area

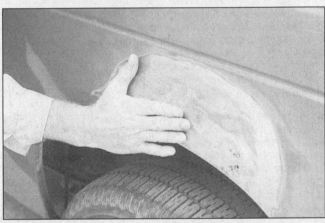

4 When the paint is removed, touch will probably be more helpful than sight for telling if the metal is straight. Hammer down the high spots or raise the low spots as necessary. Clean the repair area with wax/silicone remover

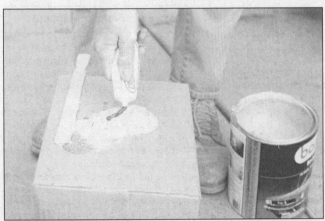

5 Following label instructions, mix up a batch of plastic filler and hardener. The ratio of filler to hardener is critical, and, if you mix it incorrectly, it will either not cure properly or cure too quickly (you won't have time to file and sand it into shape)

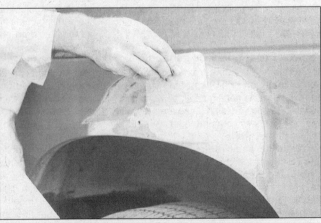

6 Working quickly so the filler doesn't harden, use a plastic applicator to press the body filler firmly into the metal, assuring it bonds completely. Work the filler until it matches the original contour and is slightly above the surrounding metal

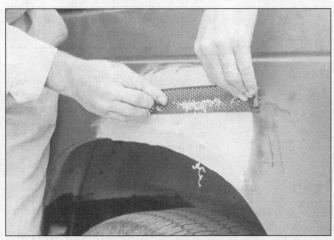

7 Let the filler harden until you can just dent it with your fingernail. Use a body file or Surform tool (shown here) to rough-shape the filler

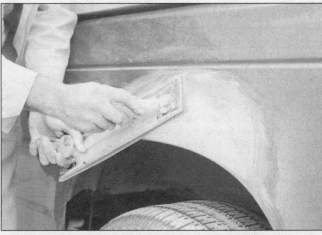

8 Use coarse-grit sandpaper and a sanding board or block to work the filler down until it's smooth and even. Work down to finer grits of sandpaper - always using a board or block - ending up with 360 or 400 grit

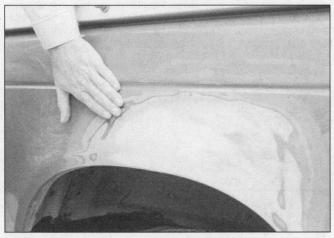

9 You shouldn't be able to feel any ridge at the transition from the filler to the bare metal or from the bare metal to the old paint. As soon as the repair is flat and uniform, remove the dust and mask off the adjacent panels or trim pieces

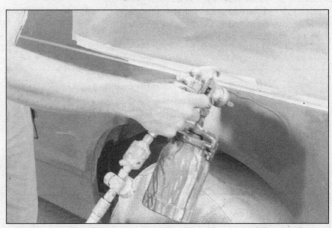

10 Apply several layers of primer to the area. Don't spray the primer on too heavy, so it sags or runs, and make sure each coat is dry before you spray on the next one. A professional-type spray gun is being used here, but aerosol spray primer is available inexpensively from auto parts stores

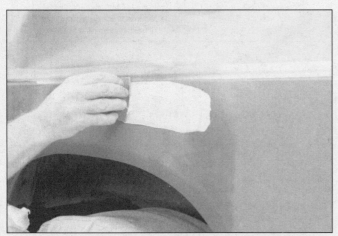

11 The primer will help reveal imperfections or scratches. Fill these with glazing compound. Follow the label instructions and sand it with 360 or 400-grit sandpaper until it's smooth. Repeat the glazing, sanding and respraying until the primer reveals a perfectly smooth surface

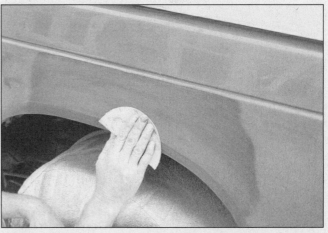

12 Finish sand the primer with very fine sandpaper (400 or 600-grit) to remove the primer overspray. Clean the area with water and allow it to dry. Use a tack rag to remove any dust, then apply the finish coat. Don't attempt to rub out or wax the repair area until the paint has dried completely (at least two weeks)

5   Fastener and trim removal

1   There is a variety of plastic fasteners used to hold trim panels, splash shields and other parts in place in addition to typical screws, nuts and bolts. Once you are familiar with them, they can usually be removed without too much difficulty.

2   The proper tools and approach can prevent added time and expense to a project by minimizing the number of broken fasteners and/or parts.

3   Trim panels are typically made of plastic and their flexibility can help during removal. The key to their removal is to use a tool to pry the panel near its retainers to release it without damaging surrounding areas or breaking-off any retainers. The retainers will usually snap out of their designated slot or hole after force is applied to them. Stiff plastic tools designed for prying on trim panels are available at most auto parts stores **(see illustration)**. Tools that are tapered and wrapped in protective tape, such as a screwdriver or small pry tool, are also very effective when used with care.

5.3 These small plastic pry tools are ideal for prying off trim panels

Fasteners

4   The illustrations below show various types of fasteners that are typically used on most vehicles and how to remove and install them. Replacement fasteners are commonly found at most auto parts stores, if necessary.

6   Upholstery, carpets and vinyl trim - maintenance

Upholstery and carpets

1   Every three months remove the floormats and clean the interior of the vehicle (more frequently if necessary). Use a stiff whiskbroom to brush the carpeting and loosen dirt and dust, then vacuum the upholstery and carpets thoroughly, especially along seams and crevices.

2   Dirt and stains can be removed from carpeting with basic household or automotive carpet shampoos available in spray cans. Follow the directions and vacuum again, then use a stiff brush to bring back the "nap" of the carpet.

3   Most interiors have cloth or vinyl upholstery, either of which can be cleaned and maintained with a number of material-specific cleaners or shampoos available in auto supply stores. Follow the directions on the product for usage, and always spot-test any upholstery cleaner on an inconspicuous area (bottom edge of a backseat cushion) to ensure that it doesn't cause a color shift in the material.

Fasteners

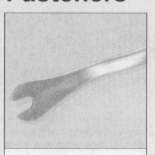

This tool is designed to remove special fasteners. A small pry tool used for removing nails will also work well in place of this tool

A Phillips head screwdriver can be used to release the center portion, but light pressure must be used because the plastic is easily damaged. Once the center is up, the fastener can easily be pried from its hole

Here is a view with the center portion fully released. Install the fastener as shown, then press the center in to set it

This fastener is used for exterior panels and shields. The center portion must be pried up to release the fastener. Install the fastener with the center up, then press the center in to set it

This type of fastener is used commonly for interior panels. Use a small blunt tool to press the small pin at the center in to release it . . .

. . . the pin will stay with the fastener in the released position

Reset the fastener for installation by moving the pin out. Install the fastener, then press the pin flush with the fastener to set it

This fastener is used for exterior and interior panels. It has no moving parts. Simply pry the fastener from its hole like the claw of a hammer removes a nail. Without a tool that can get under the top of the fastener, it can be very difficult to remove

4   After cleaning, vinyl upholstery should be treated with a protectant.
Note: *Make sure the protectant container indicates the product can be used on seats - some products may make a seat too slippery.*
Warning: *Do not use protectant on vinyl-covered steering wheels.*

5   Leather upholstery requires special care. It should be cleaned regularly with saddle-soap or leather cleaner. Never use alcohol, gasoline, nail polish remover or thinner to clean leather upholstery.

6   After cleaning, regularly treat leather upholstery with a leather conditioner, rubbed in with a soft cotton cloth. Never use car wax on leather upholstery.

7   In areas where the interior of the vehicle is subject to bright sunlight, cover leather seating areas of the seats with a sheet if the vehicle is to be left out for any length of time.

Vinyl trim

8   Don't clean vinyl trim with detergents, caustic soap or petroleum-based cleaners. Plain soap and water works just fine, with a soft brush to clean dirt that may be ingrained. Wash the vinyl as frequently as the rest of the vehicle.

9   After cleaning, application of a high-quality rubber and vinyl protectant will help prevent oxidation and cracks. The protectant can also be applied to weather-stripping, vacuum lines and rubber hoses, which often fail as a result of chemical degradation, and to the tires.

7   Hood - removal, installation and adjustment

Note: *The hood is awkward to remove and install; at least two people should perform this procedure.*

Removal and installation

1   Open the hood, then place blankets or pads over the fenders and cowl area of the

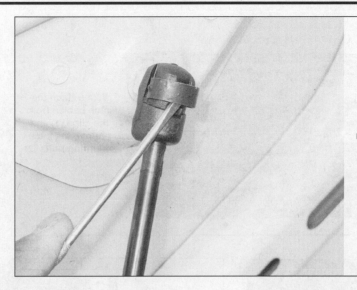

7.3 Pry out the hood strut retaining clip with a screwdriver, then pull the end off the ballstud

body. This will protect the body and paint as the hood is lifted off.

2   Make marks around the hood hinge to ensure proper alignment during installation.

3   Hold the hood up and disconnect the hood strut **(see illustration)** or lower the prop rod. Also disconnect the washer hose and any electrical connectors to the hood.

4   Have an assistant support one side of the hood. Take turns removing the hinge-to-hood nuts and lift off the hood **(see illustration)**.

5   Installation is the reverse of removal. Align the hinge bolts with the marks made in Step 2.

Adjustment

6   Fore-and-aft and side-to-side adjustment of the hood is done by moving the hinges after loosening the hinge-to-body bolts.

7   Loosen the bolts and move the hood into correct alignment. Move it only a little at a time. Tighten the hinge bolts and carefully lower the hood to check the position. Also

adjust the hood latch position to align with the striker (see Section 8).

8   Finally, adjust the hood bumpers on the radiator support so the hood, when closed, is flush with the fenders **(see illustration)**.

9   The hood latch assembly, as well as the hinges, should be periodically lubricated with white, lithium-based grease to prevent binding and wear.

8   Hood latch, release cables and interior release handle - removal and installation

Latch (primary and secondary)

Primary latch

1   Disconnect the hood ajar switch (if equipped) **(see illustration 8.4)**.

2   Disconnect the latch cables from the retaining clips on the radiator support. Use a marking pen to paint lines around the latch

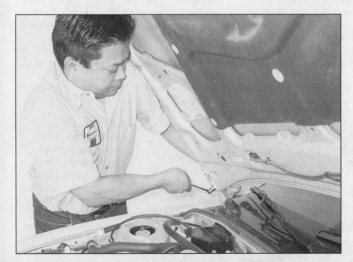

7.4 Support the hood with your shoulder while removing the hood mounting nuts (typical shown)

7.8 To adjust the vertical height of the leading edge of the hood so that it's flush with the fenders, turn each edge cushion clockwise (to lower the hood) or counterclockwise (to raise the hood)

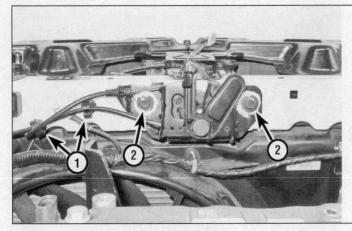

8.2a Detach the latch cables from the clips (1) and remove the latch mounting bolts (2)

8.2b Operate the lever by hand and disengage the primary cable end (1) from the slot, then squeeze the tabs and feed the cable housing through the hole (2)

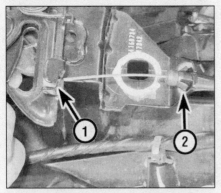

8.2c Operate the lever by hand and disengage the secondary cable end (1) from the slot, then squeeze the tabs and feed the cable housing through the hole (2)

8.4 Secondary latch mounting bolts (A) and hood ajar connector (B)

mounting bolts and latch body, then remove the bolts securing the latch to the core support. Disconnect the hood release cables by disengaging the cable housing and cable end from the latch levers **(see illustrations)**. Remove the latch assembly.

3   Installation is the reverse of removal. Align or adjust the position of the latch accordingly using the lines that were painted beforehand as a reference point.

Secondary latch

4   To remove the secondary latch, remove the mounting bolts **(see illustration)** and disconnect the cable from either latch (see Step 2).

5   Installation is the reverse of removal.

Primary cable and interior release handle

6   Unbolt and reposition the coolant expansion tank (see Chapter 3) without disconnecting the cooling hoses.

7   Disconnect the cable from the primary release latch **(see illustrations 8.2a and 8.2b)** and detach it from the cable clips along the engine upper core support and fender.

8   Push the hood release cable grommet into the firewall.

9   Pry the release handle tab with a screwdriver, sliding and detaching the handle from the knee bolster panel. Disconnect the cable from the interior release handle **(see illustration)**.

10   Tie a string or small piece of wire to the old cable before pulling the cable through the firewall.

11   Installation is the reverse of removal. Use the string or wire to pull the new cable through the firewall.

9   Bumper covers and impact beam - removal and installation

Warning: *The models covered by this manual are equipped with a Supplemental Restraint System (SRS), more commonly known as airbags. Always disable the airbag system before working in the vicinity of any airbag system component to avoid the possibility of accidental deployment of the*

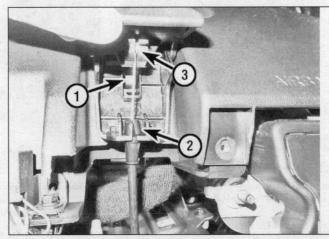

8.9 Pry the interior release handle tab with a screwdriver (1) and slide it free from the knee bolster. Squeeze the cable housing tabs (2) and pull the housing through the hole, then rotate the cable out and disconnect the cable end (3) from the handle

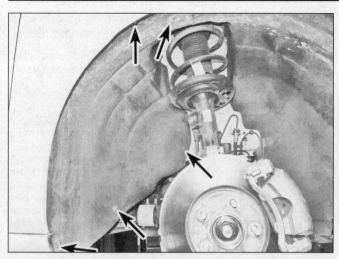

9.12a Front inner fender splash shield fastener locations (rear view)

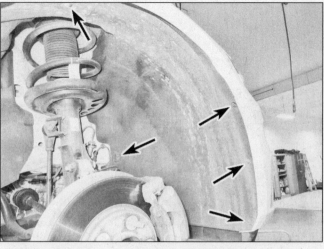

9.12b Front inner fender splash shield fastener locations (front view)

airbag, which could cause personal injury (see Chapter 12).

Note: *Disconnect the cable from the negative terminal of the battery (see Chapter 5). Refer to Section 6 for fastener and trim removal.*

Front bumper cover

2015 and earlier models (and 2016 Malibu Limited)

1   Open the hood. Apply the parking brake, raise the vehicle and support it securely on jackstands. Remove the front wheels.

Note: *The front fenderwell splash shield is comprised of two sections (front and rear).*

2   Remove the fasteners (screws and pushpins) securing the front portion of the front fenderwell splash shield, which are located in the fenderwell and beneath the vehicle. Remove the frontmost part of the front fenderwell splash shield.

3   Remove the bumper cover upper fasteners along the radiator support **(see illustration 9.16)**.

4   Remove the bumper cover lower fasteners from beneath the vehicle.

5   Remove the single fastener at each side securing the bumper cover to the fender (accessed in the fenderwells) **(see illustration 9.13)**.

6   Loosen (but DO NOT remove) the lower bumper cover impact bar rear bolts a few turns (located behind/near the foglight assemblies at each end).

7   If equipped, remove the two bolts (at each end) that retain the shutter assembly.

8   Using a plastic trim tool, gently pry between the bumper cover and the fender, working it off of the headlight housing until the bumper cover is free from the vehicle. Do this at each side, using an assistant's help to prevent the bumper cover from falling.

9   Carefully pull the bumper cover away from the vehicle while checking for and disconnecting any electrical connectors and/or hoses.

10   Installation is the reverse of removal.

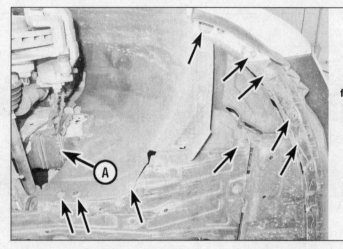

9.12c Front inner fender splash shield fastener locations (bottom-front view) - also remove the fenderwell plastic brace (A) where necessary

2016 and later models (except 2016 Malibu Limited)

11   Open the hood. Apply the parking brake, raise the vehicle and support it securely on jackstands. Remove the front wheels.

Note: *Only the front inner fender splash shield fasteners need to be removed, so the* splash shield can be pulled back and repositioned, in order for the bumper cover to be removed.

12   Remove the front inner fender splash shields from the bumper cover **(see illustrations)**.

13   Remove the bolt from inside each fenderwell area securing the bumper cover to the fender **(see illustration)**.

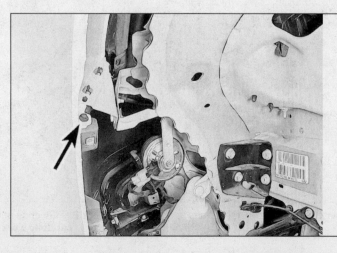

9.13 Bumper cover fenderwell bolt (left side shown, right side identical)

9.14a Remove the upper bolt where the fender meets the bumper cover. . .

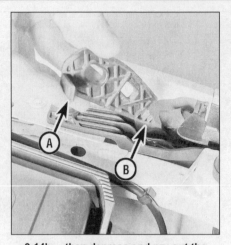

9.14b. . .then depress and pry out the tab (A) with a screwdriver, and pull the retaining brace and other tab (B) out of the slot (left side shown, right side identical)

14   Remove the upper side bolts along with the plastic retaining braces **(see illustrations)**.

15   Remove the lower radiator splash shield **(see illustrations)** that also serves as the lower bumper cover fasteners.

16   Remove the bumper cover upper mounting bolts **(see illustration)**.

Note: *Have an assistant help when pulling off the bumper cover to avoid dropping or wiring harness damage.*

17   Using a plastic trim tool, gently pry between the bumper cover and the fender, working it off of the headlight housing until the bumper cover is free from the vehicle **(see illustration)**. Do this at each side, using an assistant's help to prevent the bumper cover from falling.

18   Carefully pull the bumper cover away from the vehicle while checking for, and disconnecting, any electrical connectors.

19   Installation is the reverse of removal.

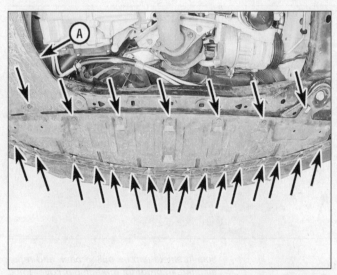

9.15a Side underbody splash shield (A - left side shown, right side removed) and lower radiator splash shield fasteners

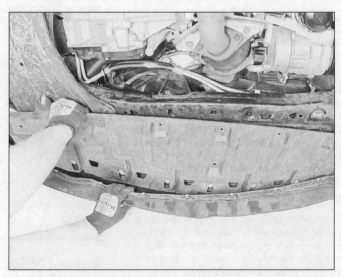

9.15b Pull down on the bumper cover to allow for enough clearance for the lower radiator splash shield to be removed

9.16 Bumper cover upper mounting bolts

9.17 Pry the ends of the bumper cover free from the fenders, then carefully work the sides off of the headlight housings

Rear bumper cover

Note: *Removal of only the rear section of the splash shield is necessary to access the bumper cover fenderwell fastener.*

20   Remove the rear inner fender splash shield fasteners **(see illustration)** at each side.
21   Remove the rear bumper cover fenderwell fastener **(see illustration)** from each side.
22   Remove the rear underbody air shield (if equipped) and the bumper cover lower fasteners **(see illustration)**.
23   Using a plastic trim tool, gently pry between the bumper cover and the rear fender, working it off of the fender bracket and taillight housing until the bumper cover is free from the vehicle **(see illustration)**. Do this at each side, using an assistant's help to prevent the bumper cover from falling.
24   Pull the bumper cover out and away from the vehicle, disconnecting any electrical connectors as necessary.
25   Installation is the reverse of removal.

Impact beam

26   Remove the front or rear bumper cover (see previous Steps).

27   If equipped, remove the pushpins retaining the air baffles, then remove the baffles from the impact beam.
28   On 2015 and earlier models, remove the right side headlight housing (see Chapter 12). **Note:** *On 2015 and earlier models, there are two impact beam mounting bolts and nuts, located on the right side of the beam and mounted vertically.*
29   Loosen the impact beam bolts **(see illustration)**, detach any wiring harnesses from the beam, then support and remove it from the vehicle.
30   Installation is the reverse of removal.

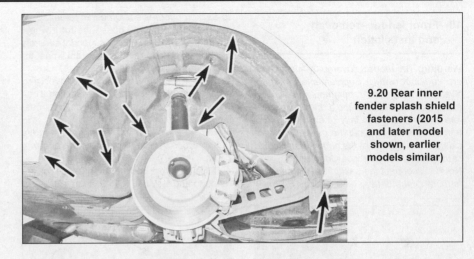

9.20 Rear inner fender splash shield fasteners (2015 and later model shown, earlier models similar)

9.21 Rear bumper cover fenderwell fastener (one each side)

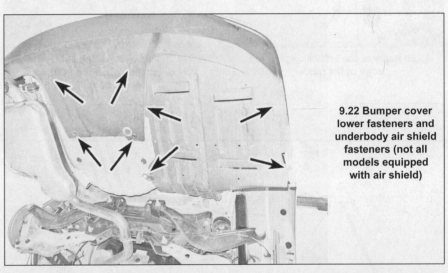

9.22 Bumper cover lower fasteners and underbody air shield fasteners (not all models equipped with air shield)

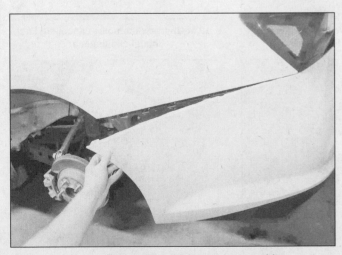

9.23 Carefully pull out the bumper cover sides from the retaining brackets

9.29 Impact beam mounting bolts and bracket retaining bolt (front shown, rear similar) - 2016 and later model shown

10   Front fender - removal and installation

Warning: *The models covered by this manual are equipped with a Supplemental Restraint System (SRS), more commonly known as airbags. Always disable the airbag system before working in the vicinity of any airbag system component to avoid the possibility of accidental deployment of the airbag, which could cause personal injury (see Chapter 12).*

Note: *Disconnect the cable from the negative terminal of the battery (see Chapter 5). Refer to Section 6 for fastener and trim removal.*

1   Open the hood. Loosen the front wheel lug nuts. Raise the vehicle, support it securely on jackstands and remove the front wheel for the fender being replaced.

2   Remove the front bumper cover and fenderwell splash shield(s) (see Section 9).

3   Remove the right or left headlight housing (see Chapter 12).

Note: *On 2015 and earlier models, remove the entire cowl cover as well as the end trim piece.*

4   Remove the cowl end trim piece for the fender being serviced (see Section 19).

5   Refer to the following illustrations and their respective captions for the removal of the fender **(see illustrations)**.

6   Lift and detach the fender, taking care not to damage or scratch any painted surfaces.

Note: *It's a good idea to have an assistant support the other end of the fender while it's being moved away from the vehicle to prevent damage to the surrounding body panels.*

7   Installation is the reverse of removal. Check the alignment of the fender to the hood and front edge of the door before final tightening of the fender fasteners.

10.5a Remove the bolts along the top edge of the fender

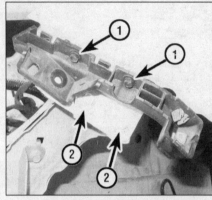

10.5b Remove the bolts securing the bracket (1), then the front edge fender bolts (2)

10.5c Remove or loosen the bolt near the hood hinge

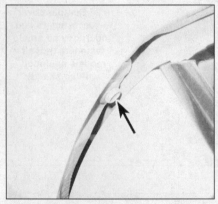

10.5d Open the door to remove this bolt

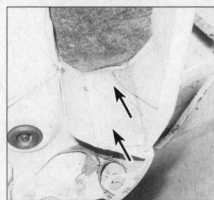

10.5e Remove the two lower bolts from inside of the fender well

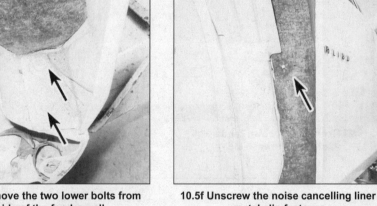

10.5f Unscrew the noise cancelling liner metal clip fastener

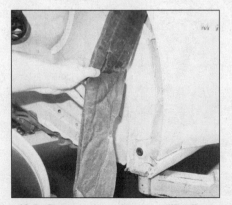

10.5g Remove the noise cancelling liner

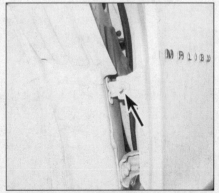

10.5h Remove or loosen the nut from inside the fenderwell

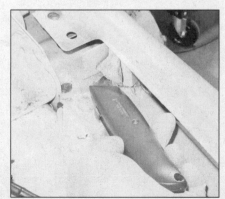

10.5i Carefully cut the adhesive foam as evenly as possible with a razorblade

11 Door trim panels - removal and installation

Warning: *Wear gloves when working inside the door openings to protect against sharp metal edges.*

Note: *This procedure applies to front doors -* *the procedure for the rear doors is similar.*

Note: *Refer to Section 6 for fastener and trim removal. Due to the variations of different trim package levels used across the models covered, some Steps may differ slightly from model to model.*

1 Disconnect the cable from the negative battery terminal (see Chapter 5).

Note: *On 2015 and earlier models, there is a decorative trim piece that is located beneath the pull handle/window switch assembly. Remove this trim piece and the retaining bolts that lie beneath, instead of the window switch assembly.*

2 For the removal of the door trim panel, refer to the following illustrations and their captions **(see illustrations)**.

11.2a Remove the trim cover and the hidden screw from the arm rest pull cup area

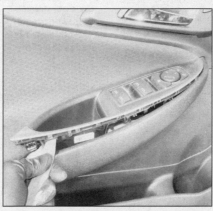

11.2b Using a plastic trim tool, pry up the pull cup and window switch assembly. . .

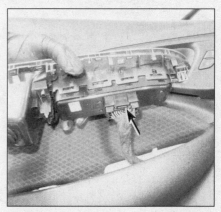

11.2c. . .then disconnect the electrical connector and remove it from the door panel

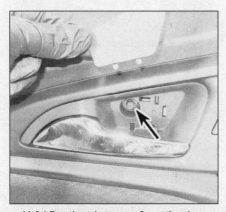

11.2d Pry the trim cover from the door release handle and remove the retaining screw

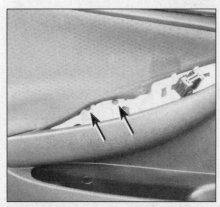

11.2e Remove the fasteners from behind the window switch assembly

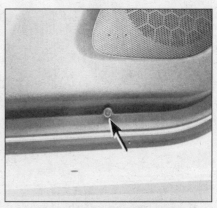

11.2f Remove the door panel lower mounting screw

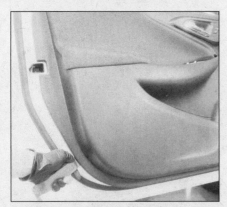

11.2g Using a plastic trim tool, carefully pry out the door trim panel along the perimeter until all the inner clips have been released. . .

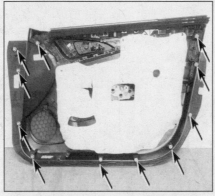

11.2h. . .locations of the door trim panel retaining clips - it's a good idea to replace any that are broken before installing the door panel

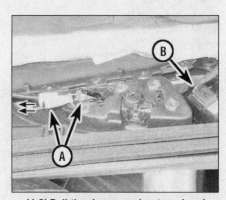

11.2i Pull the door panel outward and upward, carefully disengaging the door window sill and lifting the panel off the door - then, depress the tab **(A)** and slide off the cable bracket, disconnecting the cable end. Also release the safety tab and disconnect the electrical connector **(B)**

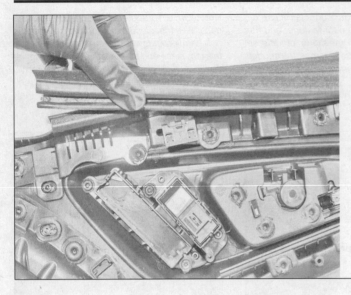

11.3 Make sure the door panel inner window sill is attached evenly across the clips

3   With the door panel removed, make sure the inner window sill fits evenly across the holding bracket clips **(see illustration)**.

4   To gain access to components inside the door, carefully peel back the watershield, noting the location routing of any cables or wiring harnesses through the shield **(see illustration)**. The remaining adhesive can be reused when installing.

5   Installation is the reverse of removal. With the pushpins aligned to their corresponding holes in the door, use the palm of your hand to "pop" the door panel into place.

Door upper window frame trim

6   Using a flat trim tool, release the push pins at each end securing the trim to the door, then carefully work the trim off the door frame **(see illustrations)**.

7   Installation is the reverse of removal.

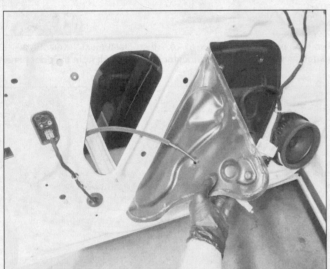

11.4 Peel back the watershield to gain access inside the door

11.6a Door window frame trim - rear pushpin location

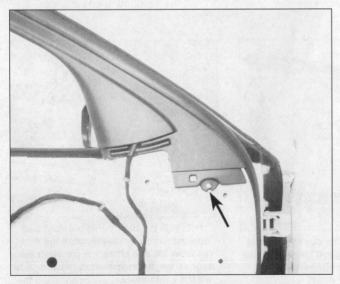

11.6b Door window frame trim - front pushpin location

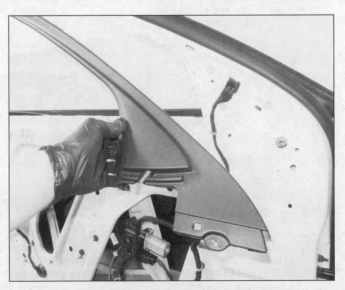

11.6c With the pushpins removed, carefully peel the trim off of the frame

12 Door - removal, installation and adjustment

Warning: *The models covered by this manual are equipped with a Supplemental Restraint System (SRS), more commonly known as airbags. Always disable the airbag system before working in the vicinity of any airbag system component to avoid the possibility of accidental deployment of the airbag, which could cause personal injury (see Chapter 12).*

Warning: *The door is heavy and somewhat awkward to remove and install - at least two people should perform this procedure.*

Note: *Make reference marks around the door hinges with a pen or a scribe to facilitate alignment during reassembly. Be aware when moving the bolts securing the hinges to the door - some paint damage may occur.*

Note: *This procedure applies to front doors - the procedure for the rear doors is similar.*

Removal and installation

1   Disconnect the cable from the negative battery terminal (see Chapter 5).

2   Open the door all the way and support it with a jack or blocks covered with rags to prevent damaging the outer surface.

3   For the removal of the door, refer to the following illustrations and their respective captions **(see illustrations)**.

4   With an assistant holding the door, completely remove the hinge-to-door bolts and lift off the door.

5   Installation is the reverse of removal. Tighten the fasteners to the torque settings listed in this Chapter's Specifications.

Adjustment

6   Having proper door-to-body alignment is a critical part of a well-functioning door assembly. First check the door hinge pins for excessive play. Fully open the door and lift up and down on the door without lifting the body. If a door has 1/16-inch or more excessive play, the hinges should be replaced.

7   Door-to-body alignment adjustments are made by loosening the hinge-to-body bolts or hinge-to-door bolts and moving the door. Proper body alignment is achieved when the top of the doors are parallel with the roof section, the front door is flush with the fender, the rear door is flush with the rear quarter panel and the bottom of the doors are aligned with the lower rocker panel. If these goals can't be reached by adjusting the hinge-to-body or hinge-to-door bolts, body alignment shims may have to be purchased and inserted behind the hinges to achieve correct alignment.

Note: *To access the front door side hinge bolts, the front wheel well liner may have to be removed or repositioned (see Section 9).*

8   To adjust the door-closed position, scribe a line or mark around the striker plate to provide a reference point, then check that

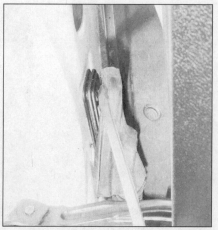

12.3a Starting at the top, use a flat screwdriver to pry the dust cover away from the electrical connector

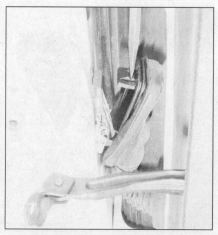

12.3b Allow the dust cover to tilt back away from the electrical connector, then depress the tab and carefully pry away the plastic connector cover

12.3c Disconnect the door harness connector by swinging the locking lever out and down, then pulling the connector straight out

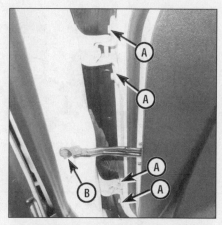

12.3d With the door supported, create marks around the door hinges, then remove the door strap bolt (B) and loosen the door mounting bolts (A)

the door latch is contacting the center of the latch striker. If not, adjust the up and down position first.

9   Finally adjust the latch striker sideways

position, so that the door panel is flush with the center pillar or rear quarter panel and provides positive engagement with the latch mechanism **(see illustration)**.

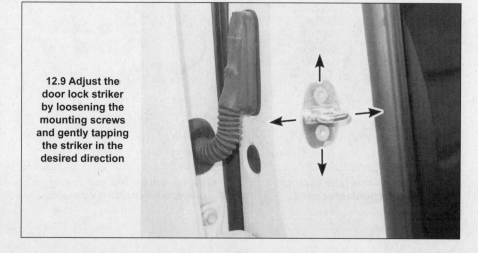

12.9 Adjust the door lock striker by loosening the mounting screws and gently tapping the striker in the desired direction

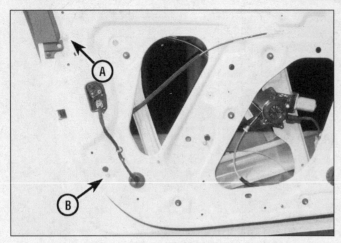

13.3a Remove the window guide rear track upper bolt (A) and loosen the lower bolt (B). . .

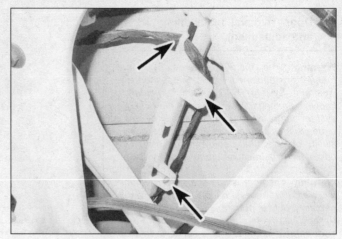

13.3b. . .then detach the wiring harness clips and remove the track

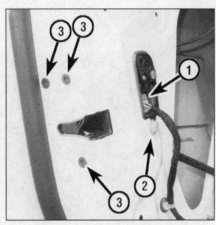

13.5a Door latch mounting details

1   *Latch assembly electrical connector*
2   *Latch assembly support fastener (loosen but don't remove)*
3   *Latch assembly mounting bolts*

13   Door latch, lock cylinder and handles - removal and installation

Warning: *The models covered by this manual are equipped with a Supplemental Restraint System (SRS), more commonly known as airbags. Always disable the airbag system before working in the vicinity of any airbag system component to avoid the possibility of accidental deployment of the airbag, which could cause personal injury (see Chapter 12).*
Note: *Disconnect the cable from the negative battery terminal before beginning (see Chapter 5).*

Door latch assembly

Note: *The door latch procedure is shown on a 2016 and later Malibu model - the procedure for 2015 and earlier models is similar.*

1   Remove door trim panel and the water-shield (see Section 11).
2   Remove the door window glass (see Section 14) and the door window glass regulator (see Section 15).
Note: *On 2015 and earlier models, remove only the window regulator left side bolts (see Section 15).*
3   Remove the window guide rear track **(see illustrations)**.
4   Remove the outside handle and handle inner bracket (see Steps 8 through 14).
5   Disconnect the electrical connector, remove the latch mounting fasteners and remove the latch **(see illustrations)**.
6   If required, disassemble the rod and cables from the latch assembly **(see illustrations)**. Transfer the rod and cables to the new latch assembly.
7   Installation is the reverse of removal. Once the components are installed, testthe operation making sure all is fully functional before installing the door trim panel.

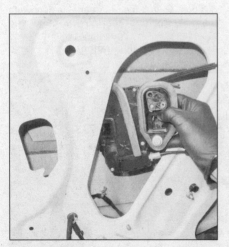

13.5b Remove the latch assembly through the door opening

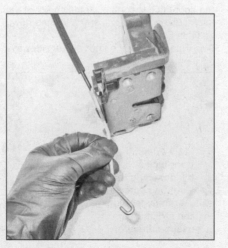

13.6a Remove the lock rod, noting the orientation in which it's installed

13.6b For cable number one: disengage the tab (1) and slide out the green cable bracket, then disconnect the cable end (2) from the lever

13.6c For cable number two: Disengage the tabs (1) and lift up the cover, then disengage the green cable bracket tab (2). . .

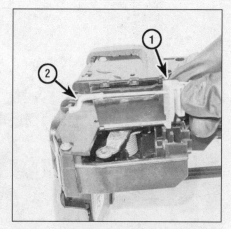

13.6d. . .slide out the green cable bracket (1) and disconnect the cable end (2) from the lever

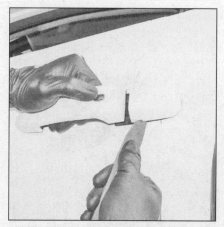

13.9a Pull the handle slightly and gently pry the plastic cover off of the lock cylinder metal cover

Door outside handle, lock cylinder and outside handle inner bracket - 2016 and later models (except Malibu Limited)

Outside handle

8　If the model being serviced is equipped with a smart key entry system, remove the door trim panel and watershield (see Section 11) and operate the window motor until the glass is rolled completely up.

9　For the removal of the outside handle, refer to the following illustrations and their respective captions **(see illustrations)**.

10　Installation is the reverse of removal. While installing the handle onto the door, you may have to manually actuate the operating mechanism (part of the inner bracket) in order for the outside handle tabs to properly catch onto the mechanism. Once the components are installed, test the operation making sure all is fully functional before installing the door trim panel.

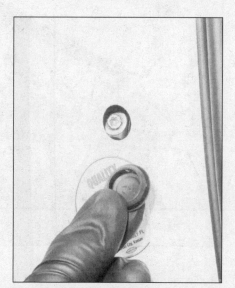

13.9b Remove the rubber cover and loosen the lock cylinder metal cover retaining screw

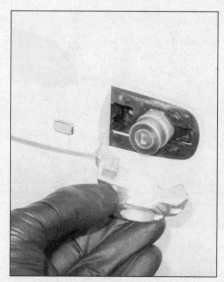

13.9c Remove the lock cylinder metal cover

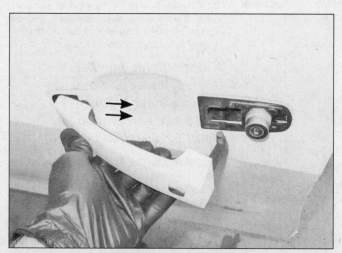

13.9d Slide the handle towards the rear of the vehicle, then rotate it outwards from the door

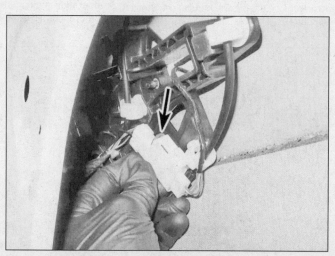

13.9e If equipped with a smart key system, disconnect the handle electrical connector from inside the door

13.14a Remove the outer molding cover

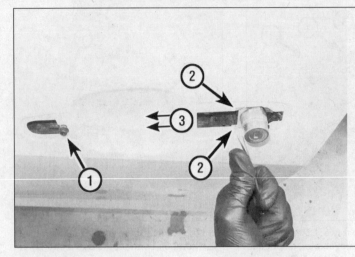

13.14b Loosen the bolt (1), depress the retaining tabs (2) and slide the inner bracket towards the front of the vehicle (3)

13.14c Working inside the door, release the latch rod from the inner bracket mechanism

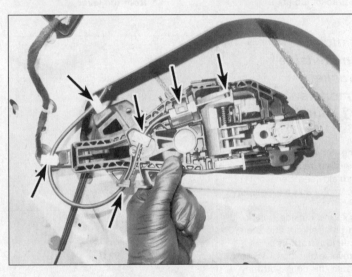

13.14d Release the cable and cable end from these retaining points

Outside handle inner bracket

11   Remove window regulator assembly (see Section 15).
12   Remove the window guide rear track (see Step 3).
13   Remove the outside handle (see Steps 8 through 9).

14   For the removal of the outside handle inner bracket, refer to the following illustrations and their respective captions **(see illustrations)**.
15   Installation is the reverse of removal. Once the components are installed, test the operation making sure all is fully functional before installing the door trim panel.

Lock cylinder

16   Remove the outside handle inner bracket (see Steps 11 through 14).
17   Depress the tabs and pull the lock cylinder out of the handle inner bracket **(see illustrations)**.
18   Installation is the reverse of removal. Once the components are installed, test the operation making sure all is fully functional before installing the door trim panel.

Door outside handle, lock cylinder and outside handle inner bracket - 2015 and earlier models (and 2016 Malibu Limited)

Outside handle and lock cylinder

19   If the model being serviced is equipped with a smart key entry system, remove the door trim panel and watershield (see Section 11) and operate the window motor until the glass is rolled completely up.
20   If equipped with a smart key system, disconnect the outside handle electrical connector from inside the door **(see illustration 13.9e)**.
Note: *If the lock cylinder still cannot be removed*

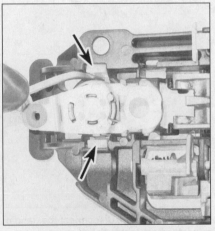

13.17a Release the retaining tabs. . .

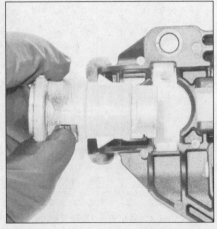

13.17b. . .then pull out the lock cylinder

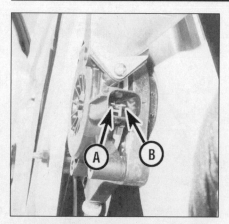

14.2 If necessary, apply a positive and negative 12V current, connected with insulated alligator clips, to the window regulator motor terminals (A, B) - reverse the polarity to operate the motor up or down

14.4a Carefully pry up the outer edge of the weatherstrip seal molding. . .

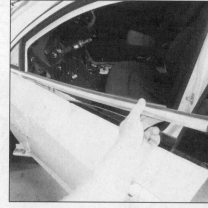

14.4b. . .then remove it from the door (be careful not to bend it)

after loosening it 10 turns, it may need to be loosened slightly more. DO NOT loosen the screw more than 2 1/2 turns past this point, or it may fall into the door and become unreachable.
21   Remove the small cover from the edge of the door. Pull the outside door handle outward (like you're opening the door), and hold it there. While the handle is held in the "opening" position, turn the lock cylinder screw **(see illustration 13.9b)** 10 revolutions counter-clockwise. The handle should now be held in this position naturally, and the lock cylinder along with the plastic cover can be pulled straight out of the door.
22   Slide the handle towards the rear of the vehicle, then rotate it outwards from the door **(see illustration 13.9d)**.
23   Installation is the reverse of removal. Once the components are installed, test the operation making sure all is fully functional before installing the door trim panel.

Outside handle inner bracket

24   Remove the door trim panel and watershield (see Section 11) and operate the window motor until the glass is rolled completely up.
25   Remove the window guide rear track (see Step 3).
26   Remove the outside handle / lock cylinder (see Steps 19 through 22).
27   Remove the outside handle bracket fastener **(see illustration 13.14b)**.
28   Working inside the door, release the plastic safety clip(s) and disconnect the rods from the handle inner bracket. Disconnect any electrical connectors (if equipped).
29   Carefully guide the handle inner bracket out from the door opening.
30   Transfer the necessary components to the new handle inner bracket. The remainder of installation is the reverse of removal. Once the components are installed, test the operation making sure all is fully functional before installing the door trim panel.

14   Door window glass - removal and installation

Warning: *The models covered by this manual are equipped with a Supplemental Restraint System (SRS), more commonly known as airbags. Always disable the airbag system before working in the vicinity of any airbag system component to avoid the possibility of accidental deployment of the airbag, which could cause personal injury (see Chapter 12).*
Warning: *Wear gloves when working inside the door openings to protect against cuts from sharp metal edges.*
Note: *Disconnect the cable from the negative battery terminal before beginning (see Chapter 5).*

Front door glass

1   Remove the door trim panel and the plastic watershield (see Section 11).
Warning: *Use caution to prevent shorting or sparks when operating the window motor by means of an electrical bypass source, which can cause injury - use insulated alligator clip*

connections through a 12-volt source ONLY.
2   Lower the window until you can access the window glass retainers, then disconnect the battery negative terminal. If the battery cannot be connected to operate the window motor, a 12V positive and negative current can be applied to the motor terminals (with the electrical connector disconnected) to operate the window up or down **(see illustration)**.
3   Remove the outside mirror (see Section 16).
Caution: *Use caution to avoid bending the weatherstrip seal outer molding when removing it - it cannot be reformed and will require replacement, which can be costly.*
4   Gently pry up and remove the door weatherstrip seal outer molding **(see illustrations)**.
Note: *When releasing the regulator-to-glass retainers, the section of the retainer behind the glass should be spread out with the trim tool.*
5   Release the window regulator-to-glass retainers (front retainer shown, rear retainer identical) while pulling up the window glass by hand at each end **(see illustration)**.

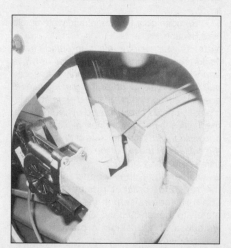

14.5 Use a plastic trim tool to release the window guide retainers at each end (one of two shown)

14.6 Carefully guide the glass out of the door

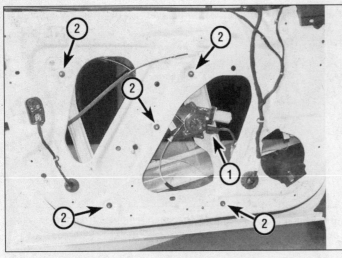

15.3 Window regulator assembly (front door shown, rear door similar) - disconnect the electrical connector (1) and remove the mounting nuts (2)

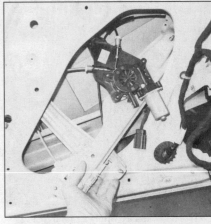

15.4 Guide the window regulator and motor through the door access opening

6   Tilt the glass with the front portion downward, then raise the back section and carefully lift the glass out of the door **(see illustration)**.
7   Installation is the reverse of removal.
8   Program the window express function (see Chapter 12).

Rear door glass
9   Remove the rear door trim panel and watershield (see Section 11).
10   Raise the window to the fully up position, then disconnect the cable from the negative battery terminal.
11   Remove the rear window guide rear track **(see illustration 13.3a)**. The bolt locations shown in the illustration may differ slightly.
12   Reconnect the negative battery cable and lower the window enough until the window glass retainer is clearly visible, then disconnect the negative battery cable.
13   Remove the door window inner belt sealing strip.
14   Gently pry up and remove the door weatherstrip seal outer molding (see Step 4). Be careful not to distort the molding.
15   Disengage the single regulator-to-glass retaining tab from the glass **(see illustration 14.5)** while pulling the glass upward by hand.
16   Carefully guide the window out of the door, tilting it as necessary.
17   Installation is the reverse of removal.

15   Door window glass regulator and motor - removal and installation

Warning: *The models covered by this manual are equipped with a Supplemental Restraint System (SRS), more commonly known as airbags. Always disable the airbag system before working in the vicinity of any airbag system component to avoid the possibility of accidental deployment of the airbag, which could cause personal injury (see Chapter 12).*
Warning: *Wear gloves when working inside the door openings to protect against cuts from sharp metal edges.*

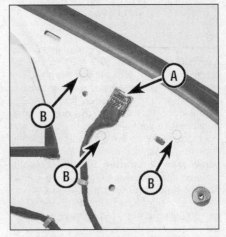

15.5 Window motor-to-regulator bolts

Note: *This procedure applies to the front and rear doors.*
Note: *Disconnect the cable from the negative battery terminal before beginning (see Chapter 5).*
1   Remove door trim panel and watershield (see Section 11).
Note: *If your window glass is tinted, avoid using tape to hold the window glass up while removing the regulator assembly. Tape can pull the tint material off of the glass. Instead, a set of suction cups attached together with a plastic coated cable is used by professional mechanics to hold the window glass up. Place one suction cup on either side of the glass with the cable over the top of the door frame (available at most part stores).*
2   Disengage the window glass from the regulator bracket retainer (see Section 14), then raise/pull the window completely to the top by hand. Securely tape the window in this position to prevent it from falling down.
3   Disconnect the regulator motor electrical connector and remove the mounting nuts **(see illustration)**.
4   Fold the cables and window tracks

16.2 Outside mirror electrical connector (A) and mounting fasteners (B)

together enough to guide the entire assembly out of the door access opening **(see illustration)**.
5   To separate the motor from the regulator, remove these bolts **(see illustration)**. Swap / transfer the necessary components.
6   Installation is the reverse of removal. Lubricate the rollers and wear points on the regulator with white lithium grease before installation.
7   Program the window express function (see Chapter 12).

16   Mirrors - removal and installation

Outside mirror assembly
1   Remove the door trim panel and upper door frame trim (see Section 11).
2   Disconnect the electrical connector, then support the mirror assembly by hand and remove the mirror mounting bolts **(see illustration)**.
3   Remove the outside mirror.
4   Installation is the reverse of removal.

16.5 Grasp the mirror glass on the outer-lower edge, then carefully, but sharply pull it out to disengage the mirror glass from the motor

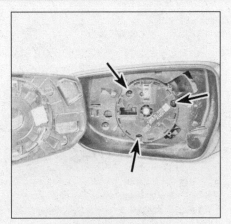

16.6 Mirror glass motor mounting fasteners

16.8a Position the mirror down, then disengage the tabs and remove the mirror outer cover. . .

16.8b. . .then, disengage the tabs and remove the mirror inner cover

16.9 Interior mirror retaining screw

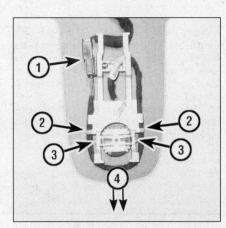

16.12 Interior moisture sensor details

1 *Disconnect the electrical connector and release the connector clip*
2 *Release the wiring harness from the retaining points*
3 *Release the sensor metal retaining tabs at each side*
4 *Remove the sensor in this direction, while guiding the wiring harness out*

Outside mirror glass and motor

Note: *On 2015 and earlier models (except Malibu Limited) - hold the pressure at the upper-inside corner with one hand, then insert a plastic trim tool at the opposite end and twist the tool to release the glass from the motor mount.*

5   To remove the mirror glass, push in the mirror at the upper-inside corner. Then, grasp the lower-outside corner and carefully pull it sharply outward to disengage it from the mirror motor **(see illustration)**. Be careful to avoid cracking the mirror glass. Disconnect the electrical connections (if equipped).

6   To remove the mirror motor, remove these mounting bolts **(see illustration)** and pull it out to disconnect the electrical connector.

7   Installation is the reverse of removal. Make sure the mirror glass plastic retainers engage completely with the motor tabs.

Interior mirror

Note: *Various inside mirror configurations and options are used across the models covered in this book. Your interior mirror may not have the exact arrangement as what is described in this procedure, however the replacement process should be similar.*

8   Remove the mirror covers **(see illustrations)**.

9   Remove the mirror screw **(see illustration)**, then disconnect the electrical connector (if equipped) and remove the mirror.

10   Installation is the reverse of removal.

Interior mirror base

Note: *The mirror base, in most cases, is removed by applying heat with a heat gun and gently prying it off from the windshield. When installing the base, a special type of rearview mirror adhesive, found at most auto parts stores, is used. Because of the risk of cracking the windshield in this tedious process, it is recommended to have this procedure performed by an automotive glass or a qualified automotive repair shop. Depending on the style of interior mirror, the replacement process may require the windshield to be removed.*

Removal

11   Remove the interior mirror (see Steps 8 and 9).

12   To gain access to remove the mirror base, any attached electrical components must be removed first - such as the forward

facing camera and windshield temperature/interior moisture sensor **(see illustration)**.

13   Draw a line on the windshield around the base with a washable-ink pen, to use as a reference point.

14   Use a heat gun on the base to carefully weaken the adhesive, then slowly pry the base loose while avoiding cracking the windshield.

Installation

15   Determine the location of the mirror mount. If the exact spot is unknown, measure the distance from left to right (A-pillar-to-A-pillar) and divide that in half; mark that spot. Then determine the up and down distances. Use the AS1* line on the windshield as a guide to where the base should be mounted.

Note: **The AS1 (rating for "approved safe-*

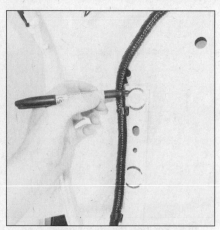

17.4 Mark around the hinge bolts for realignment purposes - then remove the retaining bolts on each side of the trunk lid

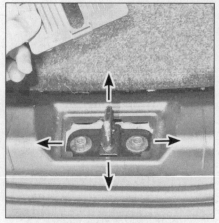

17.9 Loosen the bolts and adjust the position of the trunk latch striker

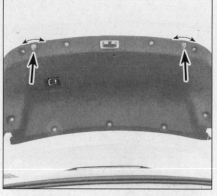

17.10 Rotate the bumpers in or out to adjust the trunk closed-position height

ty glass") line is the allowable tint line on a windshield. This line is five inches from the top of the glass. The line represents the area of windshield that, by law, allows at least 70 percent of the natural sunlight to come through.

16 Using a safety razor or utility knife, remove any glue residue from the windshield mounting area and the mirror mounting base.

17 Clean the mating surfaces with a lint free cloth saturated with brake cleaner.

18 Dry fit the mirror to the mirror mounting base, making sure that you have the mounting base in the correct orientation and the mirror is in a suitable position. Place a piece of masking tape onto the windshield just at the bottom edge of the mounting base.

19 Follow the adhesive manufacturer's procedure for the adhesive application, then press the mirror mounting base into place.

20 Hold the mounting base firmly in place for as long as the adhesive specification suggests. Allow the adhesive to cure.

21 The remainder of installation is the reverse of removal.

17 Trunk lid - removal, installation and adjustment

Removal and installation

Warning: *When the trunk lid is being replaced, be absolutely certain that the trunk hinge arms/torque rods are secured in place to prevent personal injury.*

Note: *The trunk lid is awkward to remove and install - at least two people should perform this procedure.*

1 Open the trunk lid and cover the edges of the trunk compartment with pads or cloths to protect painted surfaces when lid is removed.

2 Remove the trunk lid liner (see Section 18).

3 Disconnect any cables or wire harness connectors attached to the trunk lid that would interfere with removal.

4 Make alignment marks around the hinges with a marking pen **(see illustration)**.

5 While an assistant supports the trunk lid, remove the lid-to-hinge fasteners on both sides and lift the trunk lid off the vehicle.

6 Installation is the reverse of removal. When reinstalling the trunk lid, align the lid-to-hinge fasteners with the marks made during removal.

Adjustment

7 To adjust the position of the trunk lid in relation to the surrounding body panels, loosen the lid hinge bolts **(see illustration 17.4)**.

8 Position the trunk lid side-to-side, or forward-and-back as necessary, a little at a time, then tighten the bolts securely. Close the trunk lightly and check the gaps at each side of the trunk, repeating if necessary.

9 Remove the trim cover and loosen the bolts for the trunk lid striker **(see illustration)**, moving it into alignment with the trunk lid latch, then tighten the bolts securely.

10 The closed-position height of the trunk can also be adjusted by rotating the adjustment bumpers as necessary **(see illustration)**.

18 Trunk lid latch - removal and installation

1 Remove the plastic latch cover and trunk lid liner **(see illustrations)**.

2 Disconnect the latch electrical connector and cable, then remove the trunk lid latch mounting bolts and remove the latch **(see illustrations)**.

3 Installation is the reverse of removal.

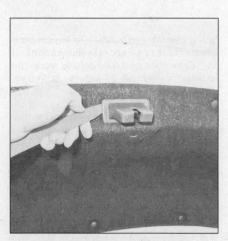

18.1a Gently pry off the plastic latch cover. . .

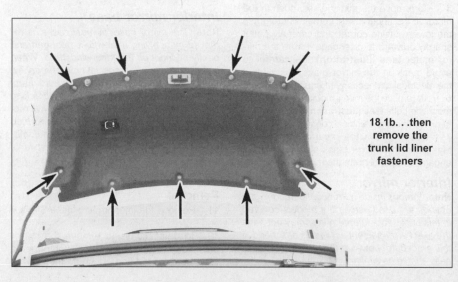

18.1b. . .then remove the trunk lid liner fasteners

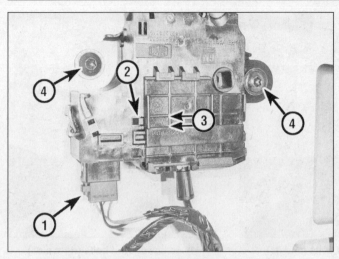

18.2a Trunk latch mounting details (later model shown, earlier models similar)

1   *Electrical connector*
2   *Depress the cover retaining tab with a screwdriver*
3   *Slide the cover in the indicated direction*
4   *Latch mounting bolts*

18.2b With the cover moved aside (1), disconnect the cable housing and end from the latch mechanism (2) - (later model shown)

19 Cowl cover - removal and installation

Note: *This procedure is shown on a later model Malibu - the procedure on earlier models is similar.*

1   Remove the wiper arms (see Chapter 1). Make sure the wipers are in the parked position and note the locations of the blades on the windshield (marking them with masking tape if necessary).

2   Remove the extension panels from each side that cover the hood hinges (**see illustrations**).

3   Remove the pushpins from the front of the cowl panel cover (**see illustration**).

4   Lift the front edge of the panel upward enough to clear the wiper motor pivot shafts, then disconnect the washer hoses and disengage the hoses from the underside retaining clips (**see illustrations**).

19.2a Pry out and remove the left cowl extension panel. . .

19.2b. . .then remove the right extension panel

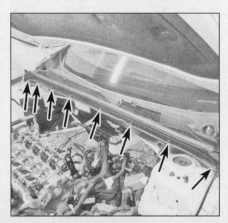

19.3 Cowl cover pushpin retaining clip locations

19.4a Lift up the front of the cowl panel cover and disconnect the washer hoses

19.4b The washer hoses are disconnected from the jets by twisting and pulling them straight off

19.6a Lower cowl bolts (left side)

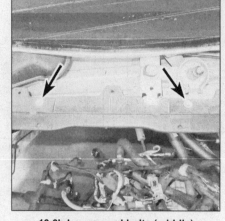

19.6b Lower cowl bolts (middle)

19.6c Lower cowl bolts (right side)

5   Pull the cowl panel cover away from the windshield and guide it out of the engine compartment.

6   To remove the lower metal cowl, remove the bolts **(see illustrations)**, then carefully guide it out of the engine.

7   Installation is the reverse of removal.

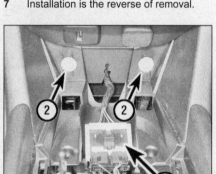

20.13a Disconnect the main console connector (1) and remove the console front bolts (2)

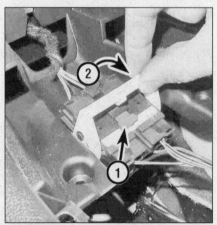

20.13b To disconnect the main connector, release the red safety tab (1) by pushing it backwards before lifting the bail arm (2)

20 Center console - removal and installation

2015 and earlier models (and 2016 Malibu limited)

1   Use a plastic trim tool to pry out the center dash trim panel / vents from around the radio and a/c control assemblies.

2   Remove the shift lever knob and boot (see Chapter 7).

3   Pry up and remove the shift indicator panel from the center console trim plate.

4   Pry out and remove the center console trim plate from along the top of the console.

5   Move the front seats all the way back, then pry out and remove the center console side trim panels.

6   Remove the four screws that secure the lowest dash control panel (directly above the center console), then pull out the panel and disconnect the electrical connector(s).

7   Pry out and remove the center console trim panel at the rear. Also remove the center console lower-rear fastener trim covers nearby.

8   Remove the center console fasteners: There are four along the bottom edges (two front, two back), and two securing the console to the dash.

9   Disconnect any electrical connectors and remove the center console from the vehicle.

10   Installation is the reverse of removal.

2016 and later models (except 2016 Malibu Limited)

11   Place the shift lever in the Neutral position, then disconnect the cable from the negative terminal of the battery (see Chapter 5).

12   Remove the shift lever knob and shift panel (see Chapter 7).

13   Disconnect the main electrical connector to the console and remove the console front bolts **(see illustrations)**.

14   Remove the dust cap, then remove the front and rear center console side screws **(see illustrations)**. Move the seat forward or back, as necessary, to access all of the fasteners.

15   Lift and slide the console slightly rearward, then remove the console and carefully guide it out of the vehicle.

16   Installation is the reverse of removal.

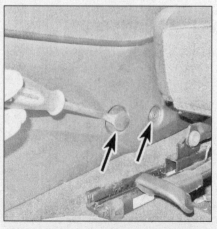

20.14a Fastener locations to the front of the seats (left side shown)

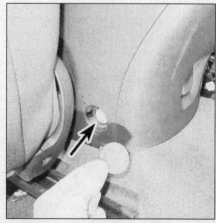

20.14b Fastener location behind the seats (left side shown)

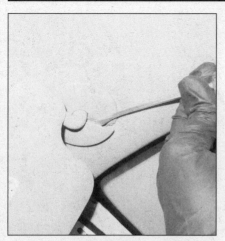

21.2a Pry off the wrap-around trim clip. . .

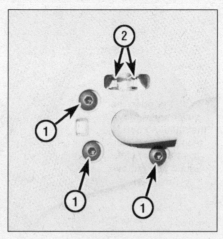

21.2b. . .then remove the screws (1) and pinch together the clip (2)

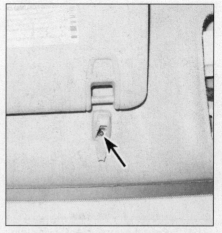

21.3 Pry open the trim cover and remove the sun visor support clip screw

21 Overhead trim components and interior trim panels - removal and installation

Warning: *These models are equipped with a Supplemental Restraint System (SRS), more commonly known as airbags. Always disable the airbag system before working in the vicinity of any airbag system component to avoid the possibility of accidental deployment of the airbag(s), which could cause personal injury (see Chapter 12).*

1   Disconnect the cable from the negative terminal of the battery (see Chapter 5).

Sun visor, grab handle and coat hanger

Sun visor and visor support clip

2   Pry off the wrap-around trim clip with a small screwdriver, then remove the screws used to fasten the sun visor to the roof **(see illustrations)**. Pinch the remaining retaining clip in with needle-nose pliers, then pull down the visor and disconnect the electrical connection for the visor light.

3   Pry open the trim cover and remove the screw that retains the sun visor support clip **(see illustration)**.

4   Installation is the reverse of removal.

Grab handle

5   Pry open the small trim covers, then remove the bolts and grab handle **(see illustration)**.

6   Installation is the reverse of removal.

Coat hanger

7   Pry open the trim cover and remove the coat hanger retaining fastener **(see illustration)**.

8   Installation is the reverse of removal.

C-pillar trim panels

9   Remove the rear seat cushion (see Section 24) and side bolster airbag (see Chapter 12).

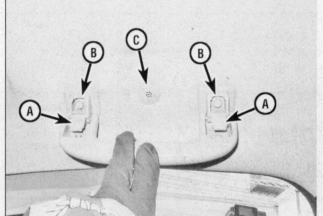

21.5 Grab handle details

A Pry open the trim covers
B Remove the grab handle mounting bolts
C If necessary, pry off this clip (if removing the headliner) - identical clip in more locations not shown

Lower C-pillar trim panel

Note: *On early models, the C-pillar trim panel is a single piece, rather than separated into three panels - it is removed in the same way by prying with a trim tool, and is not retained by any screws.*

10   Remove the lower C-pillar trim fasteners **(see illustration 21.18)**.

11   Pry the lower trim away from the vehicle body and detach the clips from the other C-pillar trim panels **(see illustration)**.

Upper-rear C-pillar trim panel

12   Remove the lower C-pillar trim panel (see previous Steps).

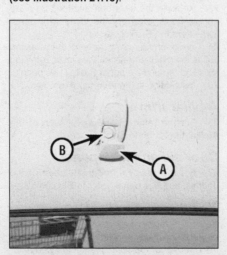

21.7 Pry open the trim cover (A) and remove the hanger fastener (B)

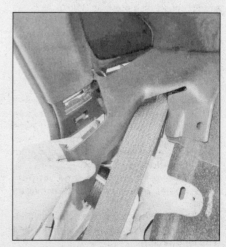

21.11 Pry out and release the lower C-pillar trim panel clips

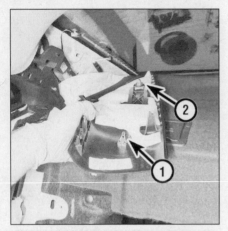

21.13 Pry out the upper-rear C-pillar trim panel - a short trim tool can be used on the outer clip (1) and an extended pry tool on the inner clip (2)

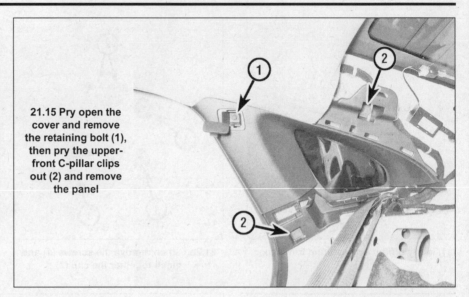

21.15 Pry open the cover and remove the retaining bolt (1), then pry the upper-front C-pillar clips out (2) and remove the panel

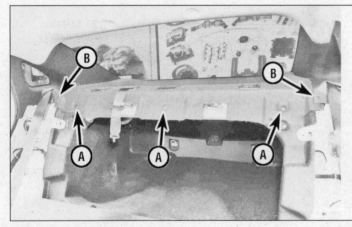

21.18 Rear parcel shelf (A) and lower C-pillar trim panel (B) retaining clips

21.20 Slide out the parcel shelf and guide it out of the vehicle interior

13   Pry the trim panel away from the side of interior **(see illustration)**. Note that an extended-arm pry tool can be used to the inner clip.

Upper-front C-pillar trim panel

14   Remove the lower and upper-rear C-pillar trim panels (see previous Steps).
15   Pry open the cover and remove the retaining bolt, then pry the upper-front C-pillar clips out to remove the panel **(see illustration)**.
16   Installation is the reverse of removal.

Rear parcel shelf

17   Remove the rear seat cushion (see Section 24) and side bolster airbag (see Chapter 12).
18   Remove the rear parcel shelf fasteners **(see illustration)**.
19   Remove the lower and upper-rear C-pillar trim panels (see previous Steps).
20   Slide out the rear parcel shelf, disconnecting any electrical connectors, if equipped **(see illustration)**.
21   Installation is the reverse of removal.

B-pillar trim

Note: *If removing the B-pillar trim panels only to remove the headliner, the seat belt anchor bolt does not need to be removed.*
22   Remove the front (see Section 22) and rear door sill scuff plates.
23   Remove the seat belt anchor trim plate and fastener, then pry the lower trim panel away from the B-pillar.
24   Pry open the cover, remove the retaining bolt at the top, then release the plastic retaining clips and remove the upper B-pillar trim panel.
25   Installation is the reverse of removal.

A-pillar trim

26   For the removal and installation of the A-pillar trim, refer to Section 22.

Door sill and kick panel

27   For the removal and installation of the door sill and kick panel, refer to Section 22.

Headliner

Note: *The factory indicates that complete removal and installation of the headliner requires the removal of the windshield - the headliner passes through the windshield opening. There*

are, however, procedures that only require partial removal of the headliner, such as lowering the rear section.
28   If equipped, remove the interior mirror / forward facing camera trim paneling where it meets with the headliner (see Section 16).
29   Remove the sun visors and supports, grab handles and coat hangers (see previous Steps). Some models may have active noise cancellation microphones in place of the clips shown in **illustration 21.5**.
30   Remove the overhead reading light console assembly (see Chapter 12 Section 20).
31   Remove the A-pillar trim panels (see Section 22).
32   Remove the B and C-pillar trim paneling (see previous Steps).
33   Remove the rear dome light assembly **(see illustration)**.
34   Move the front seats all the way forward, then operate the lever or switch to fully recline them. Release and fold down the rear seat backs.
35   Remove the headliner retaining clips at the rear, then pull down the rear of the headliner as necessary or lower it entirely for removal.
36   Installation is the reverse of removal.

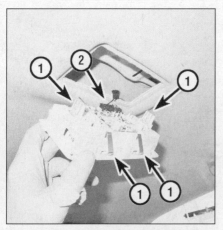

21.33 Pry out and release the retaining clips (1) for the rear dome light assembly, then disconnect the connector (2)

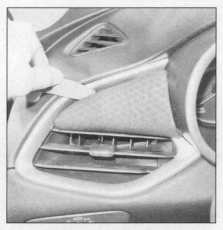

22.2a Pry off the decorative cover

22.2b Pry off the headlight switch bezel. . .

22   Dashboard trim panels - removal and installation

Warning: *These models are equipped with a Supplemental Restraint System (SRS), more commonly known as airbags. Always disable the airbag system before working in the vicinity of any airbag system component to avoid the possibility of accidental deployment of the airbag(s), which could cause personal injury (see Chapter 12).*

Note: *Refer to Section 6 for fastener and trim removal.*

Note: *The panels described in this procedure are based on a later model Malibu - The removal and installation procedures for panels on earlier models is similar.*

1   Disconnect the cable from the negative battery terminal (see Chapter 5).

Dash outer face trim panels

Headlight bezel and driver's left vent cover

2   Pry off the decorative cover and remove the headlight switch bezel (see illustrations).

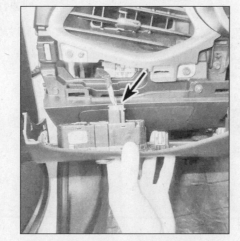

22.2c. . .then disconnect the electrical connector

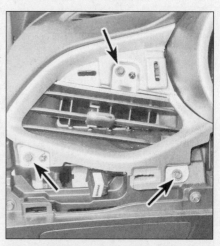

22.3 Driver's left vent cover retaining screws

3   Remove the screws and pry away the left vent cover (see illustration).

End caps

4   Pry off the dash end caps with a plastic trim tool (see illustration).

Outer and inner extended trim panels

5   Pry along the outer decorative trim panel, releasing all of the clips and disconnecting the engine start/stop switch connector (see illustrations).

22.4 Pry off the end caps (right side shown, left side similar)

22.5a Pry along the outer decorative trim panel to release all of the clips. . .

22.5b. . .disconnect the engine start/stop switch connector

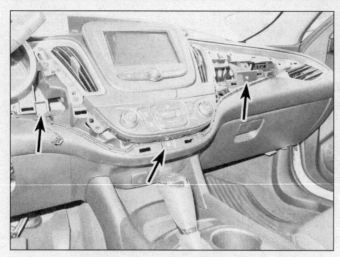

22.6a Remove the retaining screws. . .

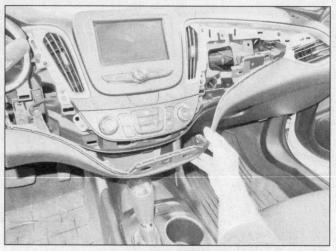

22.6b. . .then pry along the inner extended trim panel to release all the clips and remove the panel

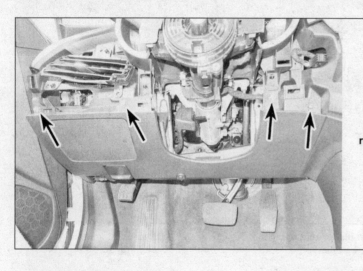

22.9a Knee bolster upper retaining screws

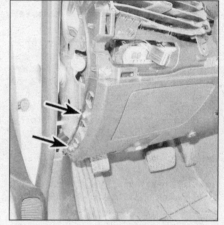

22.9b Knee bolster side retaining screws

6   Remove the screws and pry off the inner trim panel **(see illustrations)**.
7   Installation of the outer face panels is the reverse of removal.

Driver's knee bolster trim panel

8   Remove the dash outer face trim panels (see previous Steps).
9   Remove the driver's side knee bolster

trim panel fasteners, then pry out and remove the panel **(see illustrations)**. Disconnect any electrical connectors, if equipped.
10   Installation is the reverse of removal.

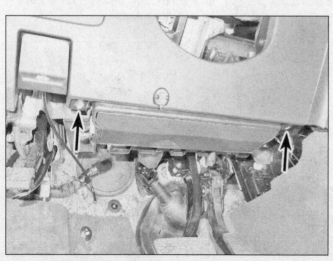

22.9c Knee bolster lower retaining screws

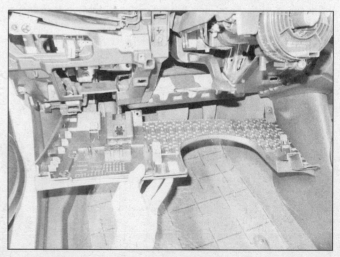

22.9d Pry out and remove the knee bolster trim panel from the dash

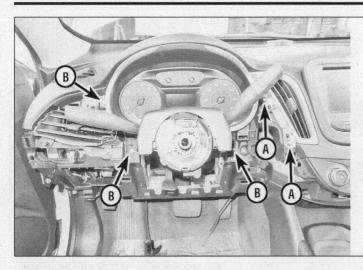

22.13 Remove the instrument cluster panel (B) and right vent cover (A) fasteners

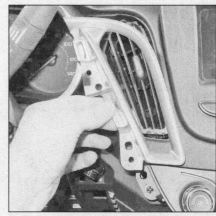

22.14a Remove the driver's right vent cover. . .

22.14b. . .then pry out the instrument cluster trim panel, starting from the top. . .

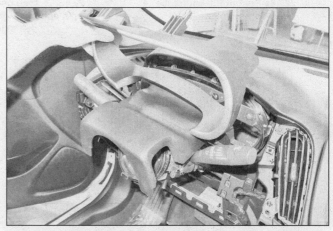

22.14c. . .remove the instrument cluster and steering column upper cover trim paneling together as an assembly

Instrument cluster trim paneling

11   Remove the dash outer face trim panels and knee bolster panel (see previous Steps).

12   Separate the upper steering column cover from the lower cover (see Section 23).

13   Remove the instrument cluster and driver's right side vent cover fasteners (see illustration).

14   Remove the vent cover, then pry out and remove the instrument cluster trim panel along with the steering column upper cover (see illustrations).

15   Installation is the reverse of removal.

Glove box
Door

16   Open the door and disconnect the dampener (see illustration).

17   Push inward on the door tray to release the stops (see illustration), then lower the door.

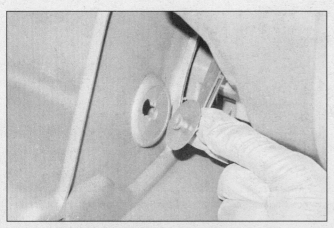

22.16 Disconnect the glove box door dampener

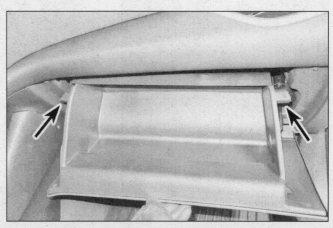

22.17 Push inward to release the door stops

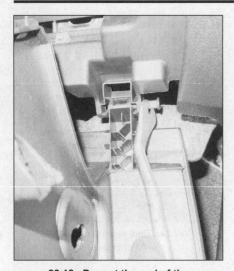

22.18a Pry out the end of the door pivot pin. . .

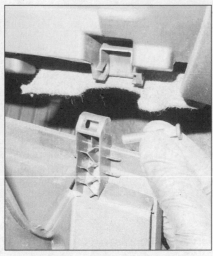

22.18b. . .then grasp and pull out the pin entirely (right side pin shown, left side similar)

18   Pry out the pivot pins on each side of the glove box door **(see illustrations)**.
19   Remove the glove box door.

Housing

20   Remove the glove box lower insulator shield **(see illustration)**.
21   Remove the necessary dash outer face trim paneling (see previous Steps).
22   Remove the passenger's side knee bolster airbag (see Chapter 12).
23   Remove the glove box housing retaining screws, then pull out the housing **(see illustrations)**.
24   Installation of the glove box housing and door is the reverse of removal.

A-pillar trim panels

25   Pry out the A-pillar trim panel to release the clips, starting from the top **(see illustration)**.
26   Pry and release the tether retaining tab, then slide the tether off the mount **(see illustration)**.

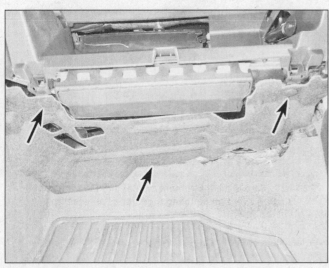

22.20 Glove box lower insulator shield fasteners

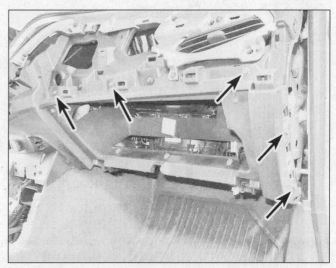

22.23a Glove box housing upper and side retaining screws

22.23b Glove box housing lower retaining screws

22.23c Pull out the glove box housing from the dash

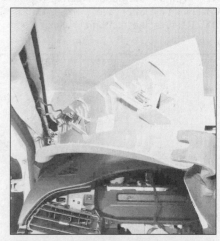

22.25 Starting from the top, use a plastic trim tool to pry out and disengage the A-pillar trim inner clips

27 Disconnect the A-pillar speaker electrical connector, if equipped **(see illustration)**.

28 Pull the A-pillar trim panel off of the instrument panel, noting the locating tabs at the bottom **(see illustration)**.

29 Installation is the reverse of removal.

Door sill lower scuff plates/ kick panel

30 Using a trim tool, pry up and remove the lower scuff plate / kick panel **(see illustrations)**. The rear door scuff plate is removed in the same manner.

31 Installation is the reverse of removal.

23 Steering column covers - removal and installation

Warning: *These models are equipped with a Supplemental Restraint System (SRS), more commonly known as airbags. Always disable the airbag system before working in the vicinity of any airbag system component to avoid the possibility of accidental deployment of the airbag(s), which could cause personal injury (see Chapter 12).*

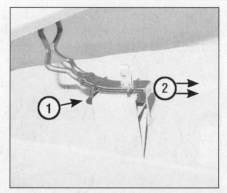

22.26 Disengage the tether by releasing the retaining tab (1) and sliding it off the mount (2)

Upper trim cover

1 Disconnect the cable from the negative terminal of the battery (see Chapter 5).

2 Using a plastic trim tool, pry up on the upper cover at each end, separating it from the lower cover **(see illustration)**.

3 Rotate the trim cover front edge upwards, releasing the rear hooks and expos-

ing the lower column cover upper retaining bolts **(see illustration)**.

4 To separate the upper column cover from the flexible trim, the instrument cluster bezel must be removed first (see Section 22). Pry the retaining tabs on each side with a screwdriver, then separate the cover from the flexible trim.

5 Installation is the reverse of removal.

22.27 Disconnect the A-pillar speaker connector, if equipped

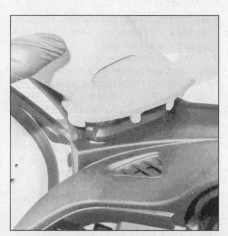

22.28 Remove the A-pillar from the top of the instrument panel, noting the tabs at the bottom

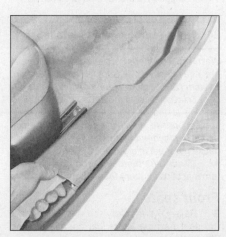

22.30a Pry up the scuff plate / kick panel with a trim tool. . .

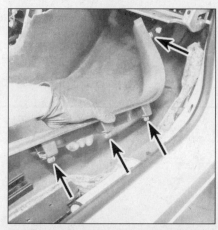

22.30b. . .and release all the retaining clips (front door shown, rear door similar)

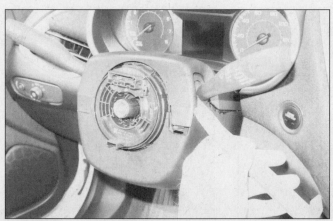

23.2 Using a plastic trim tool, separate the covers at each end (steering wheel removed for clarity)

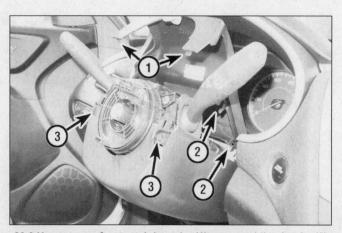

23.3 Upper cover front retaining tabs (1), rear retaining hooks (2) and lower cover upper bolts (3)

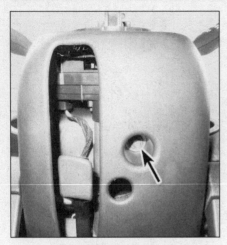

23.8 Lower column cover fastener location

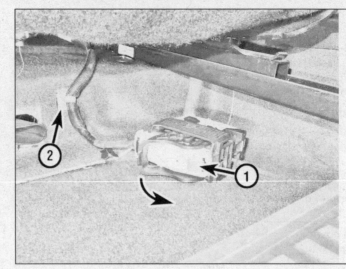

24.2 Release the safety tab (1) and rotate the connector lever outward to disconnect - also pry the wiring harness clip free (2)

Lower trim cover

6   Remove the upper trim cover first (see previous Steps).

7   Remove the lower trim cover upper fasteners **(see illustration 23.3)**. Rotate the steering wheel to gain access to the fasteners as needed.

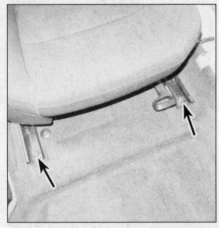

24.3a Front seat mounting bolts

8   Remove the lower cover bottom fastener **(see illustration)**.

9   Remove the trim cover off of the steering column. The steering wheel height control lever may need to be released to allow removal of the cover.

10   Installation is the reverse of removal.

---

24 Seats - removal and installation

Warning: *The models covered by this manual are equipped with a Supplemental Restraint System (SRS), more commonly known as airbags. Always disable the airbag system before working in the vicinity of any airbag system components to avoid the possibility of accidental deployment of the airbags, which could cause personal injury (see Chapter 12).*

1   Disconnect the cable from the negative terminal of the battery (see Chapter 5).

Front seats

2   Release the safety tab and disconnect the seat harness electrical connector **(see illustration)**.

3   Remove the seat mounting bolts **(see illustrations)**.

4   Carefully guide the seat out of the door opening.

5   Installation is the reverse of removal. Tighten the seat mounting bolts securely.

Rear seat cushion and seat back

Note: *If equipped with seat heaters, be sure to disconnect the seat heater connector(s) from the cushion and seat back.*

6   Release the center belt buckle anchor point with a screwdriver **(see illustration)**.

7   Position a medium-to-large size prybar under the seat (at each side), then carefully, but sharply, pry up on the seat cushion to release the cushion retaining hooks on each side **(see illustration)**.

8   With the retaining hooks released, disengage the secondary hooks at each end of the cushion **(see illustration)** by pushing down and rearward on the cushion.

9   Carry the seat cushion out of the vehicle interior.

10   For the removal of the seat back(s), first remove the side bolster airbags (see Chapter 12).

11   Fold the seat backs down, then slide the

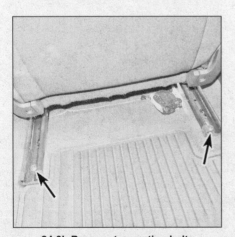

24.3b Rear seat mounting bolts

24.6 Use a screwdriver to release the center belt buckle anchor

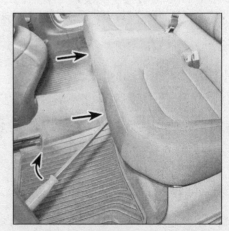

24.7 Use a prybar to help aid in releasing the seat cushion retaining hooks

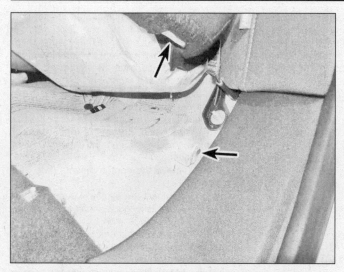

24.8 Release the seat cushion from the side hooks

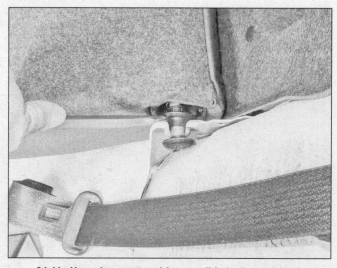

24.11a Use a large screwdriver to slide in the seat back end retaining ring. . .

end retaining ring back against spring pressure and pull the end of the seat back up out of the mount **(see illustrations)**.

12   Separate the seat backs from each other, then the center mount **(see illustrations)** and remove the seat backs.

13   Installation is the reverse of removal.

---

25   Instrument panel cover and crossbeam - removal and installation

Warning: *The models covered by this manual are equipped with a Supplemental Restraint System (SRS), more commonly known as airbags. Always disable the airbag system before working in the vicinity of any airbag system component to avoid the possibility of accidental deployment of the airbag, which could cause personal injury (see Chapter 12).*

Caution: *This is a difficult procedure for the home mechanic, involving tedious disassembly and the disconnection/reconnection of numerous electrical connectors. If you do attempt this procedure, make sure you take good notes and mark all matching connectors (and their wiring harness clip points) to aid reassembly.*

Caution: *The entire instrument panel or crossbeam assembly can be awkward and heavy. Have an assistant to help with removal.*

Note: *Disconnect the cable from the negative terminal of the battery (see Chapter 5). Refer to Section 6 for fastener and trim removal.*

2016 and later models (except 2016 Malibu Limited)

Instrument panel cover

1   Disconnect the cable from the negative battery terminal (see Chapter 5) and wait several minutes for the SRS system capacitors to fully discharge.

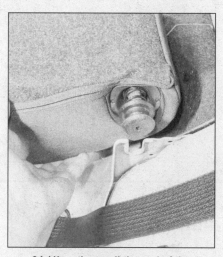

24.11b. . .then pull the end of the seat back up to disengage it from the mount

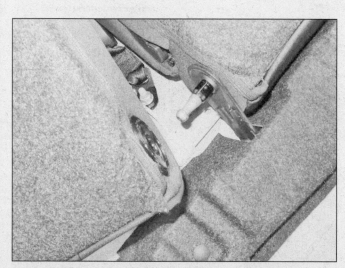

24.12a Remove the left seat back by pulling it off the stud. . .

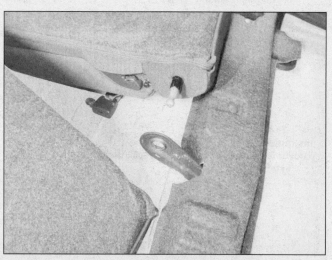

24.12b. . .then remove the right seat back from the center bracket

2   Remove the steering wheel (see Chapter 10), steering column covers (see Section 23) and steering column (see Chapter 10).
3   Remove the instrument cluster trim (see Section 22), then the instrument cluster (see Chapter 12).

4   Remove the radio (see Chapter 12).
5   Remove the glovebox (see Section 22).
6   Remove the A-pillar trim, instrument panel end caps, and remaining trim pieces on the face of the instrument panel (see Section 22).

7   Remove the ambient light sensor (see Chapter 12, Section 23).
8   If equipped, pry up and release the HUD (Heads-Up Display) from the left side of the instrument panel, then disconnect the electrical connector and remove it.
9   Remove the instrument panel air register vents from the face of the panel (see Section 26).
10   If equipped, pry up the trim cover and remove the speaker from the top-center of the instrument panel.
11   Remove the center console (see Section 20).
12   Disconnect the electrical connector and remove the passenger's airbag securing bolts (see Chapter 12).
13   Remove the instrument panel cover fasteners **(see illustrations)**.
14   With the help of an assistant, carefully lift the instrument panel cover up and towards the rear of the vehicle. DO NOT force the panel out - double-check that all wiring has been disconnected.
15   Installation is the reverse of removal.

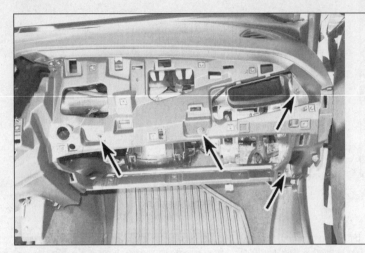

25.13a Instrument panel cover right side fasteners

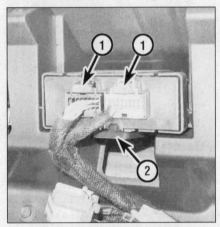

25.13b Release the safety tabs and disconnect the connectors (1) then release the module retaining tab (2). . .

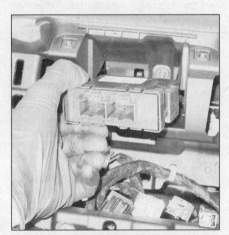

25.13c. . .and pull out the module that blocks access to the panel cover center fasteners

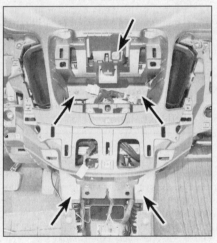

25.13d Instrument panel cover center fasteners

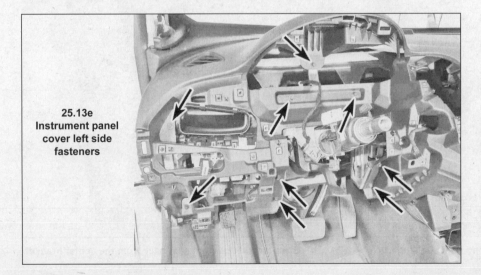

25.13e Instrument panel cover left side fasteners

25.13f Disconnect this electrical connector (center of instrument panel) and any other remaining connectors

25.13g Remove the bolts and detach the OBD2 port

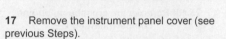

25.13h Disengage all wiring harness retaining points from the instrument panel cover using a pry tool

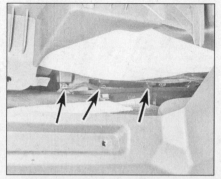

25.13i Using an extended-arm pry tool, pull up the panel and detach the ambient light sensor wiring harness from underneath (working through the instrument cluster opening)

Interior crossbeam

16 Disconnect the cable from the negative battery terminal (see Chapter 5) and wait several minutes for the SRS system capacitors to fully discharge.

17 Remove the instrument panel cover (see previous Steps).

18 Remove the various dashboard vents and ducts located under the instrument panel cover (see Section 26). Also remove the wind-shield wiper motor (see Chapter 12) and door sill/kick panel (see Section 22).

19 For the remainder of the interior cross-beam removal, refer to the following illustrations and their captions **(see illustrations)**.

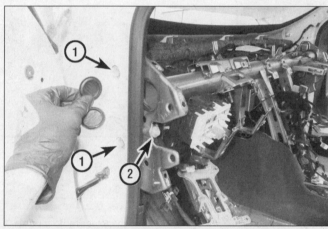

25.19a Remove the crossbeam A-pillar bolts (1) and loosen (but don't remove) the front-facing side bolts (2) - (left side shown)

25.19b Remove the crossbeam A-pillar bolts (1) and loosen (but don't remove) the front-facing side bolts (2) - (right side shown)

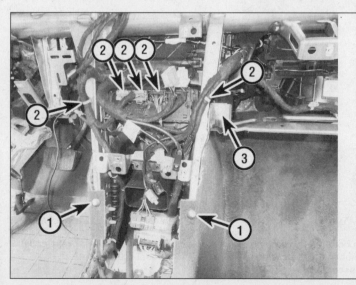

25.19c Pry out the plastic carpet clips (1), disconnect the connectors and pry off the wiring harness retainers (2) then remove the crossbeam-to-HVAC housing bolt (3)

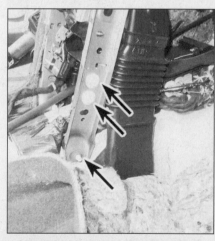

25.19d Remove the crossbeam center securing fasteners from the right side, and remove the metal bracket piece. . .

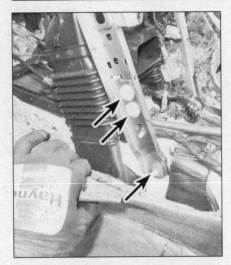

25.19e. . .then repeat this on the right side

25.19f Remove the crossbeam engine compartment bolt

25.19g Remove the HVAC housing upper securing fasteners

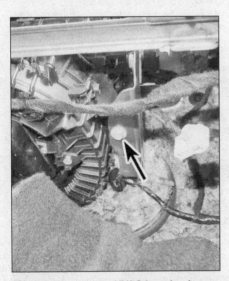

25.19h Remove the HVAC housing lower securing fastener

25.19i Remove and reposition the interior fuse block from the crossbeam

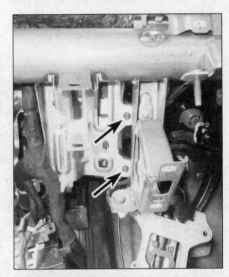

25.19j Remove the lower radio module bracket fasteners. . .

25.19k. . .then the upper fastener (also disconnecting any harness clips) and reposition the radio module

25.19l Remove the bolts for the parking brake pedal assembly and reposition the assembly

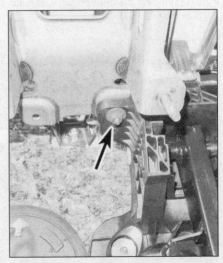

25.19m Remove the lower brake/accel pedal bracket nut. . .

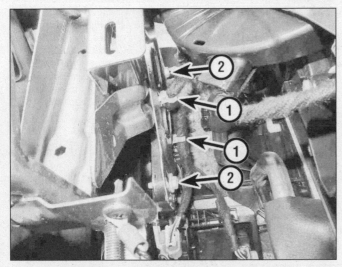

25.19n. . .then detach the wiring clips (1) and remove the bracket side bolts (2)

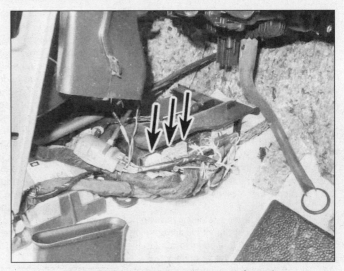

25.19o Disconnect these connectors from the passenger's side footwell. . .

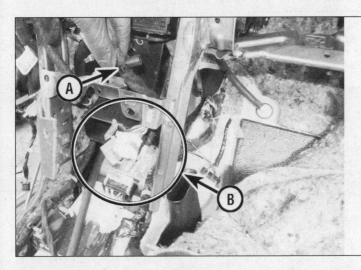

25.19p. . .then guide out the wiring harness (A) feeding the connectors (B) through the crossbeam section

25.19q Completely remove the remaining crossbeam bolts at each end, then with the help of an assistant, lift the crossbeam up and over these tabs (right side shown, left side identical)

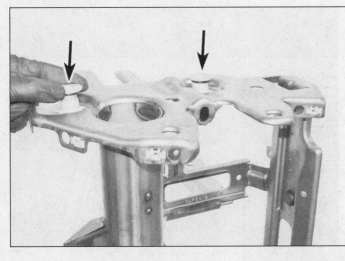

25.19r Screw-in the (reverse threaded) right side bolt mounts to allow for easier removal and installation of the crossbeam - these can be turned with a pair of pliers with the crossbeam installed in the vehicle

ward facing bolts (each end), crossbeam-to-HVAC housing fasteners, crossbeam center support fasteners, crossbeam side (A-pillar) through-bolts, crossbeam engine compartment bolt, and finally, the parking brake and module bracket fasteners.

22   The remainder of installation is the reverse of removal.

2015 and earlier models (and 2016 Malibu Limited)

Instrument panel cover and cover carrier

23   Disconnect the cable from the negative battery terminal (see Chapter 5) and wait several minutes for the SRS system capacitors to fully discharge.

24   Remove the knee bolster panel (see Section 22), steering wheel (see Chapter 10), steering column covers (see Section 23) and steering column (see Chapter 10).

25   Use a plastic trim tool to pry out the center dash trim panel / vents from around the radio and a/c control assemblies.

20   With the help of an assistant, carefully lift the crossbeam up and towards the rear of the vehicle. DO NOT force the crossbeam out - double-check that all wiring has been disconnected.

21   When installing, tighten the crossbeam fasteners to the torque settings listed in this Chapter's Specifications. Be sure to tighten the crossbeam structural fasteners to the torque settings in this order: Crossbeam for-

26 Remove the upper center instrument trim panel, located behind the defroster opening. Disconnect the speaker connector (if equipped).

27 Remove the end caps (see Section 22).

28 Pry out and remove the headlight switch trim panel and disconnect the electrical connector. Also remove the small trim panel at the opposite end of the steering wheel.

29 Pry off the instrument cluster trim panel face.

30 Remove the instrument cluster (see Chapter 12).

31 Remove the three screws that retain the pad above the instrument cluster opening.

32 Remove the A-pillar trim panels (see Section 22).

33 Remove the screws retaining the vent to the left of the the instrument cluster opening, then pry off the small trim panel located to the right of the instrument cluster opening.

34 Pry off the trim panel pad located directly above the glove box.

35 Remove the retaining screw, then pry along and release the vent and trim piece assembly from the dash (passenger's side).

36 With the A-pillar trim covers removed, remove the lower three screws (on each end) that retain the side curtain airbags. Reposition the side curtain airbags to allow for easier removal of the instrument panel cover.

37 Pry up the three instrument panel light tube assemblies from the upper end of the dash. There is no need to disconnect the electrical connectors.

38 Remove the instrument panel cover fasteners along the upper end of the cover. Also remove the hidden passenger's airbag fastener (can be seen through the hole midway between the radio and end of dash, above the glove box).

39 Disconnect any wiring harnesses attached to the instrument panel cover, noting their locations for installation.

40 With the help of an assistant, carefully lift off the cover and guide it out of the vehicle.

41 To remove the instrument panel cover carrier, first remove the center console (see Section 20).

42 Remove the glove box housing (see Section 22).

43 Remove the radio (see Chapter 12) and a/c control assembly (see Chapter 3).

44 Remove the various instrument panel cover carrier fasteners (there are twelve).

45 Disconnect any wiring harnesses attached to the instrument panel cover carrier, noting their locations for installation.

46 Installation is the reverse of removal. Tighten the fasteners securely.

Interior crossbeam

47 Remove the instrument panel cover and carrier (see previous Steps).

48 Remove the door sill scuff plates / kick panels (see Section 22).

49 Remove the fasteners that retain the electrical harnesses to the crossbeam, then position the harnesses out of the way. Disconnect any additional wiring or wiring harnesses interfering with the removal of the crossbeam, keeping track of their locations.

50 Remove the four crossbeam-to-HVAC housing nuts/bolts.

51 Remove the four brake/accel pedal assembly-to-crossbeam fasteners.

52 Remove the six crossbeam center fasteners (three each side).

53 Remove the four remaining crossbar fasteners (two at each end), then carefully remove the crossbar assembly with the help of an assistant. If the crossbar gets hung up on any wiring or brackets, do not force it out - determine where it is being held up before proceeding. Be sure to also support the HVAC assembly when removing to avoid straining any a/c lines or wiring.

54 Installation is the reverse of removal. Tighten the main crossbeam fasteners and HVAC fasteners to the torque settings listed in this Chapter's Specifications.

---

26 Dashboard ventilation air ducts - removal and installation

---

Warning: *The models covered by this manual are equipped with a Supplemental Restraint System (SRS), more commonly known as airbags. Always disable the airbag system before working in the vicinity of any airbag system component to avoid the possibility of accidental deployment of the airbag, which could cause personal injury (see Chapter 12).*

Note: *This procedure applies only to 2016 and later models (except 2016 Malibu limited)*

1 Disconnect the cable from the negative terminal of the battery (see Chapter 5).

Air register vents

2 Remove the dashboard trim paneling necessary to gain access to the register vents (see Section 22).

3 Remove the air register vent retaining screws (if any), then disengage the retaining tabs and pull the vents out of the dash. Refer to the following illustrations and their captions for specific removal details **(see illustrations)**.

4 Installation is the reverse of removal.

Air ducts (under instrument panel)

5 Remove the instrument panel cover (see Section 25).

6 Refer to the following illustrations and their captions for the removal of the ducts **(see illustrations)**.

7 Installation is the reverse of removal.

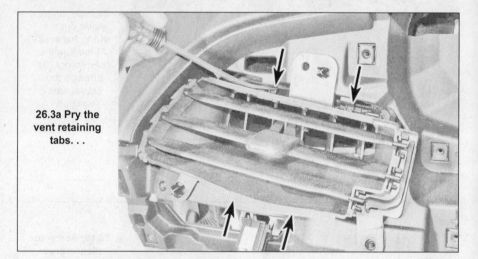

26.3a Pry the vent retaining tabs. . .

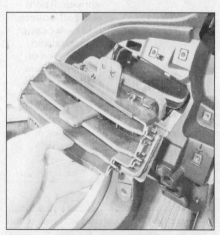

26.3b. . .while pulling it straight out of the dash (left vent shown)

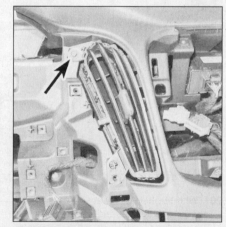

26.3c Remove the vent retaining screw and pull it out of the dash (driver's center vent shown)

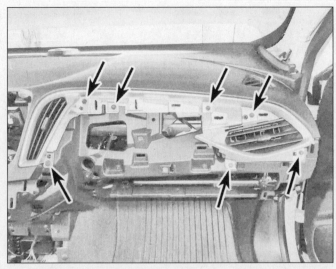

26.3d Remove the passenger's vent trim cover screws. . .

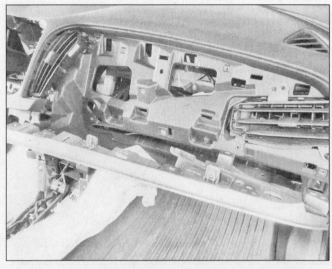

26.3e. . .then pry it off of the dash with a plastic trim tool, disengaging the clips

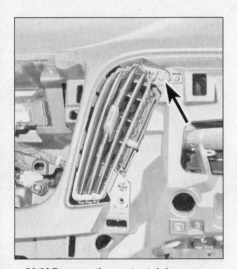

26.3f Remove the vent retaining screw and pull it out of the dash (passenger's center vent shown)

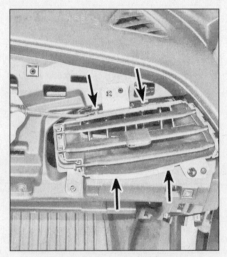

26.3g Pry the vent retaining tabs while pulling it straight out of the dash (right vent shown)

26.6a Remove the passenger's side vent screw. . .

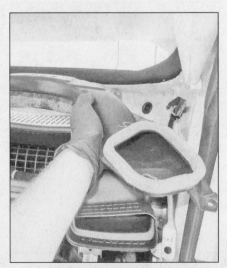

26.6b. . .then pull off the vent

26.6c Remove the driver's side vent screw. . .

26.6d. . .then pull off the vent

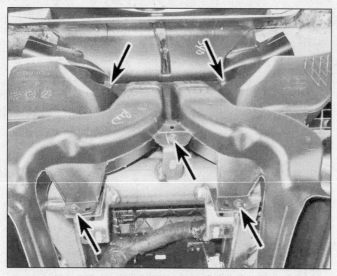

26.6e Remove the vent assembly center screws

26.6f Remove the vent assembly driver's side screws

26.6g Remove the vent assembly passenger's side screw

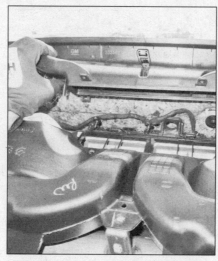

26.6h Lift off the defroster outlet vent

26.6i Remove the vent assembly from the top of the crossbeam

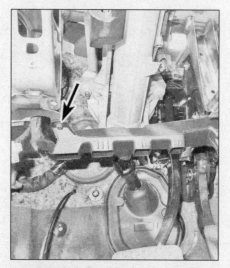

26.6j Remove the driver's side footwell vent retaining screw and pull the vent out from underneath

26.6k Remove the passenger's side footwell vent retaining screw and pull the vent out from underneath

26.6l Compress and remove the rear vents connector piece (right side shown, left side identical)

Chapter 12
Chassis electrical system

Contents

1 General information

1 The electrical system is a 12-volt, negative ground type. Power for the lights and all electrical accessories is supplied by a lead/acid-type battery that is charged by the alternator.

2 This Chapter covers repair and service procedures for the various electrical components not associated with the engine. Information on the battery, alternator, ignition system and starter motor can be found in Chapter 5.

3 It should be noted that when portions of the electrical system are serviced, the negative cable must be disconnected from the battery to prevent electrical shorts and/or fires.

Start/Stop system

4 The Start/Stop System reduces fuel consumption by turning off the engine when the vehicle comes to a complete stop, and restarting the engine when the driver takes their foot off of the brake. The system works automatically when the vehicle is driven for approximately four seconds at a minimum speed of 3 mph (5 km/h).

5 The system should be disabled when doing any type of service work on the vehicle that requires the engine running.

6 Vehicles equipped with a start/stop system use an AGM (Absorbent Glass Mat) battery instead of a traditional lead acid battery (acid flooded type). The AGM battery appearance is very similar to the standard flooded type battery. Check the part numbers for verification. Also, if you pick one up and slosh it around, the AGM type doesn't have acid in solution like the flooded type because the glass mat absorbs all the liquid in the battery.

Warning: *Vehicles equipped with the Start/ Stop System can restart at any time if the key has been left in the On position during any maintenance or repairs. Be sure to deactivate the Start/Stop system before performing any repairs. A message will be displayed in the instrument cluster indicating the Start/Stop has been disabled.*

2 Electrical troubleshooting - general information

1 A typical electrical circuit consists of an electrical component, any switches, relays, motors, fuses, fusible links or circuit breakers related to that component and the wiring and connectors that link the component to both the battery and the chassis. To help you pinpoint an electrical circuit problem, wiring diagrams are at the end of this manual.

2 Before tackling any troublesome electrical circuit, it would be wise to understand the basics of electrical theory and how a circuit in an automobile is connected. Knowing how any system works before attempting repairs will greatly reduced the possibility of replacing unneeded components. A good place to start is to study the appropriate wiring diagrams to get a complete understanding of what makes up that individual circuit. Trouble spots, for instance, can often be narrowed down by noting if other components related to the circuit are operating properly. Taking it step by step and

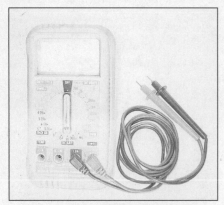

2.5a The most useful tool for electrical troubleshooting is a digital multimeter that can check volts, amps, and test continuity

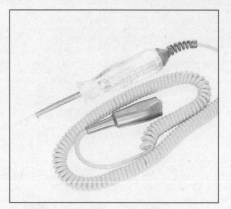

2.5b A test light is a very handy tool for checking voltage

following the guidelines provided will reduce your time in diagnosing electrical issues.

3   Electrical problems usually stem from simple causes, such as loose or corroded connections, worn or chafed wiring, a blown fuse, a melted fusible link, or faulty components. Visually inspect the condition of all fuses, wires and connections in a problem circuit before troubleshooting the circuit. Be sure to check not only the positive signals but the negative signals as well. Faulty grounds, or weak ground connections are a leading factor in system failures.

4   If test equipment and instruments are going to be utilized, be sure you understand how to use the equipment properly before attempting a repair. A bad diagnostic routine can start with bad equipment or the lack of proper use of the equipment. Use the wiring diagrams to plan ahead of time where you will make the necessary connections in order to accurately pinpoint your test connections as well as where the possible trouble could be.

5   The basic tools needed for electrical troubleshooting include a multi-meter that is capable of reading DC and AC voltage, Ohms (resistance), and Amps, a test light,

jumper wires with alligator clips at each end, a jumper wire preferably with a circuit breaker incorporated, and a few sharp pins (straight pins work well) which can be used to bypass electrical components **(see illustrations)**. Before attempting to locate a problem with test instruments, use the wiring diagram(s) to decide where to make the connections.

Voltage checks

Note: *Keep in mind that some circuits receive voltage only when the ignition key is in the Accessory or Run position.*

6   Voltage checks should be performed if a circuit is not functioning properly. Connect one lead of a circuit tester to either the negative battery terminal or a known good ground. Always check your test light before checking the actual circuit you're working on to be sure it is making good contact with the negative and the positive leads. Connect the other lead to a connector in the circuit being tested, preferably nearest to the battery or fuse **(see illustration)**. If the bulb of the tester lights, voltage is present, which means that the part of the circuit between the connector and the battery is problem free. Continue checking the rest of the circuit in the same fashion. When you reach a point at which no voltage is present, the prob-

lem lies between that point and the last test point with voltage. Most of the time the problem can be traced to a loose connection.

Finding a short

7   A short occurs when the path of electricity takes a route to ground that it was not designed for. This is usually associated with a blown fuse or melted fusible link. One method of finding shorts in a circuit is to remove the fuse and connect a test light or voltmeter in place of the fuse terminals. A fuse terminal has two connections. One is the supplied voltage to the fuse while the other is the send lead to that circuit. There should be no readable voltage at those two connectors because they should be of the same potential. Moving the wiring harness from side-to-side while watching the test light may also allow you to find any chaffed wiring that might have blown the fuse originally. If the bulb is on, there is a negative and a positive potential at the fuse connection. When the light is on, there is a short to ground somewhere in that area, probably where the insulation has rubbed through. The same test can be performed on each component in the circuit, or on a switch.

Ground check

8   Perform a ground test to check whether a component is properly grounded. Disconnect the battery and connect one lead of a continuity tester or multimeter (set to the ohms scale), to a known good ground. Connect the other lead to the wire or ground connection being tested. If the resistance is low (less than 5 ohms), the ground is good. If the bulb on a self-powered test light does not go on, the ground is bad. A more accurate method is the voltage drop test. Place the positive side of your multimeter on the positive post of the battery, then place the negative side on the chassis. Note the reading, then move the negative lead to the suspected bad ground area, such as the engine (which should have the same grounded leads to it). Take another reading. The two readings should be exactly the same.

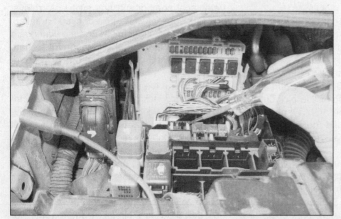

2.6 In use, a test light's lead is clipped to a known ground, then the pointed probe can test connectors, wires or electrical sockets - if the bulb lights, the circuit being tested has battery voltage

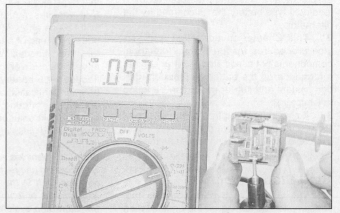

2.9 With the multimeter set to the ohm scale, resistance can be checked across two terminals - when checking for continuity, a low reading indicates continuity; a high reading or infinity indicates diminished or lack of continuity

3.2a The main fuse/relay panel is in the engine compartment; disengage the locking tabs and remove the cover for access to the fuses and relays

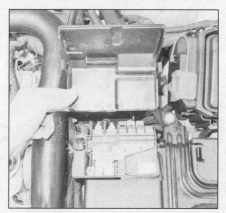

3.2b Location of the high-amperage fuse block

3.2c The passenger compartment fuse/relay panel is located at the left end of the instrument panel, behind this panel

Continuity check

9   A continuity check is done to determine if there are any breaks in a circuit - if it is passing electricity properly. With the circuit off (no power in the circuit), a self-powered continuity tester or multimeter can be used to check the circuit. Connect the test leads to both ends of the circuit (or to the power end and a good ground), and if the test light comes on the circuit is passing current properly **(see illustration)**. If the resistance is low (less than 5 ohms), there is continuity; if the reading is 10,000 ohms or higher, there is a break somewhere in the circuit. The same procedure can be used to test a switch, by connecting the continuity tester to the switch terminals. With the switch turned On, the test light should come on (or low resistance should be indicated on a meter).

Warning: *Always check your multimeter before hooking it up to any circuit so that you know you are on the right scale. If there is voltage present on a lead, and you are trying to measure resistance, you can do permanent damage to your meter if it is set on the wrong scale.*

Finding an open circuit

10   When diagnosing for possible open circuits, it is often difficult to locate them by sight because the connectors hide oxidation or terminal misalignment. Merely wiggling a connector on a sensor or in the wiring harness may correct the open circuit condition. Remember this when an open circuit is indicated when troubleshooting a circuit. Intermittent problems may also be caused by oxidized or loose connections.

11   Electrical troubleshooting is simple if you keep in mind that all electrical circuits are basically electricity running from the battery, through the wires, switches, relays, fuses and fusible links to each electrical component (light bulb, motor, etc.) and to ground, from which it is passed back to the battery. Any electrical problem is an interruption in the flow of electricity to and from the battery.

Finding a battery drain

Note: *Before attempting to find a drain, test the battery to be sure the battery itself is not the cause.*

12   Battery drain is any electrical load that is present when it shouldn't be, which will cause the battery to have insufficient amperage/voltage to restart the vehicle. Today's vehicles have what is referred to as parasitic battery drain. This is a normal process that occurs with all newer vehicles. Each of the different computer based systems in the vehicle have a certain amount of constant current required to maintain enough electricity to restart. The required voltage is very small - so small, a standard test light or volt meter will not pick up the signal correctly. An amperage meter in line with the battery negative post and negative clamp is recommended to read the amount of current being passed to the vehicle. A reading of less than 0.02 to 0.04 amps indicates a lack of battery drain. Anything above that would indicate something has been left on, or one of the computer based systems is still activated.

13   Modules all have a sleep mode; this varies with each module or system. Some will carry out their functions shortly after the last door is closed or when the key is turned off. Delay systems such as dome light entry and exit are a good example of a module cycling through the sleep mode. When the light comes on, it's awake, and when it goes out a few seconds later, it's asleep.

14   Finding a battery drain can be quite challenging. If you are hesitant in trying to locate the drain, take your vehicle to your local dealer or qualified independent shop that specializes in electrical repairs.

3   Fuses, main fuses and circuit breakers - general information

Fuses

1   The electrical circuits of the vehicle are protected by a combination of fuses, circuit breakers and fusible links. Each of the fuses is designed to protect a specific circuit, and the various circuits are identified on the fuse panel itself.

2   The underhood fuse/relay panel is in the right-front corner of the engine compartment **(see illustration)**. The battery fuse/fusible link block (main system power distribution and high-amperage fuses) is located on top of the battery **(see illustration)**. The instrument panel fuse block is located behind a panel on the driver's side knee bolster **(see illustrations)**.

3   Several sizes of fuses are employed in the fuse blocks. There are small, medium and large sizes of the same design, all with the same blade terminal design. The medium and large fuses can be removed with your fingers, but the small fuses require the use of pliers or the small plastic fuse-puller tool found in most fuse boxes.

4   If an electrical component fails, always check the fuse first. The best way to check the fuses is with a test light. Check for power at the exposed terminal tips of each fuse. If power is present at one side of the fuse but not the other, the fuse is blown. A blown fuse can also be identified by visually inspecting it **(see illustration)**.

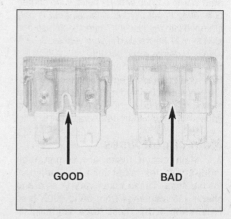

GOOD   BAD

3.4 When a fuse blows, the element between the terminals melts

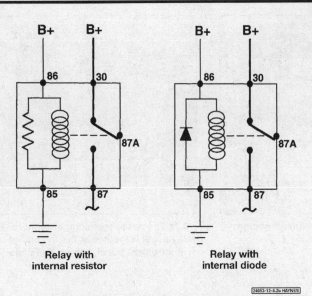

24053-12-6.2a HAYNES

4.2a Typical ISO relay designs, terminal numbering and circuit connections

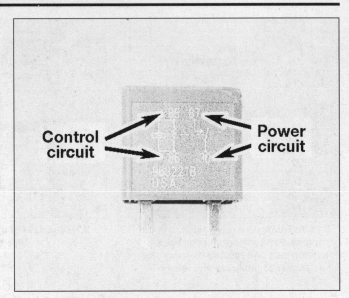

4.2b Most relays are marked on the outside to easily identify the control circuit and power circuit - this one is of the four-terminal type

5   Be sure to replace blown fuses with the correct type. Fuses (of the same physical size) of different ratings may be physically interchangeable, but only fuses of the proper rating should be used. Replacing a fuse with one of a higher or lower value than specified is not recommended. Each electrical circuit needs a specific amount of protection. The amperage value of each fuse is molded into the top of the fuse body.

Warning: *Avoid cheap "knock-off" fuses! According to a GM bulletin (# 07-08-45-002, Doc ID 2009073) some aftermarket fuses can damage your electrical system. The actual fuse amperage does not match the amperage rating embossed into them. For example, a fuse marked as a 10 amp fuse may not blow until it reaches 30 amps of electrical load. As of the date of this manual publication, it is still very easy to tell these knock-off fuses from a good quality fuse. Look at the amperage number stamped into the fuse. The number should be filled in with a white or black paint. If the amperage rating is not filled in with paint but is only stamped into the fuse it IS a knock-off fuse and should NOT be installed in your vehicle. Severe electrical damage can occur to your vehicle.*

6   If the replacement fuse immediately fails, don't replace it again until the cause of the problem is isolated and corrected. In most cases, this will be a short circuit in the wiring caused by a broken or deteriorated wire.

Main circuit fuses

7   Main circuit fuses are common on today's vehicles rather than the traditional fusible links. These fuses vary in size and shape and amperage from 5A to 400A **(see illustration 3.1b)**. These fuses can maintain current flow much more precisely than a traditional fusible link can. This avoids allowing any severe voltage spikes from entering into

sensitive electronic systems. They are generally found near or on top of the battery in most vehicles. Some of the higher amperage fuses are bolted down rather than the traditional pull-and-replace fuses. In some cases, the fuse box itself must be disassembled in order to replace a certain fuse. Always replace a main fuse with the exact same size and amperage as the original.

Circuit breakers

8   Circuit breakers protect certain circuits, such as the power windows and power seats.

9   Because the circuit breakers reset automatically, an electrical overload in a circuit-breaker-protected system will cause the circuit to fail momentarily, then come back on. If the circuit does not come back on, check it immediately.

Warning: *If there is a short in the circuit breaker wiring, the metal casing of the breaker may be extremely hot. Use caution when removing the breaker.*

10   For a basic check, pull the circuit breaker up out of its socket on the fuse/relay panel, but just far enough to probe its terminals with a voltmeter. With the voltmeter negative lead on a good chassis ground, touch each end prong of the circuit breaker with the positive meter probe. There should be battery voltage at each end. If there is battery voltage only at one end, the circuit breaker must be replaced.

4   Relays - general information and testing

General information

1   Several electrical accessories in the vehicle, such as the fuel injection system,

horns, starter, and fog lamps use relays to transmit the electrical signal to the component. Relays use a low-current circuit (the control circuit) to open and close a high-current circuit (the power circuit). If the relay is defective, that component will not operate properly. Most relays are mounted in the engine compartment and interior fuse/relay boxes. If a faulty relay is suspected, it can be removed and tested using the procedure below or by a dealer service department or a repair shop. Defective relays must be replaced as a unit.

Testing

2   Most of the relays used in these vehicles are of a type often called ISO relays, which refers to the International Standards Organization. The terminals of ISO relays are numbered to indicate their usual circuit connections and functions. There are two basic layouts of terminals on the relays used in these vehicles **(see illustrations)**.

3   Refer to the wiring diagram for the circuit to determine the proper connections for the relay you're testing. If you can't determine the correct connection from the wiring diagrams, however, you may be able to determine the test connections from the information that follows.

4   Two of the terminals are the relay control circuit and connect to the relay coil. The other relay terminals are the power circuit. When the relay is energized, the coil creates a magnetic field that closes the larger contacts of the power circuit to provide power to the circuit loads.

5   Terminals 85 and 86 are normally the control circuit. If the relay contains a diode, terminal 86 must be connected to battery positive (B+) voltage and terminal 85 to ground. If the relay contains a resistor, terminals 85

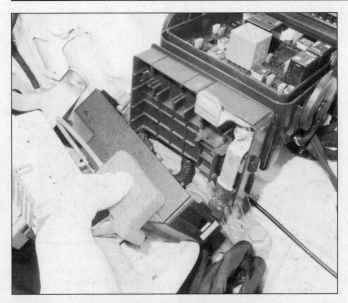

5.4 Remove the nut securing the battery positive cable to the fuse/relay box (2015 and later models shown)

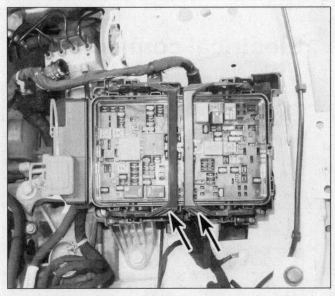

5.6a Pivot the bail arms upwards to release the fuse box. . .

and 86 can be connected in either direction with respect to B+ and ground.

6   Terminal 30 is normally connected to the battery voltage (B+) source for the circuit loads. Terminal 87 is connected to the ground side of the circuit, either directly or through a load. If the relay has several alternate terminals for load or ground connections, they usually are numbered 87A, 87B, 87C, and so on.

7   Use an ohmmeter to check continuity through the relay control coil.

a) Connect the meter according to the polarity shown in illustration 4.2a for one check; then reverse the ohmmeter leads and check continuity in the other direction.

b) If the relay contains a resistor, resistance should be indicated on the meter, and should be the same value with the ohmmeter in either direction.

c) If the relay contains a diode, resistance should be higher with the ohmmeter in the forward polarity direction than with the meter leads reversed.

d) If the ohmmeter shows infinite resistance in both directions, replace the relay.

8   Remove the relay from the vehicle and use the ohmmeter to check for continuity between the relay power circuit terminals. There should be no continuity between terminal 30 and 87 with the relay de-energized.

9   Connect a fused jumper wire to terminal 86 and the positive battery terminal. Connect another jumper wire between terminal 85 and ground. When the connections are made, the relay should click.

10   With the jumper wires connected, check for continuity between the power circuit terminals. Now, there should be continuity between terminals 30 and 87.

11   If the relay fails any of the above tests, replace it.

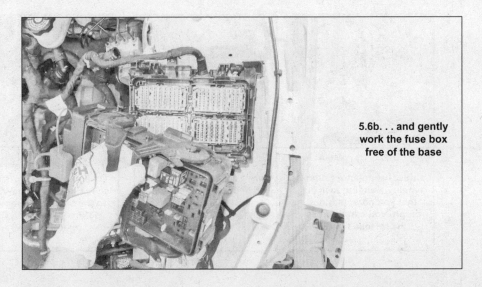

5.6b. . . and gently work the fuse box free of the base

5   Underhood fuse/relay box - removal and installation

1   Remove the battery (see Chapter 5).
2   Remove the cover from the fuse/relay box.
3   Remove the battery (see Chapter 5).
4   Open the cover, then remove the nut and detach the battery positive cable from the fuse/relay box **(see illustration)**.
5   On 2015 and earlier models (and 2016 Malibu Limited), remove the fuse/relay box mounting bolts, release the retaining tabs, and detach the box from its base.
6   On 2016 and later models (except Malibu Limited), raise the fuse box arms, swing them 90-degrees and lift the fuse box off of its base **(see illustrations)**.
7   Installation is the reverse of removal.

6   Electrical connectors - general information

1   Most electrical connections on these vehicles are made with multiwire plastic connectors. The mating halves of many connectors are secured with locking clips molded into the plastic connector shells. The mating halves of some large connectors, such as some of those under the instrument panel, are held together by a bolt through the center of the connector.

2   To separate a connector with locking clips, use a small screwdriver to pry the clips apart carefully, then separate the connector halves. Pull only on the shell, never pull on the wiring harness, as you may damage the individual wires and terminals inside the connectors. Look at the connector closely before

Electrical connectors

Most electrical connectors
have a single release
tab that you depress to
release the connector

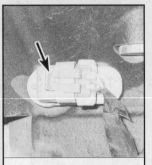

Some electrical
connectors have a
retaining tab which must
be pried up to free
the connector

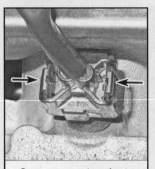

Some connectors have
two release tabs that you
must squeeze to release
the connector

Some connectors use
wire retainers that you
squeeze to release
the connector

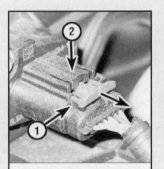

Critical connectors often
employ a sliding lock (1)
that you must pull out
before you can depress
the release tab (2)

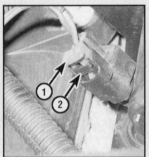

Here's another sliding-lock
style connector, with the
lock (1) and the release
tab (2) on the side of the
connector

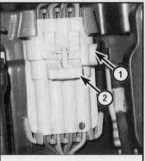

On some connectors the
lock (1) must be pulled out
to the side and removed
before you can lift the
release tab (2)

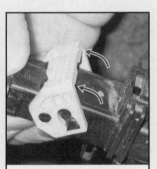

Some critical connectors,
like the multi-pin
connectors at the
Powertrain Control Module
employ pivoting locks that
must be flipped open

trying to separate the halves. Often the locking clips are engaged in a way that is not immediately clear. Additionally, many connectors have more than one set of clips.

3 Each pair of connector terminals has a male half and a female half. When you look at the end view of a connector in a diagram, be sure to understand whether the view shows the harness side or the component side of the connector. Connector halves are mirror images of each other, and a terminal shown on the right side end-view of one half will be on the left side end-view of the other half.

4 It is often necessary to take circuit voltage measurements with a connector connected. Whenever possible, carefully insert a small straight pin (not your meter probe) into the rear of the connector shell to contact the terminal inside, then clip your meter lead to

the pin. This kind of connection is called back-probing. When inserting a test probe into a terminal, be careful not to distort the terminal opening. Doing so can lead to a poor connection and corrosion at that terminal later. Using the small straight pin instead of a meter probe results in less chance of deforming the terminal connector.

7   Turn signal and hazard flashers - general information

1 The turn signal and hazard flasher system consists of bulbs, switches, and the Body Control Module (BCM). Each rear taillight housing also consists of a logic module that monitors the bulb condition. Positive voltage is supplied to the BCM from three

fuses (LT/TRN/SIG, RT/TRN/SIG, AND BCK/UP/STOP), while the ground signal is sent to the BCM from either the turn signal switch or the hazard switch. There is no external flasher to replace; the flasher is an integral part of the BCM.

2 When the flasher unit is functioning properly, an audible click can be heard during its operation. If the turn signal indicator on one side of the vehicle flashes much more rapidly than normal, a change in the amount of impedance (resistance) to the flow of current has been detected by the BCM. This can either be a faulty bulb, open wiring, and/or faulty BCM.

3 If both the front and rear turn signal bulbs on the same side are not flashing, the turn signal and hazard flasher relay function in the BCM is probably defective. Have the BCM

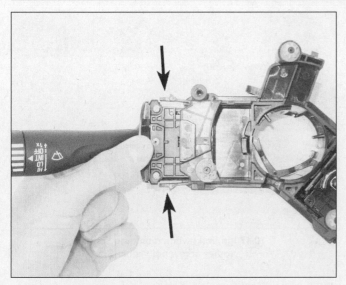

8.4 Depress the retaining tabs and pull the switch from the switch mounting bracket (removed for clarity)

8.9 Disconnect the electrical connections before removing

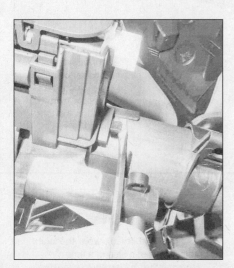

8.11 Disconnect the locking tabs. . .

8.12. . . then slide the assembly off of the steering column shaft

8.13 The clockspring is held in place by the three square shaped tabs

diagnosed (and if necessary, replaced) by a dealer service department or other repair facility equipped with the proper tools and scanners. This is not a job that you can do at home because the BCM must be programmed with a factory scan tool when it's replaced.

8   Steering column switches and mounting bracket - removal and installation

Warning: *The models covered by this manual are equipped with a Supplemental Restraint System (SRS), more commonly known as airbags. Always disable the airbag system before working in the vicinity of any airbag system components to avoid the possibility of accidental deployment of the airbags, which could cause personal injury (see Section 31).*

Multi-function switch

1   Release the tilt wheel lever and place the steering wheel in the lowest position.
2   Remove the steering column trim covers (see Chapter 11).
3   Disconnect the electrical connector from the multi-function switch.
4   Depress the multi-function switch retaining tabs, then pull the switch out of the switch mounting bracket **(see illustration)**.
5   Installation is the reverse of removal.

Switch mounting bracket

6   Remove steering wheel covers (see Chapter 11).
7   Remove the steering wheel (see Chapter 10).
8   Remove the clockspring (see Section 31).
Note: *The clockspring can remain on the*

switch mounting bracket for removal.
9   Disconnect any electrical connections to the switch mounting bracket**(see illustration)** or wire harness brackets attached to the mounting bracket.
10   On 2015 and earlier models (and 2016 Malibu Limited), remove the fasteners (two used) securing the mounting bracket to the steering column.
11   On 2016 and later models (except Malibu Limited), disengage the locking tabs **(see illustration)** on either side.
12   Slide the mounting bracket off of the steering column**(see illustration)**.
13   With the switch mounting bracket off (or can be done with it still attached to the steering column) the clockspring**(see illustration)** can be disconnected by lifting the three tabs and sliding it off of the switch mounting bracket.
14   Installation is the reverse of removal.

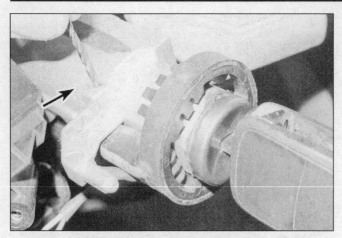

10.4 Push in the retaining pin to release the lock cylinder, then withdraw the key and cylinder

10.17 Ignition switch mounting screw (other screw not visible)

9 Steering angle sensor - centering

Note: *Steering angle sensor centering with or without electronic stability control or internal or external steering angle sensor requires the use of a scan tool. This procedure must be performed by a dealership service department or other repair facility with the proper scanning capabilities. The following procedures are an overview of the steps needed to be performed.*

1   Set the front wheels to the straight-ahead position.

2   Place selector lever in Park.

3   Connect the scan tool and turn the ignition On.

4   Follow the guidelines and scanner menu to "Steering Wheel Angle Sensor Reset" and perform the procedure as directed.

5   Complete the procedure by going to the BCM (Body Control Module) configuration/reset functions.

6   Follow the guidelines and scanner menu to relearn the steering angle sensor to the BCM.

7   Clear any codes that may have been set during the process.

10 Key lock cylinder and ignition switch - replacement

Warning: *The models covered by this manual are equipped with a Supplemental Restraint System (SRS), more commonly known as airbags. Always disarm the airbag system before working in the vicinity of any airbag system component to avoid the possibility of accidental deployment of the airbag, which could cause personal injury (see Section 31).*

Note: *For key fob battery replacement, see Section 27 .*

1   Disconnect the cable from the negative terminal of the battery (see Chapter 5).

Key lock cylinder (models with ignition key)

2   Remove the steering column covers

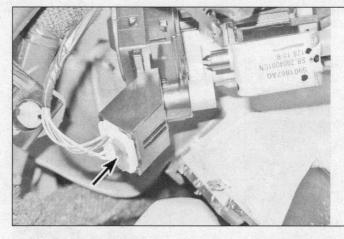

10.18 Pull out the connector lock, then disconnect the electrical connector from the ignition switch

(see Chapter 11). Using a trim tool, pry off the lock cylinder bezel.

3   Insert the ignition key into the lock cylinder and turn it to the RUN position.

4   Insert a pick or other small tool into the hole in the top of the lock cylinder housing and push it in to depress the release button **(see illustration)**. Pull the lock cylinder out of the housing.

5   To install the lock cylinder, make sure the ignition switch is still in the RUN position. If it isn't, rotate it to the RUN position with a screwdriver or needle-nose pliers. The lock cylinder won't fit all the way into the bore if the switch is in any other position.

6   Insert the lock cylinder into the housing, making sure it engages with the switch and clicks into place.

7   Verify that the ignition switch operates correctly in the Off, ACC, Run and Start positions.

Ignition switch housing (models with ignition key)

8   Remove the steering column covers (see Chapter 11).

9   Remove the steering wheel (see Chapter 10).

10   Remove the steering column switches and clockspring (see Section 8).

11   Disconnect the electrical connections to the ignition switch.

12   Using a cold chisel, work the bolts out (counterclockwise) a little at a time.

13   Remove the ignition switch housing.

14   Installation is the reverse of removal.

15   The replacement ignition switch housing comes with new shear-head bolts. Tighten the bolts until the heads of the bolts snap off. No extra torque or degree of turn is required.

Ignition switch (with or without keyless ignition)

Without keyless ignition

16   Remove the steering column covers (see Chapter 11).

17   Remove the screws and pull the ignition switch from the housing **(see illustration)**.

18   Disconnect the electrical connector from the ignition switch **(see illustration)**.

19   Installation is the reverse of removal.

With keyless ignition

20   Using a plastic flat-bladed trim tool, carefully pry off the center dash trim bezel.

21   Squeeze the retaining tabs and remove the switch from the trim bezel.

22   Installation is the reverse of removal.

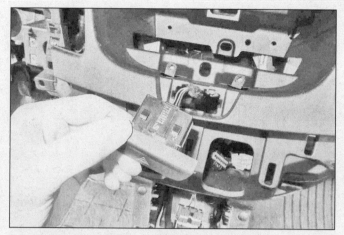

11.1 Press in on the tabs (top side shown) and the bottom tabs to release the switch from the trim panel

12.4a Remove the four instrument cluster mounting screws

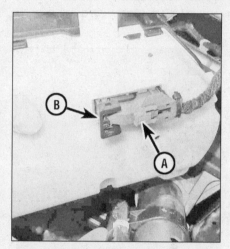

12.4b Slide back the electrical connector safety clip (A), then lift the main connector attachment lever (B). Now the connector can be removed

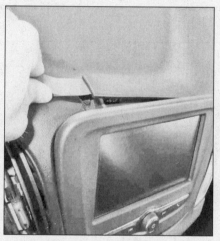

12.8a With a flat trim tool, lift the bolt close out trim to expose the fasteners

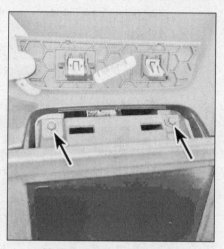

12.8b Remove the DIC upper mounting screws

11 Instrument panel switches - replacement

Warning: *The models covered by this manual are equipped with a Supplemental Restraint System (SRS), more commonly known as airbags. Always disable the airbag system before working in the vicinity of any airbag system components to avoid the possibility of accidental deployment of the airbags, which could cause personal injury (see Section 31).*

Hazard switch

1   The hazard flasher is mounted in the center dash area. Remove the trim panels, then press in on the tabs (two on the top, two on the bottom) then slide the switch out of the trim panel **(see illustration)**. When disconnecting the electrical connector, don't allow the connector to fall back into the dash.
2   Installation is the reverse of removal.

12 Instrument cluster - removal and installation

Warning: *The models covered by this manual are equipped with a Supplemental Restraint System (SRS), more commonly known as airbags. Always disable the airbag system before working in the vicinity of any airbag system components to avoid the possibility of accidental deployment of the airbags, which could cause personal injury (see Section 31).*

Instrument cluster

1   Disconnect the cable from the negative battery terminal (see Chapter 5).
2   Release the tilt wheel lever and lower the steering wheel to its lowest position.
3   Remove the instrument cluster bezel (see Chapter 11).
4   Remove the instrument cluster mounting screws and disconnect the electrical connector **(see illustrations)**.
5   Carefully remove the instrument cluster

from the instrument panel.
6   Installation is the reverse of removal.

Driver's Information Center (DIC)

Note: *This procedure covers removal and installation of the original DIC. Replacing the DIC with a new unit will require programming with a special scan tool.*
Note: *The DIC is located in the center of the dash, and can be removed without removing the cluster.*
Note: *The following procedures are for general familiarity with the process. Your actual display may have some variations to this one, but the removal and installation are similar.*
7   At some parts stores the DIC may be referred to as the "Center Stack". When ordering replacement components be sure to have the vehicle's VIN with you so the correct calibrations can be obtained.
8   The following illustrations will lead you through removal and disassembly of the DIC unit **(see illustrations)**.

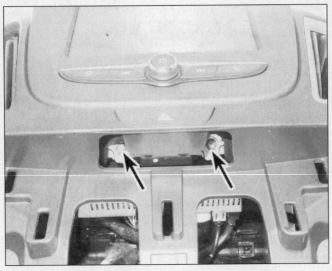

12.9 Remove the DIC lower mounting screws

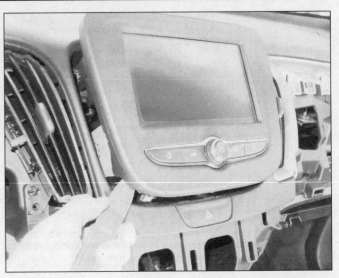

12.10 Pry near a corner to get the DIC out of the dash

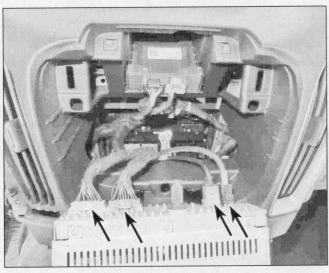

12.11 Press in on the locking tabs to release the electrical connectors

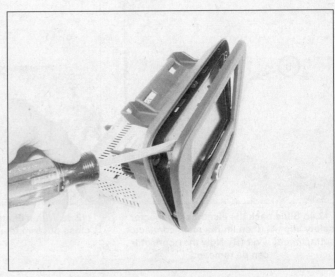

12.12a Pry the trim face off of the trim base

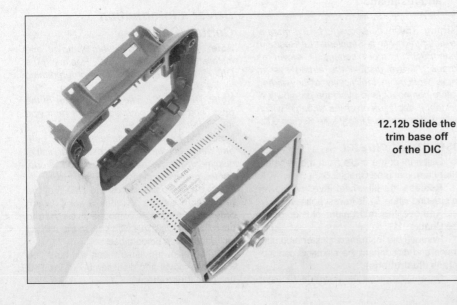

12.12b Slide the trim base off of the DIC

9   Remove the mid-level dash trim panel (see Chapter 11) to expose the lower DIC mounting screws **(see illustration)**.

10   Using the flat trim tool, work the DIC out of the dash **(see illustration)**.

11   Disconnect the electrical connectors from the back of the DIC **(see illustration)**.

12   Separate the trim from the DIC **(see illustrations)**.

13   Installation is the reverse of removal. If you are replacing the DIC, some programming will be required. Take the vehicle to a dealer service department or other properly equipped repair shop.

13   Radio and speakers - removal and installation

Warning: *The models covered by this manual are equipped with a Supplemental Restraint*

**13.3 Radio mounting screw locations
(2015 and earlier models/2016 Malibu Limited)**

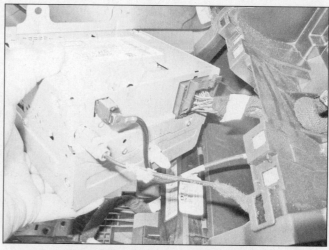

**13.4 Disconnect the antenna cable and electrical
connectors from the back of the radio**

13.8 Speaker mounting screw

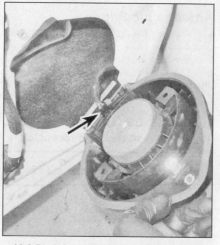

**13.9 Push in on the tab or slide out the
connector lock, as applicable, to release
the electrical connector**

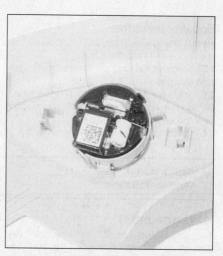

**13.17 The A-pillar speaker is held in
plastic clips molded into the A-pillar**

System (SRS), more commonly known as airbags. Always disable the airbag system before working in the vicinity of any airbag system components to avoid the possibility of accidental deployment of the airbags, which could cause personal injury (see Section 31). **Note:** On 2016 and later models (except Malibu Limited), the radio controls have all been incorporated into the DIC. Follow the DIC procedures in Section 12.

Radio

1 Disconnect the cable from the negative battery terminal (see Chapter 5).
2 Remove the center dash trim bezel (see Section 11).
3 Remove the radio mounting screws and pull the radio from the instrument panel **(see illustration)**.
4 Disconnect the electrical connectors and the antenna cable from the back of the radio **(see illustration)**.
5 Installation is the reverse of removal.

6 After installing a new or replacement factory radio, a scan tool is required to program the radio to the vehicle; this procedure must be performed by a dealer service department or other properly equipped independent repair shop.

Speakers

Door speakers
7 Remove the door trim panel (see Chapter 11).
8 Remove the speaker mounting screw(s) **(see illustration)**.
9 Pull the speaker from the door, then disconnect the electrical connector **(see illustration)**.
10 Installation is the reverse of removal.

Front (instrument panel) speaker
11 Remove the speaker grille.
12 Remove the speaker mounting screws.
13 Lift the speaker from the dash.
14 Disconnect the electrical connector.

15 Installation is the reverse of removal.

A-pillar tweeters
16 Starting from the top, carefully pry the A-pillar trim outward to detach the retaining clips. Detach the tether on models equipped with roof-rail airbags.
17 Disconnect the electrical connector, then detach the tweeter from the A-pillar trim **(see illustration)**.
18 Installation is the reverse of removal.
Warning: The manufacturer states that the tether at the top of the A-pillar trim must be replaced with a new one whenever the trim is removed.

Rear speaker
19 Remove the parcel shelf trim panel (see Chapter 11, Section 21).
20 Remove the speaker mounting screws; remove the speaker and disconnect the electrical connector.
21 Installation is the reverse of removal.

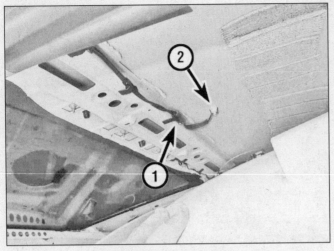

14.3 Antenna mast details

1   *Antenna electrical connector(s)*   2   *Antenna securing nut*

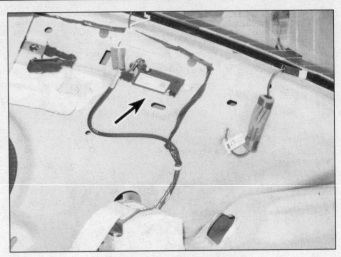

14.6 Antenna module location

Speaker amplifier

Note: *The speaker amplifier is mounted on the right side of the trunk area.*

22   Remove the luggage compartment right-side trim panel

23   Remove the screws securing the amplifier to the back of the wheel well, and disconnect the electrical connections.

24   Installation is the reverse of removal.

14   Antenna - removal and installation

Antenna mast

1   Lower the rear of the headliner just enough to access the antenna cable(s) (see Chapter 11, Section 21).

2   Disconnect the antenna cables / connector.

3   Remove the fastener, then pull the antenna from the roof, guiding the cable and wires through the hole **(see illustration)**.

Antenna module

4   Remove the right side C-pillar trim (see Chapter 11).

5   Unscrew the module from the pillar.

6   Disconnect the electrical leads **(see illustration)**.

7   Installation is the reverse of removal.

15   Audio disc and USB receptacle

1   Remove the front center console cup holder compartment.

Note: *The rear console section does not need to be removed from the front cup holder compartment to replace the receptacle.*

2   Reach in and depress the tabs on either side of the receptacle.

3   Pull out the receptacle and disconnect the electrical connectors. Remove the receptacle.

4   Installation is the reverse of removal.

16   Headlight housing - removal and installation

Warning: *Some models use High Intensity Discharge (HID) bulbs instead of conventional halogen bulbs. According to the manufacturer, the high voltages produced by this system can be fatal in the event of shock. Also, the voltage can remain in circuit even after the headlight switch has been turned to Off and the ignition key has been removed. Therefore, for your safety, we don't recommend that you try to remove one of these housings yourself. Instead, have this service performed by a dealer service department or other qualified repair shop.*

1   Remove the front bumper cover (see Chapter 11).

2   Remove the headlight housing mounting fasteners **(see illustrations)**.

3   Carefully remove the headlight housing, pulling it forward from the vehicle.

16.2a Remove the headlight lower mounting screws. . .

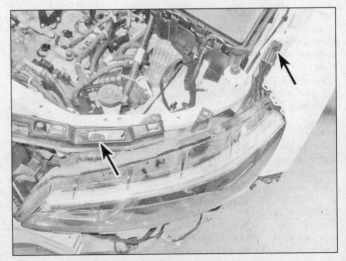

16.2b. . . and upper mounting screws

17.1 On 2015 and later models (except Malibu Limited), pry off the left-side instrument panel trim panel with a plastic trim tool. . .

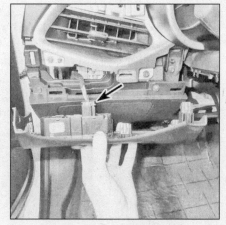

17.2. . . then disconnect the electrical connector

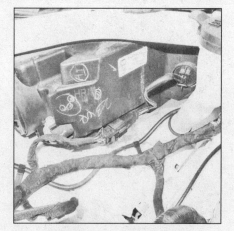

18.2 Turn the access cover counterclockwise to remove it

4   Disconnect the electrical connector and remove the housing.

5   Installation is the reverse of removal. It's a good idea to have the headlights aimed by a shop with the proper equipment. For temporary adjustment, see Section 19.

17   Headlight switch - replacement

Warning: *The models covered by this manual are equipped with a Supplemental Restraint System (SRS), more commonly known as airbags. Always disable the airbag system before working in the vicinity of any airbag system components to avoid the possibility of accidental deployment of the airbags, which could cause personal injury (see Section 31).*

1   On 2015 and earlier models/2016 Malibu Limited, remove the driver's knee bolster (see Chapter 11). Reach up behind the headlight switch, push in on the tabs on either side while applying slight pressure, then push the switch assembly out the front of the dash. On

2016 and later models (except Malibu Limited) remove the left instrument panel outer trim cover by prying it off with a trim tool **(see illustration)**.

2   With the switch removed, disconnect the electrical connection **(see illustration)**.

3   Installation is the reverse of removal.

18   Headlight bulb - replacement

Warning: *Halogen bulbs are gas-filled and under pressure and may shatter if the surface is scratched or the bulb is dropped. Wear eye protection and handle the bulbs carefully, grasping only the base whenever possible. Don't touch the surface of the bulb with your fingers because the oil from your skin could cause it to overheat and fail prematurely. If you do touch the bulb surface, clean it with rubbing alcohol.*

1   If you're replacing the left-side headlight bulb on a 2015 or earlier model/2016 Malibu Limited), remove the windshield washer tube filler neck.

2   Remove the access cover(s) from the back of the headlight housing **(see illustration)**.

3   Turn the bulb holder counterclockwise and remove it from the housing **(see illustration)**.

4   Disconnect the electrical connector from the headlight bulb **(see illustration)**.

5   Connect the electrical connector to the new bulb holder.

6   Install the access cover.

Xenon (HID) headlights

Warning: *Some models use High Intensity Discharge (HID) bulbs instead of conventional halogen bulbs. According to the manufacturer, the high voltages produced by this system can be fatal in the event of shock. Also, the voltage can remain in circuit even after the headlight switch has been turned to OFF and the ignition key has been removed. Therefore, for your safety, we don't recommend that you try to replace one of these bulbs yourself. Instead, have this service performed by a dealer service department or other qualified repair shop.*

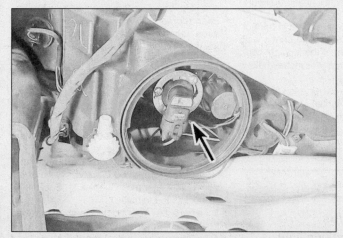

18.3 Turn the bulb holder counterclockwise and remove it from the headlight housing

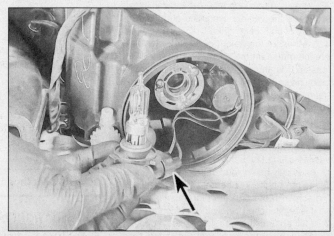

18.4 Disconnect the electrical connector from the bulb holder

19.1 Use a 6 mm hex driver to turn the adjuster screw

19 Headlights and fog lights - adjustment

Warning: *The headlights must be aimed correctly. If adjusted incorrectly, they could temporarily blind the driver of an oncoming vehicle and cause an accident or seriously reduce your ability to see the road. The headlights should be checked for proper aim every 12 months and any time a new headlight is installed or front-end bodywork is performed. The following procedure is only an interim step to provide temporary adjustment until the headlights can be adjusted by a properly equipped shop.*

Headlights

1   These models are equipped with composite headlights with adjustment screws that control up-and-down movement **(see illustration)**. Left-and-right movement is not adjustable.

2   There are several methods of adjusting the headlights. The simplest method requires a blank wall 25 feet in front of the vehicle and a level floor **(see illustration)**.

3   Position masking tape on the wall in reference to the vehicle centerline and the centerlines of both headlights.

4   Measure the height of the headlight reference marks (in the centers of the headlight lenses) from the ground. Position a horizontal tape line on the wall at the same height as the headlight reference marks.

Note: *It may be easier to position the tape on the wall with the vehicle parked only a few inches away.*

5   Adjustment should be made with the vehicle sitting level, the gas tank half-full and no unusually heavy load in the vehicle.

6   Turn on the low beams. Turn the adjusting screw to position the high intensity zone so it is eight inches below the horizontal line.

7   To ensure the headlamps are adjusted properly, have the headlights adjusted by a qualified independent repair shop or a dealer service department at the earliest opportunity.

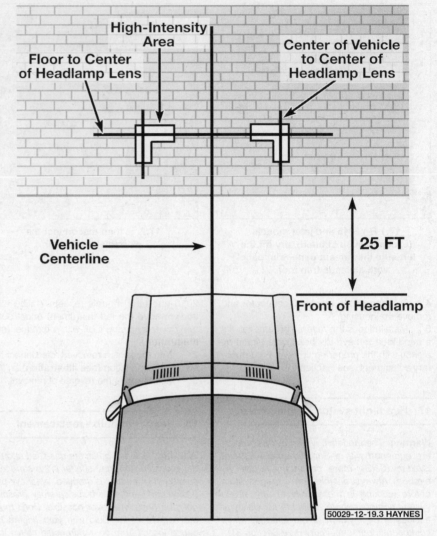

19.2 Headlight adjustment details

Fog lights

8   Some models have optional fog lights that can be aimed just like headlights. As with the headlights, there are no left-and-right adjustments.

9   Position tape on a wall 25 feet in front of the vehicle. Tape a horizontal line on the wall that represents the height of the fog light centers, and another tape line four inches below that line.

10   The adjustment screw for each fog light is accessed through the grille, just above the light. Turn the screw and adjust the pattern on the wall so that the top of the fog light beam meets the lower line on the wall.

20 Bulb replacement

Exterior light bulbs

Front turn signal/parking lights
Warning: *Some models use High Intensity Discharge (HID) bulbs instead of con-ventional halogen bulbs. According to the manufacturer, the high voltages produced by this system can be fatal in the event of shock. Also, the voltage can remain in circuit even after the headlight switch has been turned to Off and the ignition key has been removed. Therefore, for your safety, we don't recommend that you try to perform any work related to the headlight housing. Instead, have this service performed by a dealer service department or other qualified repair shop.*

1   If necessary for access to the left side bulbs on 2015 and earlier models (nd 2016 Malibu Limited), remove the windshield washer reservoir filler neck.

2   If you're working on a 2016 or later model (except Malibu Limited), remove the front fender liner (see Chapter 11, Section 10) for access to the bulb.

3   Twist the bulb holder counterclockwise to remove it from the headlight housing.

4   Remove the bulb from the holder and install the new one.

5   Installation is the reverse of removal.

Bulb removal

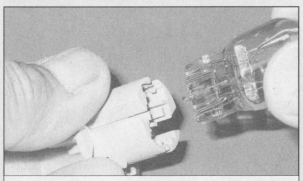

To remove many modern exterior bulbs from their holders, simply pull them out

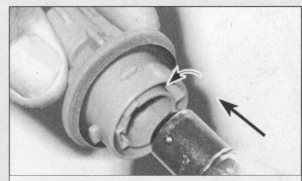

On bulbs with a cylindrical base ("bayonet" bulbs), the socket is spring-loaded; a pair of small posts on the side of the base hold the bulb in place against spring pressure. To remove this type of bulb, push it into the holder, rotate it 1/4-turn counterclockwise, then pull it out

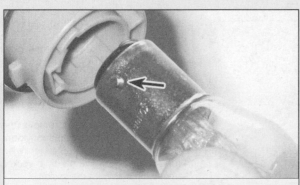

If a bayonet bulb has dual filaments, the posts are staggered, so the bulb can only be installed one way

To remove most overhead interior light bulbs, simply unclip them

Front side marker lights

6   On 2016 and later models (except Malibu Limited), remove the headlight housing (see Section 16).

7   Turn the bulb holder counterclockwise to remove it.

8   Remove the bulb from the holder and install the new one.

9   Installation is the reverse of removal.

Fog lights

Warning: *Halogen bulbs are gas-filled and under pressure and may shatter if the surface is scratched or the bulb is dropped. Wear eye protection and handle the bulbs carefully, grasping only the base whenever possible. Don't touch the surface of the bulb with your fingers because the oil from your skin could cause it to overheat and fail prematurely. If you do touch the bulb surface, clean it with rubbing alcohol.*

10   Remove the fasteners from the front portion of the inner fender splash shield (see Chapter 11), then pull the splash shield back for access to the fog light.

11   Disconnect the electrical connector from the fog light.

12   Twist the bulb counterclockwise and remove the bulb.

13   Installation is the reverse of removal.

Center High-Mounted Brake Light

Note: *The high-mounted brake light is an LED fixture and must be serviced as a complete assembly.*

2015 and earlier models
(and 2016 Malibu Limited)

14   Remove the trim panel from the trunk lid.

15   Remove the two nuts retaining the light housing, then detach the housing from the trunk lid.

16   Disconnect the electrical connector.

17   Installation is the reverse of removal.

2016 and later models
(except Malibu Limited)

18   Lower the rear section of the headliner far enough to gain access to the electrical connections and fasteners for the high mounted brake light fixture (see Chapter 11, Section 21).

19   Remove and discard the fasteners (four used) securing the high-mount brake light to the roof panel **(see illustration)**.

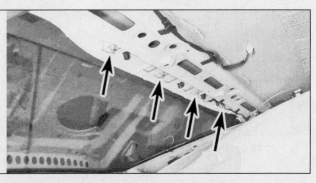

20.19 Remove the center high-mounted brake light fasteners (with the rear of the headliner lowered)

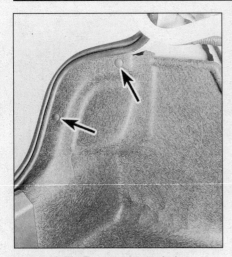

20.22a Remove the pushpins securing the trim

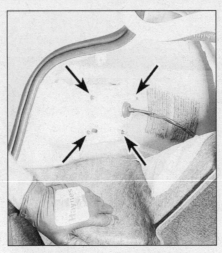

20.22b Fold the side trim down, then remove the four nuts securing the light fixture to the body

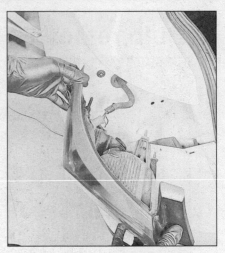

20.22c Pull the light fixture away from the body

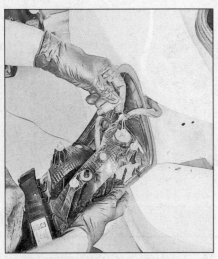

20.23a Turn the socket counterclockwise to remove it

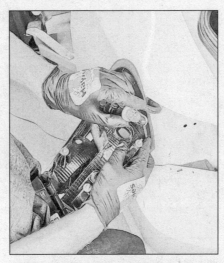

20.23b Pull the bulb out of the socket and replace it with the same type of bulb

20   Disconnect the electrical connection and remove the assembly.

21   Installation is the reverse of removal.

Brake/tail/turn signal lights

Note: *Incandescent bulbs are only used for the turn signals; the brake/tail lights are LEDs and are not replaceable.*

22   Open the trunk and remove the rear compartment side trim **(see illustrations)**.

23   Turn the socket counterclockwise **(see illustrations)**. Remove the bulb socket, then remove the bulb from the socket.

Note: *Taillights mounted on the trunk deck lid are removed in the same manner.*

24   Installation is the reverse of removal.

License plate light bulbs

25   On 2015 and earlier models (and 2016 Malibu Limited), pry down the right end of the lens. On 2016 and later models (except Malibu Limited), pry out the left end of the lens **(see illustration)**.

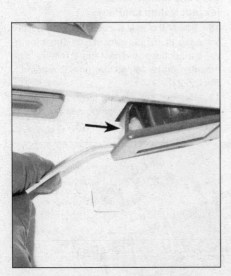

20.25 Gently pry out the lens

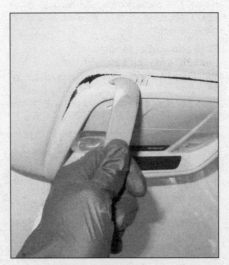

20.29a Carefully pry the housing from the headliner

20.29b Pull the entire assembly downward

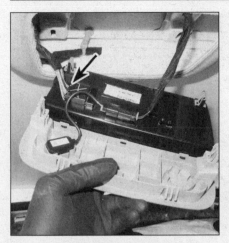

20.29c Disconnect the electrical connection

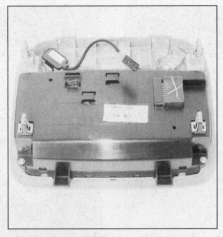

20.29d Place the fixture on a flat surface to avoid damaging the finish

20.29e Using a flat screwdriver, gently pry the trim from the fixture, working around the outer edge slowly

26   Pull the bulb out to remove it from the lens.
27   Remove the bulb from the holder and install a new one.
28   Installation is the reverse of removal.

Interior light bulbs

Reading lights

Note: *LED lights are very common for interior lighting. Most LEDs are not replaceable - the entire fixture is replaced. The following procedures reflect that process.*
29   Gently pry the overhead console from the housing **(see illustrations)**.
30   Installation is the reverse of removal.

Rear dome light

31   Pry the cover off with a small flat screwdriver to replace the bulb **(see illustrations)**.
32   Installation is the reverse of removal.

Glove box light

33   Open the glove box and carefully pry the lens off.
34   Pull down the light housing and remove the bulb.

35   Installation is the reverse of removal.

Instrument cluster light bulbs

36   Instrument cluster illumination is an inte-

gral part of the instrument cluster. Bulbs are not replaceable. If one goes out, replace the cluster (see Section 12).

20.29f The entire fixture can now be replaced

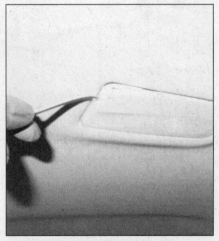

20.31a Carefully remove the trim piece

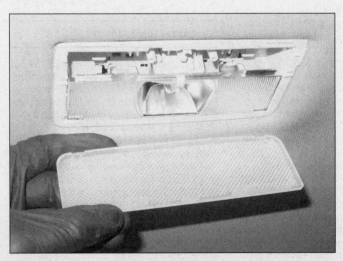

20.31b Remove the lens

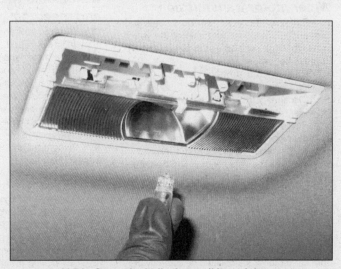

20.31c Grasp the bulb, then pull it straight out

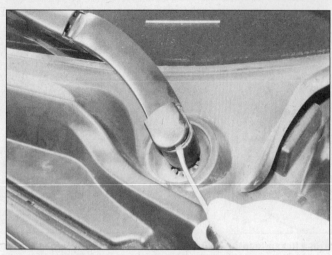

21.1 Remove the dust cap with a small screwdriver

21.4 Remove the wiper motor transmission mounting bolts

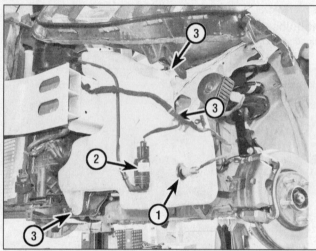

21.15 Windshield washer fluid reservoir details - 2016 and later models (except 2016 Malibu Limited)

1 Low fluid level sensor
2 Washer fluid reservoir
3 Washer fluid reservoir mounting nuts

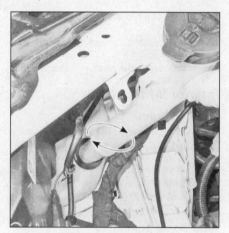

21.17 Pull and twist the filler neck out of the washer reservoir

21 Windshield wiper system - component replacement

Wiper motor transmission

1   Remove the wiper arm dust caps and nuts and mark the relationship of the wiper arms to their shafts **(see illustration)**. Remove both wiper arms.
2   Remove the cowl cover (see Chapter 11).
3   Disconnect the electrical connector from the wiper motor.
4   Remove the windshield wiper motor transmission assembly mounting bolts and remove the assembly **(see illustration)**.
5   Remove the wiper motor and transmission as one complete assembly.
6   Installation is the reverse of removal.

Wiper motor

7   Mark the transmission drive link arm to the motor shaft.
8   Separate the transmission drive link arm from the motor crank ballstud by carefully prying it off.

9   Remove the motor mounting bolts and remove the motor from the wiper transmission.
10 Installation is the reverse of removal.

Windshield washer fluid pump and reservoir

11 If you're working on a 2015 or earlier model/2016 Malibu Limited, remove the left-side inner fender liner (see Chapter 11, Section 10). If you're working on a 2016 or later model (except Malibu Limited), remove the front bumper cover (see Chapter 11, Section 9).
12 Place a drain pan under the washer fluid reservoir to collect any washer fluid that spills out.
13 Disconnect the washer hoses from the washer pump.
14 Disconnect the electrical connectors.
15 The washer pump or the low fluid level sensor can be removed by pulling and twisting it out of its grommet **(see illustration)**.
16 Always install a new grommet when replacing the washer pump.
17 Remove the filler neck to the washer reservoir by pulling the filler neck upwards **(see illustration)**.

18 Remove the fasteners that secure the washer reservoir to the chassis.
19 Transfer components to the replacement reservoir as needed.
20 Installation is the reverse of removal.

22 Horn - replacement

Note: *These models are equipped with a Body Control Module (BCM). Several systems are linked to a centralized control module that allows simple and accurate troubleshooting, but only with a professional-grade scan tool. The Body Control Module governs the door locks, the power windows, the ignition lock and security system, the interior lights, the Daytime Running Lights system, the horn, the windshield wipers, the heating/air conditioning system and the power mirrors. In the event of a malfunction with this system, have the vehicle diagnosed by a dealership service department or other qualified automotive repair facility.*
Note: *On 2015 and earlier models (and 2016 Malibu Limited), both the hig and low-note horns are mounted on the left side of the vehicle.*

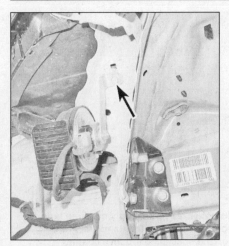

22.3 Horn mounting bolt (2016 and later models shown, except Malibu Limited)

23.1 Pry the sensor upwards to release the tabs

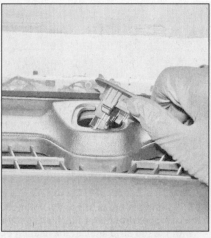

23.2 Lift the sensor up high enough to disconnect the electrical connector, without allowing the connector to fall down into the dash

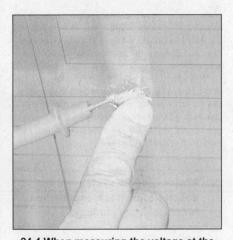

24.4 When measuring the voltage at the rear window defogger grid, wrap a piece of aluminum foil around the positive probe of the voltmeter and press the foil against the wire with your finger

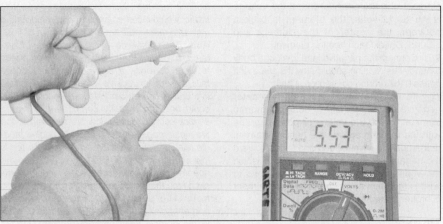

24.5 To determine if a heating element has broken, check the voltage at the center of each element - if the voltage is 5- or 6-volts, the element is unbroken; if the voltage is 10- or 12-volts, the element is broken between the center and the ground side; if there is no voltage, the element is broken between the center and the positive side

On 2016 and later models (except Malibu Limited), there is a horn mounted on each side.

1 Remove the front bumper cover (see Chapter 11).

2 Disconnect the horn electrical connector(s).

3 Remove the nut or bolt and detach the horn(s) **(see illustration)**.

4 Installation is the reverse of removal.

23 Daytime Running Lights (DRL) - general information

Note: *The Daytime Running Lights (DRL) system is a light sensitive system that observes the ambient light under all conditions, day, night, or at dusk or dawn. The system is active if the ignition is on and the parking brake is off and it is not in park, at which time the BCM will command the low-beam headlights on..*

Ambient light sensor replacement

Note: *The sensor is mounted in the top center of the instrument panel.*

1 Pry the light sensor out of the dash with a flat trim tool **(see illustration)**.

2 Disconnect the electrical connector and retaining clip, and remove the sensor **(see illustration)**.

3 Installation is the reverse of removal.

24 Rear window defogger - check and repair

1 The rear window defogger consists of a number of horizontal elements baked onto the glass surface.

2 Small breaks in the element can be repaired without removing the rear window.

Check

3 Turn the ignition switch and defogger system switches to the On position. Using a voltmeter, place the positive probe against the defogger grid positive terminal and the negative probe against the ground terminal. If battery voltage is not indicated, check the fuse, defogger switch and related wiring. If voltage is indicated, but all or part of the defogger doesn't heat, proceed with the following tests.

4 When measuring voltage during the next two tests, wrap a piece of aluminum foil around the tip of the voltmeter positive probe and press the foil against the heating element with your finger **(see illustration)**. Place the negative probe on the defogger grid ground terminal.

5 Check the voltage at the center of each heating element **(see illustration)**. If the voltage is 5 or 6-volts, the element is okay (there is no break). If the voltage is zero, the element is broken between the center of the

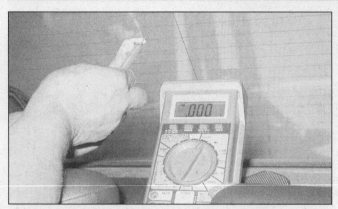

24.7 To find the break, place the voltmeter negative lead against the defogger ground terminal, place the voltmeter positive lead with the foil strip against the heating element at the positive terminal end and slide it toward the negative terminal end - the point at which the voltmeter reading changes abruptly is the point at which the element is broken

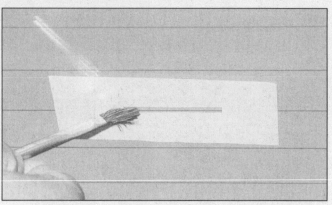

24.13 To use a defogger repair kit, apply masking tape to the inside of the window at the damaged area, then brush on the special conductive coating

element and the positive end. If the voltage is 10 to 12-volts, the element is broken between the center of the element and ground. Check each heating element.

6   Connect the negative lead to a good body ground. The reading should stay the same. If it doesn't, the ground connection is bad.

7   To find the break, place the voltmeter negative probe against the defogger ground terminal. Place the voltmeter positive probe with the foil strip against the heating element at the positive terminal end and slide it toward the negative terminal end. The point at which the voltmeter deflects from several volts to zero is the point at which the heating element is broken **(see illustration)**.

Repair

8   Repair the break in the element using a repair kit specifically recommended for this purpose, available at most auto parts stores. Included in this kit is plastic conductive epoxy.

9   Prior to repairing a break, turn off the system and allow it to cool off for a few minutes.

10   Lightly buff the element area with fine steel wool, then clean it thoroughly with rubbing alcohol.

11   Use masking tape to mask off the area being repaired.

12   Thoroughly mix the epoxy, following the instructions provided with the repair kit.

13   Apply the epoxy material to the slit in the masking tape, overlapping the undamaged area about 3/4-inch on either end **(see illustration)**.

14   Allow the repair to cure for 24 hours before removing the tape and using the system.

25 Cruise control system - description and check

Note: *The adaptive cruise control system incorporates nearly every function of the ve-*

hicle. It has the ability to sense and react to traffic, which includes braking and maintaining a certain distance from the car in front of you.
Note: *The complexity of the cruise control system also means that everything involved needs to work correctly. If any part of the process fails to send or receive information the adaptive cruise control can cease to function. This could be from a faulty component, a stored service code or even a low tire reported to the tire monitoring system. If the cruise control module is aware of the tire pressure, and the tire is low enough to cause a stability issue, then the adaptive cruise control can remain inactive until such time the tire issue is taken care of.*
Note: *The adaptive cruise control receives and analyzes data from various sources within the vehicle itself or from outside sources such as GPS. The long range radar sensors, short range radar, and front view cameras are used to identify the road, lines, obstructions, and environment. The system scans the road ahead and its surroundings to detect any possible issues in its field of view.*
Note: *Features of the adaptive cruise control system require special testers and diagnostic procedures that are beyond the scope of the home mechanic. Listed below are some general procedures that may be used to locate common problems.*

1   Check the fuses (see Section 3).

2   The Brake Pedal Position (BPP) switch (or brake light switch) deactivates the cruise control system. Have an assistant press the brake pedal while you check the brake light operation.

3   If the brake lights do not operate properly, correct the problem and retest the cruise control.

4   Is the CHECK ENGINE on? If so, have the vehicle checked for fault codes and repair as necessary.

Note: *Most problems with the adaptive cruise control will require taking your vehicle to a dealer service department or other qualified repair shop that has the proper scanning capabilities for further diagnosis.*

Note: *Many cruise control failures can be attributed to problems that are not related to the cruise control itself. Perform some basic checks. Ensure the engine and transmission are operating correctly and that no service light is on. Check the tire pressure, wipers, and cameras are functioning before assuming the problem is with the cruise control. Even a cracked windshield or heavily loaded vehicle can result in the adaptive cruise control system from operating properly.*

26 Power window system - description, check, and express function programming

Note: *These models are equipped with a Body Control Module (BCM). System diagnostic information is linked to the BCM. This allows for a quick and accurate diagnosis and in-depth troubleshooting with a professional-grade scan tool. These scan tools are expensive, and are not the type of scan tool you will find at a local parts store for code reading. Have the vehicle diagnosed by a dealership service department or other qualified repair facility.*

1   The power windows can be lowered and raised from the master control switch by the driver or by remote switches located at the individual windows. Each window has a separate motor that is reversible.

2   The window motor circuits are protected by a fuse. Each window motor is also equipped with an internal circuit breaker (the internal circuit breaker is not serviceable).

3   The master control switch (driver's door) includes a "lock-out" switch which prevents window operation from their associated door switches.

Note: *Window lock-out does not affect the driver's window.*

4   If all the power windows are not working, check the related fuses and circuit breakers.

5   If only the driver's window is operating, check the window lockout switch position.

6 If a window only works in one direction, check the related window switch for proper operation. Each switch (driver's window not included) uses the switch in the rest position as a way to complete the circuit back to its companion switch. Sometimes, the switch is not closing the loop because it is worn out or is stuck in the up or down position.

Note: *Only the driver's window requires one switch to operate correctly. All the other windows must have both the driver's window master switch and the window's individual switch in working order.*

7 If the same window works from one switch, but not the other, check the switch and/or wiring for continuity.

8 If the switch tests OK, check for an open in the circuit between the affected switch and the window motor.

9 If one window is inoperative from both switches, remove the door panel from the affected door and check for voltage (positive and negative) at the motor connection leads (refer to Chapter 11 for door panel removal). Check for the voltage signals as the switch is operated in the up or down position.

Warning: *DO NOT apply voltage or ground to any leads at the switches. There are data lines for communication between the switch and the BCM that are a very low voltage signal (5 volts or less). Applying voltage or a ground signal to the wrong leads will cause permanent damage to the BCM.*

10 If voltage is reaching the motor, disconnect the glass from the regulator (see Chapter 11). Move the window up and down by hand while checking for binding and damage to the regulator. Repair as necessary.

Note: *To verify if the motor is getting the needed voltage or ground, a simple but effective test is to sit in the car with the ignition on, open a door and look at the dome light. Then operate the switch to the faulty window. If you see the dome light dimming slightly this is a good indication that the motor is getting power and is probably a stuck motor or faulty wiring. Do not hold the switch on for very long when a motor or regulator is stuck or binding. Finally, in some cases, a good rap on the door panel in the general area of the window motor - while the key is on and the window switch is depressed in the direction the window needs to move - will free up a stuck motor temporarily. You can damage the door panel or more internal components if you hit it too hard.*

Window express down programming

Note: *Any time the battery or window motor is disconnected, you will need to perform this procedure to reestablish the auto feature.*

Warning: *All doors must be completely closed prior to normalizing the windows. Verify the doors are completely shut and the interior lighting has timed out before proceeding.*

Single window normalization programming

11 Turn the ignition to the On position.
12 Lower the appropriate window until it is in the fully Down position and continue holding the switch in the Down position for an additional five full seconds.
13 Raise the window to the full Up position (Closed). Continue holding the switch in the Up position for an additional five full seconds.
14 The window should now be programmed and normalized for the express up and down functions.
15 Verify proper operation. Repeat steps if necessary.

All window normalization programming

16 Turn the ignition to the On position.
17 Starting with the left and right rear windows in the full Up position, press and hold the appropriate window switch until the rear window is in the complete Down position. Hold the window switch for an additional five full seconds.
18 Raise the window to the full Up position and continue to hold the switch for an additional five full seconds.
19 Perform the same procedure on the remaining rear window.
20 Follow the procedure on the remaining front windows starting with the driver's side window.
21 The windows should now be programmed and normalized for the the express up and down functions.
22 Verify proper operation. Repeat steps if necessary.

---

27   Power door locks, keyless entry, key fob, transmitter, key and integrated transmitter, immobilizer, and garage door opener - description, removal and installation, and programming

---

Note: *These models are equipped with a Body Control Module (BCM). System diagnostic information is linked to the BCM. This allows for a quick and accurate diagnosis and in-depth troubleshooting with a professional-grade scan tool. These scan tools are expensive, and are not the type of scan tool you will find at a local parts store for code reading. Have the vehicle diagnosed by a dealership service department or a qualified independent automotive repair facility.*

Door locks

1 The power door lock system operates the door lock actuators mounted in each door. The system consists of the switches, actuators, lock and unlock relays, Body Control Module (BCM) and associated wiring. Diagnosis can usually be limited to simple checks of the wiring connections and actuators for minor faults that can be easily repaired.
2 Power door lock systems are operated by bi-directional solenoids located in the doors. The lock actuators are mounted as part of the door latch. Remove the door latch for access to the door lock actuator. The lock switches have two operating positions: Lock and Unlock. These switches send a signal to the BCM, which in turn sends a signal to the door lock relays, the relays then send the needed voltage to each of the door lock solenoids.
3 If you are unable to locate the trouble using the following general steps, consult your dealer service department or other qualified repair shop.
4 Always check the circuit protection first. Some vehicles use a combination of circuit breakers and fuses. Refer to the wiring diagrams at the end of this manual.
5 Check for voltage at the switches. If no voltage is present, check the fuse first. If the fuse is good then check the wiring between the fuse panel and the switches for an open lead.
6 If voltage is present, test the switch for continuity. Replace it if there's not continuity in both switch positions. There should be a voltage input and, when the switch is depressed, voltage should be going out on the appropriate lead. Follow the wiring diagram for the actual wire and position on the switch. To remove the switch, use a flat-bladed trim tool to pry out the door/window switch assembly.
7 If the switch has continuity, check the wiring between the switch, BCM, door lock relay and the door lock solenoid.
8 If all but one lock solenoids operate, remove the trim panel from the affected door (see Chapter 11) and check for voltage at the solenoid while the lock switch is operated. One of the wires should have positive voltage in the Lock position; the other lead should have positive voltage in the Unlock position.
9 If the inoperative solenoid is receiving positive voltage on one lead and negative on the other, the solenoid is most likely defective. Check the connections for good contact; if the connection is good, replace the solenoid.
10 If the inoperative solenoid isn't receiving voltage or ground, check for an open or short in the wire between the lock solenoid and the relay. A good method of non-destructive testing is to squeeze the rubber corrugated tubing and search with your fingers for an individual wire. Follow the wire as far as possible and feel for any breaks in the leads.

Note: *It's not uncommon for wires to break in the portion of the harness between the body and door (opening and closing the door fatigues and eventually breaks the wires).*

Note: *On the models covered by this manual, power door lock system communication goes through the Body Control Module. If the above tests do not pinpoint a problem, take the vehicle to a dealer or other qualified shop with the proper scan tool to retrieve trouble codes from the BCM. Replacing of some components may result in programming issues. To avoid replacing good components, always test thoroughly before any parts are deemed faulty.*

Keyless entry system

11 The keyless entry system consists of a remote control transmitter (key fob) that sends a coded signal to a receiver, which then

27.13 Separate the metal key from the key fob

27.14 Carefully separate the case halves. . .

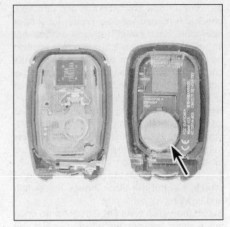

27.15. . . then pry out the battery

operates the door lock system. The receiver antennas are located in the rear bumper fascia, rear compartment, center console, instrument panel, and the front doors.

Note: *The keyless entry system requires the use of a factory level scanner to diagnose and repair. See your local dealership or other qualified repair shop for any repairs.*

12   Replace the battery in the key fob when it fails to transmit a signal to the locks at a distance of ten feet. Normal range should be about 30 feet.

Note: *To verify your key fob is transmitting correctly, or to check and see how strong the battery signal is, find a repair shop or a tire shop that has a TPMS (Tire Pressure Monitor System) scan tool. These scanners have a feature that can detect the strength of the signal produced by your key fob.*

Key fob battery replacement

13   Remove the metal key **(see illustration)** from the key fob.

14   Use a coin, a pocket screwdriver, or the metal key to carefully separate the case halves **(see illustration)**.

15   Before removing the battery, note the orientation of the positive and negative terminals **(see illustration)**.

16   Snap the case halves together.

Transmitter programming - adding keys

Note: *There are two methods of "adding keys" but only one method for programming the transmitter when erasing all the keys such as when purchasing a used car. Programming new keys requires a scanner, however, adding an additional key can be done without a scanner. The procedures that follow are for "adding" an additional key only.*

Note: *The key "adding" procedure will erase any of the keys that were previously programmed. The key "adding" feature is not a replacement for programming all new keys. This procedure will not learn any immobilizer information passed between the BCM and the ECM. This procedure only adds the latest key*

to the next available programming slot in the memory system.

Note: *A total of eight transmitters can be stored in memory.*

Note: *This procedure may be used with or without the existing learned keys present. If the original programmed keys are present, remove them from the vehicle. This procedure will unlearn all previously learned keys.*

Note: *Performing the following steps require close attention to details and the procedures. Failure to follow the steps exactly will result in the key not being programmed. Perform these steps at your own risk. If you are at all unsure of completing the tasks correctly, take your vehicle to a dealer repair shop or a other qualified repair facility.*

Note: *The following procedure is for vehicles with RPO BTM (keyless start) and without Service Programming System (SPS) only. USA models only. All other models require the use of a scanner to perform the transmitter programming and key recognition.*

With RPO BTM (without SPS)

17   Insert the correctly mechanically cut key into the door lock cylinder on the driver's door.

18   Turn the key to the unlock position 5 times within 10 seconds.

19   The Driver Information Center (DIC) will light up and display "Remote Learn Pending - Please Wait".

20   After 10 minutes the DIC will display "Press Engine Start Button to Learn".

21   Press the ignition button to start the vehicle.

22   The DIC will change display to "Remote Learn Pending - Please Wait".

23   Repeat the same steps two additional times. Actual time should be 30 minutes from initial start to the end of the programming.

24   At this point all previous keys have been erased. All keys can now be relearned during the next process.

25   The DIC will display "Ready for Remote #1".

26   Place the new key into the key pocket which is located at the rear of the center console storage area.

27   Press the ignition switch button. When the key is learned, the DIC will display that it is ready to program the next key.

28   Remove the now programmed key from the key pocket and press its unlock button.

29   Repeat the above steps for any additional keys.

30   When all the keys have been programmed, press and hold the ignition switch for five seconds. This will allow you to exit the programming mode.

With SPS and BTM

Note: *Models with SPS (Service Programming System), require the use of a factory level scanner. See your local dealership or independent repair facility for programming and repair.*

Key with Integrated transmitter - replacing or adding keys

Warning: *Replacing and Adding keys are two different things entirely. Be sure you have selected the appropriate procedure before attempting the repairs. The following procedures show the procedures "with" or "without" SPS (Service Programming System) equipped vehicles. Select the appropriate procedure that matches your vehicle.*

Replacing keys

Replacing keys (with SPS)

Note: *To replace keys with SPS requires the use of a scanner. See your local dealership or independent repair facility.*

Replacing keys (without SPS) (United States and Mexico only)

Note: *You must have two programmable keys to perform this procedure.*

Note: *A total of eight keys can be stored. This procedure will only learn the key information and not any immobilizer information.*

31   With a blank key, turn the ignition On (engine off).

32   Watch the security indicator - after 10 minutes the indicator will turn Off.

33   Now turn the ignition Off and wait 5 seconds.

34 Repeat the steps two more times (for a total of three key cycles equivalent to 30 minutes).

35 Start the vehicle with the newly "learned" key.

36 Add more keys by using the Add keys procedures.

Adding keys

Adding keys (with SPS)

Note: *To add keys with SPS requires the use of a scanner. See your local dealership or independent repair facility.*

Adding keys (without SPS) (United States - only)

Note: *Up to eight keys can be learned. All keys must be mechanically cut to match the vehicle.*

Note: *You must have two previously "learned" keys to perform this procedure.*

37 With the original "learned" key, turn the ignition On.

38 Turn the key to Off and remove the key.

39 With the second "learned" key, turn the ignition On.

40 Turn the key to Off and remove the key.

41 Within 10 seconds; insert the key that needs to be "learned".

42 Leave the key in the ignition (ignition On) for five seconds.

43 The key has now been "learned".

Garage door opener - removal and installation

44 Remove the roof console (see Chapter 11).

45 Remove the fasteners that secure the garage door opener transmitter bracket in place.

46 Pull the garage door transmitter downward and disconnect the electrical connector.

47 Transfer any components or brackets to the replacement transmitter.

48 Installation is the reverse of removal.

49 Program the garage door as described in the vehicle's owner's manual.

---

28 Electric side view mirrors - description

Note: *These models are equipped with a Body Control Module (BCM). Several systems are linked to a centralized control module that allows simple and accurate troubleshooting, but only with a professional-grade scan tool. The Body Control Module governs the door locks, the power windows, the ignition lock and security system, the interior lights, the Daytime Running Lights system, the horn, the windshield wipers, the heating/air conditioning system and the power mirrors. In the event of malfunction with this system, have the vehicle diagnosed by a dealership service department or other qualified automotive repair facility.*

1 The electric rear view mirrors use two motors to move the glass; one for up and down adjustments and one for left-right adjustments.

Some vehicles are equipped with memory mirrors as well. These mirrors are an integral part of the power seat memory unit as well as incorporated with the Body Control Module (BCM). If there is a problem with these systems it is advised to seek out a qualified independent repair facility or your local dealer.

2 The control switch has a selector portion which sends voltage to the left or right side mirror. With the ignition in the ACC position and the engine Off, roll down the windows and operate the mirror control switch through all functions (left-right and up-down) for both the left and right side mirrors.

3 Listen carefully for the sound of the electric motors running in the mirrors.

4 If the motors can be heard but the mirror glass doesn't move, there's probably a problem with the drive mechanism inside the mirror. Power mirrors have no user-serviceable parts inside - a defective mirror must be replaced as a unit (see Chapter 11).

5 If the mirrors don't operate and no sound comes from the mirrors, check the fuses (see Section 3).

6 If the fuses are OK, remove the mirror control switch. Have the switch continuity checked by a dealer service department or other qualified shop.

7 Check the ground connections.

8 If the mirror still doesn't work, remove the mirror and check the wires at the mirror for voltage.

9 If there's not voltage in each switch position, check the circuit between the mirror and control switch for opens and shorts.

Note: *If the mirror is inoperative, try holding the switch in one of the directions and swing the door open and closed. If there is a wiring harness break in the door jamb you may occasionally make contact long enough to avoid removing the mirror from the door for further testing. This will also give you some clue as to where the break is rather than testing things in one given position.*

10 If there's voltage, remove the mirror and test it off the vehicle with jumper wires. Before testing check the wiring diagram for the correct leads that have to be used for each position. Applying voltage to the wrong leads can damage the mirror drive motors. Replace the mirror if it fails this test.

---

29 Power seats - description

1 These models feature a six-way or an eight-way seat option. The six-way seat is without memory, while the eight-way seat has a four-way lumbar support, memory, heat/air conditioning functions, as well as a microprocessor for the seat memory system. The seats are powered by three reversible motors, mounted in one housing, that are controlled by switches on the side of the seat. Each switch changes the direction of seat travel by reversing polarity to the drive motor. The non-memory seat systems (6-way and non-memory passenger seats) uses direct voltage from the seat switch to the seat motors. The memory seat systems (8-way) uses data-line signals and voltages

coming from the memory processor MSM (Memory Seat Module) then to the seat motors.

Note: *To aid in your at-home diagnostics, follow these basic procedures before you need to take your vehicle to the dealer or independent repair shop for more in-depth diagnostics.*

2 Look under the seat for any objects that may be binding or causing the seat not to move at all.

3 Determine if the circuit breaker is functioning properly, (see Section 3).

4 Operate the seat controls in all directions and listen for sounds coming from the seat motors. Listen for clicks, grinding noises, and other unusual sounds that might indicate a problem with the mechanical or electrical components of the seat.

a) *A grinding sound with seat switch depressed* - indicates either a broken gear (usually plastic gears) or the cable between the motor and the seat transmission has stripped.

b) *A click or thud with seat switch depressed* - this could indicate a frozen motor or seat transmission that is in a bind or a faulty switch or motor.

c) *A dimming dome light with the seat switch depressed* - indicates stuck motor, seat transmission, or shorted wiring.

d) *One side of the seat moves but not the other* - indicates a stuck track, broken cable, broken seat frame, jammed track.

e) *Seat will not remember the preset memory positions* - faulty MSM, incorrect setting procedures used, battery was recently disconnected.

Note: *If the motor is not grinding, and there is not enough room to get under the seat and attach a multimeter to the motor leads, the next best thing is to use a scanner. A quality scanner can perform a bi-directional control and operate the seat motors without the need of removing the seat from the vehicle.*

6-way seat diagnosis

5 If the motor isn't getting voltage, remove the switch and check for voltage. If there's no voltage to the switch, check the wiring between the fuse block and the switch. If there's battery voltage at the switch, check the other terminals for voltage while moving the switch around. If the switch is OK, check for an open in the wiring between the switch and motor assembly.

8-way memory seat diagnosis

6 The Memory Seat Module (MSM) sends the necessary voltage to the seat motors by way of a circuit breaker in the instrument panel fuse box. A separate fuse sends the needed voltage for the logic circuits of the MSM. The seat switch is connected directly to the MSM. The MSM is bolted to the underside of the driver's seat cushion. The signal to and from the switch is on the GMLAN CAN data-line and is not a readable signal with a mulitmeter. Proper scanning equipment is needed to diagnose these systems efficiently. See your local independent repair shop or the nearest dealer for diagnostics.

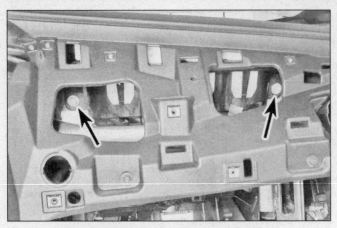

31.4a Remove the airbag upper bolts. . .

31.4b. . .then disconnect the airbag safety lock and connector (1),
release the connector from the crossbar (2) and
remove the airbag lower bolt (3)

30   Data Link Communication system - description

Note: *The vehicles covered by this manual have a complex electrical system, encompassing many power accessories, and a number of separate electronic modules. This section is an overview description of how the system works, and not intended as a guide in any repairs.*

1   All this data passes through several computer systems for different reasons and at different speeds. The data travels on a pair of wires called the CAN or Computer Adaptable Network. This twisted together pair of wires read a high and low signal between 0 and 5 volts and are continuously changing amplitude. This amplitude change allows the processor on the other end of the wire to read the coded info as to whether it is of concern to that particular processor or it needs to ignore it and allow the information to pass through and onto another processor or module.

2   The length, speed, and numerical order of the 1's and 0's that make up the data stream determine the complexity and destination of the information. The higher the number for example, would indicate that particular message needs to get to where it needs to be faster than a lower priority message would. For instance, the data from your steering wheel controls for the radio station you are seeking isn't nearly as important as a message that the engine is overheating. However, both messages travel simultaneously down the same pair of twisted wires on the data bus line.

3   The Powertrain Control Module (PCM) is responsible for engine performance, and the Transmission Control Module (TCM) (if equipped) watches over and determines the transmission/transaxle operation. Communications with these processors and other modules are all interlinked through the Data Link Communication (DLC).

4   The DLC (Data Link Connector) is the portal where you can connnect a scan tool and read the information or perform other function tests. This 16-pin DLC connector is

found below the driver's side of the dash.

5   Besides the PCM and TCM, the DLC communicates with the SDM, SRS, EBCM, TPMS, IP, SRS, TCM, HVAC, PSCM, ADAS, SMCM, TDS, BCM, HMICM, TCICM, MSM and many more systems on today's vehicles.

6   All of the modules in the vehicle have associated trouble codes, and in a lot of cases some codes cross-over to other modules or in fact, "tattletale" on each other. For example, if a certain module is not on the bus line (not communicating) a message is sent that it is not responding or another module may need part of the information from the non-communicating module and without that information it can't work correctly. Meaning - the problem isn't with the module that is providing the code, the problem is with the module that is not communicating with the module that is providing the code.

Note: *A scan tool is required to extract any stored trouble codes. Lower quality scanners have limited access to various systems and their related codes. The lower the quality of the scanner the more likely the only codes it will read are the generic type that start with the first number as a 0.*

31   Airbag system - general information and removal and installation

Warning: *Before working around or servicing any airbag or SRS component, disconnect the cable from the negative battery terminal (see Chapter 5) and wait at least 10 minutes for the airbag system capacitors to fully discharge. Accidental deployment of the system can cause injury or even death.*

1   All models are equipped with a Supplemental Restraint System (SRS), more commonly known as the airbag system. The airbag system is designed to protect the driver and the front seat passenger from serious injury in the event of a head-on or side impact collision. Airbag systems consist of the impact sensors, airbag modules (including: driver's airbag, passenger's airbag, side curtain/roof rail airbags and

side impact airbags), seat bolster and seat air bags, seat belt tensioners and a sensing/diagnostic module mounted under the center console. All of the related airbag wiring harnesses are wrapped with yellow or orange tape and have double locking tabs at their connectors. Read through this entire Section before removing and/or replacing any airbag component.

Airbag modules

Driver's airbag

Note: *See Chapter 10 for the removal/installation of the driver's airbag and clockspring.*

2   The airbag inflator module contains a housing incorporating the cushion (airbag) and inflator unit, mounted in the center of the steering wheel. The inflator assembly is mounted on the back of the housing over a hole through which gas is expelled, inflating the bag almost instantaneously when an electrical signal is sent from the system. A spiral cable (or clockspring) assembly on the steering column under the steering wheel carries this signal to the module. This clockspring can transmit an electrical signal regardless of steering wheel position.

Passenger's airbag

3   The airbag is mounted inside the right side of the instrument panel cover, in the area above the glove box. It's similar in design to the driver's airbag, except that it's larger than the steering wheel unit. The trim cover (on the side of the instrument panel that faces toward the passenger) is textured and colored to match the instrument panel and has a molded seam that splits open when the bag inflates. The passenger's airbag is designed to spread not only out towards the passenger but also to encompass the dash and windshield area to prevent the passenger from accelerating into the glass.

4   To remove it, the instrument panel cover needs to be removed first (see Chapter 11), which also requires the airbag-to-crossbar securing bolts to be removed and the airbag connector to be disconnected **(see illustrations)**. It can then be released from the instrument panel cover once the cover is on a bench.

5   Installation is the reverse of removal.

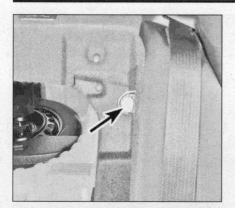

31.9a With the seat back folded down, remove the upper bolt. . .

31.9b. . .then remove the lower bolt. . .

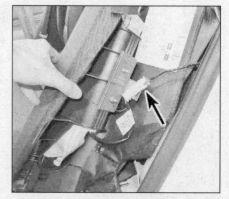

31.9c. . .pull out and rotate the side bolster airbag to disconnect the electrical connector

Passenger presence system

6 The passenger presence system is designed to determine if someone is sitting in the passenger's front seat or not. This is done by calculating the weight in the seat. Each time a person that is more than the calibrated weight sits in the seat, the passenger's airbag is activated and is ready for any collision or impact. This system prevents injury from the airbag deployment to a small child that would not meet the weight requirements that was occupying the passenger's front seat by turning off the passenger's airbag under those conditions.

Side curtain (roof rail) airbags

7 In addition to the side-impact airbags, extra side-impact protection is also provided by side-curtain airbags on some models. These are long airbags that, in the event of a side impact, come out of the headliner at each side of the vehicle between the side windows and the seats. They are designed to protect the heads of both front seat and rear seat passengers.

Side impact airbags

8 These airbags are located in the outboard sides of the front and rear seats. They are deployed during the same conditions that would trigger a roof rail airbag deployment.

9 Refer to the following illustrations and their captions for removal **(see illustrations)**. Remove the rear seat cushion first (see Chapter 11).

10 Installation is the reverse of removal.

Knee bolster airbags

11 The knee bolsters are below the steering column and the front passenger's knee area. These are designed to cushion the forward motion of the front seat occupants in a frontal collision.

12 Refer to the following illustrations and their captions for removal **(see illustrations)**. If equipped, remove the under-glovebox or under-column insulator shield (see Chapter 11).

13 Installation is the reverse of removal.

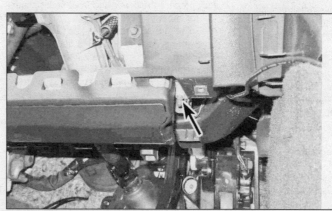

31.12a Remove the right side bolt. . .

31.12b. . .then the left side bolt (B) and disconnect the electrical connector (A) from the driver's side knee bolster airbag

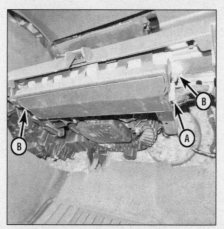

31.12c Disconnect the electrical connector (A) and remove the mounting bolts (B) from the passenger's side knee bolster airbag

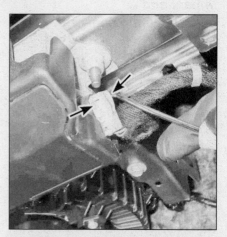

31.12d These types of SRS connectors are disconnected by pulling back the tabs at each side - using two screwdrivers or two pick tools may help ease the process

31.14 The airbag sensing and diagnostic module is located underneath the center console

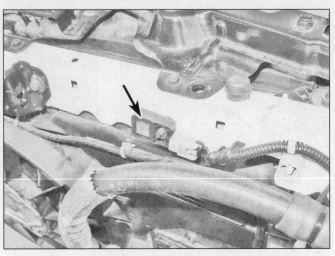

31.15 A front impact sensor, mounted on the radiator support

Sensing and diagnostic module

14   The sensing and diagnostic module supplies the current to the airbag system in the event of the collision, even if battery power is cut off. It checks this system every time the vehicle is started, causing the "AIR BAG" light to go on then off, if the system is operating properly. If there is a fault in the system, the light will go on and stay on, flash, or the dash will make a beeping sound. If this happens, the vehicle should be taken to your dealer or qualified independent shop immediately for service. This module is mounted under the center console **(see illustration)**. There is also a roll-over sensor located directly behind it on later models.

Warning: *The diagnostic module maintains a 23-volt reserve power in the unit after the key is turned off; the airbag system is still active even if the key is off. This built in safety feature is active for up to one minute after the key is turned off - keep this in mind when servicing the airbag system.*

Impact and discriminating sensors

15   Impact sensors **(see illustration)** are located in various locations in the vehicle. There are impact sensors at the front of the vehicle, in each door, and in the B- and C-pillars, depending on the vehicle. The sensing and diagnostic module uses these sensors to determine the severity of the impact or collision for airbag deployment. It is advised that no repairs are attempted on these sensors and should not be disconnected for any reason. If a sensor fails, a message is sent to the diagnostic module and the airbag warning light will illuminate.

Seat belt pre-tensioners

16   Some models are equipped with pyrotechnic (explosive) units in the front seat belt retracting mechanisms. During an impact that would trigger the airbag system, the airbag control unit also triggers the seat belt retractors. When the pyrotechnic charges go off, they accelerate the retractors to instantly take up any slack in the seat belt system to more fully prepare the driver and front seat passenger for impact.

17   The airbag system must be disabled any time work is done to or around the seats.

Warning: *Never strike the pillars or floorpan with a hammer or use an impact-driver tool in these areas unless the system is disabled.*

Disarming the system and other precautions

Warning: *Failure to follow these precautions could result in accidental deployment of the airbag.*

18   Whenever working in the vicinity of the steering wheel, steering column or any of the other SRS system components, the system must be disarmed.

To disarm the airbag system:

a) *Point the wheels straight ahead and turn the key to the Lock position.*
b) *Disconnect the cable from the negative battery terminal.*
c) *Wait at least two minutes for the back-up power supply to be depleted.*

Handling an airbag module:

19   Always keep the airbag opening (the trim side) pointed away from your body. Never place the airbag module on a bench or other surface with the airbag opening facing the surface. Always place the airbag module in a safe location with the airbag opening facing up.

20   Never measure the resistance of any SRS component. An ohmmeter has a built-in battery supply that could accidentally deploy the airbag.

21   Never use electrical welding equipment on a vehicle equipped with an airbag without first disconnecting the electrical connector for each airbag.

22   Never dispose of a live airbag module. Return it to a dealer service department or other qualified repair shop for safe deployment and disposal.

Component removal and installation

23   Refer to Chapter 10, Section 15 for the driver's airbag module and clockspring removal and installation procedures.

24   We don't recommend removing any of the other airbag modules. These jobs are best left to a professional.

---

32 Wiring diagrams - general information

---

1   Since it isn't possible to include all wiring diagrams for every year and model covered by this manual, the following diagrams are those that are typical and most commonly needed.

2   Prior to troubleshooting any circuits, check the fuses and circuit breakers (if equipped) to make sure they're in good condition. Make sure the battery is properly charged and check the cable connections (see Chapter 1).

3   When checking a circuit, make sure that all connectors are clean, with no broken or loose terminals. When disconnecting a connector, do not pull on the wires. Pull only on the connector housings themselves.

Wiring Diagrams - List

1 Starting and charging systems (without Start/Stop) - 2015 and earlier models (and 2016 Malibu Limited)
2 Starting and charging systems (with Start/Stop) - 2015 and earlier models (and 2016 Malibu Limited)
3 Starting and charging systems (without Start/Stop) - 2016 and later models (except 2016 Malibu Limited)
4 Starting and charging systems (with Start/Stop) - 2016 and 2017 models (except Malibu Limited)
5 Starting and charging systems (with Start/Stop) - 2018 and later models
6 Heating and air conditioning system (manual) - 2013 models
7 Heating and air conditioning system (automatic) - 2013 models
8 Heating and air conditioning system (manual) - 2014 and 2015 (and 2016 Malibu Limited) models
9 Heating and air conditioning system (automatic) - 2014 and 2015 (and 2016 Malibu Limited) models
10 Heating and air conditioning system (manual) - 2016 through 2018 models (except Malibu Limited)
11 Heating and air conditioning system (automatic) - 2016 and models
12 Heating and air conditioning system (automatic) - 2018 and later models
13 Heated seats - 2015 and earlier models (and 2016 Malibu Limited)
14 Heated seats - 2016 and later models (except Malibu Limited)
15 Engine cooling fans - 2015 and earlier models (and 2016 Malibu Limited)
16 Engine cooling fans - 2016 and later models (except Malibu Limited)
17 Power window system (Express Down) - 2015 and earlier models (and 2016 Malibu Limited)
18 Power window system (Express Up/Down) - 2015 and earlier models (and 2016 Malibu Limited)
19 Power window system (Express Down) - 2016 and later models (except Malibu Limited)
20 Power window system (Express Up/Down) - 2016 and later models (except Malibu Limited)
21 Power door locks - 2015 and earlier models (and 2016 Malibu Limited)
22 Power door locks - 2016 and later models (except Malibu Limited)
23 Windshield wiper and washer systems - 2015 and earlier models (and 2016 Malibu Limited)
24 Windshield wiper and washer systems (without Start/Stop) - 2016 and later models (except Malibu Limited)
25 Windshield wiper and washer systems (with Start/Stop) - 2016 and later models (except Malibu Limited)
26 Exterior lights - 2013 models (1 of 2)
27 Exterior lights - 2013 models (2 of 2)
28 Exterior lights - 2014 models (1 of 2)
29 Exterior lights - 2014 models (2 of 2)
30 Exterior lights (with halogen headlights) - 2015 and earlier models (and 2016 Malibu Limited) (1 of 2)
31 Exterior lights (with halogen headlights) - 2015 and earlier models (and 2016 Malibu Limited) (2 of 2)
32 Exterior lights (with xenon headlights) - 2015 and earlier models (and 2016 Malibu Limited) (1 of 2)
33 Exterior lights (with xenon headlights) - 2015 and earlier models (and 2016 Malibu Limited) (2 of 2)
34 Exterior lights - 2016 through 2018 models (except Malibu Limited) (1 of 2)
35 Exterior lights (without LED taillights) - 2016 through 2018 models (except Malibu Limited) (2 of 2)
36 Exterior lights (without LED taillights) - 2019 and later models (1 of 2)
37 Exterior lights (without LED taillights) - 2019 and later models (2 of 2)
38 LED taillights - 2016 and later models
39 Interior lights - 2015 and earlier models (and 2016 Malibu Limited)
40 Interior lights - 2016 and later models (except 2016 Malibu Limited)
41 Audio system - 2013 models (1 of 2)
42 Audio system - 2013 models (2 of 2)
43 Audio system - 2014 and 2015 models (and 2016 Malibu Limited) (1 of 2)
44 Audio system - 2014 and 2015 models (and 2016 Malibu Limited) (2 of 2)
45 Audio system - 2016 through 2018 models (without amplifier RPO IO5, IO6, IOA, IP1) (1 of 2)
46 Audio system - 2016 through 2018 models (without amplifier RPO IO5, IO6, IOA, IP1) (2 of 2)
47 Audio system - 2016 through 2018 models (with amplifier RPO IO5, IO6) (1 of 2)
48 Audio system - 2016 through 2018 models (with amplifier RPO IO5, IO6) (2 of 2)
49 Audio system - 2019 and later models (without amplifier RPO IOU, IOS) (1 of 2)
50 Audio system - 2019 and later models (without amplifier RPO IOU, IOS) (2 of 2)
51 Audio system - 2019 and later models (with amplifier RPO IOU, IOS) (1 of 2)
52 Audio system - 2019 and later models (with amplifier RPO IOU, IOS) (2 of 2)
53 Audio system - 2019 and later models (with amplifier RPO IOR) (1 of 2)
54 Audio system - 2019 and later models (with amplifier RPO IOR) (2 of 2)
55 Fuel pump circuit - 2015 and earlier models (and 2016 Malibu Limited)/1.5L and 2.0L models [2016 and 2017])
56 Fuel pump circuit - 1.5L models (2018 and later)
57 Fuel pump circuit - 2.0L models (2018 and later)
58 Fuses and relays (1 of 11)
59 Fuses and relays (2 of 11)
60 Fuses and relays (3 of 11)
61 Fuses and relays (4 of 11)
62 Fuses and relays (5 of 11)
63 Fuses and relays (6 of 11)
64 Fuses and relays (7 of 11)
65 Fuses and relays (8 of 11)
66 Fuses and relays (9 of 11)
67 Fuses and relays (10 of 11)
68 Fuses and relays (11 of 11)

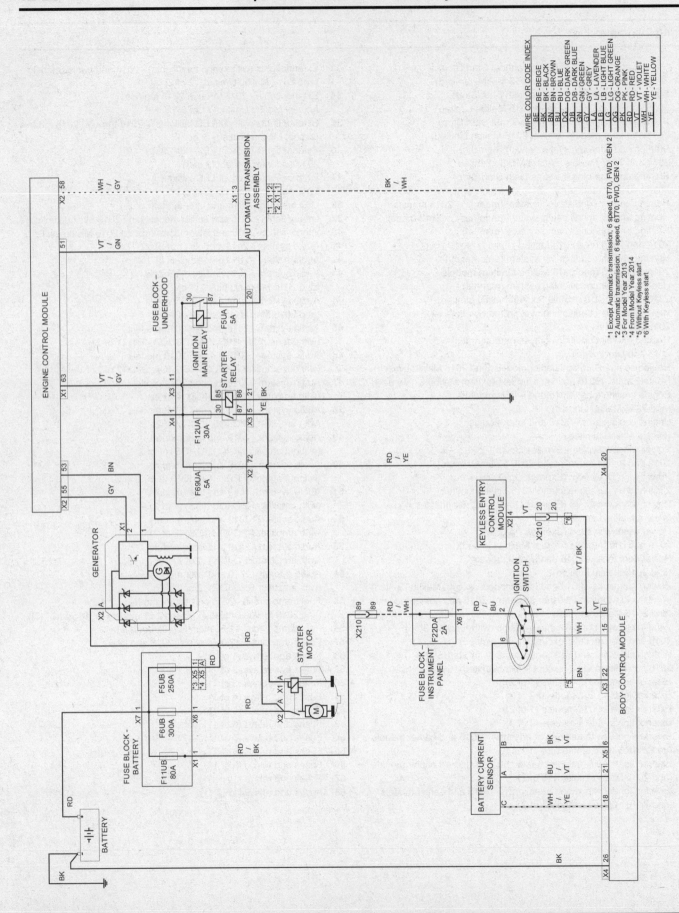

1. Starting and charging systems (without Start/Stop) - 2015 and earlier models (and 2016 Malibu Limited)

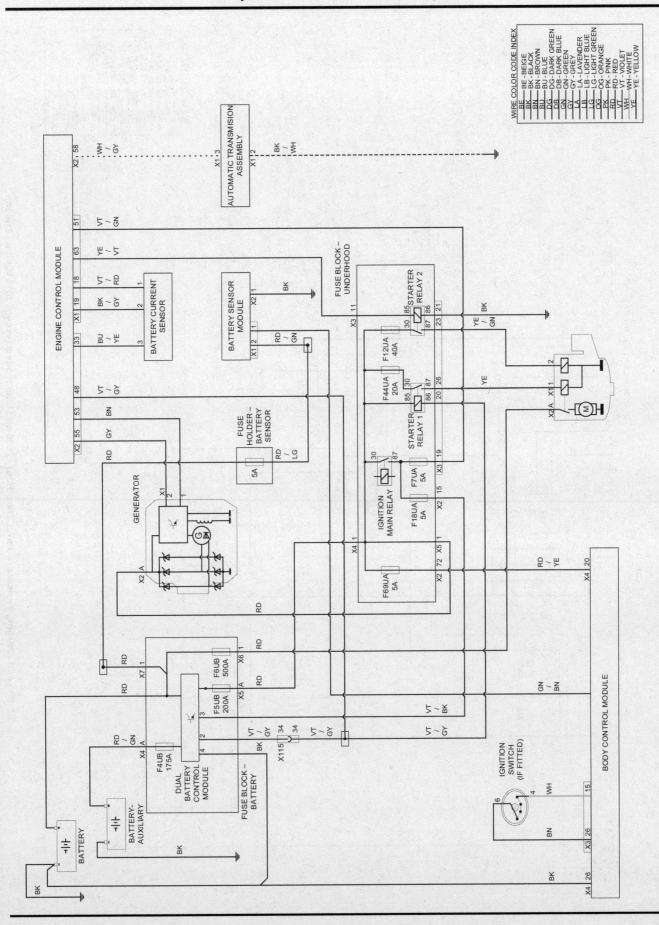

2. Starting and charging systems (with Start/Stop) - 2015 and earlier models (and 2016 Malibu Limited)

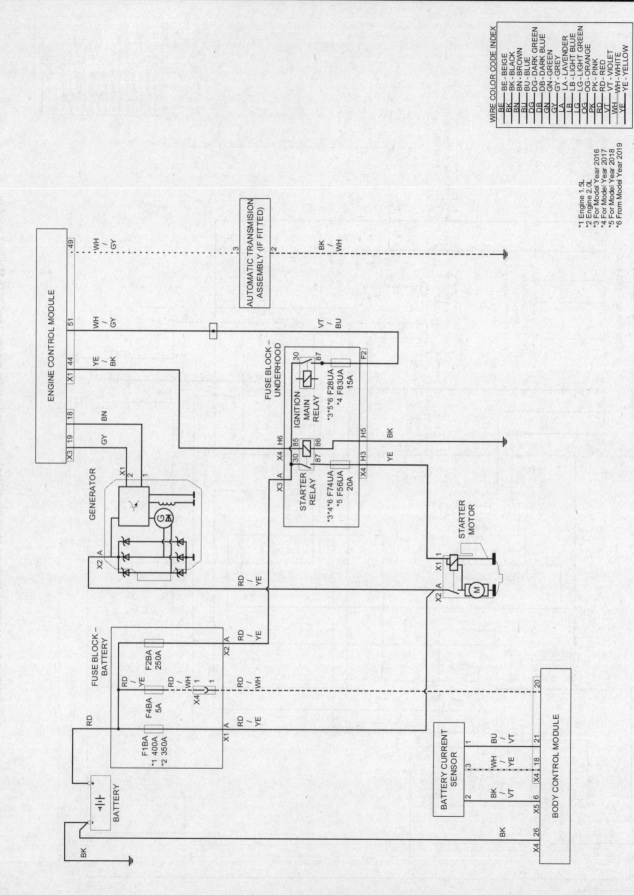

3. Starting and charging systems (without Start/Stop) - 2016 and later models (except 2016 Malibu Limited)

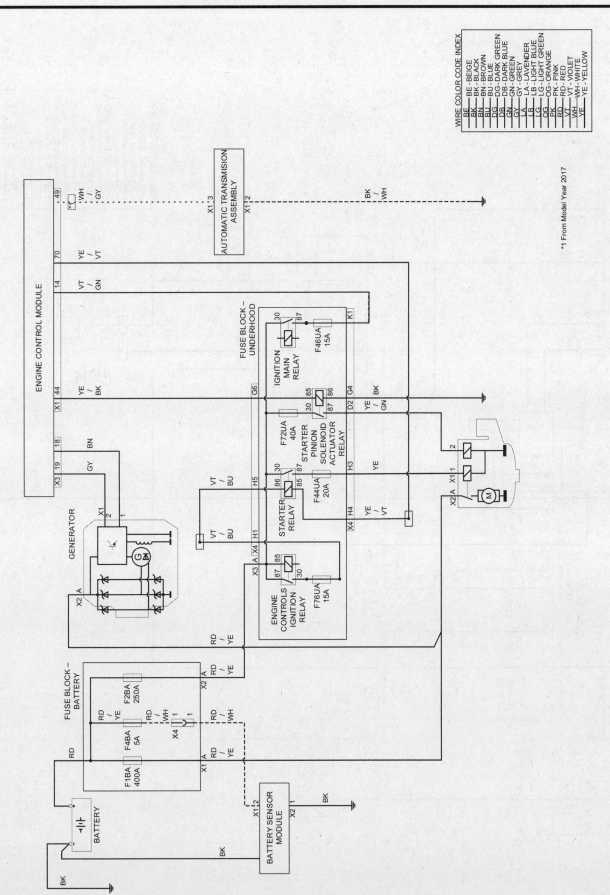

4. Starting and charging systems (with Start/Stop) - 2016 and 2017 models (except Malibu Limited)

*1 From Model Year 2017

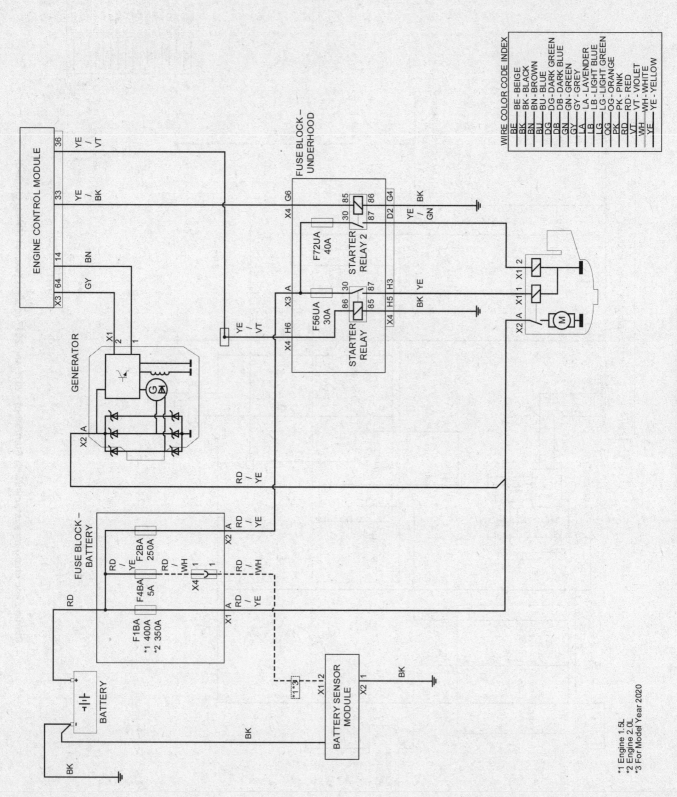

5. Starting and charging systems (with Start/Stop) - 2018 and later models

*1 Engine 1.5L
*2 Engine 2.0L
*3 For Model Year 2020

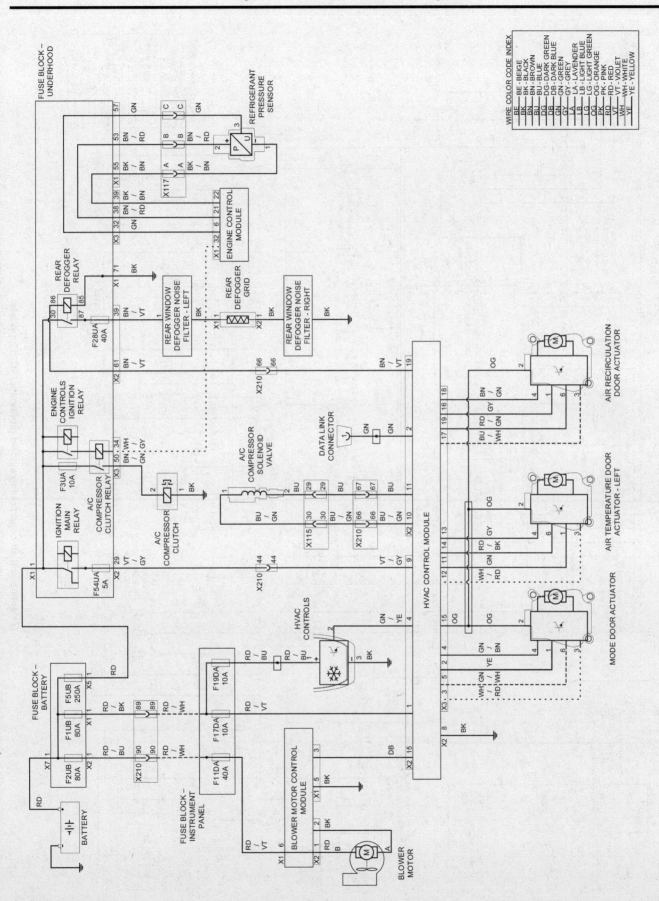

6. Heating and air conditioning system (manual) - 2013 models

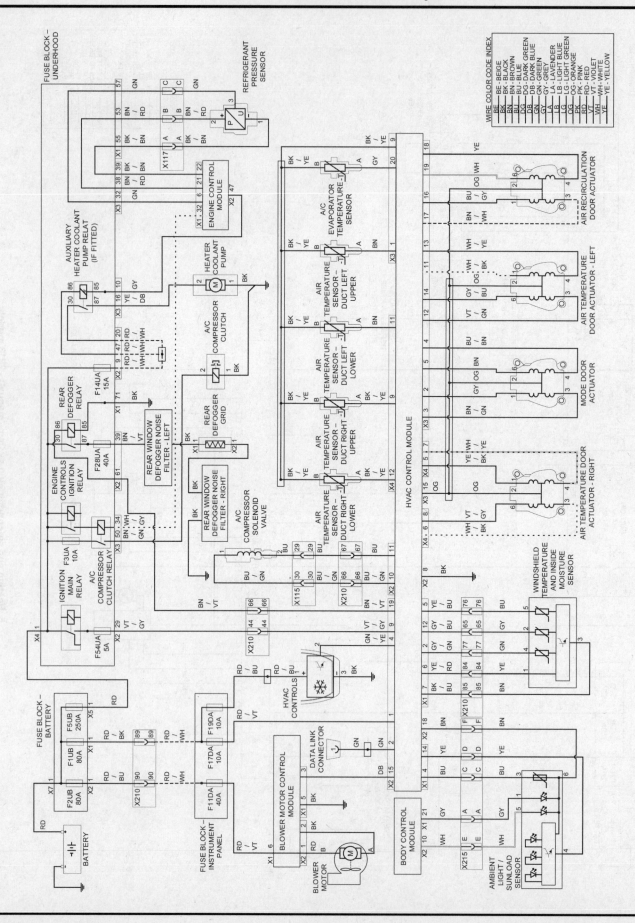

7. Heating and air conditioning system (automatic) - 2013 models

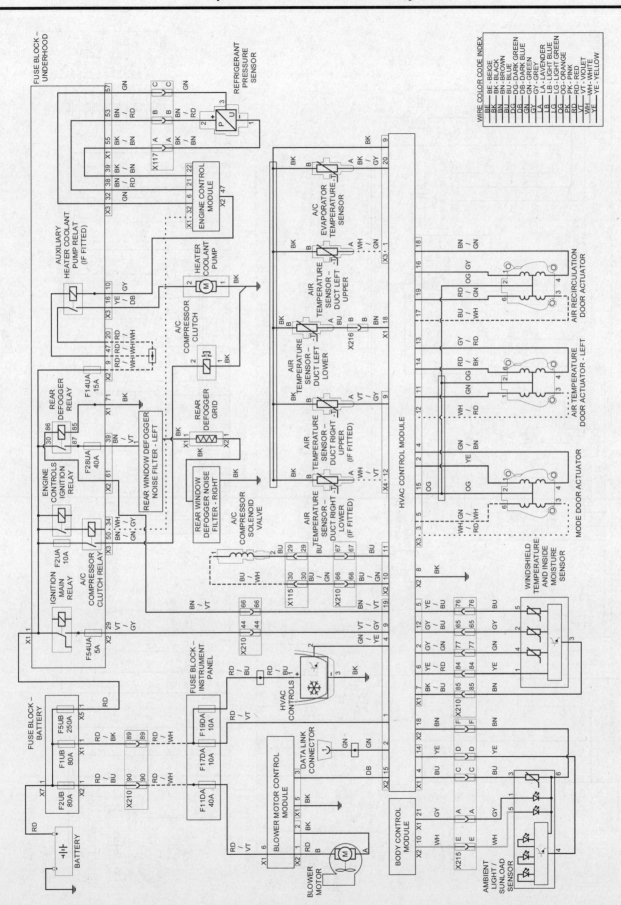

8. Heating and air conditioning system (manual) – 2014 and 2015 (and 2016 Malibu Limited) models

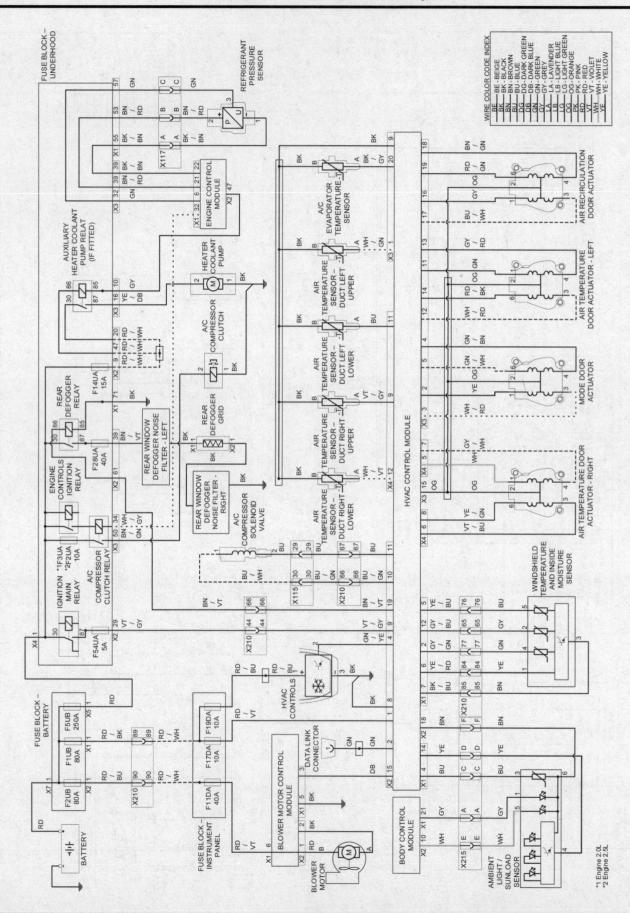

9. Heating and air conditioning system (automatic) - 2014 and 2015 (and 2016 Malibu Limited) models

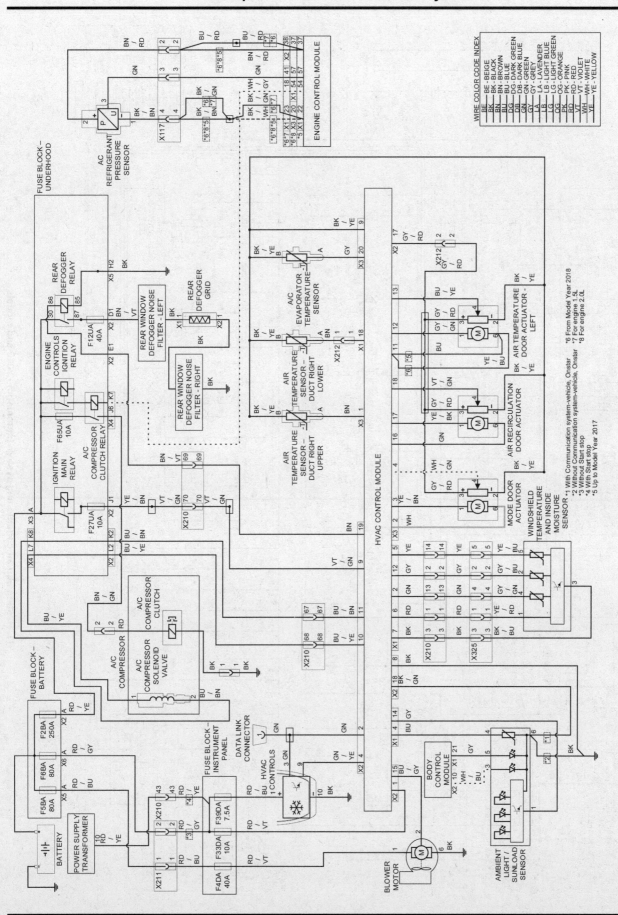

10.Heating and air conditioning system (manual) - 2016 through 2018 models (except Malibu Limited)

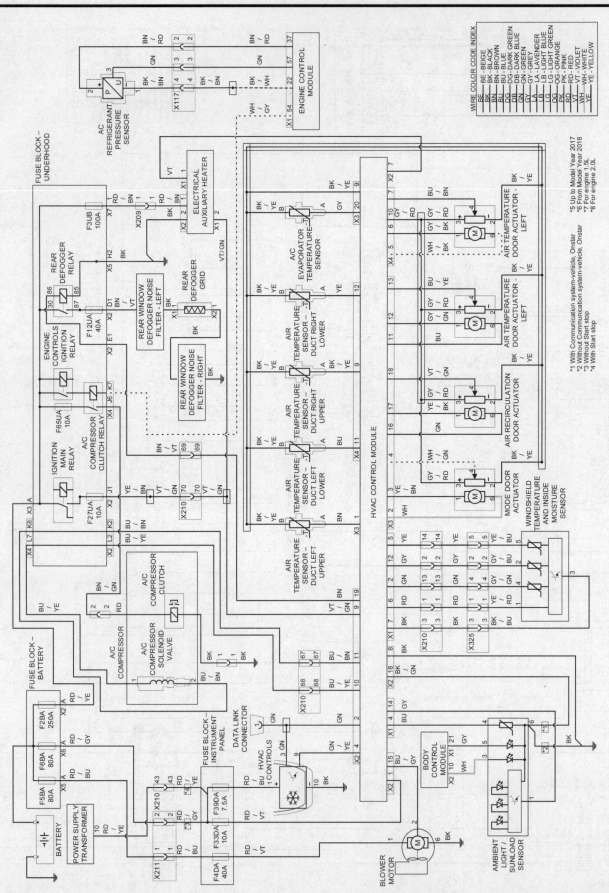

11. Heating and air conditioning system (automatic) - 2016 and models

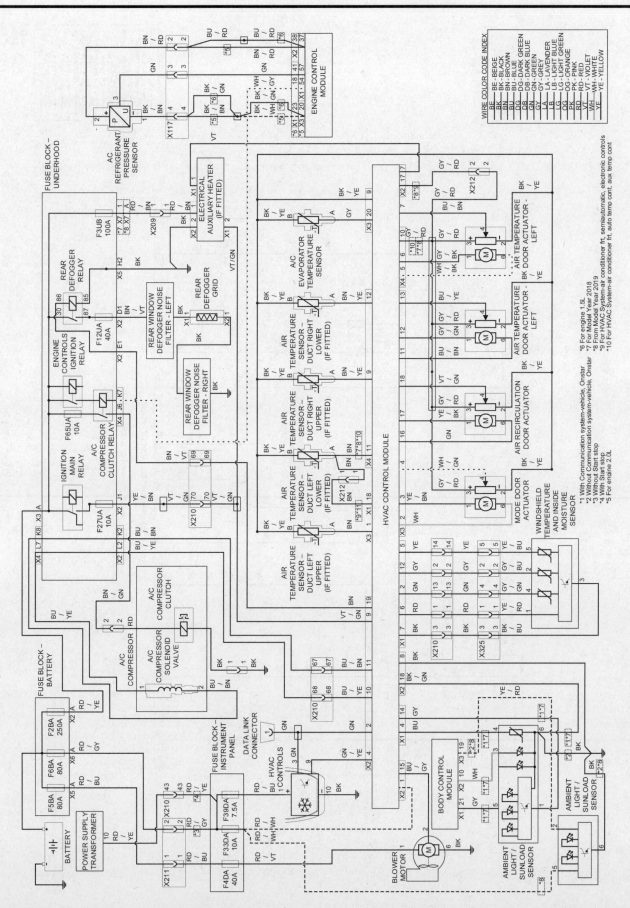

12. Heating and air conditioning system (automatic) - 2018 and later models

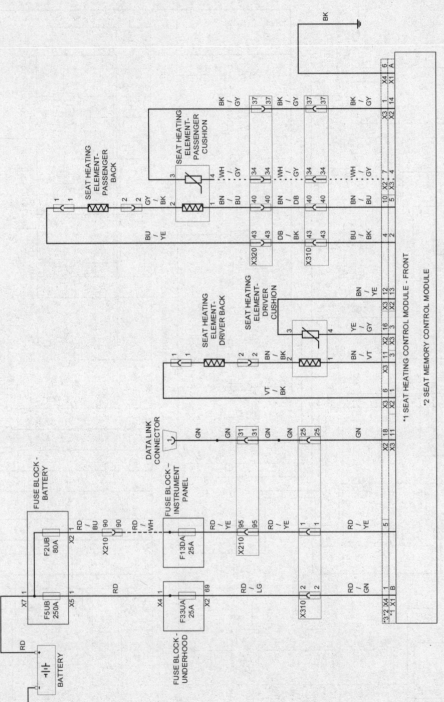

13. Heated seats - 2015 and earlier models (and 2016 Malibu Limited)

*1 Without Memory-seat, adjuster, mirror, power, driver, personalization
*2 With Memory-seat, adjuster, mirror, power, driver, personalization
*3 Up to 2015

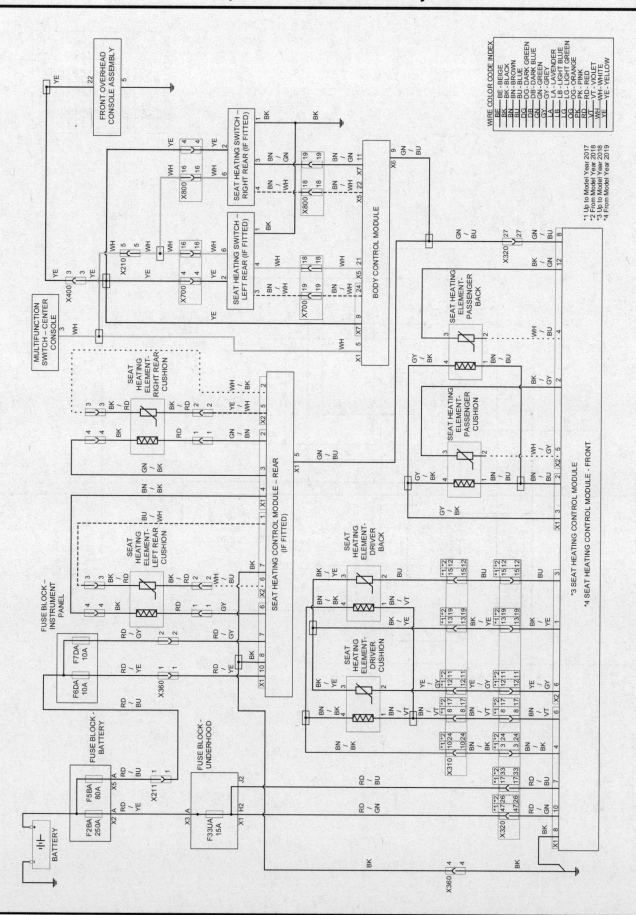

14. Heated seats - 2016 and later models (except Malibu Limited)

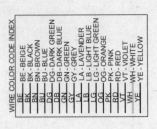

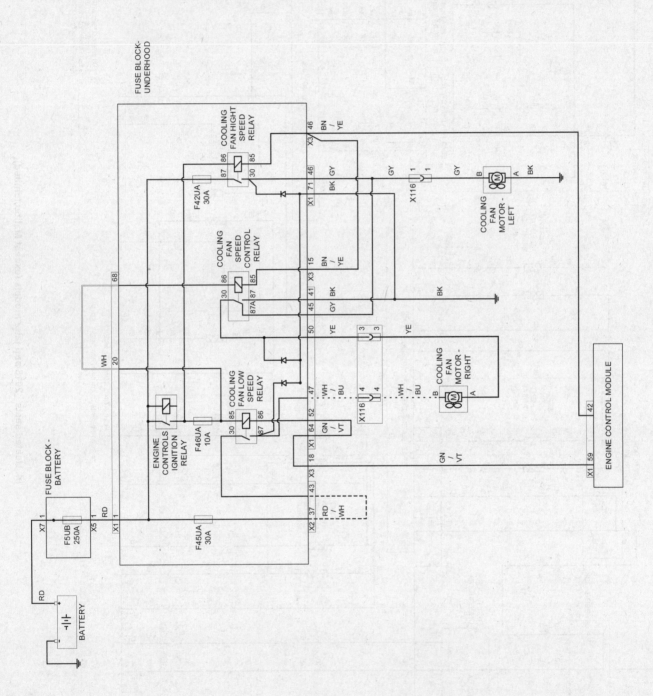

15. Engine cooling fans - 2015 and earlier models (and 2016 Malibu Limited)

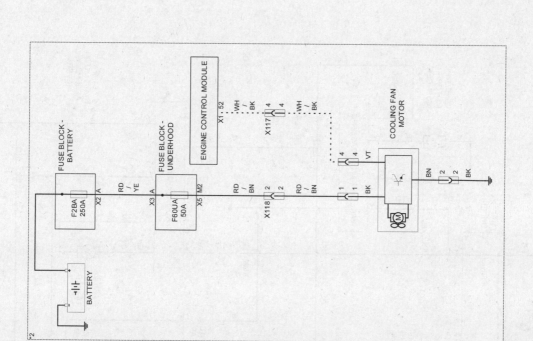

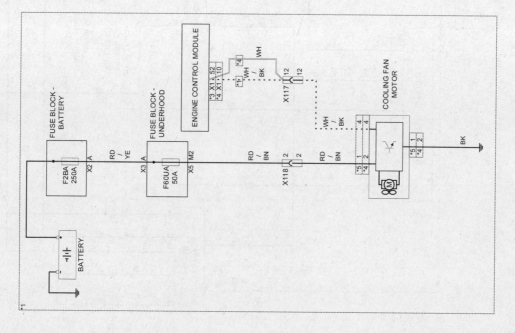

16. Engine cooling fans - 2016 and later models (except Malibu Limited)

*1 For engine 1.5L
*2 For engine 2.0L
*3 Up to Model Years 2017
*4 From Model Years 2018
*5 For Model Years 2020

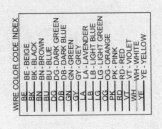

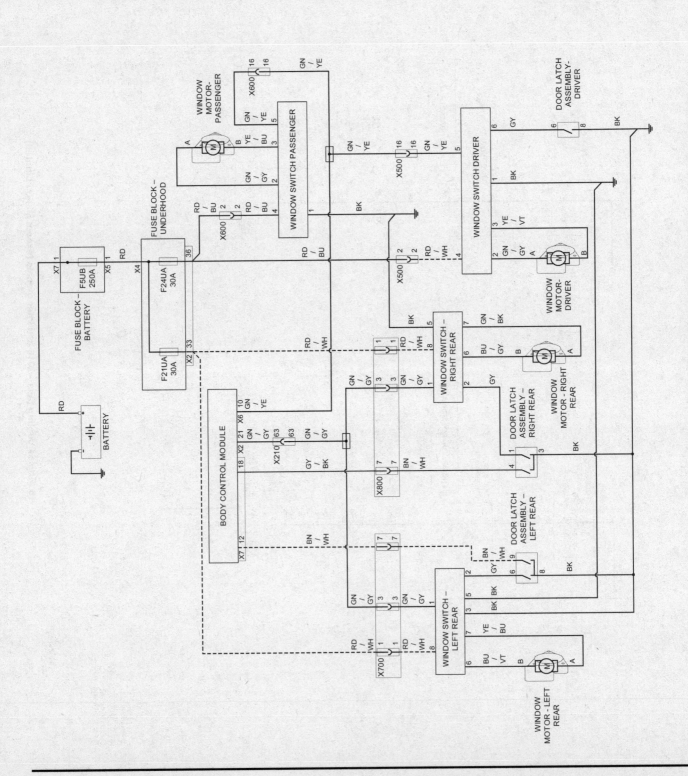

17. Power window system (Express Down) - 2015 and earlier models (and 2016 Malibu Limited)

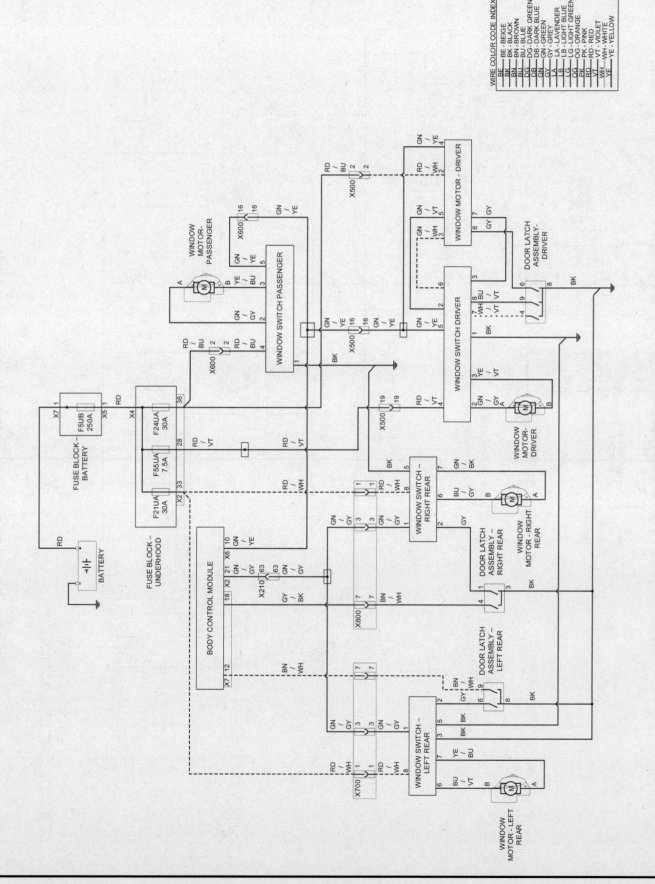

18. Power window system (Express Up/Down) - 2015 and earlier models (and 2016 Malibu Limited)

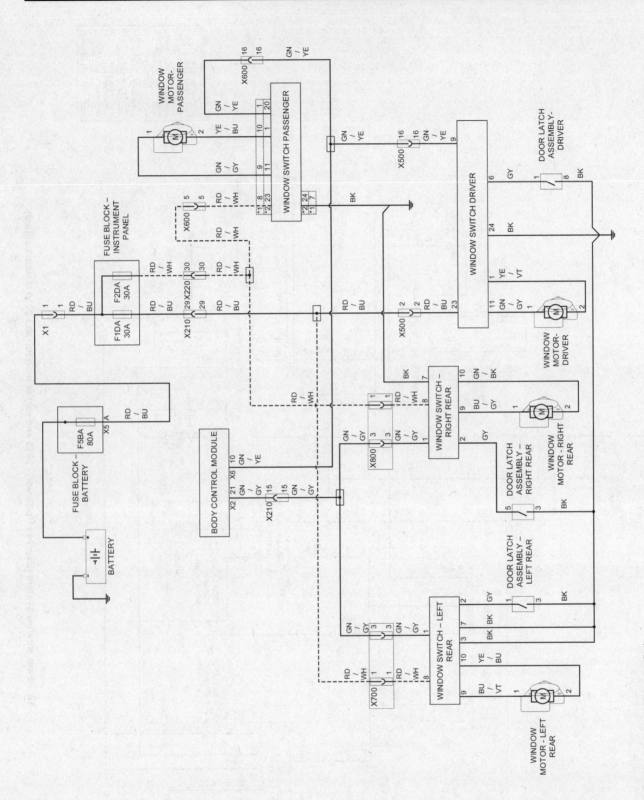

19. Power window system (Express Down) – 2016 and later models (except Malibu Limited)

*1 Without Memory-seat ajuster, mirror, power, driver, personalization
*2 With Memory-seat ajuster, mirror, power, driver, personalization

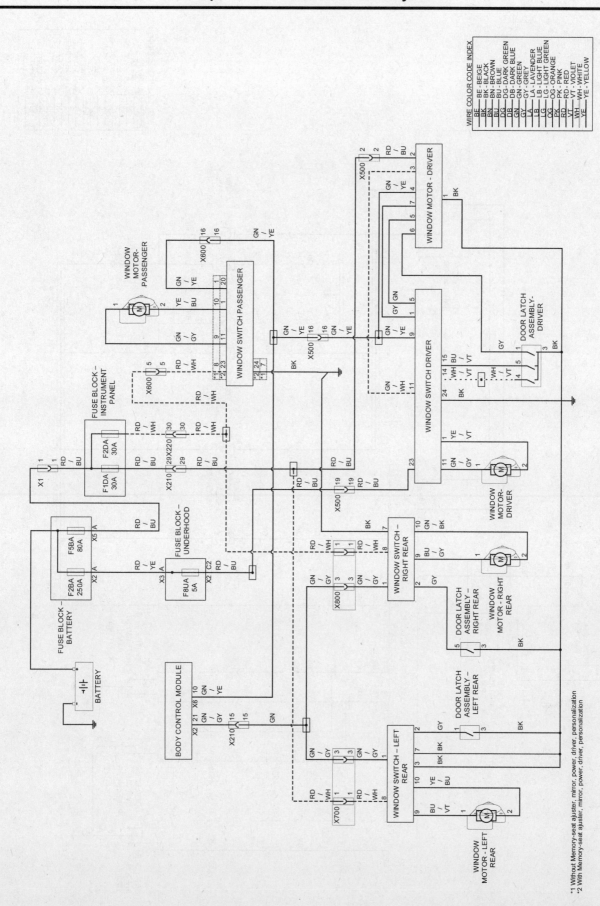

20. Power window system (Express Up/Down) - 2016 and later models (except Malibu Limited)

*1 Without Memory-seat ajuster, mirror, power, driver, personalization
*2 With Memory-seat ajuster, mirror, power, driver, personalization

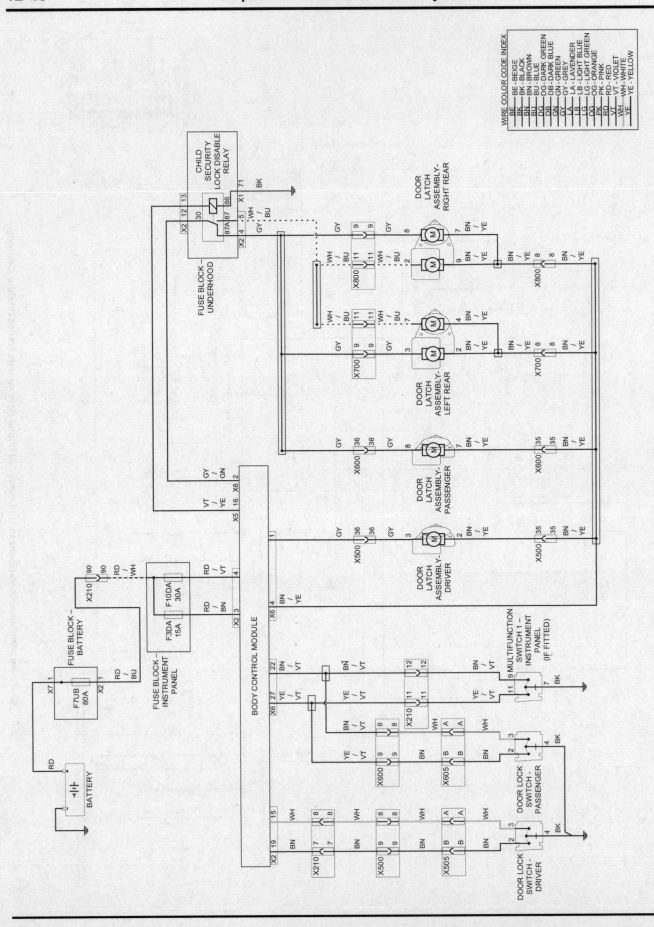

21. Power door locks - 2015 and earlier models (and 2016 Malibu Limited)

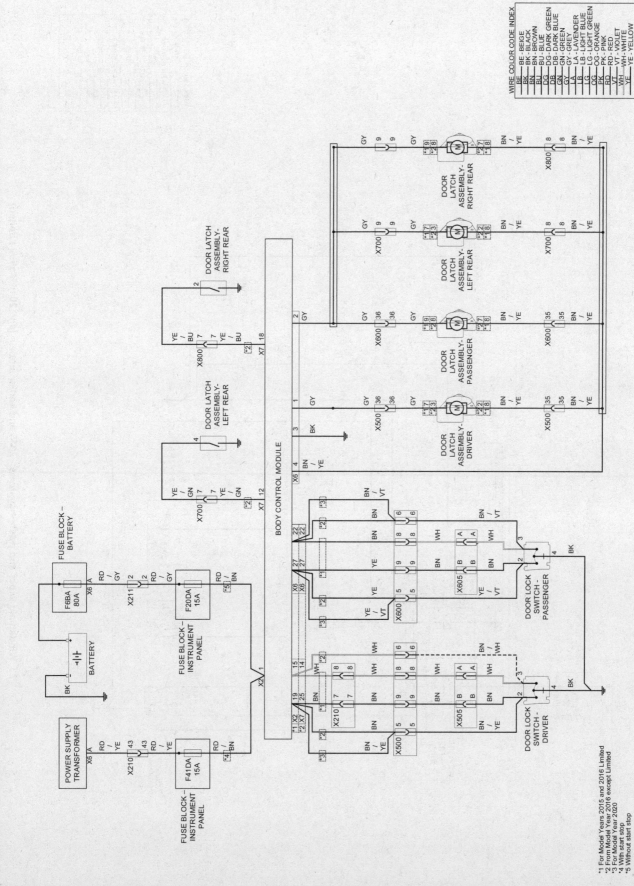

22. Power door locks - 2016 and later models (except Malibu Limited)

*1 For Model Years 2015 and 2016 Limited
*2 From Model Year 2016 except Limited
*3 For Model Year 2020
*4 With start stop
*5 Without start stop

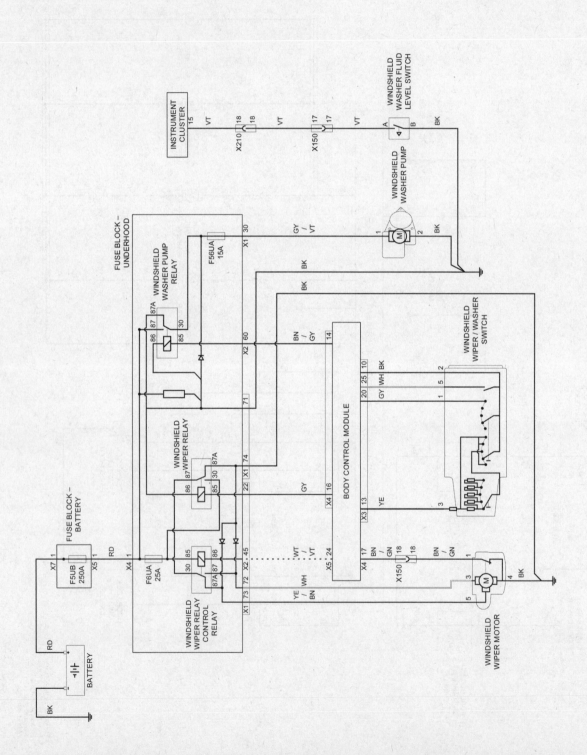

23. Windshield wiper and washer systems - 2015 and earlier models (and 2016 Malibu Limited)

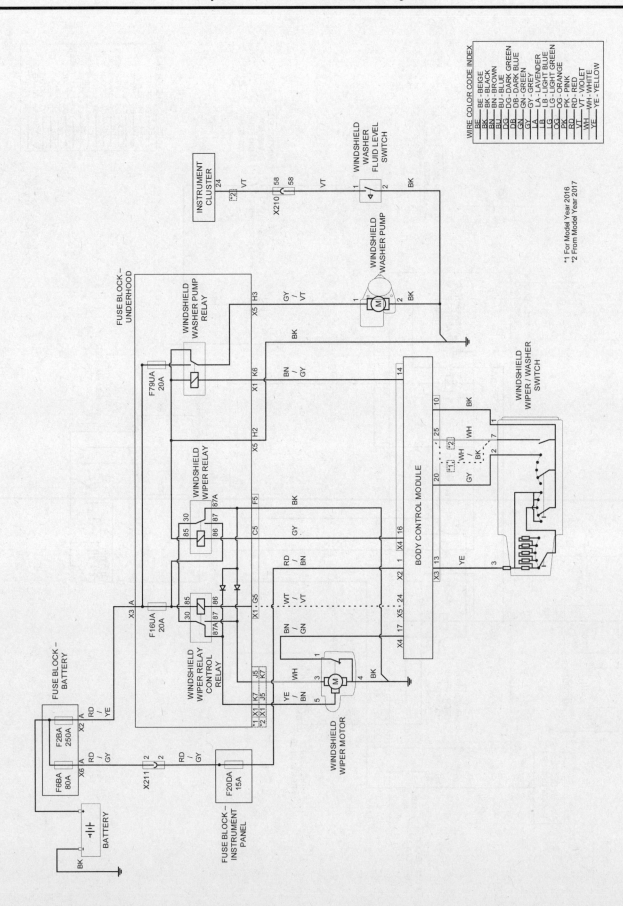

24. Windshield wiper and washer systems (without Start/Stop) - 2016 and later models (except Malibu Limited)

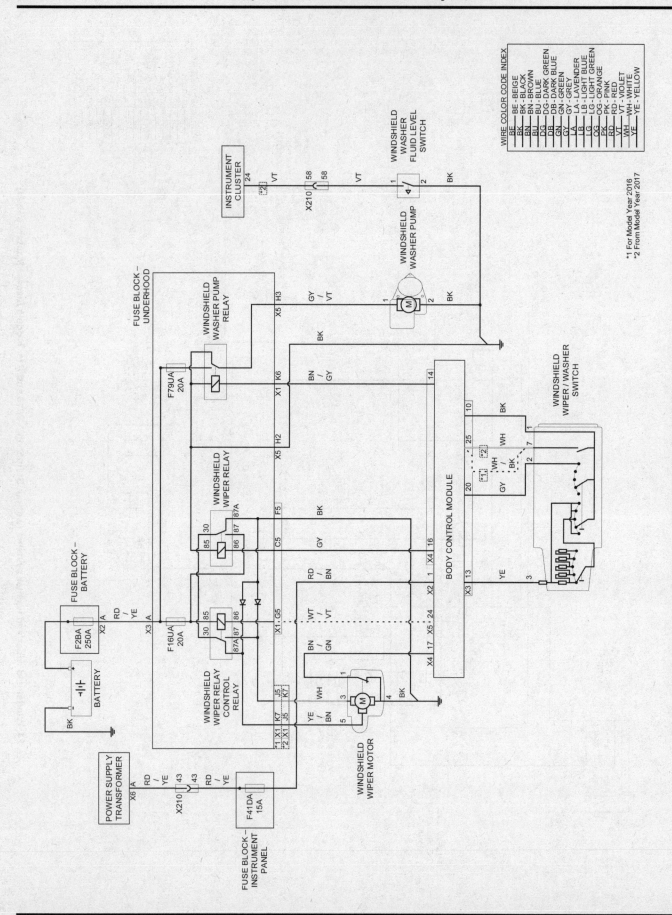

25. Windshield wiper and washer systems (with Start/Stop) - 2016 and later models (except Malibu Limited)

Notes

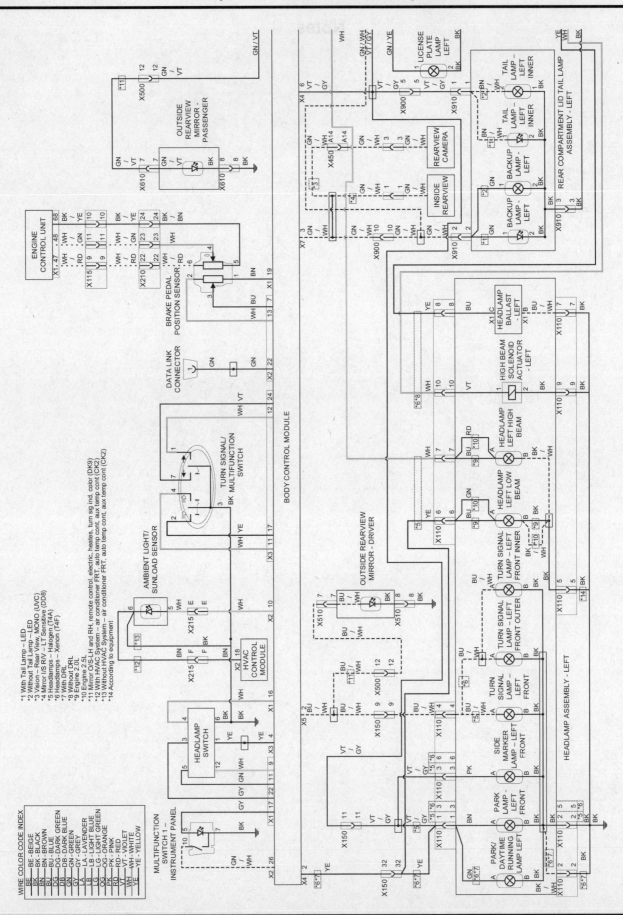

26. Exterior lights - 2013 models (1 of 2)

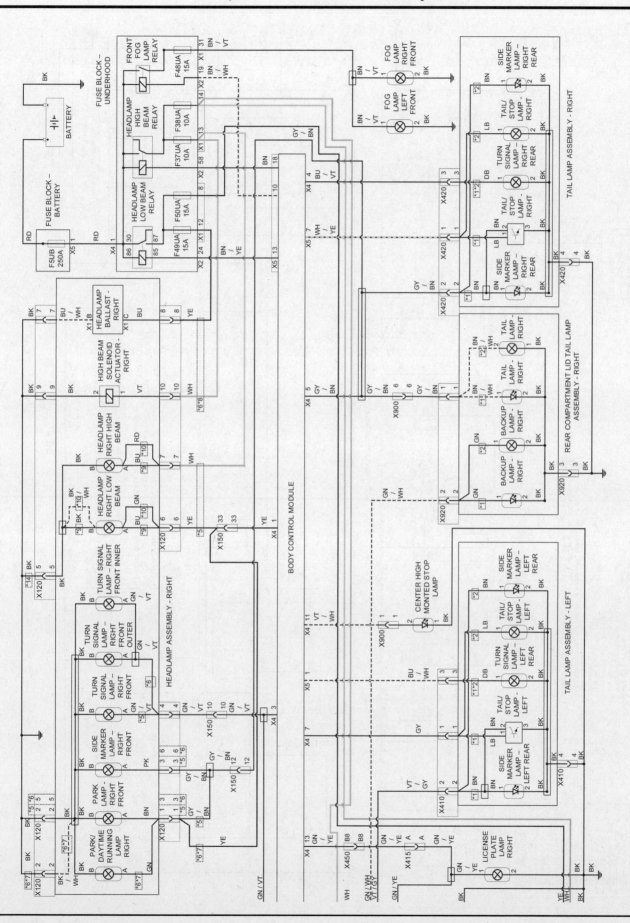

27. Exterior lights - 2013 models (2 of 2)

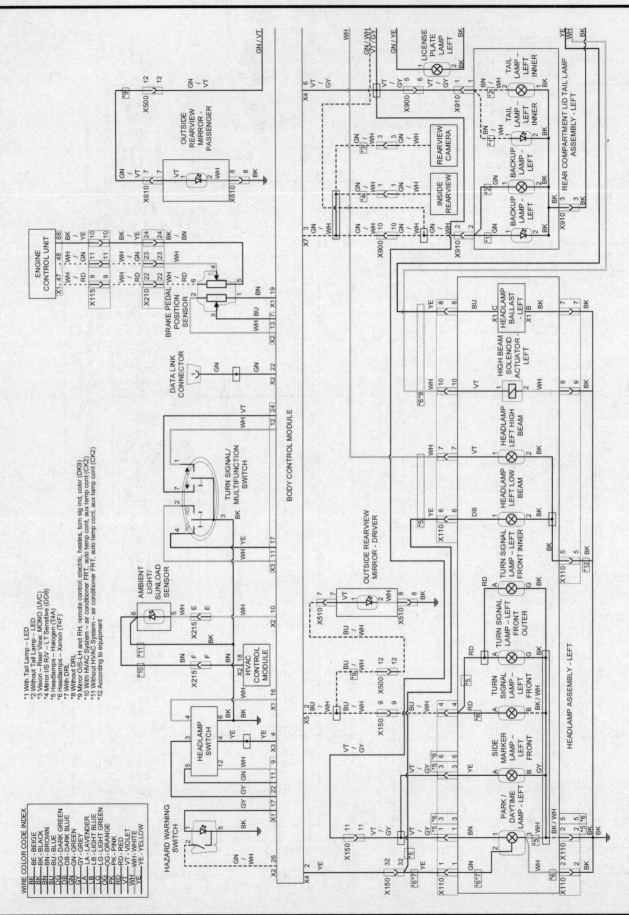

28. Exterior lights - 2014 models (1 of 2)

WIRE COLOR CODE INDEX
BE - BEIGE
BK - BLACK
BN - BROWN
BU - BLUE
DB - DARK BLUE
DG - DARK GREEN
GN - GREEN
GY - GREY
LA - LAVENDER
LB - LIGHT BLUE
LG - LIGHT GREEN
OG - ORANGE
PK - PINK
RD - RED
VT - VIOLET
WH - WHITE
YE - YELLOW

*1 With Tail Lamp – LED
*2 Without Tail Lamp – LED
*3 Vision – Rear View, MONO (UVC)
*4 Mirror I/S R/V – L.T Sensitive (DD8)
*5 Headlamps – Halogen (T4A)
*6 Headlamps – Xenon (T4F)
*7 With DRL
*8 Without DRL
*9 Mirror O/S-LH and RH, remote control; electric, heates, turn sig ind, color (DK9)
*10 With HVAC System – air conditioner FRT, auto temp cont, aux temp cont (CK2)
*11 Without HVAC System – air conditioner FRT, auto temp cont, aux temp cont (CK2)
*12 According to equipment

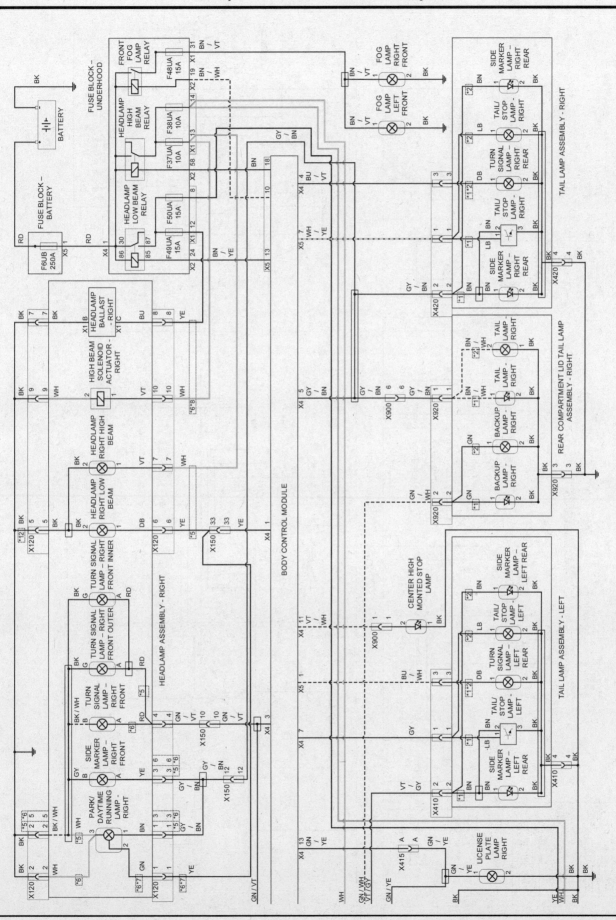

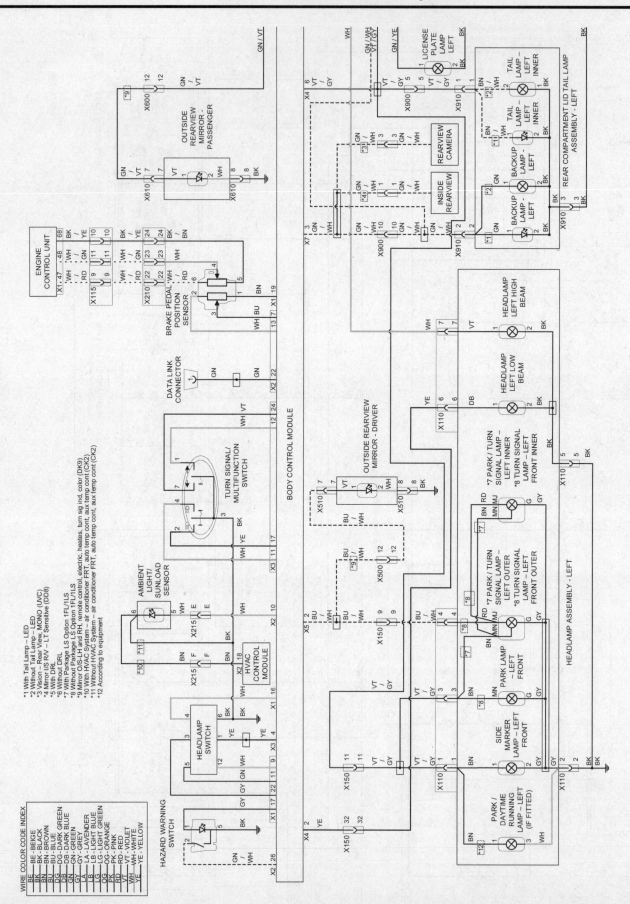

30. Exterior lights (with halogen headlights) - 2015 and earlier models (and 2016 Malibu Limited) (1 of 2)

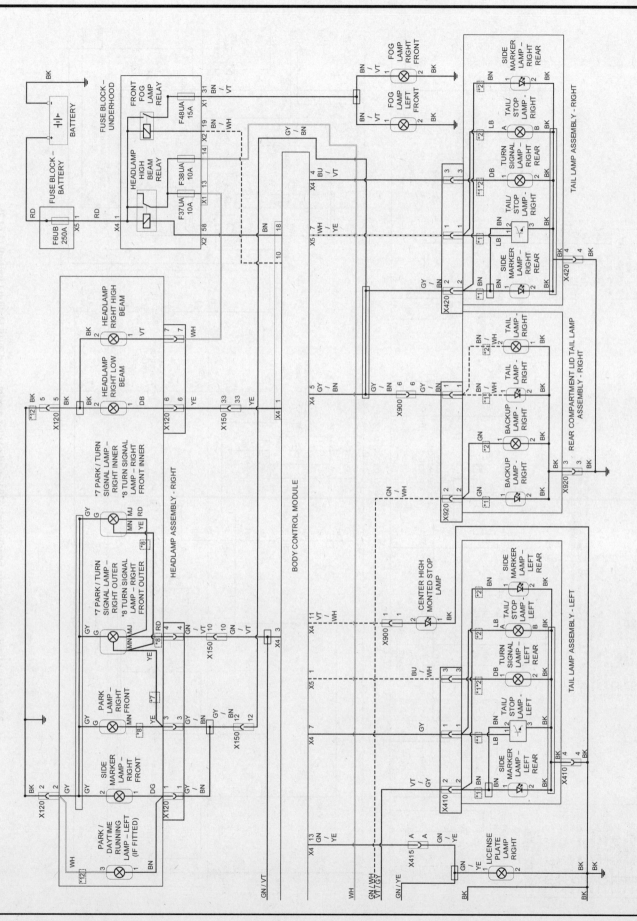

31. Exterior lights (with halogen headlights) - 2015 and earlier models (and 2016 Malibu Limited) (2 of 2)

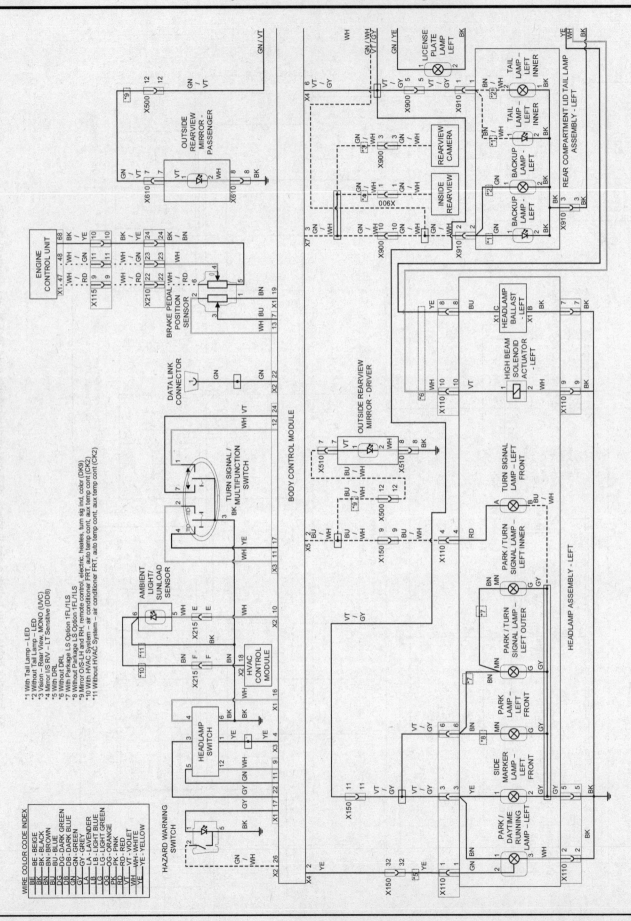

32. Exterior lights (with xenon headlights) - 2015 and earlier models (and 2016 Malibu Limited) (1 of 2)

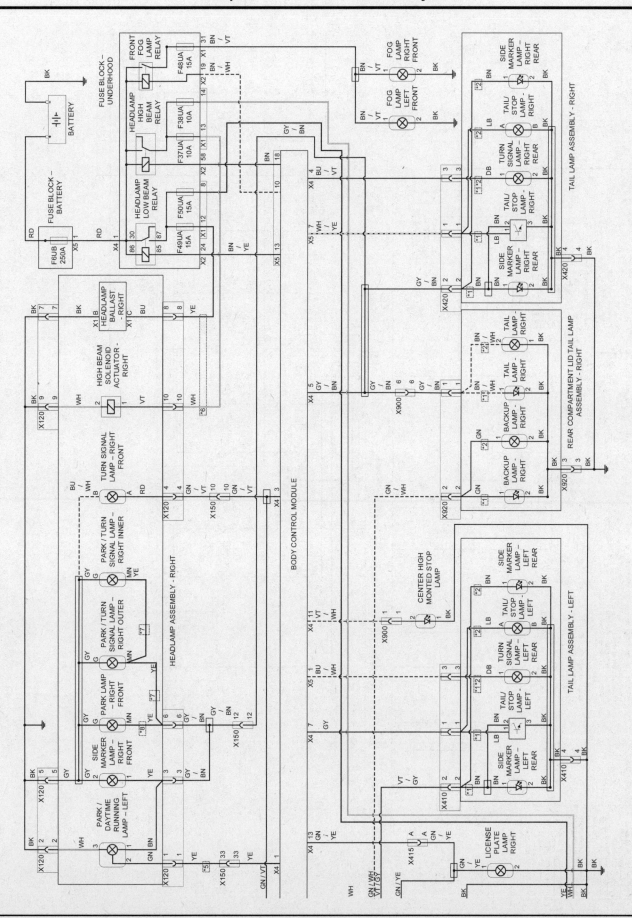

33. Exterior lights (with xenon headlights) - 2015 and earlier models (and 2016 Malibu Limited) (2 of 2)

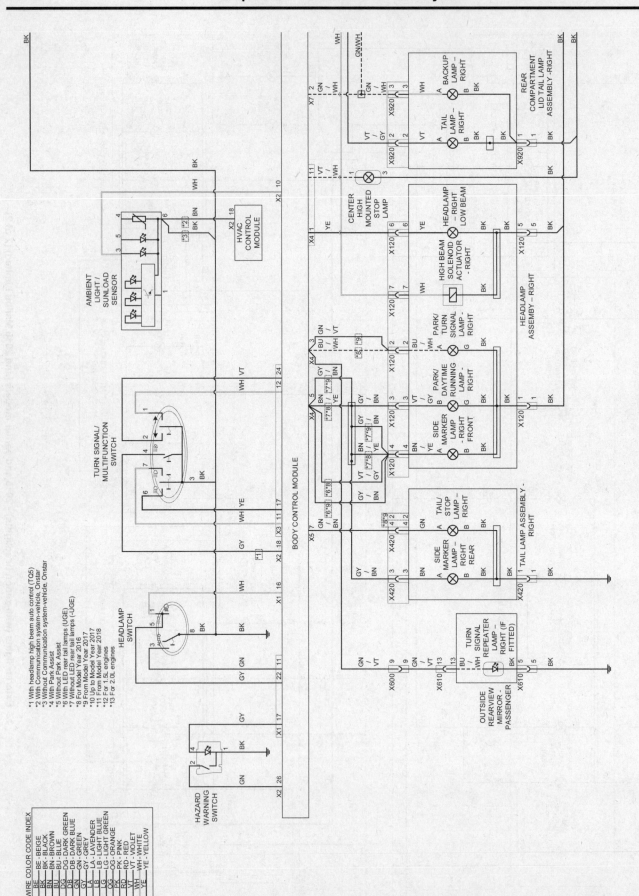

34. Exterior lights - 2016 through 2018 models (except Malibu Limited) (1 of 2)

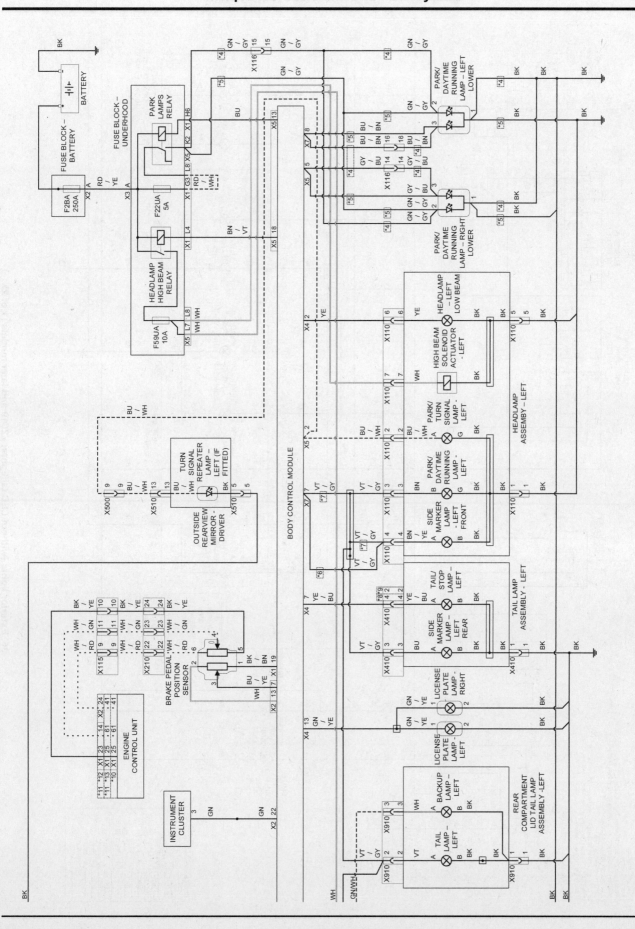

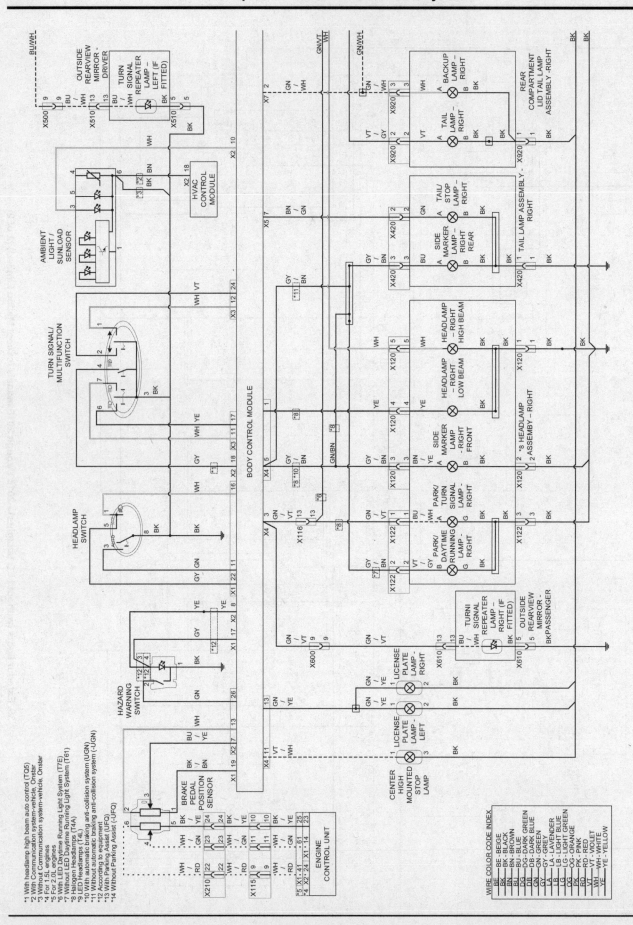

36. Exterior lights (without LED taillights) - 2019 and later models (1 of 2)

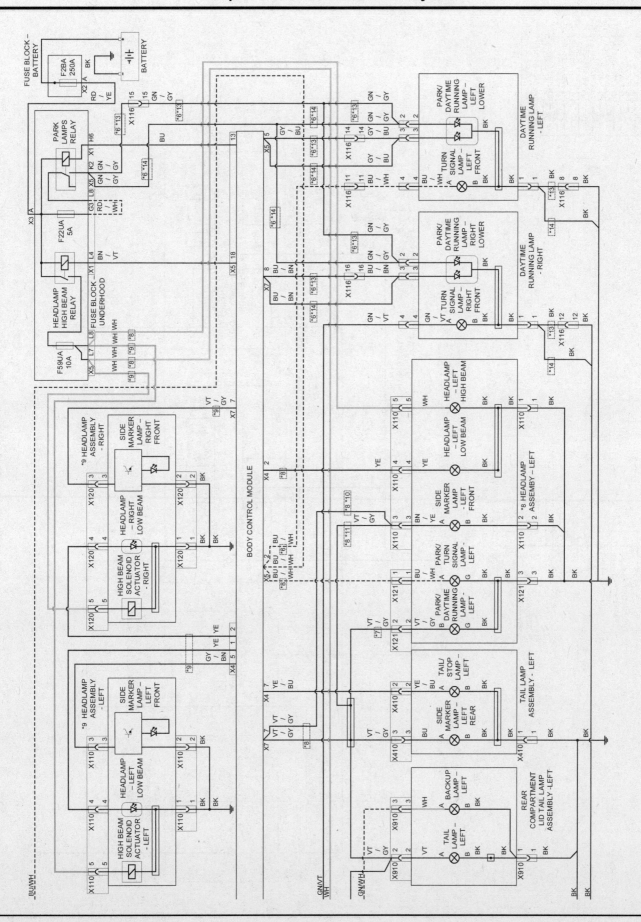

37. Exterior lights (without LED taillights) - 2019 and later models (2 of 2)

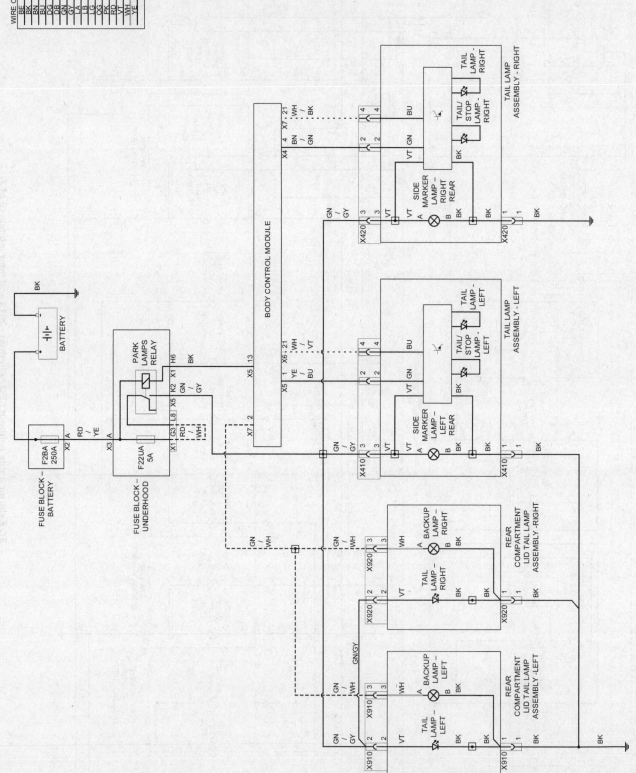

38. LED taillights - 2016 and later models

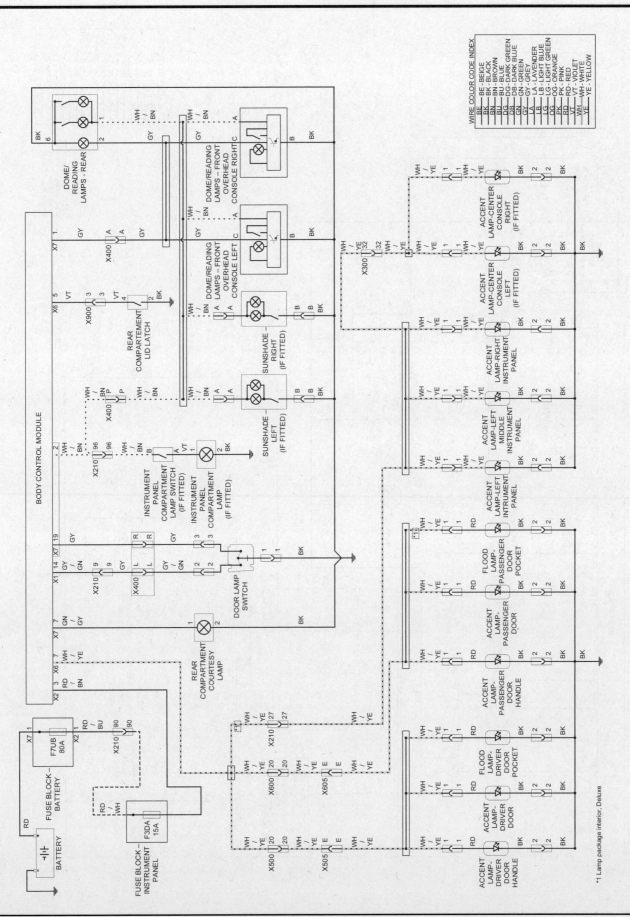

39. Interior lights - 2015 and earlier models (and 2016 Malibu Limited)

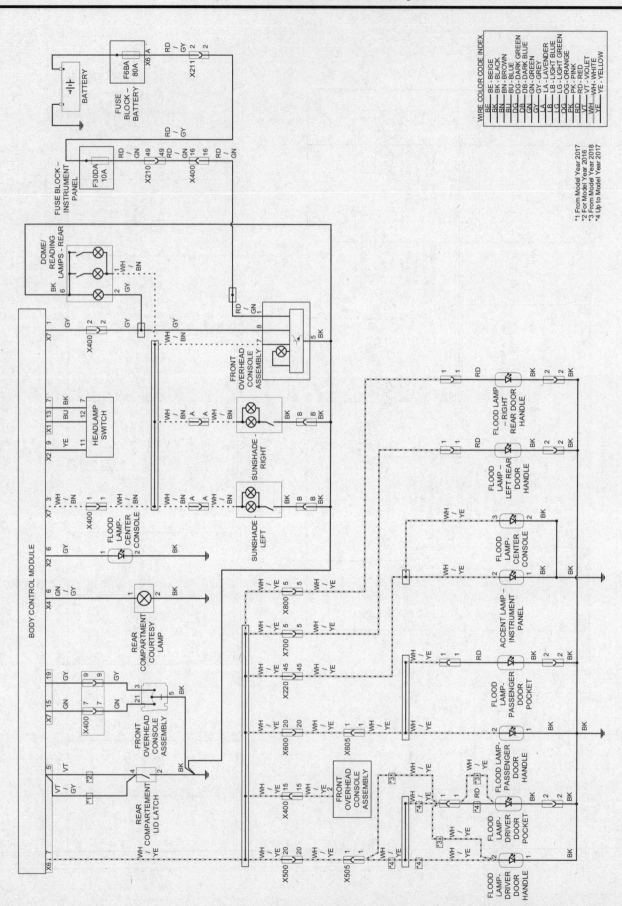

40. Interior lights - 2016 and later models (except 2016 Malibu Limited)

Notes

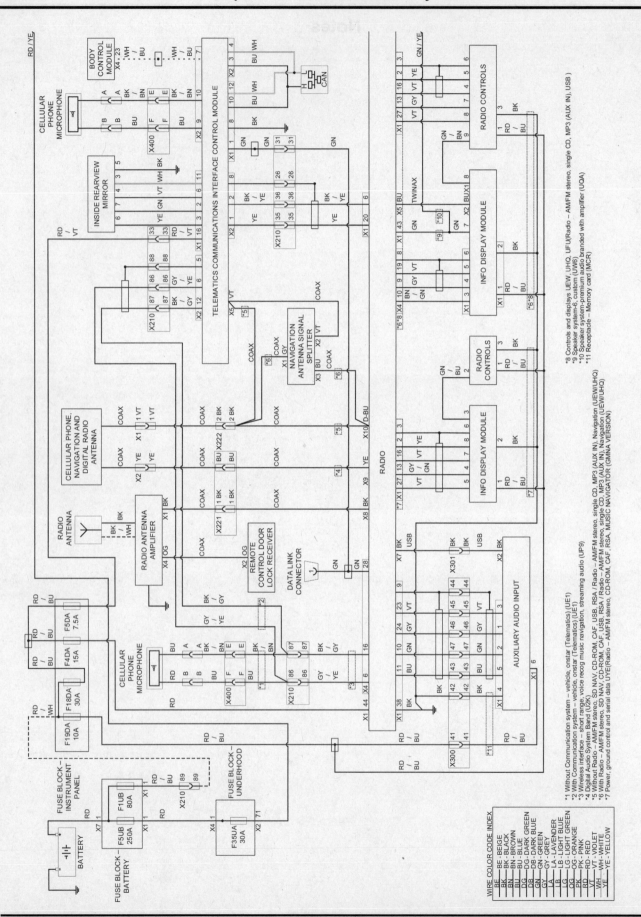

41. Audio system - 2013 models (1 of 2)

*8 Controls and displays UEW, UHQ, UFU/Radio – AM/FM stereo, single CD, MP3 (AUX IN), USB)
*9 Speaker system-6, custom (UV6)
*10 Speaker system-premium audio branded with amplifier (UQA)
*11 Receptacle – Memory card (MCR)

*1 Without Communication system – vehicle, onstar (Telematics) (UE1)
*2 With Communication system – vehicle, onstar (Telematics) (UE1)
*3 Wireless interface – short range, voice recog music navigation, streaming audio (UP9)
*4 Digital Radio System Band (U2K)
*5 Without Radio – AM/FM stereo, CD-ROM, CAF, USB, CD NAV, CD-ROM, CAF, USB, RSA / Radio – AM/FM stereo, single CD, MP3 (AUX IN), Navigation (UEW/UHQ)
*6 With Radio – AM/FM stereo, SD NAV, CD-ROM, CAF, RSA, MUSIC NAVIGATOR (GMNA VERSION)
*7 Power, ground control and serial data UYE/Radio – AM/FM stereo, CD-ROM, CAF, RSA, MUSIC NAVIGATOR (GMNA VERSION)

WIRE COLOR CODE INDEX
BE – BEIGE
BK – BLACK
BN – BROWN
BU – BLUE
DG – DARK GREEN
DB – DARK BLUE
GN – GREEN
GY – GREY
LA – LAVENDER
LB – LIGHT BLUE
LG – LIGHT GREEN
OG – ORANGE
PK – PINK
RD – RED
VT – VIOLET
WH – WHITE
YE – YELLOW

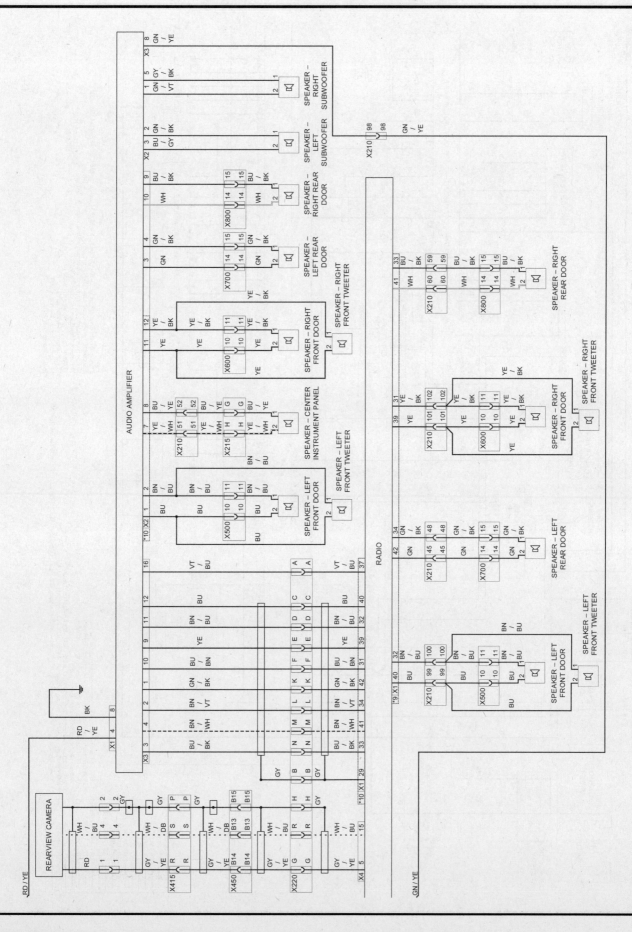

42. Audio system - 2013 models (2 of 2)

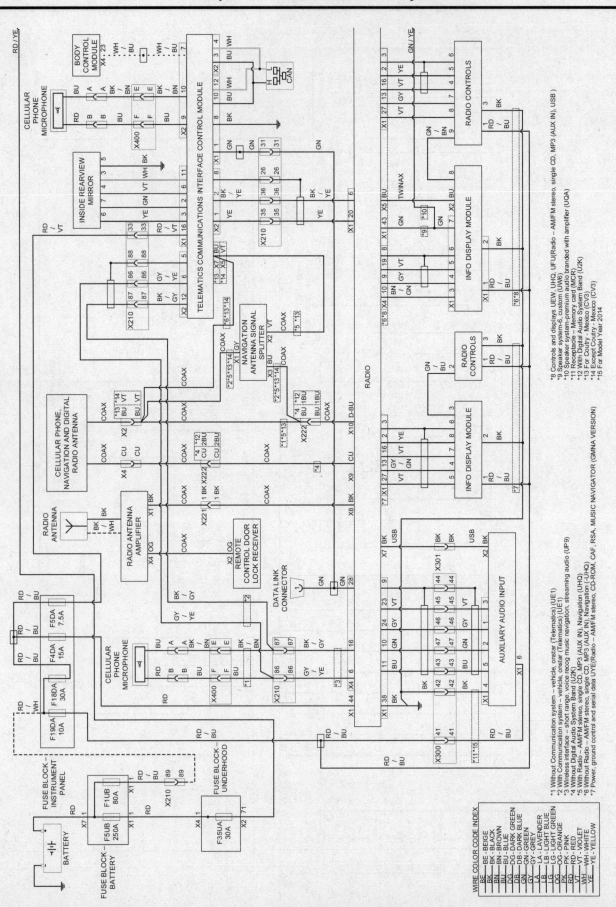

43. Audio system - 2014 and 2015 models (and 2016 Malibu Limited) (1 of 2)

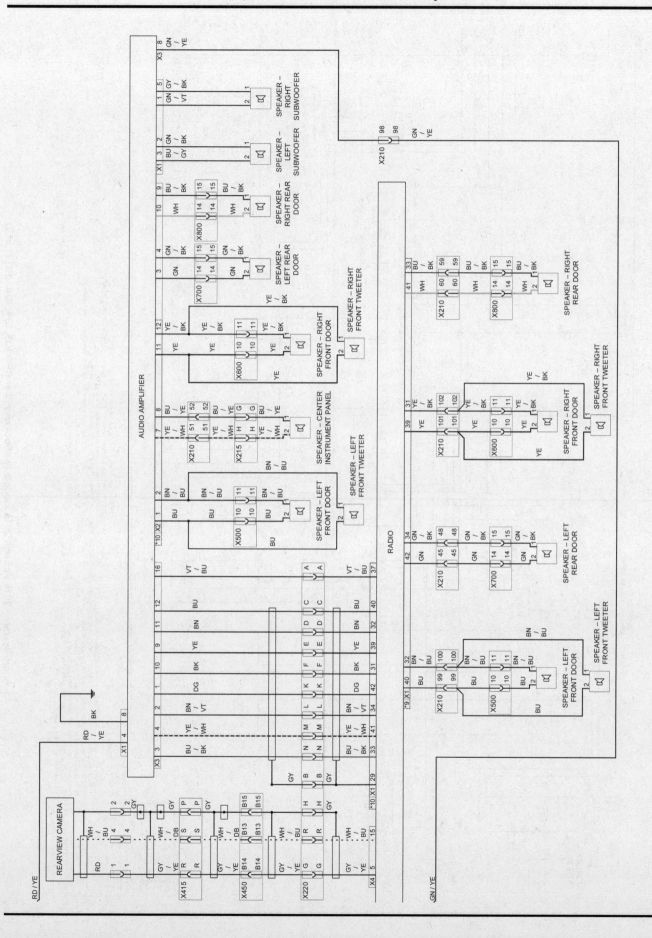

44. Audio system - 2014 and 2015 models (and 2016 Malibu Limited) (2 of 2)

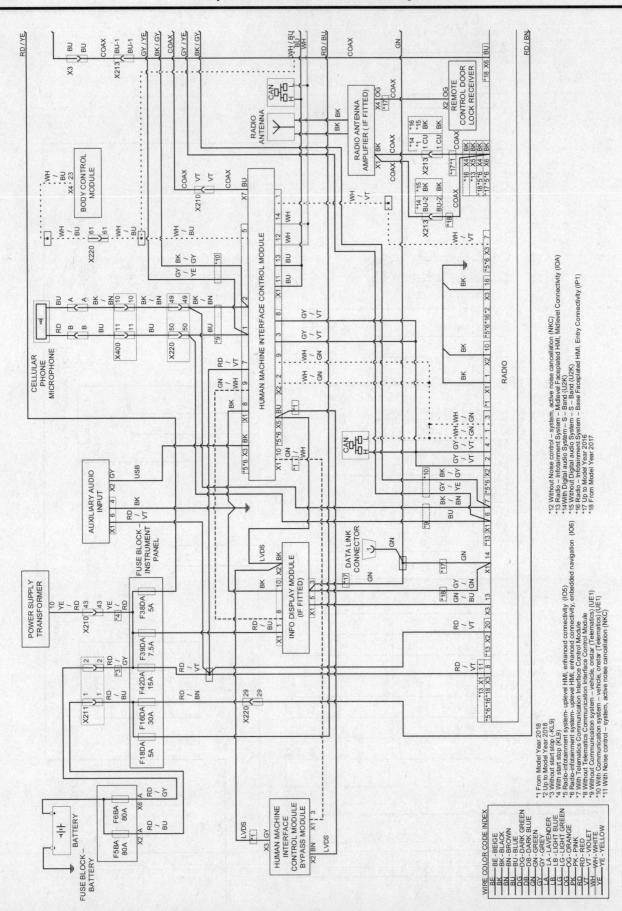

45. Audio system - 2016 through 2018 models (without amplifier RPO IO5, IO6, IOA, IP1) (1 of 2)

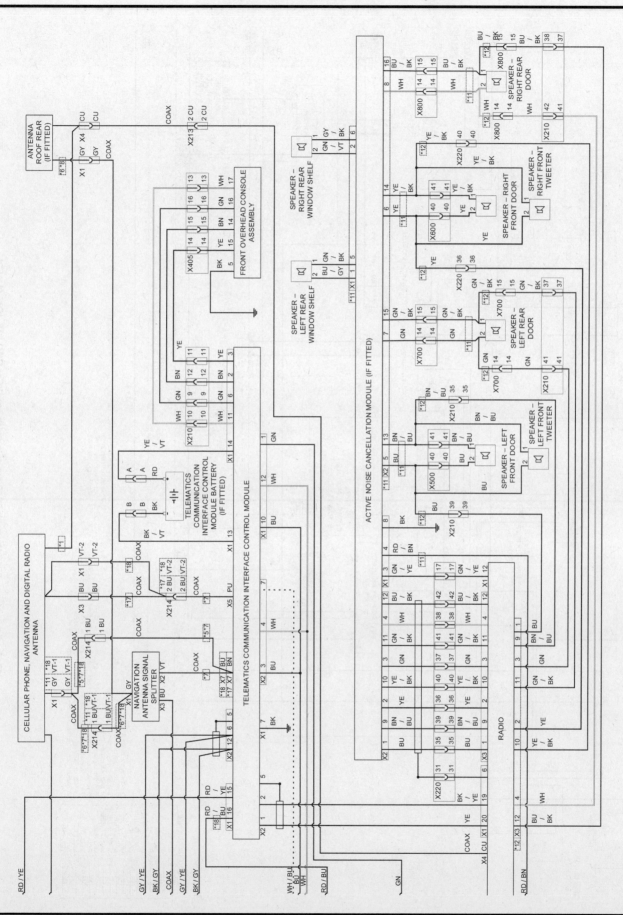

46. Audio system - 2016 through 2018 models (without amplifier RPO IO5, IO6, IOA, IP1) (2 of 2)

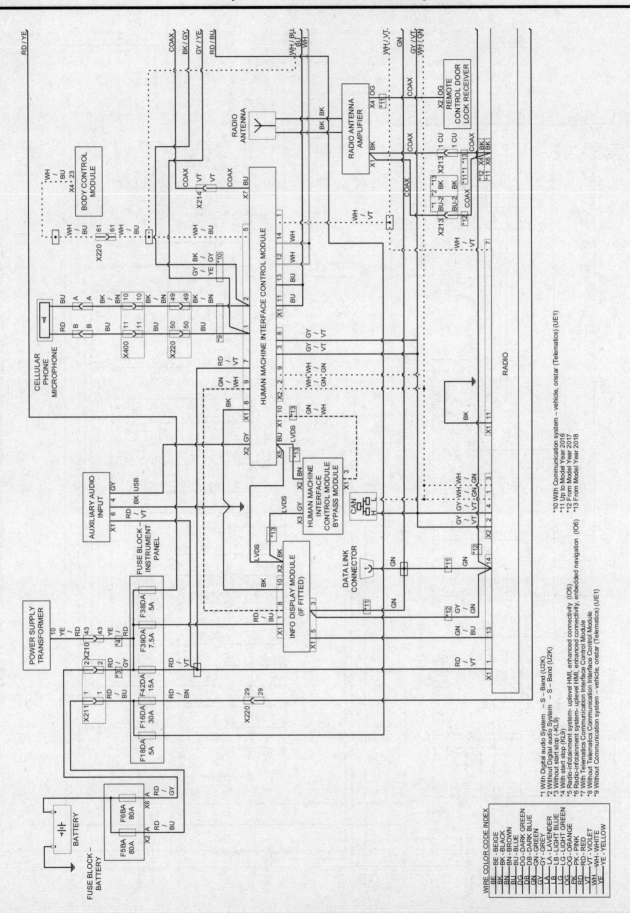

47. Audio system - 2016 through 2018 models (with amplifier RPO IO5, IO6) (1 of 2)

*1 With Digital audio System – S – Band (U2K)
*2 Without Digital audio System – S – Band (U2K)
*3 Without start stop
*4 With start stop (KL9)
*5 Radio-infotainment system- uplevel HMI, enhanced HMI, enhanced connectivity (IO5)
*6 Radio-infotainment system- uplevel HMI, enhanced HMI, enhanced connectivity, embedded navigation (IO6)
*7 With Telematics Communication Interface Control Module
*8 With Telematics Communication Interface Control Module
*9 Without Communication system – vehicle, onstar (Telematics) (UE1)
*10 With Communication system – vehicle, onstar (Telematics) (UE1)
*11 Up to Model Year 2016
*12 From Model Year 2017
*13 From Model Year 2018

WIRE COLOR CODE INDEX
BE - BEIGE
BK - BLACK
BN - BROWN
BU - BLUE
DG - DARK GREEN
DB - DARK BLUE
GN - GREEN
GY - GREY
LA - LAVENDER
LB - LIGHT BLUE
LG - LIGHT GREEN
OG - ORANGE
PK - PINK
RD - RED
VT - VIOLET
WH - WHITE
YE - YELLOW

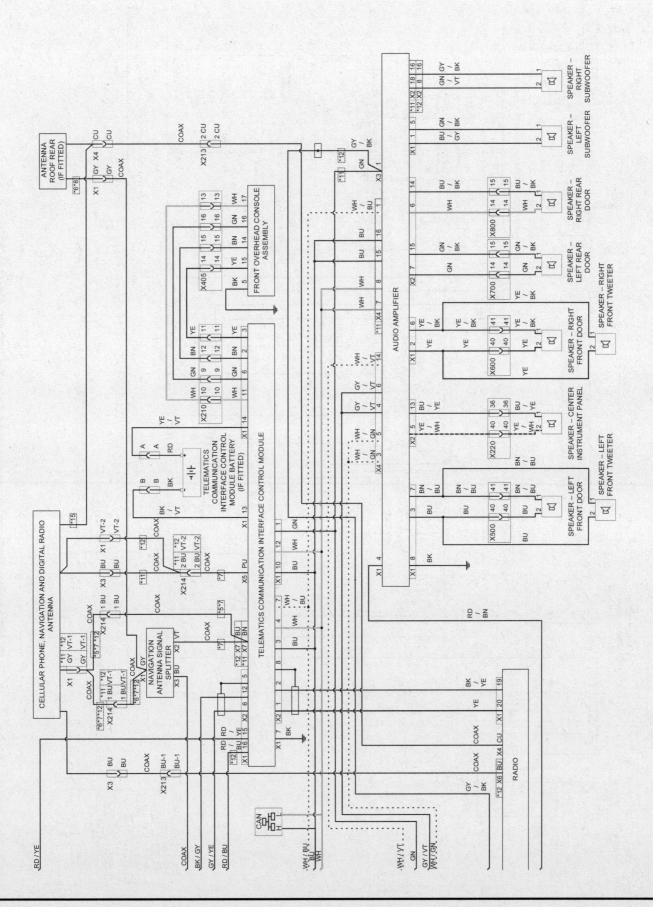

48. Audio system - 2016 through 2018 models (with amplifier RPO IO5, IO6) (2 of 2)

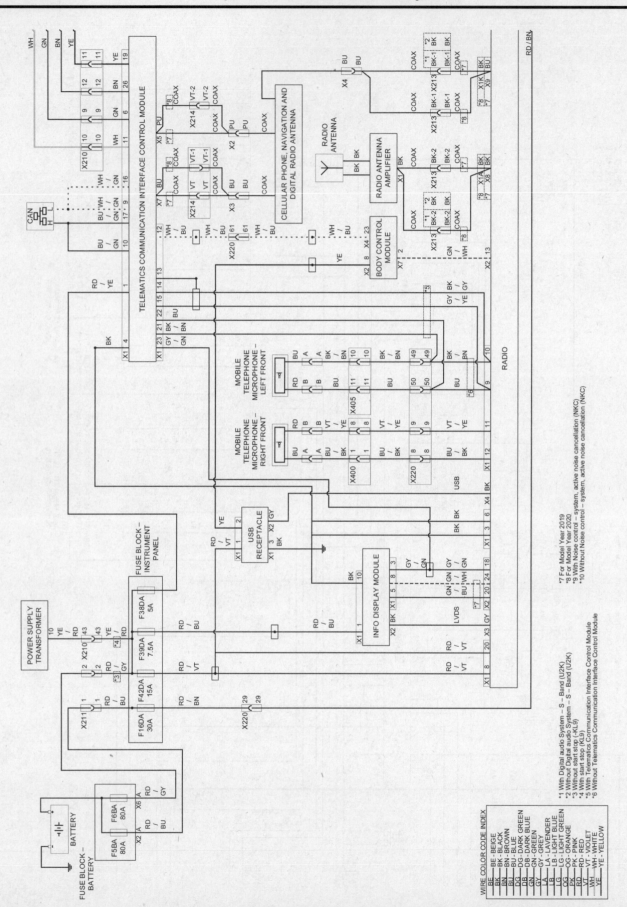

49. Audio system - 2019 and later models (without amplifier RPO IOU, IOS) (1 of 2)

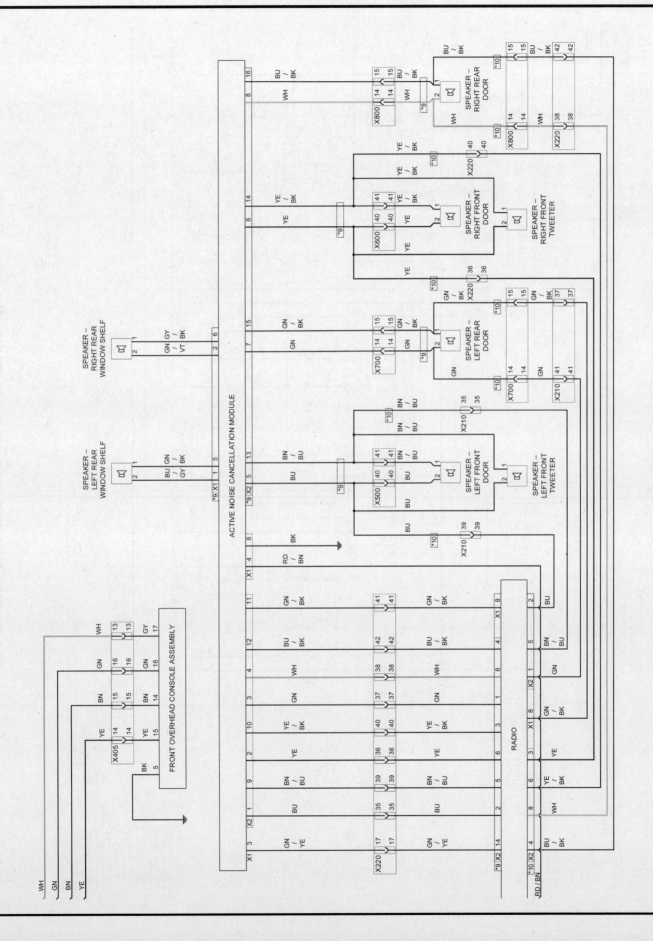

50. Audio system - 2019 and later models (without amplifier RPO IOU, IOS) (2 of 2)

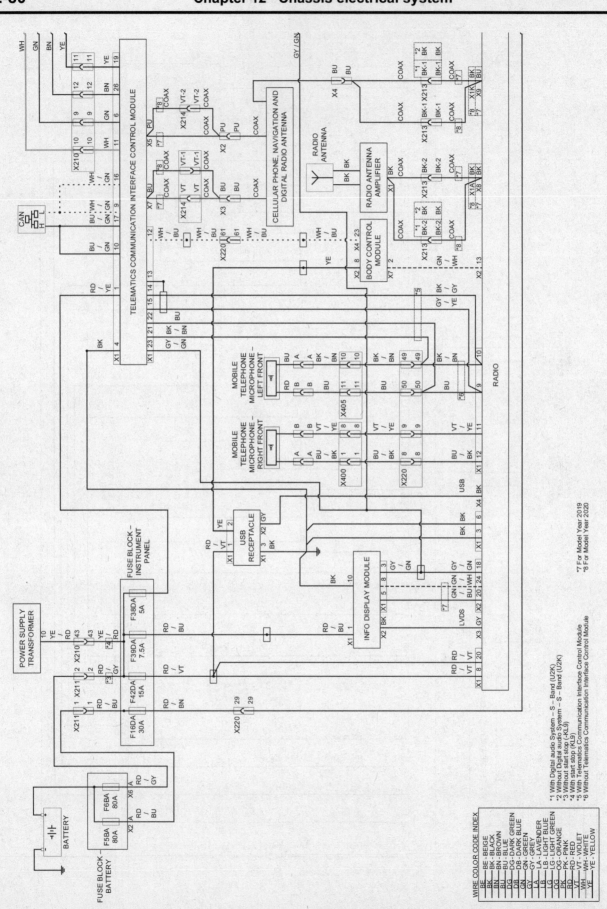

51. Audio system - 2019 and later models (with amplifier RPO IOU, IOS) (1 of 2)

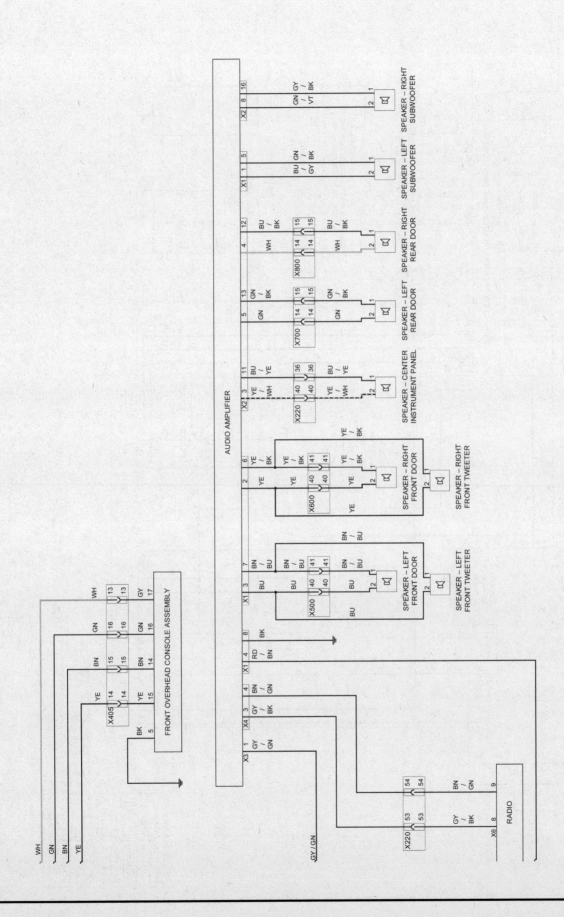

52. Audio system - 2019 and later models (with amplifier RPO IOU, IOS) (2 of 2)

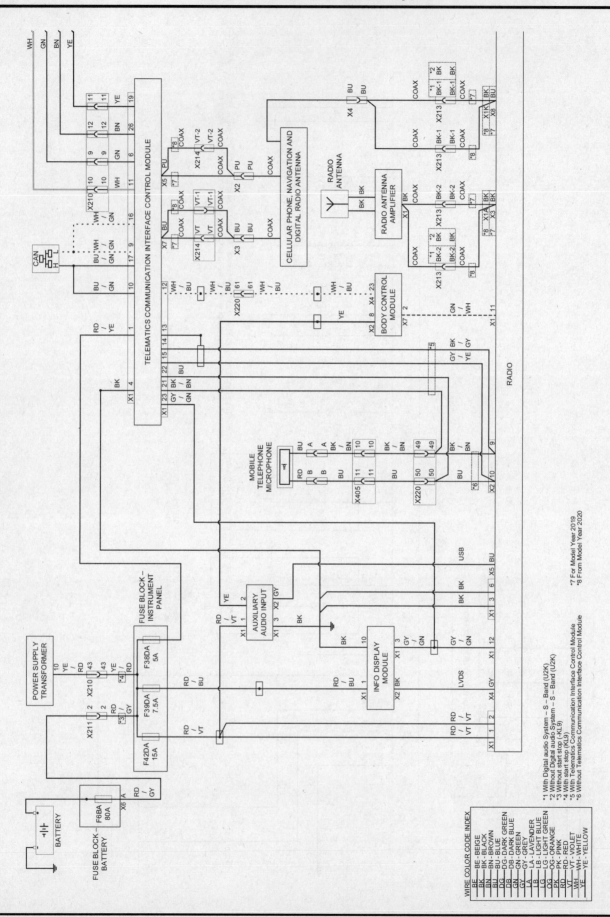

53. Audio system - 2019 and later models (with amplifier RPO IOR) (1 of 2)

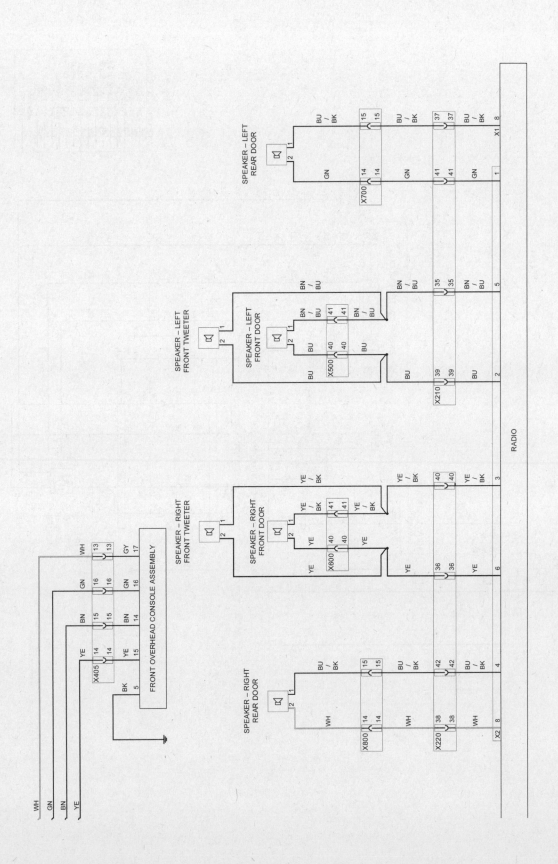

54. Audio system - 2019 and later models (with amplifier RPO IOR) (2 of 2)

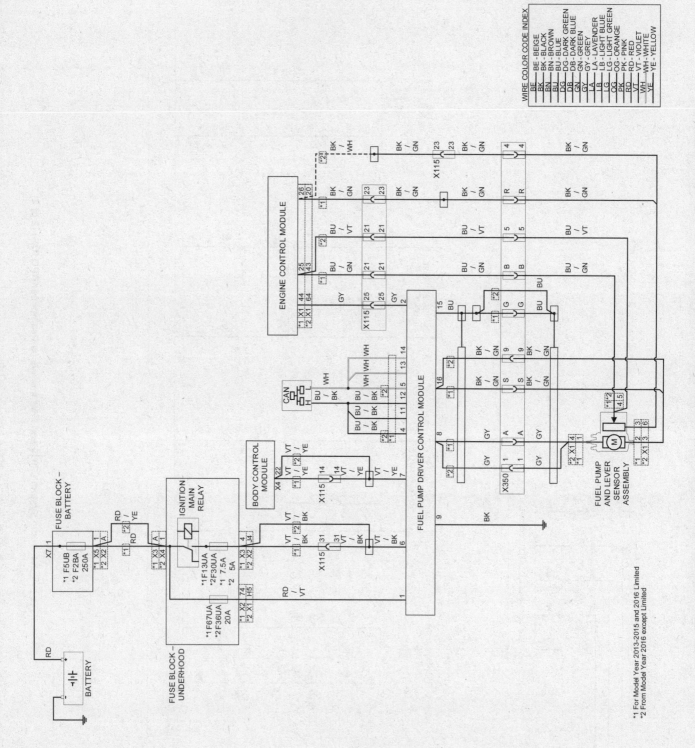

55. Fuel pump circuit - 2015 and earlier models (and 2016 Malibu Limited)/1.5L and 2.0L models [2016 and 2017])

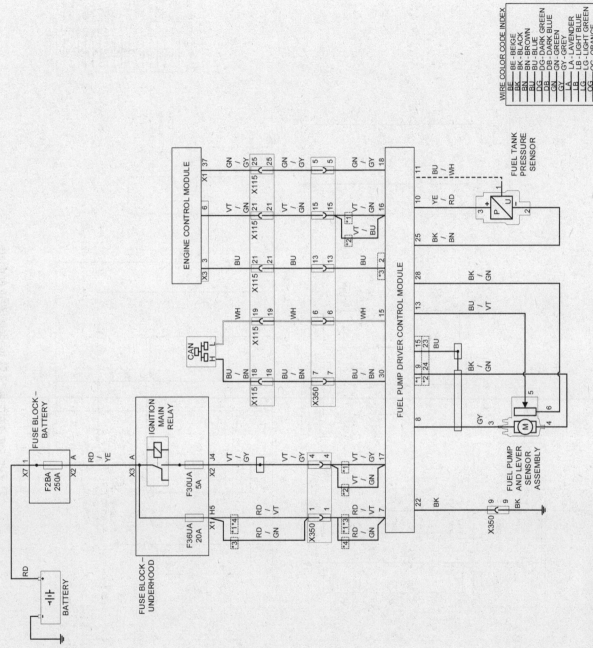

56. Fuel pump circuit - 1.5L models (2018 and later)

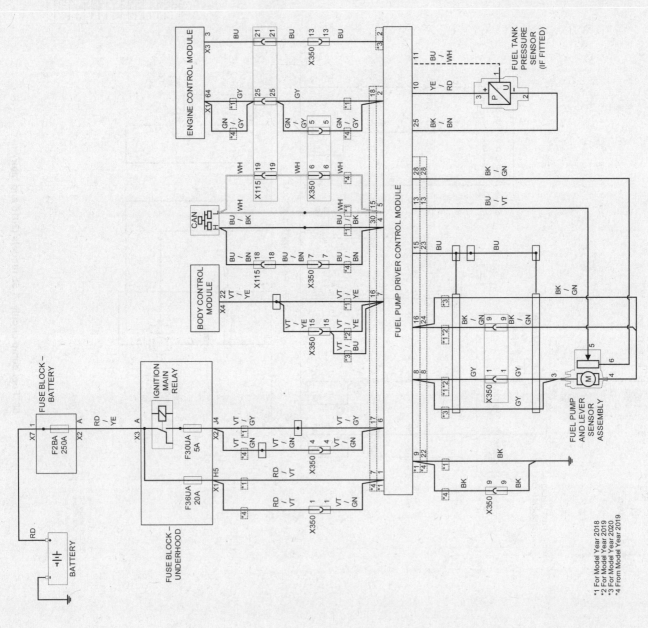

57. Fuel pump circuit - 2.0L models (2018 and later)

*1 For Model Year 2018
*2 For Model Year 2019
*3 For Model Year 2020
*4 From Model Year 2019

FUSE BOX ON THE BATTERY (FUSE BLOCK - BATTERY)

(FOR MODEL YEARS 2013-2015 AND FOR 2016 LIMITED)

WITHOUT START/STOP

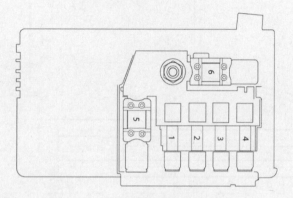

FUSE	VALUE	DESCRIPTION	OEM NAME
1	60A	Fuse box in passenger compartment (Fuse block – Instrument panel)	F1UB
2	60A	Fuse box in passenger compartment (Fuse block – Instrument panel)	F2UB
3	-	Not used (For Model Year 2013)	F3UB
	80A	Power steering control module (For Model Year 2014-2015)	
4	80A	Power steering control module (late production) (For Model Year 2013)	F4UB
	-	Not used (For Model Year 2014-2015)	
5	250A	Fuse box in engine compartment (Fuse block – Underhood)	F5UB
6	300A	Generator, Starter Motor	F6UB

WITH START/STOP

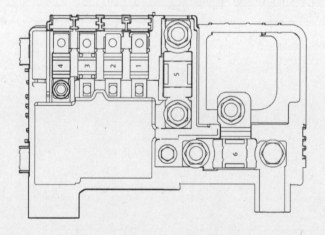

FUSE	VALUE	DESCRIPTION	OEM NAME
1	60A	Fuse box in passenger compartment (Fuse block – Instrument panel)	F1UB
2	60A	Fuse box in passenger compartment (Fuse block – Instrument panel)	F2UB
3	80A	Power steering control module	F3UB
4	175A	Battery – auxiliary	F4UB
5	200A	Fuse box in engine compartment (Fuse block – Underhood)	F5UB
6	500A	Generator, Starter Motor	F6UB

58. Fuses and relays (1 of 11)

FUSE BOX ON THE BATTERY (FUSE BLOCK - BATTERY)

(FOR MODEL YEARS 2016-2020)

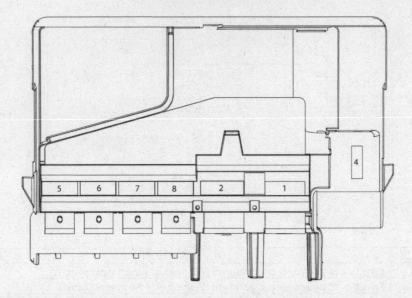

FUSE	VALUE	DESCRIPTION	OEM NAME
1	400A	Starter, Generator (1.5L engines)	F1BA
	350A	Starter, Generator (2.0L engines)	
2	250A	Fuse box in engine compartment (Fuse block – Underhood)	F2BA
3	-	Not used	F3UB
4	5A	Battery sensor module or Body control module	F4UB
5	80A	Fuse box in passenger compartment (Fuse block – Instrument panel)	F5UB
6	80A	Fuse box in passenger compartment (Fuse block – Instrument panel)	F6UB
7	100A	Power steering control module	F7UB
8	-	Not used	F8UB

FUSE AND RELAY BOX IN ENGINE COMPARTMENT (FUSE BLOCK - UNDERHOOD)

(FOR MODEL YEARS 2013-2015 AND FOR 2016 LIMITED)

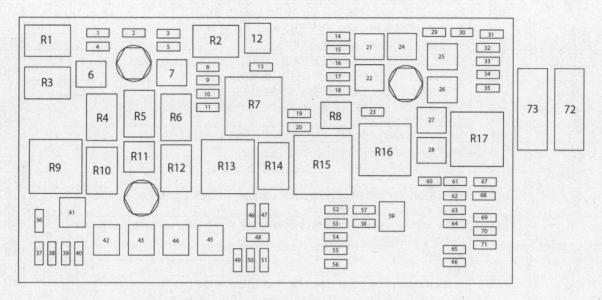

FUSE/RELAY	VALUE	DESCRIPTION	OEM NAME
1	15A	Control solenoid valve assembly	F1UA
2	10A	Engine control module or A/C compressor clutch relay, 5A also used	F2UA
3	10A	A/C compressor clutch relay or Not used	F3UA
4	5A	Engine control module or Not used	F4UA
5	5A	Engine control module or Not used	F5UA
6	25A	Windshield wiper relay, Windshield wiper speed control relay	F6UA
7	5A	Engine control module or Not used	F7UA
8	15A	Ignition coil 2, Ignition coil 4 (for Model Year 2013)	F8UA
	-	Not used (for Model Years 2014-2015 and for 2016 Limited)	
9	15A	Ignition coil 1, Ignition coil 3 (for Model Year 2013)	F9UA
	15A	Ignition coils 1-4 (for Model Years 2014-2015 and for 2016 Limited)	
10	20A	Engine control module	F10UA
11	10A	MAF/Intake Air sensor, Fuel composition sensor, Secondary air injection solenoid valve relay (if fitted) (for Model Year 2013)	F11UA
		Multifunction intake air sensor, Heated oxygen sensor, Automatic transmission accumulator solenoid valve (if fitted) (for Model Years 2014-2015 and for 2016 Limited)	
12	40A	Starter relay or Starter relay 2, 30A also used	F12UA
13	7.5A	Control solenoid valve assembly (if fitted), Fuel pump driver control module (for Model Year 2013)	F13UA
		Chassis control module, Control solenoid valve assembly, Fuel pump driver control module (for Model Years 2014-2015 and for 2016 Limited)	
14	-	Not used	F14UA
15	-	Not used	F15UA
16	7.5A	Trunk release or Active grille air shutter actuator	F16UA
17	5A	Inflatable restraint sensing and diagnostic module	F17UA
18	5A	Battery isolator control module or Not used	F18UA
19	-	Not used	F19UA
20	25A	Transmission fluid pump relay – auxiliary or Not used	F20UA
21	30A	Rear power window switches	F21UA
22	30A	Sunroof control motor	F22UA
23	-	Not used	F23UA

24	30A	Front power window switches	F24UA
25	30A	Keyless Entry control module (if fitted) or Not used	F25UA
26	60A	Electronic Brake control module	F26UA
27	30A	Parking Brake control module (for Model Year 2013)	F27UA
	-	Not used (for Model Years 2014-2015 and for 2016 Limited)	
28	40A	Left rear window defogger noise filter	F28UA
29	15A	Driver's seat lumbar support switch (if fitted)	F29UA
30	15A	Passenger's seat lumbar support switch (if fitted)	F30UA
31	15A	Fuel pump driver control module (for Model Year 2013)	F31UA
		Chassis control module (for Model Years 2014-2015 and for 2016 Limited)	
32	15A	Body control module	F32UA
33	25A	Seat heating control module, Seat memory control module	F33UA
34	25A	Electronic brake control module	F34UA
35	30A	Audio amplifier (if fitted)	F35UA
36	-	Not used	F36UA
37	10A	Right headlamp high beam (halogen headlamps) or Right high beam solenoid actuator (xenon headlamps)	F37UA
38	10A	Left headlamp high beam (halogen headlamps) or Left high beam solenoid actuator (xenon headlamps)	F38UA
39	-	Not used	F39UA
40	-	Not used	F40UA
41	20A	Brake booster pump motor relay (for Model Year 2013)	F41UA
	-	Not used (for Model Years 2014-2015 and for 2016 Limited)	
42	30A	Cooling fan high speed relay	F42UA
43	-	Not used	F43UA
44	30A	Transmission fluid pump relay – auxiliary (if fitted) (for Model Year 2013)	F44UA
	20A	Starter relay 1 or Not used (for Model Years 2014-2015 and for 2016 Limited)	
45	30A	Cooling fan low speed relay	F45UA
46	10A	Cooling fan low speed relay, Cooling fan speed control relay	F46UA
47	10A	Heated oxygen sensors, Evaporative emission purge solenoid valve, Turbocharger bypass solenoid valve, Turbocharger wastegate solenoid valve, Engine oil pressure control solenoid valve (for Model Year 2013)	F47UA
		Heated oxygen sensor 1, Evaporative emission purge solenoid valve, Turbocharger bypass solenoid valve, Turbocharger wastegate solenoid valve, Engine oil pressure control solenoid valve (2.0L engines, Model Years 2014-2015 and for 2016 Limited)	
		Heated oxygen sensor 1, Evaporative emission purge solenoid valve, Rocker arm actuator (2.5L engines, Model Years 2014-2015 and for 2016 Limited)	
48	15A	Front fog lamps (if fitted)	F48UA
49	15A	Left headlamp assembly (xenon headlamps) or Not used	F49UA
50	15A	Right headlamp assembly (xenon headlamps) or Not used	F50UA
51	15A	Horn	F51UA
52	5A	Instrument cluster	F52UA
53	10A	Inside rearview mirror, Rearview camera	F53UA
54	5A	HVAC control module, Collistion alert indicators	F54UA
55	7.5A	Outside rearview mirror switch, Driver window switch, Garage door opener	F55UA
56	15A	Windshield washer pump	F56UA
57	-	Not used	F57UA
58	-	Not used	F58UA
59	50A	Secondary air injection pump relay (if fitted) or Not used	F59UA
60	7.5A	Outside rearview mirrors	F60UA
61	-	Not used	F61UA
62	10A	Evaporative emission vent solenoid valve	F62UA
63	-	Not used	F63UA
64	-	Not used	F64UA
65	-	Not used	F65UA
66	15A	Secondary air injection solenoid valve relay or Not used	F66UA

61. Fuses and relays (4 of 11)

67	20A	Fuel pump driver control module	F67UA
68	-	Not used	F68UA
69	5A	Body control module	F69UA
70	5A	Rear parking assist control module (if fitted), Vehicle camera module (if fitted) (for Model Year 2013)	F70UA
		Side object sensor modules, Rear parking assist control module, Vehicle camera module (for Model Years 2014-2015 and for 2016 Limited)	
71	5A	Keyless entry control module (if fitted) or Not used	F71UA
72	80A	Power steering control module (early production) (for Model Year 2013)	F72UA
	-	Not used (for Model Years 2014-2015 and for 2016 Limited)	
73	-	Not used	F73UA
R1	-	A/C compressor clutch relay	-
R2	-	Starter motor relay	-
R3	-	Not used	-
R4	-	Windshield wiper speed control relay	-
R5	-	Windshield wiper relay	-
R6	-	Auxiliary heater coolant pump relay or Not used	-
R7	-	Engine controls ignition relay	-
R8	-	Transmission fluid pump relay – auxiliary or Not used	-
R9	-	Cooling fan speed control relay	-
R10	-	Cooling fan low speed relay	-
R11	-	Transmission fluid pump relay – auxiliary (for Model Year 2013)	-
		Starter pinion solenoid actuator relay or Not used (for Model Years 2014-2015 and for 2016 Limited)	
R12	-	Not used	-
R13	-	Cooling fan high speed relay	-
R14	-	Headlamp low beam relay (xenon headlamps) or Not used	-
R15	-	Ignition main relay	-
R16	-	Secondary air injection pump relay or Not used	-
R17	-	Rear defogger relay	-

The following relays are non-serviceable and are integrated in the circuit board. They are not shown in the fusebox drawing.

RELAY	VALUE	DESCRIPTION	OEM NAME
R18	-	Child security lock disable relay or Not used	-
R19	-	Starter/generator coolant pump relay or Not used	-
R20	-	Headlamp high beam relay	-
R21	-	Horn relay	-
R22	-	Front fog lamp relay	-
R23	-	Windshield washer pump relay	-
R24	-	Secondary air injection solenoid valve relay or Not used	-
R25	-	Not used	-
R26	-	Not used	-

FUSE AND RELAY BOX IN ENGINE COMPARTMENT (FUSE BLOCK - UNDERHOOD)

(FOR MODEL YEARS 2016-2020)

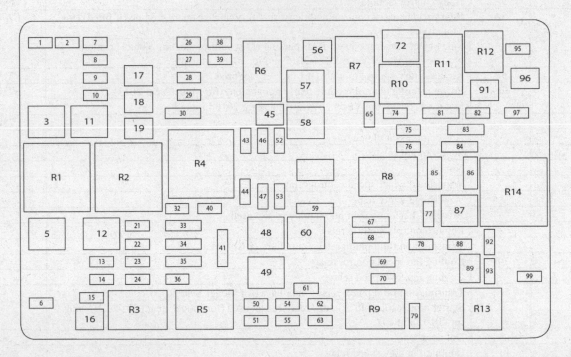

FUSE/RELAY	VALUE	DESCRIPTION	OEM NAME
1	-	Not used	F1UA
2	-	Not used	F2UA
3	60A	Electronic brake control module	F3UA
5	-	Not used	F5UA
6	7.5A	Rear compartment lid latch	F6UA
7	-	Not used	F7UA
8	5A	Driver's window switches, Seat memory control module, Passenger's driver switch	F8UA
9	-	Not used	F9UA
10	10A	Inflatable restraint sensing and diagnostic module, Passenger presence module	F10UA
11	40A	Power supply transformer (if fitted)	F11UA
12	40A	Left rear window defogger noise filter	F12UA
13	10A	Outside rearview mirrors	F13UA
14	-	Not used	F14UA
15	5A	Keyless entry control module	F15UA
16	20A	Windshield wiper motor	F16UA
17	30A	Passenger seat adjuster switch	F17UA
18	30A	Electronic brake control module	F18UA
19	30A	Seat memory control module, Driver's seat adjuster switch	F19UA
21	30A	Sunroof motor (if fitted)	F21UA
22	5A	Park lamps relay	F22UA
23	-	Not used	F23UA
24	-	Not used	F24UA
26	-	Not used	F26UA
27	10A	Inside rearview mirror, HVAC control module, Collision alert indicators (if fitted)	F27UA
28	10A	Spare fuse	F28UA
29	10A	Rearview camera, Seat blower motor – driver back (if fitted), Seat blower motor – passenger back (if fitted), Seat blower motor – driver cushion (if fitted), Seat blower motor – passenger cushion (if fitted)	F29UA

63. Fuses and relays (6 of 11)

30	-	Electronic brake control module, Power supply transformer (if fitted), Fuel pump driver control module, Instrument cluster	F30UA
32	5A	Evaporative vent solenoid valve	F32UA
33	15A	Front seat heating control module (if fitted)	F33UA
34	-	Not used	F34UA
35	10A	Body control module	F35UA
36	20A	Fuel pump driver control module	F36UA
38	-	Not used	F38UA
39	-	Not used	F39UA
40	10A	Steering column lock module	F40UA
41	-	Not used	F41UA
43	15A	Steering wheel heating control module (if fitted)	F43UA
44	-	Not used	F44UA
45	-	Not used	F45UA
46	15A	Engine control module	F46UA
47	-	Not used	F47UA
48	-	Not used	F48UA
49	40A	Power supply transformer (if fitted)	F49UA
50	-	Not used	F50UA
51	-	Not used	F51UA
52	-	Not used	F52UA
53	-	Not used	F53UA
54	-	Not used	F54UA
55	-	Not used	F55UA
56	-	Not used	F56UA
57	-	Not used	F57UA
58	-	Not used	F58UA
59	10A	High beam solenoid actuators	F59UA
60	60A	Cooling fan motor	F60UA
61	-	Not used	F61UA
62	-	Not used	F62UA
63	-	Not used	F63UA
65	10A	A/C compressor clutch relay	F65UA
67	-	Not used	F67UA
68	-	Not used	F68UA
69	-	Not used	F69UA
70	-	Not used	F70UA
72	40A	Starter pinion solenoid actuator relay (if fitted)	F72UA
74	20A	Starter motor	F74UA
75	25A	Engine control module	F75UA
76	15A	Engine control module	F76UA
77	-	Not used	F77UA
78	20A	Horns	F78UA
79	20A	Windshield washer pump relay	F79UA
81	15A	Engine control module, Transmission control module, Power inverter module	F81UA
82	-	Not used	F82UA
83	15A	Engine control module	F83UA
84	15A	Engine control module	F84UA
85	60A	Fuses 83, 84, 88 in Fuse box in engine compartment (Fuse box – Underhood)	F85UA
86	-	Not used	F86UA
87	-	Not used	F87UA
88	10A	Active grille air shutter	F88UA
89	-	Not used	F89UA
91	-	Not used	F91UA
92	-	Not used	F92UA

64. Fuses and relays (7 of 11)

93	-	Not used	F93UA
95	-	Not used	F95UA
96	-	Not used	F96UA
97	-	Not used	F97UA
99	10A	Auxiliary heater coolant pump (if fitted)	F99UA
R1	-	Not used	-
R2	-	Rear defogger relay	-
R3	-	Windshield wiper relay	-
R4	-	Ignition main relay	-
R5	-	Front wiper speed relay	-
R6	-	Not used	-
R7	-	A/C compressor clutch	-
R8	-	Engine controls ignition relay	-
R9	-	Not used	-
R10	-	Starter relay	-
R11	-	Starter motor	-
R12	-	Not used	-
R13	-	Not used	-
R14	-	Not used	-

FUSE AND RELAY BOX IN PASSENGER COMPARTMENT (FUSE BLOCK – INSTRUMENT PANEL)

(FOR MODEL YEARS 2013-2015 AND FOR 2016 LIMITED)

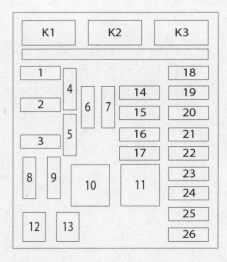

FUSE/RELAY	VALUE	DESCRIPTION	OEM NAME
1	2A	Steering wheel controls switches	F1DA
2	15A	Body control module	F2DA
3	15A	Body control module	F3DA
4	15A	Radio	F4DA
5	7.5A	Telematics communication interface control module	F5DA
6	20A	Accessory power socket – Instrument panel	F6DA
7	20A	Accessory power socket – Center console, Accessory power outlet – 110V AC	F7DA
8	15A	Body control module	F8DA
9	15A	Body control module	F9DA
10	30A	Body control module	F10DA
11	40A	Blower control module	F11DA
12	25A	Passenger's seat adjuster switch	F12DA
13	25A	Seat memory control module, Driver's seat adjuster switch	F13DA
14	7.5A	Data link connector	F14DA
15	10A	Inflatable restraint sensing and diagnostic module	F15DA
16	5A	Rear compartment lid unlatch relay	F16DA
17	10A	HVAC control module	F17DA
18	30A	Fuses 4 and 5 in fuse box in passenger compartment	F18DA
19	10A	Radio controls, HVAC controls, Info display module, Auxiliary audio input with memory card receptacle	F19DA
20	5A	Passenger presence sensor	F20DA
21	5A	Instrument cluster	F21DA
22	2A	Ignition switch	F22DA
23	15A	Body control module	F23DA
24	15A	Body control module	F24DA
25	25A	Accessory AC/DC power inverter module	F25DA
26	-	Not used	F26DA
K1	-	Rear compartment lid unlatch relay	-
K2	-	Not used	-
K3	-	Retained accessory power relay	-

FUSE AND RELAY BOX IN PASSENGER COMPARTMENT (FUSE BLOCK – INSTRUMENT PANEL)

(FOR MODEL YEARS 2016-2020)

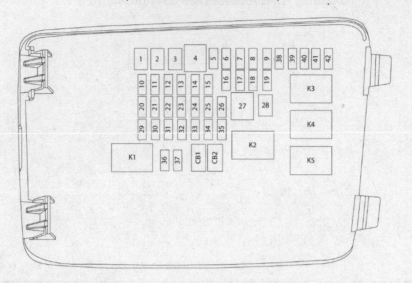

FUSE/RELAY	VALUE	DESCRIPTION	OEM NAME
1	30A	Driver's window switch	F1DA
2	30A	Right rear window switch, Passenger's window switch	F2DA
3	-	Not used	F3DA
4	40A	Blower motor	F4DA
5	15A	Body control module (without Start/Stop system)	F5DA
6	-	Not used	F6DA
7	-	Not used	F7DA
8	15A	Body control module	F8DA
9	5A	Body control module	F9DA
10	15A	Body control module	F10DA
11	-	Not used	F11DA
12	-	Not used	F12DA
13	-	Not used	F13DA
14	-	Not used	F14DA
15	20A	Transmission control module	F15DA
16	30A	Active noise cancellation module (if fitted), Audio amplifier (if fitted)	F16DA
17	15A	Seat lumbar support switches	F17DA
18	-	Not used	F18DA
19	-	Not used	F19DA
20	15A	Body control module (without Start/Stop system)	F20DA
21	15A	Body control module	F21DA
22	-	Not used	F22DA
23	-	Not used	F23DA
24	10A	Inflatable restraint sensing and diagnostic module, Passenger presence module	F24DA
25	7.5A	Data link connector	F25DA
26	-	Not used	F26DA
27	-	Not used	F27DA
28	-	Not used	F28DA
29	10A	Body control module	F29DA
30	10A	Front overhead console assembly, Garage door opener (if fitted)	F31DA
31	2A	Steering wheel controls switches	F32DA
32	-	Not used	F33DA
33	10A	HVAC control module	F34DA

67. Fuses and relays (10 of 11)

34	-	Not used	F34DA
35	-	Not used	F35DA
36	5A	Mobile device wireless charger module, USB receptacle	F36DA
37	20A	Accessory power receptacle – instrument panel	F37DA
38	5A	Telematics communication interface control module (if fitted)	F38DA
39	7.5A	HVAC controls, Instrument cluster, Info display module	F39DA
40	10A	Side object sensor modules (if fitted), Frontview camera – windshield (if fitted), Active safety control module (if fitted), Parking assist control module (if fitted)	F40DA
41	15A	Body control module	F41DA
42	15A	Radio, Human machine interface control module (if fitted), Auxiliary audio input	F42DA
CB1	-	Not used	CB1DA
CB2	20A	Accessory power receptacle – center console	CB2DA
K1	-	Not used	-
K2	-	Retained accessory power relay	-
K3	-	Not used	-
K4	-	Not used	-
K5	-	Not used	-

68. Fuses and relays (11 of 11)

Notes

Index